OPERATIONS RESEARCH

OPERATIONS RESEARCH: PRINCIPLES AND PRACTICE

DON T. PHILLIPS
DEPARTMENT OF INDUSTRIAL ENGINEERING
TEXAS A & M UNIVERSITY
COLLEGE STATION, TEXAS

A. RAVINDRAN
JAMES J. SOLBERG
SCHOOL OF INDUSTRIAL ENGINEERING
PURDUE UNIVERSITY
WEST LAFAYETTE, INDIANA

JOHN WILEY & SONS, INC.
NEW YORK LONDON SYDNEY TORONTO

Library of Congress Cataloging in Publication Date

Phillips, Don T
  Operations research.

  Includes bibliographies and index.
  1. Operations research. I. Ravindran, A., 1944–
  joint author. II. Solberg, James J.,
1942–   joint author. III. Title.

T57.6.P48   001.4'24   75-44395
ISBN 0-471-68707-3

Printed in the United States of America

10 9 8 7 6 5 4 3 2 1

PREFACE

The obvious question is, "Why another Operations Research book?" We readily admit that there is an abundance of operations research textbooks on the market, and that several of these are, at least in terms of their technical content, superb. It has been our experience, however, that students just beginning an acquaintance with the subject were less appreciative of the qualities of these books than we were. Over the years, as we subjected one after another of the published textbooks to classroom trial, it became apparent that they all left something to be desired from the students' point of view. Recurring and consistent complaints about the deficiencies forced us to develop supplementary classroom notes. It was from these notes that this book evolved.

Our principal objective was to present the material in a way that would immediately make sense to a beginning student. Often this required a juxtaposition of what might otherwise be regarded as the natural ordering of general theory followed by specific examples. We have observed that beginners rely heavily on examples and will understand the theory far more easily if it is presented as a generalization of one or more specific examples. It seems that, for the most part, students taking operations research courses have had adequate preparation in the mechanics of calculus, linear algebra, and probability. What they have greatest difficulty with is formulation and interpretation. That is, they can "do" the mathematics, but frequently do not understand the meaning of what they are doing. Hence, we have found it helpful to include quite a bit of verbal explanation of mathematical material. Purists may object to the liberties we have taken in providing loose and imprecise statements of perfectly well-defined and precise mathematics, but our embarrassment in so doing is overcome by our conviction that the student needs that kind of help. So although our presentation is far less concise and elegant than we could have made it, we feel strongly that the extra verbiage pays dividends.

Notwithstanding our desire to improve the readability of the material, we felt that it was important to keep the size of the book down. The sheer bulk of some textbooks, particularly when you consider their density, is overwhelming to beginning students. When it takes him an hour to digest what is written on one page and the book is a thousand pages long, it is not surprising that a student would feel disheartened. It is a lot easier for him to stay motivated, especially in the early stages, if he can sense that he is making substantial progress. Of course, there *is* a great deal to be learned, and as we assembled this book, we began to understand how our predecessors could have ended up with so much material. We too experienced an almost compulsive urge to include more. Even with merciless editing (which involved removing several major topics that happened to be personal favorites of the authors) the book turned out to be longer than we had originally intended. Nevertheless, we feel that it is possible to cover most of this book in one academic year.

In order to avoid creating the impression that our treatment of these subjects is conclusive, and to open the door to sources of additional information, we have provided selected references at the end of each chapter. We have also provided a few bibliographic comments to guide the reader in his research. Obviously, these brief bibliographies are only starting points, which in turn will lead to further sources.

Individual instructors will, of course, exercise their perogative to select and to rearrange certain material. Because we know this will happen, we decided at the outset that a highly integrated text would be undesirable. Thus we have deliberately sought to maintain independence among chapters to permit maximum flexibility in their use. At Purdue, for example, we use Chapters 2, 3, and 4 for a one-semester (16 week) graduate level, introductory course on linear programming. For a similar undergraduate course, we omit Chapter 4. In another graduate level course, we use Chapters 5, 6, 7, 8, and parts of 9 and 10. For the corresponding undergraduate course, we attempt to cover the same topics but must delete some of the more specialized material in each chapter. Teachers being an individualistic lot, we are confident that each will find unique ways to adapt this book to his own needs as he perceives them.

To aid the instructor in his task, there now follows a description of how we have elected to organize the material.

Chapter 1 discusses the historical origins of Operations Research (OR), and provides some loose definitions and descriptions of the OR methodology. The "philosophy" of mathematical modeling is discussed in some detail, and some important principles to be borne in mind as one engages in the practice are presented. Depending on a number of factors, the instructor may choose to employ Chapter 1 at either the beginning or the end of a course.

Chapter 2 introduces the construction of linear programming models, along with a discussion of different types of applications. The simplex method for solving linear programming problems is also developed. Although the theory is deemphasized, the economic interpretations of the simplex linear programming algorithm are clearly brought out in this chapter. The problems of degeneracy, unbounded solutions, alternate optimal solutions, and infeasible solutions are fully discussed. The use of artificial variables is illustrated with the Big M simplex method and the Phase 1-Phase 2 simplex procedure. Finally, the computer solution of linear programming problems is discussed.

Chapter 3 introduces network analysis techniques. The formulation and solutions of transportation problems, assignment problems, and least-time transportation problems are fully discussed. In the latter part of Chapter 3, the basic concepts of network theory are introduced including the max flow-min cut theorem and the labeling method for solving maximal flow problems. Utilizing these concepts, a solution to the shortest route problem by Dijkstra's algorithm is presented along with its practical applications. Finally, project management via PERT/CPM is discussed. A unique feature is the discussion of linear programming methods to solve large project management problems.

Chapter 4 introduces some advanced topics in linear programming. The computer solution of linear programs through the revised simplex method is presented. The concept of dual linear programs and the practical applications of duality theorems are also fully discussed. Finally, postoptimality analysis of linear programming solutions through sensitivity analysis and parametric programming is presented. The practical application of the dual simplex method in postoptimality analysis is also fully illustrated.

Chapter 5 contains material on basic concepts of probability that are important in Chapters 6, 7, 8, and 9. Although the treatment is reasonably complete, it is probably too concise to serve as an introduction to the topic. Students who have had no previous exposure to probability theory would be better served by one of the textbooks recommended at the end of the chapter. We have found, however, that most students electing a course in Operations Research will have had prior experience with probability theory and need only a refresher course. Following a review of the rules governing the manipulations of probabilities, the concept of a random variable, and the general properties of distributions; Chapter 5 supplies a summary of the most common discrete and continuous distribution families. It concludes with a brief commentary on the issues associated with fitting theoretical distributions to real-world data.

Chapter 6 introduces techniques for modeling random processes. The time dimension, when added to the conceptual difficulties associated with random variables, seems to give students trouble. Consequently, discrete time processes are fully developed first. An example is used to carry the development of the techniques in a plausible fashion from specific tactics to the general theory. Markov and stationarity assumptions are introduced at the point where the simplifications they produce seem necessary. The variety of structures represented by Markov chains is explored and the terminology used to describe variations is defined. Also, computational methods used to extract various kinds of information from Markov models are derived and illustrated. By the point at which continuous time models are considered, the student should already have overcome most of the conceptual difficulties. A meaningful example is used to develop the mathematics of the general continuous time Markov process, and the development parallels that of the discrete time version. Birth-death processes are mentioned briefly in preparation for Chapter 7. Finally, the Poisson process is derived as a special case of the birth-death process, and some of its useful properties are discussed.

Chapter 7 introduces queueing models. Beginning with a deterministic model to establish some of the most basic concepts, the chapter soon exploits the techniques for modeling random processes developed in the previous chapter. Useful variations of the birth-death process receive appropriate queueing interpretations, and a few results that are not dependent on the Markov assumption are mentioned. Particular emphasis is placed on the information about real-world queues that models can produce; a number of surprising insights are revealed.

Chapter 8 is devoted to inventory models. The first part of the chapter, treating deterministic models, presents the classical economic order quantity model and a number of its common variations. The second part of the chapter, dealing with probabilistic models, explores the significance of uncertainty in demand. The first example of the second part incorporates uncertainty into a single-period model. By eliminating the time dimension, we are able to concentrate on overcoming the difficulties associated with handling the probability distribution of demand. The next model restores the time dimension, to produce a probabilistic model that is comparable to the classical economic order quantity model. A numerical comparison of results from these two models establishes the importance of representing uncertainty when it is present.

Chapter 9 is a treatment of digital simulation techniques. The chapter begins with an overview of the digital simulation modeling process, along with a discussion of the design factors that must be considered in conducting simulation experiments. Monte Carlo Analysis is illustrated through two manual simulation models, and the role of (0-1) random numbers is discussed relative to simulation modeling. A complete treatment of random deviate generation is given for common statistical density functions. The chapter concludes with a discussion of simulation languages and an overview of simulation design techniques and post-simulation analysis.

Chapter 10 provides a comprehensive, straight-forward treatment of serial dynamic programming. The principle of optimality is introduced and shown to relate directly to recursive optimization solution procedures. Several representative examples are given in order to illustrate how the procedure might be used on real-world problems. Forward recursion, backward recursion, discrete-state variable problems, and continuous-state variable problems are all illustrated in Chapter 10. The chapter concludes with a treatment of the "curse of dimensionality" and remedial actions for multiple state variable problems.

Chapter 11 attempts to provide a broad overview for the field of nonlinear programming. The chapter begins with basic definitions of functions, sets, and nonlinear forms. Taylor's series expansion is developed as the cornerstone of algorithmic development, and related to the gradient, Hessian, and necessary/sufficient conditions. Starting with single-variable search techniques, the chapter treats multivariable unconstrained optimization, equality constrained optimization, inequality constrained optimization, and general nonlinear programming problems. Special techniques such as Lagrangian optimization, separable programming, quadratic programming, and geometric programming are also treated in Chapter 11.

It is perhaps obvious that the authors are indebted to the many researchers who have developed the underlying concepts which permeate this text. Although far too numerous to mention, we have tried to recognize these efforts through bibliographical references at the end of each chapter. In addition to the above, several individuals have directly contributed to the composition of this text. We are specifically indebted to Dr. J. W. Schmidt, C.B.M. Incorporated, for the second example in Chapter 9; Dr. R. S. Schecter of the University of Texas; Dr. Charles Beightler, Dr. R. M. Crisp, and Dr. W. L. Meier for the material on geometric programming in Chapter 11. Helpful comments on preliminary draft copies were received from Prof. C. C. Peterson, and P. Goel of Purdue University. Numerous graduate students were asked to endure the (seemingly) endless stream of problems, but we are particularly thankful for the inputs from B. Begenyi, V. Akileswaran, D. Hanline, P. Balasubramanian, J. Golan, D. Engi, and R. Weinberg. We are also grateful to the American Institute of Industrial Engineers for allowing us to reproduce written materials in Chapters 9, 10, and 11. Special thanks for meritorious service in typing both the preliminary and final versions of this text have been reserved for Candyce J. Phillips. Finally, we are grateful to Purdue University and also to the faculty in the School of Industrial Engineering for continuous support and encouragement of this project.

College Station, Texas   DON T. PHILLIPS
West Lafayette, Indiana   A. RAVINDRAN
                                                           JAMES J. SOLBERG

CONTENTS

CHAPTER 6. RANDOM PROCESSES

CHAPTER 7. QUEUEING MODELS

CHAPTER 8. INVENTORY MODELS

CHAPTER 1
THE NATURE OF OPERATIONS RESEARCH

1.1 THE HISTORY OF OPERATIONS RESEARCH

In order to understand what operations research (OR) is today, one must know something of its history and evolution. Although particular models and techniques of OR can be traced back to much earlier origins, it is generally agreed that the discipline began during World War II. Many strategic and tactical problems associated with the Allied military effort were simply too complicated to expect adequate solutions from any one individual, or even a single discipline. In response to these complex problems, groups of scientists with diverse educational backgrounds were assembled as special units within the armed forces. Because of the diversity of its membership, one of the earliest groups in Britain came to be known as "Blackett's circus."

Partly because the scientists involved were talented men, partly because of the pressures of wartime necessity, and partly because of the synergism generated from the interactions of different disciplines, these teams of scientists were remarkably successful in improving the effectiveness of complex military operations. Examples of typical projects were radar deployment policies, antiaircraft fire control, fleet convoy sizing, and detection of enemy submarines. By 1941, each of the three wings of the British Armed Forces were utilizing such scientific teams. As the dramatic success of the idea became amply demonstrated, other allied nations adopted the same approach and organized their own teams. Because the problems assigned to these groups were in the nature of military operations, their work became known as operational research in the United Kingdom, and as operations research elsewhere. The American effort, although it began at a later date, produced many fundamental advances in the mathematical techniques for analyzing military problems. For further details of early activities in operations research, an excellent summary is given in Trefethen (5).

After the war, many of the scientists who had been active in the military OR groups turned their attention to the possibilities of applying a similar approach to civilian problems. Some returned to universities and concentrated their efforts on providing a sound foundation for many of the techniques that had been hastily developed earlier, while others devoted renewed efforts to developing new techniques. Many individuals moved into various sectors of the private economy, where they adapted methods developed by others to the unique problems of particular industries.

1

In terms of applications, the first civilian organizations to seize upon the OR methodology were, generally, large profit-making corporations. For example, petroleum companies were among the first to make regular use of linear programming on a large scale for production planning. It was logical that "big business" would take the lead in adopting OR. To any profit-oriented organization, OR offered a way to obtain a competitive advantage; but in the early years when all OR work was in the nature of basic research, only the large companies could afford it. Later, as researchers began to recognize common categories of problems (inventory, allocation, replacement, scheduling, etc.) and the techniques for dealing with such problems became standardized, smaller companies were able to benefit from the pool of accumulated knowledge without investing heavily in research. With a few notable exceptions— such as the work on traffic control conducted at the New York Port Authority by Leslie Edie and others in the early 1950s—applications of OR in service-oriented industries and in the public sector did not begin to flourish until the mid 1960s. Today, however, service organizations such as banks, hospitals, libraries, and judicial systems recognize that OR can aid in improving the effectiveness with which they deliver their respective services. In addition, federal, state, and local government agencies are using OR, particularly in their planning and policy-making activities. In fact, work on some of these specialized applications of OR has multiplied so rapidly in recent years that subspecialties, based upon the area of application, appear to be developing. Recent operations research conferences have included special sessions on such topics as "OR in community health planning," "OR models of the criminal justice system," "mass transit studies," "travel and tourism," "energy," "education models," and "OR applications in sports."

An important factor in the rapid spread and sustained success of the OR approach to problem solving was the concurrent development of electronic computers. The computer was from the beginning an invaluable tool to the OR analyst, enabling him to perform otherwise intractable calculations. Indeed, many of the problem-solving methods now regarded as standard would be unthinkably impractical to implement without modern computers. By generating practical uses for increasingly larger and faster machines, OR has both benefited from and contributed to the explosive growth of computer capability that has occurred over the past two and a half decades.

By the early 1950s, civilian OR activities had reached a level of development that began to suggest that a unique discipline was in formation. The Operations Research Society of America (ORSA) was founded in 1952 to serve the professional needs of scientists working in the OR area. A parallel movement resulted, in 1953, in the formation of the Institute of Management Sciences (TIMS). The journals of these two organizations, *Operations Research* and *Managment Science*, as well as regular conferences of the members, helped to draw together the many diverse results into some semblance of a coherent body of knowledge.

Beginning about the same time and continuing into the early 1960s, more and more colleges and universities in the United States introduced first individual courses, then whole programs, into their curricula. Graduate programs leading to advanced degrees at both the M.S. and Ph.D. level were approved in many major universities. For good or bad, it happened that little uniformity was observed in deciding where within the academic structure OR belonged. Depending on unique development patterns at each local institution, OR programs sometimes appeared within departments of industrial engineering, sometimes in business schools, and occasionally in mathematics or economics. In keeping with the original interdisciplinary character of the work, some universities established interdisciplinary committees to administer OR programs; but because such academic "orphans" tend to be inherently unstable, they have usually been either officially or unofficially absorbed into more traditional parts of the university structure. Of course, the parent discipline tends to impart a particular unique characteristic to the OR program, and the consequent lack of uniformity in academic programs has acted against achieving "definition" in the field. Perhaps it is all for the best.

It is interesting to note that the modern perception of OR as a body of established models and techniques—that is, a discipline in itself—is quite different from the original concept of OR as an *activity*, which was performed by interdisciplinary teams. An evolution of this kind is to be expected in any emerging field of scientific inquiry. In initial formative years, there are no experts, no traditions, no literature. As problems are successfully solved, the body of specific knowledge grows to a point where it begins to require specialization even to know what has been previously accomplished. The pioneering efforts of one generation become the standard practice of the next. Still, it ought to be remembered that at least a portion of the record of success of OR can be attributed to its ecumenical nature. It is in the best traditions of the field to adopt the procedures of any discipline that can make a contribution to the solution of the problem at hand. If the initial open-mindedness of OR ever degenerates into orthodoxy, if the methods ever begin to outweigh the objectives, then the field will have lost one of its most vital precepts.

1.2 THE MEANING OF OPERATIONS RESEARCH

From the historical and philosophical summary just presented, it should be apparent that the term "operations research" has a number of quite distinct variations of meaning. To some, OR is that certain body of problems, techniques, and solutions that has been accumulated under the name of OR over the past 30 years, and we apply OR when we recognize a problem of that certain genre. To others, it is an activity or process—something we do, rather than know—which by its very nature is applied. Perhaps in time the meaning will stabilize, but at this point it would be premature to exclude any of these interpretations. It would also be counterproductive to attempt to make distinctions between "operations research" and "management science" or between the "operations research approach" and the "systems approach." While these terms are sometimes viewed as distinct, they are often conceptualized in such a manner as to defy separation. Any attempt to draw boundaries between them would in practice be arbitrary.

How, then, can we define operations research? The Operational Research Society of Great Britain has adopted the following definition:

Operational research is the application of the methods of science to complex problems arising in the direction and management of large systems of men, machines, materials and money in industry, business, government, and defense. The distinctive approach is to develop a scientific model of the system, incorporating measurements of factors such as chance and risk, with which to predict and compare the outcomes of alternative decisions, strategies or controls. The purpose is to help management determine its policy and actions scientifically.

The Operations Research Society of America has offered a shorter, but similar, description:

Operations research is concerned with scientifically deciding how to best design and operate man–machine systems, usually under conditions requiring the allocation of scarce resources.

Although both of these definitions leave something to be desired, they are about as specific as one would want to be in defining such a broad area. It is noteworthy that both definitions emphasize the *motivation* for the work; namely, to aid decision makers in dealing with complex real-world problems. Even when the methods seem to become so abstract as to lose real-world relevance, the student may take some comfort in the fact that the ultimate goal is always some useful application. Both definitions also mention *methodology*, describing it only very generally as "scientific." That term is perhaps a bit too general, inasmuch as the methods of science are so diverse and varied. A more precise description of the OR methodology would indicate its reliance on "models." Of course, that term would itself require further elaboration, and it is to that task that we now turn our attention.

1.3 MODELS IN OPERATIONS RESEARCH

The essence of the operations research activity lies in the construction and use of models. Although modeling must be learned from individual experimentation, we will attempt here to discuss it in broad, almost philosophical terms. This overview is worth having, and setting a proper orientation in advance may help to avoid misconceptions later.

First of all, one should realize that some of the connotations associated with the word "model" in common English usage are not present in the OR use of the word. A model in the sense intended here is just a simplified representation of something real. This usage does carry with it the implication that a model is always, necessarily, a representation that is less than perfect.

Why model? There are many conceivable reasons why one might prefer to deal with a substitute for the "real thing" rather than with the "thing" itself. Often, the motivation is economic—to save money, time, or some other valuable commodity. Sometimes it is to avoid risks associated with the tampering of a real object. Sometimes the real environment is so complicated that a representative model is needed just to understand it, or to communicate with others about it. Such models are quite prevalent in the life sciences, physical chemistry, and physics.

Given that one has something real, which we will call the "real system," and that there is some understandable reason for wanting to deal with it—that is, a "problem" related to the real system which calls for definite "conclusions"—the modeling process can be depicted as in Fig. 1.1. The broken line on the left represents what might be termed the "direct approach," for which we are seeking a substitute.

The first step is construction of the model itself, which is indicated by the line labeled "Formulation." This step requires a set of coordinated decisions as to what aspects of the real system should be incorporated in the model, what aspects can be ignored, what assumptions can and should be made, into what

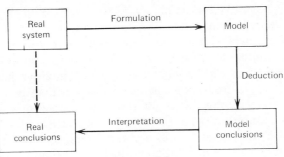

Figure 1.1

form the model should be cast, and so on. In some instances, formulation may require no particular creative skill, but in most cases—certainly the interesting ones—it is decidedly an art. The selection of the essential attributes of the real system and the omission of the irrelevant ones require a kind of selective perception that cannot be defined by any precise algorithm.

It is apparent, then, that the formulation step is characterized by a certain amount of arbitrariness, in the sense that equally competent researchers, viewing the same real system, could come up with completely different models. At the same time, the freedom to select one's assumptions cannot be taken to imply that one model is any better than another. A discussion of the boundary between reasonable and unreasonable assumptions would take us into philosophical issues which we could not hope to resolve. In fact, as one ponders the problem of model formulation, one discloses all sorts of metaphysical questions, such as how to define the precise boundary between the model and its referent, how to distinguish between what is real and what is only our perception, the implications of the resultant cause and effects of modeling procedure, and so on. These issues are mentioned only to reemphasize that it is quite meaningless to speak of the "right" way to formulate a model. The formative stages of the modeling process might be repeated and analyzed many times before the proper course of action becomes readily apparent. Once the problem formulation and definition is agreed upon, a more scientific step in the modeling process is begun.

Returning to Fig. 1.1, the step labeled "Deduction" involves techniques that depend on the nature of the model. It may involve solving equations, running a computer program, expressing a sequence of logical statements— whatever is necessary to solve the problem of interest relative to the model. Provided that the assumptions are clearly stated and well defined, this phase of modeling should *not* be subject to differences of opinion. The logic should be valid and the mathematics should be rigorously accurate. All reasonable men should agree that the model conclusions follow from the assumptions, even if they do not all agree with the necessary assumptions. It is simply a matter of abiding by whatever formal rules of manipulation are prescribed by the methods in use. It is a vital part of the modeling process to rationalize, analyze, and conceptualize all components of the deductive process.

The final step. labeled "Interpretation," again involves human judgment. The model conclusions must be translated to real-world conclusions cautiously, in full cognizance of possible discrepancies between the model and its real-world referent. Aspects of the real system which were either deliberately or unintentionally overlooked when the model was formulated may turn out to be important. Since there is no way to prove that a model has *not* omitted some important factor, there is room for reasonable men to disagree about the relevance of the model conclusions to the real system, and to what extent the interpretation phase should be tempered by direct intuitive judgments.

The most important point revealed by Fig. 1.1 is that the ties between the model and the system it represents are at best ties of plausible association, and that no one, no matter how competent, can create perfection for that situation. It is part of the nature of models as simplified representations of real systems that there can be no absolute criteria by which to determine their acceptability. In short, you cannot *prove* a model. That is not to say, of course, that there exist no criteria by which to distinguish good models from poor ones, nor to say that model validation is not an integral part of the total modeling effort. There can be more specific criteria for particular kinds of models, but generally it can be said that a model is good insofar as it is *useful*, relative to the purpose for which it was intended.

The process of acquiring the conviction that a model actually "works" is commonly called *validation*. When the people involved (the users) are persuaded that a model is useful within some basic context, they will speak of it as a valid model. Its validity is of course restricted to the understood context. Even within that context, some people may refuse to accept the model's validity because they have not yet been persuaded. Thus, "validation" is a considerably weaker term than "proof" or "verification."

To further clarify the modeling approach to problem solving, contrast it to the experimentally based "scientific method" of the natural sciences. Figure 1.2 depicts the latter approach. Here, the first step is the development of a hypothesis which is arrived at, generally by induction, following a period of informal observation. At that point an experiment is devised to test the hypothesis. If the experimental results contradict the hypothesis, the hypothesis is revised and retested. The cycle continues until a verified hypothesis, or *theory*, is obtained. The result of the process is something that purports to be "truth," "knowledge," or "a law of nature." In contrast to model conclusions, theories are independently verifiable statements about factual matters. Models are invented; theories are discovered.

It might also be noted that there exist other formalized procedures for reaching conclusions about the real world. The system of trial by jury, as a means to decide between guilt or innocence of accused criminals, is one example. The determination of policy within a group by vote according to

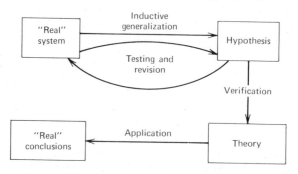

Figure 1.2

personal preference is another. Thus, modeling is a very important but certainly not unique method to assist us in dealing with complicated real-world problems.

1.4 PRINCIPLES OF MODELING

Having established a general framework for what is actually meant by modeling, let us proceed to a set of general principles useful in providing guidance to the formulation of models within the context of OR. Both developers and users of OR models should be consciously aware of the inherent limitations of the approach, and should exercise constant vigilance against falling into the common traps indicated by the following ten principles:

1. *Do not build a complicated model when a simple one will suffice.* Considering that this principle is just a restatement of Occam's Razor, which goes back to the early 14th century, it is surprising how often it is ignored. The reasons are understandable—people like to illustrate their capabilities, they want to give the client his money's worth, and so on. Even with the best of motives, it is easy to get carried away by the sheer challenge of a difficult problem, and thereby spend far more time and money on refining a model than the problem is worth. Even aside from issues of cost, it is apparent that given two models, each of which adequately performs the intended function, the simpler is the more useful and is therefore to be preferred.

   In particular, the principle implies a condemnation of brute force methods of modeling. For example, one might list every variable of possible significance to a particular system, then run an enormous regression analysis to derive a predicting equation; or a systems analyst might build enormous simulations by including every conceivable parameter. In model building, "bigger and more complicated" does not necessarily mean "better."

   The principle also seems to contradict an understood axiom of mathematical analysis which says that one should first simplify a problem by introducing as many assumptions as are necessary until the mathematics becomes tractable, then "enrich" the model by weakening the assumptions in ingenious ways until the mathematics is no longer tractable. Such a procedure will always produce the most powerful and general model, but the power and generality of a model has little to do with its usefulness in dealing with a *particular* problem. In some cases, the strongest model one can construct may fall short of what would be required to have a *useful* model; in other cases, it may give rise to far more detail than is worth having. Building the strongest model possible is a common guiding principle for mathematicians who are attempting to extend the theory or to develop techniques that have broad applicability. However, in the actual practice of building models for specific purposes, the best advice is to "keep it simple."

2. *Beware of molding the problem to fit the technique.* OR professionals are often criticized (and sometimes rightly so) of distorting reality to suit the tools they prefer to use. For example, an expert on linear programming methods may tend to view every problem he encounters as requiring a linear programming solution. In reality, not all optimization problems involve only linear functions. Furthermore, not all operations research problems involve optimization. As a matter of fact, not all real-world problems call for operations research! Of course, everyone sees reality in his own terms, so the field of operations research is not unique in this respect. Lawyers, psychologists, and political scientists are just as often guilty of "viewing the world through tinted glasses." Being human, we will tend to rely on the methods we are most comfortable in using and have been most successful with in the past. As best we can, however, we should strive not to shape the problem to preselected techniques, but rather to select the kind of model and techniques that

are most appropriate to the problem. Our freedom to operate in this fashion is restricted, of course, by the breadth of our knowledge of techniques. We certainly cannot use techniques in which we have no competence, and we cannot hope to be competent in all techniques.

We might wish to divide operations researchers into three main categories: *technique developers*, *teachers*, and *problem solvers*. Recognizing that one may play different roles at different times, as well as simultaneously, we might say that the problem solvers have an ongoing responsibility to broaden their working knowledge of available techniques in order to avoid the biases necessitated by a limited repertoire. At the same time, one should recognize that the technique developers who are seeking to extend the base of available techniques, and the teachers who bear the responsibility of conveying new developments to the practitioners and interpreting technical matters to people outside the profession, must operate according to different principles because the objectives are different. In particular, one should be prepared to tolerate the "I've-found-a-cure-but-I'm-trying-to-find-a-disease-to-fit-it" behavior in technique developers and teachers. The activity is legitimate in these circumstances because the purpose is not to produce a valid model of a real system, but to illustrate the technique or to establish its validity. Although this procedure is actually a reverse application of the scientific method, it is often a necessary step in translating theory into practice.

3. *The deduction phase of modeling must be conducted rigorously.* The reason for requiring rigorous deduction is that one wants to be sure that if model conclusions are inconsistent with reality, then the defect lies in the assumptions. In other words, if the deduction has not been carried out rigorously, the model will be unable to distinguish between external errors in formulation and internal errors in logic. One application of this principle is that one must be extremely careful when programming computers. Hidden "bugs" are particularly dangerous when they do not prevent the program from running, but simply produce results which are inconsistent with the model's intent.

4. *Models should be validated prior to implementation.* As mentioned earlier, it would be futile to attempt to establish with certainty that a model is appropriate, but this fact does not absolve one from the responsibility of checking it against reasonable standards of appropriateness. There are a number of commonly employed techniques for doing this, depending on the nature of the model.

One method for validating predictive models is "retrospective testing," in which the model is compared against some historical standard to see if it would have accurately predicted what has since been observed to occur. For example, if a model is constructed to forecast the monthly sales of a commodity, it could be tested using historical data to compare the forecasts it would have produced to the actual sales. A similar idea, useful in cases where the model is intended to represent a class of real things, is to test it against members of the class that were not used in formulating the model. For example, if a regression model is to be fit to data, some of the data might be held back for later testing. Another technique, which is sometimes useful in validating certain kinds of descriptive models, is to systematically vary parameters of the real system and observe whether the model successfully "tracks" the changes. Or, the model might be subjected to artificially constructed test situations which are deliberately designed to expose weaknesses. If it performs adequately in extreme situations, one can feel some confidence that it will work well under more normal circumstances.

If the model cannot be validated prior to implementation, then perhaps it can be implemented in phases for validation. For example, a new model for inventory control may be implemented for a certain selected group of items while the older system is retained for the majority of items. As the model proves itself, more items can be placed within its jurisdiction.

In a word of caution, it should be pointed out that validation can be carried too far. One might reach the point where an enormous amount of effort is required to increase model confidence only a small amount. Depending upon the importance of a model, it may be preferable to tolerate a lower confidence level. In some cases, it may be sufficient to know that someone else did something similar and it worked for them.

Finally, it is worth remembering that real things change in time. A highly satisfactory model may very well degrade with age. Depending on how such factors effect model performance and validity, an implemented model may require anything from constant surveillance to periodic reevaluation.

5. *A model should never be taken too literally.* This principle is obvious when the model is relatively unsophisticated, but is easily forgotten when it is elaborate. For example, suppose that one were to construct an elaborate computer model of the American economy, with many competent researchers spending a great deal of time and money installing all sorts of complicated interactions and relationships. Under these circumstances, it is easy to believe that the model duplicates the real system. Those who develop the model begin to believe it because their attention has been so directed to the model, that the model has *become* the real thing to them. In other words, they may become incapable of seeing the real problem in any terms other than those of the model. Those who are not so closely involved may be so overwhelmed by the technology and effort brought to bear that they just assume that the model is, or ought to be, "correct" because of its very complexity. As a consequence, the model may be both attacked and defended as if it were supposed to mirror reality exactly, when actually it should be evaluated in terms of its practical usefulness.

This danger continues to increase as models become larger and more sophisticated, as they must to deal with increasingly complicated problems. The deduction phase is enlarged and is perhaps spread out over a longer period of time. Aside from the fact that the likelihood of logical errors is necessarily increased, the sheer gap between the model's assumptions and its conclusions increases the likelihood that in the interpretation phase the limitations of the model will be obscured. The only preventive measures are to be meticulous in expressing the original assumptions at the time they are formulated, and again when the conclusions are reached.

6. *A model should neither be pressed to do, nor criticized for failing to do, that for which it was never intended.* Now that a vast literature of operations research has accumulated, it is both natural and sensible to seek to adapt existing models to our problems, rather than view each new problem as a totally new situation. There is nothing wrong with this approach, provided that we fully understand the model in its original context. It has already been noted that a model is shaped not only by the system it represents and the tools it employs, but also by the motivations of the model builders. Because it is so easy to attribute one's own motives to someone else, there is a definite danger of making a false presumption that some model which is reported to serve its purpose well in a different but related context will also perform well for us.

One example of this error would be the use of forecasting models to predict so far into the future that the data on which the forecasts are based have no relevance. A model might have been shown to provide excellent short-term forecasts, but that limited kind of validity provides no assurance that it is capable of producing good long-term forecasts. Another example is in the use of certain network methods to describe the activities involved in a complex project. These may provide excellent descriptive and control models for projects for which there is a good base of experience, such as construction projects. However, in describing, say, a research project in which future activities may depend on factors which are not even imagined in the present, these network models give somewhat poorer representations of reality.

Just as one must avoid stretching a model beyond its capabilities, one must also refrain from dismissing models as categorically useless when we find they do not fulfill our expectations.

7. *Beware of overselling a model.* This point is particularly significant for the OR professional because most nontechnical benefactors of an operations researcher's work are not likely to understand his methods. When a model is sold as "factual" rather than as an "integrated body of plausible assumptions that lead to useful conclusions," and it later becomes known that the implied real-world actions were somehow in error, the ensuing backlash may be out of proportion to the error. Those who deal with models professionally can shrug off such failures as cases in which some important factor was neglected or overlooked. At any rate, they have no cause to lose faith in, or to feel betrayed by, the methods they employ. Others, however, may take the simplistic view that operations research is "no good."

The increased technicality of one's methods also increases the burden of responsibility on the OR professional to distinguish clearly between his role as model manipulator and model interpreter. Despite a firm conviction that the position one advocates is right, he has an obligation to concede that models, by their very nature, cannot offer conclusive evidence of anything. Simple integrity requires that any claim of certainty be limited to the deductive phase of modeling. That is, although it may be possible to prove that the conclusions necessarily follow from the assumptions, the most one can say about the assumptions is that they are *believed* to be adequate. In those cases where the assumptions seem undeniable, the argument will not be weakened by this admission; in those cases where the assumptions can be challenged, it would be dishonest to use the model to conceal them. In either case, the OR analyst has a long-range vested interest in preserving the faith of others in the objectivity of his methods, and should therefore strive to present his conclusions with honest candor.

8. *Some of the primary benefits of modeling are associated with the process of developing the model.* Generally speaking, a model is never as useful to anyone else as it is to those who are involved in developing it. The model itself never contains the full knowledge and understanding of the real system that the builder must acquire in order to successfully model it, and there is no practical way to communicate this knowledge and understanding adequately. In extreme cases, the *sole* benefits may occur while the model is being developed; that is, the model may have no further value once it is completed. An example of an extreme case of this kind might occur when a small group of people attempts to develop a formal plan for some project. The plan is the final model, but the real problem may be to achieve a consensus on what the objectives ought to be. Once the consensus is achieved, the formal plan may be dispensable.

The obvious corollary to this principle is that it is almost always desirable for the ultimate user to be involved throughout the model construction and validation period. In addition to the extra subtleties of understanding that he may gain from the activity, his presence will help to keep the model in tune with his needs. This procedure may also help to avoid the "stillborn model syndrome," in which fine technical work is allowed to languish, unimplemented, for lack of commitment on the part of the intended user.

9. *A model cannot be any better than the information that goes into it.* A well-known maxim of computer programming stated in abbreviated form as GIGO, or "Garbage In, Garbage Out," is equally applicable to modeling. It means that a computer, or a model, can only manipulate the data provided to it; it cannot recognize and correct for deficiencies in input.

Another thing models cannot do is to *generate* information. Sometimes people get the idea that computer simulation models, for example, can produce more information than is put into them. Of course, they can produce almost unlimited quantities of data, but these data are just the direct consequences of the assumptions built into the program. Models may *condense* data, or *convert* it to more useful forms; they do not have the capacity to create it. It can certainly make one uncomfortable to be forced to make a decision without adequate information. Under these circumstances, it may be tempting to resort to modeling as an aid. It is unrealistic, however, to expect the model to supply the missing information. It is also unrealistic to expect it to somehow compensate for the absence of information and point the way to the solution that would be reached if the information were available. Although many OR models incorporate representations of uncertainty in the form of probabilities, accounting for uncertainty is not at all equivalent to eliminating it, or even reducing it. In some situations, instead of exerting one's efforts through model construction, one would be better off just gathering more information about the real system.

10. *Models cannot replace decision makers.* One of the most common misconceptions about the purpose of OR models is the idea that they are supposed to provide "optimal solutions," free of human subjectivity and error. Implicit in this notion is the concept that decision making can be automated once all the appropriate considerations have been properly defined. It is then simply a matter of finding the right formula and implementing the results. In the light of previous discussion, the falsity of this notion should be self-evident. No competent operations researcher would ever project such a view.

There are virtually always some neglected aspects to be considered, along with the output produced by the model, before committing to a course of action. In the model formulation itself, there are many decisions to be made with respect to what aspects of the problem are important, what assumptions are reasonable, and so on. All of these decisions are subjective in nature. Often a problem is influenced by nonquantifiable factors which can only be listed for consideration. Sometimes it is necessary to compromise among multiple objectives, or to trade off one human value against another when there is not even a common scale by which to measure them. All of these real-world complications call for decision-making capabilities of a uniquely human nature. Only the most routine decisions are amenable to "automation," and even these would require human overseers to monitor performance and override the system when things go wrong.

OR models can aid decision makers and thereby permit better decisions to be made. It would be going too far, however, to say that they make the job of decision making easier. If anything, the challenges are greater because of the expanded technical capabilities required to make good use of the modeling approach. Certainly, the role of experience, intuition, and judgment in decision making is undiminished.

REFERENCES

1. Ackoff, R. L., *Scientific Method: Optimizing Applied Research Decisions*, Wiley, New York, 1962.
2. Ackoff, R. L. and P. Rivett, *A Manager's Guide to Operations Research*, Wiley, New York, 1962.
3. Beer, Stafford, *Management Science: The Business Use of Operations Research*, Doubleday, New York, 1967.
4. Rivett, Patrick, *Principles of Model Building*, Wiley, New York, 1972.
5. Trefethen, Florence N., "A History of Operations Research," in *Operations Research for Management*, Joseph F. McCloskey and F. N. Trefethen, Eds., Johns Hopkins Press, Baltimore, 1954.

CHAPTER 2
LINEAR PROGRAMMING

2.1 INTRODUCTION

Programming problems in general are concerned with the use or allocation of scarce resources—labor, materials, machines, and capital—in the "best" possible manner so that costs are minimized or profits are maximized. In using the term "best" it is implied that some choice or a set of alternative courses of actions is available for making the decision. In general, the best decision is found by solving a mathematical problem. The term linear programming merely defines a particular class of programming problems that meet the following conditions:

1. The decision variables involved in the problem are nonnegative (i.e., positive or zero).
2. The criterion for selecting the "best" values of the decision variables can be described by a linear function of these variables, that is, a mathematical function involving only the first powers of the variables with no cross products. The criterion function is normally referred to as the *objective function.*
3. The operating rules governing the process (e.g., scarcity of resources) can be expressed as a set of linear equations or linear inequalities. This set is referred to as the *constraint set.*

The last two conditions are the reasons for the use of the term linear programming.

Linear programming techniques are widely used to solve a number of military, economic, industrial, and social problems. Three primary reasons for its wide use are:

1. A large variety of problems in diverse fields can be represented or at least approximated as linear programming models.
2. Efficient techniques for solving linear programming problems are available, and
3. Ease through which data variation (Sensitivity Analysis) can be handled through linear programming models.

At this point, we should point out that the solution procedures are iterative in nature, and hence even for moderate size problems, one has to resort to a digital computer for solution. This could be a serious disadvantage if the answer is not worth more than the cost to obtain it. In other words, the cost of analysis using linear programming may offset the savings that may result.

But with the advancement in computer technology, the solution of large linear programming problems by digital computer has not only become feasible but inexpensive as well.

2.2 FORMULATION OF LINEAR PROGRAMMING MODELS

The three basic steps in constructing a linear programming model are as follows:

Step I Identify the unknown variables to be determined (decision variables), and represent them in terms of algebraic symbols.

Step II Identify all the restrictions or constraints in the problem and express them as linear equations or inequalities which are linear functions of the unknown variables.

Step III Identify the objective or criterion and represent it as a linear function of the decision variables, which is to be maximized or minimized.

We shall illustrate these basic steps by formulating a number of linear programming problems. Model building is not a science but primarily an art and comes mainly by practice. Hence the reader is advised to work out many of the exercises given at the end of this chapter on problem formulation.

EXAMPLE 2.2-1 (PRODUCT-MIX PROBLEM)

The Handy-Dandy Company wishes to schedule the production of a kitchen appliance which requires two resources—labor and material. The company is considering three different models and its production engineering department has furnished the following data:

	Model		
	A	B	C
Labor (hours/unit)	7	3	6
Material (pounds/unit)	4	4	5
Profit ($/unit)	4	2	3

The supply of raw material is restricted to 200 pounds per day. The daily availability of manpower is 150 hours. Formulate a linear programming model to determine the daily production rate of the various models in order to maximize the total profit.

Formulation

Step I Identify the Decision Variables. The unknown activities to be determined are the daily rate of production for the three models.

Representing them by algebraic symbols,

x_A—Daily production of model A
x_B—Daily production of model B
x_C—Daily production of model C

Step II Identify the Constraints. In this problem the constraints are the limited availability of the two resources—labor and material.

Model A requires 7 hours of labor for each unit, and its production quantity is x_A. Hence, the requirement of manpower for model A alone will be $7x_A$ hours (assuming a linear relationship). Similarly, Models B and C will require $3x_B$ and $6x_C$ hours, respectively. Thus, the total requirement of labor will be $7x_A + 3x_B + 6x_C$, which should not exceed the available 150 hours. So, the labor constraint becomes,

$$7x_A + 3x_B + 6x_C \leqq 150$$

Similarly, the raw material requirements will be $4x_A$ pounds for Model A, $4x_B$ pounds for Model B, and $5x_C$ pounds for Model C. Thus, the raw material constraint is given by

$$4x_A + 4x_B + 5x_C \leqq 200$$

In addition, we restrict the variables x_A, x_B, x_C to have only nonnegative values. This is called the *nonnegativity constraint*, which the variables must satisfy. Most practical linear programming problems will have this nonnegative restriction on the decision variables. However, the general framework of linear programming is not restricted to nonnegative values, and methods for handling variables without sign restrictions will be discussed later.

Step III   Identify the Objective. The objective is to maximize the total profit from sales. Assuming that a perfect market exists for the product such that all that is produced can be sold, the total profit from sales becomes

$$Z = 4x_A + 2x_B + 3x_C$$

Thus, the linear programming model for our product mix problem becomes:

Find numbers x_A, x_B, x_C which will maximize

$$Z = 4x_A + 2x_B + 3x_C$$

subject to the constraints

$$7x_A + 3x_B + 6x_C \leqq 150$$
$$4x_A + 4x_B + 5x_C \leqq 200$$
$$x_A \geqq 0, \qquad x_B \geqq 0, \qquad x_C \geqq 0.$$

EXAMPLE 2.2-2 (A JOB-TRAINING PROBLEM)

A machine tool company conducts a job-training program for machinists. Trained machinists are used as teachers in the program at a ratio of one for every ten trainees. The training program lasts for one month. From past experience it has been found that out of ten trainees hired, only seven complete the program successfully (the unsuccessful trainees are released).

Trained machinists arc also needed for machining and the company's requirements for the next three months are as follows:

January	100
February	150
March	200

In addition, the company requires 250 trained machinists by April. There are 130 trained machinists available at the beginning of the year. Payroll costs per month are:

Each trainee	$400
Each trained machinist (machining or teaching)	700
Each trained machinist idle (Union contract forbids firing trained machinists)	500

Set up the linear programming problem that will produce the minimum cost hiring and training schedule and meet the company's requirements.

Formulation

First, we note that every month a trained machinist can do one of the following: (1) work a machine, (2) teach, or (3) stay idle.

Since the number of trained machinists machining is fixed, the only (unknown) decision variables are the number teaching and the number idle for each month. Thus, the variables to be determined are:

x_1—trained machinists teaching in January
x_2—trained machinists idle in January
x_3—trained machinists teaching in February
x_4—trained machinists idle in February
x_5—trained machinists teaching in March
x_6—trained machinists idle in March

The constraints require that a sufficient number of trained machinists be available each month for machining. This can be met by writing the following equation for each month:

Number machining + Number teaching + Number idle

$\qquad$ = Total trained machinists available at the beginning of the month

For example, for the month of January the constraint becomes

$$100 + x_1 + x_2 = 130$$

For February, the total number of trained machinists available will be the sum of trained machinists in January and those coming from the training program. In January, there are $10x_1$ trainees in the program, and out of those only $7x_1$ successfully complete and become trained machinists. Thus, the constraint for February becomes:

$$150 + x_3 + x_4 = 130 + 7x_1$$

Similarly, for March,

$$200 + x_5 + x_6 = 130 + 7x_1 + 7x_3$$

Since the company requires 250 trained machinists by April, we need the constraint

$$130 + 7x_1 + 7x_3 + 7x_5 = 250$$

Of course, all the variables are restricted to be nonnegative.

While writing the objective function, the cost of machinists doing machine work need not be included as it is a constant term. The relevant costs are only the cost of the training program (cost of trainees and teachers) and the cost of idle machinists. Thus, the objective function is

$$\text{Minimize:} \quad Z = 400(10x_1 + 10x_3 + 10x_5) + 700(x_1 + x_3 + x_5)$$
$$+ 500(x_2 + x_4 + x_6)$$

Thus, the linear programming problem becomes

$$\text{Minimize:} \quad Z = 4700x_1 + 500x_2 + 4700x_3 + 500x_4 + 4700x_5 + 500x_6$$

$$\begin{aligned}
\text{Subject to:} \quad x_1 + x_2 &\qquad\qquad\qquad\qquad = 30 \\
7x_1 &\quad - x_3 - x_4 \qquad\qquad = 20 \\
7x_1 &\quad + 7x_3 \quad - x_5 - x_6 = 70 \\
7x_1 &\quad + 7x_3 \quad + 7x_5 \quad = 120
\end{aligned}$$

$$x_1 \geq 0, \quad x_2 \geq 0, \quad x_3 \geq 0, \quad x_4 \geq 0, \quad x_5 \geq 0, \quad x_6 \geq 0$$

EXAMPLE 2.2-3 (ADVERTISING MEDIA SELECTION)

An Advertising Company wishes to plan an advertising campaign in three different media—television, radio, and magazines. The purpose of the advertising program is to reach as many potential customers as possible. Results of a market study are given below:

	Television			
	Day Time	Prime Time	Radio	Magazines
Cost of an advertising unit	$40,000	$75,000	$30,000	$15,000
Number of potential customers reached per unit	400,000	900,000	500,000	200,000
Number of women customers reached per unit	300,000	400,000	200,000	100,000

The company does not want to spend more than $800,000 on advertising. It further requires that (1) at least 2 million exposures take place among women; (2) advertising on television be limited to $500,000; (3) at least 3 advertising units be bought on daytime television, and two units during prime time; and (4) the number of advertising units on radio and magazine should each be between 5 and 10.

Formulation

Let x_1, x_2, x_3, and x_4 be the number of advertising units bought in daytime television, prime-time television, radio, and magazines, respectively.

The total number of potential customers reached (in thousands) = $400x_1 + 900x_2 + 500x_3 + 200x_4$. The restriction on the advertising budget is represented by

$$40,000x_1 + 75,000x_2 + 30,000x_3 + 15,000x_4 \leq 800,000$$

The constraint on the number of women customers reached by the advertising campaign becomes

$$300{,}000x_1 + 400{,}000x_2 + 200{,}000x_3 + 100{,}000x_4 \geq 2{,}000{,}000$$

The constraints on television advertising are

$$40{,}000x_1 + 75{,}000x_2 \leq 500{,}000$$

$$x_1 \geq 3$$

$$x_2 \geq 2$$

Since advertising units on radio and magazines should each be between 5 and 10, we get the following constraints:

$$5 \leq x_3 \leq 10$$

$$5 \leq x_4 \leq 10$$

The complete linear programming problem with some minor simplification is given below:

$$\text{Maximize:} \quad Z = 400x_1 + 900x_2 + 500x_3 + 200x_4$$

$$\text{Subject to:} \quad 40x_1 + 75x_2 + 30x_3 + 15x_4 \leq 800$$

$$30x_1 + 40x_2 + 20x_3 + 10x_4 \geq 200$$

$$40x_1 + 75x_2 \qquad\qquad \leq 500$$

$$x_1 \qquad\qquad\qquad \geq 3$$

$$x_2 \qquad\qquad \geq 2$$

$$x_3 \qquad \geq 5$$

$$x_3 \qquad \leq 10$$

$$x_4 \geq 5$$

$$x_4 \leq 10$$

Note: The first three constraints were simplified so that all the constraint coefficients do not have a large variation in magnitudes. This reduces the round-off errors in computer solutions.

EXAMPLE 2.2-4 (AN INSPECTION PROBLEM)

A company has two grades of inspectors, 1 and 2, who are to be assigned for a quality control inspection. It is required that at least 1800 pieces be inspected per 8-hour day. Grade 1 inspectors can check pieces at the rate of 25 per hour, with an accuracy of 98%. Grade 2 inspectors check at the rate of 15 pieces per hour, with an accuracy of 95%.

The wage rate of a Grade 1 inspector is $4.00 per hour, while that of a Grade 2 inspector is $3.00 per hour. Each time an error is made by an inspector, the cost to the company is $2.00. The company has available for the inspection job eight Grade 1 inspectors, and ten Grade 2 inspectors. The company wants to determine the optimal assignment of inspectors which will minimize the total cost of the inspection.

Formulation

Let x_1 and x_2 denote the number of Grade 1 and Grade 2 inspectors assigned for inspection. Since the number of available inspectors in each grade is limited, we have the following constraints:

$$x_1 \leq 8 \qquad \text{(Grade 1)}$$
$$x_2 \leq 10 \qquad \text{(Grade 2)}$$

The company requires at least 1800 pieces to be inspected daily. Thus, we get

$$8(25)x_1 + 8(15)x_2 \geq 1800$$

or

$$200x_1 + 120x_2 \geq 1800$$

In order to develop the objective function, we note that the company incurs two types of costs during inspection; wages paid to the inspector, and the cost of his inspection errors. The hourly cost of each Grade 1 inspector is

$$\$4 + 2(25)(0.02) = \$5 \text{ per hour}$$

Similarly, for each Grade 2 inspector

$$\$3 + 2(15)(0.05) = \$4.50 \text{ per hour}$$

Thus the objective function is to minimize the daily cost of inspection given by

$$Z = 8(5x_1 + 4.50x_2) = 40x_1 + 36x_2$$

The complete formulation of the linear programming problem thus becomes

$$\text{Minimize:} \quad Z = 40x_1 + 36x_2$$
$$\text{Subject to:} \quad x_1 \qquad\quad \leq 8$$
$$x_2 \leq 10$$
$$5x_1 + 3x_2 \geq 45$$
$$x_1 \geq 0, \qquad x_2 \geq 0$$

EXAMPLE 2.2-5 (AN INVESTMENT PROBLEM)

An investor has $100 with him on Monday. He has the following investment option available each day: "if he invests 2 units of money on one day, and 1 unit the next day, then on the following day, he can get a return of 4 units." The investor wants to determine the optimal investment policy that will maximize the money he has on Saturday of the same week.

Formulation

Since it is not given explicitly at what time of the day the various investments are made and returns are due, we will assume that any returns due that day may be used for investment immediately on the same day.

On each day, the investor has the following activities:

1. Follow up yesterday's investment with an additional 50%.
2. Initiate a fresh investment that day.
3. Save or hold cash for future investments.

Note that he has no choice regarding activity 1 if he wants to get a return from the investment initiated the previous day. But, regarding 2 and 3, he has full flexibility. So, we need two decision variables each day—one to represent fresh investment initiated that day, and the other to represent money saved that day.

x_1 = Fresh investment on Monday
s_1 = Money saved on Monday
x_2 = Fresh investment on Tuesday
s_2 = Money saved on Tuesday
x_3 = Fresh investment on Wednesday
s_3 = Money saved on Wednesday
x_4 = Fresh investment on Thursday
s_4 = Money saved on Thursday
s_5 = Money saved on Friday

No fresh investment is started on Friday since the return from that investment will not reach the investor before Sunday.

The constraints guarantee that on each day the following relationship is true: Total money invested (follow up or fresh investment) + Money saved = Total cash available.

For Monday: $x_1 + s_1 = 100$

For Tuesday: $\dfrac{x_1}{2} + x_2 + s_2 = s_1$

For Wednesday: $\dfrac{x_2}{2} + x_3 + s_3 = s_2 + 2x_1$

For Thursday: $\dfrac{x_3}{2} + x_4 + s_4 = s_3 + 2x_2$

For Friday: $\dfrac{x_4}{2} + s_5 = s_4 + 2x_3$

The total cash on hand on Saturday equals $s_5 + 2x_4$. Hence the objective function is to

$$\text{Maximize } Z = s_5 + 2x_4$$

EXAMPLE 2.2-6

Two products, A and B, are made involving two chemical operations for each. Each unit of product A requires 2 hours on Operation 1 and 3 hours on Operation 2. Each unit of product B requires 3 hours on Operation 1 and 4 hours on Operation 2. Available time for Operation 1 is 16 hours, and for Operation 2, 24 hours.

The production of product B also results in a by-product C at no extra cost. Though some of this by-product can be sold at a profit, the remainder has to be destroyed.

Product A sells for $4 profit per unit, while product B sells for $10 profit per unit. By-product C can be sold at a unit profit of $3, but if it cannot be sold, the destruction cost is $2 per unit. Forecasts show that up to 5 units of C can be sold. The company gets 2 units of C for each unit of B produced.

The problem is to determine the production quantity of A and B, keeping C in mind, so as to make the largest profit.

Formulation

This example illustrates how certain nonlinear objective functions can be handled by linear programming methods. The nonlinearity in the objective

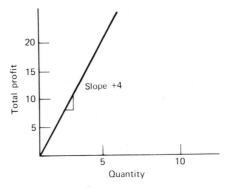

Figure 2.1

function is due to the differences in the unit profits of product C, depending on whether it is sold or destroyed. For products A and B, irrespective of the quantity produced, the unit profits are always $4 and $10, respectively. On the other hand, the unit profit of product C varies between +$3 and −$2. The nonlinearity in the objective function is apparent if a graph is plotted between total profit and production quantity. This is illustrated by Figs. 2.1 and 2.2 for products A and C, respectively. The nonlinear function shown by Fig. 2.2 is called a piece-wise linear function, since it is linear in the regions $(0, 5)$ and $(5, \infty)$. Hence, by partitioning the quantity of product C produced into two activities, namely part that is sold and part that is destroyed, the objective function could be represented as a linear function. Thus, the decision variables in this problem are:

x_1—Amount of product A produced
x_2—Amount of product B produced
x_3—Amount of product C sold
x_4—Amount of product C destroyed

The amount of product C produced $= x_3 + x_4$. Since each unit of product B produces 2 units of product C, we have

$$x_3 + x_4 = 2x_2$$

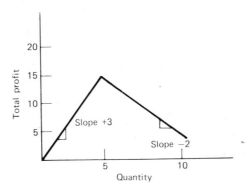

Figure 2.2

The constraint on the amount of product C sold becomes

$$x_3 \leqq 5$$

The constraint on available time on Operation 1 is given by

$$2x_1 + 3x_2 \leqq 16$$

For Operation 2,

$$3x_1 + 4x_2 \leqq 24$$

The objective function is to maximize the total profit:

$$Z = 4x_1 + 10x_2 + 3x_3 - 2x_4$$

Thus, the linear programming problem becomes

$$\text{Maximize:} \quad Z = 4x_1 + 10x_2 + 3x_3 - 2x_4$$
$$\text{Subject to:} \quad -2x_2 + x_3 + x_4 = 0$$
$$x_3 \qquad \leqq 5$$
$$2x_1 + 3x_2 \qquad \leqq 16$$
$$3x_1 + 4x_2 \qquad \leqq 24$$
$$x_1 \geqq 0, \qquad x_2 \geqq 0, \qquad x_3 \geqq 0, \qquad x_4 \geqq 0$$

It should be pointed out that product C should not be destroyed until its production exceeds 5. In other words, variable x_4 should not become positive until variable x_3 reaches its limit of 5 units. This restriction is automatically guaranteed by the objective function since the profit coefficient on x_3 is $+3$, while that on x_4 is only -2.

EXAMPLE 2.2-7

A machine shop has one drill press and five milling machines, which are to be used to produce an assembly consisting of two parts, 1 and 2. The productivity of each machine for the two parts is given below:

Part	Production Time in minutes per piece	
	Drill	Mill
1	3	20
2	5	15

It is desired to maintain a balanced loading on all machines such that no machine runs more than 30 minutes per day longer than any other machine (assume that the milling load is split evenly among all five milling machines).

Divide the work time of each machine to obtain the maximum number of completed assemblies assuming an 8-hour working day.

Formulation

Let x_1 = number of Part 1 produced per day and,
x_2 = number of Part 2 produced per day.

The load on each milling machine (in minutes) $= \dfrac{20x_1 + 15x_2}{5} = 4x_1 + 3x_2,$

whereas the load on the drill press (in minutes) $= 3x_1 + 5x_2$. Thus the time restriction on each milling machine is:

$$4x_1 + 3x_2 \leqq (8)(60) = 480$$

Similarly, for the drill press

$$3x_1 + 5x_2 \leqq 480$$

The machine balance constraint can be represented by

$$|(4x_1 + 3x_2) - (3x_1 + 5x_2)| \leqq 30$$

or

$$|x_1 - 2x_2| \leqq 30$$

This is a nonlinear constraint which can be replaced by the following two linear constraints:

$$x_1 - 2x_2 \leqq 30$$
$$-x_1 + 2x_2 \leqq 30$$

The number of completed assemblies cannot exceed the smaller value of Part 1 and Part 2 produced. Thus, the objective function is to maximize $Z = $ minimum(x_1, x_2). This is again a nonlinear function. However, another trick can be used to represent it as a linear function. Let $y = $ minimum of (x_1, x_2) where y represents the number of completed assemblies.

This means that

$$x_1 \geqq y$$
$$x_2 \geqq y$$

and the objective is to maximize $Z = y$. Thus, the complete linear programming formulation becomes

$$
\begin{aligned}
\text{Maximize:} \quad & Z = y \\
\text{Subject to:} \quad & 4x_1 + 3x_2 && \leqq 480 \\
& 3x_1 + 5x_2 && \leqq 480 \\
& x_1 - 2x_2 && \leqq 30 \\
& -x_1 + 2x_2 && \leqq 30 \\
& x_1 \quad -y && \geqq 0 \\
& x_2 - y && \geqq 0 \\
& x_1 \geqq 0, \quad x_2 \geqq 0, \quad y \geqq 0
\end{aligned}
$$

2.3   GRAPHICAL SOLUTION OF LINEAR PROGRAMS IN TWO VARIABLES

In the last section some examples were presented to illustrate how practical problems can be formulated mathematically as linear programming problems. The next step after formulation is to solve the problem mathematically to obtain the best possible solution. In this section, a graphical procedure to solve linear programming problems involving only two variables is discussed. Though in practice such small problems are usually not encountered, the graphical procedure is presented to illustrate some of the basic concepts used in solving large linear programming problems.

EXAMPLE 2.3-1

Recall the inspection problem given by Example 2.2-4:

$$\text{Minimize:} \quad Z = 40x_1 + 36x_2$$

$$\text{Subject to:} \quad x_1 \quad\quad \leq 8$$

$$x_2 \leq 10$$

$$5x_1 + 3x_2 \geq 45$$

$$x_1 \geq 0, \quad\quad x_2 \geq 0$$

In this problem, we are interested in determining the values of the variables x_1 and x_2 that will satisfy all the restrictions and give the least value for the objective function. As a first step in solving this problem, we want to identify all possible values of x_1 and x_2 that are nonnegative and satisfy the constraints. For example, a solution $x_1 = 8$, $x_2 = 10$ is positive and satisfies all the constraints. Such a solution is called a *feasible solution*. The set of all feasible solutions is called the *feasible region*. Solution of a linear program is merely finding the best feasible solution in the feasible region. The best feasible solution is called an *optimal solution* to the linear programming problem. In our example, an optimal solution is a feasible solution which minimizes the objective function $40x_1 + 36x_2$. The value of the objective function corresponding to an optimal solution is called the *optimal value* of the linear program.

To represent the feasible region in a graph, every constraint is plotted, and all values of x_1, x_2 that will satisfy these constraints are identified. The nonnegativity constraints imply that all feasible values of the two variables will lie in the first quadrant. The constraint $5x_1 + 3x_2 \geq 45$ requires that any feasible solution (x_1, x_2) to the problem should be on one side of the straight line $5x_1 + 3x_2 = 45$. The proper side is found by testing whether the origin satisfies the constraint or not. The line $5x_1 + 3x_2 = 45$ is first plotted by taking two convenient points (e.g., $x_1 = 0$, $x_2 = 15$, and $x_1 = 9$, $x_2 = 0$).

The proper side is indicated by an arrow directed above the line since the origin does not satisfy the constraint. Similarly, the constraints $x_1 \leq 8$, and $x_2 \leq 10$ are plotted. The feasible region is given by the shaded region ABC as shown in Fig. 2.3. Obviously there is an infinite number of feasible points in this region. Our objective is to identify the feasible point with the lowest value of Z.

Observe that the objective function, given by $Z = 40x_1 + 36x_2$, represents a straight line if the value of Z is fixed *a priori*. Changing the value of Z essentially translates the entire line to another straight line parallel to itself. In order to determine an optimal solution, the objective function line is drawn for a convenient value of Z such that it passes through one or more points in the feasible region. Initially Z is chosen as 600. By moving this line closer to the origin the value of Z is further decreased (see Fig. 2.3). The only limitation on this decrease is that the straight line $40x_1 + 36x_2 = Z$ contains at least one point in the feasible region ABC. This clearly occurs at the corner point A given by $x_1 = 8$, $x_2 = \frac{5}{3}$. This is the best feasible point giving the lowest value of Z as 380. Hence, $x_1 = 8$, $x_2 = \frac{5}{3}$ is an optimal solution, and $Z = 380$ is the *optimal value* for the linear program.

Thus for the inspection problem the optimal utilization is achieved by using eight Grade 1 inspectors and 1.67 Grade 2 inspectors. The fractional value $x_2 = \frac{5}{3}$ suggests that one of the Grade 2 inspectors is only utilized for 67% of the

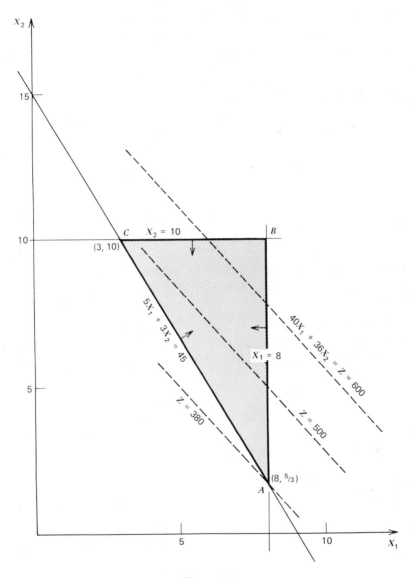

Figure 2.3

time. If this is not possible, the normal practice is to round off the fractional values to get an optimal integer solution as $x_1 = 8$, $x_2 = 2$. (In general, rounding off the fractional values will not produce an optimal integer solution.)

Unique Optimal Solution

In Example 2.3-1, the solution $x_1 = 8$, $x_2 = \frac{5}{3}$ is the only feasible point with the lowest value of Z. In other words, the values of Z corresponding to the other feasible solutions in Fig. 2.3 exceed the optimal value of 380. Hence for this problem, the solution $x_1 = 8$, $x_2 = \frac{5}{3}$ is the *unique optimal solution.*

Alternative Optimal Solutions

In some linear programming problems, there may exist more than one feasible solution such that their objective function values are equal to the optimal value of the linear program. In such cases, all of these feasible solutions are optimal solutions, and the linear program is said to have *alternative or multiple optimal solutions*. To illustrate this, consider the following linear programming problem:

EXAMPLE 2.3-2

$$\text{Maximize:} \quad Z = x_1 + 2x_2$$
$$\text{Subject to:} \qquad x_1 + 2x_2 \leq 10$$
$$x_1 + x_2 \geq 1$$
$$x_2 \leq 4$$
$$x_1 \geq 0, \qquad x_2 \geq 0$$

The feasible region is shown in Fig. 2.4. The objective function lines are drawn for $Z = 2$, 6, and 10. The optimal value for the linear program is 10, and the corresponding objective function line $x_1 + 2x_2 = 10$ coincides with side BC of the feasible region. Thus, the corner point feasible solutions $x_1 = 10$, $x_2 = 0$ (B), and $x_1 = 2$, $x_2 = 4$ (C), and all other feasible points on the line BC are optimal solutions.

Unbounded Solution

Some linear programming problems may not have an optimal solution. In other words, it is possible to find better feasible solutions continuously

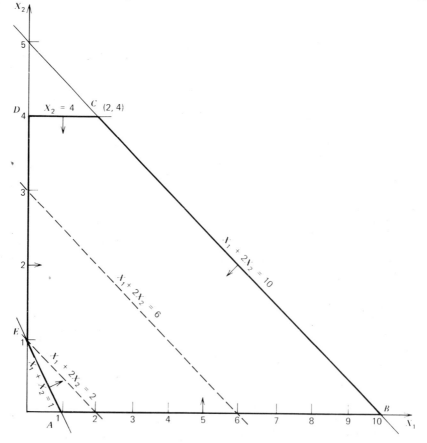

Figure 2.4

improving the objective function values. This would have been the case if the constraint $x_1 + 2x_2 \leq 10$ were not given in Example 2.3-2. In this case, moving farther away from the origin increases the objective function $x_1 + 2x_2$ and maximum Z would be $+\infty$. When there exists no finite optimum, the linear program is said to have an *unbounded solution*.

It is inconceivable for a practical problem to have an unbounded solution since this implies that one can make infinite profit from a finite amount of resources! If such a solution is obtained in a practical problem it generally means that one or more constraints have been omitted inadvertently during the initial formulation of the problem. These constraints would have prevented the objective function from assuming infinite values.

Conclusion

In Example 2.3-1, the optimal solution was unique and occurred at the corner point A in the feasible region. In Example 2.3-2, we had multiple optimal solutions to the problem which included two corner points B and C. In either case, one of the corner points of the feasible region was always an optimal solution. As a matter of fact, the following property is true for any linear programming problem:

Property 1.   If there exists an optimal solution to a linear programming problem, then at least one of the corner points of the feasible region will always qualify to be an optimal solution.

This is the fundamental property on which an iterative procedure called the *simplex method* for solving linear programming problems is based. Even though the feasible region of a linear programming problem contains an infinite number of points, an optimal solution can be determined by merely examining the finite number of corner points in the feasible region. For instance, in Example 2.3-2, the objective function was to maximize

$$Z = x_1 + 2x_2$$

The corner points of the feasible region were $A(1, 0)$, $B(10, 0)$, $C(2, 4)$, $D(0, 4)$, and $E(0, 1)$. Evaluating their Z values, we get $Z(A) = 1$, $Z(B) = 10$, $Z(C) = 10$, $Z(D) = 8$, and $Z(E) = 2$. Since the maximum value of Z occurs at corner points B and C, both are optimal solutions according to Property 1.

2.4   LINEAR PROGRAM IN STANDARD FORM

The standard form of a linear programming problem with m constraints and n variables can be represented as follows:

$$\text{Maximize (Minimize):} \quad Z = c_1 x_1 + c_2 x_2 + \cdots + c_n x_n$$

$$\text{Subject to:} \quad a_{11} x_1 + a_{12} x_2 + \cdots + a_{1n} x_n = b_1$$

$$a_{21} x_1 + a_{22} x_2 + \cdots + a_{2n} x_n = b_2$$

$$\vdots \qquad\qquad\qquad \vdots$$

$$a_{m1} x_1 + a_{m2} x_2 + \cdots + a_{mn} x_n = b_m$$

$$x_1 \geq 0, \; x_2 \geq 0, \ldots, x_n \geq 0$$

$$b_1 \geq 0, \; b_2 \geq 0, \ldots, b_m \geq 0$$

The main features of the standard form are:

1. The objective function is of the maximization or minimization type.
2. All constraints are expressed as equations.
3. All variables are restricted to be nonnegative.
4. The right-hand side constant of each constraint is nonnegative.

In matrix-vector notation, the standard linear programming problem can be expressed in a compact form as

$$\text{Maximize (Minimize):} \quad Z = \mathbf{cx}$$

$$\text{Subject to:} \qquad\qquad \mathbf{Ax} = \mathbf{b}$$

$$\mathbf{x} \geq 0$$

$$\mathbf{b} \geq 0$$

where $\mathbf{A}$ is an $(m \times n)$ matrix, $\mathbf{x}$ is an $(n \times 1)$ column vector, $\mathbf{b}$ is an $(m \times 1)$ column vector, and $\mathbf{c}$ is an $(1 \times n)$ row vector.

In other words,

$$\mathop{\mathbf{A}}_{(m \times n)} = \begin{bmatrix} a_{11} & a_{12} & \cdots & a_{1n} \\ a_{21} & a_{22} & \cdots & a_{2n} \\ \cdot & & & \\ \cdot & & & \\ \cdot & & & \\ a_{m1} & a_{m2} & \cdots & a_{mn} \end{bmatrix}, \quad \mathop{\mathbf{x}}_{(n \times 1)} = \begin{bmatrix} x_1 \\ x_2 \\ \cdot \\ \cdot \\ \cdot \\ x_n \end{bmatrix}$$

$$\mathop{\mathbf{b}}_{(m \times 1)} = \begin{bmatrix} b_1 \\ b_2 \\ \cdot \\ \cdot \\ \cdot \\ b_m \end{bmatrix}, \quad \text{and} \quad \mathop{\mathbf{c}}_{(1 \times n)} = (c_1, c_2, \ldots, c_n)$$

In practice, $\mathbf{A}$ is called the coefficient matrix, $\mathbf{x}$ is the decision vector, $\mathbf{b}$ is the requirement vector, and $\mathbf{c}$ is the profit (cost) vector of the linear program.

The standard form and its associated general notations are illustrated by the following example:

$$\text{Maximize:} \quad Z = 5x_1 + 2x_2 + 3x_3 - x_4 + x_5$$

$$\text{Subject to:} \qquad x_1 + 2x_2 + 2x_3 + x_4 \qquad = 8$$

$$3x_1 + 4x_2 + x_3 \qquad + x_5 = 7$$

$$x_1 \geq 0, \ldots, x_5 \geq 0$$

In this problem,

$$\mathop{\mathbf{A}}_{(2 \times 5)} = \begin{bmatrix} 1 & 2 & 2 & 1 & 0 \\ 3 & 4 & 1 & 0 & 1 \end{bmatrix}, \quad \mathop{\mathbf{x}}_{(5 \times 1)} = \begin{bmatrix} x_1 \\ x_2 \\ x_3 \\ x_4 \\ x_5 \end{bmatrix}$$

$$\mathop{\mathbf{b}}_{(2 \times 1)} = \begin{bmatrix} 8 \\ 7 \end{bmatrix}, \quad \text{and} \quad \mathop{\mathbf{c}}_{(1 \times 5)} = (5 \quad 2 \quad 3 \quad -1 \quad 1)$$

Reduction of a General Linear Program to a Standard Form

The simplex method for solving linear programming problems requires the problem to be expressed in standard form. But not all linear programming problems come in standard form. Very often the constraints are expressed as inequalities rather than equations. In some problems all the decision variables may not be nonnegative. Hence the first step in solving a linear program is to convert it to a problem in standard form.

Handling Inequality Constraints

Since the standard form requires all the constraints to be equations, inequality constraints have to be converted to equations. This can be done by the introduction of new variables to represent the slack between the left-hand side and right-hand side of each inequality. The new variables are called *slack or surplus variables.*

To illustrate the use of slack variables, consider Example 2.2-4. Here the constraint on the availability of Grade 1 inspectors was

$$x_1 \leq 8$$

This can be converted to an equation by introducing a slack variable, say x_3, as follows:

$$x_1 + x_3 = 8$$

Note that x_3 is also nonnegative, and it represents the number of Grade 1 inspectors not utilized. Similarly the second constraint becomes

$$x_2 + x_4 = 10, \quad \text{where} \quad x_4 \geq 0$$

To illustrate the use of surplus variables consider the third constraint on the minimum number of pieces to be inspected:

$$200x_1 + 120x_2 \geq 1800$$

By introducing a surplus variable, say x_5, the above inequality could be expressed as an equation as follows:

$$200x_1 + 120x_2 - x_5 = 1800$$

where x_5 is nonnegative and represents the number of extra pieces inspected over the daily minimum.

It should be emphasized here that slack and surplus variables are as much a part of the original problem as the variables used in the formulation of the linear program. These variables can remain positive throughout, and their values in the optimal solution give useful information about the problem.

Handling Variables Unrestricted in Sign

In some situations, it may become necessary to introduce a variable that can assume both positive and negative values. For instance, in Example 2.2-5, the total investment each day was restricted by the cash on hand that day. Suppose the investor can borrow money if necessary, there would then be a different interpretation to Monday's constraint:

$$x_1 + s_1 = 100$$

Here, s_1 can assume positive or negative values depending on whether s_1 represents money saved or money borrowed.

Since the standard form requires all the variables to be nonnegative, an unrestricted variable is generally replaced by the difference of two nonnegative variables. In other words, the following transformation of variables is used for s_1:

$$s_1 = x_5 - x_6$$

$$x_5 \geq 0, \qquad x_6 \geq 0$$

The value of s_1 is positive or negative depending on whether x_5 is larger or smaller than x_6.

As an illustration, consider the following nonstandard linear program:

EXAMPLE 2.4-1

Maximize: $Z = x_1 - 2x_2 + 3x_3$

Subject to: $x_1 + x_2 + x_3 \leq 7$

$x_1 - x_2 + x_3 \geq 2$

$3x_1 - x_2 - 2x_3 = -5$

$x_1, x_2 \geq 0$

x_3 unrestricted in sign

To convert the above problem to standard form,

1. Replace x_3 by $x_4 - x_5$ where $x_4, x_5 \geq 0$,
2. Multiply both sides of the last constraint by -1,
3. Introduce slack and surplus variables x_6 and x_7 to constraints 1 and 2 respectively, and
4. Assign zero profit for x_6 and x_7 so that the objective function is not altered.

Thus, the above problem reduces to the following standard form:

Maximize: $Z = x_1 - 2x_2 + 3x_4 - 3x_5$

Subject to: $x_1 + x_2 + x_4 - x_5 + x_6 \quad = 7$

$x_1 - x_2 + x_4 - x_5 \quad - x_7 = 2$

$-3x_1 + x_2 + 2x_4 - 2x_5 \quad = 5$

$x_1, x_2, x_4, x_5, x_6, x_7 \geq 0$

Let us review the basic definitions using the standard form of the linear programming problem given by

Maximize: $Z = \mathbf{cx}$

Subject to: $\mathbf{Ax = b},$

$\mathbf{x} \geq 0$

1. A *feasible solution* is a nonnegative vector $\mathbf{x}$ satisfying the constraints $\mathbf{Ax = b}$.
2. *Feasible region*, denoted by S, is the set of all feasible solutions. Mathematically,

$$S = \{\mathbf{x} \mid \mathbf{Ax = b}, \mathbf{x} \geq 0\}$$

If the feasible set S is empty, then the linear program is said to be *infeasible*.

3. An *optimal solution* is a vector $\mathbf{x}^o$ such that it is feasible and its value of the objective function $(\mathbf{cx}^o)$ is larger than that of any other feasible solution. Mathematically, $\mathbf{x}^o$ is optimal if and only if $\mathbf{x}^o \in S$, and $\mathbf{cx}^o \geq \mathbf{cx}$ for all $\mathbf{x} \in S$.

4. *Optimal value* of a linear program is the value of the objective function corresponding to the optimal solution. If $Z°$ is the optimal value, then $Z° = \mathbf{c}\mathbf{x}°$.
5. *Alternate optimum.* When a linear program has more than one optimal solution, it is said to have alternate optimal solutions. In this case, there exists more than one feasible solution having the same optimal value ($Z°$) for their objective functions.
6. *Unique optimum.* The optimal solution of a linear program is said to be unique when there exists no other optimal solution.
7. *Unbounded solution.* When a linear program does not possess a finite optimum (i.e., $\max Z \to +\infty$), it is said to have an unbounded solution.

2.5 SOLVING SYSTEMS OF LINEAR EQUATIONS

The central mathematical problem of linear programming is to find the solution of a system of linear equations which maximizes *or* minimizes a given linear objective function. Systems of linear equations can be solved by the classical Gauss-Jordan elimination procedure. In this section, a brief review of this procedure is given through an example.

EXAMPLE 2.5-1

Consider the following system of two equations in five unknowns denoted by

$$(S_1) \qquad \begin{aligned} x_1 - 2x_2 + x_3 - 4x_4 + 2x_5 &= 2 \qquad &(2.1) \\ x_1 - x_2 - x_3 - 3x_4 - x_5 &= 4 \qquad &(2.2) \end{aligned}$$

Since there are more unknowns than equations, this system will have more than one solution. (As a matter of fact, the existence of multiple solutions to the constraint equations make the solution of linear programs nontrivial.) The collection of all possible solutions to the system is called the *solution set*.

Definition

Two systems of equations are said to be *equivalent* if both systems have the same solution set. In other words, a solution to one system is automatically a solution to the other system and vice versa.

The method of solving a system of equations is to get an equivalent system which is easy to solve. By solving the simple system, we simultaneously get the solutions to the original system.

There are two types of elementary row operations that one can use to obtain equivalent systems.

1. Multiply any equation in the system by a positive or negative number.
2. Add to any equation, a constant multiple (positive, negative, or zero) of any other equation in the system.

An equivalent system to system S_1 can be obtained by multiplying Eq. 2.1 by -1, and adding to Eq. 2.2 as follows:

$$(S_2) \qquad \begin{aligned} x_1 - 2x_2 + x_3 - 4x_4 + 2x_5 &= 2 \qquad &(2.3) \\ x_2 - 2x_3 + x_4 - 3x_5 &= 2 \qquad &(2.4) \end{aligned}$$

From system S_2, another equivalent system can be obtained by multiplying Eq. 2.4 by 2, and adding to Eq. 2.3. This gives system S_3:

$$(S_3) \qquad \begin{aligned} x_1 - 3x_3 - 2x_4 - 4x_5 &= 6 \qquad &(2.5) \\ x_2 - 2x_3 + x_4 - 3x_5 &= 2 \qquad &(2.6) \end{aligned}$$

Since systems S_1, S_2, and S_3 are equivalent, a solution to one automatically gives a solution to the other two. In this case, it is easy to write out all the possible solutions to system S_3. For example, setting $x_3 = x_4 = x_5 = 0$ gives $x_1 = 6$, $x_2 = 2$, which is a solution to all the three systems. Other solutions to system S_3 may be obtained by choosing arbitrary values for x_3, x_4, x_5 and finding the corresponding values of x_1 and x_2 from Eqs. 2.5 and 2.6. All of these solutions are solutions to the original system. Systems like S_3 are called *canonical systems*. In Example 2.5-1, the equivalent canonical system was obtained by eliminating the coefficients of x_1 and x_2 from Eqs. 2.2 and 2.1, respectively. The variables x_1 and x_2 are called the *basic variables* of the canonical system, but any other two variables could have been made the basic variables if their coefficients were eliminated by suitable elementary operations. At times, the introduction of slack variables for obtaining the standard form automatically produces a canonical system.

Definition
A variable x_j is said to be a *basic* variable in a given equation if it appears with a unit coefficient in that equation and zeros in all other equations.

Those variables which are not basic are called *nonbasic variables*.

By applying the elementary row operations, a given variable can be made a basic variable. This is called a *pivot operation*.

Pivot Operation
A *pivot operation* is a sequence of elementary operations which reduces a given system to an equivalent system in which a specified variable has a unit coefficient in one equation and zeros elsewhere.

In order to get a canonical system, a sequence of pivot operations must be performed on the original system so that there exists at least one basic variable in each equation. The number of basic variables is decided by the number of equations in the system.

Basic Solution
The solution obtained from a canonical system by setting the nonbasic variables to zero and solving for the basic variables is called a *basic solution*.

In Example 2.5-1, a basic solution is given by $x_1 = 6$, $x_2 = 2$, $x_3 = 0$, $x_4 = 0$, and $x_5 = 0$. This is easily obtained by inspection from the canonical system S_3. Since the values of all the variables are nonnegative, this basic solution is also a feasible solution. We call such basic solutions *basic feasible solutions*.

Basic Feasible Solution
A *basic feasible solution* is a basic solution in which the values of the basic variables are nonnegative.

In Example 2.5-1, a canonical system was obtained using x_1 and x_2 as basic variables. The choice of x_1 and x_2 as basic variables was purely arbitrary. We could have obtained a different canonical system (with a different basic solution) by choosing x_3 and x_4 as basic variables. As a matter of fact, any two variables could have been selected as basic variables out of the possible five variables to obtain a canonical system and a basic solution. This means that the number of basic solutions possible is

$$\binom{5}{2} = \frac{5!}{2!\,3!} = 10$$

This can be extended to the constraint equations of a standard linear program developed in Section 2.4. With m constraints and n variables, the maximum number of basic solutions to the standard linear program is finite and is given by

$$\binom{n}{m} = \frac{n!}{m!\,(n-m)!}$$

By definition, every basic feasible solution is also a basic solution. Hence, the maximum number of basic feasible solutions is also limited by the above expression.

At the end of Section 2.3 it was pointed out that whenever there is an optimal solution to a linear program, one of the corner points of the feasible region is always optimal. It can be shown that every corner point of the feasible region corresponds to a basic feasible solution of the constraint equations. This means that an optimal solution to a linear program can be obtained by merely examining its basic feasible solutions. This will be a finite process since the number of basic feasible solutions cannot exceed $\dfrac{n!}{m!\,(n-m)!}$.

A naive approach to solve a linear program (which has an optimal solution) would be to generate all possible basic feasible solutions through canonical reduction, and determine which basic feasible solution gives the best objective function value. But, the *simplex method* for solving linear programs does this in a more efficient manner by examining only a fraction of the total number of basic feasible solutions!

The details of the simplex method will be developed in the following sections.

2.6 PRINCIPLES OF THE SIMPLEX METHOD

The *simplex method* as developed by G. B. Dantzig is an iterative procedure for solving linear programming problems expressed in standard form. In addition to the standard form, the simplex method requires that the constraint equations be expressed as a canonical system from which a basic feasible solution can be readily obtained. The general steps of the simplex method are as follows:

1. Start with an initial basic feasible solution in canonical form.
2. Improve the initial solution if possible by finding another basic feasible solution with a better objective function value. At this step the simplex method implicitly eliminates from consideration all those basic feasible solutions whose objective function values are worse than the present one. This makes the procedure more efficient than the naive approach mentioned earlier.
3. Continue to find better basic feasible solutions improving the objective function values. When a particular basic feasible solution cannot be improved further, it becomes an optimal solution and the simplex method terminates.

We shall begin by illustrating the basic principles of the simplex method with the help of an example.

EXAMPLE 2.6-1

$$\text{Maximize} \quad Z = 5x_1 + 2x_2 + 3x_3 - x_4 + x_5$$

$$\text{Subject to} \quad x_1 + 2x_2 + 2x_3 + x_4 \qquad = 8 \qquad (2.7)$$

$$3x_1 + 4x_2 + x_3 \qquad + x_5 = 7 \qquad (2.8)$$

$$x_1 \geqq 0, \qquad x_2 \geqq 0, \qquad x_3 \geqq 0, \qquad x_4 \geqq 0, \qquad x_5 \geqq 0$$

The above linear programming problem is in standard form since (1) all the variables are nonnegative, (2) all the constraints are equations, and (3) the right-hand side constants are positive. Moreover, the variable x_4 appears only in Eq. 2.7 with a unit coefficient. Hence x_4 is a basic variable in that equation. Similarly, x_5 is a basic variable in Eq. 2.8. Thus, we have a canonical system with x_4 and x_5 as basic variables. The corresponding basic solution is given by $x_1 = x_2 = x_3 = 0$, $x_4 = 8$, $x_5 = 7$. Since all the variables have nonnegative values, the above solution is also a basic feasible solution, and its objective function value is given by

$$Z = 5(0) + 2(0) + 3(0) - 1(8) + 1(7) = -1$$

It should be pointed out here that some linear-programming problems may not have a readily available canonical system and a basic feasible solution. In such problems one has to find a basic feasible solution in canonical form before initiating the simplex method. Such complications will be discussed later in Section 2.8.

Improving a Basic Feasible Solution

Given the initial basic feasible solution as $x_1 = x_2 = x_3 = 0$, $x_4 = 8$, $x_5 = 7$ with $Z = -1$, the simplex method checks whether it is possible to find a better basic feasible solution with a larger value of Z. This is done by first examining whether the present solution is optimal. In the case where it is not optimal, the simplex method obtains an *adjacent basic feasible solution* with a larger value of Z (or at least as large).

Definition

An *Adjacent Basic Feasible Solution* differs from the present basic feasible solution in exactly one basic variable.

In order to obtain an adjacent basic feasible solution, the simplex method makes one of the basic variables a nonbasic variable, and in its place a nonbasic variable is brought in as a basic variable. The problem is to select the appropriate basic and nonbasic variables such that an exchange between them will give the maximum improvement to the objective function.

In any basic feasible solution, the basic variables can assume positive values while the nonbasic variables are always held at zero. Hence, making a nonbasic variable a basic variable is equivalent to increasing its value from zero to a positive quantity. Of course, the choice is made based on which nonbasic variable can improve the value of Z. This is determined by increasing the nonbasic variable by one unit and examining the resulting change in the value of the objective function.

To illustrate, consider the nonbasic variable x_1. Let us increase its value from 0 to 1 and study its effect on the objective function. Since we are interested in examining adjacent basic feasible solutions only, the values of the other two nonbasic variables, x_2 and x_3, will not change. After setting their values to zero, Eqs. 2.7 and 2.8 can be rewritten as,

$$x_1 + x_4 \quad = 8 \tag{2.9}$$
$$3x_1 \quad + x_5 = 7 \tag{2.10}$$

As x_1 increases to 1, the value of the basic variable x_4 will decrease to 7 to satisfy Eq. 2.9. Similarly, the value of x_5 will decrease to 4 as x_1 increases to 1. Hence the new feasible solution is given by

$$x_1 = 1, \qquad x_2 = 0, \qquad x_3 = 0, \qquad x_4 = 7, \qquad \text{and} \qquad x_5 = 4$$

The new value of the objective function is

$$Z = 5(1) + 2(0) + 3(0) - 1(7) + 1(4) = 2$$

Hence, the net change in the value of Z per unit increase in x_1

$$= \text{New value of } Z - \text{old value of } Z$$
$$= 2 - (-1) = 3$$

This value is called the *relative profit* of the nonbasic variable x_1 as opposed to its actual profit of 5 units in the objective function.

Since the relative profit on x_1 is positive, the objective function can be increased further by increasing x_1. Hence the initial basic feasible solution is not optimal. The relative profit coefficient implies that Z will be increased by 3 units for every unit increase on the nonbasic variable x_1. Naturally one would like to increase x_1 as much as possible so as to get the largest increase in the objective function.

Looking back at the constraints, it is clear that x_1 cannot be increased indefinitely. As x_1 increases, both the basic variables x_4 and x_5 will decrease, and their values must remain nonnegative for the solution to remain feasible. From Eq. 2.9, we see that x_4 will become negative if x_1 is increased beyond 8. Similarly from Eq. 2.10, x_5 will turn negative if x_1 were to increase beyond 7/3. Thus x_4 limits the increase on x_1 to 8, while x_5 limits it to 7/3. In order to maintain all the variables nonnegative, the maximum increase on x_1 is given by the lower of the two limits. Thus, the maximum increase on $x_1 = \text{minimum of}$ $[8/1, 7/3] = 7/3$.

In some problems it is possible for a nonbasic variable to have a negative or zero coefficient in some constraints. In these constraints the corresponding basic variables will not decrease or become negative as we increase the nonbasic variable. Hence, these basic variables will not limit the increase of the nonbasic variable at all.

A unit increase in x_1 increases Z by 3 units. Since x_1 can be increased to a maximum of 7/3, the net increase in the objective function $= 3(7/3) = 7$. Also, when x_1 is increased to 7/3, the basic variable x_5 turns zero and is made a nonbasic variable. The nonbasic variable x_1 is made a basic variable in the second constraint. Thus the new basic feasible solution will be

$$x_1 = \frac{7}{3}, \quad x_2 = 0, \quad x_3 = 0, \quad x_4 = \frac{17}{3}, \quad x_5 = 0, \quad \text{and} \quad Z = 6$$

The new canonical system corresponding to the improved basic feasible solution is obtained by performing a pivot operation on the variable x_1 as follows:

1. Divide Eq. 2.8 by 3 to reduce the coefficient of x_1 to 1.
2. Multiply Eq. 2.8 by $-1/3$ and add it to Eq. 2.7 to eliminate x_1.

$$\frac{2}{3}x_2 + \frac{5}{3}x_3 + x_4 - \frac{1}{3}x_5 = \frac{17}{3}$$

$$x_1 + \frac{4}{3}x_2 + \frac{1}{3}x_3 \qquad + \frac{1}{3}x_5 = \frac{7}{3}$$

Once again the simplex method checks whether the above basic feasible solution is optimal by calculating the relative profits for all the nonbasic variables. If any of them turns out to be positive, then a new basic feasible solution with an improved value of Z is obtained as before. This process is repeated until the relative profits of all the nonbasic variables are negative or zero. This implies that the current basic feasible solution cannot be improved further and hence becomes an optimal solution to the linear programming problem.

Condition of Optimality

In a *maximization* problem, a basic feasible solution is optimal if the relative profits of its nonbasic variables are all *negative or zero*.

Summary of the Simplex Method

In summary, the basic steps of the simplex method for a *maximization* problem are as follows:

Step I   Start with an initial basic feasible solution in canonical form.

Step II   Check whether the current basic feasible solution is optimal. At this solution, the relative profits of all the nonbasic variables are computed. These represent the net change in the objective function value per unit increase in each nonbasic variable. If these coefficients are negative or zero, the current solution is optimal. Otherwise, go to Step III.

Step III Select a nonbasic variable to be the new basic variable in the solution. A general rule is to select the nonbasic variable with the largest relative profit so that it may give a larger increase in the value of Z.

Step IV. Determine the basic variable which will be replaced by the nonbasic variable. For this we examine each of the constraints to determine how far the nonbasic variable can be increased. For those constraints in which the nonbasic variable has a positive coefficient, the limit is given by the ratio of the right-hand side constant to that positive coefficient. For the other constraints the limit is set to ∞. The constraint with the lowest limit is determined, and the basic variable in that constraint will be replaced by the nonbasic variable. Since the determination of the variable to leave the basic set involves the calculation of ratios and selection of the minimum ratio, this rule is generally called the *minimum ratio rule*.

Step V.   Find the new canonical system and the basic feasible solution by pivot operation. Return to Step II.

2.7 SIMPLEX METHOD IN TABLEAU FORM

In the previous section, we studied the basic principles of the simplex method for solving linear programming problems. These involved successively finding improved basic feasible solutions until the optimum is reached. The various steps of the simplex method can be carried out in a more compact manner by using a tableau form to represent the constraints and the objective function. In addition, by developing some simple formulae, the various calculations can be made mechanical. The use of the tableau form has made the simplex method more efficient and convenient for computer implementation.

The tableau representation is nothing more than writing the problem in a detached coefficient form. To illustrate this, the initial basic feasible solution of Example 2.6-1 can be expressed by the following tableau:

	C_j	5	2	3	−1	1	
C_B	Basis	x_1	x_2	x_3	x_4	x_5	Constants
−1	x_4	1	2	2	1	0	8
1	x_5	3	4	1	0	1	7

Here *basis* refers to the basic variables in the current basic feasible solution. The values of the basic variables are given under the column *constants*. The symbol C_j denotes the coefficient of the variable x_j in the objective function, while C_B denotes the coefficients of the basic variables only.

From the above table, the basic feasible solution is immediately written as $x_4 = 8$, $x_5 = 7$, and $x_1 = x_2 = x_3 = 0$. The value of the objective function is given by the inner product of the vectors C_B and *constants* as follows:

$$Z = (-1, 1)\binom{8}{7} = -8 + 7 = -1$$

In order to check if the above basic feasible solution is optimal, we need the relative profits of all the nonbasic variables. These can be calculated easily by a simple formula known as the *Inner Product Rule*. The relative profit coefficient of the variable x_j, denoted by $\bar{C}_j$, is given by:

$$\bar{C}_j = C_j - \left[\begin{array}{l}\text{inner product of } C_B, \text{ and the column} \\ \text{corresponding to } x_j \text{ in the canonical system}\end{array}\right]$$

For example,

$$\bar{C}_1 = 5 - (-1, 1)\binom{1}{3} = 5 - (-1 + 3) = 3$$

$$\bar{C}_2 = 2 - (-1, 1)\binom{2}{4} = 2 - (-2 + 4) = 0$$

$$\bar{C}_3 = 3 - (-1, 1)\binom{2}{1} = 3 - (-2 + 1) = 4$$

If the above calculations were carried out for x_4 and x_5, their $\bar{C}_j$ values would be zero since they are the basic variables. It is easy to verify that the inner product rule is a compact way of doing the relative profit calculations given earlier in Section 2.6.

Note that the coefficient of x_2 in the objective function is 2, which is larger than those of the present basic variables x_4 and x_5. But any increase in x_2 will not contribute to an increase in the total profit Z because its relative profit is zero. We also note that the unit profit of x_3 is less than that of x_1; but x_3 contributes to a larger (per unit) increase in the Z value than x_1. This shows that the mere use of the objective function coefficient (C_j) to measure the worth of a nonbasic variable is incorrect. The relative profit coefficient (denoted by $\bar{C}_j$) reflects the true change in Z from its present value since it also takes into account the cost of the resources used by the nonbasic activity.

Now, the initial simplex tableau can be constructed by appending the *relative profit row* or the $\bar{C}$ row to the previous table.

Tableau 1
(INITIAL SOLUTION)

C_B	Basis	C_j x_1	x_2	x_3	x_4	x_5	Constants
		5	2	3	−1	1	
−1	x_4	1	2	2	1	0	8
1	x_5	3	4	1	0	1	7
	$\bar{C}$ Row	3	0	4	0	0	$Z = -1$

Since there are some positive values in the $\bar{C}$ row, the current basic feasible solution is not optimal. The nonbasic variable x_3 gives the greatest per unit increase in Z, and hence it will be chosen as the new variable to enter the basis.

In order to decide which basic variable is going to be replaced, we apply the minimum ratio rule as discussed in Section 2.6 by calculating the limits for each constraint as follows:

Row Number	Basic Variable	Upper Limit on x_3
1	x_4	$8/2 = 4$ (minimum)
2	x_5	$7/1 = 7$

The minimum ratio is obtained in the first row, which is generally called the *pivot row*. Thus when the nonbasic variable x_3 is increased to its maximum of 4 units, the basic variable in the pivot row (i.e., x_4) reduces to zero and becomes a nonbasic variable. The new basis contains x_3 and x_5 as basic variables. The new canonical system is obtained by performing a pivot operation as follows:

1. Divide the pivot row by 2 to make the coefficient of x_3 unity.
2. Multiply the pivot row by $-1/2$, and add it to the second row to eliminate x_3.

Tableau 2

C_B	Basis	C_j x_1	x_2	x_3	x_4	x_5	Constants
		5	2	3	−1	1	
3	x_3	1/2	1	1	1/2	0	4
1	x_5	5/2	3	0	−1/2	1	3
	$\bar{C}$ Row	1	−4	0	−2	0	$Z = 15$

From Tableau 2 the new basic feasible solution is given by $x_1 = 0$, $x_2 = 0$, $x_3 = 4$, $x_4 = 0$, $x_5 = 3$, and the value of Z is 15. In order to check whether this solution is optimal, the new relative profit coefficients have to be calculated. This can be done by applying the inner product rule as before. On the other hand, it is also possible to calculate the $\bar{C}$-row coefficients through the pivot operation. Since x_3 will be the new basic variable, its relative profit coefficient in Tableau 2 should become zero. This can be done by multiplying the first row of Tableau 1 (the pivot row) by -2, and adding it to the $\bar{C}$ row. This will automatically give the new $\bar{C}$ row for Tableau 2!

Since $\bar{C}_1$ is positive, Tableau 2 is not optimal. An improvement in the objective function may be obtained by making x_1 a basic variable. Once again the minimum ratio rule is used to determine which basic variable will leave the basis.

Row Number	Basic Variable	Upper Limit on x_1
1	x_3	$4/(1/2) = 8$
2	x_5	$3/(5/2) = 6/5$ (minimum)

The minimum ratio occurs in the second row. The basic variable x_5 will be replaced by x_1 to form the new basis. A pivot operation gives the following basic feasible solution in Tableau 3:

Tableau 3

C_B	Basis	C_j 5	2	3	-1	1	Constants
		x_1	x_2	x_3	x_4	x_5	Constants
3	x_3	0	2/5	1	3/5	$-1/5$	17/5
5	x_1	1	6/5	0	$-1/5$	2/5	6/5
	$\bar{C}$ Row	0	$-26/5$	0	$-9/5$	$-2/5$	$Z = 81/5$

All the coefficients of the $\bar{C}$ row are nonpositive. This implies that no further improvement in the objective function is possible. Hence, the current basic feasible solution $x_1 = 6/5$, $x_2 = 0$, $x_3 = 17/5$, $x_4 = 0$, $x_5 = 0$ is an optimal solution, and $Z = 81/5$ is the optimal value for the linear program.

Summary of the Computational Steps
In summary, the computational steps of the simplex method in tableau form for a *maximization problem* are as follows:

Step I.   Express the problem in standard form.

Step II.   Start with an initial basic feasible solution in canonical form and set up the initial tableau. (In Section 2.9, we discuss how to find an initial basic feasible solution in canonical form if none exists by inspection.)

Step III.   Use the inner product rule to find the relative profit coefficients ($\bar{C}$ row).

Step IV.   If all the $\bar{C}_j$ coefficients are nonpositive, the current basic feasible solution is optimal. Otherwise, select the nonbasic variable with the most positive $\bar{C}_j$ value to enter the basis.

Step V.   Apply the minimum ratio rule to determine the basic variable to leave the basis.

Step VI.   Perform the pivot operation to get the new tableau and the basic feasible solution.

Step VII.   Compute the relative profit coefficients by using the pivot operation or the inner product rule. Return to Step IV.

Each sequence of Steps IV–VII is called an *iteration* of the simplex method. Thus each iteration gives a new tableau and an improved basic feasible solution. The efficiency of the simplex method depends on the number of basic feasible solutions it examines before reaching the optimal solution. Hence the number of iterations is an important factor in simplex calculations.

EXAMPLE 2.7-1
Let us solve by the simplex method the following problem:

$$\text{Maximize:} \quad Z = 3x_1 + 2x_2$$
$$\text{Subject to:} \quad -x_1 + 2x_2 \leqq 4$$
$$3x_1 + 2x_2 \leqq 14$$
$$x_1 - x_2 \leqq 3$$
$$x_1 \geqq 0, \quad x_2 \geqq 0$$

Converting the problem to standard form by the addition of slack variables, we obtain

$$\text{Maximize:} \quad Z = 3x_1 + 2x_2$$
$$\text{Subject to:} \quad -x_1 + 2x_2 + x_3 \qquad\qquad = 4$$
$$3x_1 + 2x_2 \qquad + x_4 \qquad = 14$$
$$x_1 - x_2 \qquad\qquad + x_5 = 3$$
$$x_1 \geqq 0, \quad x_2 \geqq 0, \quad x_3 \geqq 0,$$
$$x_4 \geqq 0, \quad x_5 \geqq 0$$

We have a basic feasible solution in canonical form with x_3, x_4, and x_5 as basic variables.

The initial tableau is given below:

Tableau 1

C_B	Basis	C_j	3	2	0	0	0	
			x_1	x_2	x_3	x_4	x_5	Constants
0	x_3		−1	2	1	0	0	4
0	x_4		3	2	0	1	0	14
0	x_5		①	−1	0	0	1	3
	$\bar{C}$ Row		3	2	0	0	0	$Z = 0$

The nonbasic variable x_1 has the largest relative profit in the $\bar{C}$ row. Hence x_1 enters the basis. Applying the minimum ratio rule, the ratios are $(\infty, 14/3, 3/1)$. The minimum ratio is 3 and x_1 replaces x_5 from the basis. This is indicated by circling the coefficient of x_1 in the pivot row. The circled element is called the *pivot element.* Performing the pivot operation, we get

Tableau 2

C_B	Basis	C_j 3 x_1	2 x_2	0 x_3	0 x_4	0 x_5	Constants
0	x_3	0	1	1	0	1	7
0	x_4	0	⑤	0	1	−3	5
3	x_1	1	−1	0	0	1	3
	$\bar{C}$ Row	0	5	0	0	−3	$Z = 9$

Still the $\bar{C}$ row has a positive element indicating that the nonbasic variable x_2 can improve the objective function further. To apply the minimum ratio rule, we find the minimum of $(7/1, 5/5, \infty)$. This implies that x_2 replaces the basic variable x_4. The next basic feasible solution after the pivot operation is given below:

Tableau 3

C_B	Basis	C_j 3 x_1	2 x_2	0 x_3	0 x_4	0 x_5	Constants
0	x_3	0	0	1	−1/5	8/5	6
2	x_2	0	1	0	1/5	−3/5	1
3	x_1	1	0	0	1/5	2/5	4
	$\bar{C}$ Row	0	0	0	−1	0	$Z = 14$

Since none of the coefficients in the $\bar{C}$ row are positive, this tableau is optimal. An optimal solution is given by $x_1 = 4$, $x_2 = 1$, $x_3 = 6$, $x_4 = 0$, $x_5 = 0$, and the optimal value of Z is 14.

Alternate Optima

In Tableau 3, the nonbasic variable x_5 has a relative profit of zero. This means that any increase in x_5 will produce no change in the objective function value. In other words x_5 can be made a basic variable and the resulting basic feasible solution will also have Z as 14. By definition, any feasible solution whose value of Z equals the optimal value is also an optimal solution. Hence, we have an alternate optimal solution to this linear program. This can be obtained by making x_5 a basic variable. By the minimum ratio rule x_3 leaves the basis, and we have an alternative optimal tableau as shown below:

Tableau 4

| C_B | Basis | C_j 3 | 2 | 0 | 0 | 0 | |
		x_1	x_2	x_3	x_4	x_5	Constants
0	x_5	0	0	5/8	−1/8	`1	15/4
2	x_2	0	1	3/8	1/8	0	13/4
3	x_1	1	0	−1/4	1/4	0	5/2
$\bar{C}$ Row		0	0	0	−1	0	$Z = 14$

Thus the alternate optimal solution is given by $x_1 = 5/2$, $x_2 = 13/4$, $x_3 = 0$, $x_4 = 0$, and $x_5 = 15/4$.

In general, an alternate optimal solution is indicated whenever there exists a nonbasic variable whose relative profit ($\bar{C}_j$ coefficient) is zero in the optimal tableau.

Unique Optimum

In Example 2.6-1, the optimal solution given by Tableau 3 is unique because all the nonbasic variables have a negative value for their relative profits. This means that any increase in x_2, x_4, or x_5 will result in an immediate decrease in the objective function value. Hence it is not possible to find another feasible solution whose value of Z equals 81/5.

Minimization Problems

Let us now consider how to solve minimization problems. Recall that the coefficients in the $\bar{C}$ row give the net change in the value of Z per unit increase in the nonbasic variable. A negative coefficient in the $\bar{C}$ row indicates that the corresponding nonbasic variable (when increased) will reduce the value of the objective function. Hence in minimization problems, only those nonbasic variables with negative $\bar{C}_j$ values are eligible to enter the basis and improve the objective function. The optimal solution is obtained when all the coefficients in the $\bar{C}$ row are nonnegative. Thus all the seven steps of the simplex method outlined earlier can be used for solving minimization problems with a minor modification in Step IV as follows:

Modified Step IV.   If all the coefficients in the $\bar{C}$ row are positive or zero, the current basic feasible solution is optimal. Otherwise, select the nonbasic variable with the lowest (most negative) value in the $\bar{C}$ row to enter the basis.

An Alternative Approach to Minimization Problems

Another method of solving a minimization problem is to convert it to an equivalent maximization problem, and then use the simplex method as outlined for a maximization problem. The conversion to a maximization problem is easily done by multiplying the objective function of the minimum problem by minus one. For example, consider a minimization problem:

$$\text{Minimize:} \quad Z = 40x_1 + 36x_2$$
$$\text{Subject to:} \quad x_1 \qquad \leqq 8$$
$$x_2 \leqq 10$$
$$5x_1 + 3x_2 \geqq 45$$
$$x_1 \geqq 0, \qquad x_2 \geqq 0$$

This is equivalent to the following maximization problem:

$$\text{Maximize:} \quad Z' = -40x_1 - 36x_2$$
$$\text{Subject to:} \quad x_1 \qquad \leqq 8$$
$$x_2 \leqq 10$$
$$5x_1 + 3x_2 \geqq 45$$
$$x_1 \geqq 0, \qquad x_2 \geqq 0$$

The optimal solutions to both the problems will be the same, while their optimal values will differ by a minus sign. In other words,

the minimum value of $Z = -$(the maximum value of Z')

2.8 COMPUTATIONAL PROBLEMS

There are a number of computational problems that may arise during the actual application of the simplex method for solving a linear programming problem. Some of these problems have already been discussed. In this section, we discuss other complications that may occur and how to resolve them.

Ties in the Selection of the Nonbasic Variable

The selection of a nonbasic variable to enter the basis is done by determining which nonbasic variable gives the largest (per unit) improvement in the objective function. In other words, in a maximization problem, the variable with the largest positive value in the $\bar{C}$ row is chosen. In case there exists more than one variable with the same largest value in the $\bar{C}$ row, then we have a tie for selecting the nonbasic variable. The general rule is to select any one of them arbitrarily even though a wrong choice may increase the number of simplex tableaus or iterations. But there is no way of predicting this before hand. Hence an arbitrary choice to break the tie is generally used.

Ties in the Minimum Ratio Rule and Degeneracy

While applying the minimum ratio rule it is possible for two or more constraints to give the same least ratio value. This results in a tie for selecting which basic variable should leave the basis. This may introduce further complications leading to a reduction in the efficiency of the simplex method. To illustrate this, consider the following simplex tableau obtained for a maximization problem:

Tableau 1

C_j		0	0	0	2	0	3/2	
C_B	Basis	x_1	x_2	x_3	x_4	x_5	x_6	Constants
0	x_1	1	0	0	①	-1	0	2
0	x_2	0	1	0	2	0	1	4
0	x_3	0	0	1	1	1	1	3
$\bar{C}$ Row		0	0	0	2	0	3/2	$Z=0$

Selecting the nonbasic variable x_4 to enter the basis, we observe that the first two constraints give the same minimum ratio. This means that when x_4 is increased to 2, both the basic variables x_1 and x_2 will reduce to zero even though only one of them could be made a nonbasic variable. Deciding arbitrarily to remove x_1 from the basis, we get the new basic feasible solution as shown below:

Tableau 2

C_j		0	0	0	2	0	3/2	
C_B	Basis	x_1	x_2	x_3	x_4	x_5	x_6	Constants
2	x_4	1	0	0	1	-1	0	2
0	x_2	-2	1	0	0	②	1	0
0	x_3	-1	0	1	0	2	1	1
$\bar{C}$ Row		-2	0	0	0	2	3/2	$Z=4$

The new basic feasible solution is $x_1=0$, $x_2=0$, $x_3=1$, $x_4=2$, $x_5=0$, $x_6=0$, and $Z=4$. An interesting observation here is that a basic variable (x_2) has assumed a zero value (like a nonbasic variable). Such a basic feasible solution in which one *or* more basic variables are zero is called a *degenerate* basic feasible solution. In contrast, a basic feasible solution in which all the basic variables are positive is said to be *nondegenerate*.

A tie in the minimum ratio rule is the main cause of degeneracy in the solutions, and it introduces further complications in the simplex calculations. Continuing the simplex method, we find that variable x_5 will enter the basis. Application of the minimum ratio rule indicates that the basic variable x_2 will have to be replaced by x_5. But the minimum ratio is zero implying that x_5 cannot be increased to a positive value. This means that the objective function is not going to be improved in the next tableau as seen on p. 45.

We find that the value of Z is still 4 even though we went through a change in the basis and obtained a new basic feasible solution. Moreover Tableau 3 is nonoptimal and x_6 can improve the value of Z. Once again, we find that the minimum ratio is zero, and we will be going through another change in the basis without an increase in the value of Z!

Naturally the question arises whether it is safe to assume that Z cannot be increased any further and call the present solution optimal. Such an assumption

Tableau 3

C_B	Basis	C_j	x_1	x_2	x_3	x_4	x_5	x_6	Constants
			0	0	0	2	0	3/2	
2	x_4		0	1/2	0	1	0	1/2	2
0	x_5		−1	1/2	0	0	1	1/2	0
0	x_3		1	−1	1	0	0	0	1
	$\bar{C}$ Row		0	−1	0	0	0	1/2	$Z = 4$

will be wrong. As long as there is a positive value in the $\bar{C}$ row, an increase in the objective function is possible, and the simplex calculations have to be continued. As a matter of fact, the maximum value of Z for this problem is 5 and an optimum tableau with $Z = 5$ will eventually be obtained with all the $\bar{C}$ row coefficients nonpositive!

This example illustrated the possibility that under degeneracy new tableaus may be obtained with no real improvement in the objective function. This means that costly simplex calculations will have to be performed in the tableaus without getting any real return. This naturally reduces the computational efficiency of the simplex method. But a more important question is whether it is possible for the simplex method to go on indefinitely without improving the objective function. In fact, several examples have been constructed to show that such a thing is theoretically possible. In such situations the simplex method may get into an infinite loop and will fail to reach the optimal solution. This phenomenon is called *cycling*.

Fortunately such a thing has never happened in practice in spite of the fact that many practical problems have degenerate solutions. In other words, it is possible that the simplex method may not improve the objective function for a few iterations; but eventually it will get out of that loop and reach the optimal solution. Thus whenever ties occur in the minimum ratio rule, an arbitrary decision is made regarding which basic variable should leave, ignoring the theoretical consequences of degeneracy and cycling. But modifications to the simple minimum ratio rule have been developed to prevent the simplex method from getting into an infinite loop. Because of the extra computational efforts involved in applying these modified rules, they are not used in practice.

Unbounded Solutions

Another complication in the minimum ratio rule may occur when it is not able to determine the basic variable to leave. This happens when none of the constraint coefficients of the nonbasic variable (selected to enter the basis) is positive. This means that no finite ratios can be formed, and in effect the minimum ratio rule fails. To see the significance of such a condition, consider the following linear programming problem:

EXAMPLE 2.8-1

$$\text{Maximize:} \quad Z = 2x_1 + 3x_2$$

$$\text{Subject to:} \quad x_1 - x_2 + x_3 \qquad = 2$$

$$-3x_1 + x_2 \qquad + x_4 = 4$$

$$x_1 \geqq 0, \qquad x_2 \geqq 0, \qquad x_3 \geqq 0, \qquad x_4 \geqq 0$$

The initial tableau is given below:

C_B	Basis	C_j 2 x_1	3 x_2	0 x_3	0 x_4	Constants
0	x_3	1	−1	1	0	2
0	x_4	−3	①	0	1	4
	$\bar{C}$ Row	2	3	0	0	$Z = 0$

The nonbasic variable x_2 enters the basis to replace the basic variable x_4. The new tableau becomes

C_B	Basis	C_j 2 x_1	3 x_2	0 x_3	0 x_4	Constants
0	x_3	−2	0	1	1	6
3	x_2	−3	1	0	1	4
	$\bar{C}$ Row	11	0	0	−3	$Z = 12$

The new tableau is not optimal and the nonbasic variable x_1 can enter the basis to increase Z. But the minimum ratio rule fails as there is no positive entry in the x_1 column. In other words, as x_1 increases, both the basic variables x_3 and x_2 will also increase, and hence can never become zero to limit the increase of x_1. This means that x_1 can be increased indefinitely. Since each unit increase on x_1 increases Z by 11 units, the objective function can be increased indefinitely, and we have an unbounded solution to the linear programming problem. Thus the failure of the minimum ratio rule at any simplex tableau indicates that the problem has an unbounded solution. (Recall the practical significance of an unbounded solution discussed in Section 2.3.)

2.9 FINDING A FEASIBLE BASIS

A major requirement of the simplex method is the availability of an initial basic feasible solution in canonical form. Without it the initial simplex tableau cannot be formed. In all the examples we discussed so far, a canonical system with a basic feasible solution was readily available. This may not be so in every problem. As a matter of fact, in many practical problems one may not even know whether there exists a feasible solution to the constraints. Such problems will be discussed in this section.

There are two basic approaches to finding an initial basic feasible solution:

1. *By Trial and Error.* Here a basic variable is chosen arbitrarily for each constraint, and the system is reduced to canonical form with respect to those basic variables. If the resulting canonical system gives a basic feasible solution (i.e., the final right-hand-side constants are nonnegative), then the initial tableau can be set up to start the simplex method. It is also possible that during the canonical reduction some of the right-hand-side constants may become negative. In that case the basic solution

obtained will be infeasible, and the simplex method cannot be started. Of course, one can repeat the process by trying a different set of basic variables for the canonical reduction and hope for a basic feasible solution. Now it is clearly obvious that the trial and error method is very inefficient and expensive. In addition, if a problem does not possess a feasible solution, it will take a long time to realize this.

2. *Use of Artificial Variables.* This is a systematic way of getting a canonical system with a basic feasible solution when none is available by inspection. First the linear programming problem is converted to standard form such that all the variables are nonnegative, the constraints are equations, and all the right hand side constants are nonnegative. Then each constraint is examined for the existence of a basic variable. If none is available, a new variable is added to act as the basic variable in that constraint. In the end, all the constraints will have a basic variable, and by definition we have a canonical system. Since the right-hand-side elements are nonnegative, an initial simplex tableau can be formed readily. Of course the additional variables have no relevance or meaning to the original problem. They are merely added so that we will have a ready canonical system to start the simplex method. Hence these variables are termed as *artificial variables* as opposed to the real decision variables in the problem. Eventually they will be forced to zero lest they unbalance the equations. To illustrate the use of artificial variables, consider the following linear programming problem:

EXAMPLE 2.9-1

$$\text{Minimize:} \quad Z = -3x_1 + x_2 + x_3$$

$$\text{Subject to:} \quad x_1 - 2x_2 + x_3 \leq 11$$

$$-4x_1 + x_2 + 2x_3 \geq 3$$

$$2x_1 \qquad - x_3 = -1$$

$$x_1 \geq 0, \qquad x_2 \geq 0, \qquad x_3 \geq 0$$

First the problem is converted to the standard form as follows:

$$\text{Minimize} \quad Z = -3x_1 + x_2 + x_3$$

$$\text{Subject to} \quad x_1 - 2x_2 + x_3 + x_4 \qquad = 11 \qquad (2.11)$$

$$-4x_1 + x_2 + 2x_3 \qquad - x_5 = 3 \qquad (2.12)$$

$$-2x_1 \qquad + x_3 \qquad = 1 \qquad (2.13)$$

$$x_1 \geq 0, \qquad x_2 \geq 0, \qquad x_3 \geq 0, \qquad x_4 \geq 0, \qquad x_5 \geq 0$$

In Eq. 2.11 the slack variable x_4 is a basic variable. Since there are no basic variables in the other equations we add artificial variables x_6 and x_7 to Eqs. 2.12 and 2.13, respectively. To retain the standard form x_6 and x_7 will be restricted to be nonnegative. Thus we now have an "artificial system" given by:

$$x_1 - 2x_2 + x_3 + x_4 \qquad = 11$$

$$-4x_1 + x_2 + 2x_3 \qquad - x_5 + x_6 \qquad = 3$$

$$-2x_1 \qquad + x_3 \qquad + x_7 = 1$$

$$x_1 \geq 0, \ldots, x_7 \geq 0$$

The artificial system has a basic feasible solution in canonical form given by $x_1 = x_2 = x_3 = 0$, $x_4 = 11$, $x_5 = 0$, $x_6 = 3$, $x_7 = 1$. But this is not a feasible solution to the original problem due to the presence of the artificial variables x_6 and x_7 at positive values. On the other hand, it is easy to see that any basic feasible solution to the artificial system in which the artificial variables x_6 and x_7 are zero is automatically a basic feasible solution to the original problem. Hence the objective is to reduce the artificial variables to zero as soon as possible. This can be accomplished in two ways, and each one gives rise to a variant of the simplex method.

The Big M Simplex Method

In this approach, the artificial variables are assigned a very large cost in the objective function. The simplex method, while trying to improve the objective function, will find the artificial variables uneconomical to maintain as basic variables with positive values. Hence they will be quickly replaced in the basis by the real variables with smaller costs. For hand calculations it is not necessary to assign a specific cost value to the artificial variables. The general practice is to assign the letter M as the cost in a minimization problem, and $-M$ as the profit in a maximization problem with the assumption that M is a very large positive number.

To illustrate the *Big M Simplex Method* consider the linear program given by Example 2.9-1. In order to drive the artificial variables to zero, a large cost will be assigned to x_6 and x_7 so that the objective function becomes,

$$\text{Minimize:} \quad Z = -3x_1 + x_2 + x_3 + Mx_6 + Mx_7$$

where M is a very large positive number

The initial simplex tableau can now be constructed using x_4, x_6, and x_7 as the basic variables.

Tableau 1

C_B	Basis	C_j : x_1 (-3)	x_2 (1)	x_3 (1)	x_4 (0)	x_5 (0)	x_6 (M)	x_7 (M)	Constants
0	x_4	1	-2	1	1	0	0	0	11
M	x_6	-4	1	2	0	-1	1	0	3
M	x_7	-2	0	①	0	0	0	1	1
	$\bar{C}$ Row	$-3+6M$	$1-M$	$1-3M$	0	M	0	0	$Z = 4M$

The $\bar{C}$-row coefficients are calculated using the inner product rule as follows:

$\bar{C}_j = C_j - $ (inner product of C_B and the column corresponding to x_j in Tableau 1)

For example,

$$\bar{C}_1 = -3 - (0, M, M)\begin{pmatrix} 1 \\ -4 \\ -2 \end{pmatrix} = -3 + 6M$$

The value of Z is very high in Tableau 1 since M is very large. The $\bar{C}$ row indicates that the nonbasic variable x_3 can further reduce Z. By the application of the minimum ratio rule, x_7 leaves the basis and the new canonical system is given by Tableau 2.

Tableau 2

C_B	Basis	C_j -3 x_1	1 x_2	1 x_3	0 x_4	0 x_5	M x_6	M x_7	Constants
0	x_4	3	-2	0	1	0	0	-1	10
M	x_6	0	①	0	0	-1	1	-2	1
1	x_3	-2	0	1	0	0	0	1	1
	$\bar{C}$ Row	-1	$1-M$	0	0	M	0	$3M-1$	$Z=M+1$

Tableau 2 does not give a basic feasible solution to the original problem due to the presence of the artificial variable x_6 at positive value. Continuing the simplex calculations, we find that x_2 enters the basis to replace x_6.

Tableau 3

C_B	Basis	C_j -3 x_1	1 x_2	1 x_3	0 x_4	0 x_5	M x_6	M x_7	Constants
0	x_4	③	0	0	1	-2	2	-5	12
1	x_2	0	1	0	0	-1	1	-2	1
1	x_3	-2	0	1	0	0	0	1	1
	$\bar{C}$ Row	-1	0	0	0	-1	$M-1$	$M+1$	$Z=2$

Now both the artificial variables x_6 and x_7 have been reduced to zero. Thus Tableau 3 represents a basic feasible solution to the original problem. Of course, this is not an optimal solution since x_1 can reduce the objective function further by replacing x_4 in the basis.

Tableau 4

C_B	Basis	C_j -3 x_1	1 x_2	1 x_3	0 x_4	0 x_5	M x_6	M x_7	Constants
-3	x_1	1	0	0	1/3	$-2/3$	2/3	$-5/3$	4
1	x_2	0	1	0	0	-1	1	-2	1
1	x_3	0	0	1	2/3	$-4/3$	4/3	$-7/3$	9
	$\bar{C}$ Row	0	0	0	1/3	1/3	$M-1/3$	$M-2/3$	$Z=-2$

Tableau 4 is optimal, and the unique optimal solution is given by $x_1=4$, $x_2=1$, $x_3=9$, $x_4=0$, $x_5=0$, and minimum $Z=-2$.

REMARKS
1. An artificial variable is added merely to act as a basic variable in a particular equation. Once it is replaced by a real (decision) variable, there is no need to

retain the artificial variable in the simplex tableaus. In other words, we could have omitted the column corresponding to the artificial variable x_7 in Tableaus 2, 3, and 4. Similarly, the column corresponding to x_6 could have been dropped from Tableaus 3 and 4.

2. When the Big M Simplex Method terminates with an optimal tableau, it is sometimes possible for one or more artificial variables to remain as basic variables at positive values. This implies that the original problem is *infeasible* since no basic feasible solution is possible to the original system if it includes even one artificial variable at a positive value. In other words, the original problem without the artificial variables does not have a feasible solution. Infeasibility is due to the presence of inconsistent constraints in the formulation of the problem. In economic terms, this means that the resources of the system are not sufficient to meet the expected demands.

3. For computer solutions, M has to be assigned a specific value. Usually the largest value that can be represented in the computer is assumed.

The Two-Phase Simplex Method

This is another approach to handle the artificial variables whenever they are added. Here the linear programming problem is solved in two phases.

Phase 1. This phase consists of finding an initial basic feasible solution to the original problem. In other words, the removal of the artificial variables is taken up first. For this an artificial objective function is created which is the sum of all the artificial variables. The artificial objective is then minimized using the simplex method. If the minimum value of the artificial problem is zero, then all the artificial variables have been reduced to zero, and we have a basic feasible solution to the original problem. (Note: if the sum of nonnegative variables is zero, then each variable must be identically equal to zero). We then go to Phase 2.

In case the minimum value of the artificial problem is positive, then at least one of the artificial variables is positive. This means that the original problem without the artificial variables is infeasible, and we terminate.

Phase 2. In this phase, the basic feasible solution found at the end of Phase 1 is optimized with respect to the original objective function. In other words, the final tableau of Phase 1 becomes the initial tableau for Phase 2 after changing the objective function. The simplex method is once again applied to determine the optimal solution.

We shall illustrate the two-phase simplex method using Example 2.9-1. First the Phase 1 linear program is created with symbol W to represent the artificial objective function.

Phase 1 Problem

$$\text{Minimize:} \quad W = x_6 + x_7$$

$$
\begin{aligned}
\text{Subject to:} \quad & x_1 - 2x_2 + x_3 + x_4 && = 11 \\
& -4x_1 + x_2 + 2x_3 && -x_5 + x_6 && = 3 \\
& -2x_1 + x_3 && + x_7 = 1 \\
& x_1 \geq 0, \ldots, x_7 \geq 0
\end{aligned}
$$

The original objective function, $Z = -3x_1 + x_2 + x_3$, is temporarily set aside during the Phase 1 solution. The initial basic feasible solution for the Phase 1 problem is given below:

Tableau 1
(PHASE 1)

C_B	Basis	C_j	0	0	0	0	0	1	1	Constants
			x_1	x_2	x_3	x_4	x_5	x_6	x_7	
0	x_4		1	-2	1	1	0	0	0	11
1	x_6		-4	1	2	0	-1	1	0	3
1	x_7		-2	0	①	0	0	0	1	1
	$\bar{C}$ Row		6	-1	-3	0	1	0	0	$W = 4$

The objective function can be reduced further by replacing x_7 by x_3 as follows:

Tableau 2
(PHASE 1)

C_B	Basis	C_j	0	0	0	0	0	1	1	Constants
			x_1	x_2	x_3	x_4	x_5	x_6	x_7	
0	x_4		3	-2	0	1	0	0	-1	10
1	x_6		0	①	0	0	-1	1	-2	1
0	x_3		-2	0	1	0	0	0	1	1
	$\bar{C}$ Row		0	-1	0	0	1	0	3	$W = 1$

The above tableau is not optimal. The variable x_2 enters the basis to replace the artificial variable x_6.

Tableau 3
(PHASE 1)

C_B	Basis	C_j	0	0	0	0	0	1	1	Constants
			x_1	x_2	x_3	x_4	x_5	x_6	x_7	
0	x_4		3	0	0	1	-2	2	-5	12
0	x_2		0	1	0	0	-1	1	-2	1
0	x_3		-2	0	1	0	0	0	1	1
	$\bar{C}$ Row		0	0	0	0	0	1	1	$W = 0$

We now have an optimal solution to the Phase 1 linear program given by $x_1 = 0$, $x_2 = 1$, $x_3 = 1$, $x_4 = 12$, $x_5 = 0$, $x_6 = 0$, $x_7 = 0$ and minimum $W = 0$. Since the artificial variables x_6 and $x_7 = 0$, this tableau represents a basic feasible solution to the original problem. We now begin Phase 2 of the simplex method to find the optimal solution to the original problem. The initial tableau for Phase 2 is constructed by deleting the columns corresponding to the artificial variables, and computing the new $\bar{C}$-row coefficients with respect to the original objective function, $Z = -3x_1 + x_2 + x_3$, as shown below:

Tableau 1
(PHASE 2)

C_B	Basis	C_j $\to$ x_1	x_2	x_3	x_4	x_5	Constants
		-3 $\quad$ 1	1	1	0	0	
0	x_4	③	0	0	1	-2	12
1	x_2	0	1	0	0	-1	1
1	x_3	-2	0	1	0	0	1
	$\bar{C}$ Row	-1	0	0	0	1	$Z = 2$

In the above tableau,

$$\bar{C}_1 = -3 - (0, 1, 1)(3, 0, -2)^T = -3$$
$$\bar{C}_5 = 0 - (0, 1, 1)(-2, -1, 0)^T = 1$$

and

$$\bar{C}_2 = \bar{C}_3 = \bar{C}_4 = 0$$

Since the objective is to minimize Z, Tableau 1 is not optimal. The nonbasic variable x_1 replaces the basic variable x_4 to reduce the value of Z further.

Tableau 2
(PHASE 2)

C_B	Basis	C_j $\to$ x_1	x_2	x_3	x_4	x_5	Constants
		-3 $\quad$ 1	1	1	0	0	
-3	x_1	1	0	0	1/3	$-2/3$	4
1	x_2	0	1	0	0	-1	1
1	x_3	0	0	1	2/3	$-4/3$	9
	$\bar{C}$ Row	0	0	0	1/3	1/3	$Z = -2$

An optimal solution has been reached, and it is given by $x_1 = 4$, $x_2 = 1$, $x_3 = 9$, $x_4 = 0$, $x_5 = 0$, and minimum $Z = -2$.

Comparing the Big M simplex method and the two-phase simplex method, we observe the following:

1. The basic approach to both methods is the same. Both add the artificial variables to get the initial canonical system and then drive them to zero as soon as possible.
2. The sequence of tableaus and the basis changes are identical.
3. The number of iterations are the same.
4. The Big M method solves the linear program in one pass while the two-phase method solves it in two stages as two linear programs.

A drawback of the Big M method is the presence of unusually large numbers (M) which sometimes create computational problems in a digital computer.

2.10 COMPUTER SOLUTION OF LINEAR PROGRAMS

Many practical problems formulated as linear programs run into hundreds of constraints and thousands of decision variables. These invariably have to be solved using a digital computer. In the tableau form, the simplex method is an iterative procedure, and can be applied mechanically to any problem. Hence it is ideally suited for computer implementation.

Even though the simplex method was developed in 1947 by G. B. Dantzig, it was not formally published until 1951. Hence the solution of a linear programming problem on a digital computer did not take place until 1952. The first successful attempt on a first generation computer was made at the National Bureau of Standards in early 1952.

The first generation computers used vacuum tubes with no memory to speak of. They were capable of solving only small linear programming problems with no more than 50 constraints and 100 variables, and were also very slow computationally. For example, it took 15 minutes to solve a 10×20 linear program. (Modern-day computers solve such problems in 1 or 2 seconds!) Thus the major industrial applications of linear programming had to wait for the advancement in computer technology and, to a large extent, the advancement of linear programming and its applications have gone hand in hand with advances in computers.

The late 1950s saw the introduction of the second-generation computers. Using transistors instead of vacuum tubes, these computers were able to operate at higher speeds. Storage of data was handled by magnetic discs. The computers were able to solve moderate-size linear programming problems of the order of 300–400 constraints and 2000–3000 variables. During this phase, linear programming saw many industrial applications, but the solution of large industrial problems still had to wait for the third-generation computers.

The third generation computers were introduced in the 1960s. They employed integrated circuits, used larger magnetic core memories, and had multi-programming or time-sharing capability. These features increased their speeds of operation immensely, and the solution of large linear programming problems with thousands of constraints and an even larger number of decision variables became possible. This has resulted in the enormous success of linear programming in diverse areas like defense, industry, commercial-retail, agriculture, education, and environment.

Computer Implementation of the Simplex Method

The early computer codes for the simplex method performed calculations on the entire tableau as discussed in the earlier sections. This involved fast access to all the elements of the tableau in order to reduce the computational effort and time. This was not possible unless the entire tableau was kept in the fast memory of the computer. But the limited core memory precluded this, and the solution of large linear programs became inefficient and expensive. Further refinements in the simplex calculations were consequently carried out so that the implementation of the simplex method on a computer could be done more efficiently. This led to the development of the *Revised Simplex Method* which is currently implemented in all commercial computer codes. The revised simplex method is discussed in detail in Chapter 4. Essentially this method uses a reduced tableau which results in considerable saving in computer storage and time.

There are also a few minor modifications in the computer implementation of the simplex method. One involves the rule for selecting the nonbasic variable to enter the basis. In general, the large computer codes do not compute the entire $\bar{C}$ row, and then select the nonbasic variable with the most positive (in maximization problems) or the most negative (in minimization problems) $\bar{C}_j$ coefficient. In a large problem with thousands of nonbasic variables, this may take a considerable amount of computer time. Instead the elements of the $\bar{C}$ row are calculated one at a time, and the first nonbasic variable which shows possible improvement in Z will be selected as the variable to enter. This eliminates both further calculations on the $\bar{C}$ row and an expensive search. Of course, this may result in an increase in the total number of iterations to solve the problem, but the reduction in the time for each iteration generally offsets this deficiency.

In the early stages, when it was shown that under degeneracy the simplex method may cycle indefinitely without finding an optimal solution, elaborate modifications were introduced in the simplex procedure to overcome this problem. When practical experience showed that cycling never occurs in real problems, the expensive modifications were dropped altogether. None of the modern day computer codes worry about degeneracy. Instead the precious computer time is used to improve the accuracy and reliability of the solutions.

Computational Efficiency of the Simplex Method

It has been pointed out by many researchers in mathematical programming that the simplex method, viewed purely from a theoretical consideration, is not an efficient method since it examines adjacent basic feasible solutions only (i.e., changing one basic variable at a time). It is felt that the method can move faster to an optimal solution if it examines nonadjacent solutions as well (i.e., changing more than one basic variable at a time). But many of the suggested variants to the simplex method did not produce any appreciable change in the total computational time. Hence the basic simplex method as discussed earlier is still considered to be the best procedure for solving linear programming problems.

The computational efficiency of the simplex method depends on (1) the number of iterations (basic feasible solutions) to go through before reaching the optimal solution, and (2) the total computer time to solve the problem. Much effort has been spent to study the computational efficiency with regard to the number of constraints and the decision variables in the problem.

Empirical experience with thousands of practical problems shows that the number of iterations of a standard linear program with m constraints and n variables varies between m and $3m$, the average being $2m$. A practical upper bound for the number of iterations is $2(m + n)$ (occasionally some problems have violated this bound).

The computational time is found to vary approximately in relation to the cube of the number of constraints in the problem (m^3). For example, if Problem A has twice as many constraints as Problem B, then the computer time for Problem A will be about eight times that of Problem B.

It is to be noted that the computational efficiency of the simplex method is more sensitive to the number of constraints than to the number of variables. Hence the general recommendation is to keep the number of constraints as small as possible by avoiding unnecessary or redundant constraints in the formulation of the linear programming problem.

2.11 ADDITIONAL TOPICS IN LINEAR PROGRAMMING

In this section, we briefly discuss some of the advanced topics in linear programming. These include the *revised simplex method, duality theory*, the *dual simplex method, sensitivity analysis, parametric programming*, and *integer programming*. For a full discussion, refer to Chapter 4.

The Revised Simplex Method

The revised simplex method uses the same basic principles as the regular simplex method, but at each iteration the entire simplex tableau is never calculated. The relevant information required to move from one basic feasible solution to another is directly generated from the original system of equations. These lead to a reduction in computational effort and time in the simplex calculations. Currently all the commercial computer codes use the revised simplex method for solving linear programming problems. In addition, solution of large problems has become possible since the revised simplex method uses less central memory space in the computer. These are discussed in more detail in Section 4.1.

Duality Theory

From both the theoretical and practical points of view, the theory of duality is one of the most important concepts in linear programming. The basic idea behind the duality theory is that every linear program has an associated linear program called its dual such that a solution to one gives a solution to the other. There are a number of important relationships between the solution to the original problem and its dual. These are useful in investigating the general properties of the optimal solution to a linear program and in testing whether a feasible solution is optimal. In addition, the optimal dual solution can be interpreted as the price one pays for the constraint resources. This is known as the *shadow price*. These play an important role in postoptimality analysis. Moreover, the concept of duality and the various duality theorems are extremely useful in the study of advanced mathematical programming topics. For a complete discussion of duality theory and its application, see Section 4.2.

The Dual Simplex Method

The dual simplex method is a modified version of the simplex method using duality theory. There are instances when the dual simplex method has an obvious advantage over the regular simplex method. It plays an important part in sensitivity analysis, parametric programming, solution of integer programming problems, many of the variants of the simplex method, and solution of some nonlinear programming problems. Details of the dual simplex method are discussed in Section 4.3.

Sensitivity Analysis and Parametric Programming

In all linear programming models the coefficients of the objective function and the constraints are supplied as input data or as parameters to the model. The optimal solution obtained by the simplex method is based on the values of these coefficients. In practice their values are seldom known with absolute certainty. Each variation in their values changes the linear programming problem, which in turn may affect the optimal solution found earlier. The purpose of sensitivity analysis or postoptimality analysis is to study how the optimal solution will change with changes in the input (data) coefficients. In many instances it will not be necessary to solve the problem all over again. Sensitivity analysis considers the variations of one input parameter at a time and is discussed in detail in Section 4.4, while parametric programming considers simultaneous variations in many parameters and is discussed in detail in Section 4.5.

Integer Programming

In practice, many linear programming problems do require integer solutions for some of the variables. For instance, it is not possible to employ a fractional number of workers or produce a fractional number of cars. The term (linear) integer programming refers to the class of linear programming problems wherein some or all of the decision variables are restricted to be integers. But solutions of integer programming problems are generally difficult, too time consuming, and expensive. Hence a practical approach is to treat all the integer variables as continuous, and solve the associated linear program by the simplex method. We may be fortunate to get some of the values of the variables as integers automatically, but when the simplex method produces fractional solutions for some integer variables, they are generally rounded off to the nearest integer such that the constraints are not violated. This is very often used in practice, and it generally produces a good integer solution close to the optimal integer solution, especially when the values of the integer variables are large.

There are situations when a model formulation may require the use of binary integer variables which only can take values 0 or 1. For these integer variables, rounding off produces poor integer solutions, and one does need other techniques to determine the optimal integer solution directly. Some of these techniques and many practical applications of integer programming are discussed in Section 4.6.

Recommended Readings

For a complete history of linear programming and its developments refer to Dantzig (2). It also contains an activity analysis approach using "black-box" techniques for formulating linear programming problems. An excellent bibliography on the applications of linear programming in practice is available in Gass (5). Gale (4) discusses many linear programming models of production, exchange, and matrix games.

An excellent treatment of matrices, vectors, and matrix-vector operations is available in Hadley (7). For a mathematical treatment of the simplex method from a vector space theory, refer to Gale (4) and Hadley (6). Topics of degeneracy and its resolution are discussed at length in Dantzig.

Discussion of various computer solutions to large linear-programming problems in industries, and computational features of many LP computer codes are discussed in Driebeek (3), and Daellenbach and Bell (1).

Dantzig's is the most complete book available on linear programming, and may be referred to for any advanced material on this subject.

REFERENCES

1. Daellenbach, Hans G., and Earl J. Bell, *User's Guide to Linear Programming*, Prentice-Hall, Englewood Cliffs, New Jersey, 1970.

2. Dantzig, George B., *Linear Programming and Extensions*, Princeton University Press, Princeton, New Jersey, 1963.

3. Driebeek, Norman J., *Applied Linear Programming*, Addison-Wesley, Reading, Massachusetts, 1969.

4. Gale, David, *The Theory of Linear Economic Models*, McGraw-Hill, New York, 1960.

5. Gass, Saul I., *Linear Programming*, Fourth Ed., McGraw-Hill, New York, 1975.

6. Hadley, G., *Linear Programming*, Addison-Wesley, Reading, Massachusetts, 1962.

7. Hadley, G., *Linear Algebra*, Addison-Wesley, Reading, Massachusetts, 1961.

8. Hillier, Frederick S., and Gerald J. Liebermann, *Introduction to Operations Research*, Second Ed. Holden-Day, San Francisco, California, 1974.

9. Taha, Hamdy A., *Operations Research: An Introduction*, Macmillan, New York, 1971.

10. Wagner, Harvey M., *Principles of Operations Research*, Second Ed. Prentice-Hall, Englewood Cliffs, New Jersey, 1975.

EXERCISES

1. The Mighty Silver Ball Company manufactures three kinds of pinball machines, each requiring a different manufacturing technique. The Super Delux Machine requires 17 hours of labor, 8 hours of testing, and yields a profit of $300. The Silver Ball Special requires 10 hours of labor, 4 hours of testing, and yields a profit of $200. The Bumper King requires 2 hours of labor, 2 hours of testing, and yields a profit of $100. There are 1000 hours of labor and 500 hours of testing available.

    In addition, a marketing forecast has shown that the demand for the Super Deluxe is no more than 50 machines, demand for the Silver Ball Special no more than 80, and demand for Bumper King no more than 150.

    The manufacturer wants to determine the optimal production schedule that will maximize his total profit. Formulate this as a linear programming problem.

2. A hospital administrator has the following minimal daily requirements for nursing personnel:

Period	Clock Time (24-Hour Day)	Minimal Number of Nurses Required
1	6 AM–10 AM	60
2	10 AM– 2 PM	70
3	2 PM– 6 PM	60
4	6 PM–10 PM	50
5	10 PM– 2 AM	20
6	2 AM– 6 AM	30

    Nurses report to the hospital wards at the beginning of each period and work for 8 consecutive hours. The hospital wants to determine the minimal number of nurses to employ so that there will be sufficient number of nursing personnel available for each period. Formulate this as a linear programming problem.

3. Consider the problem of scheduling the weekly production of a certain item for the next 4 weeks. The production cost of the item is $10 for the first 2 weeks, and $15 for the last 2 weeks. The weekly demands are 300, 700, 900, and 800 units, which must be met. The plant can produce a maximum of 700 units each week. In addition the company can employ overtime during the second and third weeks. This increases the weekly production by an additional 200 units, but the cost of production increases by $5 per item. Excess production can be stored at a cost of $3 an item. How should the production be scheduled so as to minimize the total costs? Formulate this as a linear programming problem.

4. A Steel Company is faced with the problem of transporting coal from two coal mines to four of its steel plants. The amount of coal available in the coal mines are a_1 and a_2 metric tons. The amount required at the plants are b_1, b_2, b_3, and b_4 metric tons (Exactly one truck is to be used for these shipments). It is possible to ship from any mine to any plant but the truck cannot make more than one trip from a mine to a plant. The problem is to determine the minimum capacity truck which can complete all the shipments. Formulate this as a linear program.

5. The ABC Company is in the commodity trading business. It buys and sells corn for cash. It owns a warehouse with a capacity of 5000 bushels. As of January 1, it has an initial stock of 1000 bushels of corn, and cash balance of $20,000. The estimated corn prices per bushel for the next quarter is given below

	Buying Price ($)	Selling Price ($)
January	2.85	3.10
February	3.05	3.25
March	2.90	2.95

The corn is delivered in the month in which it is bought and cannot be sold until the next month. Both buying and selling corn are done strictly on "cash on delivery" basis. The company would like to have a final inventory of 2000 bushels of corn at the end of the quarter. What buying and selling policy would maximize the total net return for the three-month period? Formulate this as a linear programming problem.

6. A company manufactures three products; A, B, and C. Each unit of product A requires 1 hour of engineering service, 10 hours of direct labor, and 3 pounds of material. To produce one unit of product B, it requires 2 hours of engineering, 4 hours of direct labor, and 2 pounds of material. Each unit of product C requires 1 hour of engineering, 5 hours of direct labor, and 1 pound of material. There are 100 hours of engineering, 700 hours of labor, and 400 pounds of material available.

Since the company offers discounts for bulk purchases, the profit figures are as shown below:

Product A		Product B		Product C	
Sales (Units)	Unit Profit ($)	Sales (Units)	Unit Profit ($)	Sales (Units)	Unit Profit ($)
0–40	10	0–50	6	0–100	5
40–100	9	50–100	4	Over 100	4
100–150	8	Over 100	3		
Over 150	7				

Formulate a linear program to determine the most profitable product mix.

7. A scientist has observed a certain quantity Q as a function of variable t. He is interested in determining a mathematical relationship relating t and Q, which takes the form

$$Q(t) = at^3 + bt^2 + ct + d$$

from the results of his n experiments (t_1, Q_1), (t_2, Q_2), ..., (t_n, Q_n). He discovers that the values of the unknown coefficients a, b, c, and d must be nonnegative, and should add up to 1. To account for errors in his experiments, he defines an error term,

$$e_i = Q_i - Q(t_i)$$

He wants to determine the best values for the coefficients a, b, c, and d using the following criterion functions:

Criterion 1   Minimize: $Z = \sum_{i=1}^{n} |e_i|$

Criterion 2   Minimize: $(\text{maximum}_i |e_i|)$

where $|e_i|$ is the absolute value of the error associated with the ith experiment. Show that the scientist's problem reduces to a linear programming problem under both Criterion 1 and Criterion 2.

8. Formulate a linear program to show that all solutions of

$$x_1 + x_2 \leq 4$$
$$2x_1 - 3x_2 \leq 6$$
$$x_1 \geq 0, \qquad x_2 \geq 0$$

also satisfy

$$x_1 + 2x_2 \leq 8.$$

Verify the above graphically.

9. Consider the linear programming problem in two variables:

$$\text{Maximize:}\quad Z = x_1$$
$$\text{Subject to:}\quad x_1 + x_2 \leq \alpha$$
$$-x_1 + x_2 \leq -1$$
$$x_1 \geq 0, \qquad x_2 \geq 0$$

a. Prove that the problem is feasible if and only if $\alpha \geq 1$.
b. Find the optimum value of the linear program as a function of α for all values of $\alpha \geq 1$, using graphical means.

10. Transform the following linear program to the standard form:

$$\text{Minimize:}\quad Z = -3x_1 + 4x_2 - 2x_3 + 5x_4$$
$$\text{Subject to:}\quad 4x_1 - x_2 + 2x_3 - x_4 = -2$$
$$x_1 + x_2 + 3x_3 - x_4 \leq 14$$
$$-2x_1 + 3x_2 - x_3 + 2x_4 \geq 2$$
$$x_1 \geq 0, \qquad x_2 \geq 0, \qquad x_3 \leq 0, \qquad x_4 \text{ unrestricted in sign}$$

11. Consider a system of two equations in five unknowns as follows:

$$x_1 + 2x_2 + 10x_3 + 4x_4 - 2x_5 = 5$$
$$x_1 + x_2 + 4x_3 + 3x_4 + x_5 = 8$$
$$x_1, \ldots, x_5 \geq 0$$

a. Reduce the system to canonical form with respect to (x_1, x_2) as basic variables. Write down the basic solution. Is it feasible? Why or why not?
b. What is the maximum number of basic solutions possible?
c. Find a canonical system which will give a basic feasible solution to the above system by trial and error.

12. Consider the following linear program:

$$\text{Maximize:} \quad Z = 2x_1 - x_2 + x_3 + x_4$$

$$\text{Subject to:} \quad -x_1 + x_2 + x_3 \qquad + x_5 \qquad = 1$$

$$x_1 + x_2 \qquad + x_4 \qquad = 2$$

$$2x_1 + x_2 + x_3 \qquad\qquad + x_6 = 6$$

$$x_1, \ldots, x_6 \geq 0$$

a. Write down the initial basic feasible solution by inspection.
b. Find a feasible solution by increasing the nonbasic variable x_1 by one unit, while holding x_2 and x_3 as zero. What will be the net change in the objective function?
c. What is the maximum increase in x_1 possible, subject to the constraints?
d. Find the new basic feasible solution when x_1 is increased to its maximum value found in (c).
e. Is the new basic feasible solution obtained in (d) optimal? Why or why not?

13. Use the simplex method to solve

$$\text{Maximize:} \quad Z = x_1 + 3x_2$$

$$\text{Subject to:} \quad x_1 \qquad \leq 5$$

$$x_1 + 2x_2 \leq 10$$

$$x_2 \leq 4$$

$$x_1, x_2 \geq 0$$

Plot the feasible region using x_1 and x_2 as coordinates. Follow the solution steps of the simplex method graphically by interpreting the shift from one basic feasible solution to the next in the feasible region.

14. Find an optimal solution to the following linear program by *inspection*:

$$\text{Minimize:} \quad Z = x_1 - 3x_2 + 2x_3$$

$$\text{Subject to:} \quad -2 \leq x_1 \leq 3$$

$$0 \leq x_2 \leq 4$$

$$2 \leq x_3 \leq 5$$

15. Use the simplex method to solve:

$$\text{Minimize:} \quad Z = 3x_1 + x_2 + x_3 + x_4$$

$$\text{Subject to:} \quad -2x_1 + 2x_2 + x_3 \qquad = 4$$

$$3x_1 + x_2 \qquad + x_4 = 6$$

$$x_1, x_2, x_3, x_4 \geq 0$$

Find an alternative optimal solution if one exists.

16. Use the simplex method to solve:

$$\text{Maximize:} \quad Z = x_1 + 2x_2 + 3x_3 + 4x_4$$

$$\text{Subject to:} \quad x_1 + 2x_2 + 2x_3 + 3x_4 \leq 20$$

$$2x_1 + x_2 + 3x_3 + 2x_4 \leq 20$$

$$x_1, \ldots, x_4 \geq 0$$

Is the optimal solution unique? Why or why not?

17. Use the Big M simplex method to solve:

$$\text{Minimize:} \quad Z = 6x_1 + 3x_2 + 4x_3$$

$$\text{Subject to:} \quad x_1 \qquad\qquad \geqq 30$$
$$x_2 \qquad \leqq 50$$
$$x_3 \geqq 20$$
$$x_1 + x_2 + x_3 = 120$$
$$x_1, x_2, x_3 \geqq 0$$

18. Use the two-phase simplex method to solve:

$$\text{Maximize:} \quad Z = 3x_1 + 4x_2 + 2x_3$$

$$\text{Subject to:} \quad x_1 + x_2 + x_3 + x_4 \leqq 30$$
$$3x_1 + 6x_2 + x_3 - 2x_4 \leqq 0$$
$$x_2 \qquad\qquad \geqq 4$$
$$x_1, \ldots, x_4 \geqq 0$$

19. Given the following linear program (P-1):

$$\text{Minimize:} \quad Z = 2x_1 - x_2 + 2x_3$$

$$\text{Subject to:} \quad -x_1 + x_2 + x_3 = 4$$
$$-x_1 + x_2 - x_3 \leqq 6$$
$$x_1 \leqq 0, \qquad x_2 \geqq 0,$$
$$x_3 \text{ (unrestricted in sign)}$$

   a. Convert the given problem (P-1) to a standard linear program in nonnegative variables.
   b. Solve the standard linear program obtained in (a) by the Big M simplex method.
   c. From (b), write down the optimal solution to the given problem (P-1) carefully. (You must give the values of x_1, x_2, and x_3). What is the minimum value of Z?

20. Use the simplex method to verify that the following problem has no optimal solution:

$$\text{Maximize:} \quad Z = x_1 + 2x_2$$

$$\text{Subject to:} \quad -2x_1 + x_2 + x_3 \leqq 2$$
$$-x_1 + x_2 - x_3 \leqq 1$$
$$x_1, x_2, x_3 \geqq 0$$

From the final simplex tableau, construct a feasible solution whose value of the objective function is greater than 2000.

21. Use the two-phase simplex method to find a basic feasible solution to the following linear inequalities:

$$-6x_1 + x_2 - x_3 \leqq 5$$
$$-2x_1 + 2x_2 - 3x_3 \geqq 3$$
$$2x_2 - 4x_3 = 1$$
$$x_1, x_2, x_3 \geqq 0$$

22. Use the Big M simplex method to show that the following linear program is infeasible:

$$\text{Minimize:} \quad Z = 2y_1 + 4y_2$$
$$\text{Subject to:} \quad 2y_1 - 3y_2 \geq 2$$
$$-y_1 + y_2 \geq 3$$
$$y_1 \geq 0, \qquad y_2 \geq 0$$

23. In the tableau for the maximization problem below, the values of the six constants $\alpha_1, \alpha_2, \alpha_3, \beta, \rho_1, \rho_2$ are unknown (assume there are no artificial variables):

Basis	x_1	x_2	x_3	x_4	x_5	x_6	Constants
x_3	4	α_1	1	0	α_2	0	β
x_4	-1	-5	0	1	-1	0	2
x_6	α_3	-3	0	0	-4	1	3
$\bar{C}$ Row	ρ_1	ρ_2	0	0	-3	0	

$$x_1, \ldots, x_6 \geq 0$$

State restrictions on the six unknowns $(\alpha_1, \alpha_2, \alpha_3, \beta, \rho_1, \rho_2)$ which would make the following statements true about the given tableau:

a. The current solution is optimal but alternate optimum exists.
b. The current solution is infeasible. (State which variable.)
c. One of the constraints is inconsistent.
d. The current solution is a degenerate basic feasible solution. (Which variable causes degeneracy?)
e. The current solution is feasible but the problem has no finite optimum.
f. The current solution is the unique optimum solution.
g. The current solution is feasible but the objective can be improved by replacing x_6 by x_1. What will be the total change in the objective function value after the pivot?

24. Each of the following tableaus represents the end of an iteration to a *maximization* problem. Select *one or more* of the following conditions that best describe the results indicated by each tableau, and then answer any questions in parentheses.

a. Improvement in the value of the objective function is still possible. (Which variable should be brought into solution? Which variable should be removed? What is the total improvement in the objective function?)
b. The original problem is infeasible. (Why?)
c. The solution is degenerate. (Which variable causes degeneracy?)
d. The solution represented by the tableau is not a basic feasible solution.
e. The unique optimal solution has been obtained.
f. One of the optimal solutions has been obtained, but an alternative optimum exists. (Find the alternative optimum solution.)
g. The optimal solution to the original problem is unbounded. (Which variable causes this condition?) (Note: M is a very large positive number.)

Tableau 1

C_j	3	1	1	7	
Basis	x_1	x_2	x_3	x_4	b
x_1	1	0	1	2	2
x_2	0	1	0	1	1
$\bar{C}$ Row	0	0	-2	0	

Tableau 2

C_j	5	3	$-M$	10	
Basis	x_1	x_2	x_3	x_4	b
x_1	1	3	0	2	10
x_3	0	-1	1	-3	0
$\bar{C}$ Row	0	$-12 - M$	0	$-3M$	

Tableau 3

C_j Basis	-10 x_1	-5 x_2	-6 x_3	$-M$ x_4	b
x_4	-3	0	0	1	10
x_2	1	1	-2	0	20
$\bar{C}$ Row	$-3M-5$	0	-16	0	

Tableau 4

C_j Basis	0 x_1	0 x_2	3 x_3	-1 x_4	b
x_1	1	0	1	2	0
x_2	0	1	2	1	5
$\bar{C}$ Row	0	0	3	-1	

Tableau 5

C_j Basis	-2 x_1	-3 x_2	8 x_3	$-M$ x_4	b
x_1	1	0	-3	4	5
x_2	0	1	0	2	10
$\bar{C}$ Row	0	0	2	$-M+14$	

25. Consider the standard linear programming problem

$$\text{Minimize:} \quad Z = \mathbf{cx}$$

$$\text{Subject to:} \quad \mathbf{Ax} = \mathbf{b}, \qquad \mathbf{x} \geq 0$$

Let the vectors $\mathbf{x}^{(1)}$ and $\mathbf{x}^{(2)}$ be two optimal solutions to the above problem. Show that the vector $\mathbf{x}(\lambda) = \lambda \mathbf{x}^{(1)} + (1-\lambda)\mathbf{x}^{(2)}$ is also an optimal solution for any value of λ between 0 and 1. (Note: The above result is very useful in linear programming. Once we have two optimal solutions to a linear program, then we can generate an infinite number of optimal solutions by varying λ between 0 and 1.)

CHAPTER 3

NETWORK ANALYSIS

In this chapter we discuss a variety of flow problems in a network. A network is a system of lines or channels connecting different points. Some examples of networks are communication lines, railroad networks, pipeline systems, road networks, shipping lines, and aviation networks. In all these networks we will be interested in sending some specified commodity from certain supply points to some demand points. For example, in a pipeline system we may like to send water, oil, or gas from supply stations to demanding customers. Many of the network flow problems can be formulated as linear programs and their solutions may be obtained by using the simplex method. But a number of special network flow techniques have been developed which are generally more efficient than the simplex method. This chapter will be devoted to the discussion of some of the special network flow problems and their solution techniques.

3.1 SOME EXAMPLES OF NETWORK FLOW PROBLEMS

1. A nationwide chain store is interested in supplying a special product to its retail outlets from its various warehouses. What shipping plan would minimize the total cost of transportation?
2. In a machine shop a batch of jobs is to be assigned to a group of machines. What assignment of jobs to machines will maximize the total efficiency of the shop?
3. A pipe network distributes water from several pumping stations to various customers. If the capacities of the pipes are known, what is the maximum flow that is possible from the stations to the customers?
4. If we were to assign one-way traffic signs to a road network, what assignment would maximize the flow of traffic or the number of highway users?
5. A trucking firm has a table of distances between cities. It wants to find the shortest route and the shortest distance between all pairs of cities so as to design efficient service routes for its trucks.
6. A project consists of a large number of activities which must be done in a specified sequence. The project manager wants to determine how these activities should be scheduled and coordinated so as to minimize the project duration.

3.2 TRANSPORTATION PROBLEMS

Transportation problems are generally concerned with the distribution of a certain product from several sources to numerous localities at minimum cost.

65

Suppose there are m warehouses where a commodity is stocked, and n markets where it is needed. Let the supply available in the warehouses be a_1, $a_2, \ldots, a_m$, and the demands at the markets be $b_1, b_2, \ldots, b_n$. The unit cost of shipping from warehouse i to market j is $\$c_{ij}$. (If a particular warehouse cannot supply a certain market, we set the appropriate c_{ij} at $+\infty$.) We want to find an optimal shipping schedule which minimizes the total cost of transportation from all the warehouses to all the markets.

Linear Programming Formulation

To formulate the transportation problem as a linear program, we define x_{ij} as the quantity shipped from warehouse i to market j. Since i can assume values from $1, 2, \ldots, m$, and j from $1, 2, \ldots, n$, the number of decision variables is given by the product of m and n. The complete formulation is given below:

$$\text{Minimize:} \quad Z = \sum_{i=1}^{m} \sum_{j=1}^{n} c_{ij} x_{ij} \quad \text{(total cost of transportation)}$$

$$\text{Subject to:} \quad \sum_{j=1}^{n} x_{ij} \leq a_i \quad \begin{array}{l}\text{(supply restriction at warehouse } i) \\ \text{for } i = 1, 2, \ldots, m\end{array}$$

$$\sum_{i=1}^{m} x_{ij} \geq b_j \quad \begin{array}{l}\text{(demand requirement at market } j) \\ \text{for } j = 1, 2, \ldots, n\end{array}$$

$$x_{ij} \geq 0 \quad \begin{array}{l}\text{(nonnegative restrictions)} \\ \text{for all pairs } (i, j)\end{array}$$

The supply constraints guarantee that the total amount shipped from any warehouse does not exceed its capacity. The demand constraints guarantee that the total amount shipped to a market meets the minimum demand at the market. Excluding the nonnegativity constraints, the total number of constraints is $(m + n)$.

It is obvious that the market demands can be met if and only if the total supply at the warehouses is at least equal to the total demand at the markets. In other words, $\sum_{i=1}^{m} a_i \geq \sum_{j=1}^{n} b_j$. When the total supply equals the total demand $\left(\text{i.e., } \sum_{i=1}^{m} a_i = \sum_{j=1}^{n} b_j\right)$, every available supply at the warehouses will be shipped to meet the minimum demands at the markets. In this case, all the supply and demand constraints would become strict equations, and we have a *standard transportation problem* given by:

$$\text{Minimize:} \quad Z = \sum_{i=1}^{m} \sum_{j=1}^{n} c_{ij} x_{ij}$$

$$\text{Subject to:} \quad \sum_{j=1}^{n} x_{ij} = a_i \quad \text{for } i = 1, 2, \ldots, m$$

$$\sum_{i=1}^{m} x_{ij} = b_j \quad \text{for } j = 1, 2, \ldots, n$$

$$x_{ij} \geq 0 \quad \text{for all } (i, j)$$

We shall develop a technique for solving a standard transportation problem only. This means that any nonstandard problem, where the supplies and demands do not balance, must be converted to a standard transportation problem before it can be solved. This conversion can be achieved by the use of a dummy warehouse or a dummy market as shown below:

1. Consider an unbalanced transportation problem where the total supply exceeds the total demand. To convert this to a standard problem, a dummy market is created to absorb the excess supply available at the warehouses. The unit cost of shipping from any warehouse to the dummy market is assumed to be zero since in reality the dummy market does not exist and no physical transfer of goods takes place. Thus the unbalanced transportation problem is equivalent to the following standard problem:

$$\text{Minimize:} \quad Z = \sum_{i=1}^{m} \sum_{j=1}^{n+1} c_{ij} x_{ij}$$

$$\text{Subject to:} \quad \sum_{j=1}^{n+1} x_{ij} = a_i \qquad \text{for } i = 1, 2, \ldots, m$$

$$\sum_{i=1}^{m} x_{ij} = b_j \qquad \text{for } j = 1, 2, \ldots, n, n+1$$

$$x_{ij} \geq 0 \qquad \text{for all } (i, j)$$

Where $j = n + 1$ is the dummy market with demand $b_{n+1} = \sum_{i=1}^{m} a_i - \sum_{j=1}^{n} b_j$, and $c_{i,n+1} = 0$ for all $i = 1, 2, \ldots, m$. Note that the value of $x_{i,n+1}$ denotes the unused supply at warehouse i.

2. Consider now the situation where the total demand exceeds the total supply. Even though all the demands cannot be met, one may like to find a least-cost shipping schedule which will supply as much as possible to the markets. Here a dummy warehouse is created to supply the shortage. The equivalent standard problem becomes.

$$\text{Minimize:} \quad Z = \sum_{i=1}^{m+1} \sum_{j=1}^{n} c_{ij} x_{ij}$$

$$\text{Subject to:} \quad \sum_{j=1}^{n} x_{ij} = a_i \qquad \text{for } i = 1, 2, \ldots, m, m+1$$

$$\sum_{i=1}^{m+1} x_{ij} = b_j \qquad \text{for } j = 1, 2, \ldots, n$$

$$x_{ij} \geq 0 \qquad \text{for all } (i, j)$$

where $i = m + 1$ denotes the dummy warehouse with supply $a_{m+1} = \sum_{j=1}^{n} b_j - \sum_{i=1}^{m} a_i$, and $c_{m+1,j} = 0$ for all $j = 1, 2, \ldots, n$. Here $x_{m+1,j}$ denotes the amount of shortage at market j.

An important feature of the standard transportation problem is that it can be expressed in the form of a table, which displays the values of all the data coefficients (a_i, b_j, c_{ij}) associated with the problem. As a matter of fact, the constraints and the objective function of the transportation model can be read off directly from the table. A *transportation table* for three warehouses and four markets is shown in p. 68.

The supply constraints can be obtained by merely equating the sum of all the variables in each row to the warehouse capacities. Similarly the demand constraints are obtained by equating the sum of all the variables in each column to the market demands.

In principle, we shall solve the transportation problem by using the simplex method of linear programming. But the special structure of the transportation

		Markets				
		M_1	M_2	M_3	M_4	Supplies
	W_1	x_{11} $\quad c_{11}$	x_{12} $\quad c_{12}$	x_{13} $\quad c_{13}$	x_{14} $\quad c_{14}$	a_1
Warehouses	W_2	x_{21} $\quad c_{21}$	x_{22} $\quad c_{22}$	x_{23} $\quad c_{23}$	x_{24} $\quad c_{24}$	a_2
	W_3	x_{31} $\quad c_{31}$	x_{32} $\quad c_{32}$	x_{33} $\quad c_{33}$	x_{34} $\quad c_{34}$	a_3
Demands		b_1	b_2	b_3	b_4	

matrix (all the coefficients of the variables are 0 or 1) gives simple selection rules while choosing a nonbasic variable or dropping a basic variable.

Finding an Initial Basic Feasible Solution

The standard transportation problem has $(m+n)$ constraints and (mn) variables. In general the number of basic variables in a basic feasible solution is given by the number of constraints. But in the transportation problem, the number of variables that can take positive values is limited to $(m+n-1)$ since one of the constraints is redundant. To see this, add up all the supply constraints. This gives $\sum_{i=1}^{m}\sum_{j=1}^{n} x_{ij} = \sum_{i=1}^{m} a_i$. Summing up the demand constraints, we get $\sum_{i=1}^{m}\sum_{j=1}^{n} x_{ij} = \sum_{j=1}^{n} b_j$. Since $\sum_{i=1}^{m} a_i = \sum_{j=1}^{n} b_j$, these two equations are identical, and we have only $(m+n-1)$ independent constraints.

Because of the special structure of the transportation matrix, it is very easy to find an initial basic feasible solution to start the simplex method without the use of artificial variables. We shall illustrate this with an example.

EXAMPLE 3.2-1

Consider a transportation problem with three warehouses and four markets. The warehouse capacities are $a_1 = 3$, $a_2 = 7$, and $a_3 = 5$. The market demands are $b_1 = 4$, $b_2 = 3$, $b_3 = 4$, and $b_4 = 4$. The unit cost of shipping is given by the following table:

	M_1	M_2	M_3	M_4
W_1	2	2	2	1
W_2	10	8	5	4
W_3	7	6	6	8

Since $\sum_{i=1}^{3} a_i = \sum_{j=1}^{4} b_j = 15$, we have a standard transportation problem. The transportation table is given by

	M_1		M_2		M_3		M_4		Supplies
W_1	x_{11}	2	x_{12}	2	x_{13}	2	x_{14}	1	3
W_2	x_{21}	10	x_{22}	8	x_{23}	5	x_{24}	4	7
W_3	x_{31}	7	x_{32}	6	x_{33}	6	x_{34}	8	5
Demands	4		3		4		4		

Hereafter we shall refrain from writing the variable names (x_{ij}) explicitly in the table.

A basic feasible solution to this example will have at most six (i.e., $3+4-1$) positive variables. There are a number of ways to find an initial basic feasible solution. We shall describe two of the most important ones here.

Northwest Corner Rule. This rule generates a feasible solution with no more than $(m+n-1)$ positive values. The variables which occupy the north west corner positions in the transportation table are chosen as the basic variables. Thus x_{11} is selected as the first basic variable, and is assigned a value as large as possible consistent with the supply and demand restrictions. In other words, set $x_{11} = \min(a_1, b_1) = \min(3, 4) = 3$. This means that supply in warehouse 1 is exhausted and no further supply to the other markets is possible. Hence we set the variables x_{12}, x_{13}, x_{14} as nonbasic at zero. In addition, 3 units of market 1 demand has been satisfied. Hence the remaining demand at market 1 is only 1 unit. This is illustrated by the following table.

	M_1	M_2	M_3	M_4	
W_1	③	0	0	0	0
W_2					7
W_3					5
	1	3	4	4	

The value of the basic variable is circled for easy identification.

We then select the next northwest corner variable as a basic variable. This corresponds to x_{21}; value of $x_{21} = \min(7, 1) = 1$. Market 1 demand is now fully satisfied and supply in warehouse 2 reduces to 6 units.

	M_1	M_2	M_3	M_4	
W_1	③	0	0	0	0
W_2	①				6
W_3	0				5
	0	3	4	4	

The next northwest corner variable is x_{22} and we let $x_{22} = \min(6, 3) = 3$.

Continuing in the same manner we will finally get

	M_1	M_2	M_3	M_4
W_1	③	0	0	0
W_2	①	③	③	0
W_3	0	0	①	④

We have six positive variables in the solution. The row sums are equal to the warehouse capacities, and the column sums to market demands. Thus we have a basic feasible solution to the transportation problem as shown below:

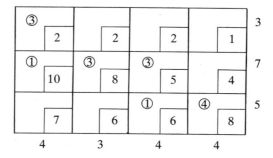

For the above basic feasible solution, the total cost of transportation is given by

$$Z = (3 \times 2) + (1 \times 10) + (3 \times 8) + (3 \times 5) + (1 \times 6) + (4 \times 8) = 93$$

The basic feasible solution obtained by the northwest-corner rule may be far from optimal since the transportation costs are completely ignored. Now we shall discuss another method of determining an initial basic feasible solution which takes into account the shipping costs as well.

The Least-Cost Rule. The only difference between the two rules is the criterion used for selecting the successive basic variables. In the least-cost rule, the variable with the lowest shipping cost will be chosen as the basic variable. We shall illustrate this rule by finding a basic feasible solution to Example 3.2-1.

The transportation table is scanned for the smallest c_{ij}, and this corresponds to the variable x_{14}. This is chosen as the first basic variable and we let $x_{14} = \min(3, 4) = 3$. Row 1 is deleted from further consideration since supply in warehouse 1 is exhausted. The resulting supply-demand configuration is given by the following table:

Out of the remaining unassigned cells, the variable x_{24} has the lowest cost, and we set $x_{24} = \min(7, 1) = 1$. Proceeding in a similar manner, the initial basic feasible solution becomes:

0		0		0		③		3
	2		2		2		1	
②		0		④		①		7
	10		8		5		4	
②		③		0		0		5
	7		6		6		8	
4		3		4		4		

The total cost of transportation equals 79. We now have a better starting solution as compared to the one obtained by the northwest-corner rule. The addition effort involved in scanning the transportation matrix for the smallest c_{ij} is generally offset by the reduction in the number of iterations required to reach the optimal solution.

In general the least cost rule provides a better starting solution as compared to the northwest corner rule. But this is not guaranteed in all problems. As a matter of fact, examples have been constructed wherein the opposite is true.

Improving the Initial Basic Feasible Solution

In Example 3.2-1, an initial basic feasible solution using the least cost rule is $x_{14} = 3$, $x_{21} = 2$, $x_{23} = 4$, $x_{24} = 1$, $x_{31} = 2$, $x_{32} = 3$, and all other $x_{ij} = 0$. The value of the objective function is 79. The corresponding transportation table is given in Table 3.1:

Table 3.1

	M_1		M_2		M_3		M_4		
W_1							③		3
		2		2		2		1	
W_2	②				④		①		7
		10		8		5		4	
W_3	②		③						5
		7		6		6		8	
	4		3		4		4		

In Table 3.1, the empty cells correspond to nonbasic variables.

The Stepping Stone Method

This determines whether the initial solution found by the least cost rule is optimum. We know from the simplex method that a given solution minimizes the objective function only if the relative cost coefficients of the nonbasic variables (net change in Z per unit increase in the nonbasic variables) are greater than or equal to zero.

The relative cost coefficients are computed by increasing a nonbasic variable by one unit, and computing the resulting change in the total transportation cost. To illustrate this let us increase the nonbasic variable x_{11} from 0 to 1. In order to satisfy the constraints (that is, row sums should add up to the various supplies, and column sums to the various demands), x_{14} will decrease by 1, x_{24} will increase by 1, and x_{21} will decrease by 1. Schematically these changes may be represented as follows:

	M_1	M_4
W_1	+1 $\longrightarrow$	−1
W_2	−1 $\longleftarrow$	+1

Note that the adjustment is done only on the values of the basic variables. This results in a change in the total shipping cost. Thus, the net change in Z per unit increase in x_{11}, denoted by $\bar{c}_{11}$, is given by

$$\bar{c}_{11} = c_{11}(\text{change in } x_{11}) + c_{14}(\text{change in } x_{14})$$
$$+ c_{24}(\text{change in } x_{24}) + c_{21}(\text{change in } x_{21})$$
$$= 2(+1) + 1(-1) + 4(+1) + 10(-1) = -5$$

This implies that the objective function will decrease by 5 units for every unit increase in the nonbasic variable x_{11}. Hence to minimize Z, x_{11} may be increased by making it a basic variable.

As a rule we calculate all the other $\bar{c}_{ij}$ coefficients, and the nonbasic variable with the lowest relative cost $(\bar{c}_{ij})$ becomes the next basic variable. Similar to the inner product rule used in the simplex method for calculating the relative costs, there is a simple way to calculate all the $\bar{c}_{ij}$ coefficients directly. This procedure is called the u-v *Method* or the *MODI* (*Modified Distribution*) *Method.**

u-v **Method**

For any basic feasible solution, find numbers u_i for warehouse i, and v_j for market j such that

$$u_i + v_j = c_{ij} \qquad \text{for every basic } x_{ij} \tag{3.1}$$

These numbers can be positive, negative, or zero. Then,

$$\bar{c}_{ij} = c_{ij} - (u_i + v_j) \qquad \text{for all nonbasic } x_{ij} \tag{3.2}$$

If all the $\bar{c}_{ij}$ are nonnegative, then the current basic feasible solution is optimal. If not, there exists a nonbasic variable x_{pq} such that $\bar{c}_{pq} = \min \bar{c}_{ij} < 0$, and x_{pq} is made a basic variable to improve the value of the objective function.

To apply the u-v method to Example 3.2-1, we have to compute seven numbers u_1, u_2, u_3, v_1, v_2, v_3, and v_4. In the current basic feasible solution

---

* The u-v method is based on the complementary slackness properties between the solutions to the transportation problem and its dual. For details, refer to Chapter 4 (Section 4.2 and Exercise 11).

(Table 3.1), the basic variables are x_{14}, x_{21}, x_{23}, x_{24}, x_{31}, and x_{32}. Using Eq. 3.1 we get the following six equations:

$$u_1 + v_4 = 1$$
$$u_2 + v_1 = 10$$
$$u_2 + v_3 = 5$$
$$u_2 + v_4 = 4$$
$$u_3 + v_1 = 7$$
$$u_3 + v_2 = 6$$

Since the system has six equations in seven unknowns, there exists an infinite number of possible solutions. To get a particular solution we can set any of the variables zero and solve for the rest.

Setting $u_1 = 0$, we get $v_4 = 1$, $u_2 = 3$, $v_1 = 7$, $v_3 = 2$, $u_3 = 0$, and $v_2 = 6$. This computation can easily be accomplished using Table 3.1 directly rather than writing the six equations separately.

Optimality Test
For every nonbasic variable x_{ij}, the unit cost c_{ij} is compared with the sum of u_i and v_j. If all the $u_i + v_j \leq c_{ij}$, then we have an optimal solution; otherwise, the nonbasic variable with the least relative cost value is chosen.

In our example,

$$\bar{c}_{pq} = \min (c_{ij} - u_i - v_j) = c_{11} - (u_1 + v_1) = -5$$

Hence the nonbasic variable x_{11} is introduced into the basis as the new basic variable. To determine the maximum increase in x_{11}, we assign x_{11} an unknown nonnegative value θ. In order to satisfy the constraints, θ has to be added or subtracted from the basic variables so that the row sums and column sums are equal to the corresponding supplies and demands. Referring to Table 3.1, we see that both the basic variables x_{14} and x_{21} are decreased by θ while x_{24} is increased by θ as shown below:

	M_1	M_2	M_3	M_4	
W_1	$+\theta$			$3-\theta$	3
W_2	$2-\theta$		4	$1+\theta$	7
W_3	2	3			5
	4	3	4	4	

Now θ is increased as long as the solution remains nonnegative. The maximum value of θ is limited by those basic variables which start decreasing with θ. The basic variable which becomes zero first is removed from the basis.* In this case the maximum θ is equal to 2, and the basic variable x_{21} is replaced by x_{11}. Table 3.2 gives the new basic feasible solution, with a new set of values for u_i and v_j.

---

* In some problems, it is possible for more than one basic variable to become zero, simultaneously. Under such cases, the rule is to select any one of them (but only one) to leave the basis.

Table 3.2

	$v_1 = 2$	$v_2 = 1$	$v_3 = 2$	$v_4 = 1$	
$u_1 = 0$	② 2	2	2	① 1	3
$u_2 = 3$	10	8	④ 5	③ 4	7
$u_3 = 5$	② 7	③ 6	6	8	5
	4	3	4	4	

The new value of the objective function is 69. The solution given by Table 3.2 is not optimal, since

$$\min (c_{ij} - u_i - v_j) = c_{33} - (u_3 + v_3) = -1 \qquad \bullet$$

Now x_{33} is introduced as a basic variable at a nonnegative value θ. This produces the following change in the values of the basic variables:

	M_1	M_2	M_3	M_4	
W_1	$2 + \theta$			$1 - \theta$	3
W_2			$4 - \theta$	$3 + \theta$	7
W_3	$2 - \theta$	3	$+\theta$		5
	4	3	4	4	

The maximum value of θ is 1, and x_{33}, replaces x_{14} in the basis. The new basic feasible solution is given by Table 3.3.

Table 3.3

	$v_1 = 2$	$v_2 = 1$	$v_3 = 1$	$v_4 = 0$	
$u_1 = 0$	③ 2	2	2	1	3
$u_2 = 4$	10	8	③ 5	④ 4	7
$u_3 = 5$	① 7	③ 6	① 6	8	5
	4	3	4	4	

The new value of the objective function is 68. Table 3.3 represents a unique optimal solution, since $\bar{c}_{ij} > 0$ for all nonbasic variables. The optimal shipping schedule is to ship

$$3 \text{ units from } W_1 \text{ to } M_1;$$
$$3 \text{ units from } W_2 \text{ to } M_3;$$
$$4 \text{ units from } W_2 \text{ to } M_4;$$
$$1 \text{ unit from } W_3 \text{ to } M_1;$$
$$3 \text{ units from } W_3 \text{ to } M_2;$$
$$1 \text{ unit from } W_3 \text{ to } M_3.$$

The least cost of shipping is 68.

Applications

A number of practical problems can be formulated as transportation problems for solution. We shall present two specific applications here.

EXAMPLE 3.2-2

A canning company operates two canning plants. Three growers are willing to supply fresh fruits in the following amounts:

Smith	200 tons at $10/ton
Jones	300 tons at $9/ton
Richard	400 tons at $8/ton

Shipping costs in dollars per ton are:

	To	
From	Plant A	Plant B
Smith	2	2.5
Jones	1	1.5
Richard	5	3

Plant capacities and labor costs are:

	Plant A	Plant B
Capacity	450 tons	550 tons
Labor cost	$25/ton	$20/ton

The canned fruits are sold at $50/ton to the distributors. The company can sell at this price all they can produce. How should the company plan its operations at the two plants so as to maximize its profits?

To formulate this as a linear program, define:

$$x_{SA} = \text{quantity shipped from Smith to Plant } A$$
$$x_{SB} = \text{quantity shipped from Smith to Plant } B$$
$$x_{JA} = \text{quantity shipped from Jones to Plant } A$$
$$x_{JB} = \text{quantity shipped from Jones to Plant } B$$
$$x_{RA} = \text{quantity shipped from Richard to Plant } A$$
$$x_{RB} = \text{quantity shipped from Richard to Plant } B$$

The supply constraints are given by

$$x_{SA} + x_{SB} \leq 200$$
$$x_{JA} + x_{JB} \leq 300$$
$$x_{RA} + x_{RB} \leq 400$$

The constraints on plant capacities are

$$x_{SA} + x_{JA} + x_{RA} \leq 450$$
$$x_{SB} + x_{JB} + x_{RB} \leq 550$$

All the variables are restricted to be nonnegative. To compute the net profit for each of the variables, we have to subtract from the selling price the cost of fresh fruits, shipping, and labor costs. For example, the profit on variable x_{SA} (fruits bought from Smith and processed at Plant A) is given by:

$$P_{SA} = 50 - (10 + 2 + 25) = \$13/\text{ton}$$

Similarly the other profits can be calculated, and the objective function is to maximize

$$Z = 13x_{SA} + 17.5x_{SB} + 15x_{JA} + 19.5x_{JB} + 12x_{RA} + 19x_{RB}$$

The above linear program is an unbalanced transportation problem where the total supply is less than the total demand. Table 3.4 gives the equivalent (standard) transportation formulation with the addition of a dummy grower.

Table 3.4

	Plant A	Plant B	
Smith	13	17.5	200
Jones	15	19.5	300
Richard	12	19	400
Dummy	0	0	100
	450	550	

Since the objective is to maximize the total profit, the variable selection rule of the transportation algorithm needs some modification. Those nonbasic variables whose $c_{ij} > u_i + v_j$ (i.e., $\bar{c}_{ij} > 0$) are eligible to enter the basis to improve the objective function. When all the $\bar{c}_{ij} \leq 0$, the solution becomes optimal. The final solution is left as an exercise.

EXAMPLE 3.2-3

Consider the problem of scheduling the weekly production of a certain item for the next 4 weeks. The production cost of the item is \$10 for the first 2 weeks, and \$15 for the last 2 weeks. The weekly demands are 300, 700, 900, and 800, which must be met. The plant can produce a maximum of 700 units each week.

In addition the company can employ overtime during the second and third week. This increases the weekly production by an additional 200 units, but the production cost increases by $5 per item. Excess production can be stored at a unit cost of $3 per week. How should the production be scheduled so as to minimize the total costs?

To formulate this as a transportation problem, we consider the production periods as warehouses, and weekly demands as markets. Since overtime production is possible during the second and third weeks, there are in all six supply points. The decision variables are

x_{1j} = Normal production in week 1 for use in week j for $j = 1, 2, 3, 4$

x_{2j} = Normal production in week 2 for use in week j for $j = 2, 3, 4$

x_{3j} = Overtime production in week 2 for use in week j for $j = 2, 3, 4$

x_{4j} = Normal production in week 3 for use in week j for $j = 3, 4$

x_{5j} = Overtime production in week 3 for use in week j for $j = 3, 4$

x_{64} = Normal production in week 4 for use in week 4

Since the total production (normal and overtime) exceeds the total demand, we create a dummy market to absorb the excess supply. Table 3.5 gives the corresponding transportation problem.

Table 3.5

Demands

	Week 1	Week 2	Week 3	Week 4	Dummy	
Week 1	10	13	16	19	0	700
Week 2 (normal)	M	10	13	16	0	700
Week 2 (overtime)	M	15	18	21	0	200
Week 3 (normal)	M	M	15	18	0	700
Week 3 (overtime)	M	M	20	23	0	200
Week 4 (normal)	M	M	M	15	0	700
	300	700	900	800	500	

Supplies (row label at left)

REMARKS

1. Some of the cost elements in the above table are set at M (an infinitely large value) to denote shipments which are not possible. For example, production during weeks 2, 3, and 4 cannot possibly supply the first week's demand.

2. Weekly storage cost of $3 per item is added to the production cost whenever an item is stored to meet future demands.

This problem can now be solved by the transportation algorithm to determine the optimal production schedule. This is left as an exercise for the reader.

3.3 ASSIGNMENT PROBLEMS

Standard Assignment Problems

A certain machine shop has n machines denoted by $M_1, M_2, \ldots, M_n$. A group of n different jobs $(J_1, J_2, \ldots, J_n)$ is to be assigned to these machines. For each job the machining cost depends on the machine to which it is assigned. Let c_{ij} represent the cost of doing job j on machine i. (If a particular job cannot be done on a machine we set the appropriate c_{ij} to a very large number.) Each machine can work only on one job. The problem is to assign the jobs to the machines which will minimize the total cost of machining.

A naive approach to solve this problem is to enumerate all possible assignments of jobs to machines. For each assignment the total cost may be computed, and the one with the least cost is picked as the best assignment. This will be an inefficient and expensive approach since the number of possible assignments is $n!$ Even for $n = 10$, there are 3,628,800 possible assignments!

To formulate this as a linear programming problem, define

$$x_{ij} = \begin{cases} 1 \text{ if job } j \text{ is assigned to machine } i \\ 0 \text{ otherwise} \end{cases}$$

Since each machine is assigned exactly to one job, we have

$$\sum_{j=1}^{n} x_{ij} = 1 \quad \text{for } i = 1, 2, \ldots, n$$

Similarly, each job is assigned exactly to one machine.

$$\sum_{i=1}^{n} x_{ij} = 1 \quad \text{for } j = 1, 2, \ldots, n$$

The objective is to minimize

$$Z = \sum_{i=1}^{n} \sum_{j=1}^{n} c_{ij} x_{ij}$$

The above is actually the formulation of a standard transportation problem with n warehouses and n markets where the supply $a_i = 1$ for $i = 1, \ldots, n$, and the demand $b_j = 1$ for $j = 1, \ldots, n$. The corresponding transportation matrix is given below:

		Jobs			
		J_1	J_2	$\cdots$	J_n	
	M_1	c_{11}	c_{12}		c_{1n}	1
	M_2	c_{21}	c_{22}		c_{2n}	1
Machines	.					.
	.					.
	.					.
	M_n	c_{n1}	c_{n2}		c_{nn}	1
		1	1	$\cdots$	1	

Nonstandard Assignment Problems

Consider a machine shop with M machines and N jobs where $M \neq N$. To convert this to an (equivalent) standard assignment problem with equal number of jobs and machines, we create dummy jobs or dummy machines.

Suppose we have more machines than jobs $(M > N)$. We then create $(M - N)$ dummy jobs so that there will be M machines and M jobs. We set the machining cost of the dummy jobs as zero so that the objective function will be unaltered. When a dummy job gets assigned to a machine, that machine stays idle. Similarly, when we have more jobs than machines $(N > M)$ then some jobs cannot be assigned. In this case, $(N - M)$ dummy machines are created whose machining cost will be zero for all jobs.

Solution by the Transportation Algorithm

Since any assignment problem can be formulated as a standard transportation problem, the transportation technique discussed in Section 3.2 can be used to find the optimal assignment. To illustrate this consider the following assignment problem:

EXAMPLE 3.3-1

Find the optimal assignment of four jobs and four machines when the cost of assignment is given by the following table:

	J_1	J_2	J_3	J_4
M_1	10	9	8	7
M_2	3	4	5	6
M_3	2	1	1	2
M_4	4	3	5	6

Solution

Since the number of jobs and machines are equal, we have a standard assignment problem given by Table 3.6.

Table 3.6

	J_1	J_2	J_3	J_4	
M_1	10	9	8	7	1
M_2	3	4	5	6	1
M_3	2	1	1	2	1
M_4	4	3	5	6	1
	1	1	1	1	

Let us use the least cost rule to find the initial basic feasible solution. In Table

3.6, both the cells (M_3, J_2) and (M_3, J_3) have the lowest cost. Arbitrarily selecting x_{32} as the first basic variable, we let $x_{32} = \min[1, 1] = 1$. Since the minimum is not unique, we could either make the remaining cells in the third row nonbasic at zero, or those in the second column nonbasic at zero. (We cannot do both because we need $4+4-1=7$ basic variables.) Since the cost elements of the second column are larger compared to those of the third row, we make the remaining cells in the second column nonbasic as shown below:

	J_1	J_2	J_3	J_4	
M_1		0			1
M_2		0			1
M_3		①			0
M_4		0			1
	1	0	1	1	

The next basic variable will be x_{33}. The maximum value for $x_{33} = $ minimum $(0, 1) = 0$ and we make the remaining cells in the third row nonbasic at zero as follows:

	J_1	J_2	J_3	J_4	
M_1		0			1
M_2		0			1
M_3	0	①	⓪	0	0
M_4		0			1
	1	0	1	1	

   The zero in cell (M_3, J_3) is circled to indicate that x_{33} is a basic variable. Hence the basic feasible solution is going to be degenerate.
   The next basic variable to be chosen is x_{21}, which has the lowest cost. Once again there is a tie and we make the elements of column 1 nonbasic. Proceeding in a similar manner, the initial basic feasible solution is obtained as shown in Table 3.7.

Table 3.7

	$v_1 = 4$	$v_2 = 6$	$v_3 = 6$	$v_4 = 7$
$u_1 = 0$	10	9	8	① 7
$u_2 = -1$	① 3	4	⓪ 5	6
$u_3 = -5$	2	① 1	⓪ 1	2
$u_4 = -1$	4	3	① 5	⓪ 6

The value of the objective function is given by $Z = 16$. Using the u-v method the u_i and v_j are calculated after setting $u_1 = 0$. The solution is not optimal since

$$\bar{c}_{22} = 4 - (6 - 1) = -1$$
$$\bar{c}_{42} = 3 - (6 - 1) = -2$$

The nonbasic variable x_{42} is introduced at a positive value θ to improve the objective function as follows:

	J_1	J_2	J_3	J_4	
M_1				1	1
M_2	1		0		1
M_3		$1-\theta$	$0+\theta$		1
M_4		$+\theta$	$1-\theta$	0	1
	1	1	1	1	

Maximum $\theta = 1$. Both the basic variables x_{32} and x_{43} reduce to 0 simultaneously when x_{42} is increased to 1. Hence either x_{32} or x_{43} could be dropped from the basis. We decide arbitrarily to drop x_{32}. Table 3.8 represents the new basic feasible solution.

Table 3.8

	$v_1 = 4$	$v_2 = 4$	$v_3 = 6$	$v_4 = 7$
$u_1 = 0$	10	9	8	① 7
$u_2 = -1$	① 3	4	⓪ 5	6
$u_3 = -5$	2	1	① 1	2
$u_4 = -1$	4	① 3	⓪ 5	⓪ 6

All the $\bar{c}_{ij}$ coefficients are nonnegative. Hence the solution given by Table 3.8 is optimal. The optimal assignment is then to assign M_1 to J_4, M_2 to J_1, M_3 to J_3, and M_4 to J_2. The least cost of machining is 14.

The transportation algorithm is generally not recommended for solving the assignment problem due to the presence of degeneracy in every basic feasible solution. As discussed earlier in Section 2.8, degeneracy can lead to non-productive basis changes and possibly cycling.

An Alternative Assignment Algorithm

A more efficient way of solving the assignment problem has been developed which takes into account the special structure of the assignment matrix. The basic principle of this procedure is that the optimal assignment is not affected if a constant is added or subtracted from any row or column of the cost matrix. For instance, if the cost of doing any job in machine 3 in Example 3.3-1 is increased by $2 so that the third row of the cost matrix becomes 4, 3, 3, 4, it can be easily verified that the optimal solution is not affected by this change.

In essence the solution procedure is to subtract a sufficiently large cost from the various rows or columns in such a way that an optimal assignment is found by inspection. We initiate the algorithm by examining each row (column) of the cost matrix to identify the smallest element. This quantity is then subtracted from all the elements in that row (column). This produces a cost matrix containing at least one 0 element in each row (column). Now try to make a feasible assignment using the cells with zero costs. If it is possible then we have an optimal assignment. Let us illustrate this with Example 3.3-1.

Examining the rows first, a reduced cost matrix can be obtained by subtracting,

1.   7 from the first row,
2.   3 from the second row,
3.   1 from the third row, and
4.   3 from the fourth row.

This produces the following cost matrix:

	J_1	J_2	J_3	J_4
M_1	3	2	1	0
M_2	0	1	2	3
M_3	1	0	0	1
M_4	1	0	2	3

From the above table a feasible assignment using only the cells with zero costs is $M_1 \rightarrow J_4$, $M_2 \rightarrow J_1$, $M_3 \rightarrow J_3$, and $M_4 \rightarrow J_2$. Hence this is an optimal assignment.

In general, it may not always be possible to find a feasible assignment using cells with zero costs. To illustrate this, consider the following assignment problem:

EXAMPLE 3.3-2
Find an optimal solution to an assignment problem with the following cost matrix:

	J_1	J_2	J_3	J_4
M_1	10	9	7	8
M_2	5	8	7	7
M_3	5	4	6	5
M_4	2	3	4	5

Solution
First the minimum element in each row is subtracted from all the elements in that row. This gives the following reduced-cost matrix.

	J_1	J_2	J_3	J_4
M_1	3	2	0	1
M_2	0	3	2	2
M_3	1	0	2	1
M_4	0	1	2	3

Since both the machines M_2 and M_4 have a zero cost corresponding to job J_1 only, a feasible assignment using only cells with zero costs is not possible. To get additional zeros subtract the minimum element in the fourth column from all the elements in that column.

	J_1	J_2	J_3	J_4
M_1	3	2	0	0
M_2	0	3	2	1
M_3	1	0	2	0
M_4	0	1	2	2

Only three jobs can be assigned using the zero cells, and so a feasible assignment is still not possible. In such cases, the procedure draws a minimum number of lines through some selected rows and columns in such a way that all the cells with zero costs are covered by these lines. The minimum number of lines needed is equal to the maximum number of jobs that can be assinged using the zero cells.

In our example, this can be done with three lines as follows.

	J_1	J_2	J_3	J_4
M_1	~~3~~	~~2~~	~~0~~	~~0~~
M_2	0	3	2	1
M_3	~~1~~	~~0~~	~~2~~	~~0~~
M_4	0	1	2	2

Now select the smallest element which is not covered by the lines. In our case it is 1. Subtract this number from all the elements which are *not covered*. Then add this number to all those *covered* elements that are at the intersection of two lines. This gives the following reduced cost matrix.

	J_1	J_2	J_3	J_4
M_1	4	2	0	0
M_2	0	2	1	0
M_3	2	0	2	0
M_4	0	0	1	1

A feasible assignment is now possible and an optimal solution is to assign $M_1 \rightarrow J_3$, $M_2 \rightarrow J_1$, $M_3 \rightarrow J_4$, and $M_4 \rightarrow J_2$. The total cost is given by $7+5+5+$

$3 = 20$. An alternate optimal solution is $M_1 \rightarrow J_3$, $M_2 \rightarrow J_4$, $M_3 \rightarrow J_2$, and $M_4 \rightarrow J_1$. In case a feasible set could not be obtained at this step, one has to repeat the step of drawing lines to cover the zeros and continue until a feasible assignment is obtained.

3.4   THE LEAST-TIME TRANSPORTATION PROBLEM

In contrast to the least-cost transportation problem discussed in Section 3.2, the least-time transportation problem is concerned with meeting the demands at the markets in the least possible time. The transportation cost is not of primary importance. Such problems arise in practice when perishable goods have to be transported without spoilage or when military supplies have to reach command posts during an emergency.

As in the regular transportation problem, we assume m warehouses with supplies $a_1, a_2, \ldots, a_m$, and n markets with demands $b_1, b_2, \ldots, b_n$ such that $\sum_{i=1}^{m} a_i = \sum_{j=1}^{n} b_j$. Let t_{ij} represent the *total* time of transportation from warehouse i to market j, *independent of the amount transported*. Assume that the shipments from the warehouses to the markets may be done simultaneously. With respect to each shipping plan, the shipment which takes the largest transportation time determines the time required to complete all the shipments. The problem is to complete all the shipments in the minimum possible time.

Mathematically, if T denotes the time required to complete all the shipments, then

$$T = \max \{t_{ij}\} \text{ over all } (i, j) \text{ for which } x_{ij} > 0$$

The objective is to find the nonnegative x_{ij} that will satisfy the supply-demand constraints and minimize the shipment time T.

The algorithm to solve the least-time transportation problem uses the same transportation table discussed in Section 3.2. The algorithm finds an initial basic feasible solution using the least-cost rule. With the help of the stepping-stone procedure an improved basic feasible solution is sought. Since the objective function here is different, the rule for selecting the nonbasic variable to enter the basis is modified. The detailed steps of the algorithm are given below:

Step I.   Find a basic feasible solution with the help of the least cost rule.

Step II.   Compute the shipment time T associated with the basic feasible solution. This is given by,

$$T = \max (t_{ij}) \qquad \text{for those } (i, j) \text{ such that } x_{ij} > 0$$

Step III.   Cross out all those nonbasic variables (cells) whose t_{ij} values are greater than or equal to T.

Step IV.   Select the basic variable whose t_{ij} equals T, and place a $-\theta$ in that cell. By the stepping-stone method, construct a closed loop using the basic cells and any one of nonbasic cells that has not been crossed out in Step III. This requires placing a $+\theta$ or a $-\theta$ in the cells such that the row sums are equal to the supplies and the column sums are equal to the demands. Care should be taken to see that the nonbasic cell contains only a $+\theta$. If no such closed loop can be found, the algorithm terminates with the

present basic feasible solution as the optimal solution. Otherwise go to Step V.

Step V. Increase θ to its maximum value such that all the variables
remain nonnegative. The basic variable which becomes zero
leaves the basis and we have a new basic feasible solution. Then
return to Step II.

We shall illustrate the procedure with the following example.

EXAMPLE 3.4-1

Find the shipping plan with the least time for the transportation problem with
three warehouses and four markets with $a_1 = 3$, $a_2 = 7$, $a_3 = 5$, $b_1 = 4$, $b_2 = 3$,
$b_3 = 4$, and $b_4 = 4$. The transportation time is given below:

	M_1	M_2	M_3	M_4
W_1	2	2	2	1
W_2	10	8	5	4
W_3	7	6	6	8

Solution

Table 3.9 gives an initial basic feasible solution using the least-cost rule.

Table 3.9

The corresponding shipping time

$$T = \max\left[t_{14}, t_{21}, t_{23}, t_{24}, t_{31}, t_{32}\right] = t_{21} = 10$$

Since all the nonbasic cells in Table 3.9 have $t_{ij} < 10$, none of them will be
crossed out. The basic variable x_{21} has the largest transportation time. A $-\theta$ is
placed in that cell and a closed loop using cells $(2, 2)$, $(3, 1)$, and $(3, 2)$ is found.
The maximum θ is 2, and the nonbasic variable x_{22} replaces x_{21} in the basis.
The new basic feasible solution is given by Table 3.10.

Table 3.10

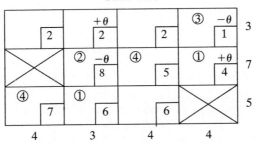

The shipment time now is 8, which corresponds to the cell $(2, 2)$. The nonbasic cells $(2, 1)$ and $(3, 4)$ of Table 3.10 are crossed out since their t_{ij}'s are not better than 8. Another closed loop is formed using cells $(2, 2)$, $(2, 4)$, $(1, 4)$, and $(1, 2)$. Maximum $\theta = 2$, and the new basic feasible solution is shown in Table 3.11.

Table 3.11

② +θ / 2	−θ / 2		2	① / 1	3
✕	✕	④ / 5	③ / 4		7
④ −θ / 7	① +θ / 6	6	✕		5
4	3	4	4		

The solution from Table 3.11 gives $T = 7$, which corresponds to the basic variable x_{31}. A closed loop using cells $(3, 1)$, $(3, 2)$, $(1, 2)$, and $(1, 1)$ is formed. Maximum $\theta = 2$, implying x_{12} leaves the basis. The basic variable with the largest transportation time, namely x_{31}, still remains in the basis. Hence the new basic feasible solution does not result in a reduction in the value of T as shown in Table 3.12.

Table 3.12

② +θ / 2	2		2	① −θ / 1	3
✕	✕	④ −θ / 5	③ +θ / 4		7
② −θ / 7	③ / 6	+θ / 6	✕		5
4	3	4	4		

The value of T is still 7. Once again a closed loop using the cells $(3, 1)$, $(1, 1)$, $(1, 4)$, $(2, 4)$, $(2, 3)$, and $(3, 3)$ is formed; maximum $\theta = 1$. The basic variable x_{14} is replaced by x_{33}. Table 3.13 gives the new shipping plan.

Table 3.13

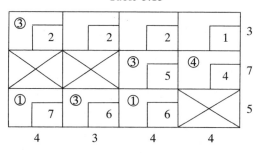

The value of T has not changed, and it corresponds to the basic variable x_{31}. Referring to Table 3.13, a $-\theta$ in cell $(3, 1)$ results in a $+\theta$ in cell $(1, 1)$. This has to be compensated by a $-\theta$ in one of the remaining cells in the first row. Since these are nonbasic variables at zero, we cannot subtract a positive value without making the solution infeasible. Hence no closed loop can be formed, and Table 3.13 represents an optimal solution.

An optimal plan is to ship

$$3 \text{ units from } W_1 \text{ to } M_1$$
$$3 \text{ units from } W_2 \text{ to } M_3$$
$$4 \text{ units from } W_2 \text{ to } M_4$$
$$1 \text{ unit from } W_3 \text{ to } M_1$$
$$3 \text{ units from } W_3 \text{ to } M_2$$
$$1 \text{ unit from } W_3 \text{ to } M_3$$

The least possible time for completing all the shipments is 7.

3.5 MAXIMAL-FLOW PROBLEMS

In this section we consider the problem of shipping a certain homogeneous commodity from a specified point, called the *source*, to a particular destination, called the *sink*. Unlike the transportation problems, there may not be a direct *link* or *arc* connecting the source and the sink. The flow network will generally consist of some intermediate nodes, known as *transshipment points*, through which the flows are rerouted.

An example of a flow network is given by Fig. 3.1. The source node is denoted by the symbol s and the sink node by n. Nodes 1 and 2 are the intermediate nodes. There are six arcs connecting the various nodes, denoted by $(s, 1)$, $(s, 2)$, $(1, 2)$, $(2, 1)$, $(1, n)$, and $(2, n)$.

Flow in arc (i, j), denoted by f_{ij}, is the quantity shipped from node i to node j. We will assume that all the arcs are *directed*. In other words, flow in arc (i, j) is possible from node i to node j only. Let f denote the total amount shipped from the source to the sink, and k_{ij} denote the *capacity* of arc (i, j) which is the maximum flow possible from i to j.

The Maximal-Flow Problem

Consider the flow network represented by Fig. 3.1. Given the capacities k_{ij} on flows on each arc (i, j), and that the flow must satisfy conservation (i.e., the total flow into a node must be equal to the total flow out of that node), we want to determine the maximum flow f that can be sent from the source node s to the sink node n.

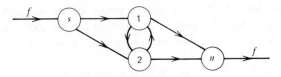

Figure 3.1

The linear programming formulation of the maximal flow problem is given:

Maximize $Z = f$
Subject to

$$f_{s1} + f_{s2} = f \tag{3.3}$$

$$f_{12} + f_{1n} = f_{s1} + f_{21} \tag{3.4}$$

$$f_{21} + f_{2n} = f_{s2} + f_{12} \tag{3.5}$$

$$f_{1n} + f_{2n} = f \tag{3.6}$$

$$0 \leq f_{s1} \leq k_{s1} \tag{3.7}$$

$$0 \leq f_{s2} \leq k_{s2} \tag{3.8}$$

$$0 \leq f_{12} \leq k_{12} \tag{3.9}$$

$$0 \leq f_{21} \leq k_{21} \tag{3.10}$$

$$0 \leq f_{1n} \leq k_{1n} \tag{3.11}$$

$$0 \leq f_{2n} \leq k_{2n} \tag{3.12}$$

Equation 3.3 represents the conservation of flow at the source node; Eqs. 3.4 and 3.5 represent the conservation of flow at the intermediate nodes 1 and 2, respectively; Eq. 3.6 represents the conservation at the sink node, while Eqs. 3.7–3.12 restrict the flows (f_{ij}) so as to be nonnegative with finite upperbounds. Although the maximal flow problem can be solved by the simplex method, there exists an efficient network method to find the maximum flow directly. We shall first introduce some basic concepts from network theory which are fundamental to the new procedure.

Definitions

Forward arcs. At any node i, all the arcs that are leaving node i are called forward arcs with respect to node i. Similarily, all the arcs entering a node are called *backward arcs* for that node. It should be noted here that an arc may be a forward arc with respect to some node, and a backward arc with respect to some other node.

In Fig. 3.1, the arcs $(1, n)$ and $(1, 2)$ are forward arcs for node 1 while the arcs $(s, 1)$ and $(2, 1)$ are its backward arcs. But for node 2, the arc $(1, 2)$ is a backward arc while $(2, 1)$ is a forward arc.

A *path* connecting the source and the sink is a sequence of arcs starting from the source node and ending in the sink node. For example, in the same figure, a path connecting s and n is given by the sequence of arcs $(s, 1)$, $(1, 2)$, $(2, n)$. Note that there exists more than one path connecting s and n in Fig. 3.1.

A *cycle* is a path whose beginning and ending nodes are the same.

Let N denote the collection of all the nodes in the network. Then, a *cut* separating the source and the sink is a partition of the nodes in the network into two subsets S and $\bar{S}$ such that the source node is in S and the sink node is in $\bar{S}$.

For example, in Fig. 3.1, a cut $(S, \bar{S})$ is given by $S = (s, 1, 2)$, $\bar{S} = (n)$. Note that $S \cup \bar{S} = N = (s, 1, 2, n)$, $S \cap \bar{S} =$ the empty set, $s \in S$, and $n \in \bar{S}$. A pictorial representation of the cut is given below:

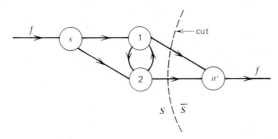

Another cut separating s and n is shown below where $S = (s, 2)$ and $\bar{S} = (1, n)$:

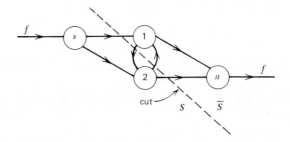

Similarly a number of other cuts may be found for the network. The *capacity* of a cut denoted by $K(S, \bar{S})$ is the sum of all the capacities of the arcs from the nodes in S to those in $\bar{S}$. For example, the capacity of the cut $(S, \bar{S})$ where $S = (s, 1, 2)$, $\bar{S} = (n)$ is $K_{1n} + K_{2n}$. But the capacity of the cut where $S = (s, 2)$ and $\bar{S} = (1, n)$ is $K_{s1} + K_{21} + K_{2n}$. (Since arc $(1, 2)$ is directed from a node in $\bar{S}$ to a node in S, it is not included in the summation.)

The cut with the smallest capacity is called a *minimal* cut. From the pictorial representation of the cuts, it is rather obvious that if all the arcs of a cut are removed from the network then there exists no path from the source to the sink; hence, no flow would be possible. In other words, any flow from s to n must flow through the arcs in the cut, and consequently the flow f is limited by the capacity of that cut. This relation between flows and cuts is given by the following lemma:

Lemma 1

For any directed network, if f is the flow from the source to the sink, and $(S, \bar{S})$ is a cut, then the value of f is less than or equal to the capacity of that cut $K(S, \bar{S})$.

Since Lemma 1 is true for *any* cut in the network, we can state that any feasible flow from source to sink cannot exceed the capacity of any cut. Thus the maximal flow across the network is limited by the capacity of the minimal cut. The following important theorem states that it is always possible to find a feasible flow from s to n *equal* to the capacity of the minimal cut.

Max-Flow Min-Cut Theorem [Ford and Fulkerson (3)]. For any network the value of the maximal flow from source to sink is equal to the capacity of the minimal cut.

Using the max-flow min-cut theorem one can find the maximal flow in a network by finding the capacities of all the cuts, and choosing the minimum capacity. Though this gives the maximal value of f, it does not specify how this flow is routed through various arcs. So we describe a different procedure known as the *maximal flow algorithm* whose validity is based on the max-flow min-cut theorem. The basic principle of this procedure is to find a path through which a positive flow can be sent from the source node to the sink node. Such a path is termed a *flow augmenting path*. This path is used to send as much flow as possible from s to n. This process is repeated until no such flow augmenting path can be found at which time we have found the maximal flow.

Labeling Routine. This is used to find a flow augmenting path from the source to the sink. We start from the source node s. We say that node j can be *labeled* if a positive flow can be sent from s to j. In general, from any node i, we can *label* node j, if one of the following conditions is satisfied:

1. The arc connecting the nodes i and j is a forward arc [i.e., the existing arc is (i, j)], and the flow in arc (i, j) is less than its capacity (i.e., $f_{ij} < K_{ij}$).
2. The arc connecting i and j is a backward arc [i.e., the existing arc is (j, i)], and the flow in arc (j, i) is greater than zero. (i.e., $f_{ji} > 0$)

We continue this labeling routine until the sink node is labeled. We then have a flow augmenting path.

Max-Flow Algorithm. The algorithm is initiated with a feasible flow on all arcs, satisfying capacity restrictions, and conservation of flows at all nodes. To improve this flow, we initially label node s, and then apply the labeling routine to label another node. When the sink is labeled, we have a flow augmenting path from s to n through which a positive flow can be sent. Now we retrace the flow augmenting path with the help of the labels on the nodes and compute the maximal flow δ that can be sent in the path. Then increase the flow by δ on all the forward arcs in the path, and decrease the flow by δ on all the backward arcs in the path. Repeat the procedure by finding another flow augmenting path from s to n using the labeling routine. The algorithm terminates when no flow augmenting path can be found, at which time we have the maximal flow possible from s to n.

We shall illustrate the max-flow algorithm through an example problem.

EXAMPLE 3.5-1

Compute the maximal flow f from s to n in the following network, where the numbers on the arcs represent their capacities:

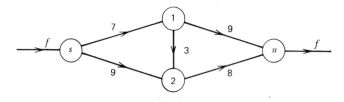

Prestep.   The max-flow algorithm is initiated with zero flows on all arcs. In Fig. 3.2, the numbers on the arcs (i, j) represent (f_{ij}, k_{ij}).

Step I (Fig. 3.2).   To find a flow augmenting path from s to n, node s is initially labeled. (Labels are denoted by asterisks.) From s, we can label node 1 since $(s, 1)$ is a forward arc, carrying a flow f_{s1}

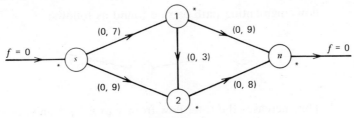

Figure 3.2

which is less than its capacity. From node 1, node 2 is labeled through the forward arc $(1, 2)$ and from node 2 the sink is labeled. We now have a flow augmenting path consisting only of forward arcs as shown below:

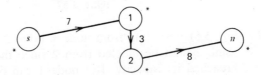

The numbers on the arcs indicate the maximum flow that is possible in each arc. Thus the maximal flow that can be sent through this flow augmenting path is 3 units. This increases f by 3 units, and the flow on all (forward) arcs in the path by 3 units. The new flow configuration is given by Fig. 3.3.

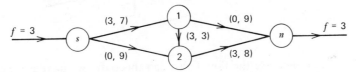

Figure 3.3

Step II (Fig. 3.3).　　Repeat the labeling routine and a new flow augmenting path is

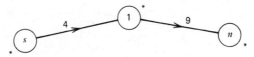

The maximum flow that can be sent through this path is 4 units. This increases the flow across the network (f) to 7 units. The new flow configuration is given by Fig. 3.4.

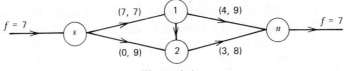

Figure 3.4

Step III (Fig. 3.4).　Now node 1 cannot be labeled from node s since $(s, 1)$ is a forward arc whose flow is equal to its capacity. But a new flow augmenting path can be found as follows:

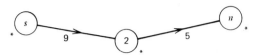

This increases the total flow from s to n by 5 units as shown in Fig. 3.5.

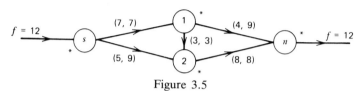

Figure 3.5

Step IV (Fig. 3.5).   Starting from node s, node 2 can be labeled, but the sink cannot be labeled from 2 since the flow in arc $(2, n)$ has reached its capacity. But node 1 can be labeled from node 2 since $(1, 2)$ is a backward arc carrying a positive flow. From node 1 the sink can be labeled using the forward arc $(1, n)$. Thus we have a new flow augmenting path consisting of two forward arcs $(s, 2)$ and $(1, n)$, and a backward arc $(1, 2)$ as shown below:

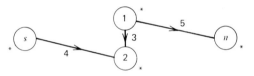

To increase the flow f through this path, we increase the flow on the forward arcs and decrease it in the backward arcs. Thus the maximum increase in f possible is 3 units, and the new assignment of flows is given in Fig. 3.6.

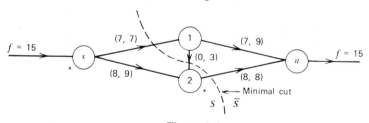

Figure 3.6

Step V (Fig. 3.6).   Even though node 2 can be labeled from node s, the sink can never be labeled. Hence no new flow augmenting paths are possible, and we have found the maximal flow possible which is 15 units.

REMARKS

In order to verify if $f = 15$ is the maximum flow, we can define a cut $(S, \bar{S})$ by placing all the labeled nodes in S and the unlabled nodes in $\bar{S}$ (see Fig. 3.6).

This gives $S = (s, 2)$, $\bar{S} = (1, n)$ and the capacity of cut $K(S, \bar{S}) = 15$. Since f cannot exceed the capacity of any cut by Lemma 1, $f = 15$ is the maximal flow possible, and the cut shown in Fig. 3.6 is the minimal cut.

Extensions

Undirected Arcs. Consider a network which contains arcs with no specified direction of flow. These arcs are generally called *undirected arcs*. When an arc connecting nodes i and j is undirected, with capacity K, we interpret that as

$$f_{ij} \leq K$$
$$f_{ji} \leq K$$
$$f_{ij} \cdot f_{ji} = 0$$

In other words, a maximum of K units of flow is possible between nodes i and j in either direction, but flow is permitted in one of the directions only. Recall that the maximal flow algorithm discussed earlier can be applied to directed networks only where the direction of flow is specified in all arcs. To find the maximal flow in an undirected network, we first convert the network to an equivalent directed network, and then apply the labeling method.

EXAMPLE 3.5-2

Consider a street network as shown below:

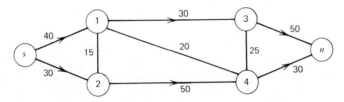

The numbers on the arcs represent the traffic flow capacities. The problem is to place one-way signs on streets not already oriented so as to maximize the traffic flow from the point s to the point n.

Solution

The trick is to replace each undirected arc by a pair of oppositely directed arcs with the same capacities. This gives a directed network as shown in Fig. 3.7:

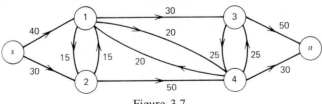

Figure 3.7

The maximal flow algorithm is applied to this network to determine the largest traffic flow from s to n. After the optimal flows have been found we cancel out the arc flows in the opposite directions so as to get the direction of flow in each of the undirected arcs. For instance, if the arc connecting i and j was undirected, and $f_{ij} > f_{ji}$, then a flow of $(f_{ij} - f_{ji})$ should be directed from i to j.

The numerical solution is left as an exercise for the reader.

Multiple Sources and Sinks (Transshipment Problems). Consider a network with several supply points and demand points. The problem is to maximize the flow from all the sources to all the destinations. The max-flow algorithm can be applied to solve this problem by converting to a single source-single sink situation. This can be done by creating an imaginary super source and an imaginary super sink. From the super source a directed arc will be created to every one of the real sources such that the super source becomes the supplier to the real sources. Similarly from each one of the real sink, a directed arc to the super sink will be created. We then apply the max-flow algorithm to maximize the flow from the super source to the super sink. This will be equivalent to maximizing the flow from all the sources to all the sinks.

To illustrate this, consider a transshipment problem wherein we have a network with multiple sources and multiple sinks with limited supplies and demands as shown below:

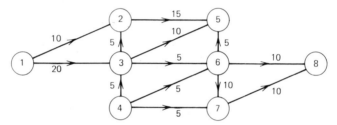

In the above network, nodes 1 and 4 are sources with supplies $s_1 = 20$, $s_4 = 20$. Nodes 5 and 8 are sinks with demands $d_5 = 15$, $d_8 = 20$. The numbers on the arcs represent the arc capacities. We wish to determine whether the transshipment problem is feasible, that is, whether it will be possible to meet the demands with the available supplies.

Solution

First the problem is converted to a problem of maximizing the flow from a single source to a single sink. An equivalent network (Fig. 3.8) is created with an imaginary source (s) and an imaginary sink (n).

In Fig. 3.8 the imaginary supply arcs $(s, 1)$ and $(s, 4)$ have capacities equal to the supplies in nodes 1 and 4, respectively. Similarly, arcs $(5, n)$ and $(8, n)$ have capacities equal to their respective demands. Even though the total supply

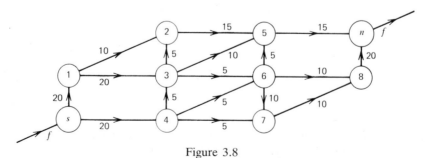

Figure 3.8

A transhipment problem as a max-flow problem.

exceeds the total demand, the transshipment problem may not be feasible due to the capacity restrictions on the intermediate arcs.

We now maximize the flow (f) from the imaginary source to the imaginary sink in the directed network of Fig. 3.8. Omitting the intermediate steps of the max-flow algorithm, the optimal distribution of flows is shown in Fig. 3.9. The numbers on arc (i, j) denote (f_{ij}, K_{ij}). The maximal flow possible is 30, and the minimal cut is given by the subsets $S = (s, 1, 2, 3, 4, 5)$ and $\bar{S} = (6, 7, 8, n)$. Since the maximum flow is less than the total demand of 35 units, it is not possible to satisfy all the demands at the sinks. Therefore the transshipment problem is not feasible.

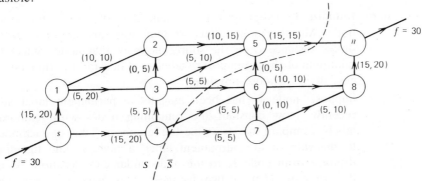

Figure 3.9
Solution of the transhipment problem.

REMARK
When the value of maximal flow f equals the sum of all the demands at the sinks, then the transshipment problem becomes feasible.

3.6 SHORTEST-ROUTE PROBLEMS
Another important network flow problem from an applied standpoint is that of determining the shortest path from the source node to the sink node. Here we are given a network of n nodes denoted by $(1, 2, \ldots, n)$. Corresponding to each arc (i, j) there is a nonnegative number d_{ij} called the distance or transit time from node i to node j. In case there is no way of getting from i to j directly, we set $d_{ij} = +\infty$. It is possible to have $d_{ij} \neq d_{ji}$. The problem is to find the length of the shortest path and the shortest route from the source node 1 to the sink node n.

One way of solving this problem is to reinterpret it as a shipping problem in which we wish to send one unit of flow from node 1 to node n, and the unit cost of shipping from i to j is d_{ij}. Then the shortest route problem can be formulated as a linear program for solution. However there are better and more elegant ways of solving the shortest-route problem. We shall describe below one of the most efficient algorithms, given by Dijkstra.

Dijkstra's Algorithm [Dreyfus (2)]
It is assumed that the direct distance between any two nodes (d_{ij}) in the network of n nodes is given, and all the distances are nonnegative. The algorithm proceeds by assigning to all nodes a *label* which is either *temporary* or *permanent*. A temporary label represents an upper bound on the shortest distance from node 1 to that node; while a permanent label is the actual shortest distance from node 1 to that node.

Initially the source node 1 is given a permanent label of zero. All other nodes $(2, 3, \ldots, n)$ are assigned temporary labels equal to the direct distance from node 1 to the node in question. Any node which cannot be reached directly from node 1 is assigned a temporary label of ∞, while all the other nodes receive temporary labels equal to d_{ij}. The algorithm then makes these tentative node labels, one at a time, permanent labels. As soon as the sink node receives a permanent label, the shortest distance from the source node to the sink node is immediately known.

Iterative Steps of the Algorithm

Prestep. Initialize by assigning a permanent label of zero to the source node. All other node labels are temporary and are equal to the direct distance from the source node to that node. Select the minimum of these temporary labels and declare it permanent. In case of ties, choose any one.

Step I. Suppose node K has been assigned a permanent label most recently. Now consider the remaining nodes with temporary labels. Compare one at a time the temporary label of each node, to the *sum* of the permanent label of node K and the *direct distance* from node K to the node under consideration. Assign the minimum of these two distances as the new temporary label for that node. (If the old temporary label is still minimal, then it will remain unchanged during this step.)

Step II. Select the minimum of all the temporary labels, and declare it permanent. In case of ties, select any one of them (*but exactly one*), and declare it permanent. If this happens to be the sink node then terminate. Otherwise return to Step I.

To find the sequence of nodes in the shortest path from node 1 to node n, a label indicating the node from which each permanently labeled node was labeled should be available. Then by retracing the path backwards from the sink node to the source node, the minimal path may be constructed. An alternative method is to determine which nodes have permanent labels that differ by exactly the length of the connecting arc. Again by retracing the path backwards from n to 1, the shortest path may be found.

We shall illustrate Dijkstra's algorithm with an example.

EXAMPLE 3.6-1

Consider an undirected network shown in Fig. 3.10, where numbers along the arcs (i, j) represent distances between nodes i and j. Assume that the distance

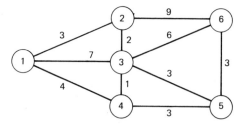

Figure 3.10

from i to j is the same as from j to i (i.e., all arcs are two-way streets). The problem is to determine the shortest distance and the length of the shortest path from node 1 to node 6.

Solution

Initially node 1 is labeled permanently as zero, and all other nodes are given temporary labels equal to their direct distance from node 1. Thus the node labels at Step 0, denoted by $L(0)$, are

$$L(0) = [0, 3, 7, 4, \infty, \infty]$$
$$\quad *$$

(An asterisk indicates a permanent label.)

At Step 1 the smallest of the temporary labels is made permanent. Thus node 2 gets a permanent label equal to 3, and it is the shortest distance from node 1 to node 2. To understand the logic behind this step, consider any other path from node 1 to node 2 through an intermediate node $j = 3, 4, 5, 6$. The shortest distance from node 1 to node j will be at least equal to 3 and d_{j2} is nonnegative since all the distances are assumed to be nonnegative. Hence any other path from node 1 to node 2 cannot have a distance less than 3, and the shortest distance from node 1 to node 2 is 3. Thus at Step 1 the node labels are

$$L(1) = [0, 3, 7, 4, \infty, \infty]$$
$$\quad * \ *$$

For each of the remaining nodes j $(j = 3, 4, 5, 6)$, compute a number which is the sum of the permanent label of node 2 and the direct distance from node 2 to node j. Compare this number with the temporary label of node j, and the smaller of the two values becomes the new tentative label for node j. For example, the new temporary label for node 3 is given by

$$\text{minimum of } (3 + 2, 7) = 5$$

Similarly, for nodes 4, 5, and 6, the new temporary labels are 4, ∞, and 12, respectively. Once again the minimum of the new temporary labels is made permanent. Thus at Step 2, node 4 gets a permanent label as shown below:

$$L(2) = [0, 3, 5, 4, \infty, 12]$$
$$\quad * \ * \quad *$$

Now using the permanent label of node 4, the new temporary labels of nodes 3, 5, and 6 are computed as 5, 7, and 12, respectively. Node 3 gets a permanent label and the node labels at Step 3 are

$$L(3) = [0, 3, 5, 4, 7, 12]$$
$$\quad * \ * \ * \ *$$

It should be emphasized here that at each step, only the node which has been recently labeled permanent is used for further calculations. Thus at Step 4 the permanent label of node 3 is used to update the temporary labels of nodes 5 and 6 (if possible). Node 5 gets a permanent label and the node labels at Step 4 are

$$L(4) = [0, 3, 5, 4, 7, 11]$$
$$\quad * \ * \ * \ * \ *$$

Using the permanent label of node 5, the temporary label of node 6 is changed to 10 and is made permanent. The algorithm now terminates, and the shortest distance from node 1 to node 6 is 10. As a matter of fact, we have the shortest distance from node 1 to every other node in the network as shown below:

$$L(5) = [0, 3, 5, 4, 7, 10]$$
$$* \quad * \quad * \quad * \quad * \quad *$$

To determine the sequence of nodes in the shortest path from node 1 to node 6, we work backwards from node 6. Node j $(j = 1, 2, 3, 4, 5)$ precedes node 6 if the difference between the permanent labels of nodes 6 and j equals the length of the arc from j to 6. This gives node 5 as its immediate predecessor. Similarly node 4 precedes node 5, and the immediate predecessor of node 4 is node 1. Thus the shortest path from node 1 to node 6 is $1 \rightarrow 4 \rightarrow 5 \rightarrow 6$.

REMARK

If we are interested in finding the shortest path between every pair of nodes in the network, then we have to repeat Dijkstra's algorithm four times taking nodes 2, 3, 4, 5 as the source node.

Applications

A number of seemingly different problems can be formulated as shortest route problems for solution. We shall present two applications here.

An Equipment Replacement Problem. Most equipment requires increased maintenance and running costs with age. By replacing the equipment at frequent intervals, this cost could be reduced. But this reduction is achieved at the expense of increased capital costs incurred during every replacement. One of the most important problems faced by the management is to decide how often to replace the equipment so as to minimize the total costs which include the capital cost, the cost of maintenance, and running costs. This can be formulated as a shortest route problem in a directed network, and Dijkstra's algorithm can be used for its solution.

As an illustration, consider a company planning its equipment replacement during the next 5 years. Let K_j represent the purchase price of the equipment in year j, and S_j the salvage value after j years of use. The maintenance and running cost of the equipment during its jth year of operation is c_j. Since costs increase with the age of the equipment, we assume $c_{j+1} > c_j$ for all $j = 1, 2, 3, 4, 5$. To formulate the problem of determining the optimal replacement policy as a shortest route problem, we construct a directed network as shown in Fig. 3.11.

Nodes 1 and 6 represent the start and the end of the planning period. Each intermediate node j $(j = 2, 3, 4, 5)$ represents the beginning of year j (or the end of year $j-1$) where an equipment replacement is possible. From every node i there exists a connecting (directed) arc to node j only if $j > i$. This corresponds to the situation where having replaced the equipment in year i, the next replacement is possible only in the later years.

The distance between node i and node j is of the form:

$$d_{ij} = K_i - S_{j-i} + \sum_{t=1}^{j-i} c_t \qquad \text{for } j > i$$

$$= \infty \qquad \text{for } j \leq i$$

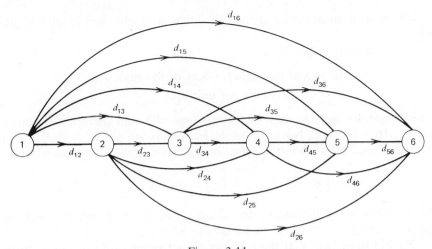

Figure 3.11
An equipment replacement problem as a shortest route problem.

The distance function d_{ij} represents the purchase cost minus any salvage value plus the maintenance and running costs of the equipment which is purchased at the start of year i, and to be replaced at the beginning of year j. (A value of ∞ indicates that there exists no arc from i to j.)

Every path from node 1 to node 6 in the network represents a possible replacement policy for the company. For example, the path $①→②→③→④→⑤→⑥$ corresponds to replacing the equipment every year so that the total cost of this policy $=\sum_{i=1}^{5} K_i - 5S_1 + 5c_1$. Another policy is to use the same equipment all 5 years, which corresponds to the path $①→⑥$, using the arc $(1,6)$. The cost of this policy is given by,

$$d_{16} = K_1 - S_5 + \sum_{t=1}^{5} c_t$$

Thus determining the shortest path from node 1 to node 6 is equivalent to finding the minimal cost policy for the equipment replacement problem.

Compact Book Storage in Libraries [9].   Consider the problem of storing books by their size. Suppose the heights and thicknesses of all books in a collection are given. Let the book heights be arranged in ascending order of its n known heights $H_1, H_2, \ldots, H_n$:

$$H_1 < H_2 < \cdots < H_n$$

(Any book of height H_i can be shelved in a shelf of height $\geq H_i$.) Since the thickness of each book is known, the required length of shelving of each height class i can be computed and is denoted by L_i.

If the books are stored upright using only one shelf height (corresponding to the tallest book) for the whole collection, then the total shelf area needed is the product of the total length, and the height of the tallest book. Instead, if the collection is divided by height into two or more groups, it can be easily seen that the total shelf area needed will be less than that of the undivided collection.

The cost of constructing shelves of different heights and lengths is given below:

For each shelf height H_i,

K_i = fixed cost independent of the shelf area

C_i = variable cost per unit area

For example, let the collection be placed in two different shelves of heights H_m and H_n ($H_m < H_n$) (i.e., books of height H_m or less are placed in shelf H_m, and the rest in shelf H_n). Then the total cost of shelving the collection will be:

$$\left[K_m + C_m H_m \sum_{i=1}^{m} L_i \right] + \left[K_n + C_n H_n \sum_{i=m+1}^{n} L_i \right]$$

The problem is to determine the optimal set of shelf heights, and their respective lengths, which will minimize the total shelving cost.

We will show here that the compact book storage problem can be formulated as a network flow problem. Consider a directed network of $(n+1)$ nodes $(0, 1, 2, \ldots, n)$ where the nodes correspond to the various book heights in the collection. (Here, node 0 corresponds to height zero and node n to the height of the tallest book.) A distance function on the set of paths connecting node 0 to node n will be proposed in terms of the shelving cost, where each intermediate node in the path is a possible partition of the set of all shelf heights. To make the network model compatible with the storage problem, the following assumptions are made:

1. $0 = H_0 < H_1 < H_2 < \cdots < H_n$

2. From every node i, there exists a connecting (directed) arc to node j, only if $j > i$. This corresponds to the situation in the book storage problem where having chosen a shelf of height H_i, the next shelf must be of height greater than H_i.

Because of this assumption, the number of arcs in the network is $n(n+1)/2$.

3. The distance function between node i and node j is of the form:

$$d_{ij} = K_j + C_j H_j \sum_{k=i+1}^{j} L_k \qquad \text{for } j > i$$
$$= +\infty \qquad \text{for } j \leq i$$

The distance function between i and j represents the fixed partition cost K_j plus the cost of shelving books of height H_j or less (but greater than H_i) in the shelf of height H_j. (A value of $+\infty$ indicates that there exists no connecting arc between those two nodes.)

It may be seen clearly that as a consequence of the Assumptions 1, 2, and 3, finding a shortest path between the source node 0 and the sink node n in the above network is equivalent to determining the number of different shelves and their respective heights which minimizes the shelving cost for a given collection. For example, a minimum path solution of the form $(0, 5, 10, n)$ means, to go from node 0 to node n, the shortest route is to use the intermediate nodes 5 and 10. This says then, store all the books of height H_5 or less on the shelf of height H_5, books of height H_{10} or less (but over H_5) on the shelf of height H_{10} and the rest on the shelf of height H_n. The shortest distance between 0 and n in the network is the sum of $d_{0,5}$, $d_{5,10}$, and $d_{10,n}$. From Assumption 3, it is equivalent to the total cost of shelving the collection using three shelves of height H_5, H_{10}, and H_n.

3.7 PROJECT MANAGEMENT

Management of big projects that consist of a large number of activities pose complex problems in *planning, scheduling,* and *control,* especially when the project activities have to be performed in a specified technological sequence. With the help of *PERT* (Program Evaluation and Review Technique), and *CPM* (Critical Path Method), the project manager can:

1. Plan the project ahead of time and foresee possible sources of troubles and delays in completion.
2. Schedule the project activities at the appropriate times to conform with proper job sequence so that the project is completed as soon as possible.
3. Coordinate and control the project activities so as to stay on schedule in completing the project.

Thus both PERT and CPM are aids to efficient project management. They differ in their approach to the problem and the solution technique. The nature of the project generally dictates the proper technique to be used.

Origin and Use of PERT

PERT was developed in the U.S. Navy during the late 1950s to accelerate the development of the Polaris Fleet Ballistic Missile. The development of this weapon involved the coordination of the work of thousands of private contractors and other government agencies. The coordination by PERT was so successful that the entire project was completed 2 years ahead of schedule. This has resulted in further applications of PERT in other weapons development programs in the Navy, Air Force, and Army. Nowadays it is extensively used in industries and other service organizations as well.

The time required to complete the various activities in a research and development project is generally not known *a priori.* Thus PERT incorporates uncertainties in activity times in its analysis. It determines the probabilities of completing various stages of the project by specified deadlines. It also calculates the expected time to complete the project. An important and extremely useful by-product of PERT analysis is its identification of various "bottlenecks" in the project. In other words, it identifies the activities which have high potential for causing delays in completing the project on schedule. Thus, even before the project has started, the project manager knows where he can expect delays. He can then take the necessary preventive measures to reduce possible delays so that the project schedule is maintained.

Because of its ability to handle uncertainties in job times, PERT is mostly used in research and development projects.

Origin and Use of CPM

Critical Path Method closely resembles PERT in many aspects but was developed independently by E. I. du Pont de Nemours Company. As a matter of fact, both techniques, PERT and CPM, were developed almost simultaneously. The major difference between the two techniques is that CPM does not incorporate uncertainties in job times. Instead it assumes that activity times are proportional to the amount of resources allocated to them, and by changing the level of resources the activity times and the project completion time can be varied. Thus CPM assumes prior experience with similar projects from which relationships between resources and job times are available. CPM then evaluates the trade-off between project costs and project completion time.

CPM is mostly used in construction projects where one has prior experience in handling similar projects.

Applications of PERT and CPM

A partial list of applications of PERT and CPM techniques in project management is given below:

1. Construction projects (e.g., buildings, highways, houses, and bridges.)
2. Preparation of bids and proposals for large projects.
3. Maintenance planning of oil refineries, ship repairs, and other large operations.
4. Development of new weapons systems and new manufactured products.
5. Manufacture and assembly of large items such as airplanes, ships, and computers.
6. Simple projects such as home remodeling, moving to a new house, and home cleaning and painting.

Project Network

Analysis by PERT/CPM techniques uses the network formulation to represent the project activities and their ordering relations. Construction of a project network is done as follows:

1. Arcs in the network represent individual jobs in the project.
2. Nodes represent specific points in time which mark the completion of one or more jobs in the project.
3. Direction on the arc is used to represent job sequence. It is assumed that any job directed toward a node must be completed before any job directed away from that node can begin.

We shall illustrate the construction of project networks with a few examples.

EXAMPLE 3.7-1

Consider seven jobs A, B, C, D, E, F, and G with the following job sequence:

Job A precedes B and C

Jobs C and D precede E

Job B precedes D

Jobs E and F precede G

The project network is shown below:

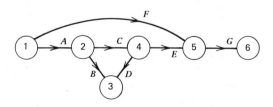

In the above network every arc (i, j) represents a specific job in the project. Node 1 represents the start of the project, while node 6 denotes the project's completion time. The intermediate nodes represent the completion of various stages of the project. The nodes of the project network are generally called *events*.

Definition. An *event* is a specific point in time which marks the completion of one or more activities, well recognizable in the project.

EXAMPLE 3.7-2

Consider a project with five jobs A, B, C, D, and E with the following job sequence:

Job A precedes C and D

Job B precedes D

Jobs C and D precede E

The completion times for A, B, C, D, and E are 3, 1, 4, 2, 5 days, respectively. The project network is shown in Fig. 3.12.

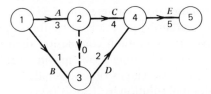

Figure 3.12

Project network for Example 3.7-2.

Arc $(2, 3)$ (dotted line in Fig. 3.12) represents a *dummy job* which does not exist in reality in the project. The dummy job is necessary so as to avoid ambiguity in the job sequence. The completion time of the dummy job is always zero and it is added in the project network whenever we want to avoid an arc (i, j) representing more than one job in the project. In Fig. 3.12, event 3 represents the completion of job B and the dummy job. Since the dummy job is completed as soon as A is completed, event 3 in essence marks the completion of jobs A and B.

Simplified Project Management Problem

The analysis of a simplified project management problem is useful to both PERT and CPM. In the simplified problem the completion times of all the project activities and their technological sequence are known. The management wants to determine the minimum time in which the project can be completed, and to identify the crucial jobs whose delay can delay the entire project.

Solution by Linear Programming

The simplified project management problem can be solved by formulating it as a linear program. To illustrate this, consider the problem given in Example 3.7-2. The project network is shown in Fig. 3.12. Let t_i represent the time at which event i occurs where $i = 1, 2, 3, 4, 5$. For example, t_5 represents when the project is completed, while t_4 represents the time at which jobs C and D are completed. Thus $(t_5 - t_1)$ represents the time of completion of the entire project, and the objective is to minimize this duration. The linear programming formulation becomes:

$$\text{Minimize:} \quad Z = t_5 - t_1$$

$$\text{Subject to:} \quad t_2 - t_1 \geqq 3$$
$$t_3 - t_1 \geqq 1$$
$$t_3 - t_2 \geqq 0$$
$$t_4 - t_2 \geqq 4$$
$$t_4 - t_3 \geqq 2$$
$$t_5 - t_4 \geqq 5$$
$$t_i \geqq 0 \qquad \text{for all } i = 1, 2, \ldots, 5$$

We have one constraint for every arc in the project network. The constraint for arc (i, j),

$$t_j - t_i \geqq t_{ij}$$

ensures that the time *available* for completing job (i, j) should be greater than or equal to the time *required* to complete job (i, j).

The above linear program may be solved by the simplex method, and the optimal value of Z gives the minimum completion time for the project. As a matter of fact, the linear programming problem can be solved by inspection by setting $t_1 = 0$, and choosing the values of t_i as small as possible to satisfy the constraints. Thus, an optimal solution by inspection is $t_1 = 0$, $t_2 = 3$, $t_3 = 3$, $t_4 = 7$, $t_5 = 12$, and minimum $Z = t_5 - t_1 = 12$ days.

Now we can identify those constraints which will be satisfied as equations in the optimal solution, and the jobs corresponding to those constraints are the *critical jobs*. For example, the constraint for arc $(1, 2)$ is satisfied as an equation by $t_2 = 3$ and $t_1 = 0$. Hence A is a critical job. For arc $(1, 3)$, the corresponding constraint is a strict inequality since $t_3 - t_1 = 3 - 0 > 1$. Hence B is not a critical job, and so in Example 3.7-2 the critical jobs are A, C, and E, while jobs B and D are not critical.

Definition.   A path in the project network connecting the starting event (node) and the ending event such that it passes through the critical jobs is called a *Critical Path.*

In Fig. 3.12, the critical path is given by

It can be shown that finding a critical path in a project network is equivalent to finding the *longest path* in the network.

For a large project, the number of constraints will be too many for an easy solution by linear programming. A direct approach using the project network is available to solve the simplified project management problem.

Solution by Network Analysis

Definition.   The *earliest time* of node j, denoted by U_j, is the earliest time at which event j can occur. We know that event j can occur as soon as all the jobs (arcs) directed towards node j are completed. For example, in the following diagram, event j occurs as soon as jobs A, B, and C are completed.

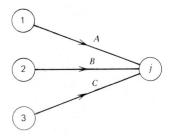

The earliest time of node j is then given by, $U_j = \max(U_1 + t_{1j}, U_2 + t_{2j}, U_3 + t_{3j})$ where t_{1j}, t_{2j}, t_{3j} are the completion times of jobs A, B, and C. Thus the general formula for calculating U_j is

$$U_j = \max_i(U_i + t_{ij})$$

where the index i ranges over all nodes for which arc (i, j) exists, and t_{ij} is the completion time of the job represented by arc (i, j). Note that the earliest time of the last event in the project network gives the earliest time of completing the project.

For the project network shown in Fig. 3.12, the U_j are calculated as follows:

Set

$$U_1 = 0$$

Then,

$$U_2 = U_1 + t_{12} = 3$$
$$U_3 = \max[(U_2 + t_{23}), (U_1 + t_{13})]$$
$$= \max(3, 1) = 3$$
$$U_4 = \max[(U_2 + t_{24}), (U_3 + t_{34})]$$
$$= \max(7, 5) = 7$$
$$U_5 = U_4 + t_{45} = 12$$

Hence the minimum duration of the project is 12 days from the start. Of course this does not identify the critical jobs nor the critical path. For that we need to calculate the *latest time* of an event.

Definition. The *latest time* of node i, denoted by V_i, is the latest time at which event i can occur without delaying the completion of the project beyond its earliest time.

To illustrate the concept of latest time, consider the following diagram:

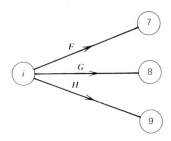

The project will not be delayed if the three jobs F, G, and H are completed by

V_7, V_8, and V_9, respectively. This is possible if we let

$$V_i = \min [V_7 - t_{i7}, \; V_8 - t_{i8}, \; V_9 - t_{i9}]$$

Hence the general formula to calculate V_i becomes

$$V_i = \min_j (V_j - t_{ij})$$

where the index j ranges over all nodes for which arc (i, j) exists.

To calculate the latest times of the events in the project network (Fig. 3.12), we set the latest time of the last event equal to its earliest time and work backwards.

Thus,

$$V_5 = U_5 = 12$$
$$V_4 = V_5 - t_{45} = 7$$
$$V_3 = V_4 - t_{34} = 5$$
$$V_2 = \min [(V_4 - t_{24}), \; (V_3 - t_{23})]$$
$$= \min (3, 5) = 3$$
$$V_1 = \min [(V_2 - t_{12}), \; (V_3 - t_{13})]$$
$$= \min (0, 4) = 0$$

The difference between the latest time and the earliest time of an event is called the *slack time* of that event. The slack time denotes how much delay can be tolerated in reaching that event without delaying the project completion date.

For the project network shown in Fig. 3.12, the slack times of events 1, 2, 3, 4, and 5 are given by 0, 0, 2, 0 and 0, respectively. Those events which have zero slack times are the *critical events*, where every care must be taken to stay on schedule if the project is to be completed on time.

The *critical path* for a project is a path through the project network such that the events on this path have zero slack times. The *critical jobs* are the arcs (jobs) in the critical path.

In Example 3.7-2, the critical path is $1 \rightarrow 2 \rightarrow 4 \rightarrow 5$, and the critical jobs are A, C, and E.

Table 3.14 summarizes the results of network analysis for Example 3.7-2.

Table 3.14

**RESULTS OF NETWORK ANALYSIS
OF EXAMPLE 3.7-2.**

Event	Earliest Time	Latest Time	Slack Time	Remark
1	0	0	0	Critical
2	3	3	0	Critical
3	3	5	2	Noncritical
4	7	7	0	Critical
5	12	12	0	Critical

In order to prepare a *project schedule* in terms of the activities, it is essential to have the starting time and the ending time of all jobs. From the event times it is possible to get the following information on each one of the activities in the project:

1. the earliest starting time,
2. the latest starting time,
3. the earliest finishing time,
4. the latest finishing time, and
5. the slack time.

To illustrate this, consider an arc (i, j) representing job J in the project as shown below:

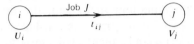

Let U_i denote the earliest occurrence time of event i, V_j denote the latest occurrence time of event j, and t_{ij} be the completion time of mob J. It is clear that job J may be started as early as U_i, but must be completed no later than V_j. Thus $(V_j - t_{ij})$ gives the latest starting time of job J, while $(U_i + t_{ij})$ is the earliest completion time of job J. In other words, $(V_j - U_i)$ is the maximum time available for job J. Thus the *slack time* of job J (maximum delay in completion) is given by $(V_j - U_i - t_{ij})$. If job J is a critical job then $V_j - U_i = t_{ij}$.

Table 3.15 gives the project schedule for the network shown in Fig. 3.12.

Table 3.15
PROJECT SCHEDULE FOR EXAMPLE 3.7-2.

Job	Expected Duration (days)	Earliest Start	Latest Start	Earliest Finish	Latest Finish	Slack Time (Maximum Delay)	Remark
A	3	0	0	3	3	0	Critical
B	1	0	4	1	5	4	Noncritical
C	4	3	3	7	7	0	Critical
D	2	3	5	5	7	2	Noncritical
E	5	7	7	12	12	0	Critical

Critical Path Method (CPM)

The basic assumption in CPM is that the activity times are proportional to the level of resources allocated to them. By assigning additional resources (capital, men, materials, and machines) to an activity, its duration can be reduced to a certain extent. Shortening the duration of an activity is known as *crashing* in the CPM terminology. The additional cost incurred in reducing the activity time is called the *crashing cost.*

We saw earlier that the duration of the critical activities determine the project completion time. Thus by crashing the critical jobs, the project duration can be reduced. Of course crashing the critical activities increases the total direct cost of the project, but the reduction in project duration may result in other advantages or returns which may offset this increased cost. These may include such indirect costs as equipment rental, supervisory personnel, supplies, and other costs which are directly proportional to the project duration. There may be other economic benefits in completing the project ahead of schedule. For instance, a new product may capture a larger share of the market if it is introduced before its competitor's. In addition some project contracts may specify bonuses or penalties for completing the project sooner or later than stipulated. Thus the total cost of the project is the sum of the direct costs (proportional to the activity times) and the indirect costs (proportional to the project duration). The critical path method essentially studies the trade-off between the total cost of the project, and its completion time.

For the critical path analysis it is assumed that every job has a *normal completion time* (maximum time) if no additional resources were assigned, and a *crash completion time* (minimum time) with the maximum amount of resources. In addition, a cost versus time relationship is available for every job in the project. The project management problem is to determine the amount by which the various jobs are to be crashed which will minimize the total cost of the project (direct and indirect).

There are two basic approaches to the CPM problem:

1. An Enumerative Method (for small projects only)
2. Mathematical Programming Methods (for large projects)

The Enumerative Method

For small projects one could determine the optimal project schedule by this method. The basic idea behind this approach is that the project length can be reduced by reducing the duration of the critical jobs. Hence the critical jobs are crashed as long as the cost of crashing is less than the reduction in overhead costs. The main difficulty with this approach is that the critical path of the project changes once we start crashing the critical jobs. There are other practical problems in applying this method to a large project, and these are discussed at the end of this section. Let us illustrate the enumerative method with an example.

EXAMPLE 3.7-3

Consider a project consisting of eight jobs (A, B, C, D, E, F, G, H). About each job we know the following:

Job	Predecessors	Normal Time (days)	Crash Time (days)	Cost of Crashing per Day ($)
A	—	10	7	4
B	—	5	4	2
C	B	3	2	2
D	A, C	4	3	3
E	A, C	5	3	3
F	D	6	3	5
G	E	5	2	1
H	F, G	5	4	4

Given the overhead costs as $5 per day, we want to determine the optimal duration of the project in terms of both the crashing and overhead costs, and develop an optimal project schedule.

Solution

The project network is shown in Fig. 3.13.

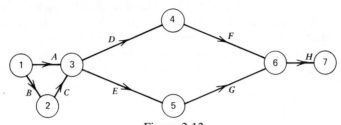

Figure 3.13
Project network for Example 3.7-3.

If all the jobs are done at their normal times, the project duration (length of the longest path) is 25 days. Hence under a "no crashing" schedule,

Total cost = overhead costs + crashing costs = $5(25) + 0 = $125.

If all the jobs were crashed to their minimum time, then the project duration is 17 days. Under this chedule, the total cost = $5(17) + 47 = $132. The project management problem is to determine the optimal duration of jobs which will minimize the total cost.

Using the normal times for the jobs, the earliest and latest occurrence times of the events (U_i, V_i) are computed as shown in Fig. 3.14. The project

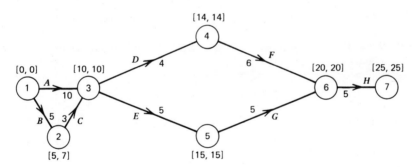

Figure 3.14

completion time is 25 days, and the project network has two critical paths as shown below:

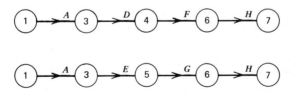

Between the nodes 3 and 6 we have *parallel critical paths*. The critical activities are jobs A, D, E, F, G, and H. The total cost of the project under normal time is $125.

In order to reduce the project duration, it is necessary to reduce the duration of the critical jobs. Consider the critical job H, which can be crashed by 1 day at a cost of $4. This reduces the project duration by 1 day at a savings of $5 in overhead costs. Hence job H is crashed to its lowest limit of 4 days and the total cost is reduced to $124.

Consider the crashing of job A now. This also results in a net savings of $1 in total cost for each day of crashing. But job A cannot be crashed to its minimum value of 7 days because when A is crashed to 8 days, jobs B and C also become critical. This results in parallel critical paths between nodes 1 and 3, and any reduction in A alone will not reduce the project duration. Hence job A is crashed only to 8 days, and the total cost is reduced to $122.

In order to reduce the project duration by one more day, we have to crash job A by 1 day and either jobs B or C by 1 day. The total cost of crashing A and B is $6 which is more than the savings in overhead costs. Similarly crashing A and C is also not economical.

Now consider the critical jobs D, E, F, and G. Since we have parallel critical paths between the nodes 3 and 6, we have to crash one job in the path

$\underbrace{3} \longrightarrow \underbrace{4} \longrightarrow \underbrace{6}$, and one job in $\underbrace{3} \longrightarrow \underbrace{5} \longrightarrow \underbrace{6}$ in order to

reduce the project length. This means we have to try four different combinations as shown below:

Jobs	Increase in Crashing Costs ($)	Decrease in Overhead Costs ($)	Net Change in Total Cost ($)
D and E	$3 + 3 = 6$	5	Increases by $1
D and G	$3 + 1 = 4$	5	Decreases by $1
F and E	$5 + 3 = 8$	5	Increases by $3
F and G	$5 + 1 = 6$	5	Increases by $1

From the above table, we find that the combination D and G alone is economical, and when we crash both jobs D and G by one day, the total cost reduces to $121. No further crashing is economical. Hence the optimal project schedule is

Crash job A to 8 days
Crash job D to 3 days
Crash job G to 4 days
Crash job H to 4 days

Jobs B, C, E, and F are completed at normal times 5, 3, 5, and 6 days, respectively. The optimal length of the project is 21 days, and the minimum project cost is $121.

Very large projects will generally contain many parallel critical paths, and each critical path may have a large number of jobs. Examining all possible combinations of jobs in the parallel paths by the enumerative method will not only be inefficient but also expensive. For example, if we have two parallel paths with 10 critical jobs in each, we will have to examine 100 combinations of jobs for possible crashing!

Mathematical Programming Methods

For large projects, the mathematical programming methods are more efficient in determining the optimal project schedule. In this section we shall discuss some linear programming models for the critical path analysis. Once again, it is assumed that a cost-versus-time relationship is available for every job in the project as shown in Fig. 3.15. We denote by k_{ij} the normal

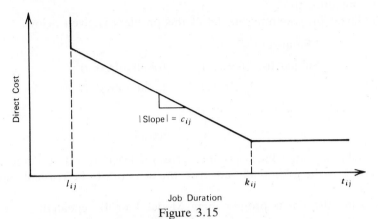

Figure 3.15
Job duration versus direct cost.

completion time of job (i, j) if no additional resources were assigned, while 1_{ij} denotes the crash completion time with the maximum amount of resources. C_{ij} represents the unit cost of shortening the duration of job (i, j). If t_{ij} is the completion time of job (i, j), then t_{ij} is an unknown variable between 1_{ij} and k_{ij}, and the cost of crashing is given by

$$C_{ij}(k_{ij} - t_{ij})$$

Let t_i be the unknown event times $(i = 1, 2, \ldots, n)$ for a project consisting of n events where events 1 and n denote the start and the end of the project.

We shall now develop three important models in the critical path analysis which are useful for project management. In all these models, we will assume that the normal time, crash time, and the crashing cost are available for all the activities in the project.

Model I. Given that the project must be completed by time T, we want to determine how the project activities are to be expedited such that the total cost of crashing is minimized. This problem can be formulated as a linear programming problem as follows:

$$\text{Minimize:} \quad Z = \sum_{(i,j)} C_{ij}(k_{ij} - t_{ij})$$

$$\text{Subject to:} \quad t_j - t_i \geq t_{ij} \qquad \text{for all jobs } (i, j)$$

$$1_{ij} \leq t_{ij} \leq k_{ij} \qquad \text{for all jobs } (i, j)$$

$$t_n - t_1 \leq T$$

$$t_i \geq 0 \qquad \text{for all } i = 1, 2, \ldots, n$$

The above problem may be solved by the simplex method. The optimal value of Z gives the minimum crashing cost. From the optimal values of t_{ij}, we can determine which jobs are expedited, and by how much. It should be pointed out here that for the above linear program to be feasible, the value of T must be greater than or equal to the length of the critical path with all the jobs at their crash (minimum) times.

Model II. Suppose an additional budget of B dollars is available for crashing the project activities. We want to determine how these additional resources may be allocated in the best possible manner so as to minimize the project completion time.

The linear programming model of this problem is given below:

$$\text{Minimize:} \quad Z = t_n - t_1$$

$$\text{Subject to:} \quad t_j - t_i \geq t_{ij} \qquad \text{for all jobs } (i, j)$$

$$1_{ij} \leq t_{ij} \leq k_{ij} \qquad \text{for all jobs } (i, j)$$

$$\sum_{(i,j)} C_{ij}(k_{ij} - t_{ij}) \leq B$$

$$t_i \geq 0 \qquad \text{for all } i = 1, 2, \ldots, n$$

The solution to this linear program gives the least project duration that can be achieved by the additional budget B, the activities to be crashed, and their durations.

By using the linear programming Model I or II repeatedly, one could obtain a relationship between the total crashing cost and the project duration. Figure 3.16 gives a typical plot of the direct (activity) costs against the project

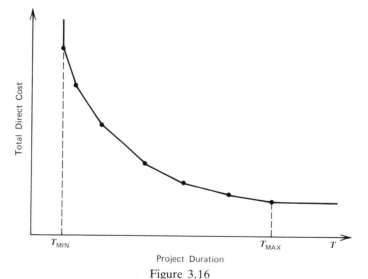

Figure 3.16

Direct cost versus project duration.

duration. T_{MAX} denotes the project duration with all the jobs at their normal times, while T_{MIN} denotes the project duration with all the jobs reduced to their crash times. The cost function shown in Fig. 3.16 is called a *piece-wise linear function*. With the help of this curve the project manager can determine

1. the minimum cost of additional resources needed to meet a given project deadline
2. the optimal allocation of scarce resources to achieve the maximum reduction in project duration

As seen in Fig. 3.16, the direct cost of completing the project activities increases when the project duration is reduced. But the indirect costs discussed earlier reduce with a reduction in project duration. Hence it will be of interest to study how the total cost (direct + indirect costs) varies with the project duration. For various project lengths the indirect cost is added to the direct cost, and a plot of points is obtained to get a relationship between the project length and the total project cost. Such a plot is shown in Fig. 3.17. This

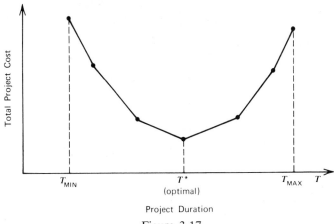

Project Duration

Figure 3.17

Project cost curve.

U-shaped curve is called a *project cost curve*. With the help of this curve, a project manager can select the *optimal project duration* (T^*) that will minimize the total costs. Corresponding to the optimal value of T, he can then determine the optimal durations of all the jobs, the cost of crashing, and the critical path. From this the *optimal project schedule* can be prepared.

    Model III. If the indirect cost of the project varies linearly with the project duration, then one can determine the optimal length of the project (T^*) and the optimal project schedule by solving a linear programming problem.

    Let the indirect (overhead) costs, proportional to the project duration, be denoted by F per unit time. Then the indirect cost is given by $F(t_n - t_1)$, where $(t_n - t_1)$ is the unknown length of the project. The direct cost is given by $\sum_{(i,j)} C_{ij}(k_{ij} - t_{ij})$, where t_{ij} is the unknown length of job (i, j). The problem is to determine the optimal schedule that will minimize the total cost. The linear programming formulation becomes

$$\text{Minimize:} \quad Z = F(t_n - t_1) + \sum_{(i,j)} C_{ij}(k_{ij} - t_{ij})$$

$$\text{Subject to:} \quad t_j - t_i \geq t_{ij} \qquad \text{for all jobs } (i, j)$$

$$1_{ij} \leq t_{ij} \leq k_{ij} \qquad \text{for all jobs } (i, j)$$

$$t_i \geq 0 \qquad \text{for all } i = 1, 2, \ldots, n$$

    We can illustrate Model III with the help of Example 3.7-3. Let t_{ij} denote the completion time of job (i, j), and t_i be the time at which event i occurs. Then the duration of the project is $(t_7 - t_1)$, and the overhead cost equals $5(t_7 - t_1)$. The direct costs are the costs of crashing each job, which are proportional to how far the jobs are expedited. For instance, the cost of crashing job A is $4(10 - t_{13})$; while for job B it is $2(5 - t_{12})$.

    Thus the linear programming formulation of the project management problem becomes

$$\text{Minimize:} \quad Z = 5(t_7 - t_1) + 4(10 - t_{13})$$
$$+ 2(5 - t_{12}) + 2(3 - t_{23}) + 3(4 - t_{34})$$
$$+ 3(5 - t_{35}) + 5(6 - t_{46}) + 1(5 - t_{56})$$
$$+ 4(5 - t_{67})$$

$$\text{Subject to:} \quad t_3 - t_1 \geq t_{13}$$
$$t_2 - t_1 \geq t_{12}$$
$$t_3 - t_2 \geq t_{23}$$
$$t_4 - t_3 \geq t_{34}$$
$$t_5 - t_3 \geq t_{35}$$
$$t_6 - t_4 \geq t_{46}$$
$$t_6 - t_5 \geq t_{56}$$
$$t_7 - t_6 \geq t_{67}$$
$$7 \leq t_{13} \leq 10$$
$$4 \leq t_{12} \leq 5$$
$$2 \leq t_{23} \leq 3$$
$$3 \leq t_{34} \leq 4$$
$$3 \leq t_{35} \leq 5$$
$$3 \leq t_{46} \leq 6$$
$$2 \leq t_{56} \leq 5$$
$$4 \leq t_{67} \leq 5$$
$$t_1, \ldots, t_7 \geq 0$$

The above linear program has 15 decision variables. Setting $t_1 = 0$, an optimal solution is found by the simplex method as $t_2 = 5$, $t_3 = 8$, $t_4 = 11$, $t_5 = 13$, $t_6 = 17$, $t_7 = 21$, $t_{13} = 8$, $t_{12} = 5$, $t_{23} = 3$, $t_{34} = 3$, $t_{35} = 5$, $t_{46} = 6$, $t_{56} = 4$, and $t_{67} = 4$. The optimal project length is 21 days, and the minimum cost of the project is $121. This means that job A is crashed by 2 days, while jobs D, G, and H are each crashed by 1 day. All the jobs in the project are critical.

Program Evaluation and Review Technique (PERT)*

So far in our analysis the probability considerations in the management of a project were not included. CPM assumed that the job times are known but can be varied by changing the level of resources. However in all the research and development projects, many activities are performed only once. Hence no prior experience with similar activities is available. The management of such projects is done by PERT which takes into account uncertainties in the completion times of the various activities.

For each activity in the project network, PERT assumes three time estimates on its completion time. They include (1) *a most probable time* denoted by m, (2) *an optimistic time* denoted by a, and (3) *a pessimistic time* denoted by b.

---

* This section assumes some knowledge of probability theory.

The most probable time is the time required to complete the activity under normal conditions. To include uncertainties, a range of variation in job time is provided by the optimistic and pessimistic times. The optimistic estimate is a good guess on the minimum time required when everything goes according to plan; while the pessimistic estimate is a guess on the maximum time required under adverse conditions such as mechanical breakdowns, minor labor troubles, shortage of or delays in delivery of material. It should be remarked here that the pessimistic estimate does not take into consideration unusual and prolonged delays or other catastrophes. Because both these estimates are only qualified guesses, the actual time for an activity could lie outside this range. (From a probabilistic view point we can only say that the probability of a job time falling outside this range is very small.)

Most PERT analysis assumes a Beta distribution for the job times as shown in Fig. 3.18, where μ represents the average length of the job duration. The value of μ depends on how close the values of a and b are relative to m.

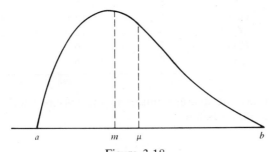

Figure 3.18
Beta distribution for job time.

The expected time to complete an activity is approximated as

$$\mu = \frac{a + 4m + b}{6} \tag{3.13}$$

Since the actual time may vary from its mean value, we need the variance of the job time. For most unimodal distributions (with single peak values), the end values lie within three standard deviations from the mean value. Thus the spread of the distribution is equal to six times the standard deviation value (σ).

Thus $6\sigma = b - a$, or $\sigma = \dfrac{b-a}{6}$. The variance of the job time equals

$$\sigma^2 = \left(\frac{b-a}{6}\right)^2. \tag{3.14}$$

With the three time estimates on all the jobs, PERT calculates the average time and the variance of each job using Eqs. 3.13 and 3.14. Treating the average times as the actual job times, the critical path is found. The duration of the project (T) is given by the sum of all the job times in the critical path. But the job times are random variables.* Hence the project duration T is also a random variable, and we can talk of the average length of the project and its variance.

The expected length of the project is the sum of all the average times of the jobs in the critical path. Similarly, the variance of the project duration is

---

* A variable whose value depends on chance.

the sum of all the variances of the jobs in the critical path assuming that all the job times are independent.

EXAMPLE 3.7-4

Consider a project consisting of nine jobs $(A, B, \ldots, I)$ with the following precedence relations and time estimates:

Job	Predecessors	Optimistic Time (a)	Most Probable Time (m)	Pessimistic Time (b)
A	—	2	5	8
B	A	6	9	12
C	A	6	7	8
D	B, C	1	4	7
E	A	8	8	8
F	D, E	5	14	17
G	C	3	12	21
H	F, G	3	6	9
I	H	5	8	11

First we compute the average time and the variance for each one of the jobs. They are tabulated below:

Job	Average Time	Standard Deviation	Variance
A	5	1	1
B	9	1	1
C	7	1/3	1/9
D	4	1	1
E	8	0	0
F	13	2	4
G	12	3	9
H	6	1	1
I	8	1	1

Figure 3.19 gives the project network, where the numbers on the arcs indicate the average job times. Using the average job times, the earliest and

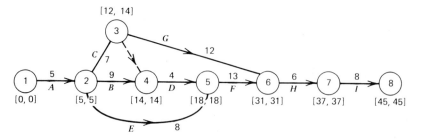

Figure 3.19
Project network of Example 3.7-4.

latest times of each event are calculated. The critical path is found as $1 \to 2 \to 4 \to 5 \to 6 \to 7 \to 8$. The critical jobs are $A, B, D, F, H,$ and I.

Let T denote the project duration. Then the expected length of the project is

$$E(T) = \text{Sum of the expected times of jobs } A, B, D, F, H, \text{ and } I$$
$$= 5 + 9 + 4 + 13 + 6 + 8 = 45 \text{ days}$$

The variance of the project duration is

$$V(T) = \text{Sum of the variances of jobs } A, B, D, F, H, \text{ and } I$$
$$= 1 + 1 + 1 + 4 + 1 + 1 = 9$$

The standard deviation of the project duration is

$$\sigma(T) = \sqrt{V(T)} = 3$$

Probabilities of Completing the Project

The project length T is the sum of all the job times in the critical path. PERT assumes that all the job times are independent, and are identically distributed. Hence by the *Central Limit Theorem*,[*] T has a normal distribution with mean $E(T)$, and variance $V(T)$. Figure 3.20 exhibits a normal distribution with mean μ and variance σ^2.

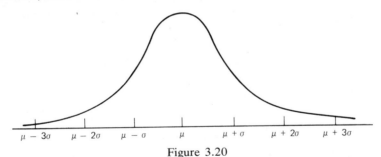

Figure 3.20
A normal distribution with mean μ and standard deviation σ.

In our example T is distributed normal with mean 45 and standard deviation 3.[†] For any normal distribution, the probability that the random variable lies within one standard deviation from the mean is 0.68. Hence there is a 68% chance that the project duration will be between 42 and 48 days. Similarly there is a 99.7% chance that T will lie within three standard deviations (i.e., between 36 and 54).

We can also calculate the probabilities of meeting specified project deadlines. For example, the management wants to know the probability of completing the project by 50 days. In other words, we have to compute $\text{Prob}(T \le 50)$ where $T \sim N(45, 3^2)$. This can be obtained from the tables of normal distribution; however, the tables are given for a standard normal only whose mean is 0 and standard deviation is 1.

---

[*] *Central Limit Theorem:* Let $X_1, X_2, \ldots, X_N$ be independent and identically distributed random variables. Then for large N, the sum of the random variables, $S_N = X_1 + X_2 + \cdots + X_N$, is normally distributed with mean $\sum_{i=1}^{N} E(X_i)$ and variance $\sum_{i=1}^{N} V(X_i)$.

[†] Theoretically this is not correct since we have a very small project and the central limit theorem does not apply. But for the sake of illustration we will assume that T is distributed normal.

From probability theory the random variable $Z = \dfrac{T - E(T)}{\sigma(T)}$ is distributed normally with mean 0 and standard deviation 1. Hence

$$\text{Prob}\,(T \leq 50) = \text{Prob}\left(Z \leq \frac{50 - 45}{3}\right) = \text{Prob}\,(Z \leq 1.67) = 0.95$$

Thus there is a 95% chance that the project will be completed within 50 days.

Suppose we want to know the probability of completing the project 4 days sooner than expected. This means we have to compute

$$\text{Prob}\,(T \leq 41) = \text{Prob}\left(Z \leq \frac{41 - 45}{3}\right) = \text{Prob}\,(Z \leq -1.33) = 0.09$$

Hence there is only a small 9% chance that the project will be completed in 41 days.

Recommended Readings

Capacitated transportation problems, and transshipment problems are discussed fully in Dantzig (1). A primal–dual network method to solve the transportation problems is available in Dantzig (1), and Ford and Fulkerson (3). Dreyfus (2) presents an excellent appraisal of the various shortest-route algorithms available in the literature. Application of network analysis to solve the compact book storage problems in libraries is fully discussed in Ravindran (9).

Project management problems with finite resources are discussed at a practical level in Wiest and Levy (12). For advanced topics in network analysis like multicommodity flows, the reader may refer to Ford and Fulkerson (3), Hu (8), and Geoffrion (6).

REFERENCES

1. Dantzig, George B., *Linear Programming and Extensions*, Princeton University Press, Princeton, New Jersey, 1963.

2. Dreyfus, Stuart E., "An Appraisal of Some Shortest-Path Algorithms," *Operations Research*, 17 (3), (1969).

3. Ford, L. R., and D. R. Fulkerson, *Flows in Networks*, Princeton University Press, Princeton, New Jersey, 1962.

4. Gale, David, *The Theory of Linear Economic Models*, McGraw-Hill, New York, 1960.

5. Gass, Saul I., *Linear Programming*, Fourth Ed., McGraw-Hill, New York, 1975.

6. Geoffrion, Arthur M., Ed., *Perspectives on Optimization: A Collection of Expository Articles*, Addison-Wesley, Reading, Massachusetts, 1972.

7. Hillier, Frederick S., and Gerald J. Lieberman, *Introduction to Operations Research*, Second Edition, Holden-Day, San Francisco, California, 1974.

8. Hu, T. C., *Integer Programming and Network Flows*, Addison-Wesley, Reading, Massachusetts, 1969.

9. Ravindran, A., "On Compact Book Storage in Libraries," *Opsearch*, 8 (4), (1971).

10. Taha, Hamdy A., *Operations Research An Introduction*, Macmillan, New York, 1971.

11. Wagner, Harvey M., *Principles of Operations Research*, Second Ed., Prentice-Hall, Englewood Cliffs, New Jersey, 1975.

12.   Wiest, Jerome D., and F. K. Levy, *A Management Guide to PERT/CPM*, Prentice-Hall, Englewood Cliffs, New Jersey, 1969.

EXERCISES

1.   We have three reservoirs with daily supplies of 15, 20, and 25 million liters of fresh water, respectively. On each day we must supply four cities A, B, C, D whose demands are 8, 10, 12, and 15, respectively. The cost of pumping per million liters is given below:

		Cities			
		A	B	C	D
	1	2	3	4	5
Reservoirs	2	3	2	5	2
	3	4	1	2	3

Use the transportation algorithm to determine the cheapest pumping schedule if excess water can be disposed of at no cost.

2.   Faced with a court order to desegregate its schools, a county school board decides to redistribute its minority students through bussing. The plan calls for bussing 50 students from each of the three cities White, Black, and Brown to the four schools East, West, North, and South. For a perfect desegregation, the schools need 20, 40, 30, and 60 minority students respectively. The dollar cost of bussing each student is given below:

		School			
		East	West	North	South
	White	7	6	5	4
City	Black	9	7	3	6
	Brown	8	8	7	3

The school board wishes to meet the court order with the least cost.
   a.   Set up the transportation table for the above problem.
   b.   Find an initial basic feasible solution by North-West corner rule.
   c.   Determine the optimal bussing plan using the u-v method.
   d.   Because of a "detour" near the East school for road construction, the bussing cost from every city to that school increases by $1. Explain how this will affect your optimal solution found in (c).

3.   Solve Example 3.2-2 using the transportation algorithm.

4.   Solve Example 3.2-3 by the transportation algorithm and interpret your solution.

5.   In order to stimulate interest and provide an atmosphere for intellectual discussion, an engineering faculty decides to hold special seminars on four contemporary topics—ecology, energy, transportation, and bioengineering. Such seminars should be held once per week in the afternoons. However, scheduling these seminars (one for each topic, and not more than one seminar per afternoon) has to be done carefully so that the number of students who could not attend is kept to a minimum. A careful study indicated that the number of students who can not

attend a particular seminar on a specific day is as follows:

	Ecology	Energy	Transportation	Bioengineering
Monday	50	40	60	20
Tuesday	40	30	40	30
Wednesday	60	20	30	20
Thursday	30	30	20	30
Friday	10	20	10	30

    a.   Show that the problem of determining the optimal schedule of seminars is equivalent to an assignment problem.

    b.   Using (a), find an optimal schedule of seminars.

6.   A group of four boys and four girls are planning on a one day picnic. The extent of mutual happiness between boy i and girl j when they are together is given by the following matrix (data obtained from their previous dating experiences):

		Girl			
		1	2	3	4
	1	11	1	5	8
Boy	2	9	9	8	1
	3	10	3	5	10
	4	1	13	12	11

The problem is to decide the proper matching between the boys and the girls during the picnic which will maximize the sum of all the mutual happiness of all the couples. Formulate this as an assignment problem and solve.

7.   A batch of four jobs can be assigned to five different machines. The set-up time for each job on various machines is given by the following table:

		Machine				
		1	2	3	4	5
	1	10	11	4	2	8
Job	2	7	11	10	14	12
	3	5	6	9	12	14
	4	13	15	11	10	7

Find an optimal assignment of jobs to machines which will minimize the total set-up time.

8.   A perishable commodity is to be shipped from four warehouses (W_1, W_2, W_3, W_4) to five retail outlets (R_1, R_2, R_3, R_4, R_5). The supplies at the warehouses are 70, 40, 60, and 30 units, respectively, while the respective demands at the retail outlets are 40, 20, 30, 60, and 50 units. The shipping time from each warehouse to every retail outlet, independent of the quantity shipped, is given below:

	R_1	R_2	R_3	R_4	R_5
W_1	7	6	5	4	2
W_2	9	7	3	6	3
W_3	8	8	7	3	1
W_4	4	3	1	2	1

Determine a shipping plan which will complete all the shipments in the least possible time.

9. Consider the following directed network where s is the source node, n is the sink node, and the numbers along the arcs denote the capacities of flows:

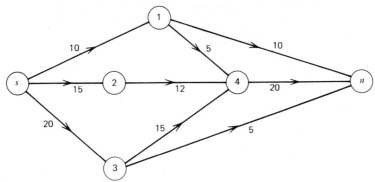

a. Illustrate the following notions with an example for the above network:
    (i)   A *path* connecting the source and the sink
    (ii) A *cut* separating the source and the sink
    (iii) The *capacity* of a cut
b. Find the maximum flow from the source to the sink using the labeling method.
c. Find the minimum cut, and verify the max-flow min-cut theorem.

10. Consider a street network as shown below:

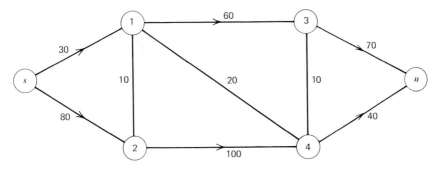

The numbers on the arcs represent the traffic flow capacities. The problem is to place one-way signs on streets not already oriented so as to maximize the traffic flow from the point s to the point n. Solve by the labeling method.

11. A certain commodity is to be shipped from three warehouses to four markets. The warehouse supplies are 20, 20, and 100 units. The market demands are 20, 20, 60, and 20 units. It is not possible to ship from all the warehouses to all the markets. The following table gives the capacities of various routes (a zero capacity implies that there exists no direct route between those two points):

		Market				
		1	2	3	4	Supplies
	1	30	10	0	40	20
Warehouse	2	0	0	10	50	20
	3	20	10	40	5	100
		20	20	60	20	
			Demands			

The problem is to determine whether it is possible to meet the market demands with the available supplies.

a.   Show that the above problem is equivalent to finding the maximum flow from a single source to a single sink in an equivalent network.

b.   Solve (a) by the labeling method, and interpret your solution.

12. Use Dijkstra's algorithm to determine the shortest distance, and the shortest path from node 0 to every other node in the network given below:

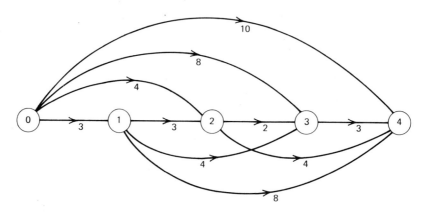

13. Consider an undirected network with 8 nodes and 13 arcs. The distance in kilometers between nodes i and j, denoted by d_{ij}, is as follows: $d_{12} = 5$, $d_{13} = 1$, $d_{14} = 7$, $d_{23} = 4$, $d_{34} = 2$, $d_{35} = 10$, $d_{36} = 9$, $d_{46} = 3$, $d_{56} = 3$, $d_{57} = 4$, $d_{67} = 9$, $d_{68} = 8$, and $d_{78} = 6$. Find the shortest distance and the shortest path between the nodes 1 and 8.

14. Use Dijkstra's algorithm to solve the compact book storage problem discussed in Section 3.6 with the following data: $H_1 = 15$ cm, $H_2 = 20$ cm, $H_3 = 25$ cm, $H_4 = 30$ cm, $L_1 = 5$ cm, $L_2 = 20$ cm, $L_3 = 45$ cm, $L_4 = 30$ cm, $K_1 = K_2 = \$100$, $K_3 = K_4 = \$200$, $C_1 = \$6$, $C_2 = \$8$, $C_3 = \$9$, and $C_4 = \$12$.

15. The following matrix (S) gives the shortest distance between all pairs of nodes in a network of six nodes.

$$\underset{(6\times6)}{S} = \begin{pmatrix} - & 10 & 20 & 5 & 12 & 6 \\ 10 & - & 25 & 12 & 2 & 15 \\ 15 & 10 & - & 15 & 20 & 10 \\ 20 & 15 & 13 & - & 11 & 9 \\ 10 & 25 & 15 & 11 & - & 15 \\ 10 & 10 & 20 & 9 & 15 & - \end{pmatrix}$$

(*Note.   The (i, j)th element in the matrix S gives the shortest distance from node i to node j.*)

If C_i denotes the length of the shortest cycle starting and ending at node i ($C_i > 0$), compute the values of C_1, C_2, C_3, C_4, C_5, and C_6.

(*Hint.   First prove that in order to compute C_i it is sufficient to consider one intermediate node.*)

16. Consider a project with eight jobs A, B, C, D, E, F, G, and H having the following job sequence ($X \rightarrow Y$ implies job X precedes job Y): $A \rightarrow C$, $B \rightarrow D$, $C \rightarrow H$, $A \rightarrow E$, $D \rightarrow F$, $B \rightarrow E$, $F \rightarrow G$, $E \rightarrow G$, $G \rightarrow H$. Draw the project network.

17. Consider a project consisting of nine jobs $(A, B, \ldots, I)$ with the following precedence relations and time estimates:

Job	Predecessor	Time (days)
A	—	15
B	—	10
C	A, B	10
D	A, B	10
E	B	5
F	D, E	5
G	C, F	20
H	D, E	10
I	G, H	15

a. Draw the project network for this problem designating the jobs by arcs and events by nodes.
b. Determine the earliest completion time of the project, and identify the critical path.
c. Determine a project schedule listing the earliest and latest starting times of each job. Also identify the critical jobs.

18. Consider the project given in Exercise 17. Discuss how the project schedule will be affected by the following events:
a. Job E is delayed, and it takes 15 days for completion.
b. Job H is delayed by 10 more days.
c. Jobs F and G are completed 1 day ahead of schedule.

19. Consider the project network given below:

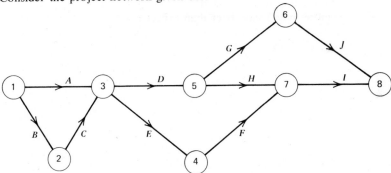

The data for normal times, crash times, and crashing costs are given as follows:

Job	Normal Time (days)	Crash Time (days)	Cost of Crashing Per Day ($)
A	10	7	4
B	5	4	2
C	3	2	2
D	4	3	3
E	5	3	3
F	6	3	5
G	5	2	1
H	6	4	4
I	6	4	3
J	4	3	3

Let T represent the earliest completion time of the project.
a. Determine the maximum and the minimum value of T.
b. Set up the linear program to solve the CPM problem if the project is to be completed in 21 days at minimum cost.
c. Given the overhead costs as $5 per day, determine the optimal duration of the project in terms of both the crashing and the overhead costs by direct enumeration method.

20. Consider a project consisting of 7 jobs $(A, \ldots, G)$ with the following precedence relations, and time estimates

Job	Predecessors	Optimistic Time (a)	Most Probable Time (m)	Pessimistic Time (b)
A	—	2	5	8
B	A	6	9	12
C	A	5	14	17
D	B	5	8	11
E	C, D	3	6	9
F	—	3	12	21
G	E, F	1	4	7

a. Draw the project network for the above problem.
b. Determine the expected duration, and variance of each job.
c. What is the expected length of the project, and its variance?
d. Compute the probabilities of completing the project
    (i)   3 days earlier than expected
    (ii) no more than 5 days later than expected

CHAPTER 4
ADVANCED TOPICS IN LINEAR PROGRAMMING

The simplex method discussed in Chapter 2 performs calculations on the entire tableau during each iteration. However updating all the elements in the tableau during a basis change is not really necessary for using the simplex method. The only information needed in moving from one tableau (basic feasible solution) to the next tableau is the following:

1. The relative profit coefficients ($\bar{c}$ row).
2. The column corresponding to the nonbasic variable entering the basis (the pivot column).
3. The current basic variables and their values (right-hand-side constants).

The information contained in the other columns of the tableau plays no role in the simplex process. Hence the solution of large linear programming problems on a digital computer will become very inefficient and costly if the simplex method were to be used in its full tableau form. Hence many refinements in the simplex calculations were carried out so that the implementation of the simplex method on a computer could be done more efficiently. This led to the development of the *revised simplex method* or *simplex method with multipliers*, which is implemented in all the commercial computer codes.

4.1 THE REVISED SIMPLEX METHOD
The revised simplex method uses the same basic principles of the regular simplex method. But at each iteration the entire tableau is never calculated. The relevant information it needs to move from one basic feasible solution to another is directly generated from the original equations.

In order to illustrate the basic principles of the revised simplex method, recall the linear program discussed in Section 2.7.

EXAMPLE 4.1-1

$$\text{Maximize:} \quad Z = 5x_1 + 2x_2 + 3x_3 - x_4 + x_5$$
$$\text{Subject to:} \quad x_1 + 2x_2 + 2x_3 + x_4 \qquad = 8$$
$$3x_1 + 4x_2 + x_3 \qquad + x_5 = 7$$
$$x_1, \ldots, x_5 \geq 0$$

For easy reference the three tableaus of the (regular) simplex method are reproduced in Table 4.1. To go from one basic feasible solution to the next, the simplex method needs the following:

1. The $\bar{c}$ row; to determine the nonbasic variable to enter the basis.
2. The pivot column, and the right-hand-side constants; to perform the minimum ratio test, and determine the basic variable to leave the basis.

Table 4.1
SIMPLEX TABLEAUS FOR EXAMPLE 4.1-1

Tableau	c_B	c_j / Basis	5 x_1	2 x_2	3 x_3	-1 x_4	1 x_5	Constants
1	-1	x_4	1	2	②	1	0	8
	1	x_5	3	4	1	0	1	7
		$\bar{c}$ row	3	0	4	0	0	$Z=-1$
2	3	x_3	$\frac{1}{2}$	1	1	$\frac{1}{2}$	0	4
	1	x_5	$\left(\frac{5}{2}\right)$	3	0	$-\frac{1}{2}$	1	3
		$\bar{c}$ row	1	-4	0	-2	0	$Z=15$
3	3	x_3	0	$\frac{2}{5}$	1	$\frac{3}{5}$	$-\frac{1}{5}$	$\frac{17}{5}$
	5	x_1	1	$\frac{6}{5}$	0	$-\frac{1}{5}$	$\frac{2}{5}$	$\frac{6}{5}$
		$\bar{c}$ row	0	$-\frac{26}{5}$	0	$-\frac{9}{5}$	$-\frac{2}{5}$	$Z=\frac{81}{5}$

For example, to go from Tableau 2 to Tableau 3 in Table 4.1, we need the value of $\bar{c}_1$, the column corresponding to x_1, and the right-hand-side constants. None of the other information contained in Tableau 1 is used. Hence there is no need to carry the entire tableau.

The revised simplex method works on the principle that any tableau corresponding to a basic feasible solution can be generated directly from the original equations by matrix-vector operations. To illustrate this, let the original columns corresponding to x_1, x_2, x_3, x_4, x_5 be denoted by column vectors $\mathbf{P}_1$, $\mathbf{P}_2$, $\mathbf{P}_3$, $\mathbf{P}_4$, $\mathbf{P}_5$, and the right-hand-side constants by the column vector $\mathbf{b}$. Thus,

$$\mathbf{P}_1 = \begin{pmatrix} 1 \\ 3 \end{pmatrix}, \quad \mathbf{P}_2 = \begin{pmatrix} 2 \\ 4 \end{pmatrix}, \quad \mathbf{P}_3 = \begin{pmatrix} 2 \\ 1 \end{pmatrix},$$

$$\mathbf{P}_4 = \begin{pmatrix} 1 \\ 0 \end{pmatrix}, \quad \mathbf{P}_5 = \begin{pmatrix} 0 \\ 1 \end{pmatrix} \quad \text{and} \quad \mathbf{b} = \begin{pmatrix} 8 \\ 7 \end{pmatrix}$$

Tableau 2 of Table 4.1 in which x_3 and x_5 are basic variables, may be generated directly by matrix theory as follows. Define a *basis matrix* $\mathbf{B}$ whose elements are the original columns corresponding to the basic variables x_3 and

x_5. Thus

$$\mathbf{B} = [\mathbf{P}_3, \mathbf{P}_5] = \begin{bmatrix} 2 & 0 \\ 1 & 1 \end{bmatrix}$$

The inverse of the basis matrix denoted by $\mathbf{B}^{-1}$ (see Appendix for a review of matrices) is given by,

$$\mathbf{B}^{-1} = \begin{bmatrix} \dfrac{1}{2} & 0 \\ -\dfrac{1}{2} & 1 \end{bmatrix}$$

Then from matrix theory any column in Tableau 2 can be obtained by premultiplying the original columns by the inverse of the basis matrix. Suppose $\bar{\mathbf{P}}_j$ denotes the updated column corresponding to the variable x_j and $\bar{\mathbf{b}}$ denotes the new constants in Tableau 2. Then, $\bar{\mathbf{P}}_j = \mathbf{B}^{-1}\mathbf{P}_j$ for all $j = 1, 2, 3, 4, 5$, and $\bar{\mathbf{b}} = \mathbf{B}^{-1}\mathbf{b}$. For example,

$$\bar{\mathbf{P}}_1 = \mathbf{B}^{-1}\mathbf{P}_1 = \begin{bmatrix} \dfrac{1}{2} & 0 \\ -\dfrac{1}{2} & 1 \end{bmatrix} \begin{bmatrix} 1 \\ 3 \end{bmatrix} = \begin{bmatrix} \dfrac{1}{2} \\ \dfrac{5}{2} \end{bmatrix},$$

$$\bar{\mathbf{P}}_2 = \mathbf{B}^{-1}\mathbf{P}_2 = \begin{bmatrix} \dfrac{1}{2} & 0 \\ -\dfrac{1}{2} & 1 \end{bmatrix} \begin{bmatrix} 2 \\ 4 \end{bmatrix} = \begin{bmatrix} 1 \\ 3 \end{bmatrix},$$

$$\bar{\mathbf{b}} = \mathbf{B}^{-1}\mathbf{b} = \begin{bmatrix} \dfrac{1}{2} & 0 \\ -\dfrac{1}{2} & 1 \end{bmatrix} \begin{bmatrix} 8 \\ 7 \end{bmatrix} = \begin{bmatrix} 4 \\ 3 \end{bmatrix}$$

Note that the vector $\bar{\mathbf{b}}$ gives the values of the basic variables x_3 and x_5.

Recall that there are two key steps in the simplex method, namely, the selection of a nonbasic variable to enter the basis and the basic variable to leave. Let us see how these key steps are carried out in the revised simplex method when it does not carry the entire tableau at each iteration.

The selection of a nonbasic variable is based on the values of the relative profit coefficients ($\bar{c}_j$). For example, in the regular simplex method, the $\bar{c}_j$ values in Tableau 2 will be calculated as follows:

$$\bar{c}_1 = c_1 - \mathbf{c_B}\bar{\mathbf{P}}_1 = 5 - (3, 1) \begin{bmatrix} \dfrac{1}{2} \\ \dfrac{5}{2} \end{bmatrix} = 1$$

$$\bar{c}_2 = c_2 - \mathbf{c_B}\bar{\mathbf{P}}_2 = 2 - (3, 1) \begin{bmatrix} 1 \\ 3 \end{bmatrix} = -4$$

$$\bar{c}_4 = c_4 - \mathbf{c_B}\bar{\mathbf{P}}_4 = -1 - (3, 1) \begin{bmatrix} \dfrac{1}{2} \\ -\dfrac{1}{2} \end{bmatrix} = -2$$

In general, for the nonbasic variable x_j,

$$\bar{c}_j = c_j - \mathbf{c_B}\bar{\mathbf{P}}_j \qquad (4.1)$$

From the matrix theory it was shown earlier that

$$\bar{\mathbf{P}}_j = \mathbf{B}^{-1}\mathbf{P}_j$$

Hence, $\bar{c}_j = c_j - \mathbf{c_B}\mathbf{B}^{-1}\mathbf{P}_j$. Let the vector $\boldsymbol{\pi}$ denote $\mathbf{c_B}\mathbf{B}^{-1}$. The elements of vector $\boldsymbol{\pi}$ are called the *simplex multipliers*. Thus Eq. 4.1 reduces to,

$$\bar{c}_j = c_j - \boldsymbol{\pi}\mathbf{P}_j \qquad \text{for all } j \qquad (4.2)$$

where c_j is the original profit coefficient, and $\mathbf{P}_j$ is the original column coefficients of the variable x_j. For example, in Tableau 2,

$$\boldsymbol{\pi} = (\pi_1, \pi_2) = \mathbf{c_B}\mathbf{B}^{-1} = (3, 1)\begin{bmatrix} \frac{1}{2} & 0 \\ -\frac{1}{2} & 1 \end{bmatrix} = (1, 1)$$

and

$$\bar{c}_1 = c_1 - \boldsymbol{\pi}\mathbf{P}_1 = 5 - (1, 1)\begin{bmatrix} 1 \\ 3 \end{bmatrix} = 1$$

$$\bar{c}_2 = c_2 - \boldsymbol{\pi}\mathbf{P}_2 = 2 - (1, 1)\begin{bmatrix} 2 \\ 4 \end{bmatrix} = -4$$

$$\bar{c}_4 = c_4 - \boldsymbol{\pi}\mathbf{P}_4 = -1 - (1, 1)\begin{bmatrix} 1 \\ 0 \end{bmatrix} = -2$$

Since $\bar{c}_1 > 0$, we select x_1 to be the new basic variable. Thus using Eq. 4.2, the $\bar{c}$ row for any tableau can be calculated directly from the original equations and the profit coefficients. The only other information needed is the inverse of the basis matrix corresponding to that tableau.

Having chosen x_1 as the variable to enter the basis, we have to find the basic variable to leave the basis by the minimum ratio rule. In order to apply this rule, we need the new right-hand-side constants, and the column corresponding to x_1 in Tableau 2. As shown earlier, these can be obtained directly from the original columns by premultiplying them by the inverse of the basis matrix. Thus, the pivot column,

$$\bar{\mathbf{P}}_1 = \mathbf{B}^{-1}\mathbf{P}_1 = \begin{bmatrix} \frac{1}{2} & 0 \\ -\frac{1}{2} & 1 \end{bmatrix}\begin{bmatrix} 1 \\ 3 \end{bmatrix} = \begin{bmatrix} \frac{1}{2} \\ \frac{5}{2} \end{bmatrix}$$

The new constants,

$$\bar{\mathbf{b}} = \mathbf{B}^{-1}\mathbf{b} = \begin{bmatrix} \frac{1}{2} & 0 \\ -\frac{1}{2} & 1 \end{bmatrix}\begin{bmatrix} 8 \\ 7 \end{bmatrix} = \begin{bmatrix} 4 \\ 3 \end{bmatrix}$$

Applying the minimum ratio rule, the minimum ratio is found in the second row, and the basic variable x_5 will be replaced by x_1. Hence the new set of basis variables are x_3 and x_1.

Once again we can form the new basis matrix

$$\mathbf{B} = (\mathbf{P}_3, \mathbf{P}_1) = \begin{bmatrix} 2 & 1 \\ 1 & 3 \end{bmatrix}$$

and compute

$$\mathbf{B}^{-1} = \begin{bmatrix} \dfrac{3}{5} & -\dfrac{1}{5} \\ -\dfrac{1}{5} & \dfrac{2}{5} \end{bmatrix}$$

The new right-hand-side constants are given by

$$\mathbf{B}^{-1}\mathbf{b} = \begin{bmatrix} \dfrac{3}{5} & -\dfrac{1}{5} \\ -\dfrac{1}{5} & \dfrac{2}{5} \end{bmatrix} \begin{bmatrix} 8 \\ 7 \end{bmatrix} = \begin{bmatrix} \dfrac{17}{5} \\ \dfrac{6}{5} \end{bmatrix}$$

In other words, the new basic feasible solution is $x_3 = 17/5$, $x_1 = 6/5$, $x_2 = x_4 = x_5 = 0$. To check the optimality of this solution, we need the $\bar{c}_j$ coefficients for x_2, x_4, and x_5. Using Eq. (4.2),

$$\bar{c}_j = c_j - \boldsymbol{\pi}\mathbf{P}_j \qquad \text{where} \qquad \boldsymbol{\pi} = \mathbf{c}_B\mathbf{B}^{-1}$$

The new simplex multipliers are given by

$$\boldsymbol{\pi} = (\pi_1, \pi_2) = \mathbf{c}_B\mathbf{B}^{-1} = (3, 5) \begin{bmatrix} \dfrac{3}{5} & -\dfrac{1}{5} \\ -\dfrac{1}{5} & \dfrac{2}{5} \end{bmatrix} = \left(\dfrac{4}{5}, \dfrac{7}{5}\right)$$

Then,

$$\bar{c}_2 = c_2 - \boldsymbol{\pi}\mathbf{P}_2 = 2 - \left(\dfrac{4}{5}, \dfrac{7}{5}\right)\begin{bmatrix} 2 \\ 4 \end{bmatrix} = -\dfrac{26}{5}$$

$$\bar{c}_4 = c_4 - \boldsymbol{\pi}\mathbf{P}_4 = -1 - \left(\dfrac{4}{5}, \dfrac{7}{5}\right)\begin{bmatrix} 1 \\ 0 \end{bmatrix} = -\dfrac{9}{5}$$

$$\bar{c}_5 = c_5 - \boldsymbol{\pi}\mathbf{P}_5 = 1 - \left(\dfrac{4}{5}, \dfrac{7}{5}\right)\begin{bmatrix} 0 \\ 1 \end{bmatrix} = -\dfrac{2}{5}$$

Since all the $\bar{c}_j$ coefficients are negative, the current solution is optimal.

To summarize, any information contained in a simplex tableau may be obtained directly from the original equations by knowing the inverse of the basis matrix corresponding to that tableau. The inverse of the basis matrix can be computed from the original equations by merely knowing the current basic variables in that tableau. Thus the revised simplex method has the capability to generate any information that is available in the regular simplex method. But it generates only the relevant information that is needed to perform the simplex steps.

In the actual implementation of the revised simplex method, the inverse of the basis is not computed explicitly by inverting the matrix of basic columns. Inverting a matrix is generally time consuming and costly on a digital computer. Hence the basis inverse at each step is obtained by a simple pivot operation on the previous inverse. To illustrate this refer to the three simplex tableaus given in Table 4.1. In the initial basic feasible solution (Tableau 1), x_4 and x_5 are the basic variables. The initial basis matrix (which correspond to the columns $\mathbf{P}_4$ and $\mathbf{P}_5$) is the identity matrix since $[\mathbf{P}_4, \mathbf{P}_5] = \begin{bmatrix} 1 & 0 \\ 0 & 1 \end{bmatrix} = \mathbf{I}$ (identity matrix).

In any subsequent tableau, the new column coefficients corresponding to x_4 and x_5 are obtained by premultiplying $\mathbf{P}_4$ and $\mathbf{P}_5$ by the inverse of the current basis matrix. That is, $\bar{\mathbf{P}}_4 = \mathbf{B}^{-1}\mathbf{P}_4$ and $\bar{\mathbf{P}}_5 = \mathbf{B}^{-1}\mathbf{P}_5$. Hence,

$$[\bar{\mathbf{P}}_4, \bar{\mathbf{P}}_5] = \mathbf{B}^{-1}[\mathbf{P}_4, \mathbf{P}_5] = \mathbf{B}^{-1}\mathbf{I} = \mathbf{B}^{-1}$$

In other words, the columns corresponding to x_4 and x_5 in any tableau contains the inverse of the basis for that tableau! For example, in Tableau 2 (Table 4.1) the columns corresponding to x_4 and x_5 is given by $\begin{bmatrix} 1/2 & 0 \\ -1/2 & 1 \end{bmatrix}$ which was the computed basis inverse for that tableau. This is true for Tableau 3 as well. This implies that the new basis inverse may be easily obtained by carrying the columns corresponding to the initial basic variables, and updating them by the pivot operation.

Similarly the right-hand-side constants of every tableau are always needed for determining the basic feasible solution, and later for the minimum ratio rule. Instead of computing it using the basis inverse, we can carry the right-hand-side constants, and update their values for each iteration by the pivot operation. Thus the revised simplex method uses a reduced simplex tableau which contains the columns corresponding to the initial basic variables, the right-hand-side constants, and the current basic variables. For example, Table 4.2 shows how the second tableau of the revised simplex method for Example 4.1-1 may look like.

Table 4.2

Basis	$\mathbf{B}^{-1}$		$\bar{\mathbf{b}}$
x_3	$\dfrac{1}{2}$	0	4
x_5	$-\dfrac{1}{2}$	1	3

From $\mathbf{B}^{-1}$, the simplex multipliers and the $\bar{c}_j$ elements are calculated. This results in selecting x_1 to enter the basis. To perform the minimum ratio test, the column corresponding to x_1 in Tableau 2 (pivot column) is required. This is computed as follows:

$$\bar{\mathbf{P}}_1 = \mathbf{B}^{-1}\mathbf{P}_1 = \begin{bmatrix} \dfrac{1}{2} & 0 \\ -\dfrac{1}{2} & 1 \end{bmatrix} \begin{bmatrix} 1 \\ 3 \end{bmatrix} = \begin{bmatrix} \dfrac{1}{2} \\ \dfrac{5}{2} \end{bmatrix}$$

Using $\bar{\mathbf{P}}_1$ and $\bar{\mathbf{b}}$, the ratio test is performed. This identifies x_5 as the basic variable to leave. Thus x_1 becomes the new basic variable in the second constraint. This means that the pivot column $\begin{bmatrix} 1/2 \\ 5/2 \end{bmatrix}$ should be reduced to $\begin{bmatrix} 0 \\ 1 \end{bmatrix}$ by pivot operation. This is done as follows:

1. Multiply the second row by $-1/5$ and add it to the first row.
2. Divide the second row by $5/2$.

The pivot operation is carried out to the reduced tableau shown in Table 4.2. The new tableau is shown in Table 4.3.

Table 4.3

Basis	$\mathbf{B}^{-1}$		$\bar{\mathbf{b}}$
x_3	$\dfrac{3}{5}$	$-\dfrac{1}{5}$	$\dfrac{17}{5}$
x_1	$-\dfrac{1}{5}$	$\dfrac{2}{5}$	$\dfrac{6}{5}$

The new basic feasible solution is $x_3 = 17/5$, $x_1 = 6/5$, $x_2 = x_4 = x_5 = 0$. The new inverse of the basis is $\begin{bmatrix} 3/5 & -1/5 \\ -1/5 & 2/5 \end{bmatrix}$. Using the new basis inverse, the simplex multipliers and $\bar{c}_j$ coefficients are computed to check the optimality of Table 4.3.

General Steps of the Revised Simplex Method
Recall the matrix form of the standard linear program given in Section 2.4.

$$\text{Minimize:} \quad Z = \mathbf{cx}$$
$$\text{Subject to:} \quad \mathbf{Ax} = \mathbf{b}$$
$$\mathbf{x} \geq 0$$

where

$$\mathbf{A}_{(m \times n)} = \begin{bmatrix} a_{11} & a_{12} & \cdots & a_{1n} \\ a_{21} & a_{22} & \cdots & a_{2n} \\ \cdot & \cdot & & \cdot \\ \cdot & \cdot & & \cdot \\ \cdot & \cdot & & \cdot \\ a_{m1} & a_{m2} & & a_{mn} \end{bmatrix}$$

$$\mathbf{b}_{(m \times 1)} = \begin{bmatrix} b_1 \\ b_2 \\ \cdot \\ \cdot \\ \cdot \\ b_m \end{bmatrix} \qquad \mathbf{x}_{(n \times 1)} = \begin{bmatrix} x_1 \\ x_2 \\ \cdot \\ \cdot \\ \cdot \\ x_n \end{bmatrix} \qquad \mathbf{c}_{(1 \times n)} = (c_1, c_2, \ldots, c_n)$$

Let the columns corresponding to the matrix $\mathbf{A}$ be denoted by $\mathbf{P}_1, \mathbf{P}_2, \ldots,$

P_n where

$$\underset{(m \times 1)}{P_1} = \begin{bmatrix} a_{11} \\ a_{21} \\ \cdot \\ \cdot \\ \cdot \\ a_{m1} \end{bmatrix} \qquad \underset{(m \times 1)}{P_{m+1}} = \begin{bmatrix} a_{1,m+1} \\ a_{2,m+1} \\ \cdot \\ \cdot \\ \cdot \\ a_{m,m+1} \end{bmatrix} \quad , \ldots , \qquad \text{and} \qquad \underset{(m \times 1)}{P_n} = \begin{bmatrix} a_{1n} \\ a_{2n} \\ \cdot \\ \cdot \\ \cdot \\ a_{mn} \end{bmatrix}$$

Suppose we have a basic feasible solution to the linear program using x_1, $x_2, \ldots , x_m$ as the basic variables. Then the basis matrix is given by,

$$\underset{(m \times m)}{B} = [P_1, P_2, \ldots , P_m] = \begin{bmatrix} a_{11} & a_{12} & \cdots & a_{1m} \\ a_{21} & a_{22} & \cdots & a_{2m} \\ \cdot & \cdot & & \cdot \\ \cdot & \cdot & & \cdot \\ \cdot & \cdot & & \cdot \\ a_{m1} & a_{m2} & & a_{mm} \end{bmatrix}$$

Let

$$\underset{(m \times m)}{B^{-1}} = \begin{bmatrix} \beta_{11} & \beta_{12} & \cdots & \beta_{1m} \\ \beta_{21} & \beta_{22} & \cdots & \beta_{2m} \\ \cdot & \cdot & & \cdot \\ \cdot & \cdot & & \cdot \\ \cdot & \cdot & & \cdot \\ \beta_{m1} & \beta_{m2} & & \beta_{mm} \end{bmatrix}$$

Let the vector x be partitioned as $\underset{(n \times 1)}{x} = \begin{bmatrix} x_B \\ x_N \end{bmatrix}$, where x_B corresponds to the basic variables, and x_N to the nonbasic variables. Thus,

$$\underset{(m \times 1)}{x_B} = \begin{bmatrix} x_1 \\ x_2 \\ \cdot \\ \cdot \\ \cdot \\ x_m \end{bmatrix} \qquad \text{and} \qquad \underset{(n-m \times 1)}{x_N} = \begin{bmatrix} x_{m+1} \\ x_{m+2} \\ \cdot \\ \cdot \\ \cdot \\ x_n \end{bmatrix}$$

The current basic feasible solution is given by

$$x_B = B^{-1}b = \begin{bmatrix} \beta_{11}b_1 + \beta_{12}b_2 + \cdots + \beta_{1m}b_m \\ \beta_{21}b_1 + \beta_{22}b_2 + \cdots + \beta_{2m}b_m \\ \cdot \\ \cdot \\ \cdot \\ \beta_{m1}b_1 + \beta_{m2}b_2 + \cdots + \beta_{mm}b_m \end{bmatrix}$$

$$= \begin{bmatrix} \bar{b}_1 \\ \bar{b}_2 \\ \cdot \\ \cdot \\ \cdot \\ \bar{b}_m \end{bmatrix}, \qquad \text{and} \qquad x_N = \begin{bmatrix} 0 \\ 0 \\ \cdot \\ \cdot \\ \cdot \\ 0 \end{bmatrix}$$

Let $\mathbf{c_B}$ denote the cost coefficients of the basic variables. Then the value of the objective with respect to the basis $\mathbf{B}$ becomes

$$Z = \mathbf{cx} = \mathbf{c_B x_B} = c_1 \bar{b}_1 + c_2 \bar{b}_2 + \cdots + c_m \bar{b}_m$$

In order to verify whether the present solution is optimal, the revised simplex method computes the simplex multipliers,

$$\underset{(1 \times m)}{\boldsymbol{\pi}} = (\pi_1, \pi_2, \ldots, \pi_m) = \mathbf{c_B B}^{-1}$$

Thus

$$\pi_1 = c_1 \beta_{11} + c_2 \beta_{21} + \cdots + c_m \beta_{m1}$$

$$\pi_2 = c_1 \beta_{12} + c_2 \beta_{22} + \cdots + c_m \beta_{m2}$$

.

.

.

$$\pi_m = c_1 \beta_{1m} + c_2 \beta_{2m} + \cdots + c_m \beta_{mm}$$

The relative cost coefficients are given by,

$$\bar{c}_j = c_j - \boldsymbol{\pi} \mathbf{P}_j \qquad \text{for } j = m+1, m+2, \ldots, n$$

Thus

$$\bar{c}_{m+1} = c_{m+1} - \boldsymbol{\pi} \mathbf{P}_{m+1} = c_{m+1} - (\pi_1 a_{1,m+1} + \pi_2 a_{2,m+1} + \cdots + \pi_m a_{m,m+1})$$

.

.

.

$$\bar{c}_n = c_n - \boldsymbol{\pi} \mathbf{P}_n = c_n - (\pi_1 a_{1n} + \pi_2 a_{2n} + \cdots + \pi_m a_{mn})$$

Since we have a minimization problem, the solution is optimal when all the $\bar{c}_j \geq 0$. Otherwise, select the nonbasic variable with the most negative value for $\bar{c}_j$ to enter the basis.

This step is sometimes called the *pricing out routine* in the computer code. During this step, the simplex multipliers are generally stored in the computer memory. The data matrix $\mathbf{A}$ and cost coefficients c_j are kept externally to the computer on a magnetic tape or disc, and are read in one column at a time to compute the $\bar{c}_j$ values. (As mentioned earlier, computer codes for large problems do not compute all the $\bar{c}_j$ elements. As soon as a negative $\bar{c}_j$ is found, the corresponding nonbasic variable x_j becomes the new basic variable.)

From the pricing out routine let us say that the nonbasic variable x_n is selected to enter the basis. Once the entering column $\mathbf{P}_n$ has been selected, it has to be transformed in terms of the current basis (tableau). This gives the pivot column which is needed in the ratio test. Thus the pivot column becomes:

$$\underset{(m \times 1)}{\bar{\mathbf{P}}_n} = \mathbf{B}^{-1} \mathbf{P}_n = \begin{bmatrix} \beta_{11} a_{1n} + \beta_{12} a_{2n} + \cdots + \beta_{1m} a_{mn} \\ \beta_{21} a_{1n} + \beta_{22} a_{2n} + \cdots + \beta_{2m} a_{mn} \\ \cdot \\ \cdot \\ \cdot \\ \beta_{m1} a_{1n} + \beta_{m2} a_{2n} + \cdots + \beta_{mm} a_{mn} \end{bmatrix}$$

$$= \begin{bmatrix} \bar{a}_{1n} \\ \bar{a}_{2n} \\ \cdot \\ \cdot \\ \cdot \\ \bar{a}_{mn} \end{bmatrix}$$

The minimum ratio test is performed to identify the basic variable to leave the basis. Suppose that

$$\frac{\bar{b}_2}{\bar{a}_{2n}} = \underset{\bar{a}_{in}>0}{\text{Minimum}}\left(\frac{\bar{b}_i}{\bar{a}_{in}}\right) \qquad \text{for } i = 1, 2, \ldots, m$$

Since the minimum ratio occurs in the second row (corresponding to the basic variable x_2), x_n replaces x_2 from the basis. A pivot operation is carried out on the basis inverse $(\mathbf{B}^{-1})$ and the right-hand-side constants $(\bar{\mathbf{b}})$ using $\bar{a}_{2n}$ as the pivot element. This gives the new basis inverse, and the constants with respect to the new basic variables $(x_1, x_n, x_3, x_4, \ldots, x_m)$.

Let the new right-hand-side constants be denoted by

$$\mathbf{b}^* = \begin{bmatrix} b_1^* \\ b_2^* \\ \cdot \\ \cdot \\ \cdot \\ b_m^* \end{bmatrix}$$

and the new inverse of the basis matrix be

$$\underset{(m \times m)}{(\mathbf{B}^*)^{-1}} = \begin{bmatrix} \beta_{11}^* & \cdots & \beta_{1m}^* \\ \cdot & & \cdot \\ \cdot & & \cdot \\ \cdot & & \cdot \\ \beta_{m1}^* & \cdots & \beta_{mm}^* \end{bmatrix}$$

The pivot operation to get $\bar{\mathbf{b}}^*$ and $(\mathbf{B}^*)^{-1}$ is described below:

$$b_2^* = \bar{b}_2/\bar{a}_{2n}$$
$$b_i^* = \bar{b}_i - (\bar{a}_{in}\bar{b}_2/\bar{a}_{2n}) \qquad \text{for all } i = 1, 3, \ldots, m$$
$$\beta_{2j}^* = \beta_{2j}/\bar{a}_{2n} \qquad \text{for } j = 1, 2, \ldots, m$$
$$\beta_{ij}^* = \beta_{ij} - (\bar{a}_{in}\beta_{2j}/\bar{a}_{2n}) \qquad \text{for } j = 1, 2, \ldots, m \text{ and } i = 1, 3, \ldots, m$$

The new basic feasible solution is $x_1 = b_1^*$, $x_n = b_2^*$, $x_3 = b_3^*, \ldots, x_m = b_m^*$, $x_2 = x_{m+1} = \cdots = x_{n-1} = 0$. With the help of the new basis inverse the simplex multipliers and $\bar{c}_j$ elements are once again computed to check the optimality of the new basic feasible solution. This process is continued until the optimal solution is reached.

We shall now illustrate the revised simplex method using the example of Section 2.9.

EXAMPLE 4.1-2

$$\begin{aligned} \text{Minimize:} \quad & Z = -3x_1 + x_2 + x_3 \\ \text{Subject to:} \quad & x_1 - 2x_2 + x_3 \leq 11 \\ & -4x_1 + x_2 + 2x_3 \geq 3 \\ & 2x_1 \qquad - x_3 = -1 \\ & x_1, x_2, x_3 \geq 0 \end{aligned}$$

In standard form, the problem reduces to

$$\text{Minimize:} \quad Z = -3x_1 + x_2 + x_3$$

$$\text{Subject to:} \quad x_1 - 2x_2 + x_3 + x_4 \qquad\qquad = 11$$

$$-4x_1 + x_2 + 2x_3 \qquad - x_5 = 3$$

$$-2x_1 \qquad + x_3 \qquad\qquad = 1$$

$$x_1, \ldots, x_5 \ge 0$$

Since there are no basic variables in the second and third equations, artificial variables x_6 and x_7 are added as shown below:

$$x_1 - 2x_2 + x_3 + x_4 \qquad\qquad = 11$$

$$-4x_1 + x_2 + 2x_3 \qquad -x_5 + x_6 \qquad = 3$$

$$-2x_1 \qquad + x_3 \qquad\qquad +x_7 = 1$$

$$x_1, \ldots, x_7 \ge 0$$

Using the Big M method, the objective function becomes

$$\text{Minimize } Z = -3x_1 + x_2 + x_3 + Mx_6 + Mx_7$$

Let $\mathbf{P}_1, \ldots, \mathbf{P}_7$ and $\mathbf{b}$ denote the columns corresponding to $x_1, \ldots, x_7$ and the right-hand side. Thus,

$$\mathbf{P}_1 = \begin{bmatrix} 1 \\ -4 \\ -2 \end{bmatrix}, \quad \mathbf{P}_2 = \begin{bmatrix} -2 \\ 1 \\ 0 \end{bmatrix}, \quad \mathbf{P}_3 = \begin{bmatrix} 1 \\ 2 \\ 1 \end{bmatrix}, \quad \mathbf{P}_4 = \begin{bmatrix} 1 \\ 0 \\ 0 \end{bmatrix}, \quad \mathbf{P}_5 = \begin{bmatrix} 0 \\ -1 \\ 0 \end{bmatrix}$$

$$\mathbf{P}_6 = \begin{bmatrix} 0 \\ 1 \\ 0 \end{bmatrix}, \quad \mathbf{P}_7 = \begin{bmatrix} 0 \\ 0 \\ 1 \end{bmatrix}, \quad \text{and} \quad \mathbf{b} = \begin{bmatrix} 11 \\ 3 \\ 1 \end{bmatrix}$$

Since (x_4, x_6, x_7) form the initial basis,

$$\mathbf{B}_{(3\times3)} = [\mathbf{P}_4, \mathbf{P}_6, \mathbf{P}_7] = \begin{bmatrix} 1 & 0 & 0 \\ 0 & 1 & 0 \\ 0 & 0 & 1 \end{bmatrix} = \mathbf{I}$$

Hence

$$\mathbf{B}^{-1} = \mathbf{I} \quad \text{and} \quad \bar{\mathbf{b}} = \mathbf{B}^{-1}\mathbf{b} = \mathbf{b}$$

The initial tableau of the revised simplex method is given below (the last two columns are added later):

Tableau 1

Basis	$\mathbf{B}^{-1}$			Constants	Variable to Enter	Pivot Column
x_4	1	0	0	11		1
x_6	0	1	0	3	x_3	2
x_7	0	0	1	1		①

The simplex multipliers are

$$\boldsymbol{\pi} = (\pi_1, \pi_2, \pi_3) = \mathbf{c_B B}^{-1} = (0, M, M)\begin{bmatrix} 1 & 0 & 0 \\ 0 & 1 & 0 \\ 0 & 0 & 1 \end{bmatrix} = (0, M, M)$$

Since $\bar{c}_j = c_j - \boldsymbol{\pi}\mathbf{P}_j$ for $j = 1, 2, 3, 5$ we get,

$$\bar{c}_1 = -3 - (0, M, M)\begin{bmatrix} 1 \\ -4 \\ -2 \end{bmatrix} = 6M - 3$$

$$\bar{c}_2 = \quad 1 - (0, M, M)\begin{bmatrix} -2 \\ 1 \\ 0 \end{bmatrix} = 1 - M$$

$$\bar{c}_3 = \quad 1 - (0, M, M)\begin{bmatrix} 1 \\ 2 \\ 1 \end{bmatrix} = 1 - 3M$$

$$\bar{c}_5 = \quad 0 - (0, M, M)\begin{bmatrix} 0 \\ -1 \\ 0 \end{bmatrix} = M$$

Since $\bar{c}_3$ is most negative, x_3 enters the basis. The pivot column is

$$\bar{\mathbf{P}}_3 = \mathbf{B}^{-1}\mathbf{P}_3 = \begin{bmatrix} 1 & 0 & 0 \\ 0 & 1 & 0 \\ 0 & 0 & 1 \end{bmatrix}\begin{bmatrix} 1 \\ 2 \\ 1 \end{bmatrix} = \begin{bmatrix} 1 \\ 2 \\ 1 \end{bmatrix}$$

(The entering variable x_3 and the pivot column elements are now entered in Tableau 1.) Applying the minimum ratio rule, the ratios are $(11/1, 3/2, 1/1)$. Hence x_3 replaces the artificial variable x_7 from the basis. This is shown by circling the pivot element in Tableau 1. Using the pivot column, the pivot operation is done on Tableau 1 as follows:

1. Multiply row 3 by -1, and add it to row 1.
2. Multiply row 3 by -2, and add it to row 2.

The new $\mathbf{B}^{-1}$, and the constants are given below:

Tableau 2

Basis	$\mathbf{B}^{-1}$			Constants	Variable to Enter	Pivot Column
x_4	1	0	-1	10		-2
x_6	0	1	-2	1	x_2	①
x_3	0	0	1	1		0

The simplex multipliers corresponding to Tableau 2 are

$$\boldsymbol{\pi} = (0, M, 1)\begin{bmatrix} 1 & 0 & -1 \\ 0 & 1 & -2 \\ 0 & 0 & 1 \end{bmatrix} = (0, M, -2M + 1)$$

The $\bar{c}_j$ elements are given by $\bar{c}_1 = -1$, $\bar{c}_2 = 1 - M$ and $\bar{c}_5 = M$. ($\bar{c}_7$ is not calculated because x_7 is an artificial variable). Since $\bar{c}_2$ is the most negative, x_2 enters the basis and the pivot column becomes

$$\bar{P}_2 = B^{-1}P_2 = \begin{bmatrix} 1 & 0 & -1 \\ 0 & 1 & -2 \\ 0 & 0 & 1 \end{bmatrix} \begin{bmatrix} -2 \\ 1 \\ 0 \end{bmatrix} = \begin{bmatrix} -2 \\ 1 \\ 0 \end{bmatrix}$$

The ratios are $(\infty, 1/1, \infty)$. Hence x_2 replaces the artificial variable x_6 from the basis. (We shall discard x_6 from further consideration.) Performing the pivot operation we obtain the new basic feasible solution shown in Tableau 3.

Tableau 3

Basis	$\mathbf{B}^{-1}$			Constants	Variable to Enter	Pivot Column
x_4	1	2	-5	12		③
x_2	0	1	-2	1	x_1	0
x_3	0	0	1	1		-2

The simplex multipliers of Tableau 3 are

$$\pi = (0, 1, 1) \begin{bmatrix} 1 & 2 & -5 \\ 0 & 1 & -2 \\ 0 & 0 & 1 \end{bmatrix} = (0, 1, -1)$$

The $\bar{c}_j$ elements of the nonbasic variables are given by,

$$\bar{c}_1 = -1 \quad \text{and} \quad \bar{c}_5 = 1$$

Thus x_1 enters the basis. The pivot column becomes

$$\bar{P}_1 = \begin{bmatrix} 1 & 2 & -5 \\ 0 & 1 & -2 \\ 0 & 0 & 1 \end{bmatrix} \begin{bmatrix} 1 \\ -4 \\ -2 \end{bmatrix} = \begin{bmatrix} 3 \\ 0 \\ -2 \end{bmatrix}$$

By the minimum ratio rule, x_1 replaces x_4 from the basis, and the new tableau after the pivot operation is given below:

Tableau 4

Basis	$\mathbf{B}^{-1}$			Constants
x_1	$\dfrac{1}{3}$	$\dfrac{2}{3}$	$-\dfrac{5}{3}$	4
x_2	0	1	-2	1
x_3	$\dfrac{2}{3}$	$\dfrac{4}{3}$	$-\dfrac{7}{3}$	9

The simplex multipliers of Tableau 4 are

$$\pi = [-3, 1, 1] \begin{bmatrix} \frac{1}{3} & \frac{2}{3} & -\frac{5}{3} \\ 0 & 1 & -2 \\ \frac{2}{3} & \frac{4}{3} & -\frac{7}{3} \end{bmatrix} = \left[-\frac{1}{3}, \frac{1}{3}, \frac{2}{3} \right]$$

and

$$\bar{c}_4 = 0 - \left[-\frac{1}{3}, \frac{1}{3}, \frac{2}{3} \right] \begin{bmatrix} 1 \\ 0 \\ 0 \end{bmatrix} = \frac{1}{3}$$

$$\bar{c}_5 = 0 - \left[-\frac{1}{3}, \frac{1}{3}, \frac{2}{3} \right] \begin{bmatrix} 0 \\ -1 \\ 0 \end{bmatrix} = \frac{1}{3}$$

Hence Tableau 4 is optimal, and the unique optimal solution is given by

$$x_1 = 4, \qquad x_2 = 1, \qquad x_3 = 9, \qquad x_4 = 0, \qquad \text{and} \qquad x_5 = 0$$

The optimal value of the objective function is

$$z = \mathbf{c_B \bar{b}} = (-3, 1, 1) \begin{pmatrix} 4 \\ 1 \\ 9 \end{pmatrix} = -2$$

Since Example 4.1-2 has been solved by the standard simplex method in Section 2.9, it is suggested that the reader compare the two to see the major differences between them.

Advantages of the Revised Simplex Method Over the Standard Simplex Method

1. There is a reduced amount of computations when the number of variables in the linear program is much larger than the number of constraints. The revised simplex method works with a reduced tableau whose size is determined by the number of constraints. Hence, the amount of computations is considerably reduced.
2. Less new information is stored in the computer memory from one iteration to the next. Since the revised simplex method works with a reduced tableau, it stores only the basic variables, the basis inverse, and the constants. The data matrix A and the objective function coefficients are kept externally on a file (tape or disc), and larger problems can be solved. Many commercial codes store even the basis inverse on tape using what is known as the *product form of the inverse.*
3. Less space is needed for recording data. The original data is usually given in fixed decimals of three or four digits. Since the revised simplex method works only with the original data, the data can be stored compactly and more accurately.
4. Less accumulation of round-off errors occurs because no calculations are done on a column until it is ready to enter the basis. Many commercial codes periodically get the basis inverse directly by inverting the original columns instead of using the pivot operation. This further reduces the accumulation of round-off errors.
5. For problems with a large percentage of zero coefficients (practical problems often have 90% or more zero elements), the revised simplex method performs fewer multiplications involving nonzero elements as compared to the standard simplex method, in which the zero elements disappear during the initial pivot operations.
6. The theory of the revised simplex method, especially the importance of the basis

inverse and the simplex multipliers, is helpful in understanding the other advanced topics in linear programming like duality theory and sensitivity analysis.

We conclude this section with the remark that the above advantages of the revised simplex method are mainly for computation by a digital computer. For hand calculations, the above may not be significant because of the amount of orderly bookkeeping, and scratch work needed in the revised simplex method.

4.2 DUALITY THEORY AND ITS APPLICATIONS

From both the theoretical and practical points of view, the theory of duality is one of the most important and interesting concepts in linear programming. The basic idea behind the duality theory is that every linear programming problem has an associated linear program called its *dual* such that a solution to the original linear program also gives a solution to its dual. Thus, whenever a linear program is solved by the simplex method, we are actually getting solutions for two linear programming problems!

We shall introduce the concept of a dual with the following linear program.

EXAMPLE 4.2-1

$$\text{Maximize:} \quad Z = x_1 + 2x_2 - 3x_3 + 4x_4$$
$$\text{Subject to:} \quad x_1 + 2x_2 + 2x_3 - 3x_4 \leqq 25$$
$$2x_1 + x_2 - 3x_3 + 2x_4 \leqq 15$$
$$x_1, \ldots, x_4 \geqq 0$$

The above linear program has two constraints and four variables. The dual of this problem is written as

$$\text{Minimize:} \quad W = 25y_1 + 15y_2$$
$$\text{Subject to:} \quad y_1 + 2y_2 \geqq 1$$
$$2y_1 + y_2 \geqq 2$$
$$2y_1 - 3y_2 \geqq -3$$
$$-3y_1 + 2y_2 \geqq 4$$
$$y_1 \geqq 0, y_2 \geqq 0$$

y_1 and y_2 are called the dual variables. The original problem is called the *primal* problem. Comparing the primal and the dual problems, we observe the following relationships:

1. The objective function coefficients of the primal problem have become the right-hand-side constants of the dual. Similarly, the right-hand-side constants of the primal have become the cost coefficients of the dual.
2. The inequalities have been reversed in the constraints.
3. The objective is changed from maximization in primal to minimization in dual.
4. Each column in the primal corresponds to a constraint (row) in the dual. Thus the number of dual constraints is equal to the number of primal variables.
5. Each constraint (row) in the primal corresponds to a column in the dual. Hence there is one dual variable for every primal constraint.
6. The dual of the dual is the primal problem.

In both of the primal and the dual problems, the variables are nonnegative and the constraints are inequalities. Such problems are called *symmetric dual linear programs.*

Definition.   A linear program is said to be in *symmetric form,* if all the variables are restricted to be nonnegative, and all the constraints are inequalities (in a maximization problem the inequalities must be in "less than or equal to" form; while in a minimization problem they must be "greater than or equal to").

Symmetric Dual Linear Programs

We shall now give the general representation of the primal–dual problems in symmetric form.

Primal

$$\text{Maximize:} \quad Z = c_1 x_1 + c_2 x_2 + \cdots + c_n x_n$$

$$\text{Subject to:} \quad a_{11} x_1 + a_{12} x_2 + \cdots + a_{1n} x_n \leq b_1$$

$$a_{21} x_1 + a_{22} x_2 + \cdots + a_{2n} x_n \leq b_2$$

$$\vdots \qquad \vdots \qquad \qquad \vdots \qquad \vdots$$

$$a_{m1} x_1 + a_{m2} x_2 + \cdots + a_{mn} x_n \leq b_m$$

$$x_1, x_2, \ldots, x_n \geq 0$$

Dual

$$\text{Minimize:} \quad W = b_1 y_1 + b_2 y_2 + \cdots + b_m y_m$$

$$\text{Subject to:} \quad a_{11} y_1 + a_{21} y_2 + \cdots + a_{m1} y_m \geq c_1$$

$$a_{12} y_1 + a_{22} y_2 + \cdots + a_{m2} y_m \geq c_2$$

$$\vdots \qquad \vdots \qquad \qquad \vdots \qquad \vdots$$

$$a_{1n} y_1 + a_{2n} y_2 + \cdots + a_{mn} y_m \geq c_n$$

$$y_1, y_2, \ldots, y_m \geq 0$$

In matrix notation the symmetric dual linear programs are:

Primal

$$\text{Maximize:} \quad Z = \mathbf{cx}$$

$$\text{Subject to:} \quad \mathbf{Ax} \leq \mathbf{b}$$

$$\mathbf{x} \geq \mathbf{0}$$

Dual

$$\text{Minimize:} \quad W = \mathbf{yb}$$

$$\text{Subject to:} \quad \mathbf{yA} \geq \mathbf{c}$$

$$\mathbf{y} \geq \mathbf{0}$$

where $\mathbf{A}$ is an $(m \times n)$ matrix, $\mathbf{b}$ is an $(m \times 1)$ column vector, $\mathbf{c}$ is a $(1 \times n)$ row vector, $\mathbf{x}$ is an $(n \times 1)$ column vector, and $\mathbf{y}$ is an $(1 \times m)$ row vector.

The general rules for writing the dual of a linear program in symmetric form are summarized below:

1. Define one (nonnegative) dual variable for each primal constraint.
2. Make the cost vector of the primal the right-hand-side constants of the dual.

3. Make the right-hand-side vector of the primal the cost vector of the dual.
4. The transpose of the coefficient matrix of the primal becomes the constraint matrix of the dual.
5. Reverse the direction of the constraint inequalities.
6. Reverse the optimization direction, that is, change minimizing to maximizing and vice versa.

Rules for writing the dual of the asymmetric linear programs will be developed later in this section.

Economic Interpretation of the Dual Problem

A midwestern manufacturer is faced with the problem of transporting his goods from two warehouses to three retail outlets at minimum cost. The supplies at the warehouses are 300 and 600 units. The demands at the retail outlets are 200, 300, and 400 units, respectively. The unit cost of transportation (in dollars) from a warehouse (W) to a retail outlet (R) is given below:

	R_1	R_2	R_3
W_1	2	4	3
W_2	5	3	4

The manufacturer's problem is to determine the least-cost shipping schedule which will meet the demands with the available supplies. The manufacturer's problem is actually a transportation problem which was discussed in detail in Section 3.2. If x_{ij} denotes the quantity shipped from warehouse i to the retail outlet j ($i = 1, 2$ and $j = 1, 2, 3$), then the linear programming formulation becomes:

Minimize: $Z = 2x_{11} + 4x_{12} + 3x_{13} + 5x_{21} + 3x_{22} + 4x_{23}$

Subject to:
$$x_{11} + x_{12} + x_{13} \leq 300$$
$$x_{21} + x_{22} + x_{23} \leq 600$$
$$x_{11} + x_{21} \geq 200$$
$$x_{12} + x_{22} \geq 300$$
$$x_{13} + x_{23} \geq 300$$

$x_{ij} \geq 0$ for all $i = 1, 2$ and $j = 1, 2, 3$

For the above linear program to be in symmetric form, all the constraints must be in "greater than or equal to" form. Hence we multiply the first two (supply) constraints by -1. The manufacturer's problem in symmetric form, which we will call the *primal* problem is given below:

Primal

Minimize: $Z = 2x_{11} + 4x_{12} + 3x_{13} + 5x_{21} + 3x_{22} + 4x_{23}$

Subject to:
$$-x_{11} - x_{12} - x_{13} \geq -300$$
$$- x_{21} - x_{22} - x_{23} \geq -600$$
$$x_{11} + x_{21} \geq 200$$
$$x_{12} + x_{22} \geq 300$$
$$x_{13} + x_{23} \geq 400$$

$x_{11}, \ldots, x_{23} \geq 0$

The dual of the above problem becomes:

Dual

Maximize: $W = -300y_1 - 600y_2 + 200y_3 + 300y_4 + 400y_5$

Subject to:

$$
\begin{aligned}
-y_1 &\qquad + y_3 &&& &\leq 2 \\
-y_1 &\qquad &+ &\ y_4 & &\leq 4 \\
-y_1 &\qquad & &&+ \ y_5 &\leq 3 \\
&-y_2 &+ y_3 &&& \leq 5 \\
&-y_2 &+ &\ y_4 & &\leq 3 \\
&-y_2 & &&+ \ y_5 &\leq 4
\end{aligned}
$$

$$y_1, y_2, y_3, y_4, y_5 \geq 0$$

Let us now give an economic interpretation of the dual problem. Imagine that a nationwide moving company approaches the manufacturer with the proposition that it will buy all the 300 units at warehouse 1 paying $\$y_1$ per unit, and all the 600 units at warehouse 2 paying $\$y_2$ per unit. It will then deliver 200, 300, and 400 units at the retail outlets 1, 2, and 3 selling them back to the manufacturer at a unit price of $\$y_3$, $\$y_4$, and $\$y_5$, respectively. The moving company then uses the dual constraints to convince the manufacturer that employing him is cheaper than transporting the goods on his own. For example, consider the transportation of goods from warehouse 1 to the retail outlet 1. The manufacturer's cost of transporting 1 unit is $2. Instead, if he employs the moving company his net cost is only $\$(y_3 - y_1)$. Since $y_3 - y_1 \leq 2$ (first dual constraint), employing the moving company seems attractive for transporting from warehouse 1 to retail outlet 1. Similarly each dual constraint implies that the transportation cost in any route is as expensive or more, than the net cost of selling and buying. Hence the manufacturer will accept the nationwide moving company's proposition with the hope that he will save some money in transportation. But, the moving company will fix the values of $y_1, \ldots, y_5$ in such a way that the dual constraints are satisfied and its net profit is maximized. The moving company's return is given by

$$-300y_1 - 600y_2 + 200y_3 + 300y_4 + 400y_5$$

which is the dual objective function. Thus the dual problem is the moving company's problem which is trying to maximize its return.

The duality theory says that the optimal values of both the primal and the dual problems are always equal. Hence, the manufacturer does not really save any money since he will be paying the minimum transportation cost to the moving company. But, he is saved from the trouble of solving the (primal) linear program to determine the least transportation cost. At the same time, the nationwide moving company has bagged the business of moving the goods at maximum profit.

Now we shall turn our attention to some of the duality theorems which give important relationships between the primal and the dual solutions.

THEOREM 1 (WEAK DUALITY THEOREM)

Consider the symmetric primal-dual linear programs, max $Z = cx$, $Ax \leq b$, $x \geq 0$, and min $W = yb$, $yA \geq c$, $y \geq 0$. The value of the objective function of the minimum problem (dual) for any feasible solution is always greater than or equal to that of the maximum problem (primal).

Proof

Let $\mathbf{x}^0$ and $\mathbf{y}^0$ be feasible solution vectors to the primal and the dual problems, respectively. We have to prove

$$\mathbf{y}^0\mathbf{b} \geqq \mathbf{c}\mathbf{x}^0$$

Since $\mathbf{x}^0$ is feasible for the primal,

$$\mathbf{A}\mathbf{x}^0 \leqq \mathbf{b}$$
$$\mathbf{x}^0 \geqq \mathbf{0} \tag{4.3}$$

Similarly, since $\mathbf{y}^0$ is feasible for the dual,

$$\mathbf{y}^0\mathbf{A} \geqq \mathbf{c}$$
$$\mathbf{y}^0 \geqq \mathbf{0} \tag{4.4}$$

Multiplying both sides of Inequality 4.3 by $\mathbf{y}^0$ (actually we take the inner product with respect to $\mathbf{y}^0$), we get

$$\mathbf{y}^0\mathbf{A}\mathbf{x}^0 \leqq \mathbf{y}^0\mathbf{b} \tag{4.5}$$

Similarly, multiplying both sides of Inequality 4.4 by $\mathbf{x}^0$,

$$\mathbf{y}^0\mathbf{A}\mathbf{x}^0 \geqq \mathbf{c}\mathbf{x}^0 \tag{4.6}$$

Inequalities 4.5 and 4.6 imply that

$$\mathbf{y}^0\mathbf{b} \geqq \mathbf{y}^0\mathbf{A}\mathbf{x}^0 \geqq \mathbf{c}\mathbf{x}^0$$

From the Weak Duality Theorem we can infer the following important results:

Corollary 1.   The value of the objective function of the maximum (primal) problem for any (primal) feasible solution is a lower bound to the minimum value of the dual objective.

Corollary 2.   Similarly the objective function value of the minimum problem (dual) for any (dual) feasible solution is an upper bound to the maximum value of the primal objective.

Corollary 3.   If the primal problem is feasible and its objective is unbounded (i.e., max $Z \to +\infty$), then the dual problem cannot have a feasible solution.

Corollary 4.   Similarly, if the dual problem is feasible, and is unbounded (i.e., min $W \to -\infty$) then the primal problem is infeasible.

To illustrate the Weak Duality Theorem, consider the following primal dual problems:

EXAMPLE 4.2-2

Primal

$$\text{Maximize:} \quad Z = x_1 + 2x_2 + 3x_3 + 4x_4$$
$$\text{Subject to:} \quad x_1 + 2x_2 + 2x_3 + 3x_4 \leqq 20$$
$$2x_1 + x_2 + 3x_3 + 2x_4 \leqq 20$$
$$x_1, \ldots, x_4 \geqq 0$$

Dual

$$\text{Minimize:} \quad W = 20y_1 + 20y_2$$

$$\text{Subject to:} \qquad y_1 + 2y_2 \geq 1$$
$$2y_1 + y_2 \geq 2$$
$$2y_1 + 3y_2 \geq 3$$
$$3y_1 + 2y_2 \geq 4$$
$$y_1, y_2 \geq 0$$

$x_1^o = x_2^o = x_3^o = x_4^o = 1$ is feasible for the primal, and $y_1^o = y_2^o = 1$ is feasible for the dual. The value of the primal objective is

$$Z = \mathbf{cx}^0 = 10$$

The value of the dual objective is

$$W = \mathbf{y}^0\mathbf{b} = 40$$

Note that $\mathbf{cx}^0 < \mathbf{y}^0\mathbf{b}$ which satisfies the Weak Duality Theorem.

Using Corollary 1, the minimum value of W for the dual objective function cannot go below 10. Similarly, from Corollary 2, the maximum value of Z for the primal problem cannot exceed 40.

The converse of the results of Corollaries 3 and 4 are also true.

Corollary 5. If the primal problem is feasible, and the dual is infeasible, then the primal is unbounded.

Corollary 6. If the dual problem is feasible and the primal is infeasible, then the dual is unbounded.

EXAMPLE 4.2-3

Consider the following primal-dual problems:

Primal

$$\text{Maximize:} \quad Z = x_1 + x_2$$

$$\text{Subject to:} \qquad -x_1 + x_2 + x_3 \leq 2$$
$$-2x_1 + x_2 - x_3 \leq 1$$
$$x_1, x_2, x_3 \geq 0$$

Dual

$$\text{Minimize:} \quad W = 2y_1 + y_2$$

$$\text{Subject to:} \qquad -y_1 - 2y_2 \geq 1$$
$$y_1 + y_2 \geq 1$$
$$y_1 - y_2 \geq 0$$
$$y_1, y_2 \geq 0$$

$x_1 = x_2 = x_3 = 0$ is a feasible solution to the primal problem. But the dual problem is infeasible since the constraint $-y_1 - 2y_2 \geq 1$ is inconsistent. (For all nonnegative values of y_1 and y_2, the left-hand side is nonpositive while the right-hand side is strictly positive.) Hence, by Corollary 5, the primal problem has an unbounded solution such that maximum Z tends to infinity. This can be easily verified by solving the primal problem by the simplex method.

THEOREM 2 (OPTIMALITY CRITERION THEOREM)

If there exist feasible solutions $\mathbf{x}^0$ and $\mathbf{y}^0$ for the symmetric dual linear programs such that the corresponding values of their objective functions are equal, then these feasible solutions are in fact optimal solutions to their respective problems.

Proof

Let $\mathbf{x}$ be any other feasible solution to the primal problem. Then by Theorem 1,

$$\mathbf{cx} \leqq \mathbf{y}^0\mathbf{b}$$

But it is given that $\mathbf{cx}^0 = \mathbf{y}^0\mathbf{b}$. Hence $\mathbf{cx} \leq \mathbf{cx}^0$ for all feasible solutions to the primal problem. Then by definition, $\mathbf{x}^0$ is optimal for the primal. A symmetrical argument proves the optimality of $\mathbf{y}^0$ for the dual problem.

Illustration

Consider the primal-dual pair given in Example 4.2-2. $x_1^0 = 0$, $x_2^0 = 0$, $x_3^0 = 4$, and $x_4^0 = 4$ is a feasible solution to the primal, while $y_1^0 = 1.2$ and $y_2^0 = 0.2$ is feasible for the dual. The value of Z for the primal $= 28 =$ the value of the W for the dual. Hence by Theorem 2, the above feasible solutions are optimal solutions to the primal and the dual problems, respectively.

THEOREM 3 (MAIN DUALITY THEOREM)

If both the primal and the dual problems are feasible, then they both have optimal solutions such that their optimal values of the objective functions are equal.

Proof

When both the primal and the dual problems are feasible, then by Corollaries 1 and 2 of Theorem 1, we have a lower bound on the minimum value of W, and an upper bound on the maximum value of Z. In other words, neither the primal nor the dual can have an unbounded solution. Therefore they both must have optimal solutions, but the difficult part of Theorem 3 is to show that at the optimum both the problems will have the same value for the objective function. The proof of this is rather involved and hence is omitted here. Interested readers may refer to Gale [2].

THEOREM 4 (COMPLEMENTARY SLACKNESS THEOREM)

Consider the symmetric dual problems in matrix form:

Primal

$$\begin{aligned} \text{Maximize:} \quad & Z = \mathbf{cx} \\ \text{Subject to:} \quad & \mathbf{Ax} \leq \mathbf{b} \\ & \mathbf{x} \geq \mathbf{0} \end{aligned}$$

Dual

$$\begin{aligned} \text{Minimize:} \quad & W = \mathbf{yb} \\ \text{Subject to:} \quad & \mathbf{yA} \geq \mathbf{c} \\ & \mathbf{y} \geq \mathbf{0} \end{aligned}$$

where $\mathbf{A}$ is an $(m \times n)$ matrix, $\underset{(m \times 1)}{\mathbf{b}}$ and $\underset{(n \times 1)}{\mathbf{x}}$ are column vectors, and $\underset{(1 \times n)}{\mathbf{c}}$ and $\underset{(1 \times m)}{\mathbf{y}}$ are row vectors. Let $\mathbf{x}^{0}$ and $\mathbf{y}^{0}$ be feasible for the primal and the dual problems respectively. Then $\mathbf{x}^{0}$ and $\mathbf{y}^{0}$ are optimal to their respective problems if and only if

$$(\mathbf{y}^{0}\mathbf{A} - \mathbf{c})\mathbf{x}^{0} + \mathbf{y}^{0}(\mathbf{b} - \mathbf{A}\mathbf{x}^{0}) = 0$$

Proof

Let the column vector $\underset{(m \times 1)}{\mathbf{u}} = \begin{pmatrix} u_1 \\ u_2 \\ \cdot \\ u_m \end{pmatrix}$ represent the slack vector for the

primal, and the row vector $\underset{(1 \times n)}{\mathbf{v}} = (v_1, v_2, \ldots, v_n)$ be the slack vector of dual.

Since $\mathbf{x}^{0}$ and $\mathbf{y}^{0}$ are feasible solutions we have

$$\mathbf{A}\mathbf{x}^{0} + \mathbf{u}^{0} = \mathbf{b}; \qquad \mathbf{x}^{0}, \mathbf{u}^{0} \geq \mathbf{0} \tag{4.7}$$

$$\mathbf{y}^{0}\mathbf{A} - \mathbf{v}^{0} = \mathbf{c}; \qquad \mathbf{y}^{0}, \mathbf{v}^{0} \geq \mathbf{0} \tag{4.8}$$

($\mathbf{u}^{0}$ and $\mathbf{v}^{0}$ represent the values of the slack variables $\mathbf{u}$ and $\mathbf{v}$ corresponding to the feasible solutions $\mathbf{x}^{0}$ and $\mathbf{y}^{0}$.)

Multiplying Eq. 4.7 by $\mathbf{y}^{0}$ (i.e., taking the inner product with $\mathbf{y}^{0}$) we get

$$\mathbf{y}^{0}\mathbf{A}\mathbf{x}^{0} + \mathbf{y}^{0}\mathbf{u}^{0} = \mathbf{y}^{0}\mathbf{b} \tag{4.9}$$

Similarly, multiplying Eq. 4.8 by $\mathbf{x}^{0}$ we get

$$\mathbf{y}^{0}\mathbf{A}\mathbf{x}^{0} - \mathbf{v}^{0}\mathbf{x}^{0} = \mathbf{c}\mathbf{x}^{0} \tag{4.10}$$

Subtracting Eq. 4.10 from Eq. 4.9, we obtain

$$\mathbf{y}^{0}\mathbf{u}^{0} + \mathbf{v}^{0}\mathbf{x}^{0} = \mathbf{y}^{0}\mathbf{b} - \mathbf{c}\mathbf{x}^{0} \tag{4.11}$$

To prove Theorem 4 we have to show that $\mathbf{x}^{0}$ and $\mathbf{y}^{0}$ are optimal to the primal and the dual problems if and only if

$$\mathbf{v}^{0}\mathbf{x}^{0} + \mathbf{y}^{0}\mathbf{u}^{0} = 0 \tag{4.12}$$

Part 1. We will assume that $\mathbf{x}^{0}$ and $\mathbf{y}^{0}$ are optimal solutions, and prove that Eq. 4.12 is true. Since $\mathbf{x}^{0}$ and $\mathbf{y}^{0}$ are optimal, $\mathbf{c}\mathbf{x}^{0} = \mathbf{y}^{0}\mathbf{b}$ by Theorem 3. Hence, Eq. 4.11 reduces to Eq. 4.12.

Part 2. We will assume that Eq. 4.12 is true and prove that $\mathbf{x}^{0}$ and $\mathbf{y}^{0}$ are optimal to the primal and the dual, respectively. Since Eq. 4.12 is true, Eq. 4.11 reduces to

$$\mathbf{y}^{0}\mathbf{b} = \mathbf{c}\mathbf{x}^{0}$$

By Theorem 2 it follows that $\mathbf{x}^{0}$ and $\mathbf{y}^{0}$ are optimal solutions.

Complementary Slackness Conditions

Equation 4.12 of the complementary slackness theorem can be further simplified to

$$v_j^{0} x_j^{0} = 0 \qquad \text{for all } j = 1, 2, \ldots, n \tag{4.13}$$

$$y_i^{0} u_i^{0} = 0 \qquad \text{for all } i = 1, 2, \ldots, m \tag{4.14}$$

by observing the following:

1. $\mathbf{x}^{0}, \mathbf{u}^{0}, \mathbf{v}^{0}, \mathbf{y}^{0} \geq 0$ and hence $\mathbf{v}^{0}\mathbf{x}^{0} \geq 0$ and $\mathbf{y}^{0}\mathbf{u}^{0} \geq 0$.
2. If the sum of nonnegative terms equals zero, then each term is zero.

Equations 4.13 and 4.14 are generally called the *complementary slackness conditions*. In words the complementary slackness conditions can be stated as follows:

1. If a primal variable (x_j^o) is positive, then the corresponding dual constraint will be satisfied as an equation at the optimum (i.e., $v_j^o = 0$).
2. If a primal constraint is a strict inequality at the optimum (i.e., $u_i^o > 0$) then the corresponding dual variable (y_i^o) must be zero at the optimum.
3. If a dual variable (y_i^o) is positive, then the corresponding primal constraint will be satisfied as an equation at the optimum (i.e., $u_i^o = 0$).
4. If a dual constraint is a strict inequality (i.e., $v_j^o > 0$), then the corresponding primal variable (x_j^o) must be zero at the optimum.

Illustration.   Consider Example 4.2-2. With the addition of slack variables, the primal-dual problems may be stated as follows:

Primal

$$\text{Maximize:} \quad Z = x_1 + 2x_2 + 3x_3 + 4x_4$$

$$\text{Subject to:} \quad x_1 + 2x_2 + 2x_3 + 3x_4 + u_1 = 20$$

$$2x_1 + x_2 + 3x_3 + 2x_4 + u_2 = 20$$

$$x_1, x_2, x_3, x_4, u_1, u_2 \geqq 0$$

Dual

$$\text{Minimize:} \quad W = 20y_1 + 20y_2$$

$$\text{Subject to:} \quad y_1 + 2y_2 - v_1 \qquad\qquad = 1$$

$$2y_1 + y_2 \quad - v_2 \qquad = 2$$

$$2y_1 + 3y_2 \qquad - v_3 \quad = 3$$

$$3y_1 + 2y_2 \qquad\qquad - v_4 = 4$$

$$y_1, y_2, v_1, v_2, v_3, v_4 \geqq 0$$

The complementary slackness conditions imply that at the optimum, $u_1^o y_1^o = 0$, $u_2^o y_2^o = 0$, $x_1^o v_1^o = 0$, $x_2^o v_2^o = 0$, $x_3^o v_3^o = 0$, and $x_4^o v_4^o = 0$. From these conditions it is possible to determine the primal optimal solution from the dual optimal solution, and vice versa.

Without the slack variables the dual problem has just two variables, and hence can be solved by the graphical methods discussed in Section 2.3. The optimal solution is found as $y_1^o = 1.2$, $y_2^o = 0.2$, and min $W = 28$. By applying the complementary slackness conditions, the primal optimal solution is determined as follows:

1. $y_1^o = 1.2 > 0$ implies that $u_1^o = 0$
2. $y_2^o = 0.2 > 0$ implies that $u_2^o = 0$
3. $y_1^o + 2y_2^o = 1.6 > 1$ implies that $v_1^o > 0$ and $x_1^o = 0$
4. $2y_1^o + y_2^o = 2.6 > 2$ implies that $v_2^o > 0$ and $x_2^o = 0$
5. $2y_1^o + 3y_2^o = 3$ implies that $v_3^o = 0$. Since $v_3^o x_3^o = 0$, x_3^o could be positive or zero.
6. Similarly $3y_1^o + 2y_2^o = 4$ and $v_4^o = 0$. Hence x_4^o is positive or zero.

In other words Conditions 5 and 6 do not give any new information in determining the primal optimal solution. But at the optimum, Conditions 1 through 4 imply that,

$$2x_3^o + 3x_4^o = 20$$

$$3x_3^o + 2x_4^o = 20$$

Solving the two equations in two unknowns, we get the optimal primal solution as $x_1^o = 0$, $x_2^o = 0$, $x_3^o = 4$, and $x_4^o = 4$. The maximum value of Z equals 28 which corresponds to the minimum value of W, verifying Theorem 3.

The complementary slackness theorem is also very useful in testing some hypotheses on the nature of optimal solutions to the linear programs. For instance, we can check the hypothesis whether both the primal constraints are strict inequalities at the optimum; in other words, all the available resources are not fully utilized.

Mathematically this implies that $u_1^o > 0$ and $u_2^o > 0$. The complementary slackness conditions imply $y_1^o u_1^o = 0$ and $y_2^o u_2^o = 0$. Hence if the hypothesis is true, $y_1^o = y_2^o = 0$ must be optimal for the dual. But we find that this is not true since $y_1^o = y_2^o = 0$ is infeasible; hence the hypothesis is false.

Applications of the Complementary Slackness Conditions

A partial list of the general applications of the complementary slackness conditions is given below:

1. Used in finding an optimal primal solution from the given optimal dual solution and vice versa.
2. Used in verifying whether a feasible solution is optimal for the primal problem. (Here we assume the given feasible solution as optimal, and try to construct an optimal dual solution using the complementary slackness conditions. If we are successful, then the given feasible solution is in fact optimal for the primal.)
3. Used in investigating the general properties of the optimal solutions to primal and dual by testing different hypotheses.
4. The Kuhn-Tucker optimality conditions of nonlinear programming are direct extensions of the complementary slackness conditions, and are extremely useful in advanced mathematical programming.

So far our discussion has been limited to symmetric primal-dual problems. Before considering the asymmetric problems, let us summarize the essential characteristics of the symmetric primal-dual pair.

	Primal	Dual
A	Constraint matrix	Transpose of the constraint matrix
b	Right-hand-side constants	Cost (price) vector
c	Price (cost) vector	Right-hand-side constants
Objective function	Maximize $Z = \mathbf{cx}$	Minimize $W = \mathbf{yb}$
Constraint inequalities	$\mathbf{Ax} \leq \mathbf{b}$	$\mathbf{yA} \geq \mathbf{c}$
Decision variables	$\mathbf{x} \geq \mathbf{0}$	$\mathbf{y} \geq \mathbf{0}$

Notes

1. If the primal problem is a minimization problem, then we have the following primal-dual relationships:

Objective function	Minimize $Z = \mathbf{cx}$	Maximize $W = \mathbf{yb}$
Constants	$\mathbf{Ax} \geq \mathbf{b}$	$\mathbf{yA} \leq \mathbf{c}$
	$\mathbf{x} \geq \mathbf{0}$	$\mathbf{y} \geq \mathbf{0}$

2. The dual of the dual is the primal problem.

Asymmetric Primal-Dual Problems

Since not all the linear programs come in symmetric form, we shall discuss the primal-dual relationships for the asymmetric problems in this section.

EXAMPLE 4.2-4

Consider a primal problem in asymmetric form as follows:

$$\text{Maximize:} \quad Z = 4x_1 + 5x_2$$

$$\text{Subject to:} \quad 3x_1 + 2x_2 \leq 20 \tag{4.15}$$

$$4x_1 - 3x_2 \geq 10 \tag{4.16}$$

$$x_1 + x_2 = 5 \tag{4.17}$$

$$x_1 \geq 0, \; x_2 \text{ unrestricted in sign}$$

Since we know how to write the dual of a symmetric problem, let us convert the above problem to symmetric form. This means that all the constraints must be "less than or equal to" type inequalities (since the primal is a maximization problem), and all the variables are nonnegative. This can be accomplished as follows:

1. Inequality 4.16 is multiplied by -1.
2. Equation 4.17 is replaced by a pair of inequalities, $x_1 + x_2 \leq 5$ and $x_1 + x_2 \geq 5$.
3. The unrestricted variable x_2 is replaced by the difference of two nonnegative variables, x_3 and x_4.

Thus the symmetric form of the primal problem becomes:

$$\text{Maximize:} \quad Z = 4x_1 + 5x_3 - 5x_4$$

$$\text{Subject to:} \quad 3x_1 + 2x_3 - 2x_4 \leq 20$$

$$-4x_1 + 3x_3 - 3x_4 \leq -10$$

$$x_1 + x_3 - x_4 \leq 5$$

$$-x_1 - x_3 + x_4 \leq -5$$

$$x_1, x_3, x_4 \geq 0$$

Symmetric Dual

$$\text{Minimize:} \quad W = 20w_1 - 10w_2 + 5w_3 - 5w_4$$

$$\text{Subject to:} \quad 3w_1 - 4w_2 + w_3 - w_4 \geq 4$$

$$2w_1 + 3w_2 + w_3 - w_4 \geq 5$$

$$-2w_1 - 3w_2 - w_3 + w_4 \geq -5$$

$$w_1, w_2, w_3, w_4 \geq 0$$

Comparing the above dual problem with the original primal given by the Eqs. 4.15, 4.16, and 4.17, we find that none of the characteristics of the primal-dual pair listed earlier is satisfied. We do not have the transpose of the coefficient matrix for the dual constraints, the original right-hand-side vector is not the cost vector of the dual, and so on.

To patch things up, suppose we let $y_1 = w_1$, $y_2 = -w_2$, $y_3 = w_3 - w_4$, and replace the last two inequalities of the dual by an equation. This gives the following modified dual problem:

$$\text{Minimize:} \quad W = 20y_1 + 10y_2 + 5y_3$$

$$\text{Subject to:} \quad 3y_1 + 4y_2 + y_3 \geqq 4$$

$$2y_1 - 3y_2 + y_3 = 5$$

$$y_1 \geqq 0, \ y_2 \leqq 0, \ y_3 \text{ unrestricted in sign}$$

Comparing the above dual with the original primal we find that all the essential characteristics of the primal-dual pair are satisfied except for the direction of inequalities on the constraints, and the sign restrictions on the variables. Thus for any linear program (symmetric or asymmetric) the dual always satisfies the following characteristics.

1. The coefficient matrix of the dual is the transpose of the coefficient matrix of the primal.
2. The cost vector of the dual is the right-hand-side vector of the primal.
3. The right-hand-side vector of the dual is the cost vector of the primal.
4. If the primal is a maximization problem, then the dual becomes a minimization problem and vice versa.

Table 4.4 summarizes the primal-dual correspondence for all linear programming problems where the primal is a *maximization* problem. (If the primal is a minimization problem, the primal-dual table should be altered accordingly.)

Table 4.4
PRIMAL-DUAL TABLE

Primal (Maximize)	Dual (Minimize)
A Coefficient matrix	Transpose of the coefficient matrix
b Right-hand-side vector	Cost vector
c Price vector	Right-hand-side vector
ith constraint is an equation	The dual variable y_i is unrestricted in sign
ith constraint is $\leqq$ type	The dual variable $y_i \geqq 0$
ith constraint is $\geqq$ type	The dual variable $y_i \leqq 0$
x_j is unrestricted	jth dual constraint is an equation
$x_j \geqq 0$	jth dual constraint is $\geqq$ type
$x_j \leqq 0$	jth dual constraint is $\leqq$ type

We shall illustrate the rules given in the primal-dual table with a few examples.

EXAMPLE 4.2-5
Write the dual of

$$\text{Maximize:} \quad Z = x_1 + 4x_2 + 3x_3$$

$$\text{Subject to:} \quad 2x_1 + 3x_2 - 5x_3 \leqq 2$$

$$3x_1 - x_2 + 6x_3 \geqq 1$$

$$x_1 + x_2 + x_3 = 4$$

$$x_1 \geqq 0, \ x_2 \leqq 0, \ x_3 \text{ unrestricted in sign}$$

Dual

$$\text{Minimize:} \quad W = 2y_1 + y_2 + 4y_3$$

$$\text{Subject to:} \quad 2y_1 + 3y_2 + y_3 \geq 1$$

$$3y_1 - y_2 + y_3 \leq 4$$

$$-5y_1 + 6y_2 + y_3 = 3$$

$$y_1 \geq 0, \ y_2 \leq 0, \ y_3 \ \text{unrestricted in sign}$$

EXAMPLE 4.2-6

$$\text{Minimize:} \quad Z = 2x_1 + x_2 - x_3$$

$$\text{Subject to:} \quad x_1 + x_2 - x_3 = 1$$

$$x_1 - x_2 + x_3 \geq 2$$

$$x_2 + x_3 \leq 3$$

$$x_1 \geq 0, \ x_2 \leq 0, \ x_3 \ \text{unrestricted}$$

Dual

$$\text{Maximize:} \quad W = y_1 + 2y_2 + 3y_3$$

$$\text{Subject to:} \quad y_1 + y_2 \qquad \leq 2$$

$$y_1 - y_2 + y_3 \geq 1$$

$$-y_1 + y_2 + y_3 = -1$$

$$y_1 \ \text{unrestricted}, \ y_2 \geq 0, \ y_3 \leq 0$$

Theorems 1, 2, 3, and 4 of the Duality Theory apply to the asymmetric primal-dual pair as well. For instance, in Example 4.2-6, $x_1^o = 2$, $x_2^o = 0$, $x_3^o = 1$ is a feasible solution to the primal; while $y_1^o = 1$, $y_2^o = 0$, $y_3^o = 0$ is feasible for the dual. By Theorem 1 (Weak Duality) the objective function value for the minimum problem should be greater than or equal to that of the maximum problem, and we find, $\mathbf{c}\mathbf{x}^o = 3 > \mathbf{y}^o\mathbf{b} = 1$. Since both the primal and dual are feasible, both must have optimal solutions by Theorem 3.

Similarly, in Example 4.2-5, $x_1^o = 0$, $x_2^o = 0$, $x_3^o = 4$ is feasible for the primal with $Z = 12$, and $y_1^o = 0$, $y_2^o = 0$, $y_3^o = 3$ is feasible for the dual with $W = 12$. The values of the objective function of the primal and dual are equal, and by Theorem 2, $\mathbf{x}^o = (0, 0, 4)$ is optimal for the primal, and $\mathbf{y}^o = (0, 0, 3)$ is optimal for the dual. Note also that complementary slackness conditions are satisfied between the primal and the dual optimal solutions. Substituting $\mathbf{x}^o = (0, 0, 4)$ in the first two inequalities of the primal, we get

1. $2x_1^o + 3x_2^o - 5x_3^o = -20 < 2$, which implies $y_1^o = 0$
2. $3x_1^o - x_2^o + 6x_3^o = 24 > 1$, which implies $y_2^o = 0$

Hence $y_3^o = 3$ is the optimal solution for the dual.

Consider the linear programming problem in standard form:

$$\text{Maximize:} \quad Z = \mathbf{c}\mathbf{x}$$

$$\text{Subject to:} \quad \mathbf{A}\mathbf{x} = \mathbf{b}$$

$$\mathbf{x} \geq \mathbf{0}$$

The dual is given by

$$\text{Minimize:} \quad W = \mathbf{y}\mathbf{b}$$

$$\text{Subject to:} \quad \mathbf{y}\mathbf{A} \geq \mathbf{c}$$

$$\mathbf{y} \ \text{unrestricted in sign}$$

The complementary slackness conditions to be satisfied at optimality are

$$(\mathbf{y}\mathbf{A} - \mathbf{c})\mathbf{x} = 0$$

Interpretation of Dual Solutions as Shadow Prices

In an economic sense, the optimal dual solution can be interpreted as the price one pays for the constraint resources. By Theorem 3 (Main Duality) the optimal values of the objective functions of the primal and dual are equal. If $\mathbf{x}^0$ and $\mathbf{y}^0$ are the respective optimal solutions then $Z_o = \mathbf{c}\mathbf{x}^0 = \mathbf{y}^0\mathbf{b} = W_o$. In other words, the optimal value of the linear program (primal or dual), is given by

$$Z_o = y_1^o b_1 + y_2^o b_2 + \cdots + y_m^o b_m$$

where $b_1, b_2, \ldots, b_m$ represent the limited quantities of the resources $1, 2, \ldots, m$, and $y_1^o, y_2^o, \ldots, y_m^o$ are the optimal values of the dual variables. Suppose we assume that the level of resource 1 (i.e., b_1) can be altered. Then, for small variations in the value of b_1, say Δb_1, the net change in the optimal value of the linear program Z_o is given by $y_1^o(\Delta b_1)$.

In other words, the optimal value of the dual variable for each primal constraint gives the net change in the optimal value of the objective function for unit increase in the right hand side constants. Hence, these are called *shadow prices* on the constraint resources. These could be used to determine whether it is economical to get additional resources at premium prices. The application of shadow price in the post optimality analysis is discussed in detail in Section 4.4.

Computing the Optimal Dual Solution

The optimal dual solution may be computed using the complementary slackness theorem as discussed earlier. It is also possible to obtain the dual solution directly from the optimal simplex tableau of the primal problem.

Consider the standard linear program.

$$\text{Minimize:} \quad Z = \mathbf{c}\mathbf{x}$$

$$\text{Subject to:} \quad \mathbf{A}\mathbf{x} = \mathbf{b}, \ \mathbf{x} \geq \mathbf{0}$$

Let $\mathbf{P}_j$ denote the jth column of the $\mathbf{A}$ matrix, and $\mathbf{B}$ denote the optimal basis matrix. Applying the principles of the revised simplex method, the optimal primal solution is given by

$$\mathbf{x}^0 = \begin{pmatrix} \mathbf{x_B} \\ \mathbf{x_N} \end{pmatrix} = \begin{pmatrix} \mathbf{B}^{-1}\mathbf{b} \\ \mathbf{0} \end{pmatrix}$$

where $\mathbf{x_B}$ and $\mathbf{x_N}$ are the basic and the nonbasic variables in the optimal solution. The minimum value of $Z = \mathbf{c}\mathbf{x}^0 = \mathbf{c_B}\mathbf{x_B} = \mathbf{c_B}\mathbf{B}^{-1}\mathbf{b}$. Since $\mathbf{B}$ represents an optimal basis, the relative cost coefficients ($\bar{c}_j$) corresponding to this basis must be nonnegative. In other words

$$\bar{c}_j = c_j - \boldsymbol{\pi}\mathbf{P}_j \geq 0 \qquad \text{for all } j \qquad (4.18)$$

where $\boldsymbol{\pi} = \mathbf{c_B}\mathbf{B}^{-1}$ is the vector of simplex multipliers. In matrix notation, the set of inequalities above can be written as

$$\mathbf{c} - \boldsymbol{\pi}\mathbf{A} \geq \mathbf{0} \qquad \text{or} \qquad \boldsymbol{\pi}\mathbf{A} \leq \mathbf{c} \qquad (4.19)$$

Inequality 4.19 is nothing but the constraints of the dual linear program. Thus the optimal simplex multipliers satisfy the dual constraints. The value of the dual objective function corresponding to this feasible solution is

$$W = yb = \pi b = c_B B^{-1} b$$

which is equal to the minimum value of Z. Hence by the Optimality Criterion Theorem, the optimal simplex multipliers of the primal problem are in fact the optimal values of the dual variables!

Illustration. Recall Example 4.1-2 from Section 4.1. Expressing it in standard form, we get:

Primal

$$\text{Minimize:} \quad Z = -3x_1 + x_2 + x_3$$

$$\text{Subject to:} \quad x_1 - 2x_2 + x_3 + x_4 \quad = 11$$

$$-4x_1 + x_2 + 2x_3 \quad - x_5 = 3$$

$$-2x_1 \quad + x_3 \quad = 1$$

$$x_1, x_2, x_3, x_4, x_5 \geq 0$$

Dual

$$\text{Maximize:} \quad W = 11y_1 + 3y_2 + y_3$$

$$\text{Subject to:} \quad y_1 - 4y_2 - 2y_3 \leq -3$$

$$-2y_1 + y_2 \quad \leq 1$$

$$y_1 + 2y_2 + y_3 \leq 1$$

$$y_1 \quad \leq 0$$

$$-y_2 \quad \leq 0$$

$$y_1, y_2, y_3 \text{ unrestricted in sign}$$

Using the revised simplex method, the optimal solution to the primal problem was obtained in Section 4.1 as $x_1 = 4$, $x_2 = 1$, $x_3 = 9$, and minimum $Z = -2$. Since x_1, x_2, x_3 are the optimal basic variables, the optimal basis matrix is given by

$$B = [P_1, P_2, P_3] = \begin{bmatrix} 1 & -2 & 1 \\ -4 & 1 & 2 \\ -2 & 0 & 1 \end{bmatrix}$$

The optimal simplex multipliers are

$$\pi = c_B B^{-1} = (-3, 1, 1) \begin{bmatrix} \frac{1}{3} & \frac{2}{3} & -\frac{5}{3} \\ 0 & 1 & -2 \\ \frac{2}{3} & \frac{4}{3} & -\frac{7}{3} \end{bmatrix} = \left(-\frac{1}{3}, \frac{1}{3}, \frac{2}{3} \right)$$

It can be easily verified that $\pi_1 = -1/3$, $\pi_2 = 1/3$, $\pi_3 = 2/3$, satisfy the dual constraints, and the value of the dual objective corresponding to this feasible solution is

$$W = 11\left(-\frac{1}{3} \right) + 3\left(\frac{1}{3} \right) + 1\left(\frac{2}{3} \right) = -2$$

which corresponds to the optimal value of primal problem. Hence the solution $y_1 = -1/3$, $y_2 = 1/3$, and $y_3 = 2/3$ is optimal for the dual. In other words, the simplex multipliers corresponding to the optimal (primal) tableau give the optimal solution to the dual problem.

4.3 THE DUAL SIMPLEX METHOD

Consider a linear program in standard form which we call the primal problem.

$$\text{Minimize:} \quad Z = \mathbf{cx}$$
$$\text{Subject to:} \quad \mathbf{Ax} = \mathbf{b}$$
$$\mathbf{x} \geq \mathbf{0}$$

where $\mathbf{A}$ is an $(m \times n)$ matrix. Let the columns of the $\mathbf{A}$ matrix be denoted by the vectors $\mathbf{P}_1, \mathbf{P}_2, \ldots, \mathbf{P}_n$.

Recall that a basis $\mathbf{B}$ for the primal problem is an $(m \times m)$ matrix consisting of any m independent columns of the $\mathbf{A}$ matrix. Let $\mathbf{x_B}$ denote the basic variables corresponding to the basis $\mathbf{B}$.

Primal Feasible Basis

A basis $\mathbf{B}$ is called a primal feasible basis if an only if $\mathbf{B}^{-1}\mathbf{b} \geq 0$. If a basis $\mathbf{B}$ is primal feasible, then the values of the basic variables are given by the vector $\mathbf{B}^{-1}\mathbf{b}$, and the basic feasible solution becomes $\mathbf{x_B} = \mathbf{B}^{-1}\mathbf{b}$ and $\mathbf{x_N} = 0$ where $\mathbf{x_N}$ denotes the nonbasic variables. The value of the objective function corresponding to this feasible basis is given by

$$Z = \mathbf{c_B}\mathbf{B}^{-1}\mathbf{b}$$

where $\mathbf{c_B}$ corresponds to the cost coefficients of the basic variables.

Optimality Conditions

In order to check whether the feasible basis $\mathbf{B}$ is an optimal basis, we have to compute the relative cost coefficients $(\bar{c}_j)$. Using the revised simplex method,

$$\bar{c}_j = c_j - \boldsymbol{\pi}\mathbf{P_j} \quad \text{for } j = 1, 2, \ldots, n \tag{4.20}$$

where $\boldsymbol{\pi} = \mathbf{c_B}\mathbf{B}^{-1}$ are the simplex multipliers. The primal feasible basis is optimal when

$$\bar{c}_j \geq 0 \quad \text{for all } j = 1, 2, \ldots, n \tag{4.21}$$

Now consider the dual of the standard linear program:

Dual

$$\text{Maximize:} \quad W = \mathbf{yb}$$
$$\text{Subject to:} \quad \mathbf{yA} \leq \mathbf{c}$$
$$\mathbf{y} \text{ unrestricted in sign}$$

The dual constraints $\mathbf{yA} \leq \mathbf{c}$ can be rewritten as

$$\mathbf{y}(\mathbf{P}_1, \mathbf{P}_2, \ldots, \mathbf{P}_n) \leq (c_1, c_2, \ldots, c_n) \quad \text{or} \quad \mathbf{yP_j} \leq c_j$$

or
$$\tag{4.22}$$
$$c_j - \mathbf{yP_j} \geq 0 \quad \text{for } j = 1, 2, \ldots, n$$

Comparing Inequality 4.22 with the Eqs. 4.20 and 4.21, we note that checking the optimality conditions in the (revised) simplex method is nothing but verifying whether the simplex multipliers satisfy the dual constraints! Thus, if the primal feasible basis **B** is also an optimal basis to the primal problem, then the simplex multipliers $\boldsymbol{\pi} = \mathbf{c_B B}^{-1}$ satisfy,

$$c_j - \boldsymbol{\pi} \mathbf{P}_j \geq 0 \qquad \text{for all } j = 1, 2, \ldots, n$$

This implies that $\boldsymbol{\pi}$ is feasible to the dual problem. The value of the dual objective function $W = \boldsymbol{\pi} \mathbf{b} = \mathbf{c_B B}^{-1} \mathbf{b}$, which is equal to the value of the primal objective function. Hence, by the Optimality Criterion Theorem (Theorem 2) $\boldsymbol{\pi}$ is optimal for the dual problem.

Dual Feasible Basis

A basis **B** to the primal problem,

$$\text{Minimize:} \qquad Z = \mathbf{cx}$$

$$\text{Subject to:} \quad \mathbf{Ax} = \mathbf{b}, \ \mathbf{x} \geq \mathbf{0}$$

is *dual feasible* if and only if

$$\mathbf{c} - \mathbf{c_B B}^{-1} \mathbf{A} \geq \mathbf{0}$$

Note that the definition of a dual feasible basis is the same as the Eqs. 4.20 and 4.21 for verifying whether a feasible basis **B** is optimal. In other words, when a basis **B** to the primal problem is both primal feasible and dual feasible, it becomes an optimal basis. The optimal solution to the primal becomes $\mathbf{x_B} = \mathbf{B}^{-1} \mathbf{b}$, and $\mathbf{x_N} = \mathbf{0}$, while the optimal solution to the dual problem becomes $\mathbf{y} = \mathbf{c_B B}^{-1}$. The optimal values of both the problems are equal since $Z^\circ = W^\circ = \mathbf{c_B B}^{-1} \mathbf{b}$, verifying the Main Duality Theorem.

To sum up, the main crux in solving a linear program is to find a basis **B** (or canonical tableau) which is both primal feasible and dual feasible. The simplex method (which we have studied up to now) does this by going from one primal feasible basis to another until the basis also becomes dual feasible. Hence this approach may be called the *primal simplex method*. Instead of searching for an optimal solution by moving from one primal feasible point to another, one can start with a dual feasible basis (a canonical tableau where the optimality conditions are satisfied), and search for a primal feasible basis by moving from one dual feasible tableau to another dual feasible tableau. This approach is called the *dual simplex method*. Generally, by simplex method, we always refer to the primal simplex method.

Details of the Dual Simplex Method

Recall the standard linear program,

$$\text{Minimize:} \qquad Z = \mathbf{cx}$$

$$\text{Subject to:} \quad \mathbf{Ax} = \mathbf{b}$$

$$\mathbf{x} \geq \mathbf{0}$$

In essence, the dual simplex method uses the same tableau as the primal simplex method. However, in all the tableaus the relative cost row ($\bar{c}_j$ coefficients) are maintained nonnegative. (In a maximization problem, the $\bar{c}_j$ coefficients will be maintained nonpositive). But the right-hand-side constants need not be nonnegative. The algorithm then proceeds to make the right-hand-side elements nonnegative, while at the same time preserving the $\bar{c}$-row coefficients as nonnegative. In other words, we always have a basic solution which is dual feasible but is not primal feasible from one iteration to the next. The algorithm terminates when all the right-hand-side constants are made nonnegative. We then have a tableau which is both primal feasible and dual feasible, and hence optimal.

Let us assume that there exists a dual feasible basis consisting of the first m columns of the $\mathbf{A}$ matrix. In other words we have a basic solution using x_1, $x_2, \ldots, x_m$ as basic variables. Table 4.5 gives the equivalent canonical system.

Table 4.5

Basis	$x_1 \cdots x_r \cdots x_m$			$x_{m+1} \quad \cdots \quad x_s \quad \cdots \quad x_n$			Constants
x_1	1			$y_{1,m+1} \cdots y_{1s}$		y_{1n}	$\bar{b}_1$
x_r		1		$y_{r,m+1} \cdots y_{rs}$	$\cdots$	y_{rn}	$\bar{b}_r$
x_m			1	$y_{m,m+1}$	y_{ms}	y_{mn}	$\bar{b}_m$
$\bar{c}$ Row	0	0	0	$\bar{c}_{m+1} \quad \cdots \quad \bar{c}_s \quad \cdots \quad \bar{c}_n$			

In the above tableau, the y_{ij}'s represent the modified coefficients of the $\mathbf{A}$ matrix after the canonical reduction. Since the tableau is dual feasible, the relative cost coefficients $\bar{c}_j$ are nonnegative. If the constants $\bar{b}_1, \ldots, \bar{b}_m$ are nonnegative, then the tableau is also primal feasible, and hence optimal. Otherwise the basic solution given by $x_1 = \bar{b}_1, \ldots, x_r = \bar{b}_r, \ldots, x_m = \bar{b}_m, x_{m+1} = \cdots = x_n = 0$, is infeasible to the given problem, and hence not optimal even though the optimality conditions are satisfied.

Now the dual simplex method moves to an adjacent basic solution (a canonical tableau) by replacing a basic variable by a nonbasic variable.

Selection of a Basic Variable to Leave the Basis

This is done by choosing a basic variable which is making the present solution infeasible; in other words, a basic variable whose solution value is negative. In general, the basic variable with the most negative value for $\bar{b}_i$ will be chosen to leave the basis.

Let $\bar{b}_r = \min_i (\bar{b}_i) < 0$. Hence the basic variable x_r is to be replaced, and row r becomes the pivot row.

Selection of a Nonbasic Variable to Enter the Basis

The pivot column is chosen such that it satisfies the following two conditions:

1. The primal infeasibility should be reduced (at least should not get worse). In other words, we want a positive right-hand-side constant at least in row r in the next tableau. This means that only those nonbasic variables (x_j) with negative coefficients in row $r(y_{rj} < 0)$ are eligible to enter the basis.
2. The next tableau after the pivot operation must still be dual feasible. This can be guaranteed if the nonbasic variable to enter the basis is selected by the following

ratio rule:

$$\underset{y_{rj}<0}{\text{Maximum}}\left[\frac{\bar{c}_j}{y_{rj}}\right] \quad \text{for } j = m+1, \ldots, n \tag{4.23}$$

Let the maximum ratio correspond to the nonbasic variable x_s. In other words,

$$\frac{\bar{c}_s}{y_{rs}} = \max_{y_{rj}<0} \frac{\bar{c}_j}{y_{rj}}.$$

This implies that x_s replaces x_r from the basis. The new tableau is obtained by a pivot operation using y_{rs} as the pivot element. Note that the new basic variable in row r is x_s whose value is $\bar{b}_r/y_{rs}$. Since both $\bar{b}_r$ and y_{rs} are negative, row r will have a positive constant as required by Condition 1.

To prove that the ratio rule satisfies condition 2, observe that the new $\bar{c}_j$ coefficients after the pivot operation are given by,

$$\text{new } \bar{c}_j = (\text{old } \bar{c}_j) - \left[\frac{y_{rj}}{y_{rs}}\right](\text{old } \bar{c}_s)$$

This can be rewritten as,

$$\text{new } \bar{c}_j = y_{rj}\left[\frac{\bar{c}_j}{y_{rj}} - \frac{\bar{c}_s}{y_{rs}}\right] \tag{4.24}$$

We have to show that if the Ratio Rule 4.23 is used, then the new $\bar{c}_j$ given by Eq. 4.24 will always be nonnegative. Consider the following two cases:

Case 1. For those $y_{rj} \geq 0$, $\bar{c}_j/y_{rj} \geq 0$, since $\bar{c}_j \geq 0$. Since y_{rs} is the pivot element, $y_{rs} < 0$, and $\bar{c}_s/y_{rs} \leq 0$. Hence the term within the brackets in Eq. 4.24 is nonnegative. This implies that the new $\bar{c}_j$ will be nonnegative.

Case 2. Now consider those y_{rj} elements which are negative. By the ratio rule,

$$\frac{\bar{c}_s}{y_{rs}} = \max_{y_{rj}<0}\left[\frac{\bar{c}_j}{y_{rj}}\right].$$

Hence the term within the brackets in Eq. 4.24 will be nonpositive. Since y_{rj} is negative, the new $\bar{c}_j$ will be nonnegative, and the ratio rule guarantees that the new tableau after the pivot operation will be dual feasible.

Once again the dual simplex method checks whether the right-hand-side constants are nonnegative. If the condition is not met, then the algorithm is continued until a tableau which is both dual feasible and primal feasible is obtained.

Let us illustrate the steps of the dual simplex method with an example.

EXAMPLE 4.3-1

$$\text{Minimize:} \quad Z = x_1 + 4x_2 \qquad + 3x_4$$
$$\text{Subject to:} \qquad x_1 + 2x_2 - x_3 + x_4 \geq 3$$
$$-2x_1 - x_2 + 4x_3 + x_4 \geq 2$$
$$x_1, x_2, x_3, x_4 \geq 0$$

Introducing x_5 and x_6 as slack variables the standard form becomes,

$$\text{Minimize:} \quad Z = x_1 + 4x_2 + 3x_4$$

$$\text{Subject to:} \quad x_1 + 2x_2 - x_3 + x_4 - x_5 \qquad = 3$$

$$-2x_1 - x_2 + 4x_3 + x_4 \qquad - x_6 = 2$$

$$x_1, \ldots, x_6 \geq 0$$

Note that we can get a canonical system using x_5 and x_6 as basic variables by simply multiplying both equations by -1. Though this basic solution is infeasible to the primal, it is feasible for the dual since the $\bar{c}_j$ coefficients will be nonnegative. Thus we have a dual feasible tableau using x_5 and x_6 as basic variables as shown below:

Tableau 1

c_B	Basis	c_j	1	4	0	3	0	0	
			x_1	x_2	x_3	x_4	x_5	x_6	constants
0	x_5		(-1)	-2	1	-1	1	0	-3
0	x_6		2	1	-4	-1	0	1	-2
	$\bar{c}$ Row		1	4	0	3	0	0	

The basic solution given by $x_5 = -3$, $x_6 = -2$, $x_1 = x_2 = x_3 = x_4 = 0$ is infeasible, though it satisfies the optimality conditions. Since the basic variable x_5 has the most negative value, it will be chosen to leave the basis. To determine the nonbasic variable to enter, we note that only x_1, x_2, and x_4 are eligible since they have negative coefficients in row 1. Forming the ratios for these nonbasic variables we get the following:

Nonbasic Variable	y_{ij}	$\bar{c}_j$	Ratios
x_1	-1	1	-1
x_2	-2	4	-2
x_4	-1	3	-3

The maximum ratio occurs corresponding to the nonbasic variable x_1. Hence x_1 replaces x_5 from the basis. This is indicated by circling the pivot element (-1). The pivot operation is performed in the usual manner as follows:

1. Divide the pivot row (row 1) by -1.
2. Multiply the pivot row by 2, and add it to the second row.
3. Multiply the pivot row by 1 and add it to the $\bar{c}$ row.

The new tableau is given below:

Tableau 2

c_B	Basis	c_j :	1 x_1	4 x_2	0 x_3	3 x_4	0 x_5	0 x_6	Constants
1	x_1		1	2	−1	1	−1	0	3
0	x_6		0	−3	(−2)	−3	2	1	−8
	$\bar{c}$ Row		0	2	1	2	1	0	

The tableau is still not feasible to the primal since the basic variable x_6 has a negative value. Hence x_6 is chosen to leave the basis. To determine the nonbasic variable to enter, the ratios are computed for the nonbasic variables x_2, x_3, and x_4 as $-2/3$, $-1/2$, and $-2/3$, respectively. The maximum ratio corresponds to x_3, and x_3 replaces x_6 from the basis. The new tableau after the pivot operation is given below:

Tableau 3

c_B	Basis	c_j :	1 x_1	4 x_2	0 x_3	3 x_4	0 x_5	0 x_6	Constants
1	x_1		1	7/2	0	5/2	−2	−1/2	7
0	x_3		0	3/2	1	3/2	−1	−1/2	4
	$\bar{c}$ Row		0	1/2	0	1/2	2	1/2	$Z = 7$

Tableau 3 is both primal feasible and dual feasible. Hence we have an optimal solution to the primal given by $x_1 = 7$, $x_2 = 0$, $x_3 = 4$, $x_4 = 0$, $x_5 = 0$, $x_6 = 0$ and the optimum value of Z is 7.

Identifying Primal Infeasibility in the Dual Simplex Method

In the dual simplex method there always exists a feasible solution to the dual. Hence, when the dual simplex method is applied to a linear program the primal problem either has an optimum solution or is infeasible. The dual simplex method recognizes the primal infeasibility when the ratio rule fails to identify the nonbasic variable to enter. In other words, when all the elements in the pivot row are nonnegative, the dual simplex method terminates with the conclusion that the primal problem has no feasible solution. To justify this, consider the dual simplex tableau in general form as shown in Table 4.5. Let the constant in row $r(\bar{b}_r)$ be negative, and all the elements of row $r(y_{rj})$ be nonnegative. Writing the constraint r in expanded form, we get

$$x_r + y_{r,m+1}x_{m+1} + \cdots + y_{rn}x_n = \bar{b}_r \tag{4.25}$$

For all nonnegative values of x_j, the left-hand-side of Eq. 4.25 is nonnegative, while the right-hand-side is negative. Hence there exists no nonnegative solution satisfying Eq. 4.25. In other words, constraint r is inconsistent, and hence the primal problem is infeasible.

Solving a Maximization Problem by the Dual Simplex Method

In a maximization problem, the relative cost efficients ($\bar{c}_j$) must be nonpositive for optimality. Assume that Table 4.5 represents a dual feasible tableau of a maximization problem. Hence all the elements of $\bar{c}$ row will be nonpositive (≤ 0). Assume that $\bar{b}_r < 0$ and x_r is chosen to leave the basis. The nonbasic variable to enter the basis is chosen in such a way that the $\bar{c}$ row elements remain nonpositive at subsequent iterations. This can be guaranteed by using the following ratio rule:

$$\min_{y_{rj} < 0} \left[\frac{\bar{c}_j}{y_{rj}} \right]$$

The minimum ratio identifies the nonbasic variable to enter. The validity of this ratio rule may be proved in a manner similar to the one used for the minimization problem.

Applications of the Dual Simplex Method

In general it is not always easy to find a dual feasible basis. Many practical problems do not have a canonical tableau which is either primal feasible or dual feasible. Hence as a rule the primal simplex method is preferred over the dual simplex method for solving the general linear programming problem. But there are instances when the dual simplex method has an obvious advantage over the primal simplex method. These are problems in which a dual feasible tableau is readily available to start the dual simplex method. A list of such applications of the dual simplex method is given below:

1. Sensitivity analysis and parametric programming (Sections 4.4 and 4.5).
2. Most of the integer programming algorithms.
3. Some nonlinear programming algorithms.
4. Some variants of the simplex method such as the primal-dual algorithm, and the self-dual parametric algorithm.

4.4   SENSITIVITY ANALYSIS IN LINEAR PROGRAMMING

In all linear programming models the coefficients of the objective function and the constraints are supplied as input data or as parameters to the model. The optimal solution obtained by the simplex method is based on the values of these coefficients. In practice the values of these coefficients are seldom known with absolute certainty because many of these coefficients are functions of some uncontrollable parameters. For instance, the future demands, the cost of raw materials, or the cost of energy resources cannot be predicted with complete accuracy before the problem is solved. Hence the solution of a practical problem is not complete with the mere determination of the optimal solution.

Each variation in the values of the data coefficients changes the linear programming problem, which in turn may affect the optimal solution found earlier. In order to develop an overall strategy to meet the various contingencies, one has to study how the optimal solution will change due to changes in the input (data) coefficients. This is known as *sensitivity analysis* or *postopti-mality analysis*. Other reasons for performing a sensitivity analysis are listed below:

1. There may be some data coefficients or parameters of the linear program which are controllable; for example, availability of capital, raw material, or machine capacities. Sensitivity analysis enables one to study the effects of changing these parameters on the optimal solution. If it turns out that the optimal value (profit/cost) changes (in our favor) by a considerable amount for a small change in the given parameters, then it may be worthwhile implementing some of these changes. For example, if increasing the availability of labor by allowing overtime contributes to a greater increase in the maximum return, as compared to the increased cost of overtime labor, then one might want to allow overtime produc-tion.

2. In many cases, the values of the data coefficient are obtained by statistical estimation procedures on past figures, as in the case of sales forecasts, price estimates, and cost data. These estimates, in general, may not be very accurate. If we can identify which of the parameters affect the objective value most, then we can obtain better estimates of these parameters. This will increase the reliability of our model and the solution.

For a discussion of the sensitivity analysis, we shall confine ourselves to the following changes in the data, and how to handle these changes:

1. Changes in the cost coefficients (c_j).
2. Changes in the right-hand-side constants (b_i).
3. Changes in the constraint or coefficient matrix ($\mathbf{A}$).
   a. Adding new activities or variables.
   b. Changing existing columns.
   c. Adding new constraints.

In this section, we shall see how to minimize the additional computations necessary to study the above changes. In many cases, it will not be necessary to solve the problem all over again. We shall present the discussion with the help of an illustrative example. The basic principles involved in performing a sensitivity analysis will be sufficiently developed so that the reader will have no difficulty in extending them to other problems or to the general case.

EXAMPLE 4.4-1 (A product-mix problem)

The Dependable Company plans production on three of their products—A, B, and C. The unit profits on these products are $2, $3, and $1, respectively, and they require two resources—labor and material. The company's operations research department formulates the following linear programming model for determining the optimal product mix:

$$\text{Maximize:} \quad Z = 2x_1 + 3x_2 + x_3$$

$$\text{Subject to:} \quad \frac{1}{3}x_1 + \frac{1}{3}x_2 + \frac{1}{3}x_3 \leq 1 \quad \text{(labor)}$$

$$\frac{1}{3}x_1 + \frac{4}{3}x_2 + \frac{7}{3}x_3 \leq 3 \quad \text{(material)}$$

$$x_1, x_2, x_3 \geq 0$$

where x_1, x_2, x_3 are the number of products A, B, and C produced.

The initial simplex tableau with the addition of slack variables x_4 and x_5 is given in Table 4.6.

Table 4.6

c_B	Basis	c_j	2 x_1	3 x_2	1 x_3	0 x_4	0 x_5	Constants
0	x_4		$\frac{1}{3}$	$\frac{1}{3}$	$\frac{1}{3}$	1	0	1
0	x_5		$\frac{1}{3}$	$\frac{4}{3}$	$\frac{7}{3}$	0	1	3
	$\bar{c}$ Row		2	3	1	0	0	$Z = 0$

Since this is already in canonical form, no artificial variables are needed. The simplex method comes out, after some iterations, with the optimal tableau shown in Table 4.7.

Table 4.7

c_B	Basis	c_j	2 x_1	3 x_2	1 x_3	0 x_4	0 x_5	Constants
2	x_1		1	0	-1	4	-1	1
3	x_2		0	1	2	-1	1	2
	$\bar{c}$ Row		0	0	-3	-5	-1	$Z = 8$

From the optimal tableau, we see that the optimal product mix is to produce 1 unit of product A and 2 units of product B for a total profit of $8. By performing a sensitivity analysis, it is possible to obtain valuable information regarding alternative production schedules in the neighborhood of the optimal solution. Quite often, this information will be more significant and useful than the determination of the optimal product mix itself. As a matter of fact, one of the reasons for the extensive use of linear programming in practice is its ability to provide a sensitivity analysis along with the optimal solution!

Variations in the Objective Function Coefficients (c_j)
Variations in the coefficients of the objective function may occur due to a change in profit or cost of either a basic activity or a nonbasic activity. We shall treat these cases separately.

Case 1.   Changing the Objective Function Coefficient of a Nonbasic Variable.   In the optimal product mix shown in Table 4.7, product C is not produced because of its low profit of $1 per unit ($c_3$). One may be interested in finding the range on the values of c_3 such that the current optimal solution remains optimal. It is clear that when c_3

decreases it has no effect on the present optimal solution. However when the profit is increased beyond a certain value, product C may become profitable to produce.

As a rule, the sensitivity of the current optimal solution can be best obtained by studying how the optimal tableau given in Table 4.7 changes due to variations in the input data. When the value of c_3 changes, the value of the relative profit coefficient of the nonbasic variable x_3 ($\bar{c}_3$) changes in the optimal tableau. Table 4.7 is optimal as long as $\bar{c}_3$ is nonpositive. In the present optimal tableau $\mathbf{c_B} = (c_1, c_2) = (2, 3)$. Hence,

$$\bar{c}_3 = c_3 - (2, 3)\begin{pmatrix} -1 \\ 2 \end{pmatrix} = c_3 - 4$$

For Table 4.7 to be optimal, $\bar{c}_3 = c_3 - 4 \leq 0$, or $c_3 \leq 4$. In other words, as long as the unit profit on product C is less than \$4, it is not economical to produce product C.

Suppose if the unit profit on product C is increased to \$6, then $\bar{c}_3 = +2$, and the current product mix is not optimal. The maximum profit can be increased further by producing product C. In other words, Table 4.7 is nonoptimal since x_3 can enter the basis to increase Z. By the minimum ratio rule, x_2 leaves the basis. The new optimal solution can be determined by applying the simplex method as shown below:

Basis	x_1	x_2	x_3	x_4	x_5	Constants
x_1	1	0	-1	4	-1	1
x_2	0	1	②	-1	1	2
			↑			
$\bar{c}$ Row	0	0	2	-5	-1	$Z = 8$
x_1	1	$\frac{1}{2}$	0	$\frac{7}{2}$	$-\frac{1}{2}$	2
x_3	0	$\frac{1}{2}$	1	$-\frac{1}{2}$	$\frac{1}{2}$	1
$\bar{c}$ Row	0	-1	0	-4	-2	$Z = 10$

Hence, the new (optimal) product mix is to produce 2 units of product A, and 1 unit of product C with a maximum profit of \$10.

In general, the new optimal solution is found in just one iteration, but it should not be taken for granted at all times.

Case 2. Changing the Objective Function Coefficient of a Basic Variable. Suppose we want to determine the effect of changes on the unit profit of product A (c_1). It is intuitively clear that when c_1 decreases below a certain level, it may not be profitable to include product A in the optimal product mix. Even when c_1 increases, it is possible that it may change the optimal product mix at some level. This happens because product A may become so profitable that the optimal mix may include only product A. Hence, there is an upper and a lower limit on the variation of c_1 within which the optimal solution given by Table 4.7 is not affected.

To determine the range on c_1, observe that a change in c_1 changes the profit vector of the basic variables ($\mathbf{c_B}$) since $\mathbf{c_B} = (c_1, c_2)$. It can be verified that the relative profit coefficients of the basic variables, namely $\bar{c}_1$ and $\bar{c}_2$, will not be affected, and they will still remain at zero value. However the relative profits of the nonbasic variables, namely $\bar{c}_3$, $\bar{c}_4$, $\bar{c}_5$, will change. But as long as these $\bar{c}_j$ remain nonpositive, Table 4.7 is still optimal. We can express the values of $\bar{c}_3$, $\bar{c}_4$, $\bar{c}_5$, as a function of c_1 as follows:

$$\bar{c}_3 = 1 - (c_1, 3)\begin{pmatrix} -1 \\ 2 \end{pmatrix} = c_1 - 5$$

$$\bar{c}_4 = 0 - (c_1, 3)\begin{pmatrix} 4 \\ -1 \end{pmatrix} = -4c_1 + 3$$

$$\bar{c}_5 = 0 - (c_1, 3)\begin{pmatrix} -1 \\ 1 \end{pmatrix} = c_1 - 3$$

From the above calculations, $\bar{c}_3 \leq 0$ as long as $c_1 \leq 5$. Similarly, each nonbasic variable puts a limit (lower or upper) on the value of c_1. Thus,

$$\bar{c}_4 \leq 0 \quad \text{implies} \quad c_1 \geq \frac{3}{4}, \text{ and}$$

$$\bar{c}_5 \leq 0 \quad \text{implies} \quad c_1 \leq 3$$

Table 4.7 will remain optimal as long as the variation on c_1 is within the limits imposed by all the nonbasic variables. Hence, if the range on c_1 is chosen as $[3/4, 3]$, then all the $\bar{c}_j$ will remain nonpositive, and the present solution $x_1 = 1$, $x_2 = 2$, $x_3 = 0$ is still optimal. Of course as c_1 changes, the optimal value of the objective function will change. For example, when $c_1 = 1$, the optimal solution is given by $x_1 = 1$, $x_2 = 2$, $x_3 = 0$, but the maximum profit $= \$7$. When the value of c_1 goes beyond the range provided by the sensitivity analysis, Table 4.7 will no longer be optimal as one of the nonbasic $\bar{c}_j$ will become positive. Once again, we can apply the simplex method to determine the new optimal solution as discussed in Case 1.

Case 3. **Changing the Price of Both the Basic and the Nonbasic Variables.** A simple case of this can be easily solved. For example, the profits on all three products are changed such that the objective function becomes $Z = x_1 + 4x_2 + 2x_3$. The effect on the optimal product mix can be determined by checking whether the $\bar{c}$ row in Table 4.7 remains nonpositive. $\bar{c}_1 = \bar{c}_2 = 0$, while

$$\bar{c}_3 = 2 - (1, 4)\begin{pmatrix} -1 \\ 2 \end{pmatrix} = -5 < 0$$

$$\bar{c}_4 = 0 - (1, 4)\begin{pmatrix} 4 \\ -1 \end{pmatrix} = 0$$

$$\bar{c}_5 = 0 - (1, 4)\begin{pmatrix} -1 \\ 1 \end{pmatrix} = -3 < 0$$

Hence the optimal solution does not change, and the optimal product mix is $x_1 = 1, x_2 = 2, x_3 = 0$, and the maximum $Z = \$9$. Of course, we now have an indication for an alternate optimal solution since $\bar{c}_4 = 0$.

Changing the Right-Hand-Side Constants (b_i)

Suppose that an additional one unit of labor is made available, and the company is interested in determining how this affects the optimal product mix.

The addition of one more unit of labor changes the vector of right-hand-side constants in the initial simplex tableau. In other words, the vector of constants in Table 4.6 change from $\binom{1}{3}$ to a vector $\binom{2}{3}$. It is clear that this change has no effect in the optimal tableau given by Table 4.7 except for changes in the values of the constants. Even after the change, if the new right-hand-side constants remain nonnegative, then the solution given by Table 4.7 is still a basic feasible solution. Because the $\bar{c}$-row coefficients are the same (namely, nonpositive) this tableau also becomes an optimal solution to the problem. Therefore in order to study the effect of variation in the right-hand-side constants, it is sufficient to verify whether the new vector of constants in the final tableau stays nonnegative. To do this, there is no need to solve the problem again. In Section 4.1 we have seen that any column in the final tableau (including the right-hand-side vector) can be obtained by multiplying the corresponding column in the initial tableau by the inverse of the basic columns. In this case, the basic columns are the columns corresponding to the variables (x_1, x_2) in the initial tableau. Hence the basis matrix corresponding to Table 4.7 is given by

$$\mathbf{B} = \begin{bmatrix} \dfrac{1}{3} & \dfrac{1}{3} \\[2mm] \dfrac{1}{3} & \dfrac{4}{3} \end{bmatrix}$$

One can compute the inverse of the basis matrix directly by the pivot method or the adjoint method. But in the discussion of the revised simplex method (Section 4.1), we have observed that the columns corresponding to the initial basic variables in any simplex tableau give the inverse of the basic matrix corresponding to that tableau. Since x_4 and x_5 are the initial basic variables (Table 4.6), the columns corresponding to x_4 and x_5 in Table 4.7 give the inverse of the basis matrix $\mathbf{B}$. This implies

$$\mathbf{B}^{-1} = \begin{bmatrix} 4 & -1 \\ -1 & 1 \end{bmatrix}$$

The values of the new right-hand-side constants in Table 4.7 due to the increased labor is given by

$$\bar{\mathbf{b}} = \begin{bmatrix} 4 & -1 \\ -1 & 1 \end{bmatrix} \begin{bmatrix} 2 \\ 3 \end{bmatrix} = \begin{bmatrix} 5 \\ 1 \end{bmatrix}$$

Thus, when the value of the constants in Table 4.6 change to $\begin{bmatrix} 2 \\ 3 \end{bmatrix}$, the new values of the constants in Table 4.7 become $\begin{bmatrix} 5 \\ 1 \end{bmatrix}$ which is a positive vector. Hence, Table 4.7 still remains optimal, and the new optimal product mix is

$x_1 = 5$, $x_2 = 1$, $x_3 = 0$, and maximum value of $Z = \$13$. Note here that both the optimal solution, and the optimal value of the objective function have changed due to a variation in the availability of labor. But, the optimal basis has not changed; in other words, it is still optimal to produce only the two products A and B. The only difference lies in the quantity of A and B produced.

Suppose the extra unit of labor can be obtained by allowing overtime which costs an additional \$4 to the company. The company may want to find out whether it is profitable to use overtime labor. This may be found by comparing the increased profit by employing overtime to its added cost. In our example, the increased profit is $\$13 - 8 = \$5$, which is more than the cost of overtime (\$4); it is therefore profitable to get the additional 1 unit of labor.

The increased profit of \$5-per-unit increase in labor availability is called the *shadow price* for the labor constraint. Knowing the shadow prices of various constraints helps in determining how much one can afford to pay for increases in the constrained resources. In Section 4.2, we showed that the optimal dual solution corresponds to the shadow prices on the various constraints. In Example 4.4-1, the optimal dual solution (y_1^o, y_2^o) is given by

$$(y_1^o, y_2^o) = \text{optimal simplex multipliers corresponding to Table 4.7}$$

$$= \mathbf{c_B B}^{-1}$$

$$= (2, 3)\begin{bmatrix} 4 & -1 \\ -1 & 1 \end{bmatrix} = (5, 1)$$

Thus the optimal dual solution is $y_1^o = 5$ and $y_2^o = 1$. In other words, the shadow price on the labor constraint is \$5 which corresponds to the one computed by the sensitivity analysis. Similarly, the shadow price on the materials constraint is \$1. It is important to note here that the shadow prices reflect the net change in the optimal value of Z per unit increase on the constraint resources, as long as the variation in the constraint resources does not change the optimal basis. Hence in order to use the shadow prices meaningfully, one has to compute the range on the variation of a constraint resource such that the optimal basis (product mix) remains the same.

To illustrate, let us compute how far the availability of labor can be varied (increased or decreased) such that the present optimal basis (product mix) still remains optimal. Let b_1 denote the amount of labor available, and $\mathbf{b}^*$ denote the new vector of constants in the initial tableau. Hence

$$\mathbf{b}^* = \begin{bmatrix} b_1 \\ 3 \end{bmatrix}$$

For the simplex tableau given by Table 4.7 to be optimal, we should have $\mathbf{B}^{-1}\mathbf{b}^* \geq 0$. Since $\mathbf{B}^{-1} = \begin{bmatrix} 4 & -1 \\ -1 & 1 \end{bmatrix}$, we get

$$\mathbf{B}^{-1}\mathbf{b}^* = \begin{bmatrix} 4 & -1 \\ -1 & 1 \end{bmatrix}\begin{bmatrix} b_1 \\ 3 \end{bmatrix} = \begin{bmatrix} 4b_1 & -3 \\ -b_1 & +3 \end{bmatrix}$$

$\mathbf{B}^{-1}\mathbf{b}^*$ is nonnegative as long as

$$4b_1 - 3 \geq 0 \qquad \text{or} \qquad b_1 \geq \frac{3}{4}$$

$$-b_1 + 3 \geq 0 \qquad \text{or} \qquad b_1 \leq 3$$

This means that x_1 and x_2 will remain in the optimal product mix as long as the labor availability varies between 3/4 of a unit and 3 units. But the optimal solution, and the maximum profit will change. Thus we have a range of optimal solutions as given below:

For all $3/4 \leq b_1 \leq 3$, the optimal solution is

$$x_1 = 4b_1 - 3$$
$$x_2 = -b_1 + 3$$
$$x_3 = 0$$

The maximum profit $Z = 2(4b_1 - 3) + 3(-b_1 + 3)$
$$= \$5b_1 + 3$$

Let us now consider the case when the labor availability is increased to 4 units. This means that the initial values of the right-hand-side constants in Table 4.6 will change to $\begin{bmatrix} 4 \\ 3 \end{bmatrix}$. The new values of the constants in the final tableau (Table 4.7) will be given by

$$\bar{\mathbf{b}} = \mathbf{B}^{-1}\begin{pmatrix} 4 \\ 3 \end{pmatrix} = \begin{bmatrix} 4 & -1 \\ -1 & 1 \end{bmatrix}\begin{bmatrix} 4 \\ 3 \end{bmatrix} = \begin{bmatrix} 13 \\ -1 \end{bmatrix}$$

This implies that Table 4.7 is no longer optimal since the basic solution $x_1 = 13$, $x_2 = -1$, $x_3 = x_4 = x_5 = 0$ is infeasible. In order to find the new optimal product mix, the simplex tableau of Table 4.7 is reproduced with the new values of the constants in Table 4.8.

Table 4.8

c_B	Basis	c_j 2	3	1	0	0	
		x_1	x_2	x_3	x_4	x_5	Constants
2	x_1	1	0	−1	4	−1	13
3	x_2	0	1	2	⊝−1	1	−1
	$\bar{c}$ Row	0	0	−3	−5	−1	

Even though the simplex tableau corresponding to Table 4.8 is infeasible for the primal problem, it is feasible for the dual since all the relative cost coefficients are nonpositive. Hence the new optimal solution can be obtained by the *dual simplex method*. Since the basic variable x_2 is negative, it will leave the basis, and since x_4 is the only nonbasic variable with a negative coefficient, it will replace x_2 in the basis. Table 4.9 gives the new tableau after the pivot operation.

Table 4.9

c_B	Basis	c_j 2	3	1	0	0	
		x_1	x_2	x_3	x_4	x_5	Constants
2	x_1	1	4	7	0	3	9
0	x_4	0	−1	−2	1	−1	1
	$\bar{c}$ Row	0	−5	−13	0	−6	$Z = 18$

Table 4.9 is optimal since the right-hand-side constants are positive. The new optimal product mix when the labor availability is increased to 4 units is given by $x_1 = 9$, $x_2 = 0$, $x_3 = 0$, and the maximum profit is $18.

Variations in the Constraint Matrix (A)

As mentioned earlier, the constraint matrix or the coefficient matrix $(\mathbf{A})$ may be changed by

1. adding new variables or activities
2. changing the resources requirements of the existing activities
3. adding new constraints

We shall discuss each of these cases separately.

Case (1): *Adding a new activity.* Suppose the company's R & D department has come out with a new product D which requires 1 unit of labor, and 1 unit of material. The new product has sufficient market and can be sold at a unit profit of $3. The company wants to know whether it is economical to manufacture product D.

Inclusion of a new product in our possible product mix is mathematically equivalent to adding a variable (say x_6), and a column $\binom{1}{1}$ in the initial tableau (Table 4.6). The present optimal product mix given by Table 4.7 is optimal as long as the relative profit coefficient of the new product, namely $\bar{c}_6$, is nonpositive. From the revised simplex method, we know that

$$\bar{c}_6 = c_6 - \pi \mathbf{P}_6$$

where $c_6 = \$3$, $\mathbf{P}_6 = \binom{1}{1}$, and π is the simplex multiplier corresponding to Table 4.7. Note that

$$\pi = \mathbf{c_B B}^{-1}$$

$$= (2, 3)\begin{bmatrix} 4 & -1 \\ -1 & 1 \end{bmatrix} = (5, 1)$$

Hence

$$\bar{c}_6 = 3 - (5, 1)\binom{1}{1} = -3$$

This indicates that producing product D will not improve the present value of the maximum profit.

In case it turns out that the new activity can contribute to an increased profit (because of its $\bar{c}_j$ value being positive), then the simplex method will be applied to determine the new optimal solution.

Case (2): *Variation in the Resources Requirements of the Existing Activities.* When the labor or the material requirements of a nonbasic activity (e.g., product C) change, its effect on the optimal solution can be studied by following the same steps as given in Case (1). On the other hand, if the constraint coefficients of a basic activity (e.g., product A or product B) change, then the basis matrix itself is affected, which in turn may affect all the quantities given in Table 4.7. It is then possible for Table 4.7 to be neither primal feasible nor dual feasible. Under such circumstances, it may be better to solve the linear program over again.

Case (3): *Adding new Constraints.* Consider the addition of an administrative services constraint to the problem wherein the products A, B, and C require 1, 2, and 1 hour of administrative services, while the available administrative hours are 10. This amounts to adding a new constraint of the form,

$$x_1 + 2x_2 + x_3 \leq 10$$

to the original formulation of the problem. To study its effect on the present optimal solution, it is sufficient to verify whether the present optimal product mix satisfies the new constraint. It can be shown mathematically that the present optimal solution stays optimal as long as it satisfies the new constraint. In our case it does satisfy the administrative services constraint, and hence the optimal product mix is not altered.

Suppose the available administrative hours are only 4, then new constraint becomes,

$$x_1 + 2x_2 + x_3 \leq 4.$$

The present optimal solution $x_1 = 1$, $x_2 = 2$, $x_3 = 0$ violates this constraint. Hence Table 4.7 is no longer optimal. In order to find the new optimal solution, let us add the new constraint as the third row in Table 4.7. Using x_6 as the slack variable in the new constraint, the modified tableau is shown below:

		c_j	2	3	1	0	0	0	
c_B	Basis		x_1	x_2	x_3	x_4	x_5	x_6	Constants
2	x_1		1	0	−1	4	−1	0	1
3	x_2		0	1	2	−i	1	0	2
0	x_6		1	2	1	0	0	1	4
	$\bar{c}$ Row		0	0	−3	−5	−1	0	

The modified tableau is not in canonical form since the basic variables x_1 and x_2 have positive coefficients in the third row. To eliminate the coefficients of x_1 and x_2, we can multiply the first row by −1, the second row by −2, and add them to the third row. Table 4.10 gives the new canonical tableau after the row operations. Note that the $\bar{c}$ row is not affected in this process since the new basic variable x_6 is slack variable.

Table 4.10

		c_j	2	3	1	0	0	0	
c_B	Basis		x_1	x_2	x_3	x_4	x_5	x_6	Constants
2	x_1		1	0	−1	4	−1	0	1
3	x_2		0	1	2	−1	1	0	2
0	x_6		0	0	−2	−2	⊖1	1	−1
	$\bar{c}$ Row		0	0	−3	−5	−1	0	

Since Table 4.10 is dual feasible, the dual simplex method is applied to find the new optimal solution. The basic variable x_6 leaves the basis. The ratios are formed for the nonbasic variables x_3, x_4, and x_5 as 3/2, 5/2, and 1 respectively. Since the minimum ratio corresponds to x_5, the basic variable x_6 is replaced by x_5. The new tableau is given in Table 4.11.

Table 4.11

c_B	Basis	c_j	2	3	1	0	0	0	Constants
			x_1	x_2	x_3	x_4	x_5	x_6	
2	x_1		1	0	1	6	0	−1	2
3	x_2		0	1	0	−3	0	1	1
0	x_5		0	0	2	2	1	−1	1
	$\bar{c}$ Row		0	0	−1	−3	0	−1	Z = 7

Table 4.11 is optimal and the new optimal product mix is to produce 2 units of product A and one unit of product B. The maximum profit has been reduced from \$8 to \$7 due to the addition of the new constraint. This is true of any linear program. In other words, whenever a new constraint is added to a linear program the old optimal value will always be better or equal to the new optimum value. Thus the addition of a new constraint cannot improve the optimal value of any linear programming problem.

The ability to add more constraints to a linear programming problem has other practical applications. We have noted earlier that the computational effort in solving a linear program varies in proportion to the cube of the number of constraints. Hence to reduce the computation time, one may be able to identify and set aside from past experience some constraints which may not be very critical in determining the optimal solution. These constraints are generally called *inactive* or *secondary constraints*. These may include resources which are under the control of the firm or those which can be obtained easily. A significant reduction in the computational time (and hence the cost of solution) can be achieved by solving the linear program without the secondary constraints. After the optimal solution has been determined, the secondary constraints are added to verify whether the optimal solution satisfies these constraints. If one or more constraints are violated, then the dual simplex method is applied to determine the new optimal solution. Of course the overall savings in computational effort will depend on how good the initial judgements are made while identifying the secondary constraints.

4.5 PARAMETRIC PROGRAMMING
The discussion of sensitivity analysis in the previous section considered the effects of variations in the input coefficients when these coefficients are changed one at a time. When simultaneous variations occur in the input data, none of the results of Section 4.4 is valid. In this section, we consider the effects of simultaneous changes in data, where the coefficients change as a function of

one parameter. Hence this is called *parametric programming*, and is simply an extension of sensitivity analysis. We shall consider the following parametric problems: (1) Parametric cost problem, and (2) parametric right-hand-side problem.

The Parametric Cost Problem

Consider a linear program of the form:

$$\text{Minimize: } Z = (\mathbf{c} + \lambda \mathbf{c}^*)\mathbf{x}$$

$$\text{Subject to: } \mathbf{Ax} = \mathbf{b}$$

$$\mathbf{x} \geq \mathbf{0}$$

where $\mathbf{c}$ is the given cost vector, $\mathbf{c}^*$ is the given variation vector, and λ is an unknown positive or negative parameter. Varying the value of λ changes the cost coefficients of all the variables. We are interested in finding the family of optimal solutions for all values of λ in the range $-\infty$ to $+\infty$.

To give a practical application of the parameteric cost problem, consider a manufacturer of different products. Each of these products require a basic raw material at varying amounts. Suppose the manufacturer knows in advance that the cost of this basic raw material is going to fluctuate widely during the coming year, and he is interested in finding the effect of this variation on the optimal product mix. In this case, the variation vector $\mathbf{c}^*$ represents the quantity of this raw material used by the different products, and λ denotes the variation in the raw material cost. As λ varies, the cost of production of all the products change by different amounts. A solution of the parametric cost problem will provide the manufacturer different optimal policies to follow depending on the cost of this raw material.

The parametric cost problem is solved by using the simplex method, and sensitivity analysis. The parametric linear program is first solved by the simplex method for a fixed value of λ which is usually taken as zero. Let $\mathbf{B}$ represent the optimal basis matrix for $\lambda = 0$. This implies that the relative cost coefficients with respect to the basis $\mathbf{B}$ are nonnegative, and are given by $\bar{c}_j = c_j - \mathbf{c_B}\bar{\mathbf{P}}_j$, where $\bar{\mathbf{P}}_j$ is the jth column (corresponding to the variable x_j) in the optimal tableau, and $\mathbf{c_B}$ is the cost vector of the basic variables. When λ varies from zero to a positive or negative value, the relative cost coefficient of the variable x_j becomes

$$\bar{c}_j(\lambda) = (c_j + \lambda c_j^*) - (\mathbf{c_B} + \lambda \mathbf{c_B^*})\bar{\mathbf{P}}_j$$

$$= (c_j - \mathbf{c_B}\bar{\mathbf{P}}_j) + \lambda(c_j^* - \mathbf{c_B^*}\bar{\mathbf{P}}_j)$$

$$= \bar{c}_j + \lambda \bar{c}_j^* \tag{4.26}$$

Since the vectors $\mathbf{c}$ and $\mathbf{c}^*$ are known, $\bar{c}_j$ and $\bar{c}_j^*$ can be computed. Then for any value of λ, the relative cost coefficients are given by Eq. 4.26. For a simplex tableau to be optimal, $\bar{c}_j(\lambda)$ must be nonnegative. In other words, for a given tableau, one can determine the range of values of λ for which that tableau is optimal.

To illustrate the parametric cost technique, consider Example 4.4–1, with the variation cost vector as $\mathbf{c}^* = (1, -1, 1, 0, 0)$.

EXAMPLE 4.5-1

$$\text{Maximize: } Z = (2+\lambda)x_1 + (3-\lambda)x_2 + (1+\lambda)x_3$$

$$\text{Subject to: } \frac{1}{3}x_1 + \frac{1}{3}x_2 - \frac{1}{3}x_3 + x_4 = 1$$

$$\frac{1}{3}x_1 + \frac{4}{3}x_2 + \frac{7}{3}x_3 + x_5 = 3$$

$$x_1, \ldots, x_5 \geq 0$$

For $\lambda = 0$, the above linear program is the same as the one given in Example 4.4-1, and its optimal solution is given in Table 4.7 (Section 4.4). Since we have a maximization problem, a basic feasible solution is optimal when the relative profit coefficients are nonpositive. For nonzero values of λ, the relative profits become linear functions of λ. To study the effect of this variation, we add a new relative profit row called the $\bar{c}^*$ row. The expanded simplex tableau is shown in Table 4.12.

Table 4.12

c_B^*	c_B	Basis	c_j^* 1	-1	1	0	0	
			c_j 2	3	1	0	0	
			x_1	x_2	x_3	x_4	x_5	Constants
1	2	x_1	1	0	-1	4	-1	1
-1	3	x_2	0	1	2	-1	1	2
		$\bar{c}$ Row	0	0	-3	-5	-1	$Z = 8$
		$\bar{c}^*$ Row	0	0	4	-5	2	$Z^* = -1$

The $\bar{c}^*$ row is calculated just like the $\bar{c}$ row except that the vector $\mathbf{c}$ is replaced by $\mathbf{c}^*$. For example,

$$\bar{c}_3 = c_3 - \mathbf{c_B}\bar{\mathbf{P}}_3 = 1 - (2, 3)\begin{pmatrix} -1 \\ 2 \end{pmatrix} = -3$$

$$\bar{c}_3^* = c_3^* - \mathbf{c_B^*}\bar{\mathbf{P}}_3 = 1 - (1, -1)\begin{pmatrix} -1 \\ 2 \end{pmatrix} = 4$$

Table 4.12 represents a basic feasible solution given by $x_1 = 1$, $x_2 = 2$, $x_3 = x_4 = x_5 = 0$, whose value of the objective function is $Z(\lambda) = Z + \lambda Z^* = 8 - \lambda$. Its relative profit coefficients are given by

$$\bar{c}_j(\lambda) = \bar{c}_j + \lambda \bar{c}_j^* \qquad \text{for } j = 1, 2, 3, 4, 5$$

For $\lambda = 0$, Table 4.12 represents an optimal tableau, and it remains optimal for other values of λ as long as the $\bar{c}_j(\lambda) \leq 0$ for $j = 3, 4, 5$. Thus, one can determine the range of λ for which Table 4.12 is optimal as follows:

$$\bar{c}_3(\lambda) = -3 + 4\lambda \leq 0 \qquad \text{or} \qquad \lambda \leq 3/4$$

$$\bar{c}_4(\lambda) = -5 - 5\lambda \leq 0 \qquad \text{or} \qquad \lambda \geq -1$$

$$\bar{c}_5(\lambda) = -1 + 2\lambda \leq 0 \qquad \text{or} \qquad \lambda \leq 1/2$$

In other words, $x_1 = 1$, $x_2 = 2$, $x_3 = x_4 = x_5 = 0$ is an optimal solution for all values of λ between -1 and $1/2$. The optimal value of Z is given by $8 - \lambda$.

As λ exceeds $1/2$, the relative profit coefficient of the nonbasic variable x_5, namely $\bar{c}_5(\lambda)$, turns positive making Table 4.12 nonoptimal. Applying the simplex method, x_5 enters the basis to replace x_2. The new tableau after the pivot operation is given in Table 4.13.

Table 4.13

c_B^*	c_B	Basis	c_j^* c_j	x_1	x_2	x_3	x_4	x_5	Constants
			1 2	−1 3	1 1	0 0	0 0		
1	2	x_1		1	1	1	3	0	3
0	0	x_5		0	1	2	−1	1	2
		$\bar{c}$ Row		0	1	−1	−6	0	$Z = 6$
		$\bar{c}^*$ Row		0	−2	0	−3	0	$Z^* = 3$

Table 4.13 represents an optimal tableau as long as $\bar{c}_2(\lambda)$, $\bar{c}_3(\lambda)$, and $\bar{c}_4(\lambda)$ remain nonpositive. They will be nonpositive if λ is not less than $1/2$. Thus for all $\lambda \geq 1/2$, the optimal solution is given by $x_1 = 3$, $x_2 = x_3 = x_4 = 0$, $x_5 = 2$, and the optimal value of $Z = 6 + 3\lambda$.

Similarly we can obtain the family of optimal solutions for $\lambda < -1$ from Table 4.12.

Figure 4.1 gives a plot of the optimal value of Z for different values of λ between -1 and ∞ for the parametric cost problem of Example 4.5-1.

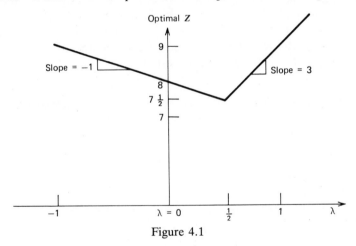

Figure 4.1

Parametric cost curve of Example 4.5-1.

Parametric Right-Hand-Side Problem

The right-hand-side constants in a linear programming problem represent the limits on the resources and the outputs. It is not necessary that all the resources be independent of one another. It is quite possible in a practical problem that a shortage of one resource may be accompanied by shortages in other resources at varying levels. This is true of the outputs as well. For example, consider a manufacturer of electrical appliances. A shortage of electricity (or increased utility cost) may affect the demands for all his products at varying degrees depending on their energy consumptions. In all these problems we are considering simultaneous changes in the right-hand-side constants when they are functions of one parameter, and study their effects on the optimal solution.

Consider a parametric right-hand-side problem of the form:

$$\text{Maximize: } Z = \mathbf{cx}$$

$$\text{Subject to: } \mathbf{Ax} = \mathbf{b} + \alpha\mathbf{b}^*$$

$$\mathbf{x} \geq \mathbf{0}$$

where

$\mathbf{b}$ is a known right-hand-side vector,
$\mathbf{b}^*$ is the variation vector, and
α is an unknown parameter

As the value of α changes, the values of the right-hand-side constants change. We are interested in determining the family of optimal solutions for all values of α from $-\infty$ to $+\infty$.

For $\alpha = 0$, let $\mathbf{B}$ be the optimal basis matrix. The optimal solution is then given by $\mathbf{x_B} = \mathbf{B}^{-1}\mathbf{b}$, and $\mathbf{x_N} = \mathbf{0}$, where $\mathbf{x_B}$ and $\mathbf{x_N}$ are the set of basic and nonbasic variables. As the parameter α is varied, the values of the basic variables change, and their new values are given by

$$\mathbf{x_B} = \mathbf{B}^{-1}(\mathbf{b} + \alpha\mathbf{b}^*) = \mathbf{B}^{-1}\mathbf{b} + \alpha\mathbf{B}^{-1}\mathbf{b}^* = \bar{\mathbf{b}} + \alpha\bar{\mathbf{b}}^*$$

A change in α has no effect on the values of the relative profit coefficients $\bar{c}_j$. In other words, the $\bar{c}_j$ values remain nonpositive. Hence as long as $\bar{\mathbf{b}} + \alpha\bar{\mathbf{b}}^*$ is a nonnegative vector, the solution $\mathbf{x_B} = \bar{\mathbf{b}} + \alpha\bar{\mathbf{b}}^*$, and $\mathbf{x_N} = \mathbf{0}$ is feasible and optimal. For a given basis $\mathbf{B}$, the values of $\bar{\mathbf{b}}$ and $\bar{\mathbf{b}}^*$ can be calculated. The basis $\mathbf{B}$ is optimal as long as $\bar{\mathbf{b}} + \alpha\bar{\mathbf{b}}^* \geq \mathbf{0}$. From this, we can determine the range of values of the parameter α for which the basis $\mathbf{B}$ is optimal.

To illustrate the parametric analysis on the right-hand-side constants, consider Example 4.4-1 with the variation right-hand-side vector as $\mathbf{b}^* = \begin{pmatrix} 1 \\ -1 \end{pmatrix}$.

EXAMPLE 4.5-2

$$\text{Maximize: } \quad Z = 2x_1 + 3x_2 + x_3$$

$$\text{Subject to: } \frac{1}{3}x_1 + \frac{1}{3}x_2 + \frac{1}{3}x_3 + x_4 = 1 + \alpha$$

$$\frac{1}{3}x_1 + \frac{4}{3}x_2 + \frac{7}{3}x_3 + x_5 = 3 - \alpha$$

$$x_1, \ldots, x_5 \geq 0$$

For $\alpha = 0$, Example 4.5-2 is the same as Example 4.4-1, for which the optimal tableau is given in Table 4.7 (Section 4.4). As α changes, the values of the right-hand-side constants will change because of the variation vector $\mathbf{b}^*$. This is shown in the expanded Tableau given by Table 4.14.

Table 4.14

C_B	Basis	c_j	2 x_1	3 x_2	1 x_3	0 x_4	0 x_5	$\bar{b}$	$\bar{b}^*$
2	x_1		1	0	-1	4	-1	1	5
3	x_2		0	1	2	-1	1	2	-2
	$\bar{c}$ Row		0	0	-3	-5	-1	$Z = 8$	$Z^* = 4$

The vectors $\bar{b}$ and $\bar{b}^*$ are computed using the inverse of the basis corresponding to Table 4.14. In other words,

$$\bar{b} = B^{-1}b = \begin{pmatrix} 4 & -1 \\ -1 & 1 \end{pmatrix}\begin{pmatrix} 1 \\ 3 \end{pmatrix} = \begin{pmatrix} 1 \\ 2 \end{pmatrix}$$

$$\bar{b}^* = B^{-1}b^* = \begin{pmatrix} 4 & -1 \\ -1 & 1 \end{pmatrix}\begin{pmatrix} 1 \\ -1 \end{pmatrix} = \begin{pmatrix} 5 \\ -2 \end{pmatrix}$$

For a fixed α, the values of the basic variables in Table 4.14 are given by

$$x_1 = \bar{b}_1 + \alpha\bar{b}_1^* = 1 + 5\alpha$$
$$x_2 = \bar{b}_2 + \alpha\bar{b}_2^* = 2 - 2\alpha$$

But the $\bar{c}_j$ values are not affected as long as the basis consists of the variables x_1 and x_2. As α varies, the values of the basic variables x_1 and x_2 will change, and Table 4.14 stays optimal as long as the basis (x_1, x_2) remains feasible. This implies that

$$x_1 = 1 + 5\alpha \geq 0 \qquad \text{or} \qquad \alpha \geq -1/5$$
$$x_2 = 2 - 2\alpha \geq 0 \qquad \text{or} \qquad \alpha \leq 1$$

In other words, Table 4.14 is optimal as long as α varies between $-1/5$ and 1. Thus for all $-1/5 \leq \alpha \leq 1$, the optimal solution is given by

$$x_1 = 1 + 5\alpha, \quad x_2 = 2 - 2\alpha, \quad x_3 = x_4 = x_5 = 0,$$

and the optimal value of $Z = 8 + 4\alpha$.

As α exceeds 1, the basic variable x_2 becomes negative. Although this makes Table 4.14 infeasible for the primal, it is feasible for the dual since all the $\bar{c}$-row coefficients are nonpositive. We can thus apply the dual simplex method to determine the new optimal solution for $\alpha > 1$. The new tableau is obtained by replacing x_2 with x_4, and is shown in Table 4.15.

Table 4.15

C_B	Basis	c_j	2 x_1	3 x_2	1 x_3	0 x_4	0 x_5	$\bar{b}$	$\bar{b}^*$
2	x_1		1	4	7	0	3	9	-3
0	x_4		0	-1	-2	1	-1	-2	2
	$\bar{c}$ Row		0	-5	-13	0	-6	$Z = 18$	$Z^* = -6$

The basic solution corresponding to Table 4.15 is given by

$$x_1 = 9 - 3\alpha, \quad x_2 = 0, \quad x_3 = 0, \quad x_4 = -2 - 2\alpha, \quad x_5 = 0,$$

and the value of $Z = 18 - 6\alpha$. The above solution is optimal as long as the basic variables x_1 and x_4 are nonnegative. This means that Table 4.15 is optimal for all values of the parameter α between 1 and 3.

For α greater than 3, the basic variable x_1 turns negative. Since there is no negative coefficient in the first row, we conclude that the primal problem is infeasible. Hence there exists no optimal solution for $\alpha > 3$ since the first constraint of Table 4.15 becomes inconsistent.*

To determine the optimal solution for α less than $-1/5$, we can apply the dual simplex method once more to Table 4.14.

4.6 INTEGER PROGRAMMING

This section will be devoted to the study of integer linear programming problems. An *integer linear programming problem*, henceforth called an *integer program*, is a linear programming problem wherein some or all the decision variables are restricted to be integer valued. A *pure integer program* is one where all the variables are restricted to be integers. A *Mixed Integer Program* restricts some of the variables to be integers while others can assume continuous (fractional) values.

The reason for considering integer programs is that many practical problems require integer solutions. In resolving such problems, one could simply solve the linear program while ignoring the integer restrictions, and then either round off or truncate the fractional values of the LP optimal solution to get an integer solution. Of course, while doing this, one has to be careful that the resulting solution stays feasible. Such an approach is frequently used in practice, especially when the values of the variables are very large so that rounding or truncating produces negligible change. But in dealing with problems where the integer variables assume small values, rounding and truncating may produce a solution far from the true optimal integer solution. In addition, for large problems such a procedure can become computationally expensive. For instance, if the optimal LP solution is $x_1 = 2.4$ and $x_2 = 3.5$, then one has to try four combinations of integer values to x_1 and x_2 which are closest to their continuous values, namely, $(2, 3)$, $(2, 4)$, $(3, 3)$, and $(3, 4)$. The one which is feasible and is closest to the LP optimal value of the objective function will be an approximate integer solution. With just ten integer variables, we have to try $2^{10} = 1024$ combinations of integer solutions! Even after examining all such combinations, we cannot guarantee an optimal integer solution to the problem.

APPLICATIONS OF INTEGER PROGRAMMING

We shall illustrate the importance of developing techniques to solve integer programs by showing how a number of real-world problems can be formulated as integer programming problems.

EXAMPLE 4.6-1 (A CAPITAL BUDGETING PROBLEM)

A company is planning its capital spending for the next T periods. There are N projects which compete for the limited capital B_i available for investment in

---

* $\alpha > 3$ corresponds to the situation where the Dependable Company's material availability becomes less than zero, and no feasible production is possible.

period i. Each project requires a certain investment in each period once it is selected. Let a_{ij} be the required investment in project j for period i. The value of the project is measured in terms of the associated cash flows in each period discounted for inflation. This is called the net present value (NPV). Let v_j denoted the NPV for project j. The problem is to select the proper projects for investment which will maximize the total value (NPV) of all the projects selected.

Formulation

To formulate this as an integer program, we introduce a binary variable for each project to denote whether it is selected or not.
Let

$$x_j = 1 \quad \text{if project } j \text{ is selected}$$

$$x_j = 0 \quad \text{if project } j \text{ is not selected}$$

It is then clear that the following pure integer program will represent the capital budgeting problem:

Maximize: $Z = \sum_{j=1}^{N} v_j x_j$

Subject to: $\sum_{j=1}^{N} a_{ij} x_j \leq B_i \quad \text{for } i = 1, \ldots, T$

$$0 \leq x_j \leq 1, \ x_j \text{ a binary variable for all } j = 1, \ldots, N$$

EXAMPLE 4.6-2 (A WAREHOUSE LOCATION PROBLEM)

A retail firm is planning to expand its activities in an area by opening two new warehouses. Three possible sites are under consideration as shown in Fig. 4.2. Four customers have to be supplied whose demands are D_1, D_2, D_3, and D_4.

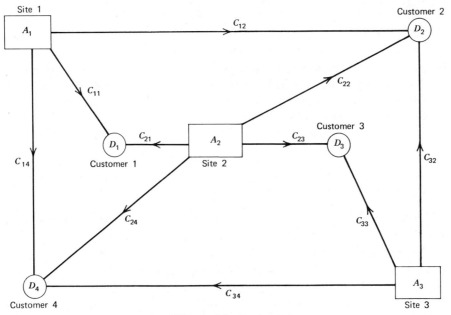

Figure 4.2
A warehouse location problem.

Assume that any two sites can supply all the demands but site 1 can supply customers 1, 2, and 4 only; site 3 can supply customers 2, 3, and 4; while site 2 can supply all the customers. The unit transportation cost from site i to customer j is C_{ij}. For each warehouse site we have the following data:

Site	Capacity	Initial Capital Investment ($)	Unit Operating Cost ($)
1	A_1	K_1	P_1
2	A_2	K_2	P_2
3	A_3	K_3	P_3

The optimization problem is to select the proper sites for the two warehouses which will minimize the total costs of investment, operation, and transportation.

Formulation

Each warehouse site has a fixed capital cost independent of the quantity stored, and a variable cost proportional to the quantity shipped. Thus the total cost of opening and operating a warehouse is a nonlinear function of the quantity stored. Through the use of binary integer variables the warehouse location problem can be formulated as an integer program.

Let the binary integer variable δ_i denote the decision to select or not to select site i. In other words,

$$\delta_i = \begin{cases} 1 & \text{if site } i \text{ is selected} \\ 0 & \text{if otherwise} \end{cases}$$

Let x_{ij} denote the quantity shipped from site i to customer j.

The supply constraint for site 1 is given by:

$$x_{11} + x_{12} + x_{14} \leq A_1 \delta_1 \text{ (site 1)}$$

When $\delta_1 = 1$, Site 1 is selected with capacity A_1 and the quantity shipped from site 1 cannot exceed A_1. When $\delta_1 = 0$, the nonnegative variables x_{11}, x_{12}, and x_{14} will automatically become zero, implying no possible shipment from site 1.

Similarly for sites 2 and 3, we obtain:

$$x_{21} + x_{22} + x_{23} + x_{24} \leq A_2 \delta_2 \text{ (site 2)}$$

$$x_{32} + x_{33} + x_{34} \leq A_3 \delta_3 \text{ (site 3)}$$

In order to select exactly two sites we need the following constraint:

$$\delta_1 + \delta_2 + \delta_3 = 2$$

Since the δ_i's can assume values 0 or 1 only, the new constraint will force two of the δ_i's to be one.

The demand constraints can be written as:

$$x_{11} + x_{21} = D_1 \quad \text{(customer 1)}$$

$$x_{12} + x_{22} + x_{32} = D_2 \quad \text{(customer 2)}$$

$$x_{23} + x_{33} = D_3 \quad \text{(customer 3)}$$

$$x_{14} + x_{24} + x_{34} = D_4 \quad \text{(customer 4)}$$

To write the objective functions, we note that the total cost of investment, operation, and transportation for site 1 is

$$K_1\delta_1 + P_1(x_{11} + x_{12} + x_{14})$$
$$+ C_{11}x_{11} + C_{12}x_{12} + C_{14}x_{14}$$

When site 1 is not selected, δ_1 will be zero. This will force x_{11}, x_{12}, and x_{14} to become zero. Similarly, the cost functions for sites 2 and 3 can be written. Thus the complete formulation of the warehouse location problem reduces to the following mixed integer program:

Minimize:

$$Z = K_1\delta_1 + P_1(x_{11} + x_{12} + x_{14})$$
$$+ C_{11}x_{11} + C_{12}x_{12} + C_{14}x_{14} + K_2\delta_2$$
$$+ P_2(x_{21} + x_{22} + x_{23} + x_{24})$$
$$+ C_{21}x_{21} + C_{22}x_{22} + C_{23}x_{23} + C_{24}x_{24}$$
$$+ K_3\delta_3 + P_3(x_{32} + x_{33} + x_{34})$$
$$+ C_{32}x_{32} + C_{33}x_{33} + C_{34}x_{34}$$

Subject to:

$$x_{11} + x_{12} + x_{14} \leq A_1\delta_1$$
$$x_{21} + x_{22} + x_{23} + x_{24} \leq A_2\delta_2$$
$$x_{32} + x_{33} + x_{34} \leq A_3\delta_3$$
$$\delta_1 + \delta_2 + \delta_3 = 2$$
$$x_{11} + x_{21} = D_1$$
$$x_{12} + x_{22} + x_{32} = D_2$$
$$x_{23} + x_{33} = D_3$$
$$x_{14} + x_{24} + x_{34} = D_4$$
$$0 \leq \delta_i \leq 1 \quad \text{and} \quad \delta_i \text{ integer for } i = 1, 2, 3$$
$$x_{ij} \geq 0 \quad \text{for all } (i, j)$$

EXAMPLE 4.6-3 (A JOB SEQUENCING PROBLEM)

Three products A, B, and C are to be produced using four machines. The technological sequence and the processing time on the machines for the three products are shown below:

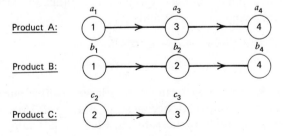

For instance, product A is processed on machine 1 first for a_1 hours, then on machine 3 for a_3 hours, and finally on machine 4 for a_4 hours. Each machine can work on only one product at a time. Moreover, each product requires a different set of tools for machining, which requires each machine to complete the processing of one product before taking up the next one.

In addition, it is required to complete product B in no more than d hours from the starting time. The problem is to determine the sequence in which the various products are processed on the machines so as to complete all the products in the least possible time.

Formulation

Let x_{Aj} denote the time (measured in hours from zero datum) when the processing of product A is started on machine j for $j = 1, 3, 4$. Similarly x_{Bj} for $j = 1, 2, 4$ and x_{Cj} for $j = 2, 3$ are defined.

The first set of constraints enforces the technological sequence in which the machining is to be done for the three products. For product A, the processing on machine 1 is done first, followed by machine 3, and then by machine 4. This means

$$x_{A1} + a_1 \leqq x_{A3} \tag{4.27}$$

and

$$x_{A3} + a_3 \leqq x_{A4} \tag{4.28}$$

Similarly, for products B and C, we need

$$x_{B1} + b_1 \leqq x_{B2} \tag{4.29}$$

$$x_{B2} + b_2 \leqq x_{B4} \tag{4.30}$$

$$x_{C2} + c_2 \leqq x_{C3} \tag{4.31}$$

The next set of pertinent constraints is the noninterference constraints which guarantee that no machine work on more than one product at a time. For instance, machine 1 can work on either product A or product B at any given time. This is equivalent to the statement that either product A precedes product B on machine 1 or vice versa. Thus we have an "either-or" type constraint for noninterference on machine 1 given by

$$x_{A1} + a_1 \leqq x_{B1}$$

or

$$x_{B1} + b_1 \leqq x_{A1}$$

With the help of a binary integer variable, the either-or constraint can be reduced to the following two constraints:

$$x_{A1} + a_1 - x_{B1} \leqq M\delta_1 \tag{4.32}$$

$$x_{B1} + b_1 - x_{A1} \leqq M(1 - \delta_1) \tag{4.33}$$

where $0 \leqq \delta_1 \leqq 1$, δ_1 is an integer, and M is a large positive number. Note that when $\delta_1 = 1$, the first constraint becomes $x_{A1} + a_1 - x_{B1} \leqq M$ and is inactive; while the second constraint reduces to $x_{B1} + b_1 - x_{A1} \leqq 0$ implying product B precedes product A on machine 1. On the other hand, when $\delta_1 = 0$, the first constraint is active implying that product A precedes product B. Thus with the help of the binary integer variable both possibilities are simultaneously included in the problem.

In like fashion, for machines 2, 3, and 4 we obtain:

$$x_{B2} + b_2 - x_{C2} \leq M\delta_2 \tag{4.34}$$

$$x_{C2} + c_2 - x_{B2} \leq M(1 - \delta_2) \tag{4.35}$$

$$x_{A3} + a_3 - x_{C3} \leq M\delta_3 \tag{4.36}$$

$$x_{C3} + c_3 - x_{A3} \leq M(1 - \delta_3) \tag{4.37}$$

$$x_{A4} + a_4 - x_{B4} \leq M\delta_4 \tag{4.38}$$

$$x_{B4} + b_4 - x_{A4} \leq M(1 - \delta_4) \tag{4.39}$$

$0 \leq \delta_2 \leq 1, 0 \leq \delta_3 \leq 1, 0 \leq \delta_4 \leq 1, \delta_2, \delta_3,$ and δ_4 are integers.
The time constraint for product B becomes:

$$x_{B4} + b_4 \leq d \tag{4.40}$$

In order to write the objective function, observe that product A will be completed at time $x_{A4} + a_4$, product B at $x_{B4} + b_4$, and product C at $x_{C3} + c_3$. If y represents the time when all the three products are completed, then the objective is to minimize y where:

$$y = \max(x_{A4} + a_4, x_{B4} + b_4, x_{C3} + c_3).$$

This nonlinear function is equivalent to the following constraints:

$$y \geq x_{A4} + a_4 \tag{4.41}$$

$$y \geq x_{B4} + b_4 \tag{4.42}$$

$$y \geq x_{C3} + c_3 \tag{4.43}$$

Thus the complete formulation of the mixed integer program is to minimize y, subject to the Eqs. (4.27) through (4.43), $0 \leq \delta_i \leq 1$, δ_i integer for $i = 1, 2, 3, 4$, and all other variables just nonnegative.

EXAMPLE 4.6–4 (HANDLING NONLINEAR 0–1 INTEGER PROBLEM)

Consider a nonlinear (binary) integer programming problem:

$$\text{Maximize:} \quad Z = x_1^2 + x_2 x_3 - x_3^3$$

$$\text{Subject to:} \quad -2x_1 + 3x_2 + x_3 \leq 3$$

$$x_1, x_2, x_3 \in (0, 1)$$

The above nonlinear integer problem can be converted to a linear integer programming problem for solution. Observe the fact that for any positive k and a binary variable x_j, $x_j^k = x_j$. Hence the objective function immediately reduces to $Z = x_1 + x_2 x_3 - x_3$. Now consider the product term $x_2 x_3$. For binary values of x_2 and x_3; the product $x_2 x_3$ is always 0 or 1. Now introduce a binary variable y_1 such that $y_1 = x_2 x_3$. When $x_2 = x_3 = 1$, we want the value of y_1 to be 1, while for all other combinations y_1 should be zero. This can be achieved by introducing the following two constraints:

$$x_2 + x_3 - y_1 \leq 1$$

$$-x_2 - x_3 + 2y_1 \leq 0$$

Note that when $x_2 = x_3 = 1$, the above constraints reduce to $y_1 \geq 1$ and $y_1 \leq 1$

implying $y_1 = 1$. When $x_2 = 0$ or $x_3 = 0$ or both are zero, the second constraint, $y_1 \leq \dfrac{x_2 + x_3}{2}$ forces y_1 to be zero.

Thus the equivalent linear (binary) integer program becomes:

$$\text{Maximize:} \quad Z = x_1 + y_1 - x_3$$

$$\text{Subject to:} \quad -2x_1 + 3x_2 + x_3 \leq 3$$

$$x_2 + x_3 - y_1 \leq 1$$

$$-x_2 - x_3 + 2y_1 \leq 0$$

$$x_1, x_2, x_3, y_1 \text{ are } (0, 1) \text{ variables.}$$

A drawback of the above procedure for handling product terms is that an integer variable is introduced for each product term. It has been observed in practice that the solution time for integer programming problems increases with the number of integer variables. An alternate procedure has been recently suggested by Glover and Woolsey (3) which introduces a continuous variable rather than an integer variable. This procedure replaces $x_2 x_3$ by a continuous variable x_{23} and introduces three new constraints as follows:

$$x_2 + x_3 - x_{23} \leq 1$$

$$x_{23} \leq x_2$$

$$x_{23} \leq x_3$$

$$x_{23} \geq 0$$

where x_{23} replaces the product term $x_2 x_3$.

Whenever x_2, x_3, or both are zero, the last two constraints force x_{23} to be zero. When $x_2 = x_3 = 1$, all the three constraints together force x_{23} to be 1. The primary disadvantage of this procedure is that it adds more constraints than the previous method.

REMARKS

The procedures for handling the product of two binary variables can be easily extended to the product of any number of variables. For example, consider the product terms $x_1 x_2 \ldots x_k$. Under the first procedure, a binary variable y_1 will replace $x_1 x_2 \ldots x_k$ and the following two constraints will be added:

$$\sum_{j=1}^{k} x_j - y_1 \leq k - 1$$

$$-\sum_{j=1}^{k} x_j + k y_1 \leq 0$$

$$y_1 \in (0, 1)$$

$$x_j \in (0, 1)$$

Under the second procedure, the product terms $x_1 x_2 \ldots x_k$ will be replaced by a nonnegative variable x_o and the following $(k + 1)$ constraints will be added:

$$\sum_{j=1}^{k} x_j - x_o \leq k - 1$$

$$x_o \leq x_j \quad \text{for all } j = 1, \ldots, k$$

SOLUTION OF INTEGER PROGRAMMING PROBLEMS

The Branch and Bound Algorithm

The Branch and Bound algorithm is the most widely used method for solving both pure and mixed integer programming problems in practice. Most commercial computer codes for solving integer programs are based on this approach. Basically the Branch and Bound Algorithm is just an efficient enumeration procedure for examining all possible integer feasible solutions.

We discussed earlier that a practical approach to solving an integer program is to ignore the integer restrictions initially and solve the problem as a linear program. If the LP optimal solution contains fractional values for some integer variables, then by the use of truncation and rounding-off procedures, one can attempt to get an approximate optimal integer solution. For instance, if there are two integer variables x_1 and x_2 with fractional values 3.5 and 4.4, then one could examine the four possible integer solutions $(3, 4)$, $(4, 4)$, $(4, 5)$, $(3, 5)$ obtained by truncation and rounding methods. We also observe that the true optimal integer solution may not correspond to any of these integer solutions since it is possible for x_1 to have an optimal (integer) value less than 3 or greater than 5. Hence in order to obtain the true optimal integer solution one has to consider all possible integer values of x_1 which are smaller and larger than 3.5. In other words, the optimal integer solution must satisfy

either $$x_1 \leq 3$$

or $$x_1 \geq 4.$$

When a problem contains a large number of integer variables, it is essential to have a systematic method which will look into all possible combinations of integer solutions obtained from the LP optimal solution. The Branch and Bound algorithm essentially does this in the most efficient manner.

Basic Principles

To illustrate the basic principles of the branch and bound method, consider the following mixed integer program (MIP):

EXAMPLE 4.6–5

$$\text{Maximize:} \quad Z = 3x_1 + 2x_2$$
$$\text{Subject to:} \quad x_1 \leq 2$$
$$x_2 \leq 2$$
$$x_1 + x_2 \leq 3.5$$
$$x_1, x_2 \geq 0 \text{ and integer}$$

The initial step is to solve the MIP as a linear program by ignoring the integer restrictions on x_1 and x_2. Call this linear program LP–1. Since we only have two variables, a graphical solution of LP–1 is presented in Fig. 4.3. The LP optimal solution is $x_1 = 2$, $x_2 = 1.5$, and the maximum value of the objective function $Z_o = 9$. Since x_2 takes a fractional value, we do not have an optimal solution for the MIP problem. But observe that the optimal integer solution cannot have an objective function value larger than 9 since the imposition of integer restrictions on x_2 can only make the LP solution worse. (Recall the fact

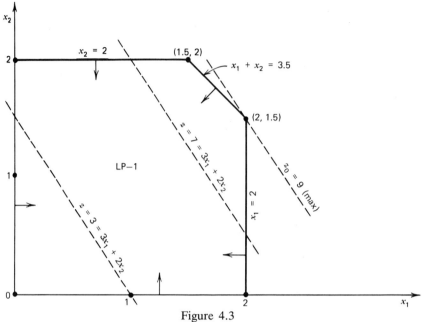

Figure 4.3
Solution to LP-1.

from Section 4.4 that addition of new constraints to a linear program cannot improve the original optimal value of Z.) Thus we have an *upper bound* on the maximum value of Z for the integer program given by the optimal value of LP–1.

The next step of the branch and bound method is to examine other integer values of x_2 which are larger or smaller than 1.5. This is done by adding a new constraint either $x_2 \leq 1$ or $x_2 \geq 2$ to the original linear program (LP–1). This creates two new linear programs (LP–2 and LP–3) as follows:

LP–2	LP–3
Maximize $Z = 3x_1 + 2x_2$	Maximize $Z = 3x_1 + 2x_2$
Subject to $x_1 \leq 2$	Subject to $x_1 \leq 2$
$x_2 \leq 2$	$x_2 \leq 2$
$x_1 + x_2 \leq 3.5$	$x_1 + x_2 \leq 3.5$
(new constraint) $x_2 \leq 1$	(new constraint) $x_2 \geq 2$
$x_1, x_2 \geq 0$	$x_1, x_2 \geq 0$

The feasible regions corresponding to LP–2 and LP–3 are shown graphically in Figs. 4.4 and 4.5, respectively (note that the feasible region for LP–3 is just the straight line AB). Observe also that the feasible regions of LP–2 and LP–3 satisfy the following:

1. The optimal solution to LP–1 ($x_1 = 2$, $x_2 = 1.5$) is infeasible to both LP–2 and LP–3. Thus the old fractional optimal solution will not be repeated.
2. Every integer (feasible) solution to the original problem (MIP) is contained in either LP–2 or LP–3. Thus none of the feasible (integer) solutions to MIP is lost due to the creation of two new linear programs.

The optimal solution to LP–2 (Fig. 4.4) is $x_1 = 2$, $x_2 = 1$, and $Z_o = 8$. Thus we have a feasible (integer) solution to the MIP problem. Even though LP–2

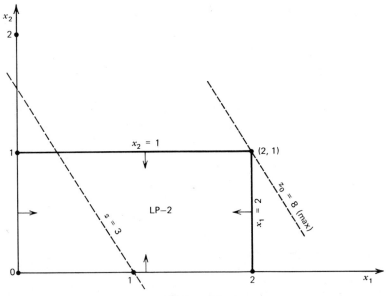

Figure 4.4
Solution to LP-2.

may contain other integer solutions, their values of the objective function cannot be larger than 8. Hence $Z_o = 8$ is a lower bound on the maximum value of Z for the mixed integer program. In other words, the optimal value of Z for the mixed integer problem cannot be lower than 8. Since we had computed earlier the upper bound as 9, we cannot call the LP–2 solution as the optimal integer solution without examining LP–3.

The optimal solution to LP–3 (Fig. 4.5) is $x_1 = 1.5$, $x_2 = 2$ and $Z_o = 8.5$. This is not feasible for the mixed integer program since x_1 is taking a fractional value. But the maximum Z value (8.5) is larger than the lower bound (8).

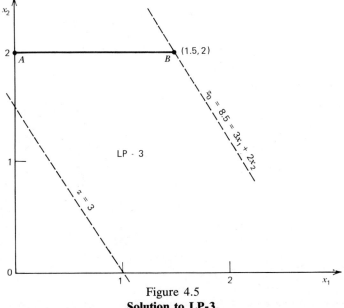

Figure 4.5
Solution to LP-3.

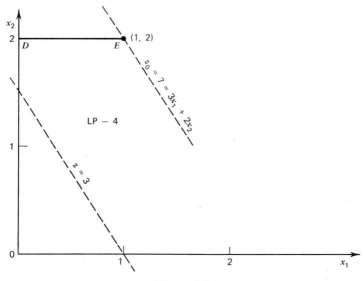

Figure 4.6
Solution to LP-4.

Hence it is necessary to examine whether there exists an integer solution in the feasible region of LP–3 whose value of Z is larger than 8. To determine this we add the constraint either $x_1 \leq 1$ or $x_1 \geq 2$ to LP–3. This gives two new linear programs LP–4 and LP–5. The feasible region for LP–4 is the straight line DE shown in Figure 4.6, while LP–5 becomes infeasible.

The optimal solution to LP–4 (Figure 4.6) is given by $x_1 = 1$, $x_2 = 2$, and $Z_o = 7$. This implies that every integer solution in the feasible region of LP–3 cannot have an objective function value better than 7. Hence the integer solution obtained while solving LP–2, namely $x_1 = 2$, $x_2 = 1$ and $Z_o = 8$, is the optimal integer solution to the mixed integer problem.

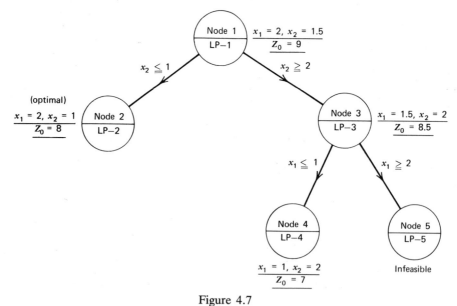

Figure 4.7
A network representation of the Branch and Bound method for Example 4.6-5.

The sequence of linear programming problems solved under the branch and bound procedure for Example 4.6–5 may be represented in the form of a *network* or *tree* diagram as shown in Figure 4.7. Node 1 represents the equivalent linear programming problem (LP–1) of the mixed integer program ignoring the integer restrictions. From node 1 we *branch* to node 2 (LP–2) with the help of the integer variable x_2 by adding the constraint $x_2 \leq 1$ to LP–1. Since we have an integer optimal solution for node 2 no further branching from node 2 is necessary. Once this type of decision can be made, we say that node 2 has been *fathomed*. Branching on $x_2 \geq 2$ from node 1 results in LP–3 (node 3). Since the optimal solution to LP–3 is fractional, we branch further from node 3 using the integer variable x_1. This results in the creation of nodes 4 and 5. Both have been fathomed since LP–4 has an integer solution while LP–5 is infeasible. The best integer solution obtained at a fathomed node (in this case, node 2) becomes the optimal solution to the mixed integer program.

Details of the Algorithm

Consider a mixed integer programming problem (MIP) of the following form:

$$\text{Maximize: } Z = \mathbf{cx}$$

$$\text{Subject to: } \mathbf{Ax} = \mathbf{b}$$

$$\mathbf{x} \geq \mathbf{0}$$

$$x_j \text{ is an integer for } j \in \mathbf{I}$$

where $\mathbf{I}$ is the set of all integer variables.

The first step is to solve the MIP problem as a linear program by ignoring the integer restrictions. Let us denote the linear program as LP–1 whose optimal value of the objective function is Z_1. Assume the optimal solution to LP–1 contains some integer variables at fractional values. Hence we do not have an optimal solution to the MIP problem. But Z_1 is an upper bound on the maximum value of Z for the MIP problem.

The next step is to partition the feasible region of LP–1 by branching on one of the integer variables at fractional value. A number of rules have been proposed to select the proper branching variable. They include:

1. Selecting the integer variable with the largest fractional value in the LP solution.
2. Assigning priorities to the integer variables such that we branch on the most important variable first. The importance of an integer variable may be based on one or more of the following criteria:
   a. It represents an important decision in the model.
   b. Its cost or profit coefficient in the objective function is very large compared to the others.
   c. Its value is very critical to the model based on the experience of the user.
3. Arbitrary selection rules; for instance, selecting the variable with the lowest index first.

Suppose that the integer variable x_j is selected for further branching and its fractional value is β_j in the LP–1 solution. Now we create two new linear programming problems LP–2 and LP–3 by introducing the constraints $x_j \leq \lfloor \beta_j \rfloor$ and $x_j \geq \lceil \beta_j \rceil$ respectively, where $\lfloor \beta_j \rfloor$ is the largest integer less than β_j, while $\lceil \beta_j \rceil$ is the smallest integer greater than β_j (see Fig. 4.8). In other words,

LP–2	LP–3
Maximize $Z = \mathbf{cx}$	Maximize $Z = \mathbf{cx}$
Subject to $\mathbf{Ax} = \mathbf{b}$	Subject to $\mathbf{Ax} = \mathbf{b}$
$x_j \leq \lfloor \beta_j \rfloor$	$x_j \geq \lceil \beta_j \rceil$
$\mathbf{x} \geq \mathbf{0}$	$\mathbf{x} \geq \mathbf{0}$

Since only one new constraint has been added, we can use the dual simplex method (discussed in Section 4.3) to find the new optimal solution to LP–2 and LP–3. Assume that the optimal solutions to LP–2 and LP–3 are still fractional, and hence infeasible to the MIP problem with integer restrictions.

The next step is to select either LP–2 or LP–3 and branch from that by adding a new constraint. Here again a number of rules have been proposed for selecting the proper node (LP problem) from which to branch. They include:

1. *Using the optimal value of the objective function.* Considering each of the nodes which can be selected for further branching, we choose the one whose LP optimal value is the largest (for a maximization problem). The rationale for this rule is that the LP feasible region with the largest Z value may contain better integer solutions. For instance any integer solution obtained by branching from LP–2 cannot have a Z value better than the optimal value of Z for LP–2.
2. *Last-in-First-Out Rule.* The LP problem which was solved most recently is selected (arbitrarily) for further branching.

Once the proper node (LP region) is selected for further branching, we branch out by choosing an integer variable with a fractional value. This process of branching and solving a sequence of linear programs is continued until an integer solution is obtained for one of the linear programs. The value of Z for this integer solution becomes a *lower bound* on the maximum value of Z for the MIP problem. At this point we can eliminate from consideration all those nodes (LP regions) whose values of Z are not better than the lower bound. We say that these nodes have been *fathomed* because it is not possible to find a better integer solution from these LP regions than what we have now.

As an illustration, consider the tree diagram given in Fig. 4.8. With the solution of LP–4 we have a lower bound on the maximum value of Z for the MIP problem given by Z_4. In other words, the optimal solution to the MIP problem cannot have a Z value smaller than Z_4. Further branching from node 4 is not necessary since any subsequent LP solution can only have a Z value less than Z_4. In other words, node 4 has been *fathomed*. Node 5 has also been fathomed since the additional constraints render the LP problem infeasible. This only leaves nodes 6 and 7 for possible branching. Suppose $Z_6 < Z_4$ and $Z_7 > Z_4$. This means node 6 has also been fathomed (implicitly), since none of the integer solutions under node 6 can produce a better value than Z_4. However, it is possible for the LP region of node 7 to contain an integer solution better than that of node 4 since $Z_7 > Z_4$. Hence we select node 7 for further branching and continue. In this manner, an intermediate node (LP problem) is explicitly or implicitly fathomed whenever it satisfies one of the following conditions:

1. The LP optimal solution of that node is integer valued; that is, it is feasible for the MIP problem.
2. The LP problem is infeasible

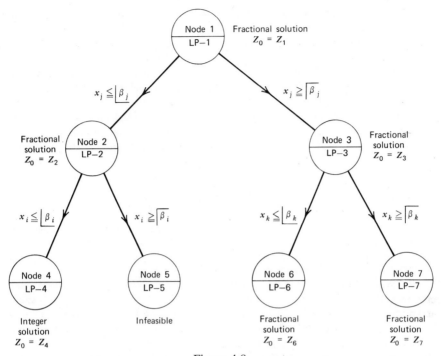

Figure 4.8
Branch and Bound algorithm.

3. The optimal value of Z for the LP problem is not better than the current lower bound.

   The branch and bound algorithm continues to select a node for further branching until all the nodes have been fathomed. The fathomed node with the largest value of Z gives the optimal solution to the mixed integer program. Hence, the efficiency of the branch and bound algorithm depends on how soon the successive nodes are fathomed. The Fathoming Conditions 1 and 2 generally take considerable time to reach. Condition 3 cannot be used until a lower bound for the MIP problem is found. However, a lower bound is not available until a feasible (integer) solution to the MIP problem is obtained (Condition 1)! Thus it is always helpful if a feasible integer solution to MIP problem can be found before the start of the branch and bound procedure. This will provide the initial lower bound to the MIP problem until a better lower bound is found by the branch and bound algorithm. In many practical problems, the present way of operating the system may provide an initial solution.

Guidelines on Problem Formulation

The solution time for solving the integer programming problem is very sensitive to the way the problem is formulated initially. From practical experience in solving a number of integer programs by the branch and bound method, the IBM research staff have come up with some suggestions on model formulations. We describe them briefly in the following points. For more information, see the IBM Reference Manual (5). The following guidelines should not be considered as restrictions but rather as suggestions which have often reduced computational time in practice.

1. Keep the number of integer variables as small as possible. One way to do this is to treat all integer variables whose values will be at least 20 as continuous variables.
2. Provide a good (tight) lower and upper bound on the integer variables when possible.
3. Unlike the general linear programming problem, the addition of new constraints to an MIP problem will generally reduce the computational time, especially when the new constraints contain integer variables.
4. If there is no critical need for obtaining an exact optimal integer solution, then considerable savings in computational time may be obtained by accepting the first integer solution which is within 3% of the continuous optimum. In other words, for a maximization problem we can terminate the branch and bound procedure whenever

$$\frac{\text{upper bound} - \text{lower bound}}{\text{upper bound}} < 3\%$$

5. The order in which the integer variables are chosen for branching affects the solution time. It is recommended that the integer variables be processed in a priority order based on their economic significance and user experience.

Recommended Readings

For an excellent discussion of duality theory and its applications to bi-matrix games, refer to Gale (2) and Murty (7). Dantzig (1) discusses a modification of the simplex method to solve linear programs with lower and upper bounds on variables. A complete discussion on the decomposition principle to solve very large linear programming problems is available in Dantzig (1) and Murty (7). Many variants of the simplex method including the primal-dual algorithm and the self-dual parametric algorithm are discussed in Hadley (4). Solution of nonlinear programming problems is discussed in Chapter 11.

For an excellent discussion of integer programming problems at an applied level, refer to McMillan (6) and Plane and McMillan (8). These also contain many practical applications of integer programming to real-world problems and some case studies.

REFERENCES

1. Dantzig, George B., *Linear Programming and Extensions*, Princeton University Press, Princeton, New Jersey, 1963.
2. Gale, David, *The Theory of Linear Economic Models*, McGraw-Hill, New York, 1960.
3. Glover, Fred, and E. Woolsey, "Converting 0–1 Polynomial Programming Problem to a 0–1 Linear Program," *Operations Research*, 22, 180–182 (1974).
4. Hadley, G., *Linear Programming*, Addison-Wesley, Reading, Massachusetts, 1962.
5. *IBM General Information Manual*, "An Introduction to Modeling Using Mixed Integer Programming," Amsterdam, 1972.
6. McMillan, Claude, *Mathematical Programming*, Wiley, New York, 1970.
7. Murty, Katta G., *Linear and Combinatorial Programming*, Wiley, New York, 1976.
8. Plane, Donald R. and Claude McMillan, Jr., *Discrete Optimization*, Prentice-Hall, New Jersey, 1971.

EXERCISES

1. The following linear program is fed to a computer for solution:

$$\text{Maximize: } Z = 3x_1 + 2x_2$$

$$\text{Subject to: } \quad -x_1 + 2x_2 + x_3 \qquad = 4$$

$$3x_1 + 2x_2 \qquad + x_4 = 14$$

$$x_1 - x_2 \qquad + x_5 = 3$$

$$x_1, \dots, x_5 \geq 0$$

Using the revised simplex method, the computer has the following information corresponding to a basis $\mathbf{B}$ at some stage:

$$\mathbf{x_B} = (x_3, x_4, x_1) \quad \text{and} \quad \mathbf{B}^{-1} = \begin{bmatrix} 1 & 0 & 1 \\ 0 & 1 & -3 \\ 0 & 0 & 1 \end{bmatrix}$$

a. Compute the current basic feasible solution and the simplex multipliers corresponding to the basis $\mathbf{B}$.
b. Show that the present solution is not optimal. Which variable should now be introduced into the basis?
c. Having chosen a variable to enter the basis, now select a variable to leave the basis and describe the selection rule. Is it possible that no variable meets the criterion of your rule? If this happens in some problem, what does that indicate about the original problem?
d. Using (c), find the new inverse of the basis and the new simplex multipliers.
e. Write down the new basic feasible solution. Is it optimal? Why or why not?

2. Solve the following linear program by the revised simplex method:

$$\begin{aligned} \text{Minimize:} \quad & Z = 40x_1 + 36x_2 \\ \text{Subject to:} \quad & x_1 \qquad\qquad \leq 8 \\ & \qquad\quad x_2 \leq 10 \\ & 5x_1 + 3x_2 \geq 45 \\ & x_1 \geq 0, x_2 \geq 0 \end{aligned}$$

3. Consider the following linear programming problem:

$$\begin{aligned} \text{Maximize:} \quad & Z = x_1 + 2x_2 + 3x_3 + 4x_4 \\ \text{Subject to:} \quad & x_1 + 2x_2 + 2x_3 + 3x_4 \leq 20 \\ & 2x_1 + x_2 + 3x_3 + 2x_4 \leq 20 \\ & x_1, x_2, x_3, x_4 \geq 0 \end{aligned}$$

Using the principles of the revised simplex method, prove that an optimal solution exists with x_3 and x_4 as basic variables.

4. Consider the following linear program which we call the primal problem:

$$\begin{aligned} \text{Maximize:} \quad & Z = 3x_1 + 2x_2 \\ \text{Subject to} \quad & -x_1 + 2x_2 \leq 4 \\ & 3x_1 + 2x_2 \leq 14 \\ & x_1 - x_2 \leq 3 \\ & x_1, \quad x_2 \geq 0 \end{aligned}$$

a. Write down the dual problem.
b. Prove using the Duality Theory that there exists an optimal solution to both the primal and dual problems.
c. Compute an upper and a lower bound on the optimal values of both the problems using the Weak Duality Theorem.

5. Prove using the Duality Theory that the following linear program is feasible but has no optimal solution:

$$\begin{aligned} \text{Minimize:} \quad & Z = x_1 - x_2 + x_3 \\ \text{Subject to:} \quad & x_1 \qquad - x_3 \geq 4 \\ & x_1 - x_2 + 2x_3 \geq 3 \\ & x_1, x_2, x_3 \geq 0 \end{aligned}$$

6. Consider the linear program given in Exercise 3.
   a. Write the dual of this problem.
   b. Using the optimal solution found in Exercise 3, compute an optimal solution to the dual by the Complementary Slackness Theorem.

7. For the standard linear program

$$\text{Minimize:} \quad Z = \mathbf{cx}$$
$$\text{Subject to:} \quad \mathbf{Ax} = \mathbf{b}$$
$$\mathbf{x} \geq \mathbf{0}$$

prove the appropriate Weak Duality Theorem, Optimality Criterion Theorem, and Complementary Slackness Theorem.

8. Consider the following primal linear program:

$$\text{Maximize:} \quad Z = x_1 + 2x_2 + x_3$$
$$\text{Subject to:} \quad x_1 + x_2 - x_3 \leq 2$$
$$x_1 - x_2 + x_3 = 1$$
$$2x_1 + x_2 + x_3 \geq 2$$
$$x_1 \geq 0, x_2 \leq 0, x_3 \text{ unrestricted in sign.}$$

   a. Write the dual of the above problem.
   b. Prove using the Duality Theory that the maximum value of Z for the primal problem cannot exceed 1.

9. Consider the bounded variable linear program:

$$\text{Maximize:} \quad Z = x_1 - x_2 + x_3 - x_4$$
$$\text{Subject to:} \quad x_1 + x_2 + x_3 + x_4 = 8$$
$$0 \leq x_1 \leq 8$$
$$-4 \leq x_2 \leq 4$$
$$-2 \leq x_3 \leq 4$$
$$0 \leq x_4 \leq 10$$

   a. Write the dual of the above problem.
   b. Show that $x_1 = 8$, $x_2 = -4$, $x_3 = 4$, and $x_4 = 0$ is an optimal solution by using the Complementary Slackness Theorem.

10. It is given that the following standard linear program has an optimal solution:

$$\text{Minimize:} \quad Z = \mathbf{cx}$$
$$\text{Subject to:} \quad \mathbf{Ax} = \mathbf{b}, \mathbf{x} \geq \mathbf{0}.$$

Suppose the requirement vector $\mathbf{b}$ is changed to another vector $\mathbf{d}$; that is, we now have a modified problem:

$$\text{Minimize:} \quad Z = \mathbf{cx}$$
$$\text{Subject to:} \quad \mathbf{Ax} = \mathbf{d}$$
$$\mathbf{x} \geq \mathbf{0}$$

Prove that if the modified problem is feasible, then it will always have an optimal solution.

11. Recall the formulation of a standard transportation problem with m warehouses

and n markets (Chapter 3):

$$\text{Minimize:} \quad Z = \sum_i \sum_j c_{ij} x_{ij}$$

$$\text{Subject to:} \quad \sum_j x_{ij} = a_i \qquad \text{for } i = 1, 2, \ldots, m,$$

$$\sum_i x_{ij} = b_j \qquad \text{for } j = 1, 2, \ldots, n,$$

where x_{ij} is the amount shipped from i to j, c_{ij} is the unit cost of shipping, and a_i and b_j are the supply and demand at warehouse i and market j, respectively.

a. Write the dual of the transportation problem.

b. Write the complementary slackness conditions to be satisfied at optimality. Compare these with the u-v method for solving the transportation problem.

12. Given the cost matrix of a transportation problem with three warehouses and four markets as:

	M_1	M_2	M_3	M_4
W_1	2	2	2	1
W_2	10	8	5	4
W_3	7	6	6	8

The supplies and demands are $a_1 = 3$, $a_2 = 7$, $a_3 = 5$, $b_1 = 4$, $b_2 = 3$, $b_3 = 4$, $b_4 = 4$. Prove, using the Complementary Slackness Theorem, that the optimal shipping schedule is to send 3 units from W_1 to M_1, 3 units from W_2 to M_3, 4 units from W_2 to M_4, 1 unit from W_3 to M_1, 3 units from W_3 to M_2, and 1 unit from W_3 to M_3.

13. Use the dual simplex method to show that the following linear program is infeasible:

$$\text{Maximize: } Z = -4x_1 - 3x_2$$

$$\text{Subject to:} \qquad x_1 + x_2 \leq 1$$

$$- x_2 \leq -1$$

$$-x_1 + 2x_2 \leq 1$$

$$x_1, x_2 \geq 0$$

14. Solve by the dual simplex method

$$\text{Minimize: } Z = x_1 + 2x_2 + 3x_3 + 4x_4$$

$$\text{Subject to:} \qquad x_1 + 2x_2 + 2x_3 + 3x_4 \geq 30$$

$$2x_1 + x_2 + 3x_3 + 2x_4 \geq 20$$

$$x_1, x_2, x_3, x_4 \geq 0$$

15. A factory manufactures three products. Three resources—technical services, labor, and administration—are required to produce these products. The following table gives the requirements on each of the resources for the three products:

Product	Resources (hours)			Unit Profit ($)
	Technical Service	Labor	Administration	
1	1	10	2	10
2	1	4	2	6
3	1	5	6	4

There are 100 hours of technical services available, 600 hours of labor, and 300 hours of administration. In order to determine the optimal product mix which will maximize the total profit, the following linear program was solved:

$$\text{Maximize: } Z = 10x_1 + 6x_2 + 4x_3$$

$$
\begin{aligned}
\text{Subject to:} \quad & x_1 + x_2 + x_3 \leq 100 \quad \text{(technical)} \\
& 10x_1 + 4x_2 + 5x_3 \leq 600 \quad \text{(labor)} \\
& 2x_1 + 2x_2 + 6x_3 \leq 300 \quad \text{(administration)} \\
& x_1, x_2, x_3 \geq 0
\end{aligned}
$$

where x_1, x_2, and x_3 are the number of product 1, product 2, and product 3 produced. The optimal solution is given by the following tableau, where x_4, x_5, and x_6 are the slack variables:

c_j Basis	10 x_1	6 x_2	4 x_3	0 x_4	0 x_5	0 x_6	Constants
x_2	0	1	5/6	10/6	−1/6	0	400/6
x_1	1	0	1/6	−4/6	1/6	0	200/6
x_6	0	0	4	−2	0	1	100
$\bar{c}$ Row	0	0	−16/6	−20/6	−4/6	0	$Z = 4400/6$

Using sensitivity analysis, answer the following with respect to the above optimal tableau:

a. What should be the profit of product 3 before it becomes worthwhile to manufacture? Find the most profitable product mix if the profit on product 3 were increased to $50/6.

b. What is the range on the profit of product 1 so that the current solution is still optimal?

c. It is believed that the estimates of the available hours of technical services might be wrong. The correct estimate is $100 + 10\lambda$ where λ is some unknown parameter. Find the range of values of λ within which the given product mix is still optimal.

d. Determine the shadow prices of all the resources.

e. The manufacturing department comes up with a proposal to produce a new product requiring 1 hour of technical service, 4 hours of labor, and 3 hours of administration. The marketing and sales department predicts that the product can be sold at a unit profit of $8. What should be the management's decision?

f. Suppose the company decides to produce at least 10 units of product 3; determine the optimal product mix.

16. A company which manufactures three products A, B, and C, requiring two raw materials—labor and material—wants to determine the optimal production schedule that maximizes the total profit. The following linear program was formulated to answer this:

$$\text{Maximize } Z = 3x_1 + x_2 + 5x_3$$

$$
\begin{aligned}
\text{Subject to} \quad & 6x_1 + 3x_2 + 5x_3 \leq 45 \quad \text{(labor)} \\
& 3x_1 + 4x_2 + 5x_3 \leq 30 \quad \text{(material)} \\
& x_1, x_2, x_3 \geq 0
\end{aligned}
$$

where x_1, x_2, x_3 are the amount of products A, B, and C. The computer prints out the following optimal tableau (x_4 and x_5 are the slacks):

c_j	$3	1	5	0	0	
Basis	x_1	x_2	x_3	x_4	x_5	Constants
x_1	1	-1/3	0	1/3	-1/3	5
x_3	0	1	1	-1/5	2/5	3
$\bar{c}$ Row	0	-3	0	0	-1	Z = 30

Answer the following with respect to the above optimal tableau:

a. Find the range on the unit profit of Product A. Find the optimal solution for $c_1 = 2$.
b. Suppose an additional 15 units of material may be obtained at a cost of \$10. Is it profitable to do so?
c. Find the optimal solution when the available material is increased to 60 units.
d. Due to a "technological breakthrough" the material requirements of product B is reduced to 2 units. Does this affect your optimal solution? Why or why not?
e. Suppose a "supervision" constraint, $2x_1 + x_2 + 3x_3 \leq 20$ is added to the original problem. How does this affect the optimal primal and dual solutions? Explain fully.

17. The following tableau gives an optimal solution to a standard linear program:

$$\text{Maximize} \quad Z = cx, \text{ Subject to } Ax = b, x \geq 0$$

c_j	2	3	1	0	0	
Basis	x_1	x_2	x_3	x_4	x_5	**b**
x_1	1	0	1	3	-1	1
x_2	0	1	1	-1	2	2
$\bar{c}$ Row	0	0	-4	-3	-4	Z = 8

Assume (x_4, x_5) was the initial identity matrix.

a. How much can c_3 be increased before the current basis is no longer optimal? Find an optimal solution when $c_3 = 6$.
b. How much can c_1 be varied so that the given basis (x_1, x_2) is still optimal?
c. Find the largest and smallest value of λ for which the given solution is still optimum if c is replaced by $c + \lambda c^*$ where $c^* = (0, 0, 1, -1, 2)$ and $-\infty \leq \lambda \leq \infty$.
d. How much can b_2 (the original value) be varied before the given basis (x_1, x_2) is no longer feasible? (Note: It is *not* necessary to compute the original value of b_2 to answer this.)
e. Find an optimal solution by the dual simplex method when b_2 is *increased by 2* units.

18. The following tableau gives an *optimal* solution to a standard linear program:

$$\text{Maximize} \quad Z = cx, \text{ Subject to } Ax = b, x \geq 0$$

c_j	2	3	1	0	0	
Basis	x_1	x_2	x_3	x_4	x_5	**b**
x_1	1	0	-1	3	-1	1
x_2	0	1	2	-1	1	2
$\bar{c}$ Row	0	0	-3	-3	-1	Z = 8

a. How much can c_2 be varied without affecting the optimal solution? Find the optimum solution when $c_2 = 1$.

b. Find the range on λ for which the given basis (x_1, x_2) is still optimal if the original **b** vector is replaced by $\mathbf{b} + \lambda \mathbf{b}^*$ where $\mathbf{b}^* = \begin{bmatrix} 1 \\ -1 \end{bmatrix}$ and $-\infty < \lambda < \infty$.

Also, find the optimal solution when $\lambda = 1/2$. (Assume that (x_4, x_5) formed the initial basis.)

c. Find the optimal solution when a new constraint

$$x_1 + x_3 \geq 2$$

is added to the *original* problem.

d. Compute the shadow prices of the constraints of the original problem.

19. A firm has four possible sites for locating its warehouses. The cost of locating a warehouse at site i is $\$K_i$. There are nine retail outlets, each of which must be supplied by at least one warehouse. It is not possible for any one site to supply all the retail outlets as shown in the following figure:

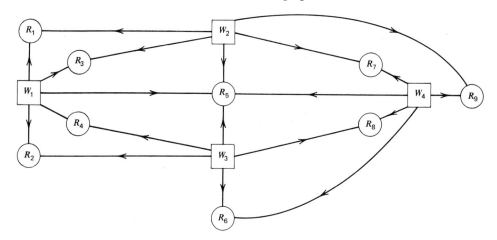

The problem is to determine the location of the warehouses such that the total cost is minimized. Formulate this as an integer program.

20. A company manufactures three products A, B, and C. Each unit of product A requires 1 hour of engineering service, 10 hours of direct labor, and 3 pounds of material. To produce one unit of product B, requires 2 hours of engineering, 4 hours of direct labor, and 2 pounds of material. Each unit of product C requires 1 hour of engineering, 5 hours of direct labor, and 1 pound of material. There are 100 hours of engineering, 700 hours of labor, and 400 pounds of materials available. The cost of production is a nonlinear function of the quantity produced as shown below:

Product A		Product B		Product C	
Production (units)	Unit Cost ($)	Production (units)	Unit Cost ($)	Production (units)	Unit Cost ($)
0–40	10	0–50	6	0–100	5
40–100	9	50–100	4	over 100	4
100–150	8	over 100	3		
over 150	7				

Formulate a mixed integer program to determine the minimum-cost production schedule.

21. An electronic system consists of three components, each of which must function in order for the system to function. The reliability of the system (probability of successful performance of the system) can be improved by installing several stand-by units for one or more of the components. The reliability of the system is given by the product of the reliability of each component, while the reliability of each component is a function of the number of stand-by units as given below:

Number of Stand-by Units	Reliability of Component		
	1	2	3
0	0.5	0.6	0.7
1	0.6	0.75	0.9
2	0.7	0.95	1.0
3	0.8	1.0	1.0
4	0.9	1.0	1.0
5	1.0	1.0	1.0

For instance, if no stand-by unit is provided, the reliability of component 2 is 0.6; with 2 stand-by units, its reliability increases to 0.95. The cost and weight of each stand-by unit for the three components are as follows:

Component	Unit Cost ($)	Weight/Unit (kilograms)
1	20	2
2	30	4
3	40	6

We have a budget restriction of $150 and a weight restriction of 20 kg for all the stand-by units. The problem is to determine how many stand-by units should be installed for each of the three components so as to maximize the total reliability of the system. Formulate this as a *linear* integer program.

22. Explain how the following conditions can be represented as linear constraints by the use of binary (0–1) integer variables:
   a. Either $x_1 + x_2 \leq 2$ or $2x_1 + 3x_2 \geq 8$
   b. Variable x_3 can assume values 0, 5, 9, and 12 only.
   c. If $x_4 \leq 4$, then $x_5 \geq 6$. Otherwise $x_5 \leq 3$.
   d. At least two out of the following four constraints must be satisfied:

$$x_6 + x_7 \leq 2$$

$$x_6 \leq 1$$

$$x_7 \leq 5$$

$$x_6 + x_7 \geq 3$$

23. Convert the following nonlinear integer program to a linear integer program:

$$\text{Minimize:} \quad Z = x_1^2 - x_1 x_2 + x_2$$
$$\text{Subject to:} \quad x_1^2 + x_1 x_2 \le 8$$
$$x_1 \le 2$$
$$x_2 \le 7$$
$$x_1, x_2 \ge 0 \text{ and integer}$$

(*Hint: Replace x_1 by $2^0\delta_1 + 2^1\delta_2$, and x_2 by $2^0\delta_3 + 2^1\delta_4 + 2^2\delta_5$, where $\delta_i \in (0, 1)$ for $i = 1, 2, \ldots, 5$*).

24. Solve the following pure integer program by the branch and bound algorithm:

$$\text{Maximize:} \quad Z = 21x_1 + 11x_2$$
$$\text{Subject to:} \quad 7x_1 + 4x_2 + x_3 = 13$$
$$x_1, x_2, x_3, \text{ nonnegative integers}$$

25. Solve the following mixed integer program by the branch and bound algorithm:

$$\text{Minimize:} \quad Z = 10x_1 + 9x_2$$
$$\text{Subject to:} \quad x_1 \le 8$$
$$x_2 \le 10$$
$$5x_1 + 3x_2 \ge 45$$
$$x_1 \ge 0, x_2 \ge 0$$
$$x_2 - \text{integer}$$

CHAPTER 5
PROBABILITY REVIEW

5.1 INTRODUCTION

Although it is likely that the student using this book will have had some previous exposure to probability theory, this chapter has been included to serve as a concise, convenient "refresher" summary of those probability concepts which are important in subsequent chapters. The student who is confident of his abilities in this area may elect to skim, or skip altogether, the entire chapter. On the other hand, the student who has had no previous exposure to the subject would be well advised to consult one of the introductory books listed at the end of the chapter.

I. BASIC DEFINITIONS

5.2 EXPERIMENTS, SAMPLE SPACES, AND EVENTS

An *experiment* is some well-understood procedure or process whose outcome can be observed but is not known with certainty in advance. The set of all possible outcomes is called the *sample space*. Whenever the sample space consists of a countable number of outcomes, it is said to be *discrete*; otherwise, it is *continuous*. An *event* is any subset of the sample space. When the result of the experiment becomes known, we would say that a specified event had *occurred* if the observed outcome is contained in the subset which is the event.

Of course, events are really no more than what you would ordinarily consider them to be. Often the most natural way to specify them is to describe them in words. However, the reason for defining them formally as sets is to establish a mathematical way to combine and manipulate them. The set theoretic union of two events produces another event. If $C = A \cup B$, we would say in words that event C had occurred if event A *or* event B occurred. Similarly, the intersection of two events corresponds to the word "and." The complement of any event is another event; we would say that $\bar{A}$ had occurred if A had not occurred. Two events are mutually exclusive if their intersection is the empty set, which can be thought of as the impossible event. In other words, two events are mutually exclusive if they could not both occur.

5.3 PROBABILITY

When the "probability of an event" is spoken of in everyday language, almost everyone has an idea of what is meant. It is fortunate that this is so, because it would be quite difficult to introduce the concept to someone who had never considered it before. There are at least three distinct ways to approach the subject, none of which is wholly satisfying.

The first to appear, historically, was the frequency concept. If an experiment were to be repeated many times, then the number of times that the event was observed to occur, divided by the number of times that the experiment was conducted, would approach a number which was defined to be the probability of the event. This definition proved to be somewhat limiting, however, because circumstances frequently prohibit the repetition of an experiment under precisely the same conditions, even conceptually.

To extend the notion of probability to a wider class of applications, the idea of "subjective" probabilities emerged. According to this idea, the probability of an event need not relate to the frequency with which it would occur in an infinite number of trials; it is just a measure of the degree of likelihood we believe the event to possess. Thus different people could attach different probabilities to the same event.

Most modern texts use a purely axiomatic definition. According to this notion, probabilities are just elements of an abstract mathematical system obeying certain axioms. This notion is at once the most powerful and the most devoid of real-world meaning. Of course the axioms are not purely arbitrary; they were selected to be consistent with the earlier concepts of probabilities and to provide them with all of the properties everyone would agree they should have.

A probability measure is a function, P ( ), mapping events onto real numbers, and satisfying

1. $0 \leq P(A) \leq 1$, for any event A.
2. $P(S) = 1$, where S is the whole sample space, or the "certain" event.
3. if A_1, A_2, $A_3 \cdots$ are a set of pairwise mutually exclusive events (finite or infinite in number), then $P(A_1 \cup A_2 \cup A_3 \cdots) = P(A_1) + P(A_2) + \cdots$.

Although probabilities have a number of other properties well worth mentioning, these three axioms are sufficient to derive the others.

It should be obvious that these three axioms are not enough to determine the probability of any event. For all but trivial sample spaces, there will exist an infinity of ways to assign probabilities to events while satisfying the three axioms. At this point, we are merely establishing properties or rules required of any way that might be chosen.

Some of the additional "basic laws" of probability (which can be proved from the above axioms) are:

4. $P(\phi) = 0$, where ϕ is the empty set, or the impossible event.
5. $P(\bar{A}) = 1 - P(A)$.
6. $P(A \cup B) = P(A) + P(B) - P(A \cap B)$, for any two events, A and B.

Another "basic law" is, in reality, a definition of the *conditional probability* of an event, A, given that another event, B, has occurred. The notation for this conditional probability is $P(A|B)$, and the defining formula is

7. $P(A|B) = \dfrac{P(A \cap B)}{P(B)}$, provided $P(B) \neq 0$.

The notion of conditional probability conforms to the intuitive concept of altering our estimate of the likelihood of an event as we acquire additional information. That is, $P(A \mid B)$ is the new probability of A after we know that B has occurred. Because it is common in modeling applications to know $P(A \mid B)$ directly, but not to know $P(A \cap B)$ axiom 7 often appears in the equivalent form

8. $P(A \cap B) = P(A \mid B)P(B)$.

Conditional probabilities are useful only when the events involved, A and B, have something to do with one another. If knowledge that B has occurred has no bearing upon our estimate of the likelihood of A, we would say that the two events are *independent*, and write

9. $P(A \mid B) = P(A)$ if and only if A and B are independent.

This rule can be taken as the formal definition of independence. Combining axioms 8 and 9, it immediately follows that

10. $P(A \cap B) = P(A)P(B)$ if and only if A and B are independent.

Alternatively, axiom 10 could be taken as the definition of independence and axiom 9 would immediately follow.

A set of events $B_1, B_2, \ldots, B_n$ constitute a *partition* of the sample space S if they are mutually exclusive, that is,

$$B_i \cap B_j = \phi \text{ for all } i \neq j$$

and collectively exhaustive, that is,

$$B_1 \cup B_2 \cup \cdots B_n = S$$

In simple terms, a partition is just any way of grouping and listing all possible outcomes such that no outcome appears in more than one group. When the experiment is performed, one and only one of the B_i will occur. It is easy to prove that

11. $\sum_{i=1}^{n} P(B_i) = 1$, for any partition $B_1, B_2, \cdots, B_n$.

One of the most useful relationships in modeling applications is the following

12. $P(A) = \sum_{i=1}^{n} P(A \mid B_i)P(B_i)$, for any partition $B_1, B_2, \cdots, B_n$.

It is not difficult to prove this relation rigorously, using only the rules of set theory and probability. However, because it is more important to understand the relation at an intuitive level in order to know how and when to use it, a verbal argument will be given here. Suppose we want to know the probability of some event A. The situation is too complicated to know $P(A)$ directly, but we *could* state the probability of A if we knew which of a number of possible conditions held. That is, we know $P(A \mid B_i)$ for a set of mutually exclusive, collectively exhaustive conditions, B_i. It would make some sense to "average" these various possible values for the probability of A. But if the conditions B_i are not all equally likely, the various $P(A \mid B_i)$ should not be given equal weight in the average; each should be weighted according to the probability that the condition B_i does in fact hold, or $P(B_i)$. This logic produces formula 12.

5.4 RANDOM VARIABLES

Although events may be directly assigned probabilities, more commonly the events are first associated with real numbers which are then in turn associated with probabilities. For example, if the experiment involves observing the number of heads appearing when four coins are tossed, it would be natural to associate the possible outcomes with the integers 0, 1, 2, 3, and 4. These integers are not, in themselves, events, but the event corresponding to each value is evident. The function which assigns numbers to events is called a *random variable*. It is interesting to note that a random variable is, technically speaking, neither random nor a variable. It is conceptually convenient, however, to suppress all references to the real-world events and to regard a random variable as an ordinary variable whose value is randomly selected. In other words, once the random variable is well defined, we may speak of any value in the range of the random variable as if it were actually the event. It makes sense, thereby, to speak of the probability that a random variable, X, equals some particular number.

In most cases, the rule which provides the value in the range of the random variable to go with each real-world event is so obvious that no special attention need be given to it. It is important to realize, however, that *values* of random variables have probabilities associated with them only because the values correspond to *events* which deserve the probabilities directly.

If the values in the range of a random variable are integers (or, more precisely, a countable subset of the real numbers), the random variable is *discrete*. If the range consists of all values over an interval of the real numbers, the random variable is *continuous*.

A word of caution is in order with respect to the use of the word "random". Occasionally, particularly in statistical applications, the word carries the connotation of equal likelihood. For example, when we say "take a random sample" we mean (among other things) that each member of the sampled population should have an equal chance of being selected. In general, however, the word "random" does not carry any such connotation.

5.5 PROBABILITY DISTRIBUTIONS

Any rule which assigns probabilities to each of the possible values of a random variable is a *probability distribution*. The term is used somewhat loosely, because there are several different ways to specify such a rule. More precise terms are used when a particular form is intended.

For discrete random variables, the most obvious and commonly used method of specifying the rule is to indicate the probability for each value separately. The function $p(x)$, defined as

$$p(x) = P(X = x)$$

is called the *probability distribution function*. An alternative, equally sufficient method is to specify the *cumulative distribution function*, $F(x)$, defined as

$$F(x) = P(X \leq x)$$

A third choice would be the complementary cumulative distribution function, $G(x)$, defined as

$$G(x) = P(X > x).$$

If any one of these is known, the others can be easily obtained in obvious ways. For example,

$$F(x) = \sum_{y=-\infty}^{x} p(y)$$

and

$$p(x) = F(x) - F(x-1)$$

For continuous random variables, the situation is somewhat complicated by the fact that range of possible values is uncountably infinite. It is not consistent with the axioms of probability to allow each individual value to have positive probability. In fact, with the possible exception of a countable number of points, each individual value must be assigned the probability zero! In contrast to the discrete case, a probability of zero does not imply that the corresponding event is impossible; it merely means that any one particular value is so unlikely, when considered next to the uncountably infinite set of alternatives, that the probability must be negligibly small. Consequently, it is fruitless to speak of the probabilities of particular values of random variables in the continuous case.

On the other hand, it makes perfect sense to speak of the probability that the value will fall within some interval. In particular, the cumulative distribution function, $F(x)$, is well defined by

$$F(x) = P(X \leq x)$$

Because the probability that X will exactly equal x is zero,

$$P(X \leq x) = P(X < x) + P(X = x) = P(X < x)$$

So $F(x)$ also describes $P(X < x)$. In other words, no distinction between strong and weak inequalities, or between open and closed intervals, need be made in the continuous case. Of course, the distinction must be scrupulously maintained in the discrete case.

From the definition, it is apparent that $F(x)$ must have the following properties

$$0 \leq F(x) \leq 1 \text{ for all } x$$

$$\lim_{x \to -\infty} F(x) = 0$$

$$\lim_{x \to \infty} F(x) = 1$$

$$F(y) \geq F(x) \text{ for any } y > x$$

In words, the function $F(x)$ must be bounded between 0 and 1, must approach zero at the left extremity of its range and one at the right extremity, and must be monotonically nondecreasing. (Actually, the last three imply the first.) Conversely, *any* function having these properties will qualify as a cumulative distribution function for some continuous random variable.

Given the cumulative distribution function, one can easily express the probability that the random variable will assume a value within any specified region. For example,

$$P(a \leq X \leq b) = P(X \leq b) - P(X < a) = F(b) - F(a)$$

The *complementary cumulative distribution function*, $G(x)$, defined by

$$G(x) = P(X > x)$$

or by

$$G(x) = 1 - F(x)$$

would also serve to describe fully the distribution.

The *probability density function*, $f(x)$, is a function which, when integrated between a and b, gives the probability that the random variable will assume a value between a and b. That is,

$$P(a \leq X \leq b) = \int_a^b f(x)dx$$

The relation between the density function and the distribution function is direct

$$F(x) = \int_{-\infty}^x f(y)dy$$

and

$$f(x) = \frac{d}{dx}F(x)$$

Although it may not seem to be the most natural way to describe a probability distribution, the density function is used more often than the cumulative or complementary cumulative distribution functions. In the case of a few distributions, only the density function can be expressed in closed form; the others must be expressed as integrals of the density function. It is important, therefore, that the student learn to think in terms of density functions. One of the first things to get straight is that the value of the density function at some point is *not* a probability. The only way to get a probability from a density function is to integrate it.

Any density function will have the properties

$$\int_{-\infty}^{\infty} f(x)dx = 1$$

$$f(x) \geq 0 \qquad \text{for all } x$$

The first property is a direct consequence of the definition, but the second requires a brief argument. If $f(x)$ were negative at any point, then there would exist two points, a and b, such that the integral of $f(x)$ between a and b was negative. This would imply that

$$P(a \leq X \leq b) < 0$$

which is impossible. Therefore $f(x)$ must be non-negative everywhere.

Any function, $f(x)$, having the two properties mentioned above will qualify as a probability density function for some continuous random variable. Notice, in particular, that there is no requirement that $f(x)$ be bounded above. The second property sometimes leads students to the mistaken presumption that $f(x) \leq 1$. In fact, $f(x)$ can be much greater than 1 over a narrow range, provided only that the *integral* over any interval does not exceed 1. Notice also that there is no requirement that $f(x)$ be continuous. Functions that are discontinuous, or abruptly "jump" from one value to another, can be integrated without difficulty, provided only that the points of discontinuity are limited in number. The method, of course, is to separate the interval that you wish to integrate into a sequence of intervals, over each of which the density function is continuous.

Although, as already noted, it is important to keep in mind that $f(x)$ is not a probability, it is useful in many applications to be able to substitute something involving $f(x)$ into expressions as if it were a probability. A generally reliable device is to think of the notation $f(x)dx$ as representing the probability that the random variable equals x. The dx part of the expression can be regarded as an interval of infinitesimal width, so the product of $f(x)$ and dx is (roughly speaking) an area under the curve, or a probability. The presence of dx will indicate that an integration must be performed before an exact expression can be inferred.

Although the distinction between the discrete and continuous random variable cases is important, there are occasions when it is convenient to have a unified terminology to cover both cases. The letters PDF may be used to refer to either the probability distribution function, in the discrete case, or the probability density function, in the continuous case. Similarly, the letters CDF will stand for the cumulative distribution function and CCDF for the complementary cumulative distribution function.

5.6   JOINT, MARGINAL, AND CONDITIONAL DISTRIBUTIONS

Whenever more than one random variable is involved in a single problem, there is a possibility that they are related. If so, it would not be sufficient to describe the probability distribution of each random variable in isolation; the relation between or among them must also be described. There are two methods in common use.

Suppose that two random variables, X and Y, are involved. The *joint cumulative distribution function*, or joint CDF, $F(x, y)$, is defined by

$$F(x, y) = P(X \leq x, Y \leq y)$$

In words, it is the probability that X takes on a value less than or equal to x and that Y takes on a value less than or equal to y. The same definition will suffice whether the random variables are both discrete, both continuous, or mixed. Conceptually the basic idea is to extend the notion of a cumulative distribution function to two dimensions. Obviously, the same basic idea can be used to extend the notion to higher dimensions.

If both X and Y are discrete, the *joint probability distribution function* is defined by

$$p(x, y) = P(X = x, Y = y)$$

If both are continuous, the *joint probability density function* is defined by

$$f(x, y) = \frac{\partial}{\partial x} \frac{\partial}{\partial y} F(x, y)$$

The latter must be integrated twice in order to obtain a probability. In particular,

$$P(a \leq X \leq b, c \leq Y \leq d) = \int_a^b \int_c^d f(x, y) \, dy \, dx$$

Each of these is just a two-dimensional extension of the appropriate function for single random variables, and can be extended to higher dimensions in the obvious way. The term "joint PDF" will describe either function.

Sometimes a joint PDF for two or more random variables is given, but one wants to know the PDF for just one of the random variables. That is, you might want to make a probability statement about, say, X, without regard to the value of Y. When both X and Y are discrete, the *marginal probability distribution* function of X is obtained from the joint PDF by

$$p(x) = \sum_{\text{all } y} p(x, y)$$

When both are continuous, the *marginal probability density function* of X is given by

$$f(x) = \int_{\text{all } y} f(x, y) dy$$

A marginal PDF is just an ordinary PDF, with all of the usual properties and interpretations. The word "marginal" merely conveys the information that it was obtained from a joint PDF.

By symmetry, the marginal PDF of Y is obtainable from the joint PDF of X and Y by summing or integrating over all values of X. If more than two random variables are involved in a joint PDF, the marginal PDF for any one can be found by summing or integrating over all values of all random variables other than the one whose marginal PDF is sought. Although it is not often used, the marginal CDF is, if anything, even easier to obtain from a joint CDF:

$$F(x) = \lim_{y \to \infty} F(x, y)$$

Dealing with the CDF also has the advantage of permitting a single expression to cover both the discrete and continuous cases.

Two random variables are *independent* if

$$F(x, y) = F(x)F(y) \qquad \text{(for all } x \text{ and } y\text{)}$$

or, in terms of PDF's,

$$p(x, y) = p(x)p(y) \qquad \text{(for all } x \text{ and } y\text{)}$$

for discrete random variables, and

$$f(x, y) = f(x)f(y) \qquad \text{(for all } x \text{ and } y\text{)}$$

for continuous random variables. When the random variables are independent, *but only then*, the joint distribution can be constructed from the marginals.

Independence of random variables is an extremely important concept. Not only must you know how to manipulate the functions in the presence or absence of the property, but also to judge whether in real-life situations the property can be reasonably assumed to hold. Because the mathematical definition may not be sufficiently revealing by itself to allow the student to grasp the concept at an intuitive level, a bit of further discussion seems warranted. When we say that the joint distribution can be obtained simply by multiplying the marginals, we are admitting that the joint distribution contains no more information than is already contained in the separate descriptions of the random variables. In other words, there is no need to account for the influence that one of the random variables might exert upon another. This would be true if and only if no such influence exists. Although the definition of independence of random variables is very similar in appearance to the definition of independence of events, it is actually a much stronger requirement. In order for X and Y to be independent, it is necessary that *every* event associated with X be independent of *every* event associated with Y.

The method of expressing joint PDF's or CDF's is just one of the ways to describe a relationship between two random variables. The other method is based on the idea of fixing a value for one and describing the subsequent distribution for the other. If both are discrete, the *conditional probability distribution function* of X given Y is defined by

$$p(x \mid y) = P(X = x \mid Y = y)$$

In $p(x \mid y)$, x is the argument of the function, and y can be regarded as a parameter. In other words, we may insert various values of x into the function to get the probability that the random variable equals x, but this probability will be contingent upon the value of y. Through its definition as a conditional probability, the conditional PDF is easily related to the joint PDF by the expression

$$p(x \mid y) = \frac{p(x, y)}{p(y)}, \qquad \text{provided } p(y) \neq 0$$

An analogous function exists for continuous random variables, but cannot be defined directly in terms of a conditional probability. The *conditional probability density function* of X given Y is most simply defined in terms of the joint density function

$$f(x \mid y) = \frac{f(x, y)}{f(y)}, \qquad \text{provided } f(y) \neq 0$$

This function must be integrated with respect to x in order to yield a probability; the y simply acts as a parameter.

The conditional PDF of X given Y reduces to the marginal PDF if and only if X and Y are independent. Notationally,

$$p(x \mid y) = p(x) \qquad \text{for all } x, y$$

or

$$f(x \mid y) = f(x) \qquad \text{for all } x, y$$

if and only if X and Y are independent. These expressions are entirely consistent with our earlier discussion of independence. If knowledge of the value of Y contributes nothing to a probability statement involving X, it must be that X and Y are unrelated.

Whenever a conditional distribution and one marginal is given, the other marginal can be obtained. The procedure is first to obtain the joint distribution and then use that to get the desired marginal. In the discrete case, the expressions would be

$$p(x, y) = p(x \mid y)p(y)$$

$$p(x) = \sum_{\text{all } y} p(x, y)$$

Therefore

$$p(x) = \sum_{\text{all } y} p(x \mid y)p(y)$$

The analogous formula in the continuous case would be

$$f(x) = \int_{\text{all } y} f(x \mid y)f(y)dy$$

Both of these expressions are very useful in modeling applications.

5.7 EXPECTATION

To describe a random variable completely requires a probability distribution in one of its various forms. If we were to require, however, a single number which best "summarized" the information contained in the distribution, we would almost certainly want to specify the "center" of the distribution. There are several ways to define "center," but the most useful is the expectation.

The *expectation* of a random variable X, denoted $E(X)$, is defined by

$$E(X) = \sum_{\text{all } x} xp(x)$$

when X is discrete, and

$$E(X) = \int_{\text{all } x} x f(x)dx$$

when X is continuous. The same quantity may be called the *expected value* of X (although this term is somewhat misleading), the *mean* of the distribution of X, or the *first moment* of the distribution of X. It should *not* be confused with an arithmetic average or a sample mean. The latter are statistical entities; we would compute them from data. An expectation is calculated from, and is an attribute of, a probability distribution. It can be regarded as a *weighted* average of the values of X, in which each possible value is weighted by the probability of its occurrence.

Although $E(X)$ is often called the expected value of X, one should be on guard against "expecting" $E(X)$ to occur as the value of X. Indeed, when X is discrete, $E(X)$ may not even be a *possible* value of X. It is true that if the experiment for which X is defined were to be repeated many times independently and the observed values of X were collected and averaged, then this average would be "close" to $E(X)$, in a certain probabalistic sense. However, this fact is a theorem of statistics (one form of the Law of Large Numbers), and has little significance for any single trial.

One of the reasons that the expectation is so useful as a measure of centrality is that it has a number of very convenient properties. For any random variable X and any constants a and b,

$$E(aX) = aE(X)$$

and

$$E(X+b) = E(X)+b$$

In words, both multiplicative and additive constants can be "pulled out" of the expectation. For any two random variables X and Y,

$$E(X+Y) = E(X)+E(Y)$$

In words, the expected value of a sum is the sum of the expected values. The same relation can be extended to sums of more than two random variables, and will hold whether or not the random variables are independent. Whenever X and Y are independent the expected value of the product will decompose; that is,

$$E(XY) = E(X)E(Y)$$

but this relation does not generally hold when the random variables are dependent.

Another convenience associated with using the expectation is the fact that the expectation of an arbitrary function of a random variable is easily expressed. Let $h(X)$ be any function of X. Then if X is discrete,

$$E(h(X)) = \sum_{\text{all } x} h(x)p(x)$$

and if X is continuous,

$$E(h(X)) = \int_{\text{all } x} h(x)f(x)dx$$

In other words, $h(x)$ merely replaces x in the definition of $E(X)$. These expressions are not a new definition, but are derived by considering a random variable $Y = h(X)$ and relating the distribution of Y to the distribution of X.

A concept used repeatedly in the next three chapters is that of *conditional expectation*. Formally, the *conditional expectation* of a random variable X given the value of a related random variable Y, is defined by

$$E(X \mid y) = \sum_{\text{all } x} xp(x \mid y)$$

or by

$$E(X \mid y) = \int_{\text{all } x} xf(x \mid y)dx$$

Usually, however, our use of the concept will be such that the conditional expectation may be known directly. For example, suppose that we are interested in an inventory problem and X represents the number of units of some good sold during a specified period. If Y represents the number of customers who purchase some number of units during the period, and if the expectation of the number of units purchased is the same for each customer, say 3.6 units, then the conditional expectation of the number of units sold *given* that the number of customers is y would be 3.6y, for any y. That is, we obtain

$$E(X \mid y) = 3.6y$$

without having to use the conditional probability distribution $p(X \mid y)$. The details of the logic involved are probably unnecessary, but, just to verify rigorously that the result is correct, we may argue as follows. The number of units sold, X, is the sum of the amounts sold to each individual customer. If the number of customers is specified to be y, then X will consist of the sum of y random variables. The expectation of a sum is the sum of the expectations; so if each of these is the same, namely 3.6, the sum of y of them is 3.6y.

The conditional expectation of X given y can be combined with the distribution of Y to yield the unconditional expectation of X. In notation,

$$E(X) = \sum_{\text{all } y} E(X \mid y)p(y)$$

or

$$E(X) = \int_{\text{all } y} E(X \mid y)f(y)dy$$

A brief way to express both of these is

$$E(X) = E[E(X \mid y)]$$

but this form does not suggest how useful the relation is as a technique for formulating an expression for $E(X)$. The other forms suggest that the expectation of X can be thought of as a weighted average of the conditional expectations of X given y, taken over all possible conditions y, with each possible $E(X \mid y)$ weighted according to the probability of occurrence. Faced with the problem of expressing $E(X)$, then, one might try to find another random variable, Y, whose distribution is known or can be found, and which has the property that when the value of Y is specified, the expectation of X is easy to obtain. If such a random variable can be found, the expectation of X can be expressed easily. The logic is very similar to that used when expressing a marginal PDF in terms of a conditional PDF, as described in Section 5.6.

5.8 VARIANCE AND OTHER MOMENTS

The nth *moment* of a random variable is defined as the expectation of the nth power of the random variable. Since X^n is just a special case of a function of X, the nth moment can be expressed as

$$E(X^n) = \sum_{\text{all } x} x^n p(x)$$

or

$$E(X^n) = \int_{\text{all } x} x^n f(x)dx$$

The first moment is, of course, the expectation. The nth *central moment*, or the nth *moment about the mean* is defined as

$$E([X - E(X)]^n) = \sum_{\text{all } x} [x - E(X)]^n p(x)$$

or

$$= \int_{\text{all } x} [x - E(X)]^n f(x)dx$$

In words, it is the expectation of the nth power of the random variable after it has been "shifted" by subtracting the expectation.

After the expectation, the next most important single number used to summarize distributions is the second moment about the mean, more commonly known as the *variance*. Denoting the variance of X by $V(X)$,

$$V(X) = \sum_{\text{all } x} [x - E(X)]^2 p(x)$$

or

$$V(X) = \int_{\text{all } x} [x - E(X)]^2 f(x)dx$$

In both the discrete and continuous case, the variance can be shown to equal the second moment minus the expectation squared. That is,

$$V(X) = E(X^2) - E(X)^2$$

The variance, being defined as a weighted average of the squared deviations from the expectation, is a measure of the spread, or dispersion, of a probability distribution. One of the objections to its use for this purpose is that the units are not those of X, but of X^2. Use of the *standard deviation*, defined as the square root of the variance, overcomes this objection.

The properties of variances are not so obvious as those of expectations. Whereas the behavior of expectations conforms to what intuition would suggest, considerable care must be exercised in dealing with variances and standard deviations. The rules for dealing with multiplicative and additive constants are

$$V(aX) = a^2 V(X)$$

and

$$V(X + b) = V(X)$$

In words, a multiplicative constant can be "pulled out" of a variance, but must be squared; an additive constant can be "dropped out." When considering a sum of random variables, the variance of the sum will be the sum of the variances, *if* the random variables are independent. For two independent random variables X and Y,

$$V(X + Y) = V(X) + V(Y)$$

On the other hand, if the random variables are dependent, this relation will not generally hold. The correct expression for the general case requires another definition.

Given two random variables X and Y, the *covariance* of X and Y is defined by

$$\text{COV}(X, Y) = E([X - E(X)][Y - E(Y)])$$

but this expression can be shown to equal

$$\text{COV}(X, Y) = E(XY) - E(X)E(Y)$$

It will be recalled that when X and Y are independent, $E(XY) = E(X)E(Y)$, so the covariance of independent random variables is zero. The converse does not always hold; that is, the mere knowledge that the covariance of random variables is zero would not be enough for one to conclude that they are independent. Indeed, examples can be constructed of dependent random variables for which the covariance equals zero. On the other hand, a nonzero covariance definitely implies a relationship between the random variables, so the covariance is used as a (somewhat imperfect) measure of the degree of dependence. Another, related, measure of dependence is the correlation coefficient between X and Y, usually denoted by ρ, which is defined as

$$\rho = \frac{\text{COV}(X, Y)}{\sqrt{V(X)V(Y)}}$$

Returning to the variance of a sum of random variables, the general equation for two random variables is

$$V(X + Y) = V(X) + V(Y) + 2\text{COV}(X, Y)$$

II. DISCRETE PROBABILITY DISTRIBUTIONS

5.9 THE DISCRETE UNIFORM DISTRIBUTION

When a random variable X has only a finite number of possible values, each of which can occur with equal likelihood, the distribution is called *discrete uniform*. Without serious loss of generality, we may assume that the range of X is $x = 1, 2, \ldots, N$, in which case the probability distribution function is

$$p(x) = \frac{1}{N}, x = 1, 2, \ldots, N$$

When X has this range, the mean and variance are

$$E(X) = \frac{N}{2}$$

$$V(X) = \frac{N^2 - 1}{12}$$

Of course, a shift or scaling of the range of X will have a concomitant effect upon the PDF, mean, and variance. In any case, the PDF is just one divided by the total number of possible values, for each value, and the expectation falls at the midpoint of the range.

Although it has many uses, the discrete uniform distribution is not so important as it is frequently thought to be by beginners in probability. Elementary textbooks often give so much emphasis to combinatorial probability—using permutations and combinations to count the number of ways that events could occur and using these counts (together with the assumption of equal likelihood) to form probabilities—that it is easy to develop a concept of probability theory that is limited to this one special case. It is important to realize that the discrete uniform distribution is just one of many useful distributions.

5.10 THE BERNOULLI DISTRIBUTION

If a random variable must assume one of two values, 0 or 1, it is said to be a Bernoulli random variable. The corresponding experiment, which has only two possible outcomes, is called a Bernoulli trial. Usually the outcome which is mapped by the random variable onto the value "1" is called a "success;" the other is called a "failure." The distribution is given by

$$p(1) = p$$

$$p(0) = 1 - p$$

where p is the only parameter of the distribution, often referred to as the "probability of success."

The distribution may seem so trivial as to be undeserving of special attention. Although it is true that direct applications are limited, it turns out that a number of more important distributions can be derived from considering a sequence of independent Bernoulli trials.

5.11 THE BINOMIAL DISTRIBUTION

Let X be a discrete random variable defined over the range $x = 0,1,2,\ldots$. If

$$p(x) = \binom{n}{x} p^x (1 - p)^{n - x}$$

then we say that X has a binomial distribution with parameters n and p, where n is a positive integer and $0 \le p \le 1$. The notation $\binom{n}{x}$ refers to the so-called "binomial coefficient" defined by $\binom{n}{x} = n!/x!(n-x)!$. Tables of binomial coefficients and the binomial distribution are readily available.

A binomially distributed random variable can usually be thought of as counting the number of successes in a sequence of n independent Bernoulli trials, where the probability of success on any trial is p.

The expectation, or mean number of successes, is np. The variance is $np(1-p)$.

5.12   THE POISSON DISTRIBUTION

Let X be a discrete variable defined over the range $x = 0, 1, 2, \ldots, \infty$. If

$$p(x) = \frac{\lambda^x e^{-\lambda}}{x!} \quad x = 0, 1, 2, \ldots$$

then we say that X has a Poisson distribution with parameter λ, where λ must be positive. The Poisson distribution has a number of convenient properties which contribute to its usefulness in modeling. The expectation and variance are equal to one another, and are given simply by the parameter of the distribution:

$$E(X) = V(X) = \lambda$$

The distribution is reproductive; that is, the sum of Poisson distributed random variables will be another Poisson distributed random variable. The parameter of the sum random variable will be just the sum of the parameters of the constituent random variables.

One of the common usages of the Poisson distribution is as an approximation to the binomial distribution when the number of trials (n) becomes large while the probability of occurrence (p) becomes small. All that is required for the approximation is to give the two distributions the same expectation. That is, let $\lambda = np$.

Another common use of the Poisson distribution is to describe the number of events occurring within some period of time. In this context, it is the usual practice to use λt as the parameter of the distribution, where t is interpreted as the length of the period and λ is now the mean "rate" at which events occur. The "Poisson process" and its properties will be discussed in some detail in the next chapter.

5.13   THE GEOMETRIC DISTRIBUTION

There are two common versions of the geometric distribution. If X is defined over the range $x = 1, 2, \ldots \infty$ and has the PDF

$$p(x) = p(1-p)^{x-1} \quad x = 1, 2, \ldots, \infty$$

where $0 \le p \le 1$, we would say that X has the geometric distribution beginning at 1. If it is defined over the range $x = 0, 1, \ldots, \infty$, and

$$p(x) = p(1-p)^x \quad x = 0, 1, \ldots, \infty$$

we would say that X has the geometric distribution beginning at 0. It is apparent that one version is just a shifted version of the other, and that other shifts could be made without altering the form of the distribution. Both of these versions appear in applications and are easily confused.

The expectations and variance for the geometric distribution beginning at 1 are, respectively,

$$E(X) = \frac{1}{p}$$

$$V(X) = \frac{1-p}{p^2}$$

When the distribution begins at 0, the variance is the same, but the expectation is $(1-p)/p$.

A possible interpretation of X, when it begins at 1, is as the number of trials, in a sequence of independent Bernoulli trials, that will occur before the first success is observed. More precisely, it is the number of the trial on which the first success occurs. If X begins at zero, it could be thought of as counting the number of failures before the first success. In either case, X counts trials, so the geometric distribution is often regarded as a "waiting time" distribution. One should not confuse this interpretation of the geometric distribution with that of the binomial distribution. The latter fixes the number of trials and counts successes.

5.14   THE NEGATIVE BINOMIAL DISTRIBUTION

Let X be a discrete random variable defined over the range $x = r, r+1, \ldots, \infty$. We would say that X follows a negative binomial distribution if

$$p(x) = \binom{x-1}{r-1} p^r (1-p)^{x-r}, \; x = r, r+1, \ldots$$

where r is an integer ≥ 1, and $0 \leq p \leq 1$. Another name for the same distribution is the Pascal distribution. When $r = 1$, the distribution reduces to the geometric. The expectation and variance are

$$E(X) = \frac{r}{p}$$

$$V(X) = \frac{r(1-p)}{p^2}$$

The explanation for this distribution just extends that of the geometric. X represents the number of the trial, in a sequence of independent Bernoulli trials, on which the rth success occurs. Thus the negative binomial distribution is another waiting-time distribution. Thinking of X in this way suggests that the waiting time for the rth success ought to be the sum of r waiting times for the one success. Because the trials are independent, this logic is valid. It is a fact that the sum of r geometrically distributed random variables will yield a random variable whose distribution is negative binomial with parameter r.

Sometimes the negative binomial distribution is used without any waiting-time interpretation, but simply because the parameters can be adjusted so as to fit a set of data. In this case, it may be desirable to have the range of X begin at zero, rather than r. If so, the appropriate PDF would be

$$p(x) = \binom{r+x-1}{x} p^r (1-p)^x \qquad \text{for } x = 0, 1, \ldots, \infty$$

The variance would be the same, but the expectation would be $r(1-p)/p$.

III. CONTINUOUS PROBABILITY DISTRIBUTIONS

5.15 THE CONTINUOUS UNIFORM DISTRIBUTION

When a continuous random variable X is restricted to a finite range, $a \leq x \leq b$, and is such that "no value is any more likely than any other," then X would be appropriately described by the continuous uniform distribution. It is the obvious analog of the discrete uniform distribution, which restricted the random variable to a finite number of equally likely values. The description "no value more likely than any other" is somewhat loose, because, of course, the probability of any one value for a continuous random variable is zero. A better, although less intuitive, description would be "the probability that x falls within any interval in the range of X depends only on the width of the interval and not on its location."

In any case, the distribution is rigorously defined by its probability density function

$$f(x) = \frac{1}{b-a} \quad a \leq x \leq b$$

The expectation is at the midpoint of the range,

$$E(X) = \frac{a+b}{2}$$

and the variance is

$$V(X) = \frac{(b-a)^2}{12}$$

5.16 THE NORMAL DISTRIBUTION

Easily the most important continuous probability distribution, the normal distribution has been useful in countless applications involving every conceivable discipline. The usefulness is due in part to the fact that the distribution has a number of properties that make it easy to deal with mathematically. More importantly, however, the distribution happens to describe quite accurately the random variables associated with a wide variety of experiments.

The range of a normally distributed random variable consists of all real numbers. The probability density function is defined by the equation

$$f(x) = \frac{1}{\sigma\sqrt{2\pi}} e^{-((x-\mu)^2/2\sigma^2)} \quad -\infty \leq x \leq \infty$$

where the parameter μ is unrestricted and the parameter σ is positive.

The two parameters, μ and σ, used to specify the distribution happen to correspond to the mean and standard deviation, respectively, of the random variable. Any linear transformation of a normally distributed random variable

Table 5.1
DISCRETE PROBABILITY DISTRIBUTIONS

Name	Range	Parameters	PDF	Expectation	Variance
Discrete uniform	$x = 1, 2, \ldots, N$	$N = 1, 2, \ldots$	$p(x) = \dfrac{1}{N}$	$\dfrac{N+1}{2}$	$\dfrac{N^2 - 1}{12}$
Bernoulli	$x = 0, 1$	$0 \leq p \leq 1$	$\begin{aligned} p(0) &= 1 - p \\ p(1) &= p \end{aligned}$	p	$p(1-p)$
Binomial	$x = 0, 1, \ldots, n$	$\begin{aligned} n &= 1, 2, \ldots \\ 0 &\leq p \leq 1 \end{aligned}$	$p(x) = \binom{n}{x} p^x (1-p)^{n-x}$	np	$np(1-p)$
Poisson	$x = 0, 1, \ldots, \infty$	$\lambda > 0$	$p(x) = \dfrac{\lambda^x e^{-\lambda}}{x!}$	λ	λ
Geometric	$x = 1, 2, \ldots \infty$	$0 \leq p \leq 1$	$p(x) = p(1-p)^{x-1}$	$\dfrac{1}{p}$	$\dfrac{1-p}{p^2}$
Negative binomial (Pascal)	$x = r, r+1, \ldots, \infty$	$\begin{aligned} r &= 1, 2, \ldots \\ 0 &\leq p \leq 1 \end{aligned}$	$p(x) = \binom{x-1}{r-1} p^r (1-p)^{x-r}$	$\dfrac{r}{p}$	$\dfrac{r(1-p)}{p^2}$

is also normally distributed. That is, if X is normal with mean μ and variance σ^2, and if $Y = aX + b$, then Y is normally distributed with mean

$$E(Y) = E(aX + b)$$
$$= aE(X) + b$$
$$= a\mu + b$$

and with variance

$$V(Y) = V(aX + b)$$
$$= a^2 V(X)$$
$$= a^2 \sigma^2$$

The significance of these facts is that every normal distribution, whatever the values of the parameters, can be represented in terms of the *standard* normal distribution which has a mean of zero and variance of 1. The linear transformation required to convert a normally distributed random variable X with mean μ and variance σ^2 to the standard normal random variable Z is

$$Z = \frac{X - \mu}{\sigma}$$

The density function of the standard normal random variable is just

$$f(x) = \frac{1}{\sqrt{2\pi}} e^{-(x^2/2)} \quad -\infty \leqq x \leqq \infty$$

Because it is so frequently used, the standard normal density function is granted the special notation $\phi(x)$. The cumulative distribution function also has its own notation, $\varphi(x)$. Unfortunately, integrals of the density function cannot be evaluated by ordinary methods of calculus, so there is no closed form expression for $\varphi(x)$, other than as an integral of $\phi(x)$. Extensive tables of $\varphi(x)$, obtained by means of numerical integration, are available. Once you have become familiar with the tables, virtually any desired probability can be evaluated with little trouble.

The normal distribution is reproductive; that is, the sum of two or more normally distributed random variables is itself normally distributed. The mean of the sum is, as always, the sum of the means. The variance of the sum is the sum of the variances, provided that the random variables are independent. Even if they are not, the variance of the sum can be expressed in terms of the variances and covariances of the constituents.

An even more remarkable result is established by the famous Central Limit Theorem, which states that (under certain broad conditions) the sum of a large number of independent *arbitrarily* distributed random variables will be (approximately) normally distributed. Since quite frequently a random variable of interest may be conceptualized as being composed of a large number of independent random effects, the Central Limit Theorem "explains" why the normal distribution appears so often in real-life applications. It also provides justification for *assuming* that certain random variables are normally distributed.

5.17 THE LOGNORMAL DISTRIBUTION

The lognormal distribution is the distribution of a random variable whose natural logarithm follows a normal distribution. The lognormal density function is given by

$$f(x) = \frac{1}{\sigma x \sqrt{2\pi}} e^{[(\ln x - \mu)^2/2\sigma^2]}$$

The range of the random variable is all $x > 0$. The parameters μ and σ may be interpreted from

$$\mu = E(\ln X)$$
$$\sigma^2 = V(\ln X)$$

but the mean and variance of X are, respectively,

$$E(X) = e^{\mu + (1/2\sigma^2)}$$
$$V(X) = e^{2\mu + \sigma^2}(e^{\sigma^2} - 1)$$

In practice, the best way to deal with a lognormally distributed random variable X is to transform it by taking its natural logarithm. That is, let $Y = \ln X$. Of course, Y would be normally distributed and is therefore easily handled. For example, suppose that you wish to evaluate

$$P(a \leq X \leq b)$$

where X is lognormally distributed. Using the fact that Y is normal,

$$P(a \leq X \leq b) = P(\ln a \leq Y \leq \ln b)$$
$$= \int_{\ln a}^{\ln b} \frac{1}{\sigma \sqrt{2\pi}} e^{-[(y - \mu)^2/2\sigma^2]} dy$$

which in turn would be evaluated by standardizing Y. Define $Z = \frac{Y - \mu}{\sigma}$, and

$$P(\ln a \leq Y \leq \ln b) = P\left(\frac{\ln a - \mu}{\sigma} \leq Z \leq \frac{\ln b - \mu}{\sigma}\right)$$
$$= \int_{(\ln a - \mu)/\sigma}^{(\ln b - \mu)/\sigma} \phi(z) dz$$

The lognormal distribution arises from the *product* of many independent nonnegative random variables, in contrast to the normal, which arises from the sum of independent random variables. It has been used to describe lifetimes of mechanical and electrical systems, incubation periods of infectious diseases, concentrations of chemical elements in geological materials, abundance of species of animals, and many other random phenomena occurring in both the social and natural sciences.

The demonstrated usefulness of the lognormal distribution immediately suggests the more general concept of fitting familiar distributions to *transformed* data rather than to the data itself. The normal distribution together with the logarithmic transformation is just one possible combination. Exponential, quadratic, square root, and trigonometric transformations could also be applied to the raw data in an attempt to find a simple distribution to describe them. This idea has become standard practice in modern data analysis.

5.18   THE NEGATIVE EXPONENTIAL DISTRIBUTION

Let X be a continuous random variable defined over the range $x \geq 0$. If

$$f(x) = \lambda e^{-\lambda x} \quad x \geq 0$$

where the parameter λ is positive, we say that X has the negative exponential distribution or, sometimes, just the exponential distribution. The cumulative distribution function has, in this case, a convenient expression

$$F(x) = 1 - e^{-\lambda x}$$

The complementary cumulative distribution function is even simpler

$$G(x) = e^{-\lambda x}$$

The expectation of a negative exponentially distributed random variable is the reciprocal of the parameter

$$E(X) = \frac{1}{\lambda}$$

and the variance is the square of the same value

$$V(X) = \frac{1}{\lambda^2}$$

The negative exponential distribution is used extensively to describe random variables corresponding to durations. In other words, it is a waiting time distribution. It has a number of useful properties, but since these are explored fully in Chapter 6, no further discussion need be included here.

5.19 THE ERLANG DISTRIBUTION

A continuous random variable defined over the range $x \geq 0$ is Erlang distributed if its density function is of the form

$$f(x) = \frac{\lambda^r x^{r-1}}{(r-1)!} e^{-\lambda x} \quad x \geq 0$$

where the parameter λ is positive and r is an integer ≥ 1. When $r = 1$ the density function reduces to that of a negative exponential distribution, so the Erlang distribution can be thought of as a generalization of the negative exponential. In fact, if we had r independent negative exponential random variables, each with the parameter λ, then the sum of these random variables would be Erlang distributed with parameters λ and r. If each of the negative exponential random variables is a waiting time, the Erlang random variable can be thought of as the time until the rth event.

The expectation is most easily found as the sum of the expectations of the negative exponential random variables

$$E(X) = \frac{r}{\lambda}$$

and the variance is found by a similar argument

$$V(X) = \frac{r}{\lambda^2}$$

In addition to its use as a waiting time for the rth event, the Erlang distribution is often considered as a candidate to fit empirical data in queueing, reliability, inventory, and replacement applications. In this case, r has no physical interpretation; it is just a parameter that may be adjusted to obtain a better fit.

5.20   THE GAMMA DISTRIBUTION

Let X be a continuous random variable defined over the range $x \geq 0$. It is gamma distributed if the density function is of the form

$$f(x) = \frac{\lambda^r x^{r-1}}{\Gamma(r)} e^{-\lambda x} \quad x \geq 0$$

where both λ and r are positive, and $\Gamma(r)$ is the gamma function, defined by

$$\Gamma(r) = \int_0^\infty x^{r-1} e^{-x} dx$$

The gamma function is tabulated, so $\Gamma(r)$ can be thought of as just a constant whose value can be easily found when r is given.

When r is an integer, $\Gamma(r) = (r-1)!$. In this case, the gamma distribution reduces to the Erlang. One way to think of the gamma is as a generalization of the Erlang in which r need not be an be an integer. The generalization permits somewhat greater flexibility in fitting empirical data.

When $\lambda = 1/2$ and $r = \upsilon/2$, where υ is an integer, the Γ density function becomes

$$f(x) = \frac{1}{2^{\upsilon/2} \Gamma(V/2)} x^{\upsilon-2/2} e^{-(1/2x)} \quad x \geq 0$$

This special form is commonly called the *chi-square density function*, and the single parameter υ is referred to as the degrees of freedom associated with the chi-square random variable. A chi-square random variable with υ degrees of freedom results when a set of υ independent standard normal random variables are each squared and then summed. The distribution has many applications in statistical hypothesis testing, but is not often used as a descriptive distribution in modeling applications. For the latter purpose, the Erlang distribution is a much more useful and special case of the gamma function.

The expectation and variance of a gamma distributed random variable X are

$$E(X) = \frac{r}{\lambda}$$

$$V(X) = \frac{r}{\lambda^2}$$

5.21   THE WEIBULL DISTRIBUTION

A continuous random variable defined over the range $x \geq 0$ has a Weibull distribution if its density function is given by

$$f(x) = \lambda \beta (\lambda x)^{\beta-1} e^{-[\lambda x]^\beta} \quad x \geq 0$$

where λ and β are positive constants. Since, when $\beta = 1$, this density function reduces to that of the negative exponential distribution, the Weibull can be thought of as a generalization of the negative exponential. Since the Erlang family generalizes the negative exponential, and the gamma in turn generalizes the Erlang, one might momentarily suspect that the Weibull and gamma distributions are the same, or that one is a special case of the other. However, there are gamma distributions that are not Weibull, and there are Weibull distributions that are not gamma. Thus, these two families are definitely distinct despite the fact that they each generalize the negative exponential family.

The mean of a Weibull distributed random variable is

$$E(X) = \frac{1}{\lambda}\Gamma\left(1 + \frac{1}{\beta}\right)$$

The variance is

$$V(X) = \frac{1}{\lambda^2}\left\{\Gamma\left(1 + \frac{2}{\beta}\right) - \left[\Gamma\left(1 + \frac{1}{\beta}\right)\right]^2\right\}$$

The gamma function $\Gamma(\ )$ appearing in these expressions can be found tabulated in most handbooks of mathematical tables.

The Weibull distribution has been found to be useful for describing lifetimes and waiting times in reliability applications. If a system consists of a large number of parts, each of which has a lifetime distribution of its own (independent of the others), and if the system fails as soon as any one of the parts does, then the lifetime of the system is the minimum of the lifetimes of its parts. Under these circumstances, there is theoretical justification for expecting a Weibull distribution to provide a close approximation to the lifetime distribution of the system.

5.22   THE BETA DISTRIBUTION

A beta-distributed random variable is defined over the range $0 \le x \le 1$ and has the density function

$$f(x) = \frac{x^{r-1}(1-x)^{s-1}}{B(r,\ s)} \qquad 0 \le x \le 1$$

where $B(r, s)$ is the beta function, which is tabulated directly or may be found from tables of the gamma function from the relation

$$B(r, s) = \frac{\Gamma(r)\Gamma(s)}{\Gamma(r+s)}$$

The mean and variance of X are, respectively,

$$E(X) = \frac{r}{r+s}$$

$$V(X) = \frac{rs}{(r+s)^2(r+s+1)}$$

These relations can be inverted to obtain interpretations of the parameters r and s in terms of the mean and variance.

$$r = E(X)\left[\frac{E(X)[1-E(X)]}{V(X)} - 1\right]$$

$$s = [1 - E(X)]\left[\frac{E(X)[1-E(X)]}{V(X)} - 1\right]$$

When it desired to define a beta-distributed random variable, say Y, having a range $a \le y \le b$, the simplest approach would be to transform Y according to

$$X = \frac{Y - a}{b - a}$$

which yields a beta-distributed random variable defined on the range $0 \leqq x \leqq 1$, and therefore has the density function mentioned above.

The beta distribution is commonly used to describe random variables that are not uniformly distributed, but whose possible values lie in a restricted interval of numbers. Sometimes the range is restricted by the very nature of the random variable, such as when it represents a fraction or a percentage. Other times, the range is restricted by choice. In project-scheduling networks (PERT and CPM), the durations of activities are often assumed to follow a beta distribution, where the minimum and maximum possible times are supplied by people who are familiar with the activity.

IV. USING DISTRIBUTIONS

5.23 FITTING DISTRIBUTIONS TO DATA

Given the necessity of selecting a distribution to describe a particular random phenomenon, one would ordinarily attempt to acquire data representing a large number of independent samples of the random variable one has in mind. Sometimes, of course, the acquisition of adequate data may be economically infeasible or even physically impossible. In these cases, there may exist theoretical justification for believing that a certain distribution family is appropriate. For example, if the phenomenon can be thought of as the number of successes in a sequence of independent Bernoulli trials, a binomial distribution would be appropriate; or if it can be thought of as consisting of the sum of a large number of independent random variables, the Central Limit Theorem would suggest the normal distribution. On other occasions, the choice of distribution is influenced by a need for particular mathematical properties. The beta distribution in PERT and CPM applications and the negative exponential distribution in Markov process models are selected for reasons that have little to do with observed data.

Preferably, however, one would like to have real-world data to provide assurance that the distribution selected really does describe the real-world phenomenon. Because it is difficult to see any pattern in a raw list of values, one would ordinarily plot a histogram as a first step in identifying an appropriate distribution. The next step, that of selecting one or more candidate distribution types, requires a familiarity with the characteristics of various distribution families. In particular, one has to know what "shapes" a PDF is capable of assuming, in order to decide whether there is any hope of adjusting the parameters to get a PDF that looks like the histogram. The book by Derman et al. [3] provides especially good descriptions of all of the distribution types summarized only briefly here, as well as a number of others that have not even been mentioned. It also provides guidance on how to fit each distribution to particular data, and gives examples.

Once a distribution type is at least tentatively selected, the next problem is to set values for the parameters that fix the distribution within the family. Unless other, external factors intervene, one would usually use the data to estimate, in the formal statistical sense, values for the parameters. In a few cases, the statistics to use are obvious. For example, the parameter λ in a Poisson distribution is estimated by the sample mean, and μ and σ^2 in a normal distribution are estimated by the sample mean and sample variance,

Table 5.2
CONTINUOUS PROBABILITY DISTRIBUTIONS

Name	Range	Parameters	PDF	Expectation	Variance
Continuous uniform	$a \leq x \leq b$	a, b	$f(x) = \dfrac{1}{b-a}$	$\dfrac{a+b}{2}$	$\dfrac{(b-a)^2}{12}$
Normal	$-\infty < x < \infty$	μ $\sigma^2 > 0$	$f(x) = \dfrac{1}{\sigma\sqrt{2\pi}} e^{-[(x-\mu)^2/2\sigma^2]}$	μ	σ^2
Lognormal	$0 \leq x$	μ $\sigma^2 > 0$	$f(x) = \dfrac{1}{\sigma x\sqrt{2\pi}} e^{-[(\ln x - \mu)^2/2\sigma^2]}$	$e^{\mu+1/2\sigma^2}$	$e^{2\mu+\sigma^2}(e^{\sigma^2}-1)$
Negative exponential	$0 \leq x$	$\lambda > 0$	$f(x) = \lambda e^{-\lambda x}$	$\dfrac{1}{\lambda}$	$\dfrac{1}{\lambda^2}$
Gamma (Erlang when r is an integer; χ^2 when $\lambda = 1/2$, $r = \nu/2$)	$0 \leq x$	$\lambda > 0$ $r > 0$	$f(x) = \dfrac{\lambda^r x^{r-1}}{\Gamma(r)} e^{-\lambda x}$	$\dfrac{r}{\lambda}$	$\dfrac{r}{\lambda^2}$
Weibull	$0 \leq x$	$\lambda > 0$ $\beta > 0$	$f(x) = \lambda\beta(\lambda x)^{\beta-1} e^{-[\lambda x]^\beta}$	$\dfrac{1}{\lambda}\Gamma\left(1+\dfrac{1}{\beta}\right)$	$\dfrac{1}{\lambda^2}\left[\Gamma\left(1+\dfrac{2}{\beta}\right) - \left\{\Gamma\left(1+\dfrac{1}{\beta}\right)\right\}^2\right]$
Beta	$0 \leq x \leq 1$	$r > 0$ $s > 0$	$f(x) = \dfrac{x^{r-1}(1-x)^{s-1}}{B(r,s)}$	$\dfrac{r}{r+s}$	$\dfrac{rs}{(r+s)^2(r+s+1)}$

respectively. In other cases, however, the appropriate statistic is not so obvious. The parameters r in a gamma distribution, or β in a Weibull, require additional statistical work before proper estimation formulas become apparent. Again, the book by Derman et al. is useful in providing this kind of information.

After the parameters are adjusted so as to provide the best fit to the data that a selected distribution type can provide, one is still left with the question of whether the fit is good enough. In other words, you should validate your model by checking the goodness of fit. As a bare minimum, one could graph the precise PDF over the histogram (using vertical scales that permit comparison), and observe the discrepancies. A more formal procedure would be to perform any of several available statistical tests for goodness of fit. The chi-square and the Kolmogorov-Smirnov goodness-of-fit tests are probably the best known. Descriptions of these two tests can be found in almost all intermediate-level statistics textbooks. The handbook by Phillips (9) describes several others as well, and contains a quite thorough discussion of the practical aspects affecting the choice of test. Computer programs written in Fortran are also provided.

One of the basic points to bear in mind about statistical goodness-of-fit testing is that the null hypothesis assumes that the candidate distribution is correct. Only if the discrepancies between the data and the candidate distribution are significantly large will the test lead you to reject the candidate. In other words, the test is, by its very nature, biased in favor of whatever distribution you have selected to test. The mere fact that the test does not reject the distribution should not be taken as strong evidence that the selected distribution is correct. Someone else might have selected a different distribution and come up with just as much confirmation that his choice was correct. This is particularly likely to occur when the data base is small.

The word to describe the capability of a statistical test to detect that a null hypothesis is false is *power*. Other factors being equal, a greater amount of data will make for a more powerful test. To obtain a very powerful test, however, may require truly enormous quantities of data—orders of magnitude greater than would be required for good hypothesis tests about parameters. It is easy to see why this is so if you think about how many total observations are required to provide enough information about the "tails" of a distribution to ensure that you have obtained a proper fit.

As a final philosophical point, it is well to keep in mind that no amount of data can confirm absolutely that you have selected the correct distribution. Ultimately, there is no escape from having to make assumptions. On the other hand, there is no need for a model to represent its real-world referent perfectly. It can be useful despite acknowledged imperfections if it represents the significant aspects adequately.

Recommended Readings

If any of the topics mentioned in this chapter seems hazy, or if you would just feel more confident about proceeding if you had worked some problems, you should by all means devote some time to an elementary textbook on probability. There are many fine ones available. Unfortunately for the purposes of this book, the orientation of many leans toward statistical, as opposed to modeling, applications. However, any of the books [Clarke (1), Cramer (2), Drake (4), Meyer (7), or Parzen (8)] should serve the purpose adequately. If one does not suit your taste, feel free to select another. Feller's two volumes, (5) and (6), are classics familiar to everyone seriously interested in probability. Even beginners can find much of interest in them. The first volume deals with discrete, the second, with continuous distributions

REFERENCES

1. Clarke, B., and R. Disney, *Probability and Random Processes for Engineers and Scientists*, Wiley, New York, 1970.

2. Cramer, H., *The Elements of Probability Theory and Some of Its Applications*, Wiley, New York, 1955.

3. Derman, C., L. J. Gleser, and I. Olkin, *A Guide to Probability Theory and Application*, Holt, Rinehart, and Winston, New York, 1973.

4. Drake, A. W., *Fundamentals of Applied Probability Theory*, McGraw-Hill, New York, 1967.

5. Feller, W., *An Introduction to Probability Theory and Its Applications*, Vol. I, 2nd ed., Wiley, New York, 1957.

6. Feller, W., *An Introduction to Probability Theory and Its Applications*, Vol. II, Wiley, New York, 1966.

7. Meyer, P. L., *Introductory Probability and Statistical Applications*, Addison-Wesley, Reading, Mass., 1965.

8. Parzen, E., *Modern Probability Theory and Its Applications*, Wiley, New York, 1960.

9. Phillips, D. T., *Applied Goodness of Fit Testing*, OR Monograph No. 1, American Institute of Industrial Engineers, Inc., Norcross, Ga., 1972.

EXERCISES

1. Suppose that an experiment has five possible outcomes, which are denoted $\{1, 2, 3, 4, 5\}$. Let A be the event $\{1, 2, 3\}$ and let B be the event $\{3, 4, 5\}$. For each of the following relations, tell whether it could possibly hold. If it could, say why or give an example; if it could not, explain why not.

   a. $P(A) = P(B)$
   b. $P(A) = 2P(B)$
   c. $P(A) = 1 - P(B)$
   d. $P(A) + P(B) > 1$
   e. $P(A) - P(B) < 0$
   f. $P(A) - P(B) > 1$

2. The sample space of a particular experiment is given by $S = \{0, 1, 2, 3, 4, 5\}$. Let three events be defined as $A = \{0, 1, 2\}$, $B = \{0, 2, 4\}$, and $C = \{1, 3, 5\}$. Assuming that the probabilities of A, B, and C are given, but no further information is available, express the probabilities of as many of the following events as you can.

   a. $A \cap B$
   b. $B \cup C$
   c. $\bar{A}$
   d. $B \cap \bar{C}$
   e. $\overline{(A \cap B \cup C}$

3. If two events are known to be mutually exclusive, could they also be independent? If they are known to be independent, could they also be mutually exclusive? If they are *not* mutually exclusive, could they be independent? If they are *not* independent, could they be mutually exclusive?

4. Prove Properties 4, 5, and 6, using only the axioms 1, 2, and 3, and the rules of set theory.

5. Prove relation 12, using 3, 8, 'and the rules of set theory.

6. Let X be a discrete random variable whose CDF is $F(x) = 1 - \left(\frac{1}{3}\right)^{x+1}$ for $x = 0, 1, 2, \ldots$. What is $P(X = 3)$?

7. Show how $G(x)$, the complementary cumulative distribution function, may be used to obtain $p(x)$, when X is discrete, and $f(x)$, when X is continuous.

8. Let X be a continuous random variable having a density function of the form

$$f(x) = a - \frac{x}{10}, \quad \text{for } 0 < x < b$$

$$= 0 \quad \text{elsewhere}$$

where a and b are constants which have to be determined so as to make $f(x)$ a legitimate density function.
a. Select an appropriate pair of values for a and b.
b. Using these values, find $P\left(X < \frac{b}{2}\right)$.

9. Suppose that the life length in hours of a certain light bulb is a continuous random variable with density function

$$f(x) = \frac{100}{x^2} \quad \text{for } x > 100$$

$$= 0 \quad \text{elsewhere}$$

What is the probability that the bulb will last less than 200 hours if it is known that it was still functioning after 150 hours?

10. X and Y are discrete random variables defined on the ranges $x = 0, 1, 2$ and $y = -1, 0, 1$. The joint probability distribution is indicated in the table below, where the entry in any cell gives the probability of the corresponding combination of values of X and Y.

Y \ X	0	1	2
−1	$\frac{1}{9}$	$\frac{1}{6}$	$\frac{1}{18}$
0	$\frac{1}{6}$	0	$\frac{1}{6}$
1	$\frac{1}{9}$	$\frac{1}{6}$	$\frac{1}{18}$

Find the marginal distributions of X and Y, the conditional distribution of Y given $X = 0$, and the conditional distribution of X given $Y = 0$.

11. Let the joint PDF of a discrete two-dimensional random variable (X, Y) be given by

$$p(x, y) = k\left(\frac{1}{2}\right)^{x+y+1} \quad \text{for } x = 0, 1, 2 \text{ and } y = 1, 2, 3$$

$$= 0 \quad \text{elsewhere}$$

where k is some constant having whatever value is necessary to make the function a joint PDF. What is $P(X = 1 \mid Y = 2)$?

12. Using the definition of expectation (either discrete or continuous) and algebraic manipulation, prove the properties
     a. $E(aX) = aE(X)$
     b. $E(X+b) = E(X)+b$
     c. $E(X+Y) = E(X)+E(Y)$

13. Using the definition of variance and algebraic manipulation, prove the properties
     a. $V(X) = E(X^2) - E(X)^2$
     b. $V(aX) = a^2V(X)$
     c. $V(X+b) = V(X)$
     d. $V(X+Y) = V(X) + V(Y) + 2\ \text{cov}(X,\ Y)$

14. Using the properties of expectation and variance, show that if c is any constant,

$$E\{(X-c)^2\} = V(x) + (E(X)-c)^2$$

15. Prove that if X is a nonnegative random variable,

$$E(X) = \int_0^\infty G(x)\,dx \qquad \text{in the continuous case, and}$$

$$E(X) = \sum_{x=1}^\infty G(x) \qquad \text{in the discrete case}$$

16. Let the joint density function of X and Y be

$$f(x,\ y) = \frac{1}{5}(8 - 2x - y) \qquad \text{for } 0 \le x \le 2$$

$$3 \le y \le 4$$

$$= 0 \qquad \text{elsewhere}$$

Find $E(X)$, $E(Y)$, $E(XY)$, and cov(X, Y).

17. Let the joint density function of X and Y be

$$f(x,\ y) = e^{-y} \qquad \text{for } 0 < x < y$$

$$= 0 \qquad \text{elsewhere}$$

Find $E(X\,|\,y)$, and verify that $E(X) = E(E(X\,|\,y))$.

18. Verify that the X and Y of problem 10 are dependent random variables, but that their dependence is not apparent from the value of the covariance.

19. In problem 11, obtain the marginal distributions of X and Y, and determine whether X and Y are independent by seeing if the product of the marginals is the same as $p(x,\ y)$, for all x and y.

CHAPTER 6
RANDOM PROCESSES

6.1 INTRODUCTION

This chapter is concerned with the techniques of modeling random processes— processes which evolve through time in a manner that is not completely predictable. With a description this general, it should be obvious that real-world examples exist in abundance. Indeed, almost any conceivable context can provide an opportunity to use the tools presented here.

Whenever a mathematical technique has many potential applications, there is a danger in presenting it in terms so oriented to one application or one category of applications that others cannot be envisioned. Yet a purely abstract presentation is just as likely to leave the reader unappreciative of the potential applicability of the mathematics. Every teacher knows that students need concrete examples; the real dilemma occurs in deciding whether it is better to present the general, abstract concepts first and then illustrate them, or to give a concrete example first and then attempt to generalize.

Some very fine textbooks (particularly those intended for mathematics students) take the first approach. Presumably the authors feel that it is most important that the concepts be understood in their full abstract generality, even if that means that some students may encounter difficulty in relating the abstractions to their real-world referents. Other textbooks (often those intended for business school students or other "practitioners") take the second approach, preferring to sacrifice generality, if necessary, to ensure that whatever *is* learned can be directly applied.

Although this chapter will adopt the second approach—that of example first, theory second—the contention held here is that it is extremely important to achieve both goals. We have elected to make continuous use of one concrete example, referring to it each time a new concept is introduced. This is done only to provide a temporary pedagogical crutch in the early phases of understanding the concepts. The student should earnestly try to get beyond the example as soon as possible by imagining other situations which could be handled in the same way. The problems should help considerably in this effort.

The objective for the student should be to acquire the *skills* to model *new* situations. It is important that he understand the techniques well enough to recognize appropriate opportunities to use them, while at the same time appreciating their limitations enough to be conservative in their use. That is, he should know when and how to use them, but also when *not* to use them.

The basic methodology presented here was developed initially by the Russian mathematician, A. A. Markov, around the beginning of the 20th century. "Markov processes" form a subclass of the set of all random processes—a subclass with enough simplifying assumptions to make them easy to handle. More complicated (non-Markovian) processes are beyond the scope of this text, but certainly warrant further study by the interested student.

The first major section of the chapter deals with Markov processes in which time is measured discretely, or "counted". The concepts seem to be easier to learn when this restriction is made, perhaps because the only mathematics used is algebra. Many of the concepts established in the discrete time case hold also for continuous time Markov processes, which are the subject of the second major section. The mathematics is more difficult, however; calculus is required where algebra previously sufficed.

I. DISCRETE TIME PROCESSES

6.2   AN EXAMPLE

Imagine that you are anticipating graduation and are considering an offer of employment by the Reeves and Newton Dependable Old Manufacturing Corporation. It happens that the Random Corporation, as it is better known has a policy of reassigning its white-collar personnel every 6 months in order to keep them in touch with all phases of the business. They have three divisions: engineering, production, and sales. There is no set pattern of rotation; in fact, one never knows in which division one will work next. It is even possible to be reassigned to the same division one has been in for the past 6 months. On the other hand, not all possibilities are equally likely; where one goes next depends to some extent on where one has been before.

Now there are many questions one might pose for this process. The following gives just a sample:

1. If a man enters the engineering division, what is the probability that after three reassignments he will again be in engineering?
2. If a man starts in engineering, how many months will pass (on the average) before he is first assigned to sales?
3. After a man has spent 5 years in the company, how many times, on the average, will he have been assigned to the production division?
4. If a man is now in sales and you were to return at some distant time in the future, what is the probability that you would find the man in engineering?
5. In the long run, what percentage of a man's assignments will be to production?

These are examples of some very practical questions which you might want to answer in order to evaluate your potential satisfaction with a position in the Random Corporation. Some of these questions require probabilities as answers; others require expected values. Some pertain to the probability of being in a particular division at a specified time; others pertain to the time required to reach a division.

6.3   MODELING THE PROCESS

Because reassignment occurs only at fixed 6-month intervals, the passage of time may be recorded by counting the number of reassignments that have occurred. Starting at an arbitrary time, denote a particular 6-month interval by

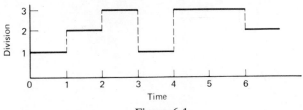

Figure 6.1
A realization.

the number zero. The first reassignment will occur at the end of that interval, so the following interval will be denoted by the number one, and so on. The nth reassignment occurs at the beginning of the nth 6-month interval.

It is also convenient to number the divisions, so let engineering be denoted by 1, production by 2, and sales by 3. This particular arrangement is obviously arbitrary.

A *realization*, or time history, of the process can now be drawn as a graph, as in Fig. 6.1. This would show that at time 0 (and for the next 6 months) the man was in division 1 (engineering), was then assigned to division 2 (production), next to division 3 (sales), and so on. Of course, this is a record of the past; the future is unknown. If time zero is the present and we wish to predict the future, we would have to say that it is represented by the set of all possible such graphs, each graph having a certain probability associated with it.

If we specify a particular interval in the future and ask what division the man will be at that time, we would have to say that it is given by a random variable which can take on the values 1, 2, and 3, according to some probability distribution. Since this is true for any specified time interval, one way to describe the future of the whole process is to say that it is given by a sequence of random variables, $\{X_1, X_2, X_3, \ldots\}$. The random variable X_n would be interpreted as the (uncertain) assignment that the man will have during the nth interval.

Virtually any random process for which time can be measured discretely can be represented as such a sequence of random variables. In fact, we may take the following as formal definitions: A *discrete time stochastic process* is any sequence of random variables indexed by time. The set of all possible values for the random variables is called the *state space*; the value assumed by X_n is called the *state of the process at time n*. Changes of state are called *transitions*.

If you focus not on time but on the structure of allowable transitions, it is natural to construct the *transition diagram*. This is a pictorial map of the process in which states are represented by points and transitions by arrows. An arrow from state 1 to state 2, for example, would mean that if the process is in state 1 at some time n, then it is possible for it to be in state 2 at time $n+1$. In our example there are three states with no restrictions on possible transitions, so the transition diagram would be as shown in Fig. 6.2.

Instead of thinking of a random process as a sequence of random variables, one can visualize it as the random walk of a particle over the transition diagram. Occupying a state is equivalent to the particle being at a particular point; a transition corresponds to a "jump" or an instantaneous movement of the particle along one of the arrows.

There is a slight deliberate ambiguity in the term "transition." In some applications, we will want a transition to occur each time that the time index is

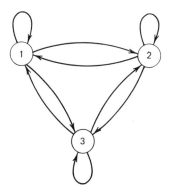

Figure 6.2
A transition diagram.

incremented, even if the new state is the same as the old. Such transitions, to give them a name, are called *virtual transitions*, and are represented by loops in the transition diagram. On other occasions, we want to consider only genuine changes of state, or *real transitions*. If so, the transition diagram would have no loops.

So far we have no data nor probability distributions. Because the process is described by a sequence of random variables, $\{X_1, X_2, X_3, \ldots\}$, we must *at least* specify the probability distribution of each X_i. However, this will not be enough. We have mentioned in the Random Corporation example that where a man is assigned next depends on where he has been assigned before. In other words, the random variables, X_i, are not independent. Whenever one has two or more dependent random variables, either a joint distribution function or a conditional distribution function is necessary to completely express the relationship. The marginal distributions of the random variables taken individually do not do the whole job. At worst, then, the complete specification of a stochastic process would require joint distribution functions, taken jointly over all of the random variables. But this would be absurdly impractical to attempt for any real-world process.

At this point we need Markov's simplifying assumption. In the case of our example, the assumption is made that where a man will be assigned next depends *only* on his present assignment. We thereby eliminate all previous experience of the man as a factor in determining the next assignment. More generally, a *Markov chain* is a discrete time stochastic process in which each random variable, X_i, depends only upon the previous one, X_{i-1}, and affects only the subsequent one, X_{i+1}. The term "chain" suggests the linking of the random variables to their immediately adjacent neighbors in the sequence.

Compared to stochastic processes in general, Markov chains are very simple. Without completely eliminating the dependence between random variables (which would severely curtail our ability to represent real-life processes realistically), we have avoided the necessity of having to express joint distributions of everything all at once. Instead, it will be sufficient to express joint or conditional distributions of just two neighboring random variables at a time.

Suppose that X_0 represents the man's present assignment and we are interested in X_1, his next assignment. What we want is a probability distribution over the three possible values for X_1. But these probabilities depend on what division the man is in now. Suppose he is in engineering (i.e., $X_0 = 1$). Then, for his next assignment, he will be kept in engineering ($X_1 = 1$) or transferred to production ($X_1 = 2$) or transferred to sales ($X_1 = 3$). The probabilities of these *transitions* give the probabilities for the *state* at time 1, provided that the man is now in engineering. Of course, if the man is now in production, the probabilities will be different, and if he is in sales they will be different yet.

One convenient way to record these different probabilities is in matrix form:

$$\mathbf{P} = \begin{bmatrix} p_{11} & p_{12} & p_{13} \\ p_{21} & p_{22} & p_{23} \\ p_{31} & p_{32} & p_{33} \end{bmatrix}$$

The first row of this matrix represents the probabilities that the man will next be in engineering, production, or sales, respectively, if he is now in engineering. The second row gives the same probabilities if he is now in production; the third row, if he is in sales. Each row is, individually, a probability distribution for X_1; the appropriate one to use depends on which value X_0 has. Incidentally, the fact that each row is a probability distribution implies that the elements of each row must sum to 1.

The element p_{ij} means the probability that $X_1 = j$ if you know that $X_0 = i$. Formally, it is the conditional probability, $p_{ij} = P\{X_1 = j \mid X_0 = i\}$. A handy, though somewhat inaccurate, way to think of it is as the probability of "going" from state i to j, or of making the transition from i to j. The p_{ij}'s are, in fact, called (one-step) *transition probabilities*, and the matrix $\mathbf{P}$ is called the *transition matrix*.

Instead of using the matrix, we could have just labeled the arrows of the transition diagram. The arrow from i to j would receive the label p_{ij}, which can then be thought of as the probability that that arrow is used when the particle leaves point i. Row i of $\mathbf{P}$ would correspond to the set of arrows leaving point i, so the sum of the probabilities taken over this set must equal 1. For our example, the transition diagram would be as in Fig. 6.3. Of course, if any of these p_{ij} are zero (indicating that a direct transition from i to j is not possible) the arrow from i to j would simply not appear in the diagram.

It should be apparent that the labeled transition diagram contains exactly the same information that the matrix $\mathbf{P}$ does. Given a transition matrix, we can construct a unique transition diagram; given a transition diagram we can

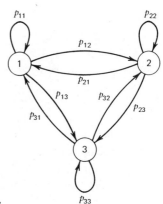

Figure 6.3
A transition diagram.

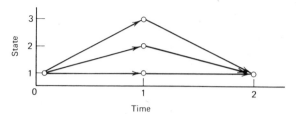

Figure 6.4
The three possible sequences.

construct a unique transition matrix. To construct either one, in order to model some real-life process, it is necessary to imagine every possible transition from one state to another and then to find the probability that is associated with each possible transition.

We have now expressed everything necessary to describe X_1, the state at time 1, taking into account the dependence upon X_0, the state at time 0. By the Markov assumption, no further information about previous states is required. We now turn our attention to X_2, the state at time 2. Suppose once again that our man is initially in engineering, $X_0 = 1$, and we want to know the probability that he will be in engineering at time 2, $X_2 = 1$. Although X_2 is not directly dependent upon X_0, it is dependent on X_1, which in turn is dependent on X_0.

There are three distinct ways that the event we are interested in could come about, corresponding to the three alternative possibilities for the state at time 1. The man could stay in engineering the whole time; he could be transferred to production at time 1 and then back to engineering; or he could be transferred to sales and then back to engineering. Figure 6.4 shows these three possible sequences of transitions. There is no way other than these that the event could occur, and the three ways are mutually exclusive. In other words, if the man is to be in engineering at time 2 when he was in engineering at time 0, then he must get there by exactly one of the three alternative paths enumerated.

Consequently, the probability that he will be in engineering at time 2 given that he was in engineering at time 1 can be broken into the sum of three probabilities, one for each possible path. Using an inefficient, but natural, notation, we might write

$$P\{X_0 = 1 \rightarrow X_2 = 1\} = P\{X_0 = 1 \rightarrow X_1 = 1 \rightarrow X_2 = 1\}$$
$$+ P\{X_0 = 1 \rightarrow X_1 = 2 \rightarrow X_2 = 1\}$$
$$+ P\{X_0 = 1 \rightarrow X_1 = 3 \rightarrow X_2 = 1\}$$

(This actually represents an abuse of conventional probability notation, but will be corrected in due course.) The problem now is to express "path" probabilities, such as $P\{X_0 = 1 \rightarrow X_1 = 3 \rightarrow X_2 = 1\}$.

We have, of course, notation to express the probability for the first leg of the path, namely p_{13}. Furthermore the probability for the second leg, the probability of going from state 3 to 1, is (by the Markov assumption) independent of the state at time 0. Hence we can multiply the probabilities of the two legs to get the probability of the path:

$$P\{X_0 = 1 \rightarrow X_1 = 3 \rightarrow X_2 = 1\} = P\{X_0 = 1 \rightarrow X_1 = 3\}P\{X_1 = 3 \rightarrow X_2 = 1\}$$
$$= p_{13}P\{X_1 = 3 \rightarrow X_2 = 1\}$$

A similar expression can be written for the other paths.

An additional simplifying assumption becomes convenient at this point. Because $\{X_1 = 3 \to X_2 = 1\}$ is a transition from state 3 to 1, it would be nice to be able to use the notation p_{31} for its probability, but up until now p_{31} has referred to the probability of making the transition from 3 to 1 at the *first* transition and we are now talking about the *second* transition. The obvious thing to do is to assume that transition probabilities do not change with the passage of time. The term used to describe this assumption is *stationarity*. For a stationary Markov chain, the matrix $\mathbf{P}$ will provide the one-step transition probabilities for any time, and (as we shalll see) is sufficient to describe the entire process. If our process were not stationary, it would be possible to continue; but we would require a new transition matrix for each transition. The stationarity assumption is discussed later. For now, it is expedient to make the assumption and continue the development.

With the assumption of stationarity,

$$P\{X_0 = 1 \to X_1 = 3 \to X_2 = 1\} = p_{13}p_{31}.$$

In words, the two-step path probability is given by the product of the two one-step transition probabilities comprising the path. Finding the corresponding probabilities for the other two paths, and collecting results gives

$$P\{X_0 = 1 \to X_2 = 1\} = p_{11}p_{11} + p_{12}p_{21} + p_{13}p_{31}.$$

This expresses, in terms of values already known, the probability that the man will be in engineering at time 2, given that he was in engineering at time 0.

By similar logic, we may obtain the probabilities for being in production and sales at time 2, given that he started in engineering:

$$P\{X_0 = 1 \to X_2 = 2\} = p_{11}p_{12} + p_{12}p_{22} + p_{13}p_{32}$$

$$P\{X_0 = 1 \to X_2 = 3\} = p_{11}p_{13} + p_{12}p_{23} + p_{13}p_{33}$$

The three expressions together give the probability distribution of the random variable X_2, given that $X_0 = 1$.

If the man is not initially in engineering, but in production, we get three different expressions for the distribution of X_2, and three more for when he begins in sales. There are a total of nine expressions required to specify the distribution of X_2 under the various possible initial conditions. As it was for X_1, it is convenient to use a matrix arrangement. Let $\mathbf{P}^{(2)}$ denote the matrix of these probabilities, and let $p_{ij}^{(2)}$ represent the i, jth entry.

$$\mathbf{P}^{(2)} = \begin{bmatrix} p_{11}^{(2)} & p_{12}^{(2)} & p_{13}^{(2)} \\ p_{21}^{(2)} & p_{22}^{(2)} & p_{23}^{(2)} \\ p_{31}^{(2)} & p_{32}^{(2)} & p_{33}^{(2)} \end{bmatrix}$$

$\mathbf{P}^{(2)}$ is called the two-step transition matrix; its elements, two-step transition probabilities. They give conditional probabilities for the states at time 2 under varying possible conditions for the state at time zero. Each row is a probability distribution. Loosely speaking, $p_{ij}^{(2)}$ is the probability of "going" from state i to state j in two steps. It is also the probability which we previously designated $P\{X_0 = i \to X_2 = j\}$. The briefer notation is clearly more efficient (once you know what it means), so at this point we drop the old notation.

We know how to express the $p_{ij}^{(2)}$ in terms of the one-step transition probabilities. For example,

$$p_{11}^{(2)} = p_{11}p_{11} + p_{12}p_{21} + p_{13}p_{31}.$$

We got this by considering all the ways that the event could occur. It would be preferable to have a systematic method that would yield the correct expressions without requiring a detailed consideration of the process.

One method that will work utilizes the transition diagram. Each line of the diagram represents a one-step transition. Because of stationarity, the probability associated with each line remains constant as time progresses. So a particular sequence of transitions is represented by a sequence of arrows in the transition diagram, and the probability of taking that sequence of transitions is given by the product of probabilities associated with the arrows. (Independence of events is required in order to multiply probabilities, but this independence is assured by the Markov assumption.) Of course, in order to represent a legitimate sequence of transitions, the arrows must be arranged "head-to-tail." The graph theoretic term for such a sequence is a *walk*. One can obtain a walk by placing a pencil at any point of the diagram and, without lifting the pencil, following arrows from point to point, always moving *with* the direction of the arrows. Arrows may be traversed more than once in a walk.

Thus, a short-cut way to obtain the expressions for the two-step transition probabilities is to examine the transition diagram for all two-step walks starting at the initial state and ending at the state of interest. For each walk, you multiply the probabilities associated with the arrows in that walk, then add all of the products. You should verify that this method works by using it to obtain the expressions we derived earlier.

There is another systematic way to get the two-step transition probabilities—a way so automatic that it lends itself to computer implementation. The method is based on the simple observation that the expressions previously derived are exactly what would be obtained if the matrix **P** were multiplied by itself (using, of course, matrix multiplication). In symbols,

$$\mathbf{P}^{(2)} = \mathbf{PP} = \mathbf{P}^2$$

In words, the matrix of two-step transition probabilities is equal to the square of the matrix of one-step transition probabilities. This is not obvious; it is a derived relation, requiring both the Markov and stationarity assumptions. It is a most fortuitous relation because it means that a familiar, well-known matrix operation can be used to compute the probabilities for X_2.

So far we have described X_1 and X_2. To get the distributions of X_3 under varying possible conditions at time 0, we again have to consider the ways in which the states could occur. For example, suppose the man starts in engineering ($X_0 = 1$) and we are interested in the probability that he is in engineering at time 3 ($X_3 = 1$). Then at time 2, he must have been in engineering, production, or sales, and have made the transition to engineering at time 3. Since these are mutually exclusive, collectively exhaustive possibilities,

$$p_{11}^{(3)} = p_{11}^{(2)}p_{11} + p_{12}^{(2)}p_{21} + p_{13}^{(2)}p_{31}$$

By this logic, we can write all three-step transition probabilities in terms of the two-step and one-step transition probabilities, which are of course already known. Furthermore, we may observe that the same results would be obtained by multiplying the two-step transition matrix by the one-step transition matrix. That is,

$$\mathbf{P}^{(3)} = \mathbf{P}^{(2)}\mathbf{P}$$

But since $\mathbf{P}^{(2)} = \mathbf{P}^2$,

$$\mathbf{P}^{(3)} = \mathbf{P}^2\mathbf{P} = \mathbf{P}^3$$

So the three-step transition matrix is just the one-step matrix cubed. The elements of this matrix completely describe X_3, the random variable describing the state at time 3.

By now it should be apparent how to continue. In general, the n-step transition matrix equals the one-step transition matrix raised to the nth power,

$$\mathbf{P}^{(n)} = \mathbf{P}^n$$

This is the single most important result for Markov chains. By raising $\mathbf{P}$ to the appropriate power, we can answer any question pertaining to the probability of being in a particular state at a particular time. The complete sequence of random variables $\{X_1, X_2, X_3, \ldots\}$ which characterize the process is now fully described.

The method of finding walks in the transition diagram also generalizes. The probability of a walk of any number of steps is given by the product of the transition probabilities associated with the arrows in the sequence. The n-step transition probability $p_{ij}^{(n)}$ is given by the sum of the probabilities of all walks of length n from i to j. If the transition diagram is large, complicated, or both; if the number of steps is large, it is impractical to try to enumerate every such walk. Nevertheless, it is worthwhile to realize that the raising of $\mathbf{P}$ to the nth power accomplishes something which is precisely equivalent.

There is one minor extension to be considered now. We have all of the random variables $\{X_1, X_2, X_3, \ldots\}$ characterized *provided* that the state at time zero is known. Occasionally it happens that the value of X_0 is not known with certainty, but is given by a probability distribution. Suppose that such is the case, and let $p_i^{(0)}$ denote the probability that $X_0 = i$. For example, $p_1^{(0)}$ would be the probability that the man is in engineering at time 0. Suppose we want to know the probability that he will be in, for example, production at some later time, say $n = 5$. Having the matrix $\mathbf{P}^{(5)}$, we can read off $p_{12}^{(5)}$, $p_{22}^{(5)}$, and $p_{32}^{(5)}$ from the second column. These are all probabilities of being in state 2 at time 5, but differ in the assumed state at time 0. The obvious thing to do is to take a weighted average of $p_{12}^{(5)}$, $p_{22}^{(5)}$, and $p_{32}^{(5)}$, weighting each according to the likelihood that the initial state it assumes is, in fact, the correct one. This logic would yield the expression

$$p_1^{(0)}p_{12}^{(5)} + p_2^{(0)}p_{22}^{(5)} + p_3^{(0)}p_{32}^{(5)}$$

which is, indeed, the probability that $X_5 = 2$.

Extending the notation a bit, let $p_i^{(n)} = P\{X_n = i\}$. Such a probability is called a *state probability* to distinguish it from a transition probability. It would give the probability of being in a particular state at a particular time, regardless of the state at time zero. Since matrix notation has proved so convenient for the transition probabilities, let $\mathbf{p}^{(n)}$ be the row vector of state probabilities. (Note that this is a lower-case $\mathbf{p}$; the upper case is reserved for the transition matrix.)

Using the new notation, we may observe that the expressions we would obtain for the elements of $\mathbf{p}^{(5)}$—one of which was derived above—can also be obtained from

$$\mathbf{p}^{(5)} = \mathbf{p}^{(0)}\mathbf{P}^{(5)}$$

Furthermore, the logic will generalize to give the state probabilities at any time:

$$\mathbf{p}^{(n)} = \mathbf{p}^{(0)} \mathbf{P}^{(n)}$$

In words, the vector of state probabilities for time n is given by the vector of initial state probabilities multiplied by the n-step transition matrix.

The right-hand side of this relation involves matrix multiplication, which is ordinarily not commutative (i.e., $AB \neq BA$), so the order is important. Also it is important to remember that the $\mathbf{p}^{(n)}$ are *row* vectors. If, for reasons of convenience in writing the expressions on paper, one prefers column vectors, everything must be transposed. This would in turn reverse the order of multiplication on the right-hand side. That is,

$$\mathbf{p}^{(n)T} = \mathbf{P}^{(n)T} \mathbf{p}^{(0)T}$$

6.4   SOME NUMERICAL RESULTS

Let us now put some specific numbers into our example and perform the calculations we have prescribed. Suppose that the policies of the Random Corporation dictate that a man who is in engineering cannot be assigned to sales, but may be reassigned to engineering or transferred to production, with equal likelihood. A man in the production division is equally likely to stay there or to change to sales, but could not go to engineering. A man in sales is certain to be transferred out, with engineering being 3 times as likely as production to be the new assignment.

The transition diagram resulting from these assumptions is shown in Fig. 6.5.

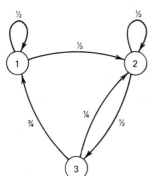

Figure 6.5
The transition diagram.

The one-step transition matrix is:

$$\mathbf{P} = \begin{bmatrix} 0.5 & 0.5 & 0 \\ 0 & 0.5 & 0.5 \\ 0.75 & 0.25 & 0 \end{bmatrix}$$

Because one number looks pretty much like another, we will have to infer the meaning of an element from its position in the matrix.

We get the matrix of two-step transition probabilities, $\mathbf{P}^{(2)}$, by squaring $\mathbf{P}$:

$$\mathbf{P}^{(2)} = \mathbf{P}^2 = \begin{bmatrix} 0.250 & 0.500 & 0.250 \\ 0.375 & 0.375 & 0.250 \\ 0.375 & 0.500 & 0.125 \end{bmatrix}$$

This says, for example, that a man who starts in engineering has a probability of 0.25 of being in sales after two reassignments. If the initial department is not known with certainty, but is given by a probability distribution, we would have recourse to the formula

$$\mathbf{p}^{(2)} = \mathbf{p}^{(0)}\mathbf{P}^{(2)}$$

If, for example, the man were equally likely to be assigned to any of the three divisions initially, then

$$\mathbf{p}^{(0)} = [p_1^{(0)}, p_2^{(0)}, p_3^{(0)}] = \left[\frac{1}{3}, \frac{1}{3}, \frac{1}{3}\right]$$

and

$$\mathbf{p}^{(2)} = \left[\frac{1}{3}, \frac{1}{3}, \frac{1}{3}\right] \begin{bmatrix} 0.250 & 0.500 & 0.250 \\ 0.375 & 0.375 & 0.250 \\ 0.375 & 0.500 & 0.125 \end{bmatrix}$$

$$= [0.3333, 0.4583, 0.2083]$$

In words, if the man is equally likely to be assigned to any of the three divisions initially, then the probability that he will be in engineering after two transitions is 0.3333. The probability that he will be in production is 0.4583; and in sales, 0.2083.

The transition matrices of higher order are:

$$\mathbf{P}^{(3)} = \mathbf{P}^3 = \mathbf{P}^2\mathbf{P} \ (\text{or } \mathbf{P}\mathbf{P}^2) = \begin{bmatrix} 0.3125 & 0.4375 & 0.2500 \\ 0.3750 & 0.4375 & 0.1875 \\ 0.28125 & 0.46875 & 0.2500 \end{bmatrix}$$

$$\mathbf{P}^{(4)} = \mathbf{P}^4 = \mathbf{P}^3\mathbf{P} \ (\text{or } \mathbf{P}\mathbf{P}^3 \text{ or } \mathbf{P}^2\mathbf{P}^2) = \begin{bmatrix} 0.34375 & 0.4375 & 0.21875 \\ 0.328125 & 0.453125 & 0.21875 \\ 0.328125 & 0.4375 & 0.234375 \end{bmatrix}$$

$$\mathbf{P}^{(5)} = \mathbf{P}^5 = \mathbf{P}^4\mathbf{P} \ (\text{or other ways}) = \begin{bmatrix} 0.3359375 & 0.4453125 & 0.21875 \\ 0.328125 & 0.4453125 & 0.2265625 \\ 0.33984375 & 0.44140625 & 0.21875 \end{bmatrix}$$

and so on.

Later, we shall want to explore the behavior of the transition probabilities viewed as functions of time and will resurrect this numerical example at that time.

6.5   THE ASSUMPTIONS RECONSIDERED

Although it is easy to remember *how* to compute state and transition probabilities, it can be tempting to forget about *why* the methods work. In particular, one can easily forget that the Markov and stationarity assumptions are crucial. While it is true that many real-life processes satisfy these two assumptions (or, at least well enough for the models to be considered useful), it is also true that many do not. There are no automatic safeguards built into the methods to prevent their misuse. Even if a process does *not* satisfy the Markov and stationarity assumptions, it is still possible to define a one-step transition matrix and use it to compute "answers." The answers would simply be meaningless. Thus, a certain amount of vigilance is required to avoid applying these methods when the circumstances are inappropriate.

Although there exist certain statistical tests to verify the reasonableness of making the Markov and stationarity assumptions (cf. Bhat(3) pp. 96–102), the best protection is provided by *understanding* the assumptions and what they imply and by *thinking* about whether they seem appropriate to the situation.

The Markov assumption is basically an independence assumption. It says that knowledge of the state at any time is sufficient to predict the future of the process from that point on; information about how that state was reached (the sequence of prior states) is superfluous. Simpler but less precise ways to say the same thing are "given the present, the future is independent of the past," and "the process is forgetful." In the case of the example we have been using, the process would *not* be Markovian if a man's record of past assignments are taken into account when determining his next. Suppose, for example, that a man who is now in engineering was previously in sales. If the fact that he was previously in sales has any bearing on the likelihood of being assigned next to production, the Markov assumption would be violated. It is easy to imagine that such might be the case. On the other hand, if records of previous assignments are not kept, the man himself is not consulted, and new assignments are made by a computer using a random number generator, the Markov assumption might be precisely satisfied. More commonly, it is satisfied (if at all) in the weaker sense that one is unable to *detect* any relationship between new assignments and past ones. One may sometimes suspect that a relationship could exist but at the same time be satisfied that it is so weak that one is content to make use of the Markov assumption.

The stationarity assumption is one of "constancy" over time. It suggests stability of the process, although of course it does not imply that the process remains in a fixed state or even that there is a sluggishness in the rate at which transitions occur. It is the *probability mechanism* that is assumed stable. Again, it is easy to imagine cases for which the assumption does not hold. If the time scale of the model is very long, that process may undergo such fundamental changes—growth, evolution, ageing, policy change, and the like—that one would hesitate to call it the same process. Even over the short run, many real-life processes have "peak periods" or "slow times" during which they exhibit behavior that is different from the norm. Such changes can occur gradually or all at once, but in either case would violate the stationarity assumption. In the case of the example, one might be conscious of an increasing tendency to assign men who have been in production to engineering rather than to sales. If so, the transition matrix that accurately described the transition probabilities at one time would not be accurate at a later time.

The Markov and stationarity assumptions are unrelated to one another; either could hold in the absence of the other.

6.6   FORMAL DEFINITIONS AND THEORY

The development of Markov modeling techniques has so far been heuristic. Although the formulas were made to sound plausible, no proofs were given to assure that they really are consistent with the rules of probability theory and require *only* the Markov and stationarity assumptions. Furthermore, we still lack formal definitions that are general enough to cover every conceivable application, yet specific enough to be used in proofs. This section remedies these deficiencies. At the same time, it concisely summarizes everything done so far.

Let $\{X_n, n = 0, 1, 2, \ldots\}$ be a family of real valued random variables indexed by n. The family is called a *discrete parameter* (or discrete time) *stochastic process*. The value of X_n for a specific realization of the process is called the *state of the process at the nth step*. If the random variables X_n are discrete random variables—that is, if they take on only integer values—we call the process a *discrete state* process. Although it is possible to consider continuous state processes, this discussion will be confined to discrete state and discrete parameter processes.

In general the random variables are dependent on one another, so one must describe the process in terms of either joint or conditional probabilities. The index n typically denotes something akin to time, so at worst X_n will be dependent on $X_{n-1}, X_{n-2}, \ldots, X_0$ (that is, the "past history" of the process), but not upon $X_{n+1}, X_{n+2}, \ldots$ (the "future" of the process).

If for all n,

$$P\{X_n = j_n \mid X_{n-1} = j_{n-1}, X_{n-2} = j_{n-2}, \ldots, X_0 = j_0\} = P\{X_n = j_n \mid X_{n-1} = j_{n-1}\}$$

the process is said to be a discrete state, discrete parameter Markov process, or a *Markov chain*. In other words the conditional distribution of X_n given the whole past history of the process must equal the conditional distribution of X_n given X_{n-1}. The conditional probability $P\{X_n = j \mid X_{n-1} = i\}$ is referred to as the one-step transition probability from i to j at step n. If for all m and n, $P\{X_n = j \mid X_{n-1} = i\} = P\{X_m = j \mid X_{m-1} = i\}$, the Markov chain is said to be *stationary*. In this case, the one-step transition probabilities do not depend explicitly on the step number. For such a process, it is sufficient to specify the *one-step transition probabilities*, $p_{ij} = P\{X_1 = j \mid X_0 = i\}$, because the one-step transition probabilities at any step number are the same. The square matrix $\mathbf{P}$ whose elements are the p_{ij}'s is called the *one-step transition matrix*, or just the transition matrix when there is no likelihood of confusion.

The n-step transition probabilities, $p_{ij}^{(n)}$, are defined by $p_{ij}^{(n)} = P\{X_n = j \mid X_0 = i\}$. In words, $p_{ij}^{(n)}$ is the probability that the process is in state j at time n, given that it was in state i at time 0. Of course, $p_{ij}^{(1)}$ is just p_{ij}. In addition, it can easily be seen from the definition that $p_{ij}^{(0)}$ must be 1 if $i = j$, and 0 otherwise.

We may derive an important relationship as follows:

$$
\begin{aligned}
p_{ij}^{(n)} &= P\{X_n = j \mid X_0 = i\} && \text{(definition)} \\
&= \sum_k P\{X_n = j, X_{n-1} = k \mid X_0 = i\} && \text{(marginal from joint)} \\
&= \sum_k P\{X_n = j \mid X_{n-1} = k, X_0 = i\}P\{X_{n-1} = k \mid X_0 = i\} && \text{(joint from conditional)} \\
&= \sum_k P\{X_n = j \mid X_{n-1} = k\} P\{X_{n-1} = k \mid X_0 = i\} && \text{(Markov assumption)} \\
&= \sum_k P\{X_1 = j \mid X_0 = k\} P\{X_{n-1} = k \mid X_0 = i\} && \text{(stationarity)} \\
&= \sum_k p_{kj}p_{ik}^{(n-1)} && \text{(definition)}
\end{aligned}
$$

In conclusion, then,

$$p_{ij}^{(n)} = \sum_k p_{ik}^{(n-1)}p_{kj}$$

Observing that the right-hand side looks like the definition of matrix multiplication, we note that the same equation can be represented in matrix form by

$$\mathbf{P}^{(n)} = \mathbf{P}^{(n-1)}\mathbf{P}$$

where $\mathbf{P}^{(n)}$ is the matrix whose elements are the n-step transition probabilities. This fundamental relationship specifying the n-step transition probabilities of lower order is called the *Chapman-Kolmogorov equation*. It should be apparent from the derivation that the equation would not hold if either the Markov or stationarity properties were absent. On the other hand, these are the *only* assumptions required.

As a matter of fact, what has been derived is just a special case of the general form of the Chapman-Kolmogorov equations. (It is, however, the most frequently used form.) The general form, which can be proved by an argument similar to that given for the special case, is given by

$$p_{ij}^{(n)} = \sum_k p_{ik}^{(n-m)} p_{kj}^{(m)}$$

for any m between 1 and n, or in matrix representation,

$$\mathbf{P}^{(n)} = \mathbf{P}^{(n-m)}\mathbf{P}^{(m)}$$

Applying the Chapman-Kolmogorov equations iteratively, it is easy to prove that $\mathbf{P}^{(n)} = \mathbf{P}^n$. That is, the matrix of n-step probabilities is just the matrix of one-step transition probabilities raised to the nth power (using, of course, matrix multiplication).

If the unconditional probabilities $P\{X_n = j\}$ (called the *state probabilities*) are desired, the initial conditions must be specified. Of course, if the process is known with certainty to have started in a certain state, say i, at time zero, we have only to read off the elements of the ith row of $\mathbf{P}^{(n)}$, because the condition $X_0 = i$ is known to hold. More generally, the initial conditions may be given by a distribution over the possible states at time zero. Let $p_i^{(n)} = P\{X_n = i\}$, and let $\mathbf{p}^{(n)}$ denote the row vector whose elements are the $p_i^{(n)}$. (There is a slight possibility for confusion among elements, vectors, and matrices because of the similarity of notation, but in every case the number of subscripts provides the tell-tale clue.) Then the initial conditions are given by the vector $\mathbf{p}^{(0)}$. To get $\mathbf{p}^{(n)}$, we may use the following argument.

$$\begin{aligned} p_j^{(n)} &= P\{X_n = j\} \\ &= \sum_i P\{X_n = j \mid X_0 = i\}P\{X_0 = i\} \\ &= \sum_i p_{ij}^{(n)} p_i^{(0)} \end{aligned}$$

Therefore,

$$p_j^{(n)} = \sum_i p_i^{(0)} p_{ij}^{(n)}$$

Recognizing the right-hand side as multiplication of vectors, we see that

$$\mathbf{p}^{(n)} = \mathbf{p}^{(0)}\mathbf{P}^{(n)}$$

In words, the vector of state probabilities for time n is given by the vector of initial state probabilities multiplied by the n-step transition matrix. Thus, we see that a Markov chain is completely specified when its transition matrix $\mathbf{P}$ and the initial conditions $\mathbf{p}^{(0)}$ are known.

6.7   STEADY-STATE PROBABILITIES

To introduce the concepts of this section, consider once again the job assignment example. If we fix the initial state, say $X_0 = 3$, and observe how the

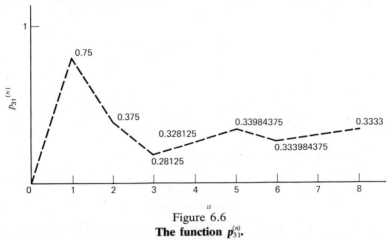

Figure 6.6
The function $p_{31}^{(n)}$.

transition probability to a particular state, say 1, behaves as a function of time, we would see the pattern of Fig. 6.6. The numerical values to plot the graph are drawn from successive powers of the transition matrix (see page 239). The graph plots the probability of the man being in the engineering division at various times in the future, assuming that he starts in sales. For $n = 0$, the probability is, of course, zero. It then jumps up to 0.75, then drops to 0.375, falls some more to 0.28125, rises slightly to 0.328125, and so on.

After some rather wide fluctuations when n is small, the probability seems to stabilize about the value 1/3. It is typical of processes of this kind that the transition probabilities do stabilize as n grows large. It is logical that they should do so, for as you consider the future at more and more distant times, the fact that the man is now in sales tends to lose significance. Put another way, if you had to estimate the likelihood of finding him in engineering 10 years from now and also the likelihood for 11 years from now, the numbers would be very nearly the same.

The same logic suggests that if the man is now in engineering or production, rather than sales, the distinction should lose relevance over time. Examination of the transition probability functions $p_{11}^{(n)}$ and $p_{21}^{(n)}$ verifies that they do indeed converge to the same value, 1/3 (See Fig. 6.7 and 6.8). The three graphs just drawn all relate to the probability of being in state 1 at time n; they differ in the initial state assumed. It appears that, for large n, the probability of being in

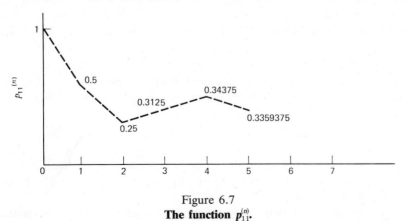

Figure 6.7
The function $p_{11}^{(n)}$.

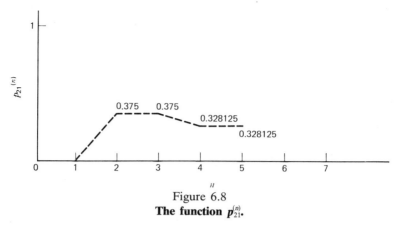

Figure 6.8
The function $p_{21}^{(n)}$.

state 1 is 1/3, regardless of where the process started. This makes intuitive sense if you think of the initial state as information about the process which is of some value in predicting the future of the process. As one projects further and further into the future (i.e., as n grows large), the value of this information decreases to the point of virtual irrelevance.

Because the value converged to is 1/3 and there are three states, one might also conjecture that as n grows large, all states become equally likely. This conjecture, however, is false. As we may see from the transition matrices, the probability of being in state 2 stabilizes at the value $0.4444\ldots$, or 4/9, and the probability of being in state 3 stabilizes at the value $0.2222\ldots$, or 2/9, regardless of the initial state.

To summarize our observations with respect to this example, then, we would say that if we were to assign the man to one of the three departments, and allow the process to operate for many transitions, then the probability of finding the man in each of the three departments would be independent of where he began, but would not be equal for the three departments. In more mechanistic terms, as we raise **P** to higher and higher powers, the rows will necessarily become identical but the columns will not.

We now generalize on the preceding remarks by discussing formally the behavior of a Markov chain as n, the number of transitions, goes to infinity. There are several terms in common use to describe the asymptotic values of the state or transition probability functions. We will call them *steady-state prob-abilities*. Other books may call them equilibrium probabilities, limiting values, or the stationary distribution—not to be confused with the stationarity assumption. The steady-state distribution is formally defined as the set of Π_j, where

$$\Pi_j = \lim_{n \to \infty} p_j^{(n)} = \lim_{n \to \infty} P\{X_n = j\}$$

In most of the cases you will encounter (but not all), the initial state will become less and less relevant to the n-step transition probability as n increases. In such cases,

$$\lim_{n \to \infty} P\{X_n = j \mid X_0 = i\} = \lim_{n \to \infty} P\{X_n = j\} = \Pi_j$$

so we can obtain the unconditional steady-state distribution from the n-step transition probabilities by taking n to infinity. We need not consider the initial conditions *in these cases.*

Whenever it is true that the steady-state probabilities are independent of the initial state, the matrix $\mathbf{P}^{(n)}$ becomes, as n goes to infinity, a matrix whose rows are identical. Each row is, in fact, the row vector $\mathbf{\Pi} = (\Pi_1, \Pi_2, \ldots)$. Hence we can obtain an equation for the steady-state distribution as follows:

$$\mathbf{P}^{(n)} = \mathbf{P}^{(n-1)}\mathbf{P}$$

$$\lim_{n \to \infty} \mathbf{P}^{(n)} = \lim_{n \to \infty} \mathbf{P}^{(n-1)}\mathbf{P}$$

$$\begin{bmatrix} \Pi_1, \Pi_2, \Pi_3, \ldots \\ \Pi_1, \Pi_2, \Pi_3, \ldots \\ \Pi_1, \Pi_2, \Pi_3, \ldots \\ \cdot \quad \cdot \quad \cdot \\ \cdot \quad \cdot \quad \cdot \\ \cdot \quad \cdot \quad \cdot \end{bmatrix} = \begin{bmatrix} \Pi_1, \Pi_2, \Pi_3, \ldots \\ \Pi_1, \Pi_2, \Pi_3, \ldots \\ \Pi_1, \Pi_2, \Pi_3, \ldots \\ \cdot \quad \cdot \quad \cdot \\ \cdot \quad \cdot \quad \cdot \\ \cdot \quad \cdot \quad \cdot \end{bmatrix} [\mathbf{P}]$$

This represents many replications of the same set of equations

$$\mathbf{\Pi} = \mathbf{\Pi}\mathbf{P}$$

or, if we wish to express this equation in terms of the more conventional column vectors

$$\mathbf{\Pi}^T = \mathbf{P}^T\mathbf{\Pi}^T$$

It turns out that this set of linear equations, though it has as many equations as unknowns, is a dependent set and therefore possesses an infinite number of solutions. (The dependency derives from the fact that every row of $\mathbf{P}$ sums to 1.) Only one of the infinite number of solutions, however, will qualify as a probability distribution. This one solution can be "forced" by requiring that the Π_i sum to 1. That is, we append the linear equation

$$\sum_{\text{all } i} \Pi_i = 1$$

to those previously expressed, and the resulting set of linear equations will possess a unique solution satisfying all the requirements of a probability distribution.

This last equation is called the *normalizing equation*. The usual practice is first to obtain an "unnormalized" solution by manipulating the $\mathbf{\Pi} = \mathbf{\Pi}\mathbf{P}$ equations to express all of the Π_i in terms of one of them; then to use the normalizing equation to fix the value of this last one; and finally to substitute this value into the expressions for the others.

Referring once again to our numerical example, the steady-state equation would be given by

$$(\Pi_A \Pi_B \Pi_C) = (\Pi_A \Pi_B \Pi_C) \begin{bmatrix} 0.5 & 0.5 & 0 \\ 0.0 & 0.5 & 0.5 \\ 0.75 & 0.25 & 0 \end{bmatrix}$$

or, in column vector form,

$$\begin{bmatrix} \Pi_A \\ \Pi_B \\ \Pi_C \end{bmatrix} = \begin{bmatrix} 0.5 & 0 & 0.75 \\ 0.5 & 0.5 & 0.25 \\ 0 & 0.5 & 0 \end{bmatrix} \begin{bmatrix} \Pi_A \\ \Pi_B \\ \Pi_C \end{bmatrix}$$

$$\Pi_A = 0.5\Pi_A \qquad\qquad + 0.75\Pi_C$$

$$\Pi_B = 0.5\Pi_B + 0.5\Pi_B + 0.25\Pi_C$$

$$\Pi_C = \qquad\quad 0.5\Pi_B$$

Note that when written in this form, the coefficient matrix is the *transpose* of **P**. The first equation is sufficient to solve for Π_C in terms of Π_A:

$$\Pi_A = \frac{1}{2}\Pi_A + \frac{3}{4}\Pi_C$$

$$\frac{1}{2}\Pi_A = \frac{3}{4}\Pi_C$$

$$\Pi_C = \frac{2}{3}\Pi_A$$

The last equation will give Π_B in terms of Π_C which is in turn expressible in terms of Π_A

$$\Pi_C = \frac{1}{2}\Pi_B$$

$$\Pi_B = 2\Pi_C$$

$$\Pi_B = \frac{4}{3}\Pi_A$$

If we attempt to use the remaining (second) equation to determine Π_A, we get nowhere:

$$\Pi_B = \frac{1}{2}\Pi_A + \frac{1}{2}\Pi_B + \frac{1}{4}\Pi_C$$

$$\frac{4}{3}\Pi_A = \frac{1}{2}\Pi_A + \left(\frac{1}{2}\right)\left(\frac{4}{3}\right)\Pi_A + \left(\frac{1}{4}\right)\left(\frac{2}{3}\right)\Pi_A$$

$$\frac{4}{3}\Pi_A = \frac{3}{6}\Pi_A + \frac{4}{6}\Pi_A + \frac{2}{6}\Pi_A$$

$$\frac{4}{3}\Pi_A = \frac{4}{3}\Pi_A$$

Thus, this last equation is consistent with the other two, but provides no additional information.

Resorting, then, to the normalizing equation, we have

$$\Pi_A + \Pi_B + \Pi_C = 1$$

$$\Pi_A + \frac{4}{3}\Pi_A + \frac{2}{3}\Pi_A = 1$$

$$\Pi_A\left(1 + \frac{4}{3} + \frac{2}{3}\right) = 1$$

$$\Pi_A(3) = 1$$

$$\Pi_A = \frac{1}{3}$$

And finally, by resubstitution, we get Π_B and Π_C

$$\Pi_B = \frac{4}{3}\Pi_A = \frac{4}{9}$$

$$\Pi_C = \frac{2}{3}\Pi_A = \frac{2}{9}$$

Notice that the ease with which these exact steady-state probability values were obtained using the linear equations contrasts rather sharply with the effort required to raise the transition matrix to higher and higher powers, the latter yielding only approximations to the same steady-state values.

There is a sort of "physical" analog to the determination of the steady-state probabilities, which uses the transition diagram. The trick is to think of the points as small reservoirs and the arcs as connecting pipes through which liquid can flow, with valves to ensure that the flow goes only in the direction of the arrows. The probability p_{ij} associated with any arc is to be thought of as the fraction of the liquid in reservoir i that will pass to reservoir j in one transition time unit.

One unit of liquid is poured into the system according to $p^{(0)}$. If, for example, $p_1^{(0)} = 1/4$, then $1/4$ of the liquid is poured in at point 1. After a while, a dynamic equilibrium is attained; the liquid continues to flow, but the amount in every reservoir remains constant. When this happens, the amount in each reservoir gives the steady-state probability for the corresponding state. They are proper probabilities because they are nonnegative and sum to 1.

The analogy can be made more exact by thinking of the liquid in terms of its molecules. The trajectory of an individual molecule describes a realization of the stochastic process. The effect of pouring in many molecules is to consider many realizations simultaneously. So we are using, in effect, a statistical mechanics approach. This technique is used in chemical diffusion models, in electronics, and elsewhere.

Now when is equilibrium reached? Certainly a necessary condition is that the flow into any reservoir must equal the flow out, because if the two were not equal, the amount in the reservoir would be changing. If this condition is met for *all* reservoirs, it is sufficient. For any i,

$$\text{flow out} = \sum_j \Pi_i p_{ij} = \Pi_i \sum_j p_{ij} = \Pi_i, \quad \text{since} \quad \sum_j p_{ij} = 1$$

$$\text{flow in} = \sum_k \Pi_k p_{ki}$$

Hence, $\Pi_i = \sum \Pi_k p_{ki}$ for all i; or, in matrix form $\mathbf{\Pi} = \mathbf{\Pi P}$.

The steady-state probabilities have several useful interpretations. If you fix a point in time in the distant future, Π_j is the probability that you will find the process in state j at that time. This is the most obvious interpretation. It can also be viewed as a time average; if you ran the process for a long time, Π_j would be the fraction of time that the process spent in state j. Or it can be viewed as an ensemble average; if you ran many identical processes simultaneously, Π_j would be the fraction of processes that you would find in state j (after a long period of time). Finally, it can be viewed as the reciprocal of the mean number of transitions between recurrences of the state. For example, in the job reassignment process, $\Pi_1 = 1/3$, so an average of three transitions will occur before a man in engineering will again be in engineering.

6.8 FIRST-PASSAGE AND FIRST-RETURN PROBABILITIES

The probabilities treated so far answer questions of the general form, "What is the probability of being in a certain state at a certain time?" Another type of question which is frequently of interest is, "How long will it take to reach a certain state?" The answer must involve probabilities, but the random variable is the number of transitions that occur before a specified state is reached rather than the state after a specified number of transitions.

One might be tempted to interpret $p_{ij}^{(n)}$ as the probability that n steps are required to reach state j given that the process starts in state i. If this were a correct interpretation, then the set $\{p_{ij}^{(1)}, p_{ij}^{(2)}, p_{ij}^{(3)}, \ldots\}$ would give the probability distribution of the number of steps to get from i to j. However, this is not a correct interpretation of $p_{ij}^{(n)}$.

To see what is wrong, consider $p_{ij}^{(3)}$ and suppose the event to which this probability refers does indeed happen. That is, suppose the process is in state j three steps after it was in state i. But this does not mean that you have waited three steps for state j to be reached. It might have been reached after only one or two steps, after which the process either stayed in state j or changed to another state and then returned to state j. Any of the possibilities could result in the event indicated by $X_3 = j$.

When we speak of the number of steps required to reach state j, we mean the number of steps required to reach state j *for the first time*. So to get the distribution of this time, we must consider the first passage probability, $f_{ij}^{(n)}$, defined to be

$$f_{ij}^{(n)} = P\{X_n = j, X_{n-1} \neq j, X_{n-2} \neq j, \ldots, X_1 \neq j \mid X_0 = i\}$$

In words, $f_{ij}^{(n)}$ is the probability that the process is in state j at time n *and not before*, given that it was in state i at time 0. This may be correctly reinterpreted as the probability that n steps are required to reach state j for the first time given that the process starts in state i.

Clearly $f_{ij}^{(0)} = 0$ and $f_{ij}^{(1)} = p_{ij}$. By extending the logic of the explanation of $p_{ij}^{(3)}$, one can show that

$$f_{ij}^{(n)} = p_{ij}^{(n)} - \sum_{k=1}^{n-1} f_{ij}^{(k)} p_{ij}^{(n-k)}$$

Thus the $f_{ij}^{(n)}$ can be obtained iteratively if the $p_{ij}^{(n)}$ are known.

The set of the $f_{ij}^{(n)}$ (for fixed i, j and varying n) do give the distribution of the number of steps to get from i to j (the "first passage"), so if N_{ij} is the random variable defined to be the number of steps required,

$$P\{N_{ij} = n\} = f_{ij}^{(n)}$$

The above discussion tacitly assumed that i and j were distinct. If they are not, the formal definition would be exactly the same, but we would speak of *first return* rather than first passage. Formally,

$$f_{ii}^{(n)} = P\{X_n = i, X_{n-1} \neq i, X_{n-2} \neq i, \ldots, X_1 \neq i \mid X_0 = i\}$$

The equation relating $f_{ii}^{(n)}$ to the $p_{ii}^{(n)}$ would also be the same, except that $f_{ii}^{(0)} = 1$, since $f_{ii}^{(0)} = P\{X_0 = i \mid X_0 = i\} = 1$. In this case N_{ii} would be a random variable whose value is the *recurrence time* for state i; that is, the number of steps between recurrences of state i.

For purposes of displaying some numerical results, let $\mathbf{F}^{(n)}$ be the matrix whose elements are $f_{ij}^{(n)}$. Then, for the job assignment example we have been using,

$$\mathbf{F}^{(1)} = \begin{bmatrix} 0.50 & 0.50 & 0 \\ 0 & 0.50 & 0.50 \\ 0.75 & 0.25 & 0 \end{bmatrix}$$

$$\mathbf{F}^{(2)} = \begin{bmatrix} 0 & 0.25 & 0.25 \\ 0.375 & 0.125 & 0.25 \\ 0 & 0.375 & 0.125 \end{bmatrix}$$

$$\mathbf{F}^{(3)} = \begin{bmatrix} 0.1875 & 0.125 & 0.250 \\ 0.1875 & 0.1875 & 0.125 \\ 0.09375 & 0.1875 & 0.250 \end{bmatrix}$$

$$\mathbf{F}^{(4)} = \begin{bmatrix} 0.09375 & 0.0625 & 0.1875 \\ 0.140625 & 0.046875 & 0.0625 \\ 0.1 & 0.09375 & 0.21875 \end{bmatrix}$$

$$\mathbf{F}^{(5)} = \begin{bmatrix} 0.0703125 & 0.03125 & 0.125 \\ 0.09375 & 0.0703125 & 0.03125 \\ 0.00859375 & 0.049125 & 0.15625 \end{bmatrix}$$

The first passage probabilities are useful in expressing a number of other values of interest. Because the $f_{ij}^{(n)}$ give the distribution of N_{ij}, the passage time from i to j, the *mean first passage time* from i to j, denoted m_{ij}, is given by

$$m_{ij} = E(N_{ij}) = \sum_{n=1}^{\infty} n f_{ij}^{(n)}$$

Of course, higher moments can be expressed also. In the case where $i = j$, m_{ii} would be called the *mean recurrence time*. Recall that in the discussion of steady-state probabilities, it was pointed out that Π_i can be interpreted as the reciprocal of the mean recurrence time of state i. In symbols,

$$\Pi_i = \frac{1}{m_{ii}}$$

While it is possible to get the first passage probabilities, and hence the distribution of first passage times, the calculation is at best tedious. If all that is desired is the *mean* first passage times, a rather simple calculation will suffice. Formally, m_{ij} is given by

$$m_{ij} = \sum_{n=1}^{\infty} n f_{ij}^{(n)}$$

but this would require the complete first passage time distribution. Instead, we may obtain a formula for m_{ij} by conditioning on the state at step 1. Given that the process is in state i at time 0, either the next state is j, in which case the passage time is exactly 1, or it is some other state k, in which case the passage time will be 1 plus the passage time from that state k to j. Weighting the possibilities by the appropriate probabilities gives

$$m_{ij} = 1 p_{ij} + \sum_{k \neq j} (1 + m_{kj}) p_{ik}$$

which then manipulates

$$m_{ij} = p_{ij} + \sum_{k \neq j} p_{ik} + \sum_{k \neq j} p_{ik} m_{kj}$$

$$m_{ij} = \sum_{\text{all } k} p_{ik} + \sum_{k \neq j} p_{ik} m_{kj}$$

to produce the formula

$$m_{ij} = 1 + \sum_{k \neq j} p_{ik} m_{kj}$$

This expresses m_{ij} as a linear function of the m_{kj}. By using the same relation for other m_{ij}'s, a set of linear equations may be expressed. The solution to the set gives the mean first passage times from any state into state j. Mean first recurrence times are also available in this way, but it is just as easy to get them as inverses of steady-state probabilities.

To illustrate the method, consider again the three-department job assignment model. One of the questions posed when that model was first discussed was "how many assignments will occur, on the average, before a man who is first assigned to engineering will be assigned to sales?" In terms of present notation, the question asks for the value of m_{13}.

Using the formula, we obtain the relation

$$m_{13} = 1 + p_{11} m_{13} + p_{12} m_{23}$$

But to solve this requires knowledge of m_{23}. Using the formula for m_{23},

$$m_{23} = 1 + p_{21} m_{13} + p_{22} m_{23}$$

We now have two linear equations in the two unknowns m_{13} and m_{23}. Substituting the particular values of the p_{ij} from the transition matrix,

$$m_{13} = 1 + 0.5 m_{13} + 0.5 m_{23}$$
$$m_{23} = 1 + \qquad 0.5 m_{23}$$

and solving, we obtain

$$m_{23} = 2$$
$$m_{13} = 4$$

The latter value answers the question originally posed.

6.9 CLASSIFICATION TERMINOLOGY

Up until now it has been tacitly assumed that the processes have whatever properties are necessary to make the methods work. Now we must consider what these properties are and develop the terminology to distinguish between Markov chains that have the properties and those that do not.

The method of raising a transition matrix to higher powers to obtain n-step transition probabilities or state probabilities will always work. So also will the recursive formula for the first-passage and first-return probabilities. However, the linear equation methods for obtaining steady-state probabilities and mean first-passage times may fail. In fact, the steady-state, first-passage probabilities, or both, may not even exist for certain kinds of processes.

To get an indication of what can happen, suppose we are dealing with the process characterized by the following transition matrix and corresponding diagram Fig. 6.9. If the process starts in the first state it will either stay in that state, with probability 1/2, or change to either of the two states, each with probability 1/4. Once either the second or third state is entered, the process will remain in that state ever after. Hence, if the initial state is the second state,

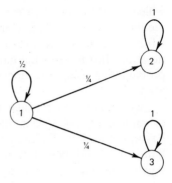

Figure 6.9
A transition diagram.

the n-step transition probability for the transitions to state 1 or 3 is zero for all n. Similarly if the initial state is 3, then $p_{31}^{(n)}$ and $p_{32}^{(n)}$ are zero for all n. If the process begins in state 1, then it may stay in that state for awhile, but ultimately it must enter state 2 or 3 and remain there forever. By symmetry, one may conclude that the process is equally likely to end up in state 2 or 3. So, as n goes to infinity

$$p_{11}^{(n)} \to 0$$

$$p_{12}^{(n)} \to \frac{1}{2}$$

$$p_{13}^{(n)} \to \frac{1}{2}$$

This discussion has been heuristic, but the conclusions can be verified by raising **P** to higher powers, for example:

$$\mathbf{P}^{(2)} = \mathbf{P}^2 = \begin{bmatrix} \frac{1}{4} & \frac{3}{8} & \frac{3}{8} \\ 0 & 1 & 0 \\ 0 & 0 & 1 \end{bmatrix}$$

$$\mathbf{P}^{(3)} = \mathbf{P}^3 = \begin{bmatrix} \frac{1}{8} & \frac{7}{16} & \frac{7}{16} \\ 0 & 1 & 0 \\ 0 & 0 & 1 \end{bmatrix}$$

$$\mathbf{P}^{(4)} = \mathbf{P}^4 = \begin{bmatrix} \frac{1}{16} & \frac{15}{32} & \frac{15}{32} \\ 0 & 1 & 0 \\ 0 & 0 & 1 \end{bmatrix}$$

$$\mathbf{P}^{(5)} = \mathbf{P}^5 = \begin{bmatrix} \frac{1}{32} & \frac{31}{64} & \frac{31}{64} \\ 0 & 1 & 0 \\ 0 & 0 & 1 \end{bmatrix}$$

If we persist in these calculations, we can see that the limiting matrix is

$$\lim_{n \to \infty} \mathbf{P}^{(n)} = \begin{bmatrix} 0 & \frac{1}{2} & \frac{1}{2} \\ 0 & 1 & 0 \\ 0 & 0 & 1 \end{bmatrix}$$

which verifies our heuristic discussion. The rows of $\mathbf{P}^{(n)}$ do *not* become identical. Since the behavior of the process as n goes to infinity depends on which state the process started in, it would not make sense even to use the Π_i notation. Just to see what happens, the reader should try to obtain steady-state probabilities using the linear equation method when $\mathbf{P}$ is the matrix given above.

The mean first passage times are also of questionable meaning. For the example above, it is clear that passage from state 2 to state 3 can *never* occur. Passage from 1 to 2 might not ever occur. In such cases, there cannot exist any finite mean number of transitions required to take the process from i to j. Again, the reader should try the linear equation method anyway, just to see what happens.

What we need now is the terminology and criteria to distinguish between processes of the kind just examined. There are a whole series of words and accompanying concepts to be introduced. For the most part, the words are suggestive and the concepts, intuitive. First, we consider some words to describe the structure of processes, in terms of how states relate to one another. Later, we will develop terms to describe individual states.

One state j is *reachable* from another i if there exists some sequence of possible transitions which would take the process from state i to state j. In the previous example, every state was reachable from state 1, but only state 2 was reachable from 2, and only state 3 from 3. Two states *communicate* if each is reachable from the other. No two states communicate in the example. In terms of the transition diagram, state j is reachable from i if there is a walk from point i to point j. Two states communicate if there are walks going in both directions.

A *closed set* of states is a set such that no state outside the set is reachable from any state in the set. That is, once a closed set is entered, it cannot be left. Using the transition diagram, a rough method to determine whether a set is closed is to encircle the points in the set and see if there are any arrows penetrating the boundary in an outward direction. Notice that finding closed sets by this method depends somewhat on your ability to perceive them and perhaps on the way the diagram is drawn. (Ponder these questions: Is it always possible to encircle the points of a closed set with just one circle? And how do you handle a diagram like the one in Fig. 6.10?)

If a single state forms a closed set, as in the example treated earlier, the state is called an *absorbing* state. A *minimal* closed set is one which has no proper closed subsets. Every state in a minimal closed set communicates with every other state in the set (for, if not, the closed set would not be minimal). For this reason, the minimal closed sets are sometimes called *communicating*

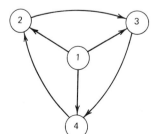

Figure 6.10
A transition diagram.

classes. If all of the states of a process belong to a single communicating class, the process is said to be *irreducible.* Otherwise, the process is *reducible.*

To illustrate a number of these concepts, consider the following transition matrix:

$$
\mathbf{P} = \begin{array}{c} \\ 1 \\ 2 \\ 3 \\ 4 \\ 5 \\ 6 \\ 7 \\ 8 \end{array}
\begin{array}{c}
\begin{array}{cccccccc} 1 & 2 & 3 & 4 & 5 & 6 & 7 & 8 \end{array} \\
\left[\begin{array}{cccccccc}
\frac{1}{5} & \frac{1}{5} & \frac{1}{5} & \frac{1}{5} & \frac{1}{5} & 0 & 0 & 0 \\
\frac{1}{2} & & & & & \frac{1}{2} & & \\
& & \frac{1}{2} & & & & \frac{1}{2} & \\
& & & \frac{1}{3} & \frac{1}{3} & & & \frac{1}{3} \\
& & & \frac{1}{3} & \frac{1}{3} & & & \frac{1}{3} \\
& & & & & 1 & & \\
& & \frac{1}{2} & & & & \frac{1}{2} & \\
& & & \frac{1}{3} & \frac{1}{3} & & & \frac{1}{3}
\end{array} \right]
\end{array}
$$

It is a bit difficult to see the structure of the process in this form, but Fig. 6.11 reveals it clearly (the probabilities are omitted for clarity). It is apparent that states 3 and 7 form a minimal closed set, as do the states 4, 5, and 8. Either of these closed sets can be entered from state 1, but not from states 2 or 6. States 2 and 6 form a closed set—once entered, the process cannot leave the set—but they do not form a *minimal* closed set. State 6 alone is a closed set; in fact, it is an absorbing state. (Notice that an absorbing state is recognizable by the "1" on the diagonal.) In summary, then, the minimal closed sets are {6}, {3, 7}, and {4, 5, 8}. States 1 and 2 are "left over"; they do not belong to any minimal closed set.

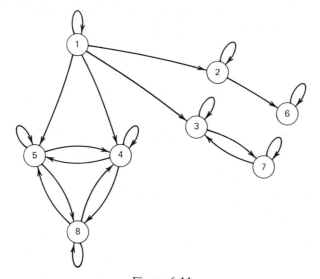

Figure 6.11
A transition diagram.

A state belonging to a minimal closed subset is called *recurrent*; the others—the left-over ones—are called *transient*. These terms make sense when you realize that a transient state might occur a number of times, but once the process enters a closed set, it could never again occur. Once a recurrent state occurs, (indicating that the process has entered the minimal closed set to which that state belongs), then it is certain to go on reoccurring time after time. Notice that it is not necessary that a recurrent state ever occur because it could belong to a minimal closed set which the process never enters. But once it does occur, it will necessarily reoccur.

If the process is reducible, as the example above was, the transition matrix can be written in the form

$$
\mathbf{P} =
\begin{array}{|c|c|c|c|}
\hline
\mathbf{P}_1 & & & \\
\hline
 & \mathbf{P}_2 & & \\
\hline
 & & \ddots & \\
 & & \mathbf{P}_c & \\
\hline
\mathbf{Q}_1 & \mathbf{Q}_2 & \cdots\ \mathbf{Q}_c & \mathbf{Q}_{c+1} \\
\hline
\end{array}
$$

where $\mathbf{P}_i$ is a square submatrix containing the probabilities governing the transitions within the *i*th minimal closed set of states, $\mathbf{Q}_{c+1}$ is a square submatrix of probabilities of transitions among the transient states, and the other $\mathbf{Q}_i$ are matrices (not necessarily square) containing probabilities of transitions from transient states to states within the *i*th minimal closed set. Of course to accomplish this expression of $\mathbf{P}$ may require the reordering of rows and columns. In the case of the example treated above, appropriate reordering of states yields the following transition matrix:

$$
\mathbf{P} =
\begin{array}{c}
\ \\ 6 \\ 3 \\ 7 \\ 4 \\ 5 \\ 8 \\ 1 \\ 2
\end{array}
\begin{array}{c}
\begin{array}{cccccccc} 6 & 3 & 7 & 4 & 5 & 8 & 1 & 2 \end{array} \\
\left[
\begin{array}{cccccccc}
1 & & & & & & & \\
 & \frac{1}{2} & \frac{1}{2} & & & & & \\
 & \frac{1}{2} & \frac{1}{2} & & & & & \\
 & & & \frac{1}{3} & \frac{1}{3} & \frac{1}{3} & & \\
 & & & \frac{1}{3} & \frac{1}{3} & \frac{1}{3} & & \\
 & & & \frac{1}{3} & \frac{1}{3} & \frac{1}{3} & & \\
0 & \frac{1}{5} & 0 & \frac{1}{5} & \frac{1}{5} & 0 & \frac{1}{5} & \frac{1}{5} \\
\frac{1}{3} & 0 & 0 & 0 & 0 & 0 & 0 & \frac{1}{2}
\end{array}
\right]
\end{array}
$$

There are definite advantages to expressing the transition matrix of a reducible process in this way. One is that the minimal closed sets become visably distinguishable. More importantly, the powers of the transition matrix assume a predictable form. To see what happens, square such a matrix in partitioned form:

$$\mathbf{P}^2 = \begin{bmatrix} \mathbf{P}_1 & \mathbf{O} & \mathbf{O} & \mathbf{O} \\ \mathbf{O} & \mathbf{P}_2 & \mathbf{O} & \mathbf{O} \\ \mathbf{O} & \mathbf{O} & \mathbf{P}_3 & \mathbf{O} \\ \mathbf{Q}_1 & \mathbf{Q}_2 & \mathbf{Q}_3 & \mathbf{Q}_4 \end{bmatrix} \begin{bmatrix} \mathbf{P}_1 & \mathbf{O} & \mathbf{O} & \mathbf{O} \\ \mathbf{O} & \mathbf{P}_2 & \mathbf{O} & \mathbf{O} \\ \mathbf{O} & \mathbf{O} & \mathbf{P}_3 & \mathbf{O} \\ \mathbf{Q}_1 & \mathbf{Q}_2 & \mathbf{Q}_3 & \mathbf{Q}_4 \end{bmatrix}$$

$$= \begin{bmatrix} \mathbf{P}_1^2 & \mathbf{O} & \mathbf{O} & \mathbf{O} \\ \mathbf{O} & \mathbf{P}_2^2 & \mathbf{O} & \mathbf{O} \\ \mathbf{O} & \mathbf{O} & \mathbf{P}_3^2 & \mathbf{O} \\ \mathbf{Q}_1\mathbf{P}_1+\mathbf{Q}_4\mathbf{Q}_1 & \mathbf{Q}_2\mathbf{P}_2+\mathbf{Q}_4\mathbf{Q}_2 & \mathbf{Q}_3\mathbf{P}_3+\mathbf{Q}_4\mathbf{Q}_3 & \mathbf{Q}_4^2 \end{bmatrix}$$

The points to notice are that the product retains the same partitioned format and that the matrices along the diagonal are just the squares of the diagonal matrices of $\mathbf{P}$. Higher powers, as the reader may verify, possess similar properties. Aside from the terms in the bottom row of matrices, which are complicated, $\mathbf{P}^n$ can be constructed by raising $\mathbf{P}_1, \mathbf{P}_2, \ldots, \mathbf{P}_c$, and $\mathbf{Q}_{c+1}$ to the nth power *separately*. The minimal closed sets behave almost as if they were unrelated irreducible Markov chains. Intuitively, once the process is within a closed set, it cannot leave; so it is just as if the other states did not exist. Of course, there are still questions to be answered, such as "*when* will the process enter one of the minimal closed sets?" and "*which* minimal closed set will it enter?" These questions are taken up in Section 6.10.

If a process is reducible, it contains one or more minimal closed sets (or communicating classes) of recurrent states, plus (usually) some transient states. If it is irreducible, (i.e., does not contain a proper subset which is a minimal closed set), one might assume that all states must be recurrent. Although this is usually the case, it is technically possible for all states to be transient! A transition matrix having this property is given below:

$$\mathbf{P} = \begin{bmatrix} \frac{1}{2} & \frac{1}{2} & 0 & 0 & 0 & \cdot & \cdot & \cdot \\ 0 & \frac{1}{2} & \frac{1}{2} & 0 & 0 & \cdot & \cdot & \cdot \\ 0 & 0 & \frac{1}{2} & \frac{1}{2} & 0 & \cdot & \cdot & \cdot \\ 0 & 0 & 0 & \frac{1}{2} & \frac{1}{2} & \cdot & \cdot & \cdot \\ & \cdot & \cdot & \cdot & & & & \\ & \cdot & \cdot & \cdot & & & & \\ & \cdot & \cdot & \cdot & & & & \end{bmatrix}$$

The dots indicate that the matrix is infinite. No state of this process, once left, can occur again. There are many closed sets, in fact, an infinite number. But there is no *minimal* closed set. Consequently, all states are transient. The oddity derives from the nature of infinity. In any process having a finite number of states, at least one would have to be recurrent. So if a process is finite and irreducible, every state is recurrent.

Notice that whether a state is transient or recurrent depends only on the structure of the process, not on values of transition probabilities. We can, however, characterize the categories in terms of probabilities. Recall that the first return probability $f_{ii}^{(n)}$ gives the probability that state i is revisited for the first time after n steps. Consequently the sum $\sum_{n=1}^{\infty} f_{ii}^{(n)}$ gives the probability that state i is ever revisited. Let $f_i = \sum_{n=1}^{\infty} f_{ii}^{(n)}$, and call it the *probability of recurrence of state i*. Then it can be shown that state i is recurrent if and only if $f_i = 1$, and is transient if and only if $f_i < 1$.

If the process is in a transient state i at time 0 the probability that it will ever occupy that state again is f_i, which is less than 1. If it does occupy state i again, then the probability that it will return once again is still f_i. Each time it returns to i, there is a positive probability, $1-f_i$, that it will never happen again. Thus, the process may return some finite number of times to a transient state, but eventually it will return no more. Over an infinite period of time, the probability of being in any transient state goes to zero.

If the process is in a recurrent state at time 0, it is certain that the state will occur again, because $f_i = 1$. Once it does, it is certain to occur once again, and so on. Over an infinite period of time, a recurrent state which has occurred once will occur an infinite number of times.

On the other hand, a peculiar anomaly can occur. It is possible for a recurrent state to have infinite mean recurrence time. Mathematically it is possible that the infinite series,

$$m_{ii} = \sum_{n=1}^{\infty} n f_{ii}^{(n)}$$

does not converge, even though the infinite series

$$f_i = \sum_{n=1}^{\infty} f_{ii}^{(n)}$$

sums to 1. A recurrent state having infinite mean recurrence time is called a *null state*. Over an infinite period of time, null states occur so infrequently that—even though they occur an infinite number of times—the probability of being in one falls to zero. Null states are of rare practical use; but because they can occur, they must be considered when categorizing states. Recurrent states having finite mean recurrence times—the usual case—are called *nonnull* or *positive*.

Another anomaly occasionally shows up in applications. For discussion purposes consider the following transition matrix:

$$\mathbf{P} = \begin{bmatrix} 0 & 0 & \frac{1}{2} & \frac{1}{2} \\ 0 & 0 & \frac{1}{2} & \frac{1}{2} \\ \frac{1}{2} & \frac{1}{2} & 0 & 0 \\ \frac{1}{2} & \frac{1}{2} & 0 & 0 \end{bmatrix}$$

The states now fall into two classes, $\{1, 2\}$ and $\{3, 4\}$, which are such that the process alternates between the two sets. If the process is in state 1 or 2, then at the next step it must be in state 3 or 4. At the following step, it must be in state

1 or 2, and so on. In other words, state 1, if it occurs at step 0, could occur again only at steps 2, 4, 6, 8, 10, and so on. A state which can occur only at steps m, $2m$, $3m$, and so on, where m is some integer greater than 1, is called a *periodic state of period m*. Therefore all of the states of the above example are *periodic of period* 2. A state for which no such m, greater than 1, exists is called *aperiodic*.

A state i is periodic if *all* walks in the transition starting from i and returning to i are of length m, or $2m$, and so on where m is greater than 1. If you can find a walk of length 1 (i.e., a loop) or if you can find two walks which have relatively prime lengths (i.e., there is no number other than 1 which divides both of them), you are assured that the state is aperiodic. Furthermore, periodicity is a class property; that is, if one state of a communicating class is periodic of period m, then they all are. So if you can determine that one state is aperiodic, you know that the other states of the same class are too.

The trouble with periodic states, at least insofar as steady-state probabilities are concerned, is that the limits of the transition probability functions do not exist. To see this, square the transition matrix of the example above.

$$\mathbf{P}^2 = \begin{bmatrix} \frac{1}{2} & \frac{1}{2} & 0 & 0 \\ \frac{1}{2} & \frac{1}{2} & 0 & 0 \\ 0 & 0 & \frac{1}{2} & \frac{1}{2} \\ 0 & 0 & \frac{1}{2} & \frac{1}{2} \end{bmatrix}$$

When we cube $\mathbf{P}$, we get

$$\mathbf{P}^3 = \begin{bmatrix} 0 & 0 & \frac{1}{2} & \frac{1}{2} \\ 0 & 0 & \frac{1}{2} & \frac{1}{2} \\ \frac{1}{2} & \frac{1}{2} & 0 & 0 \\ \frac{1}{2} & \frac{1}{2} & 0 & 0 \end{bmatrix}$$

which is the same as $\mathbf{P}$. By induction, we can conclude that

$$\mathbf{P}^n = \mathbf{P} \quad \text{if } n \text{ is odd}$$
$$= \mathbf{P}^2 \quad \text{if } n \text{ is even}$$

The transition probabilities all continue to alternate between the two values 0 and 1/2; they do not approach any limits.

Because the difficulty is more theoretical than practical, the subject of periodic states will not be pursued further in this text. If you should encounter a problem with them, they are treated fully in Feller (6).

Now that we have words to describe the exceptions, we may consider the processes for which the steady-state probabilities may be found by the method of solving the linear equations discussed earlier. A state which is not transient, not periodic, and not null is called an *ergodic state*. An irreducible process consisting of ergodic states is called an *ergodic process*. Notice that the category is defined by what it is *not*, so it covers every case except those specifically excluded. It can be shown that an ergodic process possesses a unique steady-state distribution which is independent of the initial state and is given by the unique solution to the linear equations,

$$\Pi = \Pi P$$

$$\sum \Pi_j = 1$$

The theorem assures that a solution to the equations always exists, is unique, and has the properties to qualify as a probability distribution.

There is no need for a method to determine limiting probabilities for transient or null states; the probability of being in such a state tends to zero. Periodic states do not possess steady-state probabilities as we have defined them. All other states are ergodic and are covered by the linear equation method, provided that the process is irreducible. If it is not, we will have to know the probability that the minimal closed set to which a state belongs is ever entered. Once entered, the class will behave like an irreducible process.

6.10 TRANSIENT PROCESSES

Although null states and periodic states can be regarded as unusual, "nuisance" cases, it would be a mistake to dismiss transient states as being of little practical significance. Although real-life processes which continue to operate for long periods of time would ordinarily be modeled as irreducible ergodic processes, there are many processes which terminate after a relatively short period of time. Such processes may be conveniently modeled as reducible Markov chains having one or more absorbing states and a number of transient states.

It is possible to model the same physical process both ways, depending on the point of view taken and the questions you want answered. For example, in a production situation, you could look at a particular machine processing different types of parts (in a random sequence) and view the process as a continuing one. You might then ask how many parts of a given type would be processed in a given time. Alternatively, you could look at a particular part going through a sequence of operations on different machines and view the process as a terminating one. You might want to know the mean number of operations required to complete the part.

Among all reducible processes, the special case of greatest interest is that in which all minimal closed sets consist of single (absorbing) states. In this special case, the transition matrix, when expressed in the partitioned form discussed earlier, would look like this:

$$P = \begin{bmatrix} 1 & 0 & 0 & \vdots & \\ 0 & 1 & 0 & \vdots & \\ 0 & 0 & 1 & \vdots & 0 \\ & & \cdot & \vdots & \\ & & \cdot & \vdots & \\ & & \cdot & \vdots & \\ \hline Q_1 & Q_2 & Q_3 \cdots & \vdots & Q_{C+1} \end{bmatrix}$$

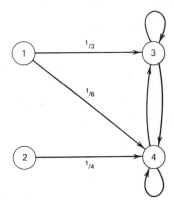

Figure 6.12
A transition diagram.

That is, all of the matrices previously designated $\mathbf{P}_i$ are just ones, and the matrices $\mathbf{Q}_i$, $i = 1, 2, \ldots, C$, are column vectors. To simplify the notation in this special case, let the set of column vectors $\mathbf{Q}_i$, $i = 1, 2, \ldots C$, be redesignated as the matrix $\mathbf{R}$, and drop the subscript from matrix $\mathbf{Q}_{C+1}$. Using this notation,

$$\mathbf{P} = \left[\begin{array}{c|c} \mathbf{I} & \mathbf{O} \\ \hline \mathbf{R} & \mathbf{Q} \end{array}\right]$$

The identity matrix $\mathbf{I}$ is of dimension equal to the number of absorbing states. $\mathbf{Q}$ is a square matrix containing all of the transition probabilities from one transient state to another transient state. $\mathbf{R}$ is a matrix—not necessarily square—containing the transition probabilities from transient states to absorbing states.

Now if you have a reducible process which is not of this form—that is, if the minimal closed sets are not single states—it may be advantageous to "shrink" or "collapse" the minimal closed sets to single states in order to achieve this form. To see how this could be done, consider Fig. 6.12, which might represent only a portion of a transition diagram. States 1 and 2 are transient states; 3 and 4 form a minimal closed set. Collapsing states 3 and 4 into a single state would produce Fig. 6.13. Notice that the single state ends with a loop of value 1 regardless of the transition probabilities within the closed set in the original diagram. The two lines from 1 to 3 and from 1 to 4 become a single line of value equal to the sum of the values of the original lines. The same kind of transformation can, of course, be carried out within the transition matrix.

When a transformation of this kind (technically known as a "homomorphism") is carried out, information is obviously lost. The resulting process, though

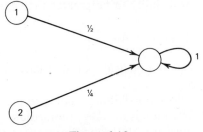

Figure 6.13
The collapsed diagram.

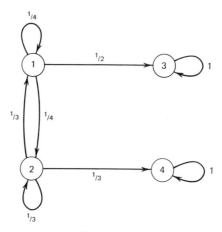

Figure 6.14
A transition diagram.

smaller, simpler, and easier to handle, is not as complete in its representation as the original. On the other hand, the derived process is identical in its behavior to the original until the time it enters a minimal closed set. So any questions having to do with transitions among the transient states can be answered as well by the derived process as by the original.

The first question we will address is which absorbing state (or minimal closed set, represented by an absorbing state) will be entered. Of course, if a process has only one, the answer is trivial. If there is more than one possibility, the question is answered by a probability distribution over all of the possible absorbing states. Figure 6.14 gives a transition diagram that will illustrate the problem. States 1 and 2 are transient; 3 and 4 are both absorbing. Over a short period, states 1 and 2 may be visited a number of times; but ultimately, the process will enter either state 3 or state 4 and remain there. If chance determines that state 3 is entered, then state 4 will never occur, and vice versa. What we need is a method to determine the probability that state 3 is *ever* entered (as opposed to state 4, since one of the two must eventually occur). This is called an *absorption probability*.

Now it should be apparent from the diagram that the probability of ever entering state 3 is greater if we start in state 1 than if we start in state 2. We are saying, then, that the absorption probabilities, unlike steady-state prob-abilities in an ergodic chain, *do* depend upon the initial state.

Let a_{ij} represent the probability that the process ever enters absorbing state j given that the initial state is i. It is easy to see that i must be a transient state in order for this probability to be greater than zero. Formally,

$$a_{ij} = \sum_{n=1}^{\infty} f_{ij}^{(n)}$$

but this is not computionally practical. An alternative method is available via the following argument.

There are two immediate possibilities leading to the ultimate occurrence of state j. Either the first transition is to state j (immediate absorption), or the first transition is to some *transient* state k and the process ultimately enters state j from that state. The probability of the first event is just p_{ij}, of the second is

$\sum_k p_{ik}a_{kj}$, where the sum is over all transient states k. Since the two possibilities are mutually exclusive,

$$a_{ij} = p_{ij} + \sum_{\text{transient } k} p_{ik}a_{kj}.$$

This is one linear equation in several unknown absorption probabilities. A complete set of independent linear equations will be obtained if the same formula is reapplied to all possible transient states, regarding each in turn as the initial state.

By way of example, if we want a_{13} for the process illustrated in Fig. 6.14, our first equation would be

$$a_{13} = p_{13} + p_{11}a_{13} + p_{12}a_{23}.$$

This is an equation in two unknowns, a_{13} and a_{23}. If we now write the equation for a_{23},

$$a_{23} = p_{23} + p_{21}a_{13} + p_{22}a_{23}$$

we get another equation in the same two unknowns. Substituting numerical values, our equations are

$$a_{13} = \frac{1}{2} + \frac{1}{4}a_{13} + \frac{1}{4}a_{23}$$

$$a_{23} = 0 + \frac{1}{3}a_{13} + \frac{1}{3}a_{23}$$

Solving these, we obtain

$$a_{13} = \frac{4}{5}$$

$$a_{23} = \frac{2}{5}$$

Notice that even if we have no direct interest in a_{23}, it was necessary to obtain it in order to find a_{13}. Notice also that a_{13} and a_{23} do not sum to 1; there is no reason that they should. On the other hand, if the initial state is fixed, then the process must ultimately enter one of the two absorbing states, so

$$a_{13} + a_{14} = 1$$

and

$$a_{23} + a_{24} = 1$$

From this, we can deduce that

$$a_{14} = \frac{1}{5}$$

$$a_{24} = \frac{3}{5}$$

Alternatively, we could have used the formula to get two linear equations in a_{14} and a_{24} and solved for them directly.

It is convenient to express the equations for the absorption probabilities in matrix form. Let **A** be the matrix of the a_{ij}. It will not necessarily be square, but will have as many rows as there are transient states, and as many columns as there are absorbing states. Thus, it has the same dimension as $\mathbf{R}$ does. In fact, examination of the equations for the a_{ij} reveals that

$$\mathbf{A} = \mathbf{R} + \mathbf{QA}.$$

Manipulation of this matrix equation gives $\mathbf{A}$ in terms of $\mathbf{R}$ and $\mathbf{Q}$, which are just portions of the transition matrix $\mathbf{P}$.

$$\mathbf{A} - \mathbf{QA} = \mathbf{R}$$
$$(\mathbf{I} - \mathbf{Q})\mathbf{A} = \mathbf{R}$$
$$\mathbf{A} = [\mathbf{I} - \mathbf{Q}]^{-1} \mathbf{R}$$

It can be shown that $(\mathbf{I} - \mathbf{Q})$ is nonsingular, so the inverse exists, and this method can be used if all of the a_{ij} are desired. If only one or two are sought, it would be more efficient to solve the equations for them than to invert the entire $(\mathbf{I} - \mathbf{Q})$ matrix.

To illustrate the matrix method for the example previously calculated, observe that $\mathbf{R}$ and $\mathbf{Q}$ are, respectively,

$$\mathbf{R} = \begin{bmatrix} \frac{1}{2} & 0 \\ 0 & \frac{1}{3} \end{bmatrix}$$

$$\mathbf{Q} = \begin{bmatrix} \frac{1}{4} & \frac{1}{4} \\ \frac{1}{3} & \frac{1}{3} \end{bmatrix}$$

The matrix $\mathbf{I} - \mathbf{Q}$ is

$$\mathbf{I} - \mathbf{Q} = \begin{bmatrix} \frac{3}{4} & -\frac{1}{4} \\ -\frac{1}{3} & \frac{2}{3} \end{bmatrix}$$

and its inverse is

$$(\mathbf{I} - \mathbf{Q})^{-1} = \begin{bmatrix} \frac{8}{5} & \frac{3}{5} \\ \frac{4}{5} & \frac{9}{5} \end{bmatrix}$$

Finally, the matrix of absorption probabilities is

$$\mathbf{A} = (\mathbf{I} - \mathbf{Q})^{-1} \mathbf{R} = \begin{bmatrix} \frac{4}{5} & \frac{1}{5} \\ \frac{2}{5} & \frac{3}{5} \end{bmatrix}$$

which agrees with our previous calculation.

The matrix $(\mathbf{I} - \mathbf{Q})^{-1}$ is also useful in answering a question of a different sort. Suppose that you want to know how many times a transient state will be occupied before absorption occurs. This would, of course, be a random variable which depended on the initial state. Let e_{ij} be the *mean number of times that transient state j is occupied given that the initial state is i*, and let **E** be the matrix of the e_{ij}. Because i and j each range over the transient states, **E** is a square matrix.

To develop an expression for the e_{ij}, we may use the same logic already used several times—that of conditioning on the state at time 1. If $i \neq j$,

$$e_{ij} = \sum_{\text{transient } k} p_{ik} e_{kj}$$

because j will be occupied a mean of e_{kj} times if the first transition is to any transient state k, and 0 times if the first transition is to any of the absorbing states. If $i = j$,

$$e_{ii} = 1 + \sum_{\text{transient } k} p_{ik} e_{ki}$$

because i will be occupied once (it spends the first time interval in i) plus a mean of e_{ki} times if the first transition is to any transient state k. Putting these relations into matrix form,

$$\mathbf{E} = \mathbf{I} + \mathbf{Q}\mathbf{E}$$

and solving for the matrix **E**,

$$\mathbf{E} - \mathbf{Q}\mathbf{E} = \mathbf{I}$$
$$(\mathbf{I} - \mathbf{Q})\mathbf{E} = \mathbf{I}$$
$$\mathbf{E} = (\mathbf{I} - \mathbf{Q})^{-1}$$

In words, then, the i, jth entry of the matrix $(\mathbf{I} - \mathbf{Q})^{-1}$ gives the mean number of times that the state j will be occupied before absorption occurs, given that the process starts in state i. For example, in the numerical example treated earlier, if the process begins in state 1, it will occupy state 2 an average of 3/5 times before absorption occurs.

When **E** is available, the mean total number of transitions until absorption is easily obtained. This will obviously depend upon the initial state, so let d_i represent this mean, given that i is the initial state. In many practical applications, d_i will represent the mean duration of the process. The total expected number of transitions will equal the total number of times that any of the transient states are occupied, so

$$d_i = \sum_{\text{transient } j} e_{ij}$$

which is just the sum of elements across row i of **E**. In the numerical example, if the process begins in state 1, it makes an average of 11/5 transitions before being absorbed in one of the two absorbing states.

It is quite a different question if one specifies a particular absorbing state and asks how many transitions will occur before it is entered. This question would be answered by something like a mean first passage time. In fact, if there is only one absorbing state, so that ultimate passage to that state is certain, then an ordinary mean first passage time will do. In other cases, when it is not certain that passage will ever occur, the ordinary mean first-passage time would be infinite. In these cases, what is really desired is the *conditional* mean first-passage time, given that passage does occur.

We have previously used the notation m_{ij} for the mean first-passage time from i to j in an ergodic process. Because there is little possibility of confusion, let the same notation be used for the *conditional* mean first passage time in a reducible process. Then it can be shown that

$$a_{ij}m_{ij} = a_{ij} + \sum_{k \neq j} p_{ik}a_{kj}m_{kj}$$

Notice that if passage to j is certain to occur, as in an irreducible process, then $a_{kj} = 1$ for all k, and the equation reduces to the one derived earlier.

Assuming that the absorption probabilities a_{kj} are known, the above equation is linear in the unknowns m_{kj}. By writing a complete set, one such equation for each transient state i, a sufficient number of independent equations will be available to determine the m_{kj}.

To illustrate, suppose that we want to know the mean number of transitions that would occur in the process we used to illustrate absorption probabilities, if we know that it started in state 1 and ultimately reached state 3. We want m_{13}, so writing the associated equation,

$$a_{13}m_{13} = a_{13} + p_{11}a_{13}m_{13} + p_{12}a_{23}m_{23}$$

Since this equation has the two unknowns m_{13} and m_{23}, we need another equation. Writing the one for m_{23},

$$a_{23}m_{23} = a_{23} + p_{21}a_{13}m_{13} + p_{22}a_{23}m_{23}$$

Substituting the values of the p_{ij} and the a_{ij}, which were previously calculated, we have the two equations

$$\frac{4}{5}m_{13} = \frac{4}{5} + \left(\frac{1}{4}\right)\left(\frac{4}{5}\right)m_{13} + \left(\frac{1}{4}\right)\left(\frac{2}{5}\right)m_{23}$$

$$\frac{2}{5}m_{23} = \frac{2}{5} + \left(\frac{1}{3}\right)\left(\frac{4}{5}\right)m_{13} + \left(\frac{1}{3}\right)\left(\frac{2}{5}\right)m_{23}$$

These can be solved to yield

$$m_{13} = 1.9$$

$$m_{23} = 3.4$$

To answer our original question, then, it will take a mean of 1.9 transitions to get from state 1 to state 3, assuming that it does occur.

II. CONTINUOUS TIME PROCESSES

6.11 AN EXAMPLE

Continuous time stochastic processes are similar in most respects to discrete time stochastic processes. Additional complexities occur, however, because each infinitesimal instant is available as a possible transition time. For example, it will not make sense to speak of a one-step transition matrix because time is not measured in steps.

In order to facilitate understanding, a simple two-state example will be solved in its entirety before the formal development is presented. Consider,

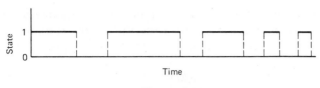

Figure 6.15
A realization.

then, for purposes of illustration the following situation which concerns the operation of an automatic loom used to weave cloth. Normally, the loom will operate without human intervention. Occasionally, however, a thread breaks and the shuttle may jam. There is an attendant standing by whose sole responsibility is to unjam the shuttle, tie threads, and put the loom back into operation.

Ignoring shift changes, lunch hours, and coffee breaks, the system will always be in one of two states: 0—the loom is shut off, the man is working to repair it; 1—the loom is operating, the man is idle. A typical realization of the process would resemble Fig. 6.15. The upper lines, representing continuous intervals of time during which the loom is working, could be called "operating times". The lower lines could be called "repair times." One way to approach the problem of modeling this system would be to describe the operating and repair times as continuous random variables having some particular distribution. Here, we shall pursue an alternative approach.

Let $p_{ij}(t)$ represent the probability that the system is in state j at time t given that it was in state i at time 0. Since there are only two states in this example, we are speaking of four functions: $p_{00}(t)$, $p_{01}(t)$, $p_{10}(t)$, and $p_{11}(t)$. The development of the equations which determine the $p_{ij}(t)$ functions can be simplified if the following four assumptions are made:

1. The process satisfies the Markov property.
2. The process is stationary.
3. The probability of a transition from 0 to 1 (a repair) or from 1 to 0 (a breakdown) in a short interval, Δt, is proportional to Δt.
4. The probability of two or more changes of state in a short interval Δt is zero.

Before using these assumptions, let us pause to consider what they mean. When we assume that the process satisfies the Markov property, we are asserting that if at *any* time we know whether the loom is operating or shut off, we can determine all probabilities associated with the process from that time on. We do not need to know, nor does it even help us to know, the sequence of states leading up to the present one, how long the process spent in each of these states, or even how long it has been in the present state. It is common to personify this property and say that the process has no memory, or is forgetful at every point of time.

The process will be stationary if the breakdown and repair rates do not depend on the time of day. It would not be stationary if, for example, the attendant worked slower at certain times.

Assumptions 3 and 4 could not strictly hold. If Δt is small enough, however, they will be acceptable approximations. Later Δt will be reduced to zero; at this time, they will become precise. At any rate, the results will be correct, and the development is aided considerably by making these assumptions. To make assumption 3 even more specific, let the constants of proportionality be 3 for the repair transition and 2 for the breakdown transition. That is, let

$$p_{01}(\Delta t) = 3\Delta t$$

$$p_{10}(\Delta t) = 2\Delta t$$

These constants of proportionality are called the "repair rate" and "breakdown rate"; they receive further interpretation later.

Consider now the function value $p_{01}(t+\Delta t)$, or the probability that the loom is in state 1 (operating) at time $t+\Delta t$, given that it was in state 0 (being repaired) at time zero. Either the loom was being repaired at time t and was put into operation during the interval Δt, or the loom was operating at time t and continued to operate for the short interval Δt.

In symbolic terms,

$$p_{01}(t+\Delta t) = p_{00}(t)p_{01}(\Delta t) + p_{01}(t)p_{11}(\Delta t)$$

This expression, a special case of the Chapman-Kolmogorov equations for the continuous time case, requires the Markov assumption to permit multiplication of the probabilities referring to events during t and to events during Δt. It also requires stationarity to permit use of the same probability functions for the interval t and for the later interval Δt.

We now substitute our linear approximations for $p_{01}(\Delta t)$ and $p_{11}(\Delta t)$, and manipulate

$$p_{01}(t+\Delta t) = p_{00}(t)3\Delta t + p_{01}(t)[1-2\Delta t]$$

[because $p_{11}(\Delta t) = 1 - p_{10}(\Delta t)$]

$$p_{01}(t+\Delta t) = 3p_{00}(t)\Delta t + p_{01}(t) - 2p_{01}(t)\Delta t$$

$$p_{01}(t+\Delta t) - p_{01}(t) = 3p_{00}(t)\Delta t - 2p_{01}(t)\Delta t$$

$$\frac{p_{01}(t+\Delta t) - p_{01}(t)}{\Delta t} = 3p_{00}(t) - 2p_{01}(t)$$

Taking the limit of both sides as Δt goes to zero, we recognize the definition of a derivative

$$\lim_{\Delta t \to 0}\left[\frac{p_{01}(t+\Delta t) - p_{01}(t)}{\Delta t}\right] = \lim_{\Delta t \to 0}[3p_{00}(t) - 2p_{01}(t)]$$

and obtain the differential equation

$$\frac{dp_{01}(t)}{dt} = 3p_{00}(t) - 2p_{01}(t)$$

If were were to go through the corresponding derivations for the other three transition functions, we would get

$$\frac{dp_{00}(t)}{dt} = -3p_{00}(t) + 2p_{01}(t)$$

$$\frac{dp_{10}(t)}{dt} = -3p_{10}(t) + 2p_{11}(t)$$

$$\frac{dp_{11}(t)}{dt} = 3p_{10}(t) - 2p_{11}(t)$$

Thus, we have a system of linear first-order differential equations with constant coefficients. In this particular case, they are simple enough to solve directly. Making use of whatever manipulations or solution technique we find most convenient, and using the initial conditions $p_{ij}(0) = 0$ for $i \neq j$ and $p_{ij}(0) = 1$ for $i = j$, we obtain the solutions:

$$p_{00}(t) = \frac{2}{5} + \frac{3}{5} e^{-5t}$$

$$p_{01}(t) = \frac{3}{5} - \frac{3}{5} e^{-5t}$$

$$p_{10}(t) = \frac{2}{5} - \frac{2}{5} e^{-5t}$$

$$p_{11}(t) = \frac{3}{5} + \frac{2}{5} e^{-5t}$$

These are conveniently expressed in the matrix form

$$\mathbf{P}(t) = \begin{bmatrix} p_{00}(t) & p_{01}(t) \\ p_{10}(t) & p_{11}(t) \end{bmatrix} = \begin{bmatrix} \frac{2}{5} + \frac{3}{5} e^{-5t} & \frac{3}{5} - \frac{3}{5} e^{-5t} \\ \frac{2}{5} - \frac{2}{5} e^{-5t} & \frac{3}{5} + \frac{2}{5} e^{-5t} \end{bmatrix}$$

If we graph these solutions as functions of time, using the same matrix ordering, we obtain the four graphs shown in Fig. 6.16.

Notice that the functions behave as they should in order for them to represent probabilities. They lie uniformly within the interval $[0, 1]$ for all values of $t \geq 0$; the sum over the second subscript equals 1 for all values of $t \geq 0$; and the initial conditions are satisfied. Observe also that the limit of each function as t goes to infinity is immediately apparent, both in the function itself and in the graph. Convergence to this value is smooth and monotonic (as opposed to discontinuous, oscillating, or both), and functions with the same

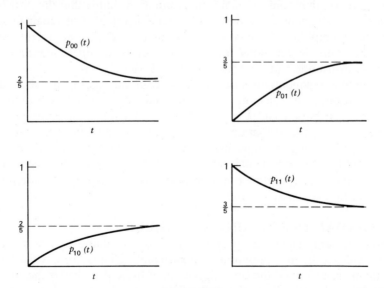

Figure 6.16
The four functions graphed.

second subscript but different first subscripts converge to the same value. These points, as illustrated by this particular example, are generally true in processes of this kind.

The solution is complete, but we do not yet have an interpretation of the "rates" which is sufficient to enable us to measure or estimate the rates in a real-world situation. Heretofore, we have assumed they were *given* as 2 and 3. In order to get this interpretation, as well as some other information about the process, consider now the repair process in isolation. We will imagine that the process begins a repair time at $t = 0$, remains in state 0 until the repair is complete, then changes to and remains in state 1. There are no breakdowns in this modified version of the process. Using the same method of derivation as before,

$$p_{00}(t + \Delta t) = p_{00}(t)p_{00}(\Delta t)$$
$$= p_{00}(t)[1 - 3\Delta t]$$
$$p_{00}(t + \Delta t) - p_{00}(t) = -3\Delta t p_{00}(t)$$
$$\frac{p_{00}(t + \Delta t) + p_{00}(t)}{\Delta t} = -3p_{00}(t)$$

$$\frac{dp_{00}(t)}{dt} = -3p_{00}(t)$$

This is immediately solvable (again using the initial condition $p_{00}(0) = 1$) as:

$$p_{00}(t) = e^{-3t}$$

Now $p_{00}(t)$ is the probability that, given the loom is not operating at time zero, it is not operating at time t. Since breakdowns are not allowed, this event can also be described as "the repair time exceeds t." So the probability that the repair time is less than or equal to t, that is, the cumulative distribution function of the repair time, is $1 - e^{-3t}$. This describes a *negative exponential* distribution.

In summary, then, our original four assumptions imply that the distribution of repair time is negative exponential. *No other distribution* of repair times will satisfy the assumptions. Of course, by means of a similar argument, we can deduce the same implications for the distribution of operating times. The cumulative distribution of operating times is $1 - e^{-2t}$.

A negative exponentially distributed random variable having the cumulative distribution $1 - e^{-\lambda t}$ has an expected value of $1/\lambda$. In this example, the repair time distribution had $\lambda = 3$, so the expected repair time would be $1/3$. The operating time distribution had $\lambda = 2$, so the expected operating time would be $1/2$. Turning the logic around, we can say that the "rates" of 3 and 2 that we used for the original derivation can be interpreted as the reciprocals of the mean repair and operating times, respectively. In a real-world situation, the latter could be estimated statistically.

6.12   FORMAL DEFINITIONS AND THEORY

A continuous time stochastic process $\{X(t)\}$ is an infinite family of random variables indexed by the continuous real variable t. That is, for any fixed t, $X(t)$ is a random variable, and the collection of all of these (for all t) is the stochastic process. We ordinarily think of t as time, so we may expect $X(t_1)$ the random variable at time t_1 to be dependent on $X(t_0)$, where $t_0 < t_1$, but not upon $X(t_2)$, where $t_2 > t_1$. We refer to the value of $X(t_1)$ as *the state of the process at time t_1*. Here we will assume that the $X(t)$ are discrete random variables, so we will be speaking of discrete-state, continuous-time stochastic processes.

If for all t_n, $t_{n-1}, \ldots,$ t_0 satisfying $t_n > t_{n-1} > \ldots > t_0$, we have that $P[X(t_n) = j_n \mid X(t_{n-1}) = j_{n-1}, \ldots, X(t_0) = j_0] = P[X(t_n) = j_n \mid X(t_{n-1}) = j_{n-1})]$ we say that the process has the *Markov property*, or is a (continuous time) *Markov process*. This property is an independence property. It says that if you have information as to the state of the process at a sequence of points in time $(t_0, t_1, \ldots, t_{n-1})$ and wish to predict the state at some future time (t_n), that only the information as to the most recent state is of value. If we think of t_{n-1} as the present, t_n as any future time, and the $t_0, \ldots, t_{n-2}$ as any times in the past, we may say that the future of a Markov process is dependent only on the present, and not at all upon the past. It is sometimes said that "a Markov Process is forgetful."

A Markov process is said to be *time homogeneous* or *stationary* if

$$Pr[X(t_2) = j \mid X(t_1) = i] = Pr[X(t_2 - t_1) = j \mid X(0) = i]$$

for all i, all j, all t_1 and t_2 such that $t_1 < t_2$. In words, the process is stationary if these conditional probabilities depend only on the *interval* between the events rather than upon absolute time. The words "time homogeneous" and "stationary" suggest "invariance" or "sameness" in time. This connotation is correct if we apply it to the *probability* mechanism of the process. The state of the process does, of course, change in time.

A stationary Markov process is completely described by its *transition probability functions*, denoted $p_{ij}(t)$, where

$$p_{ij}(t) = Pr[X(t) = j \mid X(0) = i]$$

The sufficiency of these functions (to describe everything of interest having to do with the stochastic process) is a consequence of both the Markov and stationarity assumptions. That only one state need be known follows from the Markov assumption, and that we may arbitrarily call the time at which that state known as "zero" time follows from stationarity.

A fundamental equation for stationary Markov processes, known as the Chapman-Kolmogorov equation, will now be derived. One could argue the validity of the equation more directly, but it is given here in full detail to emphasize its reliance upon the assumptions.

$p_{ij}(t+s) = Pr[X(t+s) = j \mid X(0) = i]$ (definition)

$\quad = \sum_k Pr[X(t+s) = j, X(t) = k \mid X(0) = i]$ (marginal from joint)

$\quad = \sum_k Pr[X(t+s) = j \mid X(t) = k, X(0) = i] Pr[X(t) = k \mid X(0) = i]$

                (joint from conditional)

$\quad = \sum_k Pr[X(t+s) = j \mid X(t) = k] Pr[X(t) = k \mid X(0) = i]$

                (Markov assumption)

$\quad = \sum_k Pr[X(s) = j \mid X(0) = k] Pr[X(t) = k \mid X(0) = i]$ (Stationarity)

$\quad = \sum_k p_{kj}(s) p_{ik}(t)$ (definition)

$p_{ij}(t+s) = \sum_k p_{ik}(t) p_{kj}(s)$

This final line is the Chapman-Kolmogorov equation in general form. It will be used shortly in the more specialized form

$$p_{ij}(t+\Delta t) = \sum_k p_{ik}(t)p_{kj}(\Delta t)$$

which is known as the "forward" Chapman-Kolmogorov equation. There is also the somewhat less useful "backward" equation,

$$p_{ij}(\Delta t + t) = \sum_k p_{ik}(\Delta t)p_{kj}(t).$$

Now a fair amount can be known about these $p_{ij}(t)$ functions just as a consequence of the fact that they are, for all t, probabilities. For example, they are nonnegative, bounded functions, because a probability must lie between 0 and 1. The values of the functions at $t = 0$ can be deduced because $p_{ij}(0) = Pr[X(0) = j \mid X(0) = i]$. Clearly, for i different from j, $p_{ij}(0) = 0$, and for i equal to j, $p_{ij}(0) = 1$. If we fix i and vary j over all states, the sum of the $p_{ij}(t)$ must equal 1 (for all t), because

$$\sum_j p_{ij}(t) = \sum_j Pr[X(t) = j \mid X(0) = i]$$

$$= Pr[X(t) = \text{any of its possible states} \mid X(0) = i]$$

$$= 1$$

So these transition probability functions are not just arbitrary functions of time, but are quite restricted in the sense that they must satisfy all of these properties. Notice also that these properties are not *assumed*, but are a direct consequence of what the notation means.

Under the reasonable assumption that the $p_{ij}(t)$ are continuous functions (since the probabilities are not likely to suddenly jump), we may express p_{ij} for small Δt by use of MacLaurin's series,

$$p_{ij}(\Delta t) = p_{ij}(0) + p'_{ij}(0)\Delta t + \rho(\Delta t^2)$$

where $\theta(\Delta t^2)$ represents all terms of the order of $(\Delta t)^2$ or higher. If we consider this expression for $i \neq j$, and let $\lambda_{ij} = p'_{ij}(0)$, we obtain

$$p_{ij}(\Delta t) = \lambda_{ij}\Delta t + \rho(\Delta t^2).$$

We may think of this as a linear approximation to $p_{ij}(t)$ which is a good approximation as long as Δt is small. The λ_{ij} is called the *transition rate* from i to j. This terminology is, of course, entirely consistent with its definition as a time derivative of the transition function. Since $p_{ij}(0) = 0$ and this is its minimum value, we may be certain that λ_{ij} is nonnegative.

For $i = j$, the MacLaurin's series expansion yields

$$p_{ij}(\Delta t) = 1 + p'_{ij}(0)\Delta t + \rho(\Delta t^2),$$

and if we again let $\lambda_{jj} = p'_{jj}(0)$, we get the linear approximation

$$p_{jj}(\Delta t) = 1 + \lambda_{jj}\Delta t + \rho(\Delta t^2)$$

Since we know that $p_{jj}(0) = 1$ and that this is its maximum value, we may be certain that λ_{jj} is nonpositive.

If we now consider the forward Chapman-Kolmogorov equation,

$$p_{ij}(t+\Delta t) = \sum_k p_{ik}(t)p_{kj}(\Delta t)$$

for small Δt, and substitute our linear approximation, we get

$$p_{ij}(t+\Delta t) = p_{ij}(t)[1+\lambda_{jj}\Delta t + o(\Delta t^2)] + \sum_{k \neq j} p_{ik}(t)[\lambda_{kj}\Delta t + o(\Delta t^2)]$$

Manipulating slightly,

$$\frac{p_{ij}(t+\Delta t)-p_{ij}(t)}{\Delta t} = p_{ij}(t)\lambda_{jj} + \frac{p_{ij}(t)o(\Delta t^2)}{\Delta t} + \sum_{k \neq j}\left[p_{ik}(t)\lambda_{kj} + \frac{p_{ik}(t)o(\Delta t^2)}{\Delta t}\right]$$

$$= \sum_k p_{ik}(t)\lambda_{kj} + \sum_k \frac{p_{ik}(t)o(\Delta t^2)}{\Delta t}$$

Taking the limit as $\Delta t \to 0$,

$$\frac{dp_{ij}(t)}{dt} = \sum_k p_{ik}(t)\lambda_{kj}$$

The terms of the order of $(\Delta t)^2$ go to zero faster than Δt, so these terms drop out. The result is an *exact* (not approximate) differential equation for $p_{ij}(t)$ in terms of the $p_{ik}(t)$. It is a linear, first-order differential equation with constant coefficients—the λ_{ki}'s.

Recognizing the above sum as matrix multiplication, we may express all of the differential equations at once in the matrix form

$$\frac{d\mathbf{P}(t)}{dt} = \mathbf{P}(t)\mathbf{\Lambda},$$

where $\dfrac{d\mathbf{P}(t)}{dt}$ is the matrix whose (i,j)th element is $\dfrac{dp_{ij}(t)}{dt}$, $\mathbf{P}(t)$ is the matrix whose (i,j)th element is $p_{ij}(t)$, and $\mathbf{\Lambda}$ is the matrix whose (i,j)th element is λ_{ij}.

The elements of $\mathbf{\Lambda}$ may be further related by extending the properties of $\mathbf{p}(t)$. In particular, since for each i,

$$\sum_j p_{ij}(t) = 1$$

then

$$\frac{d}{dt}\left[\sum_j p_{ij}(t)\right]\bigg|_{t=0} = \frac{d}{dt}[1]\bigg|_{t=0}$$

$$\sum_j \frac{d}{dt}p_{ij}(t)\bigg|_{t=0} = 0$$

$$\sum_j \lambda_{ij} = 0$$

In words, each row of $\mathbf{\Lambda}$ must sum to zero. Since every off-diagonal element is nonnegative, the diagonal element, λ_{ii}, must be equal in magnitude and opposite in sign to the sum of the others in the same row. That is,

$$\lambda_{ii} = -\sum_{j \neq i}\lambda_{ij}$$

For the two state example studied earlier, λ_{01} was 3 and λ_{10} was 2. In this case, the matrix Λ would be given by

$$\Lambda = \begin{bmatrix} -3 & 3 \\ 2 & -2 \end{bmatrix}$$

and the four differential equations could be obtained from

$$\frac{d\mathbf{P}(t)}{dt} = \mathbf{P}(t)\Lambda.$$

The elements λ_{ij} for $i \neq j$, may be interpreted (and hence measured) as the parameters of negative exponential distributions. For a particular λ_{ij}, the distribution referred to is the distribution of time spent in state i when j is the next state. If T_{ij} is the random variable, $E(T_{ij}) = \frac{1}{\lambda_{ij}}$, so λ_{ij} can be estimated by the inverse of a sample mean.

6.13   THE ASSUMPTIONS RECONSIDERED

As was the case in discrete time, the derivation emphasizes the assumptions, but the result is in a form which permits use without understanding. That is, the λ_{ij}'s could be measured and the equations could be expressed and solved in the complete absence of understanding—or, for that matter, awareness—of the assumptions. Furthermore, to state the assumptions is not enough. You must be sufficiently cognizant of their implications to judge whether or not they are reasonable in particular contexts. The Markov and stationarity assumptions are both strong assumptions—especially so when time is treated as continuous; there are, however, many, many situations where they are inappropriate. In fact, as you begin to appreciate how strong they are, you may begin to doubt whether any real-life process behaves as a stationary Markov process. It is an empirical fact, however, that many such real-life processes do exist. So the object now is to develop sufficient understanding to be able to distinguish between those processes which might properly be modeled as stationary Markov processes and those which should not.

We have already seen that the Markov and stationarity assumptions imply that the times between events must be negative-exponentially distributed. The parameters of these distributions, the λ_{ij}, may be dependent on the state occupied, i, and the next state, j, but all of the distributions must be of the negative exponential form. No other distribution family can even be considered as a candidate for describing the times between events.

Recall that the negative exponential density function is of the form $f(t) = \lambda e^{-\lambda t}$. Figure 6.17 plots this function for three values of λ. Notice that the

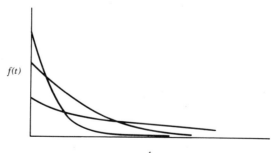

Figure 6.17
The negative exponential density function.

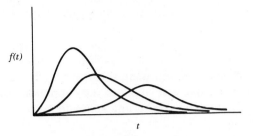

Figure 6.18
Other possible density functions.

function intercepts the vertical axis at λ, that it diminishes monotonically to zero (asymptotically), and that the rate of convergence is proportional to λ. The total area under the curve is, of course, always equal to 1, as it must be for any density function. Varying λ, the only parameter of the distribution, cannot alter the basic form shown in Fig. 6.17. The mean is $1/\lambda$ and the variance is $(1/\lambda)^2$. Thus the mean and variance are not separately adjustable, as one may frequently desire.

In many applications, by contrast, the times between events are most naturally conceived of as having a density function of the general form shown in Fig. 6.18 (perhaps a gamma or Weibull). That is, one tends to think in terms of some nominal value, the mean, plus or minus some relatively minor variation. Or, put another way, the most likely values are considered to be clustered about the mean, and large deviations from the mean are viewed as increasingly unlikely. However, the form of the negative exponential density function implies that the most likely times are close to *zero*, and very *long* times are increasingly unlikely. If this characteristic of the negative exponential distribution seems incompatible with the application you have in mind, perhaps a Markov model is inappropriate.

Another characteristic of the negative exponential distribution which may help you decide whether it is appropriate is the "forgetfulness" property. To use a specific example, suppose that you want to represent some process in which the time between a change of state corresponds to the lifetime of an automobile tire. The state changes when the tire fails. Now there are at least two distinct kinds of tire failure. If what you have in mind is the kind of failure that is due to road hazards, that is, "blow-outs", then the distribution can legitimately be assumed to be negative exponential. There is no logical connection between road hazards and the age of the tire, so the fact that a blow-out has not yet occurred would not carry the connotation that the remaining time to failure is any more or less than when the tire was new. In other words, the lifetime distribution is forgetful, but the only forgetful distribution is the negative exponential. On the other hand, if you are interested in "wear-out" failures, the process would not be forgetful. How long the tire has been in use, as well as its age, would affect our estimate of its remaining life. In this case, a Markov model would be questionable.

6.14 STEADY-STATE PROBABILITIES
In most cases involving more than a few states, the differential equations expressing the $p_{ij}(t)$ cannot be solved without expending impractical efforts.

However their limiting values can be found indirectly. In many practical situations, these will be sufficient.

As in the discrete time case, the states must be ergodic in order for the procedure to work. All of the state classification terms (reachable, communicating, minimal closed sets, transient, recurrent, null, ergodic, irreducible) developed for the discrete-time case apply to the continuous-time case as well, with one exception: It does not make any sense to speak of periodic states when time is continuous.

Assuming, then, that the process at hand is irreducible and all states are ergodic, we may derive a set of linear equations determining the steady-state probabilities. These are defined, as you should expect, by

$$\Pi_j = \lim_{t \to \infty} p_{ij}(t).$$

The argument goes as follows:

$$\frac{dp_{ij}(t)}{dt} = \sum_k p_{ik}(t)\lambda_{kj}$$

$$\lim_{t \to \infty} \frac{dp_{ij}(t)}{dt} = \lim_{t \to \infty} \sum_k p_{ik}(t)\lambda_{kj}$$

$$\frac{d}{dt} \lim_{t \to \infty} p_{ij}(t) = \sum_k \lim_{t \to \infty} p_{ik}(t)\lambda_{kj}$$

$$\frac{d}{dt} \Pi_j = \sum_k \Pi_k \lambda_{kj}$$

$$0 = \sum_k \Pi_k \lambda_{kj}$$

In matrix form, the final result is

$$\mathbf{0} = \mathbf{\Pi\Lambda},$$

where $\mathbf{0}$ is a row vector of zeros, $\mathbf{\Pi}$ is the row vector of steady-state probabilities, and $\mathbf{\Lambda}$ is the matrix of transition rates.

Actually the argument above contains a flaw. It is not generally true that the limit of a derivative is equal to the derivative of the limit. However, these $p_{ij}(t)$ functions are suitably well behaved to ensure that the equality will hold in this case.

There will be an equal number of equations and unknowns in the system of linear equations $\mathbf{0} = \mathbf{\Pi\Lambda}$, but, as in the discrete case, the equations will be dependent. Still assuming that the process is irreducible and the states ergodic, there will be exactly one dependency. The additional equation necessary to determine the unique solution is again as it was in the discrete time case,

$$\sum \Pi_i = 1,$$

and this is still called the normalizing equation.

To illustrate the solution procedure, consider once again the loom example. In that case, the matrix of transition rates was

$$\mathbf{\Lambda} = \begin{bmatrix} -3 & 3 \\ 2 & -2 \end{bmatrix}$$

so the steady-state equations would be

$$(0, 0) = (\Pi_0, \Pi_1)\begin{bmatrix} -3 & 3 \\ 2 & -2 \end{bmatrix}$$

or

$$0 = -3\Pi_0 + 2\Pi_1$$

$$0 = 3\Pi_0 - 2\Pi_1$$

It is immediately apparent that these two equations are dependent. Using either one, we can conclude that

$$\Pi_1 = \frac{3}{2}\Pi_0$$

Now by the normalizing equation,

$$\Pi_0 + \Pi_1 = 1$$

$$\Pi_0 + \frac{3}{2}\Pi_0 = 1$$

$$\Pi_0\left(1 + \frac{3}{2}\right) = 1$$

$$\Pi_0 = \frac{2}{5}$$

And, finally,

$$\Pi_1 = \frac{3}{5}, \qquad \Pi_0 = \frac{2}{5}.$$

6.15 BIRTH-DEATH PROCESSES

Nearly all simple queueing models (as well as a number of nonqueueing models) are special cases of the birth-death process, which is itself a special case of the general continuous-time Markov process. A birth-death process is characterized as a Markov process in which all transitions are to the next state immediately above (a "birth") or immediately below (a "death") in the natural integer ordering of states. That is, a birth-death process does not "jump" states.

The transition diagram of a birth-death process would look like Fig. 6.19. There may be either a finite or an infinite number of states, and the transition rates associated with the lines shown are arbitrary.

The transition rate matrix is also of recognizable form. Because "jumps" are forbidden, $\lambda_{ij} = 0$ except when $|i - j| \leq 1$. This implies that Λ is tridiagonal:

$$\Lambda = \begin{bmatrix} \lambda_{00} & \lambda_{01} & & & & \\ \lambda_{10} & \lambda_{11} & \lambda_{12} & & & 0 \\ & \lambda_{21} & \lambda_{22} & \lambda_{23} & & \\ & & \lambda_{32} & \lambda_{33} & \lambda_{34} & \\ 0 & & & \cdot & \cdot & \cdot \\ & & & & \cdot & \cdot & \cdot \\ & & & & & \cdot & \cdot & \cdot \end{bmatrix}$$

Figure 6.19
The transition diagram of a birth-death process.

Furthermore, since the diagonal terms must equal "minus-the-sum-of-the-other-elements-in-the-same-row", we must have

$$\lambda_{ii} = -(\lambda_{ii-1} + \lambda_{ii+1})$$

That is, the matrix must be of the form

$$\Lambda = \begin{bmatrix} -\lambda_{01} & \lambda_{01} & & \\ \lambda_{10} & -(\lambda_{10}+\lambda_{12}) & \lambda_{12} & \\ & \lambda_{21} & -(\lambda_{21}+\lambda_{23}) & \lambda_{23} \\ & & \cdot & \cdot & \cdot \\ & \cdot & & \cdot & & \cdot \\ & & \cdot & & \cdot & & \cdot \end{bmatrix}$$

Again, there may be either a finite or an infinite number of states, and the specific values for the transition rates are arbitrary.

It is fairly common to simplify the notation, using λ_i for the birth rate λ_{ii+1} and μ_i for the death rate λ_{ii-1}. No generality is lost, but the special notation does tend to conceal the fact that the birth-death process is just a special case of the general Markov process.

The steady-state equations for the birth-death process have the characteristic form

$$0 = -\lambda_{01}\Pi_0 + \lambda_{10}\Pi_1$$
$$0 = \lambda_{01}\Pi_0 - (\lambda_{10}+\lambda_{12})\Pi_1 + \lambda_{21}\Pi_2$$
$$0 = \lambda_{12}\Pi_1 - (\lambda_{21}+\lambda_{23})\Pi_2 + \lambda_{32}\Pi_3$$

$$\cdot \qquad \cdot \qquad \cdot \qquad \cdot$$
$$\cdot \qquad \cdot \qquad \cdot \qquad \cdot$$
$$\cdot \qquad \cdot \qquad \cdot \qquad \cdot$$

6.16   THE POISSON PROCESS

The Poisson process is a special case of the birth-death process. It might be more descriptive to call it a pure birth process, since the death rates, μ_i, are all zero. The birth rates, the λ_i, are all equal to a constant value λ. Thus the behavior of the Poisson process is governed by the single parameter λ, and the structure is such that the state index can only increase (see Fig. 6.20).

The Poisson process is often used to model the kind of situation in which a count is made on the number of events occuring in a given time. For example, it is used in the next chapter, "Queueing Models," to represent the arrivals of customers to a service facility. The state at time t would correspond to the number of arrivals by time t.

The matrix of transition rates Λ would be:

$$\Lambda = \begin{bmatrix} -\lambda & \lambda & & \\ & -\lambda & \lambda & & 0 \\ & & -\lambda & \lambda & \\ & & & \cdot & \cdot \\ 0 & & & & \cdot & \cdot \\ & & & & \cdot & \cdot \end{bmatrix}$$

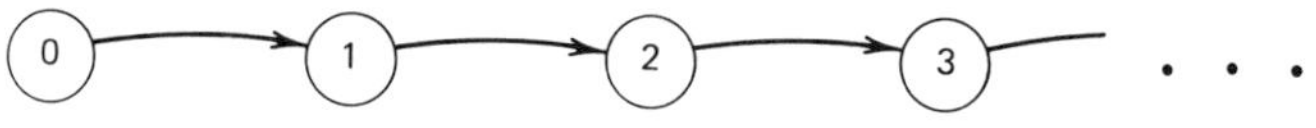

Figure 6.20
The transition diagram of a Poisson process.

Since the applications usually involve counting events, and the count would ordinarily begin at zero, we will assume that the initial state is zero. The differential equations determining the $p_{0j}(t)$ would be

$$\frac{dp_{00}(t)}{dt} = -\lambda p_{00}(t)$$

$$\frac{dp_{01}(t)}{dt} = \lambda p_{00}(t) - \lambda p_{01}(t)$$

$$\frac{dp_{02}(t)}{dt} = \lambda p_{01}(t) - \lambda p_{02}(t)$$

.
.
.

In general,

$$\frac{dp_{0j}(t)}{dt} = \lambda p_{0j-1}(t) - \lambda p_{0j}(t) \qquad \text{for } j > 0,$$

but note that the first equation, for $j = 0$, is a special case.

The first equation involves only $p_{00}(t)$ and is of a particularly simple form. It can be integrated directly to yield the solution

$$p_{00}(t) = e^{-\lambda t}$$

(The constant of integration is evaluated from $p_{00}(0) = 1$.) This solution can be substituted into the next equation, giving

$$\frac{dp_{01}(t)}{dt} = \lambda e^{-\lambda t} - \lambda p_{01}(t)$$

This now involves only $p_{01}(t)$. Tables of standard differential equations or integration by parts will yield the solution

$$p_{01}(t) = \lambda t e^{-\lambda t}$$

This can then be substituted into the next equation to give

$$\frac{dp_{02}(t)}{dt} = \lambda^2 t e^{-\lambda t} - \lambda p_{02}(t)$$

which can be solved to give

$$p_{02}(t) = \frac{(\lambda t)^2}{2} e^{-\lambda t}$$

Continuing in this manner, we find that the general solution is

$$p_{0j}(t) = \frac{(\lambda t)^j}{j!} e^{-\lambda t} \qquad j \geq 0$$

(To verify that it is, indeed, the general solution, it can be substituted into the general differential equation).

The form of the expression is that of a Poisson distribution, which accounts for the name given to the model. One way to interpret the result is to fix t, which has the effect of making λt a fixed parameter. Then the set $\{p_{00}(t), p_{01}(t), p_{02}(t), \ldots\}$ would give the probability distribution of the state at the fixed time

t, which has been identified as Poisson. In terms of a count of events, we would say that the number of events occuring in a fixed time interval t is Poisson distributed with parameter λt. Furthermore, since the mean of a Poisson distribution is equal to the parameter, λt can be interpreted as the expected number of events occuring in time t.

There are other ways to characterize the same process. Suppose that T_n represents the random variable corresponding to the time between the $(n-1)$th and nth event. In particular T_1 would be the time until the first event. Then

$$p_{00}(t) = P\{\text{no events in time } t\}$$
$$= P\{T_1 > t\}$$

So

$$P\{T_1 \leq t\} = 1 - p_{00}(t)$$
$$= 1 - e^{-\lambda t}$$

This distribution can be recognized as the negative exponential distribution with parameter λ. By a similar argument, it can be shown that

$$p\{T_n \leq t\} = 1 - p_{n-1,n-1}(t)$$

and, by solution of the appropriate differential equation, it can further be shown that

$$p_{n-1,n-1}(t) = e^{-\lambda t}$$

Consequently,

$$P\{T_n \leq t\} = 1 - e^{-\lambda t} \qquad \text{for all } n$$

In words, the times between events in a Poisson process are all negative-exponentially distributed with the same parameter λ. Since the mean of a negative-exponential random variable is the reciprocal of the parameter, λ can be interpreted as the reciprocal of the expected time between events.

The Poisson process has a number of mathematically convenient properties that contribute to its usefulness in modeling. First, imagine that we have two independent processes operating simultaneously, and consider the effect of "merging" these processes as shown in Fig. 6.21. More precisely, what we mean by merging the processes is technically called "superposition." The superposition of two processes, A and B, produces a third process, C, in which an event occurs whenever an event occurs in either A or B. Figure 6.22 shows how events in both A and B are "copied" in C.

The convenient fact is that the superposition of two independent Poisson processes produces a Poisson process. This fact can be quite tricky to prove if you think in terms of the times between events, but becomes almost trivial if you think in terms of counting the number of events occurring in time t. Let $N_A(t)$, $N_B(t)$, and $N_C(t)$ be the random variables counting the number of events occurring in

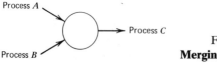

Figure 6.21
Merging two processes.

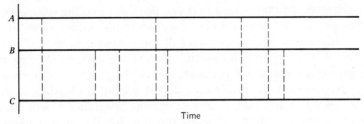

Time

Figure 6.22
The superposition of two processes.

processes A, B, and C, respectively, over the same time interval t. Then since process C counts events occurring in either A or B,

$$N_C(t) = N_A(t) + N_B(t)$$

Of course, both $N_A(t)$ and $N_B(t)$ are Poisson distributed random variables. But we already know that the sum of independent Poisson random variables is a Poisson random variable. Since this is true for all t, C is a Poisson process.

Furthermore we know that the expectation of a sum is the sum of the expectations. Consequently, if λ_A and λ_B are the parameters or rates of occurrence of the A and B processes,

$$E[N_A(t)] = \lambda_A t$$
$$E[N_B(t)] = \lambda_B t$$

and, therefore,

$$E[N_C(t)] = E[N_A(t) + N_B(t)]$$
$$= E[N_A(t)] + E[N_B(t)]$$
$$= \lambda_A t + \lambda_B t$$
$$= (\lambda_A + \lambda_B)t$$

In other words, the rate of occurrence in process C is equal to the sum of the rates of occurrence in processes A and B. One could not ask for a nicer result. It should also be apparent from the argument used that the result extends in the obvious way to the superposition of more than two independent Poisson processes.

This "mergibility" property of the Poisson process is useful in a variety of contexts. The processes A and B might represent, for example, the arrivals of orders for some good to each of two different stores that are supplied from the same inventory. The superposition process would represent the total demands from inventory. Or, in a queueing problem, the component processes may represent arrivals from two different sources, or perhaps of two different types (e.g., male and female). The superposition would represent all of the arrivals to the system.

Since Poisson processes merge so nicely, it is logical to ask whether they may be "separated", as in Fig. 6.23. Although we will make no attempt to

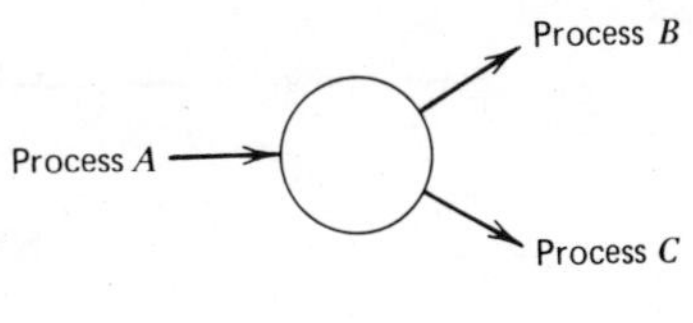

Process B

Process A

Figure 6.23
Separating two processes.

Process C

prove it, the answer to this question is yes, provided that the separation is done in a particular way. Whenever an event occurs in the parent, or input, process, it will be assigned to one or the other of the output processes. The rule that determines whether a particular event is assigned to process B or to process C must be probabilistic and independent of everything else. In other words, it is as if the assignment were determined by the toss of a (possibly biased) coin. Other conceivable rules, such as alternating the assignments, will not produce Poisson processes as outputs. If λ_A is the rate for the input stream, and p_B denotes the probability that an event is assigned to stream B, then the rate for process B is $p_B \lambda_B$, just as you would probably suspect. It is also true, as you might imagine, that the result can be extended to the separation of a Poisson process into more than two processes.

There are several useful ways to interpret the "separability" property of Poisson processes. If the input process represents arrivals of customers to a bank, then the output processes might be the arrivals to individual tellers. Of course, in order to preserve the Poisson process, the customers must be separated on a completely random basis. In particular we could not allow the customers to choose their tellers on the basis of how long the lines are. Another possible interpretation of the separating device is that of a filter. Perhaps the input process represents parts arriving at an inspection station which separates them into acceptable parts and rejects. Provided that the probability of acceptance is independent of everything, both the stream of accepted parts and the stream of rejects would retain the Poisson character.

Perhaps the most remarkable property of the Poisson process is indicated by a rather deep limit theorem formulated by Khintchine (9). Consider a number of independent processes, each of which generates events over time. Within each process, the times between successive events are assumed to be independent, identically distributed random variables. In Fig. 6.24, the inter-event times for the first process are indicated by T_1, T_2, and so on. It is these random variables that are assumed to be identically distributed. We do not assume that the interevent times for different processes have the same distribution. Of course, if the interevent times are negative-exponentially distributed for any process, then that process would be a Poisson process, but we specifically refrain from making any such assumption. The forms of the

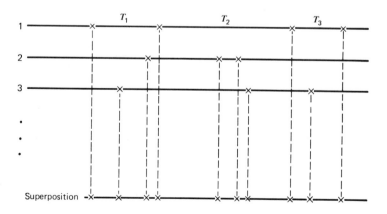

Figure 6.24
Khintchine's theorem.

interevent time distributions are arbitrary. The technical terminology for a process of the kind described—that is, one with independent, identically distributed interevent times—is a *renewal process.*

Khintchine's theorem states that, provided certain reasonable conditions are satisfied, the superposition of a large number of independent renewal processes is approximately a Poisson process. Because we already know that the superposition of Poisson processes is a Poisson process, the real point of the theorem is that the component processes need not be Poisson. Regardless of the distributions of the times between events within processes, if there are enough of them, the superposition is approximately Poisson.

This theorem is somewhat analogous to the Central Limit Theorem. It will be recalled that the latter ensures that the sum of a sufficiently large number of independent random variables will be approximately normally distributed regardless of what the distributions of the constituent random variables may be. Khintchine's theorem states that the superposition (a kind of sum) of a sufficiently large number of independent renewal processes will produce a Poisson process regardless of what the distributions of the constituent renewal processes may be. Like the Central limit Theorem, Khintchine's theorem "explains" why such a remarkably simple process with such convenient properties should happen to occur so often in real life. It also serves to justify the Poisson assumption in cases where the process of interest can be thought of as consisting of the superposition of a large number of independent renewal processes.

To illustrate this last point, consider the arrivals of customers to a supermarket. If you think in terms of an individual customer, the process describing his arrivals is almost certainly not Poisson. That is, it seems very unlikely that a negative-exponential distribution would adequately serve to describe the times between one customer's visits to the supermarket. On the other hand, it does not seem unreasonable to assume that successive intervals between visits are independent and identically distributed, and that the arrival patterns for different customers are independent. Since the arrivals to the store are given by the superposition of the arrival processes of all of the customers, Khintchine's theorem provides reason to expect that the arrivals do indeed form a Poisson process.

6.17 CONCLUSIONS

We have seen that the behavior over time of a stationary Markov process is completely characterized by, in the discrete case, the one step transition matrix, P, and in the continuous case, the matrix of instantaneous transition rates, Λ. Given the elements of the appropriate matrix (plus, in some cases, information about the initial conditions), it is possible to calculate virtually everything of interest about the process. For the most part, the mathematics required is no worse than linear algebra. Even in the continuous case, in which differential equations may appear, they are first-order, linear differential equations with constant coefficients. In short, there are no theoretical barriers to solving practically any kind of problem that can be phrased in terms of stationary Markov processes.

While there is some danger of overextending the techniques to model situations where the stationarity, Markov assumptions, on both, are not warranted, the methods are sufficiently robust to permit an enormous variety of real-world processes to be represented and studied. The next chapter develops just one category of application.

Recommended Reading

For many years, most of the literature of random processes was so mathematically advanced that a beginner would have difficulty in gaining access to the methods. This problem, however, has been remedied in recent years; there is now a selection of good introductory textbooks available. Bhat (3), Clarke and Disney (4), Cox and Miller (5), Parzen (10), and Ross (11) all offer the basic fundamentals of random processes as used in operations research. The styles of treatment, and the depths to which they probe, vary considerably; but one could begin with any of these books. Howard (7) and Kemeny and Snell (8) are also suitable for beginners; however, their treatments are so unique that there is a danger of obtaining a misleading image of the subject as a whole. Used in conjunction with one of the more standard textbooks, they have a great deal to offer. Although not introductory in nature, Bailey (1) and Bartholomew (2) are useful in suggesting applications.

REFERENCES

1. Bailey, N. T. J., *The Elements of Stochastic Processes with Applications to the Natural Sciences*, Wiley, New York, 1964.
2. Bartholomew, D. J., *Stochastic Models for Social Processes*, Wiley, New York, 1967.
3. Bhat, U. N., *Elements of Applied Stochastic Processes*, Wiley, New York, 1972.
4. Clarke, A. B., and R. Disney, *Probability and Random Processes for Engineers and Scientists*, Wiley, New York, 1970.
5. Cox, D. R., and H. D. Miller, *Theory of Stochastic Processes*, Wiley, New York, 1965.
6. Feller, W., *An Introduction to Probability Theory and Its Applications*, Vol. I, 2nd ed., Wiley, New York, 1957.
7. Howard, R., *Dynamic Probablistic Systems*, Vols. I and II, Wiley, New York, 1971.
8. Kemeny, J. G., and L. Snell, *Finite Markov Chains*, Van Nostrand, New York, 1960.
9. Khintchine, A. Y., *Mathematical Methods in the Theory of Queueing*, Hafner, New York, 1960.
10. Parzen, E., *Stochastic Processes*, Holden-Day, New York, 1962.
11. Ross, S., *Introduction to Probability Models*, Academic, New York, 1972.

EXERCISES

1. A naturalist is observing the behavior of a frog in a small lily pond. There are four lily pads in the pond, and the frog jumps from one to another. The pads are numbered arbitrarily; the state of the system is the number of the pad that the frog is on. Transitions occur only when he jumps. Although he can jump from any pad to any other, the probability of jumping to any given pad from the one he is on is inversely proportional to the distance (that is, he is more likely to jump to a near

pad than a far one). The distances are:

> between 1 and 2—6/5 feet
> between 1 and 3—2 feet
> between 1 and 4—3/2 feet
> between 2 and 3—6/7 feet
> between 2 and 4—1/2 feet
> between 3 and 4—3/4 feet

a. Set up the transition matrix.
b. If the frog starts on pad 2, what is the probability that he is on pad 3 two jumps later?
c. Interpret the steady-state probabilities in terms of the behavior of the frog.
d. Explain in terms of the frog, his motivation, his behavior, and so forth, what the Markov and stationarity assumptions mean.

2. A self-service elevator in a four-story building operates solely according to the buttons pushed inside the elevator. That is, a person on the outside cannot "call" the elevator to the floor he is on. Consequently, the only way to get on the elevator is for someone else to get off at your floor. Of the passengers entering the building at the ground floor and wishing to use the elevator, half go the second floor, and the other half divides equally between the third and the fourth. Passengers above the ground floor want to go to the ground floor in 80% of the cases. Otherwise, they are equally likely to want to go to the other floors.

a. If you walk into the building, what is the probability that you will find the elevator at the ground floor?
b. If it is not at the ground floor, but at the second floor, how many stops will it make (on the average) before coming to the ground floor?
c. Assuming that each stop takes 30 seconds (including travel time even if it is between floors of maximum separation) and the elevator is at the second floor, what is the probability of having to wait at the ground floor for more than 2 minutes?

3. Classify the states of the Markov chains characterized by the following transition matrices.

a.
$$\begin{bmatrix} 0 & \frac{1}{2} & \frac{1}{2} \\ \frac{1}{2} & 0 & \frac{1}{2} \\ \frac{1}{2} & \frac{1}{2} & 0 \end{bmatrix}$$

b.
$$\begin{bmatrix} 0 & 0 & 0 & 1 \\ 0 & 0 & 0 & 1 \\ \frac{1}{2} & \frac{1}{2} & 0 & 0 \end{bmatrix}$$

c.
$$\begin{bmatrix} 0 & 0 & 1 & 0 & 0 \\ \frac{1}{2} & 0 & \frac{1}{2} & 0 & 0 \\ \frac{1}{4} & \frac{1}{2} & \frac{1}{4} & 0 & 0 \\ \frac{1}{2} & 0 & \frac{1}{2} & 0 & 0 \\ 0 & 0 & 0 & \frac{1}{2} & \frac{1}{2} \\ 0 & 0 & 0 & \frac{1}{2} & \frac{1}{2} \end{bmatrix}$$

d.
$$\begin{bmatrix} 0 & \frac{1}{2} & \frac{1}{2} & 0 & 0 & 0 \\ 0 & 0 & 0 & \frac{1}{3} & \frac{1}{3} & \frac{1}{3} \\ 0 & 0 & 0 & \frac{1}{3} & \frac{1}{3} & \frac{1}{3} \\ 1 & 0 & 0 & 0 & 0 & 0 \\ 1 & 0 & 0 & 0 & 0 & 0 \\ 1 & 0 & 0 & 0 & 0 & 0 \end{bmatrix}$$

4. Construct a transition matrix for a six-state Markov chain which contains an absorbing state and a closed set consisting of three states.

5. The following is the transition matrix for some Markov chain. Without calculating, determine what the steady-state probability for each state must be, and explain why.

$$\begin{bmatrix} 0 & \frac{1}{2} & 0 & \frac{1}{2} & 0 \\ \frac{1}{3} & 0 & 0 & 0 & \frac{2}{3} \\ 0 & 0 & 1 & 0 & 0 \\ \frac{1}{2} & 0 & \frac{1}{8} & 0 & \frac{3}{8} \\ 0 & \frac{3}{4} & 0 & \frac{1}{4} & 0 \end{bmatrix}$$

6. Given below is the transition matrix for a four-state Markov chain. For each state, find the steady-state probability. Note that the matrix is reducible.

$$\begin{bmatrix} \frac{1}{2} & \frac{1}{2} & 0 & 0 \\ \frac{1}{3} & \frac{2}{3} & 0 & 0 \\ \frac{1}{4} & \frac{1}{4} & \frac{1}{4} & \frac{1}{4} \\ \frac{1}{5} & \frac{1}{5} & \frac{1}{5} & \frac{2}{5} \end{bmatrix}$$

7. Some questions on state classification:
   a. Can a state be simultaneously recurrent and null?
   b. Can a state be transient and ergodic?
   c. If a process has only one minimal closed set, must all the states be recurrent?
   d. If a state i is transient, what is $\lim_{n} p_{ii}^{(n)}$?
   e. Can a state be recurrent and periodic?
   f. Can a state be transient and periodic?
   g. If some states of a process are periodic, must they all be?
   h. If a process is irreducible and some states are periodic, must they all be?
   i. If a process has two minimal closed sets and states of both are periodic, must they have the same period?
   j. Can a state be transient and null?
   k. If a process is irreducible, must all states be recurrent?
   l. If a process has a finite number of states and is irreducible, must all states be recurrent?
   m. If a process has a finite number of states and is irreducible, must all states be ergodic?

8. Three bellboys, Matthew, Mark, and Luke, share the night-shift duty at the Paradise Hotel. On any given night, only two are on duty; the other has the night off. Rather than maintain a fixed schedule, they have adopted the following procedure: the one who is off-duty one night will be on-duty the following night, and the two who are on-duty will flip a fair coin to determine which will get the next night off. The question on everyone's mind is, of course, "When is Mark off?" To answer this question more specifically, do the following.
   a. Construct a mathematical model which describes the "duty roster" (i.e., who is

on duty) as it changes over time. State your assumptions and comment on their reasonableness. You may use previously defined notation freely, but be sure to relate your model to the particular situation described (for example, you will have to define your states and your time parameter).

b. Assuming that today is Thursday and Mark had last night (Wednesday night) off, find the probability that he will have Saturday night off.

c. Still assuming that Mark had last night off, we can be sure that he will be working tonight, but he may have tomorrow night off. If so, we would say that he worked only one night in succession. It is possible that he will have to work two, three, or even more nights in succession. Explain how you would find the probability distribution which describes the number of nights in succession that Mark will work.

9. Paper currency is initially issued by a bank. It will then be circulated throughout the economy, changing hands perhaps many times before it is ultimately judged by a bank teller to be worn out and is removed from circulation. There are three questions we want to answer:

a. How many times, on the average, will a particular dollar bill be deposited in banks during its lifetime?

b. How many times, on the average, will it be in the hands of private citizens (as opposed to banks or other institutions such as businesses and corporations)?

c. Counting each transfer of the bill as a usage, what is the probability distribution of the number of usages obtained from the bill over its entire lifetime?

Set up a Markov model which is capable of answering these questions. Indicate its structure by drawing a transition diagram. Define your states and time scale. State your assumptions and comment on them. Indicate what data is needed.

Explain how to use your model to answer the questions.

10. A market survey has been conducted to determine the movements of people between types of residences. Two hundred apartment dwellers were asked if their previous residence was an apartment, a townhouse, their own home, or a rented home. Similarly, 200 townhouse dwellers were asked about their previous residences, and so on. The results of the survey are tabulated below.

		Previous Residence				
		Apt.	Townhouse	Own House	Rented House	Total
	Apt.	100	20	40	40	200
Present	Townhouse	150	40	0	10	200
Residence	Own House	50	20	120	10	200
	Rented House	100	20	20	60	200
	Total	400	100	180	120	800

The data are believed to be representative of the behavior of the population at large. Develop a model and answer the following:

a. What is the probability that someone who is now in an apartment will own his own home after two moves?

b. What is the probability that the same person will own his own home after two moves but not sooner?

c. How many moves will occur, on the average, before a homeowner will live in a townhouse?

d. What, if anything, can you say about the long-term demand for townhouses, relative to the other residence types?

e. Consider the validity of your assumptions.

11. The accounting department of a large firm is interested in modeling the dynamics

of its accounts receivable (i.e., the money that is owed to it by its customers). When a "charge" sale occurs, a bill is sent out at the end of the month. Payment is due within 30 days, but may not occur in that time. If it is late, a penalty charge of 4% of the amount due is added. If no payment is received within 6 months of the billing date, the amount is classified as a bad debt. Thus, an individual account is described by its age in months, or by "paid," or by "bad debt."

Realizing that data would have to be collected to determine, for example, the percentage of bills that are paid on time, make whatever assumptions seem reasonable or necessary, and model the process. You may use symbols to represent the probabilities, or you may feel free to insert some invented numerical values. Using the model,

a. Calculate the probability that a new sale will ultimately be paid for.
b. Calculate the probability that a bill which is not paid within the 30 day period will never be paid.
c. Calculate the average time that a bill is outstanding (for those that are paid).
d. If a bill for $100 is sent out, what is the expected amount of the return?

12. The Dept. of Agriculture wants a model to predict crop yields in Indiana. Of course, weather and other factors will have to be taken into account, but the main factor affecting how much corn (for example) will be produced is how many acres are planted with corn. Other things being equal, individual farmers try to plant those crops for which they think the market price at harvest time will be best, but other considerations are also important. They have to take into account soil conditions, crop rotation, opportunity for irrigation, and so forth. Because of the variability in the decisions made by individual farmers, the Department of Agriculture feels that a random process model would be appropriate.

There are two major crops, corn and soybeans. All other marketable crops can be lumped into a single class called "other"; land not used for marketable crops is called "fallow." Information is available on the acreage devoted to each of the four categories during 1975 and what was planted on the same acreage during 1974. For example, of the 8 million acres planted with corn during 1975, 6 million acres were planted with corn in 1974, 1 million were planted with soybeans, one-half million were planted with some other crop, and one-half million were left fallow.

1975 Agricultural Land Usage (in millions of acres)	1974 Usage (in millions of acres)			
	Corn	Soybeans	Other	Fallow
Corn 8	6	1	0.5	0.5
Soybeans 3.2	1	1.2	0.6	0.4
Other 4	1	1	1.3	0.7
Fallow 2	1	0.8	0.2	nil

a. Develop a model for the Department of Agriculture describing the sequence of uses of a randomly selected acre of farm land. Define states, time, transitions, and show how to use the available data. State your assumptions and comment on their reasonableness.
b. Explain how the model could be used to:
   1. calculate the amount of land devoted to each category at some distant future time
   2. predict 1977 acreages
   3. estimate the average number of years between fallow years.

13. This problem asks you to develop a Markov chain model to represent aging of

automobiles. Let there be a set of states representing the age of a car in years:

$$0 = \text{car is new}$$
$$1 = \text{car is 1 year old}$$

.

.

.

$$10 = \text{car is 10 years old}$$

(No doubt 10 years is enough to cover the lifetimes of nearly all American-made cars.) Let state 11 represent "car is junked." Because of accidents, even a new car has some changce of being junked during its first year. Ordinary wear and tear, however, has the effect of increasing the likelihood that a car will be junked during the next year as the car gets older.

a. Show what the transition matrix would look like.

b. If one were contemplating buying a two-year-old car to keep for three years, how would you calculate the probability that the car would last that long?

c. How would you calculate the average lifetime of a car, if you had the numerical data to fill in the transition matrix?

d. Critique the model.

14. The Auditor's Manual for the Internal Revenue Service dictates the following review procedures for tax returns from private individuals.

a. All submitted returns are subjected to a computer check for arithmetic errors and "unusual" deviations from typical returns. Seventy percent pass the test; 10% must be returned to the taxpayer for correction of errors; the remainder are sent to trained auditors for review. In addition, a spot check is made on those returns that passed the test by selecting 5% at random to be audited.

b. Of those returns selected for audit, 40% are judged satisfactory without involving the taxpayer. The others require that the taxpayer be contacted to provide additional information or substantiation. After hearing the taxpayer's case, the department may assess additional taxes, which happens in seven out of ten cases, or it may accept the return as submitted.

c. If a taxpayer is assessed additional taxes and wants to appeal, he may do so by applying for review by the IRS District Appeal Board. The chance that the Appeal Board will overturn the auditor's decision is only 1 in 50. Nevertheless a third of such taxpayers do appeal.

d. As a last resort, a taxpayer may go to court to obtain a favorable ruling, but his chances are only 1 in 100 of emerging without any additional tax assessment. Of those who could go to court, half do.

1. Of a million submitted returns, how many (on the average) go to court?

2. If a return is audited, what is the probability that the taxpayer will have to pay additional taxes?

3. Including the computer check, what is the expected number of times that a return will be reviewed?

4. What is the expected number of times that an *audited* return will be reviewed?

15. You are to model the process about to be described as a continuous-time Markov process. The process concerns arrivals to and departures from a Saturday night college mixer. Obviously, such a process will not be stationary; however, we will assume that "once it gets going," we can get a reasonably good model by assuming that it *is* stationary. The state is the number of people at the mixer, ignoring distinctions of gender. Assume in part a that the room will hold a maximum of 200 people. People come to the mixer individually and, if they are lucky, leave in pairs. There is an arrival every 3 minutes on the average, and a couple leaves every 5/3 minutes on the average. However, some people fail to connect and leave, in

disgust, alone. One such person leaves every 5 minutes on the average. The departure of a pair is to be regarded as a single transition.
  a. Set up the differential equations describing the state at time t. Be sure you have enough equations to cover every case.
  b. The steady-state probabilities for the finite capacity case are complicated. However, if we assume that the room is infinitely large, they will turn out to be fairly decent. Make this assumption, and solve for the steady-state probabilities. You will find it helpful to know that $\Pi_2 = \frac{1}{3}\Pi_1$. You should be able to sum the infinite series that appears when you introduce the normalizing equation.

16. Consider an investment opportunity which has the following characteristics:
  1. The value of the investment increases or decreases by $1 at a time. There are no larger jumps, nor are there fractional changes.
  2. If the current value is n, the rate of increase is $n\lambda$, and the rate of decrease is n, the time between changes being negative-exponentially distributed.
  3. Profits are unlimited, but losses are limited to the amount of the original. investment. That is, the value cannot go below zero.
    a. Assuming the investment starts with a value of i dollars, how would you determine the probability distribution of the worth at time t?
    b. Assuming you could do that, how would you express the expected profit at time t?
    c. What are the steady-state probabilities, and what do they mean?

17. To show that the parameter identified as "time" need not be taken literally, consider the following model. Suppose that government expenditures for cancer research produce results which are only probabilistically related to the amount of expenditure. To be more specific, suppose that we have defined an index for the state of medical technology in the area of cancer. Say that the present value of this index is ten, and higher values are better. To achieve an increase of one point in this index will require an amount of research whose *expected* cost is $5 million, but because of the uncertain nature of research, the actual cost is a random variable. Suppose that this random variable is negative-exponentially distributed.
  a. Show how to obtain the expected cost and the distribution of cost necessary to achieve an increase of three points in the index.
  b. Show how to obtain the expected value and distribution of the index that would be achieved from an expenditure of $18 million.

18. A truck trailer has four wheels on one axle, two on each side. Each tire is independently subject to failure (blowouts) at the rate of one failure per 20,000 miles, on the average. Assume that the failure process is Markovian, and let $R(m)$ denote the probability that none of the tires has blown after m miles.
  a. Explain how to obtain $R(m)$.
  b. What is the expected number of miles until the first blowout? At least one tire on each side must *not* have failed in order to keep going. That is, one blowout on either or both sides is acceptable, but two on the same side forces a stop. Assume that flat tires are not repaired, and let $Q(m)$ denote the probability that the trailer is still operable after m miles.
  c. Explain how to obtain $Q(m)$.
  d. What is the expected number of miles until the first forced stop?
  e. How reasonable is the Markov assumption?

CHAPTER 7
QUEUEING MODELS

7.1 INTRODUCTION

Most of the chapters of this book are oriented toward providing the reader with an understanding of and familiarity with *techniques*, so that he may be able to devise his own models to fit his own particular problems. This chapter, in contrast, considers a class of *problems*, and, drawing upon whatever techniques are appropriate, attempts to provide an understanding of the real-world phenomena that characterize the class.

The subject is queues, or waiting lines. More generally, the intent is to study the causes of and cures for congestion. It hardly seems necessary to say that such a study is worthwhile. The increasing role that congestion plays in our daily lives should lend a sense of urgency to our efforts to understand the phenomena that contribute to delays. Moreover, the phenomena are not simple; queues are not just the predictable consequence of too many people or not enough servers. As we shall see, there is little hope of accounting for queues without considering variability. Although unaided human intuition is often quite reliable when dealing with averages, common sense is just not very good when it comes to dealing with variability. Consequently the models of queues that we develop using random process techniques produce a number of surprises. The models are all the more valuable for having this property; they reveal truths that we do not learn as a matter of course from ordinary experience. With the deeper understanding thus obtained, we are better able to contend with real-life congestion.

7.2 A DETERMINISTIC MODEL

We begin with a naive deterministic model of a situation which is later modeled in a more sophisticated manner, using Markov process methods. There are two reasons for doing this: One is to introduce some of the concepts of queueing theory without involving mathematical complications; the other is to exhibit the kinds of results that you might come up with if you knew nothing about random processes, in order to show later how these results can be misleading.

Suppose that we have a man (called the "server") who performs some task on parts or assemblies (called "items") which "arrive" at his work station at periodic intervals. We say, initially, that one item arrives every 3 minutes. The task that the man performs requires some length of time (called the "service time"), and we suppose that this time is 2 minutes. We have no interest in what happens to the items before they arrive or after they are serviced.

If we were to graph the activity of the man over time, starting at an instant when an item has just arrived, we would see the pattern depicted in Fig. 7.1. In

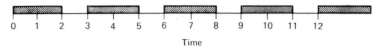

Time

Figure 7.1
Server activity.

this graph, the dark lines indicate the times during which the man is working and the gaps indicate when he is idle. It is apparent that, over the long run, the man is idle one-third of the time. With only a little reflection, one can conclude that the server will be idle $(a - s)/a$ or $1 - (s/a)$ of the time, where s is the service time and a is the interarrival time. Or if one prefers to think in terms of utilization, the server will be busy s/a of the time. This, of course, assumes that $s \leqq a$.

Now certainly ordinary common sense, not to mention traditional management principles, would suggest that this server is underutilized. If the process is subject to control through, for example, the interarrival times, it would make intuitive sense to speed up the arrivals (i.e., reduce the interarrival time) until the idleness is reduced to 0 or, equivalently, the utilization is increased to 1. This would occur when $a = s$; that is, when the time between arrivals exactly matches the service time. Any attempt to further reduce interarrival times would result in a "bottleneck" situation; the items would be arriving faster than they could be serviced and would therefore form a continually growing queue.

In summary, then, our model tells us

if $s < a$, the server will be idle $[1 - (s/a)]$ of the time

if $s = a$, the server will be fully occupied and no queue will form

if $s > a$, a continually increasing queue will form

A manager using this model (perhaps without realizing it) may view the first and third alternatives as equally undesirable and exert his efforts toward maintaining a "balance" between the arrival and service rates. Indeed, this concept underlies much of industrial engineering. Later, upon completion of a Markov model of the same situation, this apparently optimal operating principle will be reexamined.

Before getting into a formal stochastic model, let us consider informally the effect of introducing random variations into the arrival and service processes. Now, instead of arrivals at fixed intervals, we will assume that they occur at randomly varying intervals whose *average* is 3 minutes (or, more generally, a minutes). Similarly, we will assume that services take an *average* of 2 minutes (or s minutes). A new phenomenon occurs—when the time between two arrivals happens to be less than the time required to complete service on the first, the second arrival will have to wait for some period of time before it can begin service. In other words, a queue will form. The average times being what they are, this kind of event may not happen very often; but it *will* occasionally occur. Furthermore, the same kind of thing can happen two or more times in succession, so it is conceivable that the queue could occasionally get quite long.

Note that, *on the average*, the arrival and service processes are just as they were in our first model. The queue we are talking about now is a temporary, fluctuating waiting line resulting from random variations in the times and is quite unlike the constantly worsening bottleneck situation which prevails when the server is overloaded. When the interarrival and/or service times are random, we can have a queue even if the mean service time, s, is much less than the mean interarrival time, a. The phenomenon is a consequence of the *variability* of the service and/or interarrival times, and simply does not occur when both times are fixed. Because variability is complicated, there is a natural temptation to overlook it and to deal with the service and interarrival times as if they were fixed values, justifying the simplifications with the idea that "average" behavior of the two interacting factors ought to be sufficient to predict average behavior of the system. To do so, however, would in this case eliminate the very phenomenon we are seeking to understand.

7.3 QUEUE PARAMETERS

Queueing theory is the study of the randomly fluctuating waiting lines that occur in situations such as that described in the example above. Before developing a Markov process model to apply to the same example, let us pause to consider what elements are essential to a queue, and what variations can occur.

Starting with the example at the beginning of the chapter, it should be apparent that the "server" need not have been a man and that the "arrivals" need not have been parts or assemblies. Indeed, the only aspects of the process that will matter are time aspects. The so-called "services" can be virtually anything that occupy a man or facility or location for some period of time in a way that prevents use by a subsequent arrival until the service is completed. Similarly, the "arrivals" can be anything that appear at particular times and require use of the server. In addition to the obvious queueing situations, such as at ticket windows and supermarket registers, the class of queues would include telephone calls waiting to be connected at a switchboard, airplanes awaiting access to a runway, letters waiting to be typed, and computer programs waiting to be run.

The arrival process could be described in a number of ways. Usually the most convenient way is to designate the random variables corresponding to the times between arrivals (see Fig. 7.2). It is almost always assumed that these

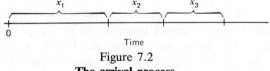

Figure 7.2
The arrival process.

random variables are independent and identically distributed, in which case it is sufficient to name the form of the distribution (e.g., negative exponential, Erlang, general) and to specify the parameters.

Similarly, the service process is usually described by specifying the random variables S_i, where S_i denotes the service time of the ith arrival. It is almost always assumed that the S_i are independent and identically distributed, so that it will be sufficient to name a distribution form and its parameters. The service process is assumed to be independent of the arrival process in the sense that the *duration* of a service time does not depend on when the arrival occurs (nor do arrival times depend on service durations), but note that the service process *is* dependent on the arrival process in the sense that a service S_i cannot begin until the arrival has occurred.

Figure 7.3 shows a commonly employed pictorial representation of a queue with a single server. Frequently, a system may possess multiple servers, which

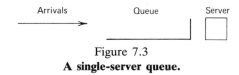

Figure 7.3
A single-server queue.

would be pictured as shown in Fig. 7.4. There exists a special notation for queues of the types discussed so far, known as Kendall's notation. Under his

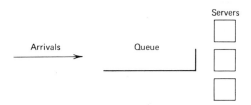

Figure 7.4
A multiple-server queue.

conventions, a queue is described by $(i/j/c)$, where i and j are alphabetic characters, each denoting one of several possible types of distribution. The first letter specifies the arrival process; the second, the service process. The last term, c, is a numerical symbol specifying the number of servers. The letters used to specify distributions are:

M for negative exponential

E_k for Erlang-k

D for deterministic, or fixed

GI for general distribution of interarrival times

G for general distribution of service times

Thus the queue with negative exponential times between arrivals, and three servers, each with Erlang-2 service times would be designated $M/E_2/3$.

In some cases, it is important to limit the length of the queue to some predetermined capacity; in other cases, the capacity can be considered to be infinite. Kendall's notation does not distinguish between these cases. Additionally, the population from which the arrivals come may be infinite, in which case the rate of arrivals is unaffected by how many are already waiting for service. Or it may be finite, in which case the rate of arrivals must decrease as the number waiting for service increases. (In the extreme case, the arrivals must cease when all of the members of the population are already within the system.) We refer to the two cases as the infinite and finite "source" cases, respectively. Unless otherwise indicated, the infinite source case is assumed.

As the pictures are drawn, it may appear that arrivals are always served in the order in which they arrived, but it need not be so. The rule by which the next job or customer or whatever is selected for service is called the *queue discipline.* Among the common ones are:

> FCFS—First come, first served
> LCFS—Last come, first served
> RSS—Random selection for service
> PR—Priority

The last designation is not very precise; there are many possible priority schemes.

To cover these additional common variations, a conference on Standardization of Notation in Queueing Theory agreed in 1971 to extend Kendall's notation by adding three more terms. It should now read:

$$\left(\frac{\text{Arrival}}{\text{Process}} \Big/ \frac{\text{Service}}{\text{Process}} \Big/ \frac{\text{Number of}}{\text{Servers}} \Big/ \frac{\text{Limit on Number}}{\text{In System}} \Big/ \frac{\text{Number in}}{\text{The Source}} \Big/ \frac{\text{Queue}}{\text{Discipline}} \right)$$

The last two or the last three terms may be omitted if they are

$$(./././\infty/\infty/\text{FCFS})$$

In other words, these terms are assumed to take their standard values unless otherwise stated.

Even this lengthy notation is inadequate to describe the variety of possibilities you might want to model. For example, if you have multiple servers, you may want to give them different service rates, but there is no provision within the notation to indicate that you have done so. Furthermore the notation describes only *one* queue, but in practice service systems frequently involve multiple queues. Despite its shortcomings, the notation does cover a considerable variety of useful cases.

There are a number of different outputs that might be desired from a queueing model. Among the more common are:

$L =$ Expected number in the system (including the units served) under steady-state conditions.

$L_q =$ Expected number in the queue (excluding the units being served) under steady-state conditions.

$W =$ Expected time spent in the system (including service time) by a unit at steady state.

$W_q =$ Expected time spent in the queue (excluding service time) by a unit at steady state.

All four of these are related in such a way that if any one is known, the others can be easily obtained.

7.4   THE *M*/*M*/1 QUEUE

We turn now to a random process model of the single server case treated deterministically at the beginning of the chapter. Because the model is the most straightforward of many possible queueing models, the development will be carried out in considerable detail. A thorough understanding of this one model will lay the foundation for many useful variations.

Recall that parts or assemblies were assumed to arrive at regular intervals of a minutes, and service times were fixed at s minutes. We will now assume that the interarrival times and service times are each random variables, having means of a and s minutes, respectively. In order to satisfy the Markov property, we are forced to assume that these random variables are each negative-exponentially distributed. Other distributions might be desirable, but would not permit use of the simple continuous time Markov techniques. If λ is the parameter of the interarrival time distribution (i.e., the arrival rate) and μ, that of the service time distribution (i.e., the service rate), then $a = 1/\lambda$ and $s = 1/\mu$. In a real-world situation, a and s can be estimated by sampling and averaging interarrival and service times. The values for λ and μ would be given by their reciprocals, and these values would then be sufficient to characterize the distribution completely.

We will define the state of our Markov process to be the number of parts present in the system at any time, including the one being serviced. We will not limit the capacity of the system, so the possible states are $0, 1, 2, 3, \ldots$, extending to infinity. Because arrivals occur one at a time and have the effect of increasing the number in the system by 1, and because service is completed on one part at a time, which has the effect of decreasing the number in the system by one, the process will be a birth-death process. Furthermore because the arrival rate and service rate are not influenced by the number present in the system, the transition rates remain constant. In short, the transition diagram is as shown in Fig. 7.5.

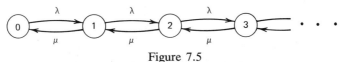

Figure 7.5
The M/M/1 transition diagram.

From this point on, the Markov process is well defined and the analysis should be routine. It is worth pausing to consider, however, some of the assumptions inherent in the formulation of the model. First, observe that if we ignore service completions and maintain a count of the total number of arrivals, we would have an ordinary Poisson process. Hence, we could describe the arrival process, in isolation, as a Poisson process. We could not, however, do the same with the service process, since it would not make sense to consider it in isolation. The service process operates only when there is something in the system to be serviced. Note that the transition diagram indicates the difference between the processes automatically; there is an arrow corresponding to an arrival transition leaving every point, but there is an arrow corresponding to a service completion only for those points greater than zero.

When the process is in any state other than zero, the next state is uncertain. One could say that which way the process will go is the result of a competition between the arrival and service processes. Suppose that the system started empty and the first item has just arrived. What happens next will depend on whether the server can complete the service on the first item before the next arrival occurs. Suppose he does not quite do so; the second item arrives before the first is completed. What happens after that will depend on whether the server can complete the service on the *first* item before the *third* arrives. Now the temptation might well be to assume that because the first item has been receiving service prior to the time that the second arrived, the *remaining* service time will be short and it is relatively more likely that the server will finish before the next arrival occurs. But the Markov assumption specifically contradicts this statement. Once the second item arrives (i.e., state 2 is entered), the server "forgets" that he has already spent time on the first, and the distribution of remaining service time is identical to the distribution of the entire service time. If this sounds preposterous, then we should not be attempting to employ a Markov model. On the other hand, if we insist on allowing the passage of time to influence the distribution of remaining service time (or remaining time until the next arrival), then we shall have to expect *much* more complicated mathematical descriptions. Even the transition diagram would lose its meaningfulness, because you would have to know how a state was entered before you can determine how it will be left.

Returning to the computation, the matrix of transition rates is of the form:

$$\Lambda = \begin{bmatrix} -\lambda & \lambda & & 0 \\ \mu & -(\lambda+\mu) & \lambda & \\ & \mu & -(\lambda+\mu) & \lambda \\ & & \cdot & \cdot & \cdot \\ 0 & & \cdot & \cdot & \cdot \\ & & \cdot & \cdot & \cdot \end{bmatrix}$$

It extends infinitely to the right and to the bottom. The fact that it is infinite does not, in itself, pose any problem, because the structure is very regular.

It is easy enough to express the differential equations for the state transition functions, the $p_{ij}(t)$. They are given by two equation forms:

$$\frac{dp_{i0}(t)}{dt} = -\lambda p_{i0}(t) + \mu p_{i1}(t), \qquad \text{for any } i \geq 0$$

$$\frac{dp_{ij}(t)}{dt} = \lambda p_{ij-1}(t) - (\lambda + \mu)p_{ij}(t) + \mu p_{ij+1}(t)$$

$$\text{for any } i \geq 0, \text{ any } j > 0$$

These are obtainable from the general form equations for any continuous-time Markov process, $\frac{dP(t)}{dt} = P(t)\Lambda$. In this context, $p_{ij}(t)$ would represent the probability that there are j items in the system at time t, given that there were i at time zero. From the $p_{ij}(t)$ we could determine virtually everything else of interest.

Unfortunately, despite their apparent simplicity the differential equations do not solve easily. The solution is known, but it involves modified Bessel Functions and is so complicated that it provides no intuitive insight into the behavior of the queue. Generally speaking, it is neither feasible nor worthwhile to obtain $p_{ij}(t)$ functions for queueing models. As a result, nearly all known results are for steady-state behavior. This is regrettable on those occasions when you want to know what might happen over the short term. On the other hand, most decision-making with respect to design or operation of a queueing system would involve comparative behavior over the long run, for which steady-state results are sufficient.

The steady-state equations for the model under consideration are:

$$0 = -\lambda \Pi_0 + \mu \Pi_1$$
$$0 = \lambda \Pi_0 - (\lambda + \mu)\Pi_1 + \mu \Pi_2$$
$$0 = \qquad \lambda \Pi_1 - (\lambda + \mu)\Pi_2 + \mu \Pi_3$$

The general form is

$$0 = \lambda \Pi_{j-1} - (\lambda + \mu)\Pi_j + \mu \Pi_{j+1} \qquad \text{for } j > 0$$

but the first equation is a special case. Since the first equation involves only Π_0 and Π_1, it can be used to obtain a solution for Π_1 in terms of Π_0.

$$\Pi_1 = \left(\frac{\lambda}{\mu}\right) \Pi_0$$

Substituting this in the second equation leaves an equation involving only Π_0 and Π_2, which can be manipulated to yield

$$\Pi_2 = \left(\frac{\lambda}{\mu}\right)^2 \Pi_0$$

Continuing in this manner, we find that, in general,

$$\Pi_j = \left(\frac{\lambda}{\mu}\right)^j \Pi_0$$

(To be certain that this form is, indeed, the solution for the entire, infinite set of equations, it should be tested by substituting it into the general equation.)

The remaining unknown, Π_0, is evaluated by imposing the normalizing equation:

$$1 = \Pi_0 + \Pi_1 + \Pi_2 + \cdots$$
$$1 = \Pi_0 + \left(\frac{\lambda}{\mu}\right) \Pi_0 + \left(\frac{\lambda}{\mu}\right)^2 \Pi_0 + \cdots$$
$$1 = \Pi_0 \left[1 + \left(\frac{\lambda}{\mu}\right) + \left(\frac{\lambda}{\mu}\right)^2 + \cdots \right]$$
$$1 = \Pi_0 \left[\frac{1}{1 - \frac{\lambda}{\mu}} \right] \qquad \left(\text{provided that } \frac{\lambda}{\mu} < 1 \right)$$
$$\Pi_0 = 1 - \frac{\lambda}{\mu}$$

Note that convergence of the infinite series requires that λ/μ be less than 1. The implications of this requirement are considered shortly.

In conclusion, then, the steady-state probabilities are given by:

$$\Pi_0 = \left(1 - \frac{\lambda}{\mu}\right)$$

$$\Pi_1 = \left(\frac{\lambda}{\mu}\right)\left(1 - \frac{\lambda}{\mu}\right)$$

$$\Pi_2 = \left(\frac{\lambda}{\mu}\right)^2\left(1 - \frac{\lambda}{\mu}\right)$$

$$\cdot$$
$$\cdot$$
$$\cdot$$

or by:

$$\Pi_j = \left(\frac{\lambda}{\mu}\right)^j\left(1 - \frac{\lambda}{\mu}\right) \qquad j \geq 0$$

This distribution is of the geometric form.

Because the two parameters λ and μ appear only together as a ratio, it is conventional to replace them by the single parameter, ρ, where $\rho = \lambda/\mu$. The steady-state probabilities simplify to

$$\Pi_j = \rho^j(1 - \rho)$$

The new parameter, ρ, is called the traffic intensity. It is, of course, the ratio of the arrival rate to the service rate, but there are also some other ways to view it. It is the arrival rate, λ, times the mean service time, $1/\mu$, so ρ can be thought of as the expected number of arrivals during a period equal to the mean service time. In terms of the a and s that we began with, that is, the mean interarrival and service times, respectively,

$$\rho = \frac{\lambda}{\mu} = \frac{(1/\mu)}{(1/\lambda)} = \frac{s}{a}$$

Recall that the deterministic model at the beginning of the chapter revealed that, in order to avoid a continually growing queue, the ratio s/a would have to be less than or equal to 1. The requirement in the Markov model that λ/μ (or ρ) be less than 1, which was necessary to obtain a solution to the normalizing equation, amounts to almost the same thing. The difference is that the deterministic model suggests that the case $s/a = 1$ is not only feasible but desirable. It would represent the condition of exact "balance" of arrival and service rates. But the solution we have for the Markov model does not include the case $\rho = 1$. We investigate this case further a bit later.

Another interpretation of ρ can be obtained from the steady-state solution. Π_0 is the steady-state probability that the system is empty, which can also be thought of as fraction of time (over the long run) that the server is idle. So $1 - \Pi_0$ would be the fraction of time that the server is busy. Since $1 - \Pi_0 = 1 - (1 - \rho) = \rho$, we can interpret ρ as the utilization rate for the server. Once again, the model apparently suggests that, if control is possible, the parameters should be adjusted to make ρ approach 1, in order to achieve full utilization of the server.

Now that we have the probability distribution of the number in the system (in steady state), we may calculate the mean, L.

$$L = \sum_{j=0}^{\infty} j\Pi_j$$

$$= 0\Pi_0 + 1\Pi_1 + 2\Pi_2 + \cdots$$

$$= 0(1-\rho) + 1\rho(1-\rho) + 2\rho^2(1-\rho) + \cdots$$

$$= (1-\rho)[\rho + 2\rho^2 + 3\rho^3 + \cdots]$$

$$= \frac{\rho}{1-\rho}$$

The infinite series converges to a finite sum only if $\rho < 1$, but this is already presupposed.

We can also use the Π_j to calculate the steady-state mean number in the queue, L_q. Since there is only one server, the probability that there are j parts in the queue is equivalent to the probability that there are $j+1$ in the system. The one exception to this statement occurs when there are none in the queue. In this case, there may be either zero or 1 in the system. Consequently,

$$L_q = 0(\Pi_0 + \Pi_1) + 1\Pi_2 + 2\Pi_3 + \cdots$$

$$= 1\rho^2(1-\rho) + 2\rho^3(1-\rho) + \cdots$$

$$= (1-\rho)[\rho^2 + 2\rho^3 + 3\rho^4 + \cdots]$$

$$= (1-\rho)\frac{\rho^2}{(1-\rho)^2}$$

$$= \frac{\rho^2}{(1-\rho)}$$

Note that the difference between L, the mean number in the system, and L_q, the mean number in the queue, is

$$L - L_q = \frac{\rho}{1-\rho} - \frac{\rho^2}{1-\rho}$$

$$= \frac{\rho(1-\rho)}{1-\rho}$$

$$= \rho$$

This might have been expected, for ρ has already been interpreted as the fraction of time that the server is occupied.

Figure 7.6 graphs both L and L_q as a function of the traffic intensity (or utilization rate), ρ, over the full range of permissible values, $0 \leq \rho < 1$. This figure reveals what happens as we attempt to obtain full utilization of the server—the expected number in the queue and in the system grows to infinity. It would be bad enough if the queue might occasionally grow to infinity, or if there were some probability that it might grow to infinity, but this result is even worse. It says that the *mean* queue length grows to infinity.

If this result seems so extraordinary that it casts doubt on the model, you must realize that there is a good reason why we do not witness infinite queues in everyday life. Whenever they start to grow too long, people intercede and alter the system. In other words, even if we manage to achieve $\rho = 1$, we will

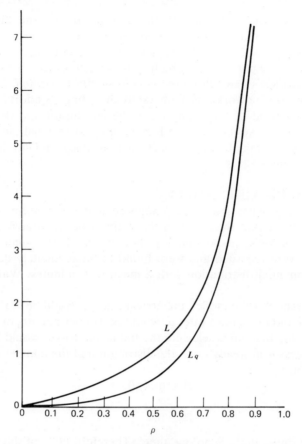

Figure 7.6
L and L_q as functions of ρ.

never see that system reach steady state. The model does correctly reflect what *would* happen *if* the system were allowed to operate.

Closer examination of the curves reveals even further cause for concern. In order to limit the mean queue length to a reasonably small size, say 5, the utilization must be a disappointingly low 0.85. That is, we must be prepared to tolerate 15% idleness of the server in order to avoid a queue which averages more than 5. Of course, even with a *average* queue length of 5, it may, occasionally, be considerably longer. Furthermore, the mean queue length is very sensitive to small changes in ρ in this range.

Thus the stochastic model has revealed that there is an unavoidable conflict between the desire to obtain full utilization of a server and the desire to keep the mean queue length short. The conflict was not at all apparent from the deterministic model. Our earlier tentative conclusion that the system is "in balance" when the arrival rate is equal to the service rate is clearly wrong. The ideal ratio of arrival rate to service rate is something less than one; its specific value depends on the relative costs of idleness versus congestion.

A misunderstanding of the queueing phenomenon has undoubtedly been the source of a good many disputes between labor and management, between customers and agents, and so on. Most people encountering a queue interpret the situation too narrowly. For example, a manager who sees that a worker is idle on one occasion may jump to the conclusion that the "feed" rate is unnecessarily small, and attempt to increase it. He may very well discover later that a very long queue has developed, and be forced to reduce it again. Over a period of time, as he persists in trying to achieve a "balance" between the feed rate and the worker's capability, and is consistently frustrated, he may reach the conclusion that the worker is deliberately thwarting his efforts. The worker, over the same period of time, may reach the conclusion that the manager is attempting to run a "sweatshop." In fact, both the occasional idleness and the occasional backlogs may be attributable solely to the *variability* in interarrival and/or service times.

7.5   A NUMERICAL EXAMPLE

Consider a single-pump gas station. Suppose that observation of the arrival process has shown that the distribution of times between arrivals is at least approximately negative exponential with a mean of 10 minutes. Similarly, service times were recorded and were found to be adequately described by a negative exponential distribution with a mean of 6 minutes. Waiting space is unlimited.

In the notation of the model, the arrival rate, λ, would be 1/10 per minute, or 6 per hour, and the service rate, μ, would be 1/6 per minute, or 10 per hour. Regardless of the time units selected, the traffic intensity ρ would be $\lambda/\mu = 0.6$. Once the process is in steady state, the distribution of the number of cars at the station is given by

$$\Pi_j = (0.4)(0.6)^j$$

In particular,

$$\Pi_0 = 0.4$$

So 40% of the time there is no one there. Therefore 60% of the time there is at least one customer at the station, and this can also be interpreted as the probability that an arriving customer will have to wait, or as the utilization of the server.

$$P(\text{Delay}) = \text{Utilization} = \rho = 0.6$$

The steady-state mean number of customers at the station would be

$$L = \frac{\rho}{1-\rho} = 1.5$$

and the steady-state mean number waiting (i.e., not yet receiving service) would be

$$L_q = \frac{\rho^2}{1-\rho} = 0.9$$

There are several ways in which this model could prove inadequate. One obvious possibility is that the waiting space may in fact be limited. Given the usual dimensions of gas station driveways and of automobiles, a queue of more than five or six might be impossible (finite-capacity queues are treated in the next section). Another possibility is that the arrival rate is state dependent. That is, potential customers are discouraged from entering the station if they observe a long line at the time they drive by. This variation can also be modeled by a method indicated in one of the problems at the end of the chapter.

Another practical possibility is that the arrival process is not stationary. It is very possible, perhaps even likely, that the gas station would experience "peak periods" and "slack periods" during which the arrival rate λ is higher and lower, respectively, than the overall average. These could occur at particular times during a day, particular days during the week, or particular weeks during a year. There is not a great deal one can do to account for nonstationarity without complicating the mathematics enormously. Even the statistical problems of parameter estimation are complicated.

Perhaps the simplest escape from the difficulty, if one knows that the process is not stationary, is to isolate certain periods during which the process is relatively stationary and to restrict the model and its conclusions to these periods. For example, if one is worried about the worst case from the point of view of the length of queue, one could measure λ from observations taken during peak periods. If one is concerned about utilization, one could use data from slack periods. In neither case would the model provide accurate descriptions of the actual process operating in real time, but it might still be useful in providing "conservative" upper or lower bounds on the quantities of interest.

Another point worth mentioning is that it would be pointless to use this model merely to determine Π_0 or L for an existing facility. Since statistics had to be collected to estimate λ or μ, it would have been just as easy to collect statistics for the quantities we were really interested in; in short, there is no need to model what we can measure directly. The real value of the model would be in evaluating the effect of a change in the system. For example, suppose that the station owner wants to improve his service by installing a more powerful, faster pump or by hiring an extra man. If he could reduce the mean service time from 6 minutes to 5 minutes, what effect would that change have on the probability of delay and upon the mean queue size? The model can answer questions of this kind in advance, whereas a statistical approach would require that the change be made and the effect observed. In this case, the new ρ would be 0.5, so the probability of delay would drop from 0.6 to 0.5 and the mean number of cars at the station, L, would drop from 1.5 to 1.0. The mean number of waiting cars, L_q, would drop from 0.9 to 0.5. If these improvements are not sufficient, in the opinion of the owner, to warrant the added expense of a new pump or extra man, he still has the opinion of not making the change. The other approach might leave him in the position of discovering after making the change that it was not worthwhile.

7.6 LIMITED QUEUE CAPACITY

When waiting space is limited, a number of minor modifications must be made to the previously developed model. In terms of the queueing notation introduced earlier, we are now concerned with the $M/M/1/N$ system, in which N represents the maximum number of units or customers allowed in the system. Because the arrival process would ordinarily continue to generate arrivals even when the system was full, we must assume that these "blocked" arrivals are lost to the system.

A schematic version of the finite queue is shown in Fig. 7.7; the associated transition diagram is given in Fig. 7.8. The latter is identical to Fig. 7.5, except

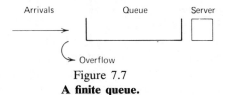

Figure 7.7
A finite queue.

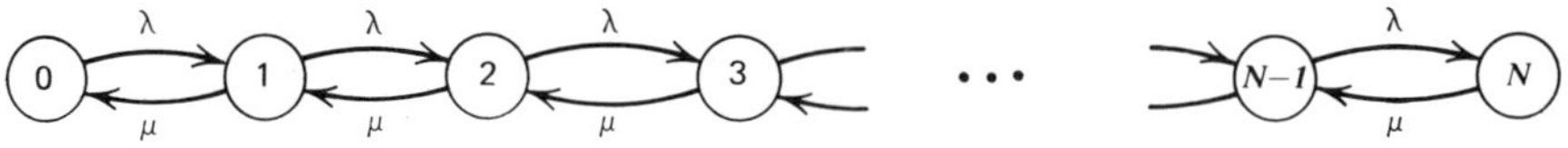

Figure 7.8
The transition diagram for a finite queue.

that it is finite. Similarly, the transition matrix is similar to that used before, except that it is finite.

$$
\Lambda = \begin{bmatrix}
-\lambda & \lambda \\
\mu & -(\lambda+\mu) & \lambda \\
& \mu & -(\lambda+\mu) & \lambda \\
& & & \cdot & \cdot & \cdot \\
& & & & \cdot & \cdot & \cdot \\
& & & & & \cdot & \cdot & \cdot \\
& & & & & & \mu & -\mu
\end{bmatrix}
$$

The steady state equations are identical to those used previously, except that the last equation is now a special case:

$$0 = -\lambda \Pi_0 + \mu \Pi_1$$
$$0 = \lambda \Pi_{j-1} - (\lambda+\mu)\Pi_j + \mu \Pi_{j+1} \qquad \text{for } 0 < j < N$$
$$0 = \lambda \Pi_{N-1} - \mu \Pi_N$$

The fact that the last equation is of an altered form does not influence the solution for the Π_j in terms of Π_0, because the equations contain a dependency. That is, we do not require the last equation. We obtain, as before,

$$\Pi_j = \left(\frac{\lambda}{\mu}\right)^j \Pi_0 \qquad j = 0, 1, \ldots, N$$

(It is easy to verify that this solution is consistent with the neglected last equation.) So far, then, the limitation on system capacity has not made any difference.

At this point, however, we must apply the normalizing equation to determine Π_0.

$$1 = \Pi_0 + \Pi_1 + \Pi_2 + \cdots + \Pi_N$$

$$1 = \Pi_0 + \frac{\lambda}{\mu}\Pi_0 + \left(\frac{\lambda}{\mu}\right)^2 \Pi_0 + \cdots + \left(\frac{\lambda}{\mu}\right)^N \Pi_0$$

$$1 = \Pi_0 \left[1 + \frac{\lambda}{\mu} + \left(\frac{\lambda}{\mu}\right)^2 + \cdots + \left(\frac{\lambda}{\mu}\right)^N \right]$$

$$1 = \Pi_0 \left[\frac{1 - \left(\frac{\lambda}{\mu}\right)^{N+1}}{1 - \frac{\lambda}{\mu}} \right]$$

$$\Pi_0 = \frac{1 - \frac{\lambda}{\mu}}{1 - \left(\frac{\lambda}{\mu}\right)^{N+1}} = \frac{1 - \rho}{1 - \rho^{N+1}}$$

This time the series is finite, so no convergence requirement appears to restrict the value of ρ. The formula given is valid for any value of ρ, with the exception of $\rho = 1$, in which case the sum is trivially $N + 1$, so $\Pi_0 = 1/N + 1$. In summary,

$$\Pi_j = \rho^j\left(\frac{1-\rho}{1-\rho^{N+1}}\right) \qquad j = 0, 1, \ldots, N$$

unless $\rho = 1$, in which case,

$$\Pi_j = \frac{1}{N+1} \qquad j = 0, 1, \ldots, N$$

The mean number in the system, L, can be obtained from the distribution, using well known finite-sum formulas

$$L = \frac{\rho}{1-\rho}\left(\frac{1-\rho^N}{1-\rho^{N+1}}\right) - \frac{N\rho^{N+1}}{1-\rho^{N+1}} \qquad \text{for } \rho \neq 1$$

$$= \frac{N}{2} \qquad \text{for } \rho = 1$$

If the traffic intensity, ρ, is low and N is large, L will be close to $\frac{\rho}{1-\rho}$, as you would expect. If ρ is much greater than one, L approaches N. This, too, makes sense. A heavily overloaded system will tend to remain nearly full. This is one way to get good utilization of the server. Of course, when the arrival rate is much greater than the service rate, most arrivals will be blocked and therefore never be served by the system. Depending on the application, this loss may be anything from perfectly acceptable to intolerable.

Incidentally, the fraction of customers or items lost due to blocking is easily quantified. Π_N gives the probability that the system is full.

$$\Pi_N = \rho^N\left(\frac{1-\rho}{1-\rho^{N+1}}\right) \qquad \text{for } \rho \neq 1$$

$$= \frac{1}{N+1} \qquad \text{for } \rho = 1$$

The same quantity can be interpreted as the fraction of time, over the long run, that an arriving customer will find the system full; hence, it is the fraction of arriving customers who are blocked. The *number* blocked per unit time would be this fraction times the number of arrivals per unit time, or $\Pi_N\lambda$. This number may be useful in determining how many more customers would be served if the waiting space, N, were increased. One of the problems at the end of the chapter explores the idea further.

The case $\rho = 1$ is interesting, in that it can provide additional insight into why a balance between the arrival rate and service rate is generally not desirable. When $\rho = 1$, the distribution of the number in the system is uniform; that is, all states are equally likely. The mean would be "half full." For any finite N, items are being blocked. In an industrial setting where the items are workpieces that *must* be processed, the only recourse (short of unbalancing the arrival and service rates) is to increase the waiting room. But as N is increased, the states remain equally likely and the mean is still "half full." In the limit, as N goes to infinity, the probability of being in any particular state goes to zero and the mean goes to infinity (or half of infinity, which is the same thing). In the terminology of Markov processes, the states remain recurrent, but become null.

7.7 MULTIPLE SERVERS

Another important and easily handled variation involves multiple servers drawing from a single queue, as depicted in Fig. 7.4. Such a system would be designated by $M/M/C/N$, where C is the number of servers. The system capacity N would certainly have to be at least C. One important special case occurs when $N = C$; that is, when the maximum number permitted in the system equals the number of servers. We will call this the "no waiting" case. Another special case occurs when $N = \infty$, or when there is infinite waiting room so that all arrivals may ultimately be served.

Assuming that all servers operate at the same mean rate, μ, there is no need to keep track of which servers are busy. It will be sufficient, in describing the state of the system, to indicate the number of customers in the system. Despite the fact that service may take place on a number of customers simultaneously, departures will occur one at a time. (The probability of two or more services being completed at exactly the same instant is zero.) Consequently it will still be appropriate to model this system as a birth-death process. What is different now is that the transition rates will be state dependent. If there is only one customer in the system, he will receive service from one of the servers at the rate μ. The other servers will stand idle. So the transition rate from state 1 to state zero is μ. If there are two customers present, they will both receive service, *each* at the rate μ. The transition from state 2 to state 1 will occur as soon as *either* completes service, so the rate at which this occurs is twice as great as the rate would be if only one server were working, or 2μ. Similarly, the transition rate from 3 to 2 is 3μ, and so on. (If you find it difficult to think in terms of rates, you may wish to convince yourself that these rates are correct by translating them to mean times between transitions.) The transition rates corresponding to service completions continue to increase in this way until all C servers are occupied, after which they remain at the value $C\mu$. The transition diagram is shown in Fig. 7.9.

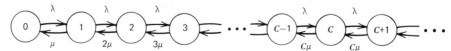

Figure 7.9
The transition diagram for multiple servers.

If we now restrict attention to the "no waiting" case, or the $M/M/C/C$ system, the transition diagram would extend only to the state C. The steady-state equations are:

$$0 = -\lambda \Pi_0 + \mu \Pi_1$$
$$0 = \lambda \Pi_0 - (\lambda + \mu)\Pi_1 + 2\mu \Pi_2$$
$$0 = \lambda \Pi_1 - (\lambda + 2\mu)\Pi_2 + 3\mu \Pi_3$$

$$\vdots$$

$$0 = \lambda \Pi_{C-1} - C\mu \Pi_C$$

These can be solved in the usual way for birth-death equations to yield

$$\Pi_j = \frac{1}{j!}\left(\frac{\lambda}{\mu}\right)^j \Pi_0 \qquad \text{for } j = 0, 1, \ldots, C$$

Defining $\rho = \lambda/\mu$, as in the $M/M/1$ queue,

$$\Pi_j = \frac{\rho^j}{j!}\,\Pi_0$$

Using the normalizing equation to evaluate Π_0, we find

$$\Pi_0 = \frac{1}{\displaystyle\sum_{i=0}^{C}\frac{\rho^i}{i!}}$$

The sum in the denominator does not simplify any further, but it might be helpful to observe that it is the first $C+1$ terms of the infinite series expression of e^ρ. If C is very large relative to ρ, so that the remaining terms in the infinite series are small, we can say that Π_0 is approximately $e^{-\rho}$, and

$$\Pi_j = \frac{\rho^j}{j!}\,e^{-\rho}$$

is, approximately, the distribution of the number of occupied servers. This distribution is, of course, Poisson. The approximation becomes exact as C goes to infinity. One way in which a real-life system could have an unlimited number of servers is for each arrival to serve himself.

More generally, when C is finite and the approximation is not appropriate,. the steady-state distribution is

$$\Pi_j = \frac{\dfrac{\rho^j}{j!}}{\displaystyle\sum_{i=0}^{C}\frac{\rho^i}{i!}}$$

and this distribution has been called a truncated Poisson distribution.

One term, in particular, is of special interest. The probability that all servers are occupied, or that the system is full, is given by

$$\Pi_N = \frac{\dfrac{\rho^N}{N!}}{\displaystyle\sum_{i=0}^{C}\frac{\rho^i}{i!}}$$

This formula, known variously as *Erlang's lost call formula*, the *Erlang B-formula*, or the *first Erlang function*, has been used extensively in the design of telephone systems. Tables and graphs are readily available in, for example, ref. 2.

The mean number of occupied servers, or customers in the system is given by

$$L = \rho[1 - \Pi_N]$$

This relation has a number of interesting verbal interpretations. The reader is encouraged to try to think of some.

Of course, all of these results were derived from a Markov model. In particular, service times were assumed to be negative-exponentially distributed. Perhaps surprisingly, exactly the same results occur when the service time distribution is arbitrary. A. K. Erlang, who first obtained all of these results (for the negative-exponential service time case) as early as 1917, conjectured that they would hold for arbitrary service times. The conjecture was confirmed, however, only as recently as 1969 (12). As you might expect, the mathematics used is beyond the level of this text, but it is useful to know that the solution for the $M/G/C/C$ system (including the case $C = \infty$) is the same as for the $M/M/C/C$ system.

The solutions just discussed were for the "no waiting" case. Returning now to the more general case in which some, perhaps infinite, waiting capacity is available, the steady-state equations would be:

$$0 = -\lambda \Pi_0 + \mu \Pi_1$$

$$0 = \lambda \Pi_{j-1} - (\lambda + j\mu)\Pi_j + (j+1)\mu \Pi_{j+1} \qquad \text{for } j = 1, \ldots, C-1$$

$$0 = \lambda \Pi_{j-1} - (\lambda + C\mu)\Pi_j + C\mu \Pi_{j+1} \qquad \text{for } j = 0, C+1, \ldots$$

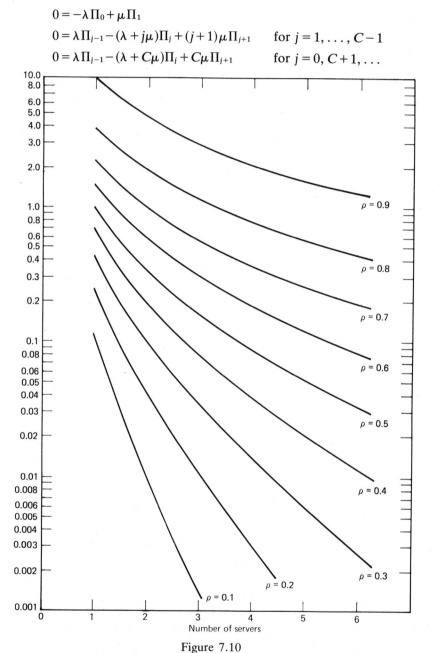

Figure 7.10

Mean delay in multiples of mean service time, $1/\mu$, for $M/M/C$, $C = 1, 2, \ldots, 6$ and $\rho = \lambda/C\mu = 0.1, 0.2, \ldots, 0.9.$

If the total system capacity, N, is finite, there would be one more equation for the last state.

$$0 = \lambda \Pi_{N-1} - C\mu\Pi_N$$

The solution of these equations offers no difficulties in principle, but the solutions are cumbersome to express. A chart, Fig. 7.10, has been provided as an alternative. This chart, which was constructed from solutions to the equations above, for $N = \infty$ and $C = 1, 2, 3, 4, 5,$ and 6, graphs W_q, the mean time spent waiting to begin service, in multiples of the mean service time. Other quantities, such as L and L_q, can be deduced from W_q by methods to be discussed in Section 7.10. It should be noted that the solution for this infinite state case produces the convergence requirement $(\lambda/C\mu) < 1$.

7.8 POOLED VERSUS SEPARATE SERVERS

To illustrate use of the chart just given and at the same time to reveal an interesting principle, consider the following application. Two businessmen, working in adjacent offices, each require secretarial service. They each produce an average of four letters a day to be typed, and a secretary can be expected to require an average of 1/5 day to type one letter. The question is, should each man have his own secretary, or should they get together and form a two-person secretarial pool?

Considering the separate systems first, we see that each would be an $M/M/1$ system with $\lambda = 4$ and $\mu = 5$, or $\rho = 0.8$, as shown in Fig. 7.11. We

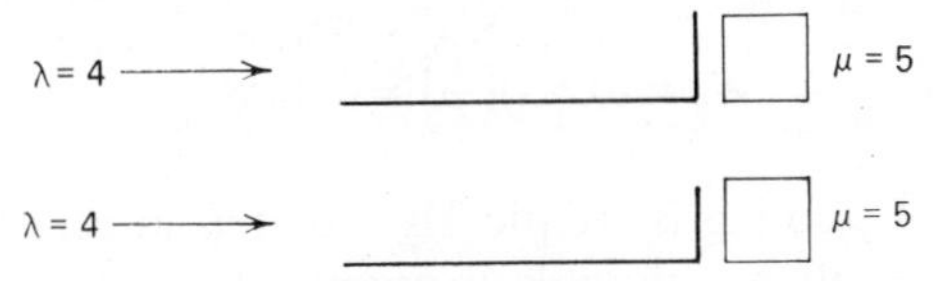

Figure 7.11
Parallel systems.

have formulas to cover this case; but using the chart, we find that for $\rho = 0.8$ and $c = 1$, the mean delay, W_q, is 4.0 times the mean service time, or

$$W_q = 4.0\left(\frac{1}{5}\right) = 0.8 \text{ day}$$

On the average, then, a letter will sit on the secretary's desk for 4/5 day before typing begins. This same result applies for each of the two systems.

The alternative, pooled system would establish a single queue with two servers as in Fig. 7.12. As soon as a secretary finished one letter, the next one

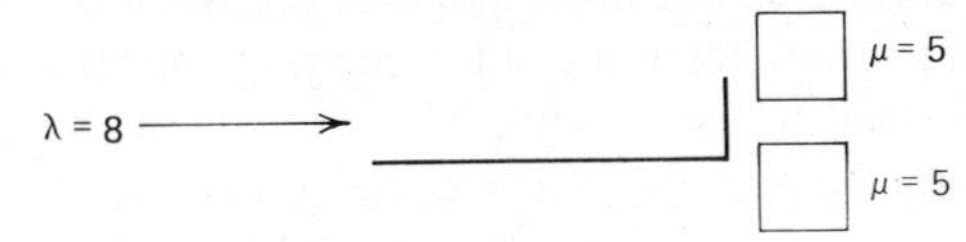

Figure 7.12
The pooled system.

in the queue is begun, regardless of which businessman wrote it. This would constitute on $M/M/2$ system. The effective arrival rate to the system would be $\lambda = 8$ per day, but the service rate per server, μ, would still be 5 per day. The ρ used in the chart is $\lambda/C\mu$ (*not* λ/μ as in the single server and multiple server with no waiting models), so ρ is again 0.8. For $\rho = 0.8$ and $C = 2$, the chart shows the mean delay is 1.75 times the mean service time.

$$W_q = 1.75\left(\frac{1}{5}\right) = 0.35 \text{ day}$$

In other words, the average delay is reduced by more than half, just by pooling the work.

The same conclusion is valid for any value of ρ, and the principle extends to more than two servers. This fact can be confirmed by comparing the mathematical expressions for W_q, or perhaps more simply, by realizing that the downward slope of the curves in the chart as C increases implies that pooling is always advantageous.

The principle is remarkable in that intuition would seem to lead to the opposite conclusion. Businessmen would ordinarily expect to get better service if they did not have to share access to a secretary. Even the example above may not convince them otherwise if the workloads generated by the two men are not equal. For example, suppose that one of the two men generates a mean of only two letters a day instead of four. With a secretary of his own, he will experience a mean delay (from the chart) of only 0.13 days. Surely, he might feel, there is nothing to be gained by pooling his work load with the other office. The other fellow would be better off, but it would be at his expense. In fact, however, pooling the work load would benefit both men! The combined λ would be 6, and the mean delay would be

$$W_q = (0.55)\left(\frac{1}{5}\right) = 0.11 \text{ days}$$

The principle of pooling is frequently violated in real-life service systems; banks and supermarkets are notable examples. Separate queues are provided for each server, and a customer must commit himself to a particular server at the time he arrives. The "take a number" system commonly used in some shops, such as bakeries, is significantly better from the standpoint of customer delay. Of course, it must be admitted that there are other factors to be considered in the design of any system. Customers may prefer to choose the teller or clerk they want; questions of jurisdiction may prevent pooling; and so on. Nevertheless it can be said quite firmly that, from the standpoint of the waiting time and assuming all other things equal, it is always best to pool.

7.9   FINITE SOURCES

The next variation to be developed models the situation that occurs when the potential arrivals form a fixed, finite population. Such a situation would occur if, for example, the server were an office copying machine which only a dozen people were authorized to use. Figure 7.13 depicts the situation. It is assumed that when a customer completes service, he returns to the source.

The queueing nomenclature for this model is $M/M/1/N/N$. The second N refers to the number of items in the source, or the maximum number of arrivals. The first N represents the capacity of the system. Although the capacity could conceivably differ from the maximum number of arrivals, there is no point in considering a greater capacity—it would never be used—and it will be obvious how to treat a lesser capacity.

The difference between this model and previous ones is in the arrival rates.

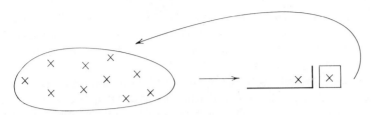

Figure 7.13
The transition diagram for the finite source queue.

It is intuitively clear that when most of the population are in the queue, the arrival rate should be lower than when most are in the source. Certainly, when *all* are in the queue, the arrival rate should be zero.

Let λ represent the mean arrival rate *per customer*. This would be statistically estimated by recording the times spent in the source by each customer, that is, the durations of the intervals beginning when a customer returns to the source after completing service and ending when the same customer reappears at the queue requiring another service. Assuming these times fit a negative exponential distribution with a common mean for all customers, λ would be the reciprocal of the average time. Note that λ *cannot* be estimated by recording times between arrivals to the queue, because these times will be dependent on the number already in the queue.

If there is only one customer in the source, and the other $N-1$ are in the system, the arrival rate will obviously be λ. If there are two in the source, the arrival rate will be twice as great, or 2λ. The logic here is similar to that used to obtain the service transition rates when there were multiple servers. Continuing in this manner, we obtain the transition diagram shown in Fig. 7.14. As in

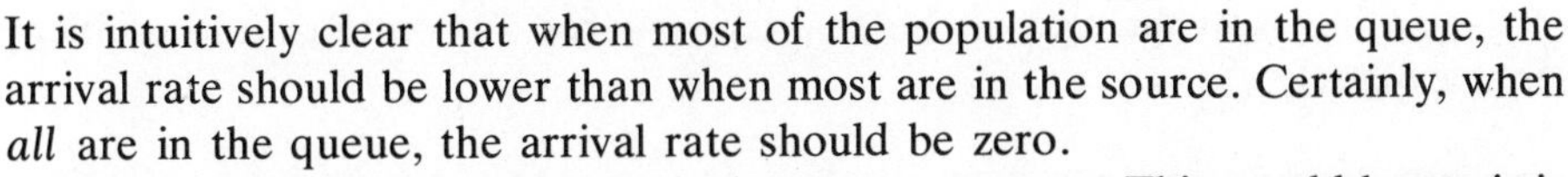

Figure 7.14
The transition diagram for the finite source queue.

previous models, the state represents the number in the system (queue plus server), but it would also be possible in this case to use the number in the source as the indicator.

The steady-state equations are

$$0 = -N\lambda\,\Pi_0 + \mu\,\Pi_1$$
$$0 = (N-j+1)\Pi_{j-1} - [(N-j)\lambda + \mu]\Pi_j + \mu\,\Pi_{j+1} \qquad \text{for } j = 1, 2, \ldots, N-1$$
$$0 = \lambda\,\Pi_{N-1} - \mu\,\Pi_N$$

The general solution, obtained in the usual way, is

$$\Pi_j = \frac{N!}{(N-j)!}\left(\frac{\lambda}{\mu}\right)^j \Pi_0$$

The expressions for Π_0, L, and L_q are obtainable in a straightforward manner, but do not reduce to simple formulas that could provide additional insight.

The finite source arrival rates can be combined with the multiple server service rates to provide a useful model which is commonly called the "machine interference model" or the "N machine, R repairmen" model. In this application, the N machines form the source population, and the repairmen are the servers. The breakdown of a machine constitutes an "arrival" (not to imply, necessarily, that broken machines are physically moved to a repair shop). A repair restores the machine to operation and, in that sense, returns it to the source. Formally the model is $M/M/R/N/N$.

The problem usually posed is, "given the failure and repair rates, λ and μ, and a fixed number of machines, N, what is the optimal number of repairmen, R, to service the machines?" The method of solution is, of course, to model the various alternatives and to select that one which achieves the most advantageous trade-off between the cost of repairmen and the cost of idle machines. One of the problems at the end of the chapter explores this optimization problem more explicitly.

7.10   WAITING TIMES

In each of the queueing models presented so far, the state has been defined as the number in the system. From the steady-state distribution, the Π_j, it was possible to calculate such measures of system performance as L and L_q. Sometimes, however, the number in the system or queue is not, in itself, of direct interest. Instead, the concern may be for waiting times. Of course, intuitively, the two are closely related; when one is large so will the other be.

As a matter of fact, there exists a fundamental identity, known as *Little's formula*, which directly relates the steady-state mean number in the system to the mean waiting time in the system (including service time). The relation is

$$L = \lambda W$$

There also exists an analogous result relating the mean number in the queue to the mean waiting time in the queue:

$$L_q = \lambda W_q$$

These relations, particularly the first, have enjoyed a long history. They have been proved many times under increasingly weaker assumptions. A recent reference on the subject is Stidham (11). The relations are now known to be valid for arbitrary arrival and service processes, for any number of servers and for any queue discipline.

In both relations, λ represents the effective arrival rate to the system, or the reciprocal of the mean time between arrivals to the system. The notation is not intended to imply that the arrival process need be Poisson. Some care must be taken in certain cases to obtain the *effective* arrival rate. When system capacity is finite, as in the $M/M/1/N/\infty/FCFS$ or the $M/M/C/C/\infty/FCFS$ models, some potential arrivals do not actually enter the system. In these cases, the original λ must be reduced appropriately. For example, in the single-server finite-capacity model, the fraction Π_N does not enter, so the effective arrival rate is

$$\lambda[1 - \Pi_N] = \lambda\left[1 - \rho^N\left(\frac{1-\rho}{1-\rho^{N+1}}\right)\right]$$

$$= \lambda\left[\frac{1-\rho^N}{1-\rho^{N+1}}\right]$$

A further simple relation can be used to tie W to W_q. In words,

$$E(\text{time in system}) = E(\text{time in queue} + \text{service time})$$

$$= E(\text{time in queue}) + E(\text{service time})$$

Translating to symbols,

$$W = W_q + \frac{1}{\mu}$$

where $1/\mu$ represents the mean service time, without necessarily implying that it is negative-exponentially distributed. If both sides of this relation between W and W_q are multiplied by λ, we obtain a relation between L and L_q:

$$\lambda W = \lambda \left[W_q + \frac{1}{\mu} \right]$$

$$\lambda W = \lambda W_q + \frac{\lambda}{\mu}$$

$$L = L_q + \frac{\lambda}{\mu}$$

In summary, the four quantities L, L_q, W, and W_q are all simply related. As soon as one is known, the others follow easily. Ordinarily the easiest one to find first would be L. A possible exception would occur in the case of the $M/M/C/\infty/\infty/FCFS$ model, for which the chart provides W_q.

The quantities W and W_q are only *mean* values. In some applications it may be desirable to have the *distribution* of waiting time in the system or queue. For example, one may wish to know the probability of having to wait longer than some particular time. The subject of waiting-time distributions has provoked a good deal of attention from queueing theorists, but the mathematics required tends to be quite advanced.

There is one case for which the mathematics is elementary and the result is interesting. That case is the $M/M/1$ model—the single server, infinite capacity model with which we initiated our study of queues. Let $\bar{W}$ denote the random variable corresponding to the total time spent in the system (in steady state). That is, the waiting time experienced by a randomly chosen customer arriving at a time long after commencement of the process would be a sample value of $\bar{W}$. Consider the probability that $\bar{W}$ exceeds t, and condition on the number of customers present at the time this randomly chosen customer arrives.

$$P(\bar{W} > t) = \sum_{k=0}^{\infty} P(\bar{W} > t \mid k \text{ customers present}) P(k \text{ customers present})$$

Now the probabilities of finding k customers already in the system are known; they are the steady-state probabilities, $\Pi_k = \rho^k (1 - \rho)$. The conditional probabilities can be developed by a verbal argument. If the newly arrived customer finds k customers ahead of him, and assuming that the first-come, first-served discipline is adhered to, he will not begin service until k negative-exponential service times are completed. He will not complete his stay in the system until $k + 1$ service times are completed. He will still be there at time t if the number of services in time t is less than $k + 1$. In abbreviated notation,

$$P(\bar{W} > t \mid k \text{ customers}) = P(k + 1 \text{ service times} > t)$$

$$= P(\text{number of services in } t < k + 1)$$

But since the service times are negative exponential, the number completed in time t (assuming no interruptions, of course) would be Poisson distributed, so

$$P(\bar{W} > t \mid k \text{ customers}) = \sum_{i=0}^{k} \frac{(\mu t)^i}{i!} e^{-\mu t}$$

Substituting this, along with the Π_k, into the original expression for $P(\bar{W}>t)$ and manipulating,

$$P(\bar{W}>t)=\sum_{k=0}^{\infty}\left(\sum_{i=0}^{k}\frac{(\mu t)^{i}}{i!}e^{-\mu t}\right)\rho^{k}(1-\rho)$$

$$=e^{-\mu t}(1-\rho)\sum_{i=0}^{\infty}\frac{(\mu t)^{i}}{i!}\sum_{k=i}^{\infty}\rho^{k}$$

$$=e^{-\mu t}(1-\rho)\sum_{i=0}^{\infty}\frac{(\mu t)^{i}}{i!}\left(\frac{\rho^{i}}{1-\rho}\right)$$

$$=e^{-\mu t}\sum_{i=0}^{\infty}\left(\frac{(\rho\mu t)^{i}}{i!}\right)$$

$$=e^{-\mu t}e^{\rho\mu t}$$

$$=e^{-(1-\rho)\mu t}$$

But $P(\bar{W}>t)$ is a complementary cumulative probability distribution, and $e^{-\alpha t}$ is the complementary cumulative form of a negative-exponential distribution. Consequently the waiting time in the system is negative exponential in form and has the mean

$$E(\bar{W})=\frac{1}{(1-\rho)\mu}$$

Of course, the mean waiting time is W, which could have been obtained more easily from the $L=\lambda W$ relation. What we did not know before is the form of the distribution.

7.11 QUEUE DISCIPLINES
It has been natural to assume throughout previous sections that the queues operated according to the first-come, first-served (FCFS) rule. Most systems serving human customers are at least intended to operate by this rule, simply because anything else would be perceived of as "unfair." Occasionally, however, practical constraints prevent strict adherence to a FCFS rule. Or sometimes the arrivals are not human customers for whom the order of service is an issue. For example, they might be workpieces which are to be operated on by a machine. In such cases there is no obvious incentive to hold to the FCFS discipline. In fact, if the workpieces are stacked on one another, the last-come, first-served (LCFS) discipline is a natural one. If they are spread out in no particular arrangement, the random selection for service (RSS) discipline may be appropriate.

   At first glance it may appear that differences of this kind would immediately invalidate all previous results; however, such is not the case. A bit of reflection about the logic that went into the construction of the transition diagrams will convince the reader that the steady-state distribution of the number in the system is the same for any queue discipline which does not depend on service times. That is, the server could choose the next customer arbitrarily, as long as his choice is not biased by a prediction of the customer's service times, and the transition rates would be the same. The corresponding steady-state equations, and therefore the solution, would also remain the same. Since the distributions are the same, the mean (as well as other moments) of the number in the system or of the number in the queue would be the same. In other words, the L's and the L_q's that have been calculated for the FCFS cases are also applicable for the LCFS and RSS cases.

Furthermore, because the $L = \lambda W$ and $L_q = \lambda W_q$ relations apply for any queue discipline, the mean waiting times in the system and in the queue are the same for all three cases. On the average, it will take just as long to pass through a first-come, first-served system as it will through a last-come, first-served system—a fact that is certainly not intuitively obvious.

What measures *are* affected by the queue discipline? The primary one is the distribution of waiting times. Just because the mean waiting times are unaffected by the discipline, there is no cause to infer that, say, variances are also unaffected. In fact it can be shown that, among the three disciplines mentioned so far, the FCFS rule will produce the smallest variance in waiting times, the LCFS rule will produce the largest, and the RSS rule will produce an intermediate value. In a sense, the risk of a very long wait is minimized if customers are served in the order of their arrival. By the same token, the chance of a very short wait is also minimized by the same policy. Thus the policy has the effect of tending to equalize waiting times, relative to other policies. It is in this sense, but in this sense only, that the first-come, first-served policy is "fairer" than other methods. Despite virtually universal acceptance of and insistence on the FCFS rule when a queue consists of human beings, there is no quantitative indication that *average* waiting times are any better under this rule.

One way to reduce average waiting times for *selected* customers is to use a priority (PR) discipline. There are many possible priority schemes, at least some of which can be modeled as Markov systems. The interested reader should consult a specialized textbook on queueing theory, such as Refs. 2, 4, 6, and 10.

Some of the more difficult priority schemes to model happen to yield some of the most useful results. Recall that the arguments leading to the conclusion that mean waiting times were unaffected by the queue discipline contained the qualification, "provided that the discipline is independent of service times." It may be correctly inferred that queue disciplines that *are* dependent on service times *will* influence the mean waiting times, W and W_q. This fact, in turn, suggests that wise selection of a service-time dependent queue discipline can *reduce* mean waiting time. Providing "express" service for customers whose predicted service times are short would be one way to implement such an idea.

In many industrial applications of queueing theory, the arrivals are not customers but jobs. Processing (service) times, or at least estimates of them, are available for use in scheduling. It is possible to imagine many seemingly reasonable scheduling concepts, such as "give highest priority to the job with the greatest work content," or "give highest priority to the job with the nearest due date." Out of all of these rules-of-thumb, one has been shown to produce surprisingly good results (i.e., small mean waiting times) under widely varying circumstances. This rule, which is briefly stated as the shortest processing time (SPT) rule, attributes highest priority to jobs requiring the least amount of time to complete. The rule can be applied strictly—even to the extent of interrupting or "preempting" a job being serviced whenever a job which could be finished in less time comes along—or only weakly. A method that separated arrivals into long and short jobs and then gave priority to the short ones would implement the SPT rule in a weak way. Even this method can achieve dramatic reductions in mean waiting time. In fact, almost any way of implementing the SPT idea will perform with surprising efficacy. For a more complete discussion, along with tables demonstrating comparative results for various queueing disciplines, see Ref. 1, Chapter 8.

7.12 NON-MARKOVIAN QUEUES

Aside from a few more general results which have been cited without proof, all of the queueing theory in this chapter has been based on Markov models. A remarkably rich variety of useful models was obtainable merely through suitably adjusting the transition rates. In each case, however, the probability distributions involved were negative exponential. This assumption, although certainly convenient, is not always realistic. Service-time distributions, in particular, frequently lack the "forgetfulness" property that is characteristic of the negative-exponential family. Thus there is a practical need for models that do not rely on strict Markov assumptions.

The Erlang family of distributions, a subclass of the Gamma family (see Chapter 5), is representable in terms of Markov processes if a certain trick is employed. The trick is based on the fact that an Erlang-k distributed random variable is equivalent to the sum of k negative exponentially distributed random variables. To show how the trick would work in a specific example, suppose that we wish to model an $M/E_3/1$ system. Each service time, which is actually Erlang-3 distributed, can then be thought of as consisting of three negative exponentially distributed "stages." A supplementary variable will have to be incorporated into the state definition to keep track of which stage the service process is in; but once this is done, the process becomes Markovian. The states would be designated as follows:

> "0"   means the system is empty
> "(i, j)"   means the system contains i customers and the server is
> currently in stage j

The transition diagram, for the $M/E_3/1$ system, would look like Fig. 7.15. In this diagram, each arrow directed to the right represents a possible "arrival" transition, and each one directed down or to the upper left represents a

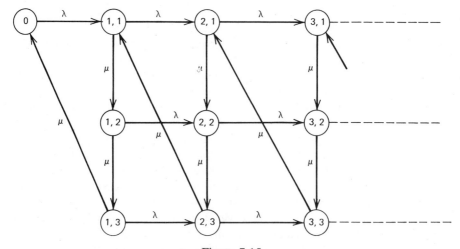

Figure 7.15
The transition diagram for $M/E_3/1$.

"service stage" completion. The times between any such transitions are, of course, negative exponential. Although the resulting process is not of the birth-death type, as were most of the queueing models, it *is* a continuous-time Markov process.

The same idea can be exploited to model systems with Erlang-distributed interarrival times. With two supplementary variables, it is even possible to model the system in which both the arrival process and service process are of the Erlang type. Although no difficulties in principle occur, in practice the steady-state solution is tedious to obtain and the expressions are rather nasty. Solutions for the $M/E_k/1$ and $E_k/M/1$ systems are derived in Ref. 10, pp. 164–169.

Another device is commonly used when either the service times or interarrival times are arbitrarily distributed but the other is negative-exponentially distributed. The idea is known as "embedding a Markov chain," and is generally attributed to D. G. Kendall. The basic concept is to view the process only at selected moments, ignoring the dynamic behavior of the process at intermittent times. The moments at which the process is viewed—the embedding points—are chosen so that the discrete-time Markov assumption will hold. That is, given the state at one of these points, enough information is available to predict (probabilistically) the state at the next point, and any additional information is superfluous.

In the case of the $M/G/1$ system, for example, we may embed a Markov chain at the moments of service completions. At these times, and at these times only, it will be sufficient to know the number in the system to predict the future. At any other times, one would also have to know something like "elapsed service time on the customer currently in service." Because the arrival process is assumed to be negative exponential, it does not matter how long it has been since the last arrival. The same idea can be used to model the $GI/M/1$ queue, embedding at the moment when arrivals occur. It does not work for the $GI/G/1$ queue because the only possible embedding points at those moments at which an arrival and a service completion exactly coincide, but these moments are so rare that they may be considered useless for modeling purposes.

The embedded Markov chain method leads to a very useful and important result for the $M/G/1$ queue. It turns out that, for this system, the four measures L, L_q, W, and W_q depend on no more than the mean and variance of the service time distribution. The formula for L, known as the Pollaczek-Khintchine formula, is:

$$L = \frac{2\rho - \rho^2 + \lambda^2 V(S)}{2(1-\rho)}$$

where $\rho = \lambda/u$, or the arrival rate times the mean service time, and $V(S) =$ the variance of the service time. The formulas for L_q, W, and W_q can be obtained from this one by the methods of Section 7.10. For example,

$$L_q = L - \rho = \frac{\rho^2 + \lambda^2 V(S)}{2(1-\rho)}$$

It is convenient to have such a powerful result. As mentioned earlier, it is frequently the case that service time distributions are clearly not negative exponential. The Pollaczek-Khintchine formula covers arbitrary service-time distributions. Moreover, it does not even require that the form of the distribution be identified; the mean and variance of the distribution are sufficient. Of course, the statistical problem of obtaining good estimates of the mean and variance from empirical data is much easier than the problem of fitting an appropriate distribution to the the same data. Because L, L_q, W, and W_q are independent of any queue discipline which does not depend on service times, the Pollaczek-Khintchine formula is not limited to the FCFS case. The restrictions to remember are that it applies only to single server, infinite capacity systems with Poisson arrivals.

One quick application of the formula yields an interesting insight. Consider the $M/D/1$ system, in which service times are constant. For this system, $V(S) = 0$, so

$$L_q = \frac{\rho^2}{2(1-\rho)}$$

Recalling the analogous result for the $M/M/1$ system,

$$L_q = \frac{\rho^2}{1-\rho}$$

we see that the average number in the queue would be reduced by exactly one half if the variability were eliminated from the service times. In a sense, half of the queue can be attributed to service-time variability. The other half can be charged to arrival-time variability.

7.13   CONCLUSIONS

It would be satisfying to be able to claim that most important queueing models have now been covered, and that the student, upon completing the chapter, should be equipped to handle the majority of situations he is likely to encounter. Such, regrettably, is not the case. Real-life problems typically involve complexities not even touched on here. For example, queues often interact within networks of servers, but nothing has been said about how to model such systems. In fact, the present state-of-the-art of queueing theory does not have much to contribute to the network problem. The need is obvious, but the mathematical problems have proved difficult. Consequently if one has a specific requirement for results for some particular real-life system involving multiple, interacting queues, digital simulation will usually be called for.

On the other hand, mathematical models for many simpler systems exist in abundance, and considerable insight can be gained into complex situations from studying simpler ones. This insight is particularly valuable because unaided human intuition is frequently defective when dealing with queueing phenomena.

Recommended Readings

Hopefully, this introduction has provided some motivation to study the subject more thoroughly. Any of the textbooks listed below would provide an entry into the queueing theory literature. Either Cox and Smith (3) or Morse (9) would be a good place to begin a formal study of the field. Each emphasizes techniques which have since become standard. When it was new, Saaty (10) was a thorough catalog of the state-of-the-art. The bibliography is particularly extensive. Cooper (2), Gross and Harris (4), Kleinrock (6), and Kosten (7), are recent additions to the literature emphasizing theory. For an emphasis on applications, complete with detailed case studies, see Lee (8).

REFERENCES

1. Conway, R. W., W. L. Maxwell, and L. W. Miller, *Theory of Scheduling*, Addison-Wesley, Reading, Mass., 1967.
2. Cooper, Robert B., *Introduction to Queueing Theory*, MacMillan, New York, 1972.
3. Cox, D. R. and Walter L. Smith, *Queues.*, Wiley, New York, 1961.
4. Gross, D. and C. M. Harris, *Fundamentals of Queueing Theory*, Wiley, New York, 1974.
5. Khintchine, A. Y., *Mathematical Methods in the Theory of Queueing*, Hafner Publishing Company, New York, 1960.
6. Kleinrock, Leonard, *Queueing Systems*, Vol. I, Wiley, New York, 1975.
7. Kosten, L., *Stochastic Theory of Service Systems*, Pergamon Press, Oxford, 1973.
8. Lee, Alec M., *Applied Queueing Theory*, St. Martin's Press, New York, 1966.
9. Morse, Philip M., *Queues, Inventories, and Maintenance*, Wiley, New York, 1958.
10. Saaty, Thomas L., *Elements of Queueing Theory*, McGraw-Hill, New York, 1961.
11. Stidham, Shaler, Jr., "A Last Word on $L = \lambda W$", *OR 22*, (2), 417–421 (1974).
12. Takacs, L., "On Erlang's Formula", *Am. Math. Stat.*, **40**, (1969), 71–78.

EXERCISES

1. Consider a barbershop with two chairs, two barbers, and no room for customers to wait. Say that the state of the system is the number of customers in the shop: 0, 1, or 2. If there is an empty chair when a customer arrives, he enters the shop and his haircut begins. If both chairs are occupied when he arrives, he does not enter the shop. As soon as a customer's haircut is completed, he leaves the shop instantaneously. The barbers do not assist one another when there is only one customer in the shop. On the average, a customer arrives every 10 minutes, and each haircut takes an average of 15 min.
   a. Set up the differential equations.
   b. Solve the steady-state equations for the distribution of the number of customers in the shop.
   c. Calculate the expected number of busy barbers.
   d. Calculate the expected number of customers turned away per hour.
   e. Notice in the above problem that some potential customers are turned away. If the shop had another barber, it might be able to profit from additional paying customers. On the other hand, the extra barber would have to be paid. Describe how you might determine whether it would be worthwhile for the shop to hire another barber.

2. A parking lot for a small shopping center has spaces for 100 cars. Assume that cars arrive according to a Poisson process, and that the durations of shopping trips are negative exponentially distributed. Also assume that a car will not wait for a parking space if the lot is full.
   a. Identify an appropriate queueing model.
   b. Write the steady-state equations and give the solution.
   c. Interpret, in this context, the steady-state probabilities, L, W, L_q, and W_q. That is, explain what these mean in terms of the parking lot.
   d. Explain how you would determine whether spaces for more cars would be worth having.
   e. Explain what, if anything, could be done to model the situation if the shopping-trip durations were not negative exponential.

3. An executive must establish a secretarial staff. He has been allocated enough money to hire either two "class A" secretaries or three "class B" secretaries. In this company, secretaries are classified and paid according to their work efficiency. One "class A" secretary can complete the same job in an average of 2/3 the time that a "class B" secretary can, and is paid accordingly. Thus, at first glance, the

two alternatives seem equal. Develop a Markovian queueing model (where the secretaries are the servers and the jobs submitted to them form a single queue with a FCFS discipline), to evaluate which, if either, alternative is preferable to the other in terms of keeping the backlog of work to a minimum.

4. In order to model a single server, infinite capacity queueing system in which customers are "discouraged" from entering when the queue grows long, let the arrival rate be dependent on the state in the following way: when there are i customers in the system, let the arrival rate be $\frac{\lambda}{i+1}$. Make the usual Markov and stationarity assumptions.

   a. Show the steady-state equations and solve them if you can. Be sure to note any convergence requirement.
   b. Explain in words what the parameter λ represents in this model, and how it could be measured. (Note: discouraged customers are never seen.)
   c. Show an expression for W_q, the steady-state mean time spent in the queue. Be as precise as you can.

5. Moonshine Max is in the business of buying and selling illegally produced whisky. When he gets a jug from his supplier, he dilutes it with spring water to obtain two jugs of "city strength" moonshine. The time between customer requests for his merchandise is negative exponentially distributed with a mean of 1/3 day. He receives the pure stuff on an understandably irregular schedule. The time between his inventory replenishments is also negative-exponentially distributed, but with a mean of 2 days. He gets only one jug at a time; he sells one diluted jug at a time.

   a. The situation described has aspects of an inventory problem, but see if you can interpret it as a queueing problem (i.e., identify the arrivals, the queue, the service process, etc.). If you cannot see it, continue anyway.
   b. Using a continuous time Markov model, explain in detail how to determine (1) the percentage of customer requests, over the long term, that Max is forced to reject because he is out of stock, and (2) his long-term average inventory.

6. Imagine a closed stack library system which operates as follows. Customers arrive individually at the rate of one every 10/7 minutes, on the average. When they arrive at the desk, they have already recorded on a piece of paper the names of the books they want. The librarian (assume there is only one) must take a book request, go back into the stacks, get the book or books if it or they are available, and return to the desk. At this point, the customer departs, the librarian takes another request, and so on. Operating as just described, the librarian requires an average of 1.25 minutes to service a request. We are thinking about ways to improve the system.

   It occurs to us that, since most of the service time is spent walking around in the stacks, a librarian ought to be able to handle two requests simultaneously in less total time than he would require for the two requests separately. A quick study confirms this: a "double" service requires an average of only $1\frac{7}{8}$ minutes. For purposes of comparison to the present system, we want to predict the performance of the system if the librarian is instructed to take two requests at a time, provided that two or more customers are waiting. Of course, if there is only one customer at the desk, he is to handle that request individually.

   For *each* of the two cases (the system as first described and the "double-service" proposed system), do the following:

   a. Exhibit the steady-state equations.
   b. Find the steady-state distributions, assuming infinite waiting room. For the second case, you may use the information that $\Pi_2 = (3/4)\Pi_1$.
   c. Find the average number of customers in each system.
   d. Find the average waiting time in each system.
   e. Discuss the assumptions inherent in your models, and consider whether any recommendations to the library staff are justified.

7. A job shop has four numerically controlled machine tools which are capable of operating on their own (i.e., without a human operator) once they are set up with the proper cutting tools and all adjustments are made. Each set-up requires the skills of an experienced machinist, and the time needed to complete a set-up is negative-exponentially distributed with a mean of 1/2 hour. When the set-up is complete, the machinist just pushes a button, and the machine requires no further attention until it has finished its lot size and is ready for another set-up. The lot size production times are negative exponentially distributed with a mean of 1 hour. The question is, "how many machinists should there be to tend the machines?" At opposite extremes, there could be one machinist tending all four machines, or there could be one machinist for each of the machines. The optimal number to have obviously depends upon a trade-off between the cost of machinists and the cost of idle machines. Of course, machinists are paid the same regardless of how much work they do, but each machine incurs idle-time costs only when it is idle.

   a. Assume that the cost of a machinist (including fringe benefits, overhead, and the like) is $20 per hour, and that the cost of an idle machine (including lost revenues and interest on the capital invested in the machine) is $60 per hour of idleness. Using the finite source model suggested in Section 7.9 for each of the possible numbers of machinists, 1, 2, 3, or 4, evaluate the total cost for each alternative and select the optimal number of machinists.

   b. Assume that the cost of a machinist is fixed at some arbitrary value (such as $20 per hour), and let the cost of an idle machine be expressed as some multiple, k, of that value. Generalize the results of part a, by finding the ranges over which k may vary to produce the same optimal number of machinists. In other words, for what values of k would one machinist be optimal, for what values would two be optimal, and so on.

8. Consider an airport with two runways, one of which is used solely for take-offs and the other solely for landings. Assume that a plane, whether landing or taking off, will occupy a runway for an average of 2 minutes, where by occupy we mean "prevent use by any other plane." Delay on the ground, although unpleasant for passengers, does not pose a safety hazard; delay in the air, on the other hand, is of serious concern. Suppose that F.A.A. regulations specify that the mean delay in the air (i.e., W_q) must not exceed 10 minutes. Assume that planes arrive according to a Poisson process, and construct a model from the information given above to answer the following questions.

   a. What is the maximum tolerable load on the airport in terms of the mean number of planes that can arrive per hour?

   b. Would it make much difference if you were told that the standard deviation of the time that a plane will occupy a runway is 1 minute?

   c. Suppose that the F.A.A. has another regulation requiring that the probability of having to spend more than 20 minutes from time of arrival to completion of landing cannot exceed 0.05. What is the maximum load when this regulation is taken into account? [$\ln(0.05) = -3.0$]

   d. What practical suggestion can you make as to what might be done to increase the load capacity of the airport, short of building new runways?

9. Assuming that we are talking about an $M/M/1$ queue, suppose that a particular customer arrives at time t to find four customers in the system ahead of him (one of these in the process of being served). How much can you say about the length of time that the newly arrived customer will spend in the system? For example, what is the distribution, the mean, and the variance? To what extent does your answer depend on the specific characteristics of the $M/M/1$ queue? What other queues would give the same result?

10. A new hospital is to be built in a particular location. Restricting attention to just

one section of the hospital, the maternity wing, imagine that the following information has been obtained:

1. For the population that the hospital is intended to serve, we may expect an average of 12 deliveries per day. (This estimate is based on the national birth rate, but is confirmed by local data.)

2. Recovery rooms are no problem. If necessary, rooms outside the maternity wing can be used. Delivery rooms are also not a problem because they are used only briefly for the actual delivery. The potential "bottleneck" is the availability of labor rooms.

3. The average time that a labor room will be occupied by a patient is 3.5 hours, but of course there is considerable variability in this time. Preparation of a room for the next patient can be accomplished in half an hour, if necessary.

4. If all labor rooms are occupied, an arriving maternity patient will be directed to another hospital. This is done very reluctantly, but state laws necessitate such action.

a. Provide a formula for the fraction of maternity patients who are turned away, as a function of the number of labor rooms designed into the hospital.

b. Provide a formula for the occupancy rate of the labor rooms, that is, the long-term average fraction occupied. (This figure is to be multiplied by the room rate to predict annual income from the labor rooms.)

c. Formulate a reasonable optimization problem, the solution to which would indicate the appropriate number of labor rooms to provide. (Introduce whatever cost parameters and the like that you feel are needed.)

d. Suppose that additional data were to reveal that the standard deviation of the labor room occupancy time is 1 hour. What effect would this information have on your analysis?

CHAPTER 8
INVENTORY MODELS

8.1 INTRODUCTION

Similar to the chapter on queueing models, and unlike other chapters that are technique oriented, this chapter is devoted to an area of application. The subject is inventory control. By inventory, we mean the measured amount of some good which varies in quantity over time in response to a "demand" process, which operates to diminish the stock, and a "replenishment" process, which operates to increase it. Usually the demand is not subject to control, but the timing and magnitude of the replenishments can be regulated. Figure 8.1 represents an inventory system in its broadest sense.

It is worthwhile to attempt to achieve a very broad perspective of the problems that are addressed in inventory theory. In addition to the obvious applications to stocks of physical goods—lightbulbs, toothpaste, raw materials to be used in some production process, and the like—there exist many less obvious opportunities to use the models developed in this chapter. For example, the number of engineers employed by a company or the number of students enrolled in a college can be regarded as inventories. Various modes of natural attrition would comprise what we have called the demand process, and hiring or recruitment would constitute replenishment. The amount of equity capital available for corporate growth can be regarded as inventory. As it is used up, it must be replenished through issuance of new stocks or bonds. Sometimes it is useful to think not of the physical items but of the space they occupy as the inventory. For example, the space available for new books in a library can be thought of as an inventory. As it is consumed, it must be replenished. These examples only begin to indicate the wealth of opportunity for application of the models and insights obtainable from the study of inventory theory.

I. DETERMINISTIC MODELS

Among the reasons for holding inventory is to avoid the time, cost, nuisance, and so on, of constant replenishment. On the other hand, to replenish only infrequently would imply large inventories. It is apparent that some sort of trade-off is involved, and the models of this section make this trade-off explicit.

Figure 8.1
An inventory system.

These are not the only justifications for inventory control because, of course, there are other reasons as well for holding inventory.

A common feature of these models is that they assume demand to be completely predictable. In those situations where it is *not* (perhaps a majority), they fall far short of representing proper trade-offs. The models should not be criticized on this account—they simply are not intended to represent those situations. At the same time, one should be aware of this limitation. Probabilistic models will be dealt with later in the chapter.

8.2 THE CLASSICAL ECONOMIC ORDER QUANTITY

We begin with the simplest possible version. We assume a single commodity. We penalize frequent replenishment by saying that a set-up or ordering charge of $a is incurred each time an order is placed. We penalize excessive inventory by saying that each unit will cost $h to store for 1 unit of time (typically, the time unit is 1 year, but may be anything provided that other time units are consistent.) The "driving force" of the system—the process for which the inventory is held—is a steady demand for d units per unit time. All demand must be met without delay. To keep things simple, we assume that replenishment occurs instantaneously whenever an order for replenishment is made (*zero lead time*).

We now give a verbal argument for how the system should operate. Starting at any time with an inventory of y, the inventory will decrease at the rate d until it reaches zero or an order is placed. If it reaches zero, an order must be placed immediately in order to satisfy all demand without delay.

Would there be any reason to order before inventory reaches zero? No, because that would imply that the remaining items were held in inventory (thereby accumulating carrying costs) unnecessarily. If they were needed at all, they could have been ordered in the next shipment and the carrying cost would have been saved. Figure 8.2, graphically illustrates the pattern of inventory. We call the order quantity for the first order Q_1. By repetition of the same

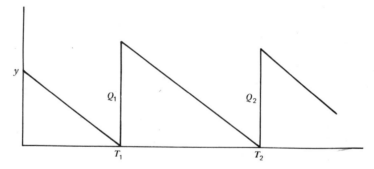

Figure 8.2
The inventory pattern.

argument, we can be sure that inventory will again fall to zero (at the same rate, of course) before the second order, of size Q_2, is placed.

Will Q_2 be larger than, smaller than, or equal to Q_1? Without even knowing what determines Q_1 and Q_2, we may argue that they must be equal. Q_1 is determined at time T_1 by taking into account costs and revenues for (possibly) the entire future of the process. But because the future is infinite, and the process is not changing in time, the entire future looks the same at time T_2 as it did at time T_1. Therefore, *however* Q_1 is determined, Q_2 will be determined in the same way and will therefore have the same value. By induction, all order sizes are equal, and the inventory level will behave as in Fig. 8.3. This "sawtooth" pattern is typical of inventory models.

Since the order size is always the same, we will use Q (without a subscript) to denote the common value, and use T to denote the common length of time between orders. T is just the length of time required to deplete Q units at the rate d, so

$$T = \frac{Q}{d}$$

The only remaining problem is to determine Q. There are a number of ways to set up a cost function to show how costs depend on Q, some of which are fruitless. One approach that will not work is to try to write the sum of all future costs. Because the time horizon is infinite, the sum of all future costs will be infinite no matter what Q is. An alternative would be to "discount" future costs, but since this would involve an additional parameter, it will not be pursued here. Another alternative would be to minimize the cost *per cycle*. This makes some sense, since these cycles are all the same and if you minimize the cost of one, you have minimized them all.

Following up on this idea, we could write

$$\text{cost/cycle} = \text{order cost} + \text{inventory holding cost}$$

$$\text{cost/cycle} = a + \left(\frac{Q}{2}\right)(h)\left(\frac{Q}{d}\right)$$

Here $Q/2$ is the average inventory over the length of the cycle, h is the cost per unit per unit of time, and Q/d is the duration of the cycle. To minimize this function, we differentiate with respect to Q, set equal to zero, and solve for Q.

$$\frac{d}{dQ}(\text{cost/cycle}) = \frac{Qh}{d} = 0$$

$$Q = 0$$

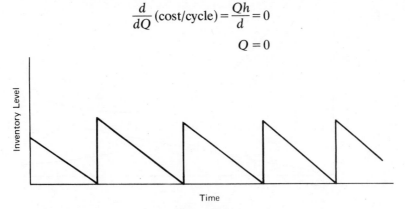

Time

Figure 8.3
The inventory pattern.

This apparent oddity for a solution is not the result of improper mathematics. The minimum of the cost function written does, indeed, occur at $Q = 0$. The intuitive reason is that we lower carrying costs by reducing Q and shortening the length of the cycle. The set-up or order charge remains, of course, and as we shorten the cycle, we incur more and more of these charges over the same period of time. The problem is that we do not really want to minimize the cost *per cycle*, but rather the cost over some fixed interval of time.

Beginning again, we write:

$$\frac{\text{cost}}{\text{unit time}} = \left(\frac{\text{order cost}}{\text{cycle}}\right)\left(\frac{\text{no. of cycles}}{\text{unit time}}\right) +$$

$$(\text{average inventory})\left(\frac{\text{holding cost}}{\text{unit time}}\right) = a\frac{d}{Q} + \frac{Q}{2}h$$

This expression can be justified on its own, or it may be obtained from the cost/cycle by multiplying by the number of cycles per unit time, which is d/Q.

We are interested in this expression as a function of Q. In particular, we wish to select Q so as to minimize the cost rate. (See Fig. 8.4.) The first term behaves like the reciprocal function, decreasing monotonically to zero; the second term is linear in Q, increasing monotonically from zero. Hence the sum will possess a unique minimum and that minimum will occur where the derivative vanishes. Setting the derivative to zero,

$$\frac{dC}{dQ} = -\frac{ad}{Q^2} + \frac{h}{2} = 0$$

and solving for Q, the optimum value of Q,

$$Q = \sqrt{\frac{2ad}{h}}$$

This is the famous economic order quantity, or EOQ formula. It is also known

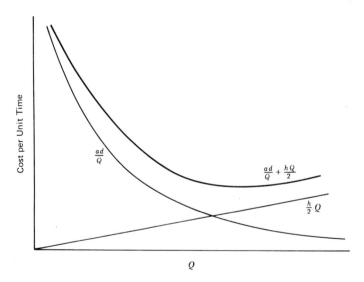

Figure 8.4
The cost rate as a function of Q.

as the *Wilson-Harris formula, the economic lot size,* the *"square-root"* law and other names.

Since $T = Q/d$, the optimal time between replenishments, or the duration of a cycle, is

$$T = \sqrt{\frac{2a}{dh}}$$

and by substituting the optical Q in the cost function, we find that the minimum cost per unit time is $C = \sqrt{2adh}$. This expression, of course, neglects the cost of the goods. If the latter is desired, it is $d \times$ (cost per item).

Close examination of the EOQ formula reveals that the optimal-order quantity behaves about the way you would expect. Since a is in the numerator, the optimal-order quantity increases when the ordering cost does. Similarly, since h is in the denominator, the optimal-order quantity decreases when the holding cost increases. If the demand rate, d, increases then so does Q. Thus it is not surprising that the formula contains the ratio ad/h. (Incidentally, it should not be necessary to memorize this form, since a little brief reflection along the lines described should be sufficient to reconstruct it.) The only possibly surprising parts to the formula are the 2 in the numerator and the square-root sign. However, even the square-root sign could have been predicted if one considered the dimensions of ad/h:

$$\frac{ad}{h} = \frac{\text{(units/time)($)}}{\text{($/units)/time}} = \frac{\text{units} \cdot \$}{\text{time}} \cdot \frac{\text{units} \cdot \text{time}}{\$} = (\text{units})^2$$

Thus, the square-root sign must appear in order to make the dimension of ad/h consistent with that of Q. The 2 in the numerator originated from the fact that the average inventory is $Q/2$. A simple mnemonic way to account for it is to say that "the numerator is twice as significant as the denominator because it has two parameters in it."

8.3   A NUMERICAL EXAMPLE

One can hardly begin to appreciate the generality of the model just developed until one has seen the variety of possible applications. Some of the problems at the end of the chapter are designed to suggest this versatility by using situations which do not obviously involve inventory at all. For now, we will use a rather prosaic, typical inventory situation to illustrate the model concretely.

Consider a newspaper publishing concern that must periodically replenish its supply of paper stock. We will suppose that the paper comes in large rolls and that the printers use it up at the rate of 32 rolls per week. The cost of replenishment (which includes the cost of bookkeeping, trucking, and handling) will be taken to be $25 plus the cost of the paper. The cost of keeping the paper on hand, including rent for the space occupied, insurance, and interest on the capital tied up, will be $1 per roll per week. In terms of the notation of the EOQ model, then,

$$d = 32$$
$$a = 25$$
$$h = 1$$

Consequently, the optimal number of rolls to order at a time would be

$$Q = \sqrt{\frac{2(32)(25)}{1}} = 40 \text{ rolls}$$

The time between orders would be

$$T = \frac{Q}{d} = \frac{40}{32} = 1.25 \text{ weeks}$$

and the cost of operating the system would be $C = \$40$ per week.

8.4 SENSITIVITY ANALYSIS

One of the important characteristics of the EOQ model is its "robustness." It tends to give reasonably good results even when parameter values are in error. To see why this is so, imagine that one of the values in the example just given were in error by as much as 100 percent. Say, for example, that the order cost a were really $50 instead of $25. Then the correct value of Q should be

$$Q = \frac{\sqrt{(2)(32)(50)}}{1} = \frac{\sqrt{(2)(2)(32)(25)}}{1}$$

$$= (\sqrt{2})40$$

or about 1.41 times as great as the answer previously obtained. In other words, an error of 100 percent in the input produced only a 41 percent error in the result. Similar errors in d or h give similar results, as the reader may verify for himself. Overestimation is no more serious than underestimation. The cost function is also similarly insensitive to parameter errors. It is, of course, the square-root form that provides this very desirable quality.

The conclusion, then, is that the EOQ model may be applied with some confidence even in those situations which do not permit much confidence in the parameter values. This is perhaps the predominant case. Holding costs are very difficult to isolate from fixed overhead costs; some contributions to order costs may be hidden, and so on. It is reassuring to know that the parameter values do not need to be known very precisely to get reasonably good (i.e., close to optimum) results.

On the other hand, the above argument provides no assurance whatsoever that the EOQ formula will give good results when the *assumptions* of the model are not met. This point has been frequently overlooked, or misunderstood, with potentially disastrous consequences. Sometimes students remember that the EOQ formula is "robust" and use that fact to justify its use when, for example, demand is not really predictable. Later, when a probabilistic demand model is developed, an example will be given to illustrate the perils of using the EOQ model for that case.

8.5 NONZERO LEAD TIME

If an order for replenishment must be placed some fixed time in advance—that is, if there is a delay between placement of the order and receipt of the goods—then it is only necessary to anticipate sufficiently far in advance when the inventory will be exhausted and to place the order at that time which is such that the goods will arrive exactly when the inventory runs out. Since (in this model) the demand rate is fixed and known, this presents no problem.

If the lead time is denoted by L, then the quantity dL will be consumed

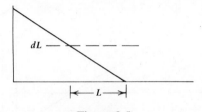

Figure 8.5
Lead-time demand.

during the lead time. Hence the order for replenishment should be placed when the stock falls to the level dL. (See Fig. 8.5.)

8.6   THE EOQ WITH SHORTAGES ALLOWED

If shortages are not prohibited, but merely penalized, it is possible that the optimal policy is deliberately to run out and accumulate back orders before replenishment occurs. Intuitively, the idea is that the cost of running out may be sufficiently small relative to the cost of holding inventory that the cost trade-off results in doing both. The pattern of inventory would still be "saw-toothed" (see Fig. 8.6), but would drop below the zero level. Here, negative inventory represents goods which are "sold" but not "delivered." In addition to notation already used, we need

b = backorder penalty cost, proportional to both the
   number of backorders and time (like h)

S = inventory level just after replenishment (a portion of Q)

Figure 8.7 may help to identify the terms in the cost function. The cost per unit time is as follows:

$$\frac{\text{cost}}{\text{unit time}} = \left(\frac{\text{order cost}}{\text{cycle}}\right)\left(\frac{\text{no. cycles}}{\text{unit time}}\right) + \left(\frac{\text{holding cost}}{\text{unit time}}\right)(\text{ave. inventory})$$

$$+ \left(\frac{\text{backorder cost}}{\text{unit time}}\right)(\text{ave. backorder}) = a\left(\frac{d}{Q}\right) + h\left(\frac{S^2}{2Q}\right) + b\left(\frac{(Q-S)^2}{2Q}\right)$$

Taking the partial derivatives with respect to Q and S, setting equal to zero, and solving yields the following results:

$$Q = \sqrt{\frac{2ad}{h}\left(\frac{h+b}{b}\right)}$$

$$S = \sqrt{\frac{2ad}{h}\left(\frac{b}{h+b}\right)}$$

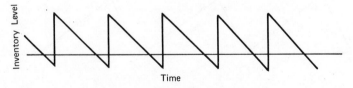

Figure 8.6
Inventory pattern with shortages.

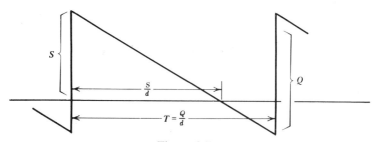

Figure 8.7
The terms identified.

Resubstituting, the minimum cost per unit time will be

$$C = \sqrt{2adh\left(\frac{b}{h+b}\right)}$$

which is smaller by the factor $\sqrt{b/h+b}$ than the optimal cost when back orders are prohibited.

8.7 THE PRODUCTION LOT-SIZE MODEL

Sometimes the replenishment of stock occurs gradually, rather than all at once. Such would be the case if the item is produced internally instead of purchased from an outside supplier. Because this result is more aptly described as a lot size than an order quantity, the model is referred to as the *production lot size*, or PLS, model.

The modification required in the EOQ model is relatively minor. Assuming no shortages are permitted, the inventory pattern would be as shown in Fig. 8.8. Production occurs during the intervals shown as darkened line segments and labeled T_p. Of course, usage also occurs during these intervals, so the inventory never reaches a level equal to the production lot size. Let p denote the production rate, which must be greater than d, the usage rate, in order for the model to make any sense. Starting from an inventory level of zero, production begins and demand continues, so the net rate of increase is $p-d$. This rate of increase continues for the time T_p, which is the time required to produce the total lot size, Q. But $T_p = Q/p$, so the maximum level of inventory reached is

$$T_p(p-d) = Q\left(1-\frac{d}{p}\right)$$

Once the maximum inventory level is established, it is a straightforward matter

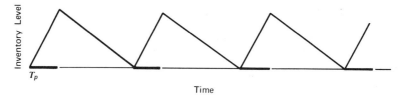

Figure 8.8
The PLS inventory pattern.

to formulate the average inventory expression and, thereby, the cost function. After differentiating with respect to Q and solving, the optimal PLS turns out to be

$$Q = \sqrt{\frac{2ad}{h}\left(\frac{p}{p-d}\right)}$$

If, as would often be the case, p is much greater than d, this formula would produce a result not significantly different from that produced by the ordinary EOQ formula.

8.8 THE EOQ WITH QUANTITY DISCOUNTS

In previous models, the cost of the goods held in inventory did not appear in any of the formulas. Of course, if this cost is independent of the order size Q, it cannot have any influence on Q. (More directly, if one adds a term to the total cost function representing the cost of goods per unit time, this term will not contain the variable Q. Therefore when one differentiates with respect to Q, that term drops out.) However, there are many situations in real life in which the order size *should* be influenced by the fact that a lower per unit price may be offered on larger-order quantities. This section will explain how to modify previous results to accommodate quantity discounts. Although the explanation will be heuristic, the reader may be assured that the method has been rigorously justified. See, for example, Ref. 3, p. 62.

Suppose that all of the assumptions of the simplest EOQ model are satisfied, but that the per unit cost of the goods stocked depends on order quantity as follows:

$$\text{if} \qquad 0 \leq Q < k_1, \text{ then goods cost } \$c_0 \text{ per unit}$$
$$k_1 \leq Q < k_2, \text{ then goods cost } \$c_1 \text{ per unit}$$
$$k_2 \leq Q < k_3, \text{ then goods cost } \$c_2 \text{ per unit}$$
$$\vdots \qquad\qquad \vdots$$
$$k_n \leq Q \qquad \text{ then goods cost } \$c_n \text{ per unit}$$

Here the k_i represent price "break" points, and (ordinarily) $c_0 > c_1 > c_2 \dots$.

If we were to ignore the quantity discount factor, we would use $Q = \sqrt{(2ad/h)}$. If this Q falls within the range (k_i, k_{i+1}), then the total cost per unit time of the inventory system plus the goods would be $\sqrt{2adh} + c_i d$. It is apparent that we do not wish to order less than Q because both costs (cost of inventory system and cost of goods) would be higher. However, if we were to order more than Q, it is possible that the increase in the inventory system cost would be more than compensated for by the savings in the cost of the goods. If, indeed, it were desirable to increase the order size to obtain the price break, then the increase should be just barely enough to get the lower price; anything more would incur unnecessarily high inventory costs. Hence, k_{i+1} is a candidate for the optimal order quantity, as are k_{i+2}, k_{i+3}, and so on.

In summary, then, the procedure involves comparing the total cost per unit time if Q is ordered to the total cost per unit time if k_{i+1}, $k_{i+2}, \dots$, or k_n is ordered. The order size which gives the lowest total cost is selected.

A numerical example may better convey the logic of the technique. Consider once again the example of the newspaper publisher who is purchasing paper stock. Suppose that the supplier offers quantity discounts according to the following schedule:

$12.00 per roll for 1–9 rolls

10.00 per roll for 10–49 rolls

9.50 per roll for 50–99 rolls

9.00 per roll for 100 or more

We solve for the EOQ as before (i.e., ignoring the cost of the stock), and find that the inventory system costs will be minimized if $Q = 40$. If the publisher orders this quantity, he will pay $10.00 per roll, and his total cost per week will be

$$C(Q) = \sqrt{2adh} + \$10.00d$$
$$= \$40 + \$320$$
$$= \$360 \text{ per week}$$

It is clear that there is no incentive to order less than 40 rolls, but there is a price break at 50 rolls that may be worth exploiting. To continue, we consider the cost per week if 50 are ordered:

$$C(50) = \frac{ad}{50} + \frac{50h}{2} + \$9.50d$$
$$= \$41 + \$304$$
$$= \$345 \text{ per week}$$

We observe that, although the inventory system costs are higher ($41 per week), the price advantage for the stock is more than sufficient to compensate, and the total cost is lower. There is no incentive to order 51, 52, 53, . . . , 99, but there may be a reason to order 100. The total cost per week would be

$$C(100) = \$58 + 288$$
$$= \$346$$

Since there is no advantage to ordering larger quantities, the optimal order size is 50.

8.9   THE EOQ WITH CONSTRAINTS

Sometimes one of the preceding models produces a result that is infeasible for reasons not yet considered. For example, in the numerical example just given, we determined that there was an advantage to ordering 50 rolls at a time, but did not consider whether there was a capacity to store that many rolls. Another common constraint is one on the total amount of capital invested in inventory.

   If there is only one item under consideration, the necessary adjustments are fairly obvious. Suppose, for example, that space and/or capital constraints result in the requirement that the order quantity Q may not exceed some constant k. Then the procedure would be to determine Q, the optimal-order quantity ignoring the constraint. If Q is feasible, that is, $Q \leq k$, then order Q. If it is not, that is, $Q > k$, then order k, the maximum feasible quantity. Figures 8.9 and 8.10 show the two cases and clearly indicate that this procedure yields the optimal feasible-order quantity. Of course if the cost function were not convex ("bowl" shaped), the procedure could fail, but this property is present in virtually every inventory model.

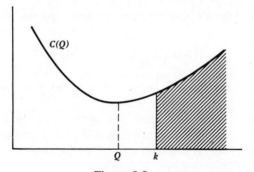

Figure 8.9
The EOQ when $Q \leqq k$.

On the other hand, if multiple items are competing for the same space or capital (or whatever resource is constrained), the necessary adjustments are not quite so obvious. To deal with a specific case, suppose there are three items to be ordered. Use subscripts to indicate which item a parameter refers to. For example, h_1 would be the holding cost for the first item. Then we would formulate the inventory costs for each of the three items and add them to obtain the total combined cost.

$$C(Q_1, Q_2, Q_3) = C(Q_1) + C(Q_2) + C(Q_3)$$

where $C(Q_i) = a_i d_i / Q_i + h_i Q_i / 2$.

Notice that this expression requires that the three items be independent of one another. If there is no constraint to relate them, the optimal solution for the whole problem would simply consist of the three solutions to the three problems taken separately.

To express the constraint, suppose that the maximum available storage space is S square feet and that each unit of item i requires s_i square feet. (Here we assume that "stacking" is impossible—if not, we could deal with volumes rather than areas.) The constraint is then:

$$s_1 Q_1 + s_2 Q_2 + s_3 Q_3 \leqq S$$

There are two cases to consider. It is possible that the optimal solution to the problem results in less than full usage of the available storage space. That is, the constraint may not be binding. If this is so, then the solution must be that which would be obtained if the constraint were not present. So as a first

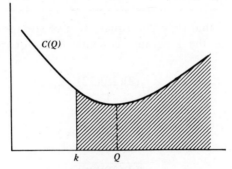

Figure 8.10
The EOQ when $Q > k$.

step, we should obtain the three (unconstrained) optimal order quantities,

$$Q_i = \sqrt{\frac{2a_i d_i}{h_i}} \qquad i = 1, 2, 3$$

substitute them into the capacity constraint, and determine whether or not the constraint is satisfied. If it is, we are done.

If the constraint is violated, then one or more of the Q_i will have to be adjusted downward until the total quantity will just fit into the space available. The mathematical problem becomes one of minimizing the total-cost function subject to the *equality* constraint

$$s_1 Q_1 + s_2 Q_2 + s_3 Q_3 = S$$

This optimization can be accomplished through the method of Lagrange multipliers (see Section 11.6).

Introduce the Lagrange multiplier, λ, and form the function

$$L(Q_1, Q_2, Q_3, \lambda) = C(Q_1) + C(Q_2) + C(Q_3) + \lambda[s_1 Q_1 + s_2 Q_2 + s_3 Q_3 - S]$$

Then differentiate this function with respect to each of the unknowns, Q_1, Q_2, Q_3, and λ, set each partial derivative equal to zero, and solve the equations simultaneously. The theory of Lagrange multipliers assures that the resulting values solve the original problem. (Actually, vanishing of the partial derivatives is only a necessary condition for an optimum, but the form of the objective and constraint functions provides additional sufficiency conditions.) The equations to be solved are nonlinear. Although the way to solve them may not be obvious, no serious problems will be encountered. A numerical example may help to illustrate the procedure.

Suppose that the newspaper publisher of previous examples must purchase three kinds of paper stock. The appropriate parameter values are given in Table 8.1.

Table 8.1
DATA FOR THE NUMERICAL ILLUSTRATION.

	Type I	Type II	Type III
	$d_1 = 32$ rolls/week	$d_2 = 24$	$d_3 = 20$
	$a_1 = \$25$	$a_2 = 18$	$a_3 = 20$
	$h_1 = \$1$/roll/week	$h_2 = 1.5$	$h_3 = 2$
	$s_1 = 4$ sq. ft./roll	$s_2 = 3$	$s_3 = 2$

It is further assumed that only 200 square feet of storage space is available.

Determination of the separate economic order quantities, ignoring the constraint, yields

$$Q_1 = \sqrt{\frac{(2)(25)(32)}{1}} = 40$$

$$Q_2 = \sqrt{\frac{(2)(18)(24)}{1.5}} = 24$$

$$Q_3 = \sqrt{\frac{(2)(20)(20)}{2}} = 20$$

But these quantities would require

$$s_1Q_1 + s_2Q_2 + s_3Q_3 = 4(40) + 3(24) + 2(20) = 272 \text{ square feet}$$

as opposed to the 200 square feet available. Consequently, these Q_i are not feasible, and must be adjusted downward.

The Lagrangean function, written in its complete form is:

$$L(Q_1, Q_2, Q_3, \lambda) = \frac{a_1d_1}{Q_1} + \frac{h_1Q_1}{2} + \frac{a_2d_2}{Q_2} + \frac{h_2Q_2}{2} + \frac{a_3d_3}{Q_3} + \frac{h_3Q_3}{2}$$
$$+ \lambda(s_1Q_1 + s_2Q_2 + s_3Q_3 - S)$$

The partial derivatives are

$$\frac{\partial L}{\partial Q_1} = -\frac{a_1d_1}{Q_1^2} + \frac{h_1}{2} + \lambda s_1$$

$$\frac{\partial L}{\partial Q_2} = -\frac{a_2d_2}{Q_2^2} + \frac{h_2}{2} + \lambda s_2$$

$$\frac{\partial L}{\partial Q_3} = -\frac{a_3d_3}{Q_3^2} + \frac{h_3}{2} + \lambda s_3$$

$$\frac{\partial L}{\partial \lambda} = s_1Q_1 + s_2Q_2 + s_3Q_3 - S$$

Setting these equal to zero and solving the first three for Q_1, Q_2, and Q_3, respectively, gives

$$Q_1 = \sqrt{\frac{2a_1d_1}{h_1 + 2\lambda s_1}}$$

$$Q_2 = \sqrt{\frac{2a_2d_2}{h_2 + 2\lambda s_2}}$$

$$Q_3 = \sqrt{\frac{2a_3d_3}{h_3 + 2\lambda s_3}}$$

The last partial derivative, when set equal to zero, merely reexpresses the original constraint.

It is instructive to note, before proceeding, that the new formulas for the Q_i are similar to the old. The effect of the constraint is to introduce into each formula an additional term in the denominator. It is "as if" the holding costs h_i had each been increased. The amount of increase is proportional to the space occupied (the s_i), and the Lagrange multiplier, λ, plays the role of a proportionality constant. It may be observed that the units of λ must be in dollars per square foot, so λ is something very much like a rental rate for space.

The problem is not yet solved, because λ is still unknown. Substituting the expressions for the Q_i into the last equation

$$s_1\sqrt{\frac{2a_1d_1}{h_1 + 2\lambda s_1}} + s_2\sqrt{\frac{2a_2d_2}{h_2 + 2\lambda s_2}} + s_3\sqrt{\frac{2a_3d_3}{h_3 + 2\lambda s_3}} - S = 0$$

or, after substituting the values of the known parameters and simplifying,

$$160\sqrt{\frac{1}{1 + 8\lambda}} + 72\sqrt{\frac{1}{1 + 4\lambda}} + 40\sqrt{\frac{1}{1 + 2\lambda}} - 200 = 0$$

This is the equation that must be solved to determine the value of λ.

The left-hand side of the equation is a monotonically decreasing function of λ—that is, the larger λ is, the smaller the left-hand side will be. The case $\lambda = 0$ is equivalent to the no-constraint situation already considered, at which the value would be 72. It is clear that the function will cross zero at exactly one value of λ, and that this value is greater than zero. If we try $\lambda = 1$, we find that the function value is -91.4. So we know that the desired value of λ is between 0 and 1. Further trial-and-error attempts to locate the desired value are summarized in Table 8.2

Table 8.2
SOLVING FOR λ.

Value of λ	Value of $160\left(\dfrac{1}{1+8\lambda}\right)+72\left(\dfrac{1}{1+4\lambda}\right)+40\left(\dfrac{1}{1+2\lambda}\right)-200$
0.5	-91.374
0.25	-58.593
0.1	$+16.623$
0.15	-0.125
0.149	$+0.170$
0.1496	-0.007

More sophisticated methods, such as Newton's method, could be used to find the value of λ at which the function value is zero. Such methods might be worth employing when the problem involves many items and a computer routine is to be implemented. The above table, however, required only a few minutes with a calculator to produce. Each successive choice of λ was just a reasonable guess based on the information produced by prior guesses. Since three-digit accuracy was achieved in just a few steps, it would appear that the trial-and-error approach is perfectly adequate for a problem of this order of magnitude.

The conclusion, then, is that λ is very close to 0.1496. Substitution of this value into the formulas for the Q_i gives as the optimum *feasible* values,

$$Q_1 = 26.988$$
$$Q_2 = 18.983$$
$$Q_3 = 17.547$$

The cost per week of running the inventory system with these order quantities would be

$$C(Q_1, Q_2, Q_3) = C(27.988) + C(18.983) + C(17.547)$$
$$= 43.137 + 36.994 + 40.343 = \$120.474$$

as opposed to the cost if no-capacity constraint were present

$$C(Q_1, Q_2, Q_3) = C(40) + C(24) + C(20)$$
$$= 40 + 36 + 40 = \$116$$

This example illustrates the conventional approach to finding the EOQ subject to constraints. But perhaps this was a bit hasty. Because the Lagrange multiplier technique was available as a way to extend the classical method of optimization by differentiation to a similar problem subject to constraints, it was an obvious step to take. What we failed to consider, however, was whether the objective function should really be the same in the constrained case as it was in the unconstrained case. More specifically, the model just presented contained the implicit assumption that the order size for each item must remain constant, or that the order for replenishment is for the same quantity every time the order is placed. When no constraint was present, there was no advantage to varying the order size; whatever was optimal one time would be optimal the next. But the constraint which is operative when all three items are ordered simultaneously (at $t = 0$ and on rare occasions, thereafter) will ordinarily not be operative—or at least not to the same degree—at other times. Because the stocks will ordinarily run out at different times, it is only when the cycles are relatively "in phase" that the constraint has to be considered.

One of the problems at the end of the chapter asks you to graph the fluctuations in the amount of space occupied over time and asks you to consider better policies. It is not at all obvious what *is* optimal, but the fixed-order sizes produced by the Lagrange multiplier technique are certainly *not* optimal when variable-order sizes are an option. After struggling to express the objective function in the more general case, you may be led to the conclusion that, in the absence of anything better, one might as well use the simply stated results of the fixed-order-size model. The real moral to be drawn from this critique is that one has to watch out for hidden assumptions, particularly when modifying an existing model to fit a slightly different situation.

8.10   OTHER DETERMINISTIC INVENTORY MODELS

Hansmann (4) gives a variation of the PLS model in which the holding cost is proportional to production costs which are in turn a function of the lot size Q. He also considers a model in which holding cost is a step function related to Q, representing the situation in which additional space must be rented in fixed increments. A third variation makes the demand rate price dependent. Starr and Miller (7) have an interesting analysis of when items should be aggregated and ordered as a group. Buffa (1) addresses the problem of coordinating production-lot sizes for multiple items requiring the same production facilities.

Having seen classical optimization methods used to advantage in determining optimal inventory policies, the reader may already have wondered whether there is not some way to make use of linear programming for the same general purpose. Of course, there is. Example 3.2-3 on p. 76 suggests one such approach. Although it was convenient in that example to use wording indicating that replenishment of stock occurred through production, it could just as well be purchased externally. As a matter of fact, when the structure of the linear programming problem is that of a transportation problem and, further, when the costs are such that the "below diagonal" costs in the transportation tableau are all prohibitively large (as they are in Example 3.2-3 and would be whenever back orders are prohibited), it is possible to obtain the optimal solution by hand in a single pass; that is, no iterations will be required. When applicable, this model could be implemented on quite a large scale even without the aid of a computer. The method is described and proved optimal in Johnson (5).

Linear programming models enjoy considerable versatility. They can readily accommodate multiple items, changing demand rates (to represent, say, seasonal variations), and several kinds of constraints. Because large linear programming problems can be solved economically, there is little resistance to embellishing the model with additional aspects of the real-world problem. Of course, the solution will not appear as a closed-form expression, as it did in the models we have seen in this chapter.

There is one significant variation that linear programming models will *not* readily accept. A set-up (or order) cost is a fixed charge which is incurred whenever production (or a purchase) occurs, but is not incurred in any period for which the production or order quantity is zero. To incorporate such a cost would destroy the linearity of the objective function, and thereby remove the problem from the realm of linear programming. Dynamic programming, described in Chapter 10, is well suited to such problems; Section 10.9 contains an example.

II. PROBABILISTIC MODELS

The principle objective of the remainder of this chapter is to reveal, through a sequence of models, the significance of uncertainty in inventory decisions. There will be no attempt to be complete in cataloging the possible variations that can occur, nor even to be very rigorous in deriving the models that are presented. The mathematics required to incorporate aspects of uncertainty is much more difficult than that required for any of the deterministic models already treated. The temptation to dismiss those aspects—perhaps with the loose justification that variations will average out in the long run anyway—is strong. The major point of this section is that it is perilous to do so.

The first probabilistic model to be considered introduces the uncertainty aspects while dropping the dynamic aspects. The resulting model has a number of direct applications, but also serves as a transition to the more important and more complicated model subsequently considered.

8.11   THE NEWSBOY PROBLEM: A SINGLE PERIOD MODEL
One class of inventory problems requires that the order quantity decision be made only once for the entire demand process. That is, the opportunity to replenish the stock as it becomes depleted does not occur. Given that the total demand over the period in question is uncertain, the dilemma is to order *enough*, so that the full potential for profit may be realized, but not *too much*, so as to avoid losses on the excess. A streetcorner newsboy faces this dilemma. Although his problem recurs daily, each day's paper is unique and cannot be sold the following day. Hence his decision on how many to buy may be made without regard to any day but the current one. In fact, since it will not matter when within the day he sells each paper, but only how many are sold by the end of the day, all aspects having to do with the passage of time may be safely neglected.

The model we develop to solve the problem will be oriented toward the newsboy's problem, but there are many inventory problems of a similar nature. Just to list a few suggestive examples, consider how to determine:

1. How many hot dogs to have on hand to sell at a particular ball game;
2. How many Christmas trees to stock for the Christmas season;
3. How much fresh bread to bake for a given day;
4. How many Easter lilies to plant for next spring;
5. How many swimsuits of a currently fashionable style to produce.

The major distinguishing characteristics of the newsboy-type problem are that the order quantity decision is a "one shot" affair and that, despite uncertainty in the demand, a proper trade-off must be achieved between the consequences of too much and too little.

Let c denote the cost per item and s the selling price per item. Then $s - c$ will represent the profit per item actually sold. Let v be the salvage value per item. v may be zero if excess items are utterly worthless, or even negative if it actually costs something to dispose of them. In any case, v is assumed to be less than c, for if it is not, one could profit even from the excess and would therefore desire unlimited quantities. The amount $c - v$ could be called the potential loss per unsold item.

As in earlier models, the order quantity will be represented by Q, and the fixed cost of placing an order by a. With negligible extra effort, we can include a provision for goodwill lost when customers' demands are not met, so let p represent the "lost sales penalty". The units of p will be dollars per item. The demand, being uncertain, will be described by a random variable D whose probability distribution is specified by $p_D(x)$. We may think of $p_D(x)$ as the probability that total demand will equal x.

To aid in formulating an expression for profit in terms of Q, temporarily imagine that x is fixed. There will be two expressions for profit depending on whether x, the amount demanded, is less than or greater than Q, the amount available. In the former case, all x units will be sold for s dollars each, the remainder $Q - x$ will be sold for v dollars each, and no sales will be lost. The cost of ordering the Q items will be $a + cQ$. This leads to the profit expression

$$P(Q \mid x) = sx + v(Q - x) - a - cQ \qquad \text{if} \qquad x < Q$$

On the other hand, if demand exceeds supply, all Q items will be sold for v dollars each, there will be no excess items to dispose of at the salvage rate, but there will be a cost of p for each of the $(x - Q)$ demands not met. The cost of ordering the goods would remain the same as before. Consequently,

$$P(Q \mid x) = sQ - p(x - Q) - a - cQ \qquad \text{if} \qquad x > Q$$

Now, to get an overall expression for total *expected* profit, each possible profit, as given by the above two expressions, must be weighted by the probability of occurrence and the results summed. The new expression is

$$EP(Q) = \sum_{x=0}^{Q} (sx + vQ - vx - a - cQ)p_D(x) + \sum_{x=Q+1}^{\infty} (sQ - px + pQ - a - cQ)p_D(x)$$

which simplifies slightly to

$$EP(Q) = \sum_{x=0}^{Q} [(s - v)x + vQ]p_D(x) + \sum_{x=Q+1}^{\infty} [(s + p)Q - px]p_D(x) - a - cQ$$

The problem now remaining is to find the value of Q that maximizes this expression.

Although it has been logical up to this point to treat x and Q as integer valued, it will be easier to obtain and to express the solution if they are treated as continuous. Specifically, we would like to be able to differentiate the expected profit function to obtain the maximum. To do so, the sums must be replaced by integrals and $p_D(x)$ by $f(x)$, which must be interpreted as a density function. The revised expression is

$$EP(Q) = \int_0^Q [(s-v)x + vQ]f(x)\, dx + \int_Q^\infty [(s+p)Q - px]f(x)\, dx - a - cQ$$

This is now a continuous function of Q, having a shape something like that of Fig. 8.11.

To find the maximum will necessitate taking the derivatives of integral terms involving Q in the limits of integration. There is no difficulty posed by this; the formula is well known as *Leibniz's* rule. Because it may not be familiar to some readers, the rule is given here.

If

$$g(u) = \int_{a(u)}^{b(u)} h(u, x)\, dx$$

then

$$\frac{dg}{du} = \int_{a(u)}^{b(u)} \frac{dh}{du}\, dx + h[u, b(u)]\frac{db}{du} - h[u, a(u)]\frac{da}{du}$$

Application of Leibniz's rule to $EP(Q)$ gives for the derivative

$$\frac{dEP(Q)}{dQ} = v\int_0^Q f(x)\, dx + (s+p)\int_Q^\infty f(x)\, dx - c$$

Because $f(x)$ is a density function, the two integrals sum to 1. Setting the derivative equal to zero and simplifying,

$$0 = v\left[1 - \int_Q^\infty f(x)\, dx\right] + (s+p)\int_Q^\infty f(x)\, dx - c$$

$$c - v = (s+p-v)\int_Q^\infty f(x)\, dx$$

$$\int_Q^\infty f(x)\, dx = \frac{c-v}{s+p-v}$$

This is about as close as we can come to a closed-form expression for Q, unless we have further information about the nature of $f(x)$. It is not very satisfying as a solution, but it does specify a value for Q. The left-hand side can be interpreted as the probability that demand will exceed Q. In words, then, Q must be selected so that the probability of running out is equal to the value given by the right-hand side.

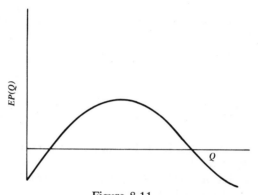

Figure 8.11
The expected profit as a function of Q.

A solution of this kind is not uncommon among inventory models. We shall encounter it again in the next section. Whenever Q is determined by requiring the complementary cumulative distribution of demand to equal a certain expression, such as above, the solution is called a *critical ratio* policy.

Before illustrating the model with numerical values, let us devote some thought to the meaning of the critical ratio expression in this case. The numerator, $c - v$, is just what we earlier identified as the potential loss per unsold item. The denominator, $s + p - v$, can be more easily interpreted by adding and subtracting c in the appropriate places to yield the equivalent $(s - c) + p + (c - v)$. It can now be seen to equal the sum of the potential profit per item sold, the potential loss per unmet demand, and the potential loss per unsold item. The reader may want to reflect on what happens to the critical ratio, and hence to Q, as these unit profits or losses increase or decrease one at a time. Such reflection will be of aid in understanding the nature of the critical ratio solution, as well as in assuring that the results make sense.

Incidentally, if you are bothered by the continuity assumption which was made for the sake of mathematical convenience, you may be assured that the final result in the discrete case is completely analogous. That is Q is selected so that

$$\sum_{x=Q}^{\infty} p_D(x) = \frac{c - v}{s + p - v}$$

(or, if exact equality cannot be achieved, Q is the largest value such that the left-hand side barely exceeds the right). Details of the discrete case treatment may be found in Hadley and Whitin (3, p. 298).

To illustrate the model, suppose that the newsboy pays 8 ¢ per paper and sells them for 15 ¢ each. If he has any left, he can return them for 1 ¢ credit each. Lost sales involve no direct cost, so $p = 0$. Assume that demand is normally distributed with a mean of 150 papers and a standard deviation of 25. According to the model, Q should be selected so that

$$\int_{Q}^{\infty} f(x)\, dx = \frac{c - v}{s + p - v} = \frac{8 - 1}{15 + 0 - 1} = 0.5$$

In other words, Q should be chosen so that half of the area under the density function should lie to the right of Q. Since the normal distribution is symmetric, this would imply $Q = 150$. In this particular case, it is optimal to order a quantity equal to the mean demand.

But now suppose that the newsboy finds an alternative buyer who is willing to pay 5 ¢ per paper late in the day. That is, suppose that v increases from 1 to 5 ¢. Then the critical ratio becomes

$$\frac{8 - 5}{15 + 0 - 5} = 0.3$$

and the optimal Q increases to where only three-tenths of the area under the normal density curve lies to the right. From normal tables, the implied Q is $150 + (0.52)(25) = 163$.

Hadley and Whitin (3) have several numerical examples worked out (pp. 299–303). They also show how to extend the model to cover multiple items subject to a common constraint, using dynamic programming (pp. 304–307).

The reader may have observed that the fixed cost of ordering, a, does not appear in the critical ratio and will therefore not affect the value of Q. However, there is a situation in which this cost can play an important role. If a is large enough, the optimal profit may be negative, in which case it may be best not to engage in the business at all. Suppose, for example, that the newsboy has fixed daily costs of $10, independent of how many papers he orders or sells. In the first case calculated above, according to which he should order 150 papers, his expected total profit would be $a - 90$ ¢. (This is, of course, found by substituting $Q = 150$, along with the other parameter values, into the expected profit function.) In other words, if he engages in selling papers at all, the *best* he can do is to lose an average of 90 ¢ a day. Clearly, he would be better off in some other business. In the second case, when the salvage value is much better and the optimal Q is 163, one would expect that his expected profits would be higher. They are indeed, but not enough to justify staying in business. They turn out to be -37 ¢ per day.

8.12 A LOT SIZE, REORDER POINT MODEL

Having, to this point, examined the deterministic economic lot-size model (with variations) and a probabilistic model in which time plays no role, the objective of this section is to incorporate both probabilistic and time aspects into a single model. The result will share characteristics with each of the aforementioned models, but will obviously be more complicated than either.

To begin, we assume that the status of the inventory is known at all times. In many real-life situations, this assumption would not hold. The kind of inventory system in which inventory is "taken" and therefore is of known quantity only at periodic intervals is called a *periodic review* system. In the current discussion, the system is one of *continuous review*.

There will be a lead time for replenishment, denoted by L. Although it will initially be assumed that L is fixed, we will eventually want to consider the effect of making L a random variable. Even when there is no uncertainty in L, the fact that demand during L is unpredictable implies that the order for replenishment must be initiated in anticipation of the *possibility* of running out. The policy assumed for this model is that the replenishment order will be initiated the moment that the inventory level falls to a certain value called the *reorder point*, and denoted r. The value of r is one of the quantities to be determined.

The other decision variable is Q, the order quantity. Because orders always occur when the inventory level is r, and everything else is the same, there is no reason to vary the order quantity from one time to the next.

Regardless of what L, r, and Q may be, there will be a positive probability that the inventory will be depleted before the lead time expires. Consequently, what happens when this occurs must be specified. There are two obvious choices: demands that occur when the stock is out are accumulated as back orders and fulfilled when the order arrives, or such demands are simply never fulfilled. The former case is called the *back-orders case*; the latter is referred to as the *lost sales case*. Both are treated here. In either case, p will be used as the penalty cost per item. That is, if the inventory is exhausted, each unit demanded up until the stock is replenished will cost p dollars. Notice that this penalty is independent of the duration of the stockout period.

In keeping with previous models, the fixed cost of placing an order will be

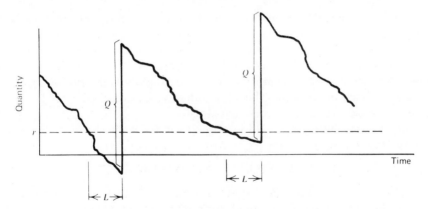

Figure 8.12
Inventory pattern in backorders case.

denoted by a, and the holding cost per item per unit time by h. The demand rate will be denoted by d, although this must now be understood to be an expected value of a random variable. The units of d are items per unit time, usually taken to be per year. The probability distribution of demand during a lead time L is given by the density function $f(x)$. The mean of this probability distribution will be represented by μ.

Although it is not apparent in the notation, there is an implicit relation among d, L, and μ. If, for example, d is 600 units per year, and the lead time L is 2 months, or $\frac{1}{6}$ year, then μ would have to be 100 units. More generally, the relation $dL = \mu$ must hold; for if it did not, the expected demand during a lead time would be either greater or less than at other times. Since the three parameters are all related, any one could be expressed in terms of the other two, and we could get by with one less symbol. However, there is little incentive to eliminate any one of the three when you consider their separate, individually useful interpretations. Consequently all three will be retained.

A graph of one possible pattern of the varying inventory level over time is shown in Fig. 8.12. This particular graph would apply to the back-orders case, since the inventory level does go negative at one point. Notice that while L and Q are the same for each cycle, the cycles are not of equal duration nor are the inventory levels just after replenishment (i.e., the peaks) of equal height. For contrast, Fig. 8.13 shows a lost-sales case, in which the inventory can never go

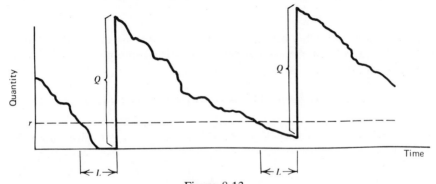

Figure 8.13
Inventory pattern in lost sales case.

below zero. Notice that relative to the back-orders case, the peaks will be higher by an amount equal to the lost sales. In other words, the full order quantity Q goes into inventory in the lost-sales case, whereas some may be allocated to filling prior demands in the back-orders case. Other factors being equal, then, the average inventory level will be slightly higher in the lost-sales case than in back-orders case. This observation will be recalled when formulating an expression for the average inventory.

The first step in the formulation of the expected annual-cost function is to identify the separate components of cost. Accordingly, let

$$EAC(Q, r) = OC + SC + HC$$

where $EAC(Q, r)$ stands for Expected Annual Cost, as a function of the decision variables Q and r, OC stands for Ordering Cost, SC for Stockout Cost, and HC for Holding Cost. The three terms on the right can now be developed separately.

The ordering cost is quite easy to obtain. It is a, the cost per order, times the expected number of cycles per year. Since d is the expected demand per year and Q is the amount sold per cycle, the expected number of cycles per year is d/Q, provided that all demand is met. So, at least in the back-orders case,

$$OC = a \frac{d}{Q}$$

In the lost-sales case, this expression is not exactly correct. If we assume, however, that p is sufficiently large to ensure that the policy ultimately used will result in few lost sales, the same expression will suffice as a close approximation to the expected ordering cost even in the lost-sales case.

The expected stockout cost, in either the back-orders or lost-sales case, will be p, the cost per back order or lost sale, times the expected number of back orders or lost sales per cycle, times the average number of cycles per year. The average number of cycles per year is d/Q, by the argument just given, so the only remaining problem is to determine the expected number of back orders or lost sales per cycle. Of course, it is only during a lead time that a stockout situation might occur. It will occur if the demand during that lead time exceeds r, which is the quantity on hand when the lead time begins. So if x represents the demand during a lead time, then the number of back orders or lost sales is:

$$
\begin{array}{lll}
0 & \text{if} & x \leq r \\
x - r & \text{if} & x > r
\end{array}
$$

To get the expected value of this function of x, we must weight the values by their probability of occurrence and sum. Let $B(r)$ denote the expected number of back orders or lost sales per cycle. Then

$$B(r) = \int_0^r 0 f(x)\, dx + \int_r^\infty (x - r) f(x)\, dx = \int_r^\infty (x - r) f(x)\, dx$$

Further comments will be made later on the subject of how to compute $B(r)$, but for now it will suffice to represent the total expected stockout cost per year as

$$SC = p \frac{d}{Q} B(r)$$

It remains to express the expected annual holding cost. The argument to be employed now is far from rigorous, but it does yield the correct expression and gives a plausible explanation of where the terms come from. A properly cautious development can be found in Hadley and Whitin (3, pp. 175–188). The expected holding cost per year will be h, the holding cost per item per year, times the average inventory over a year. But the average inventory over a year will be the same as the average inventory over a "typical" cycle, where by a typical cycle we mean one whose behavior is identical to the expected behavior of all cycles. That is, it begins at an inventory level equal to the expected level at the beginning of all cycles, lasts a duration equal to the expected duration, and so on. We cannot hope to observe such a cycle in reality; it is merely a conceptual device to aid in formulating the expression for the average inventory level. The device "works" only because expected values, or averages, behave pretty much as intuition would suggest.

Imagine, then, this typical cycle, and consider the back-orders case. The cycle begins when an order arrives. Our only definite information about the inventory level is that it was r when this arriving order was initiated. Since that time, for the period L, demand has continued in its random fashion. The expected demand during L is μ, so the expected inventory level just before the order arrives is $r - \mu$ (which may conceivably be negative), and the expected inventory level at the start of our cycle is $Q + r - \mu$. The demand process then depletes the inventory, another replenishment order is placed, and the cycle ends with an expected inventory level of $r - \mu$ (see Fig. 8.14), The average inventory over this cycle is midway between $Q + r - \mu$ and $r - \mu$, or

$$\frac{Q + r - \mu + r - \mu}{2} = \frac{Q}{2} + r - \mu$$

By this argument, the expected annual holding cost expression is

$$HC = h\left(\frac{Q}{2} + r - \mu\right)$$

But this argument was for the back-orders case. It is apparent from Figs. 8.12 and 8.13 that, other things being equal, the average inventory in the lost-sales case will be slightly higher than in the back orders case. The expected inventory level just before the order arrives is not quite $r - \mu$, because now the inventory is not allowed to go negative. To see what it is instead, let x be the

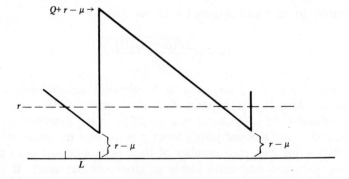

Figure 8.14
The typical cycle.

demand during the lead time L. Then the inventory level is

$$
\begin{array}{lll}
r - x & \text{if} & x \leq r \\
0 & \text{if} & x > r
\end{array}
$$

Taking the expected value of this function of x gives for the expected inventory level:

$$
\int_0^r (r-x)f(x)\, dx + \int_r^\infty 0 f(x)\, dx = \int_0^r (r-x)f(x)\, dx
$$

$$
= \int_0^\infty (r-x)f(x)\, dx - \int_r^\infty (r-x)f(x)
$$

$$
= r \int_0^\infty f(x)\, dx - \int_0^\infty x f(x)\, dx + \int_r^\infty (x-r)f(x)\, dx
$$

$$
= r - \mu + B(r)
$$

In words, the expected inventory level just before replenishment is greater by an amount equal to the expected number of lost sales. The average inventory can be found as in the back-orders case. It works out to give for the expected annual holding cost in the lost-sales case

$$
\mathrm{HC} = h\left(\frac{Q}{2} + r - \mu + B(r)\right)
$$

The total expected annual cost is therefore

$$
\mathrm{EAC}(Q,\, r) = \frac{ad}{Q} + \frac{pd}{Q} B(r) + h\left(\frac{Q}{2} + r - \mu\right)
$$

in the back-orders case, and the same expression plus $hB(r)$ in the lost-sales case. This is the function of Q and r which is to be minimized; that is, the order quantity and reorder point that yield the smallest expected annual cost have to be found. The function happens to be convex. Barring extraordinary circumstances, the minimum will occur for values of Q and r which are nonnegative and finite, and will occur at that point where the partial derivatives with respect to Q and r both vanish.

So, taking the derivative with respect to Q,

$$
\frac{\partial \mathrm{EAC}(Q,\, r)}{\partial Q} = -\frac{ad}{Q^2} - \frac{pd B(r)}{Q^2} + \frac{h}{2}
$$

setting it equal to zero and solving for Q, we find

$$
Q = \sqrt{\frac{2d[a + pB(r)]}{h}}
$$

Note the similarity of this expression to the classical, deterministic economic-order quantity formula. It appears that the optimal-order quantity when demand is probabilistic is the same as it would be in the deterministic case if a were increased by the amount $pB(r)$. Since p is the cost per back order or lost sale and $B(r)$ is the expected number of back orders or lost sales per cycle, $pB(r)$ is the expected cost attributable to stockouts per cycle. If you think about it, the addition of this quantity to a makes some sense. Of course, r and therefore $B(r)$ are still unknown.

Returning, then, to the expected annual-cost function and taking the partial derivative with respect to r, we get

$$\frac{\partial \text{EAC}(Q, r)}{\partial r} = h + \frac{pd}{Q}\frac{dB(r)}{dr}$$

in the back-orders case, or

$$\frac{\partial \text{EAC}(Q, r)}{\partial r} = h + \left(\frac{pd}{Q} + h\right)\frac{dB(r)}{dr}$$

in the lost-sales case. Recalling that

$$B(r) = \int_r^\infty (x - r)f(x)\,dx$$

and making use of Leibniz' rule to differentiate the integral (as in the newsboy problem),

$$\frac{dB(r)}{dr} = -\int_r^\infty f(x)\,dx$$

Substituting this back into the partial derivative, setting it equal to zero, and solving, we get

$$\int_r^\infty f(x)\,dx = \frac{hQ}{pd}$$

in the back-orders case, or

$$\int_r^\infty f(x)\,dx = \frac{hQ}{pd + hQ}$$

in the lost-sales case.

As occurred in the newsboy problem, the best expression for r that we can obtain is a critical ratio solution. The left-hand side is the complementary cumulative distribution of lead-time demand evaluated at r, or the probability that the demand during L exceeds r. In words, then, the reorder point r must be set high enough so that the probability of running out is just equal to the critical ratio. It would be worthwhile for the reader to verify to his own satisfaction that the critical ratios make sense. For example, if p is very large, the critical ratio will tend to be small, which will in turn force the reorder point to be large enough to provide a generous margin of safety against stockouts.

Although we now have expressions for both Q and r, the problem is not solved because evaluation of each of the expressions requires knowledge of the value of the other. To get Q we need r, and to get r we need Q. Fortunately, there is an iterative approach which works out quite nicely in practice. It proceeds as follows:

1. As an initial, temporary value, let $B(r) = 0$, and solve for $Q_1 = \sqrt{2d[a + pB(r)]/h}$. This would amount to solving for the deterministic optimal-order quantity.
2. Using Q_1, find r_1 from the critical ratio rule:

$$\int_{r_1}^\infty f(x)\,dx = \frac{hQ}{pd} \qquad \text{(back-orders case)}$$

$$= \frac{hQ}{pd + hQ} \qquad \text{(lost-sales case)}$$

3. Using r_1, evaluate

$$B(r_1) = \int_{r_1}^{\infty} (x - r_1) f(x) \, dx$$

4. Using $B(r_1)$, solve for Q_2 as in step 1.
5. Using Q_2, find r_2 as in step 2.
6. Continue in this manner until no change occurs in the values of Q_i and r_i. The final values obtained are the optimal-order quantity and reorder point.

In practice, convergence is usually rapid. Often Q_2 and r_2 will be so close to optimal that further iterations are not worth the trouble.

Still, compared to the immediately calculable formula available for the deterministic case, the solution procedure required for this model is cumbersome. Although it would pose no difficulty for implementation as a computer algorithm, it would not seem realistically practical for use as a hand method in a day-to-day real-world setting. On the other hand, it is not inconceivable that an abbreviated procedure, simply and carefully explained with appropriate tables provided, could be made operational as an everyday decision tool. Here the solution is to be employed more as a pedagogical tool, to help in reaching a deeper understanding of the significance of uncertainty in demand to inventory systems. Once we know how important a factor it is, we can decide intelligently how to (or indeed, whether to) include it in our considerations. It may be, at least under certain conditions, that the error introduced by ignoring demand uncertainty is so minor that the considerable effort necessary to include it is unwarranted.

Because we do not have a closed-form solution, but only an iterative approach for obtaining it, a direct evaluation is difficult. For the most part, we will resort to numerical examples to show what difference it makes to include uncertainty. First, however, it is necessary to devote some attention to the evaluation of the integral involved in $B(r)$.

Recall that

$$B(r) = \int_{r}^{\infty} (x - r) f(x) \, dx$$

where $f(x)$ is the lead-time demand density function. When $f(x)$ is complicated, as it may reasonably be expected to be most of the time, the integration may not be trivial. Perhaps the most important special case occurs when the lead-time demand distribution is normal, in which case

$$B(r) = \int_{r}^{1} (x - r) \frac{1}{\sigma \sqrt{2\pi}} \exp\left[-\frac{1}{2}\left(\frac{x - \mu}{\sigma}\right)^2 \right] dx$$

Fortunately this rather imposing expression can be translated to an expression involving only the Standard Normal density and cumulative distribution functions, which are readily available in tables. After some preliminary manipulation,

$$B(r) = \int_{r}^{\infty} [(x - \mu) + (\mu - r)] \frac{1}{\sigma \sqrt{2\pi}} \exp\left[-\frac{1}{2}\left(\frac{x - \mu}{\sigma}\right)^2 \right] dx$$

$$= \int_{r}^{\infty} \left[\frac{x - \mu}{\sigma} + \frac{\mu - r}{\sigma} \right] \frac{1}{\sqrt{2\pi}} \exp\left[-\frac{1}{2}\left(\frac{x - \mu}{\sigma}\right)^2 \right] dx$$

a change of variable from x to $y = (x - \mu)/\sigma$ produces

$$B(r) = \int_{(r-\mu)/\sigma}^{\infty} y \frac{1}{\sqrt{2\pi}} e^{-(1/2)y^2} \sigma \, dy + \int_{(r-\mu)/\sigma}^{\infty} \left(\frac{\mu - r}{\sigma}\right) \frac{1}{\sqrt{2\pi}} e^{-(1/2)y^2} \sigma \, dy$$

$$= \sigma \int_{(r-\mu)/\sigma}^{\infty} y \frac{1}{\sqrt{2\pi}} e^{-(1/2)y^2} \, dy + (\mu - r) \int_{(r-\mu)/\sigma}^{\infty} \frac{1}{\sqrt{2\pi}} e^{-(1/2)y^2} \, dy$$

Now the first integral is easy to evaluate.

$$\int_{(r-\mu)/\sigma}^{\infty} y \frac{1}{\sqrt{2\pi}} e^{-(1/2)y^2} \, dy = \frac{1}{\sqrt{2\pi}} \int_{(r-\mu)/\sigma}^{\infty} y e^{-(1/2)y^2} \, dy$$

$$= \frac{1}{\sqrt{2\pi}} \left[-e^{-(1/2)y^2} \, \Big|_{(r-\mu)/\sigma}^{\infty} \right]$$

$$= \frac{1}{\sqrt{2\pi}} \exp\left[-\frac{1}{2}\left(\frac{r - \mu}{\sigma}\right)^2 \right]$$

$$= f\left(\frac{r - \mu}{\sigma}\right)$$

where $f(x)$ is the Standard Normal density function. The second integral is even easier; it is already tabulated as the complementary cumulative of the Standard Normal. In summary,

$$B(r) = \sigma f\left(\frac{r - \mu}{\sigma}\right) + (\mu - r) G\left(\frac{r - \mu}{\sigma}\right)$$

where $G(x)$ is the complementary cumulative distribution function for the Standard Normal. (Just to be sure there is no confusion, the lower-case f refers to the height of the density function, and the upper-case G refers to the area under the right-hand tail of the density function.) Of course, this expression is valid only when the lead-time-demand distribution is normal. If it is, say, gamma distributed, some other method of evaluating $B(r)$ must be found.

The assumption that lead-time demand is in fact normal is frequently justified by the Central Limit Theorem. The total demand can be written as a sum of the demands of individual customers, so if there are enough of them, the total should approach a normally distributed random variable. There are some weaknesses in this argument, but it provides some reassurance that the normality assumption is not completely arbitrary, in many real-world problems.

8.13 SOME NUMERICAL EXAMPLES

For the first illustration of the lot-size, reorder-point model, suppose that a large department store chain sells blank recording tape under its own brand name. The tape itself is identical to that of a well-known recording tape manufacturer, and is in fact supplied to the chain by that manufacturer. Because of the special labeling and packaging, however, there is a lead time of 5.2 weeks, or 1/10 year. Assume that the demand during a period of this length is normally distributed with a mean of 1000 tapes and a standard deviation of 250. By implication, the mean annual demand must be 10,000 tapes. The cost of paper work and handling associated with placing an order is $100, and the holding cost is 15 ¢ per tape per year. Although we shall want to see what happens in the lost-sales case as well, assume for now that back orders are taken. The penalty is assumed to be $1.00 per tape backordered.

According to the iterative procedure, we first find

$$Q_1 = \sqrt{\frac{2da}{h}} = \sqrt{\frac{2(10,000)(100)}{0.15}} = 3651.5$$

This would, of course, suffice as the economic-order quantity if demand were deterministic. Proceeding, we next find

$$\int_{r_1}^{\infty} f(x)\, dx = \frac{Q_1 h}{pd} = 0.055$$

where $f(x)$ is normal with mean 1000 and standard deviation 250. Standardizing to permit use of the Standard Normal tables,

$$\int_{(r_1-1000)/250}^{\infty} f(x)\, dx = 0.055$$

we find

$$\frac{r_1 - 1000}{250} = 1.60$$

$$r_1 = 1400$$

Now, to find $B(r_1)$, the expected number of backorders if the reorder point is 1400, we have recourse to the formula

$$B(r) = \sigma f\left(\frac{r-\mu}{\sigma}\right) + (\mu - r)G\left(\frac{r-\mu}{\sigma}\right)$$

which in this case is

$$B(1400) = 250f(1.60) + (1000 - 1400)G(1.60)$$
$$= 250(0.111) - 400(0.055)$$
$$= 5.822$$

This is an accurate result, in the sense that if the reorder point is 1400, then the expected number of back orders per cycle will be 5.82. Of course, the reorder point has not yet achieved its final value.

Beginning the second iteration, the revised-order quantity is

$$Q_2 = \sqrt{\frac{2d[a + pB(r_1)]}{h}}$$

$$= \sqrt{\frac{2(10,000)[100 + 5.822]}{0.15}}$$

$$= 3756.27$$

which is slightly larger than the previous value. The critical ratio increases just a little

$$\int_{r}^{\infty} f(x)\, dx = \frac{Q_2 h}{pd} = 0.05634$$

so the reorder point is only slightly lower

$$\frac{r_2 - 1000}{250} = 1.586$$

$$r_2 = 1396.5$$

With a lower reorder point, the expected number of back orders will increase.

$$B(1397.5) = 250f(1.586) - 397.5G(1.586)$$
$$= 250(0.113) - 397.5(0.056)$$
$$= 5.99$$

But this time when we reevaluate Q

$$Q_3 = 3759.86$$

we find that the change in the order quantity is only about 1 unit (versus a change of about 100 units previously). In fact the change in the next reorder point is not detectable,

$$r_3 = 1396.5$$

At this point, convergence may be considered complete. Since, from a practical standpoint, the order quantity and reorder point must be integers, there is no sense in trying to achieve accuracy beyond the first decimal figure.

The computations are summarized in Table 8.4.

Table 8.4
SOLVING FOR Q AND r.

Iteration Number	Q	Critical Ratio	r	$B(r)$
1	3651.5	0.055	1400	5.82
2	3756.3	0.0563	1396.5	5.91
3	3757.9	0.0563	1396.5	5.91

From this table, it is easy to see the direction and magnitudes of the changes that occur from one iteration to the next. It is apparent that the first value for r was close to optimal, but was just a bit too large. One might be content to use this value, particularly since it happens to be a nice round number. The second value for Q appears to be close to optimal; further iterations increase it only slightly. As a practical procedure for hand computation, then, one might suggest finding r only once and Q only twice. Because the convergence of both Q and r to their respective optimal values is monotonic, we may be confident that r_1 is above its optimum and Q_2 is beneath its optimum. Consequently, the reorder point and order quantity could be rounded down and up, respectively, to operationally convenient values. In this case, $r = 1400$ and $Q = 3760$ would be good, realistic answers.

It would be a good idea for the student to attempt to duplicate the above calculations. A certain degree of delicacy is required to avoid computational errors. The expression for $B(r)$ is particularly sensitive to errors which may be introduced almost casually when r is rounded off or a value is interpolated from the normal tables.

The calculations for the lost-sales version of the same problem are, of course, very similar; only the expression for the critical ratio is different. Table 8.5 summarizes the values obtained.

A careful examination of the formulas will reveal that, other things being equal, the order quantity must be lower and the reorder point higher in the lost-sales case as compared to the back-orders case. On the other hand, as the

Table 8.5
LOST-SALES CASE.

Iteration Number	Q	Critical Ratio	r	B(r)
1	3651.5	0.052	1407.5	5.31
2	3747.2	0.053	1402.5	5.67
3	3753.5	0.053	1402.5	5.67

tables for this example show, the differences may be so small as to be negligible. Inasmuch as many real-life situations cannot be classified as either pure back-orders or pure lost-sales cases, but lie somewhere between the two, it is reassuring to know that these variations are not very important. Having made this point, our further examination of the results will be limited to the back-orders case.

The minimum cost for the example has not yet been exhibited. To obtain it requires only that the optimal values of Q and r be resubstituted into the cost function.

$$EAC(Q, r) = \frac{(100)(10,000)}{Q} + \frac{(1)(10,000)B(r)}{Q} + (0.15)\left[\frac{Q}{2} + r - 1000\right]$$

$$EAC(3757.9, \; 1397.5) = \$266.10 + 15.73 + 341.31$$
$$= \$623.15$$

Just to verify the intuitive notion that it "shouldn't make much difference" if rounded-off values are used instead of the optimal ones, the cost expression can be evaluated at $Q = 3760$ and $r = 1400$:

$$EAC(3760, \; 1400) = \$265.96 + 15.48 + 342.00$$
$$= \$623.44$$

As expected, the difference is not worth being concerned about.

An interesting cost comparison can be made between the above expected annual cost and the annual cost that would be incurred if the demand were deterministic. For the latter, the optimal-order quantity would be the first Q_1 found, or

$$Q = 3651.5$$

and the (deterministic) cost associated with operating the system would be $547.72. It is apparent that a substantial portion of the expected annual cost is attributable solely to the fact that demand is uncertain. In other words, uncertainty is expensive. As the reader may verify, the difference between the two costs is accentuated as σ, a measure of the unpredictability of demand, increases. It is also a fact that (as one would expect) the difference diminishes to zero as σ does.

An even more dramatic comparison can be made between the expected annual cost using the optimal values for the probabilistic model and the expected annual cost using the values that would be obtained from the deterministic model. In other words, what would the penalty be if one used the simple model when, in fact, the more complicated one were appropriate? If uncertainty in the demand is ignored, the optimal Q would be 3651.5 and the r would be 1000. Using these values in the expected annual-cost function from the probabilistic model,

$$EAC(3651.5, 1000) = \$820.86$$

Compared to the minimum cost of $623.15, this cost represents a serious departure from the optimum.

8.14 VARIABLE LEAD TIMES

We have seen that the reorder point (and hence the cost) is quite sensitive to the variance of the lead-time demand. This was all done under the assumption that the lead time was itself known with certainty. That is, all variability in lead-time demand was due to the demand process, and none to the supply process. It would be more realistic, surely, to allow for variability in both.

There is not too much additional required in the way of theory. Let $y(x \mid t)$ be the conditional density function of demand, given that the lead time is t. Let $g(t)$ be the density function for the lead time t. Then $f(x)$, the lead-time-demand density function (as used in the previous models) is just the marginal density

$$f(x) = \int_0^\infty y(x \mid t)g(t) \, dt$$

So if $y(x \mid t)$ and $g(t)$ are known separately, they can—in principle, at least—be combined to give the $f(x)$ used before.

From the practical standpoint, there are not too many cases for which the $f(x)$ will be a familiar, tabulated distribution. One case that can be handled is that in which $y(x \mid t)$ is Poisson and $g(t)$ is of the gamma family. In this case, $f(x)$ turns out to be negative binomial [see Hadley and Whitin (3, p. 117)].

Because the payoff, in terms of added insight, to be obtained from pursuing the general case is meager, an alternative course will now be taken. Suppose that, whatever distributions are involved in $y(x \mid t)$ and $g(t)$, the resulting $f(x)$ is normal. If the demand quantities are sufficiently large and consist of a sufficient number of individual orders, the Central Limit Theorem can be used to justify this assumption. But if $f(x)$ is normal, only the first two moments are required. We are interested now in how these two moments are affected by the variability in lead time.

Let $E(Y)$ and $V(Y)$ represent the mean and the variance, respectively, of the demand per day. Similarly, let $E(L)$ and $V(L)$ represent the mean and variance of the lead time in days. Finally, let μ and σ^2 denote the mean and variance of the lead-time demand, which are the only parameters required when $f(x)$ is normal. Then using the relation above it can be shown that

$$\mu = E(Y)E(L)$$

which is exactly what one would expect. For example, if the expected demand per day is 50 units and the expected lead time is 16 days, then the expected lead-time demand would be 800 units. However, it can also be shown [Feller (2, p. 164)] that

$$\sigma^2 = E(L)V(Y) + E(Y)^2 V(L)$$

which is perhaps more than one would expect. The first term is not surprising; it is just what you would get if the lead time were fixed. For example, if the

Table 8.6
FIXED AND RANDOM LEAD TIMES.

	Fixed Lead Time	Random Lead Time
$E(Y)$, mean demand per day	50	50
$\sqrt{V(Y)}$, stan. dev. of same	5	5
$E(L)$, mean lead time	16	16
$\sqrt{V(L)}$, stan. dev. of same	0	2
μ, mean lead-time demand	800	800
σ, stan. dev. of same	20	102

variance of the demand per day were 25, then over a 16-day lead time the variances for each day would add up to a total lead-time demand variance of 400. The squaring of $E(Y)$ in the second term, however, tends to accentuate the effect of $V(L)$, the lead-time variance. If the lead time is not fixed, but has a variance of 4, then the total lead-time demand variance would be

$$\sigma^2 = (16)(25) + (50)^2(4)$$
$$= 400 + 10,000$$
$$= 10,400$$

It can be seen that the second term has contributed much more to the total than the first term. The implication is that variability in lead times can have a surprisingly significant impact on lead-time demand variability. The latter, it will be recalled, had a surprisingly significant impact on cost.

To get a better feel for the magnitude of the variability generated when both demand and lead time are random variables, it would be preferable to compare standard deviations. Table 8.6 does so for the numerical examples just presented.

Notice in the second column that the standard deviations are small relative to the means for each of the two random variables considered separately. If one did not know better, it would be easy to assume that the combined effect would be small, and therefore to neglect to consider lead-time variability. But as the table shows, the standard deviation of lead-time demand is more than 5 times as large when lead-time variability is included than it is when this variability is neglected.

In more physical terms, the risk of running out of stock is greatly increased when one is unsure of how long it will be until replenishment occurs. The reorder point and (to a lesser extent) the order quantity should reflect this greater risk. The consequences of failing to account for this source of variability can be severe.

8.15 THE IMPORTANCE OF SELECTING THE RIGHT MODEL

Imagine the following scenario, which has doubtlessly occurred in real life many times. A young engineer, fresh out of college and armed with a whole arsenal of textbook techniques, joins an old, established company. He immediately notices that order quantities and reorder points are determined solely by the subjective judgements of an "old hand" who never even graduated from high school. Eager to make an impression and confident that he can improve upon the status quo, the engineer proposes the institution of a modern, computerized system of inventory control based on the (deterministic) EOQ formula. In selling the proposal to his superiors, he goes so far as to predict the savings that could be expected. Taking the one item used in the numerical example given in Section 8.14 as representative, he might predict an annual cost, for this one item, of $547.22. Compared to an experienced cost of, say, $750.00 for the same item under the existing system, the proposal seems quite attractive. The young engineer is patted on the back, and his system is implemented.

About a year later, when the new costs are accumulated, it is discovered that the actual cost under the new system has been, for the one item, $900.00. Similarly disappointing costs are experienced for the other items. As soon as his superiors figure out that the computer is not to blame, that it has operated as it was supposed to, the young engineer is fired. The responsibility for inventory control is restored to the "old hand," who emerges as the hero and only benefactor of the whole chain of events. For ever after, the company management is suspicious of bright young engineers bearing mathematical models. For his own part, the young engineer has "matured" as a result of his tragic experience; he will never again place his faith in models. Thus the "young" engineer becomes an "old" engineer.

The story is a sad one. It is sadder yet because no one in the story ever detected the true culprit. The unrecognized villain in the story is variability or, more precisely, the neglect of it. There was nothing inherently wrong with the model used; the flaw was in using it inappropriately. The EOQ was never intended to apply to situations in which demand is other than completely predictable.

Had the young engineer used the model of Section 8.13 for the item in question, he would have obtained a different order size and reorder point and a less optimistic predicted cost of $623.44. Of course, when uncertainty is present, there is risk associated with any course of action, so he should have been careful to explain that the predicted cost was only an expected value. By exploring the sensitivity of the cost function to various possible demand patterns, he could even place a sort of confidence interval on his prediction. With the right model, the chances are that he *could* improve upon the existing system.

To be sure, it is not always so. The "old hand," with years of experience to develop a feel for the trade-offs involved, is sometimes hard to surpass. An ordinary man, given no special training but plenty of time to learn from his mistakes, can evolve into a very sophisticated self-adaptive control system. The most serious objection to becoming dependent on such a man is that he cannot be replaced. If his only method depends on an unquantifiable "sixth sense" which cannot be expressed or conveyed to anyone else, his successor will have to repeat the same mistakes in order to develop the same ability. One reason to turn to more objective methods of decision making is to avoid some of the inevitable disruptions that occur when personnel change.

The correct moral to draw from the story is that mathematical models in general, or inventory models in particular, *can* contribute to impressive improvements in systems, but there is no guarantee that they will do so. A perfectly good model incompetently applied can lead to grossly misleading conclusions. In any case, a model should not be considered an adequate substitute for good judgement.

8.16 CONCLUSIONS

At the conclusion of the last chapter, it was pointed out that it would be a serious mistake to believe that queueing models exist to cover most real-life situations. The same statement must be made with regard to inventory models. It is easy to find real-world problems for which no appropriate model has yet been developed. For example, situations in which the stocks of tens of thousands of individual, but interrelated, parts must be controlled are commonplace. Often the interrelations are so complicated that mere record keeping is a massive task requiring sophisticated information organizing systems. The models of this chapter—indeed, nearly all of the inventory models that appear in the literature—treat only the simplest kinds of interactions. As a consequence, inventory theory has been severely criticized by many practitioners faced with real-world problems; it has even been dismissed as wholly useless by some. But to draw such a conclusion would be just as wrong as to believe that it can solve all problems.

What inventory models *can* do is to provide quantitative decision making aids in a limited number of cases, and valuable qualitative insights in many other cases. Often, the understanding of the real-world system that is revealed through the construction of a model would not be obtained even from years of direct experience with the system.

Recommended Readings

One of the best resources with which to continue your study of inventory theory would be the book by Hadley and Whitin (3). For a quick survey, see Chapter 7, entitled "A Survey of Analytic Techniques in Inventory Theory," in the compendium edited by Scarf, Guilford, and Shelly (6). Another, somewhat more recent, survey is the article by Veinott (8). Buffa (1), Hanssmann (4), and Starr and Miller (7) are examples of a number of available books which attempt to straddle the "theory-versus-practice" issue.

REFERENCES

1. Buffa, Elwood S., *Production-Inventory Systems: Planning and Control*, Irwin, Homewood, Illinois, 1968.

2. Feller, William, *An Introduction to Probability Theory and Its Applications*, Vol. II, Wiley, New York, 1966.

3. Hadley, G. and T. M. Whitin, *Analysis of Inventory System*, Prentice-Hall, Englewood Cliffs, New Jersey, 1963.

4. Hanssman, F., *Operations Research in Production and Inventory Control*, Wiley, New York, 1962.

5. Johnson, S. M., "Sequential Production Planning Over Time at Minimum Cost," *Man. Sci.*, 3, 435–437, 1957.

6. Scarf, Herbert, E., Dorothy Guilford, and Maynard W. Shelly (eds.), *Multistage Inventory Models and Techniques*, Stanford University Press, Stanford, California, 1963.

7. Starr, Martin K. and David W. Miller, *Inventory Control: Theory and Practice*, Prentice-Hall, Englewood Cliffs, New Jersey, 1962.

8.   Veinott, Arthur F., Jr., "The Status of Mathematical Inventory Theory," *Man. Sci.*, *12*, 745–777, 1966.

EXERCISES

1.   Two roommates, Bud Wiser and Mick O'Loeb, drink enough beer between them to have an inventory problem. They do not have a refrigerator themselves, but find they are able to rent space in various neighbors' refrigerators at the rate of 2¢ per can per week. Being minors, they have to drive to another state to buy their beer, where they also get a better price than they could locally. Each trip costs them $21 for gas, oil, turnpike tolls, and so on, plus the cost of the beer, which is 20¢ per can. They quaff their brew at the steady rate of a six-pack per man per day. If they run out, they just must suffer until the next trip; they cannot get it any other way. How often do they make their shopping excursions, and how much do they buy at a time? How much do their vices cost them (per month, per week, or per year), counting the total cost of purchasing and keeping the beer? Suppose they found two more people who consumed at the same rate and would like to "join forces." How much would they buy on each trip?

2.   A company which has a definite plan for expansion will need to hire and train 60 new engineers per year. The cost of running a training program is $10,000, independent of the number of trainees. These engineers earn annual salaries of $12,000, so the company prefers not to hire and train them before they are needed. On the other hand, they *must* be available when they are needed; and since it costs so much to train them, they will be trained in advance of the time they are needed and in groups. They receive full salary while in the pool of trained, but not yet needed, engineers. What should the training-group size be, how often will the six-week training sessions be held, and how much will this program cost the company?

3.   A pizza delivery man makes regular runs to a particular dormitory each evening. He hates to make a separate trip for each order because of the time it would take, the gas for the truck, and so on. On the other hand, he cannot deliver all at once because the orders come in at various times and the customers want quick service. He figures the orders (from the same dorm) come in at a rate of eight per hour in the evening. The cost of a trip is considered to be 60¢. A pizza sells for $2.00. The cost of delaying a pizza beyond the normal preparation time, which the customer expects, is estimated to be 1¢ per pizza per minute. The cost has something to do with the reduction of future business from dissatisfied customers. Treating the prepared pizzas as inventory, and the delay cost as a holding cost, determine the optimal number of pizzas to deliver in each trip. What is the average delay? What is the maximum delay?

4.   A company retains its cash reserves primarily in the form of short-term certificates of deposit which earn at the rate of 8%. Periodically, however, withdrawals are made in order to meet payroll and other cash requirements. These outflows occur through a checking account which earns no interest. The transfer of funds from the certificates of deposit involve penalties and service charges amounting to $150 each time a transfer is made. If the outflow of cash from the checking account is $300 per day, how often should the transfers be made? Suppose that an option is available to borrow cash from the bank at an interest rate of 0.033¢ per dollar per day (or 12% per year). It is suggested that it may sometimes be cheaper to meet immediate cash requirements by borrowing, rather than by transferring funds from the certificates of deposit. Would it ever be advantageous to do so? Explain why it would or would not. If so, how often would transfers from the certificates of deposit occur?

5.   Formulate the production-lot size cost function and verify that the solution given

in Section 8.7 is correct. Also verify the comment that if p is much greater than d, one might as well use the ordinary EOQ, by calculating the ratio of the PLS to the EOQ when $p = 10d$.

6. Section 8.6 presents a variation of the EOQ in which back orders are penalized at the rate b, which is proportional to both the quantity of back orders and their duration. Suppose, as an alternative, that the back orders are penalized only in proportion to their quantity. Formulate the appropriate cost function, and minimize it to obtain the optimal order quantity, the peak inventory level, and the resulting minimum cost. (Note: This is a tricky problem. In seeking the minimum of the cost function, it is important to realize that S is bounded by $0 \leq S \leq Q$. A solution on the boundary $S = Q$ would correspond to a policy of "no back orders"; one on the boundary $S = 0$ would correspond to "every order back ordered.")

7. For the numerical example used in Section 8.9 to illustrate the EOQ with a capacity constraint, graph the total square footage occupied by all three items as a function of time, assuming that the order sizes are kept constant from one order to the next. Extend the time axis far enough to include five or six cycles for each item. Observe that, although the 200 square feet of available space is fully occupied at $t = 0$, it will not fill up again for a very long time. Can you suggest a policy, involving nonconstant order sizes, that would make better use of the space and also lower the cost per year?

8. A certain vending machine dispenses sandwiches. Each morning, fresh sandwiches are put in, and the excess, if any, from the previous day are removed. Sandwiches cost the vendor 15¢, and are sold for 35¢. Day-old sandwiches are sold for 5¢ apiece to a skid-row soup kitchen. Assuming that daily demand is Poisson distributed with a mean of 25, determine the number of sandwiches to put into the machine each day.

9. In Section 8.11, the solution to the newsboy problem was expressed as a critical ratio policy. Suppose that demand is uniformly distributed over the range $[a, b]$. That is,

$$f(x) = \frac{1}{b-a} \quad \text{for} \quad a \leq x \leq b$$

$$= 0 \quad \text{elsewhere}$$

Derive an explicit, closed-form expression for Q.

10. In planning a conference to be held next year, the Operations Research Society of America must decide on an appropriate number of hotel rooms to reserve for its members. We cannot be sure how many rooms will be required, but judging from previous conferences, the distribution is approximately normal with a mean of 1000 and a standard deviation of 200. Rooms at the conference hotel normally rent for $35 per night, but have been offered to ORSA for $25. If ORSA reserves too many rooms for its members, the excess rooms may be released to the hotel for possible use by other guests, but a charge of $8 will be assessed for each such room. On the other hand, if not enough rooms are reserved, some members will at least have to pay the higher rate, and may even be forced to stay at another hotel. The inconvenience to a member who does not obtain one of the prereserved rooms is valued at $7 (this is in addition to the higher room cost). How many rooms should ORSA reserve? Hint: Although ORSA, as an organization, does not profit, one can think of the collective benefits received by the members as profit.

11. In Section 8.12, a method was given for evaluating $B(r)$ when lead-time demand is normally distributed. Derive a method for evaluating $B(r)$ when lead-time demand is Poisson distributed, using tables of the complementary cumulative Poisson distribution.

12. Determine Q, r, and EAC (optimal order size, reorder point, and expected cost per year) under the assumptions:

   a. Deterministic demand at the rate 2000 per year; lead time is $\frac{1}{10}$ year; and no back orders are permitted.

   b. Same, but back orders are permitted, with penalty cost of $160 per back order (independent of time, as in Problem 6).

   c. Probabilistic demand; Normally distributed (mean = 200, standard deviation = 40) during fixed lead time of $\frac{1}{10}$ year (so mean annual demand is 2000); back orders permitted with penalty cost of $160 per back order.

   d. Same as part c but back orders not permitted; lost sales penalty is $160 per lost sale. In each case, the holding cost is $16 per item per year, and the ordering cost is $4000.

13. Solve for the optimal reorder point and order quantity using the data of the example in Section 8.12, but substituting for the lead-time demand distribution the data of Table 8.6. That is, find r and Q when lead-time demand is normal with $\mu = 800$ and $\sigma = 20$, then resolve with $\mu = 800$ and $\sigma = 102$. Substitute the optimal values into the cost function to contrast the cost of fixed versus random lead time.

CHAPTER 9
SIMULATION

I. BASIC CONCEPTS

9.1 INTRODUCTION

Simulation analysis is a natural and logical extension to the analytical and mathematical models inherent in operations research. The previous eight chapters of this text have been concerned with formulating decision models which not only closely approximate the real-world environment, but also produce answers through standard numerical and/or mathematical manipulations of the resulting equations. It is evident that there are many situations which cannot be represented mathematically due to the stochastic nature of the problem, the complexity of problem formulation, or the interactions needed to adequately describe the problem under study. For many situations defying mathematical formulation, simulation is the only tool that might be used to obtain relevant answers.

The word simulation has been used rather loosely in the preceding discussion, so before we proceed it will be necessary to develop a working definition of this term. The following definition has been adopted from Naylor et al. (41).

Simulation is a numerical technique for conducting experiments on a digital computer, which involves certain types of mathematical and logical relationships necessary to describe the behavior and structure of a complex real-world system over extended periods of time.

Simulation has often been described as the process of creating the essence of reality without ever actually attaining that reality itself. Within the context of this chapter, simulation will involve the construction, experimentation, and manipulation of a complex model on a digital or analog computer. For the sake of discussion purposes, the techniques described in this chapter are directly applicable to a high-speed digital computer, although they certainly will not be restricted to this mode of operation.

Although simulation is often viewed as a "method of last resort," often to be employed when all else fails, recent advances in simulation methodologies, software availability, and technical developments have made simulation one of the most widely used and accepted tools in systems analysis and operations research. In addition to the reasons previously stated, Naylor (57) has suggested that simulation analysis might be appropriate for the following reasons.

1. Simulation makes it possible to study and experiment with the complex internal interactions of a given system whether it be a firm, an industry, an economy, or some subsystem of one of them.
2. Through simulation, one can study the effects of certain informational, organizational, and environmental changes on the operation of a system by making alterations in the model of the system and by observing the effects of these alterations on the system's behavior.
3. A detailed observation of the system being simulated may lead to a better understanding of the system and to suggestions for improving it, which otherwise would be unobtainable.
4. Simulation can be used as a pedagogical device for teaching both students and practitioners basic skills in theoretical analysis, statistical analysis, and decision making.
5. The experience of designing a computer simulation model may be more valuable than the actual simulation itself. The knowledge obtained in designing a simulation study frequently suggests changes in the system being simulated. The effects of these changes can then be tested via simulation before implementing them on the actual system.
6. Simulation of complex systems can yield valuable insight into which variables are more important than others in the system and how these variables interact.
7. Simulation can be used to experiment with new situations about which we have little or no information, so as to prepare for what may happen.
8. Simulation can serve as a "preservice test" to try out new policies and decision rules for operating a system, before running the risk of experimenting on the real system.
9. For certain types of stochastic problems the sequence of events may be of particular importance. Information about expected values and moments may not be sufficient to describe the process. In these cases, simulation methods may be the only satisfactory way of providing the required information.
10. Monte Carlo simulations can be performed to verify analytical solutions.
11. Simulation enables one to study dynamic systems in either real time, compressed time, or expanded time.
12. When new elements are introduced into a system, simulation can be used to anticipate bottlenecks and other problems that may arise in the behavior of the system.

Simulation analysis always begins with a representation of the system which needs to be studied. In digital computer simulation this step is accomplished through the construction of a computer program which "describes" the system under study to the appropriate computer configuration. This representation might be in the form of a FORTRAN program, graphical interactive displays, or a complex simulation language. Once this step has been completed, the model of the system is acted upon and the results of these actions are observed over long simulated periods of time. In essence, the experimenter is acting upon the created model rather than the actual system itself. Although simulation analysis is usually performed via high speed computer, such a representation is not always needed to study complex problems in operations research. Examples 9.1 and 9.2 in this chapter clearly illustrate this premise through two "hand" simulations. Regardless of the mode used to perform simulation analysis, a great deal of experience is desirable in order to adequately exploit the real powers of simulation. This background is often best gained through modeling experience, enabling a simulation analyst to create unique skills in this area. For this reason, simulation modeling is often more of an "art" than a science. This art is best cultivated rather than taught, although the basic tools and modeling logic can be gained through diligent study of simulation methodologies.

9.2   THE PHILOSOPHY, DEVELOPMENT, AND IMPLEMENTATION OF SIMULATION MODELING

Simulation is one of the easiest tools of management science to use, but probably one of the hardest to apply properly and perhaps the most difficult from which to draw accurate conclusions. With the widespread installation of digital computers, simulation is readily available to most managers and engineers engaged in operations research activities. With a reasonably knowledgeable programmer, a general purpose simulation language like GASP IV (45) (which costs less than $200 for the manual and master deck of cards), and a FORTRAN compiler, the manager is ready to attack complex problems with digital simulation. However the skills required to develop and operate an *effective* simulation model are substantial. The variability or dispersion of simulation results is a significant problem in itself and may require long and complex simulation analysis in order to draw meaningful conclusions from the simulation.

Regardless of these drawbacks, simulation is a useful technique and one that is particularly appropriate for complex operations research and systems analysis. Many of the recent textbooks on simulation give example applications of simulation to a wide variety of operational types of problems. [See Chorafas (6), Emshoff and Sisson (8), Martin (35), Meier, Newell, and Pazer (38) and Pritsker and Kiviat (44), for examples.]

It is the purpose of this chapter to examine the process of simulation and the necessary tools to perform such analysis. A special emphasis will be placed upon the problems associated with the mechanics of simulation modeling itself.

The Simulation Process

It is appropriate to examine the entire process by which simulation analysis is planned and performed. Design of the simulation model itself is a critical portion of any study, but not the only one with which the user must be concerned. The activities shown in Figs. 9.1, 9.2, and 9.3 are the major ones in any simulation study. Figure 9.1 covers the presimulation tasks while Figs. 9.2 and 9.3 are the actual simulation activities, broken down into design and operational groups of activities.

Presimulation Activities

In any general view of situations in which systems simulation is used, the first activity is a recognition of the problem. This recognition leads directly to the study and analysis of the system itself and culminates in the establishment of an objective directed toward solving the problem. Typical objectives could be categorized as follows:

Characterization of System Performance
- Selection of operation parameters for an existing system
- Selection of operation parameters for a proposed system
- Exploration of System Behavior
Modification of an existing system
Design of a new system

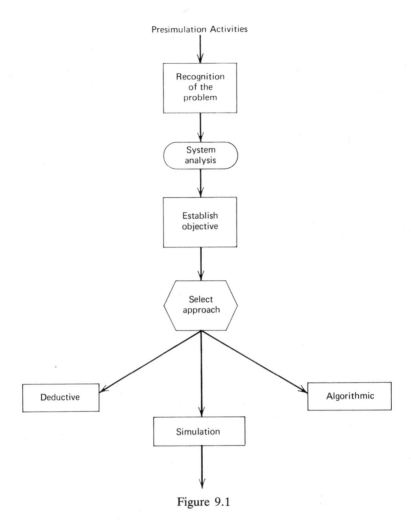

Figure 9.1

At this stage in the process, the user must evaluate the different tools or techniques available to him relative to his objective and the system with which he is dealing. If the problem is one of establishing optimal parameters and the system fits or can be made to fit one of the available techniques previously discussed in this text, then this is obviously the most appropriate technique to use. The user could also develop his own mathematical model if none of the textbook methods apply to his problem. These models are generally developed along two main lines of thought; *deductive* models and *algorithmic* models. Economic order quantities (EOQ) in inventory control techniques are examples of deductive solution methods. Algorithmic techniques are inductive, iterative techniques for developing numerical solutions to specific problems. Linear programming is an example of a technique in which an algorithm, usually the simplex algorithm, leads to an optimal solution. If the problem is inherently an optimization problem, and can be cast in a framework for which there is such an algorithm, then that approach might be preferred over simulation. Still another alternative is to experiment with the operating system itself. There are techniques, such as evolutionary operation (EVOP) which provide a means of systematically evaluating changes in the operating parameters of the

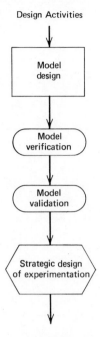

Figure 9.2

system. This approach should be appropriate in dealing with systems that are highly responsive to parameter changes.

Simulation is the appropriate technique where it is not feasible to experiment on the system itself or where direct analytic techniques are not available. In the first case, it may be too expensive to experiment with the existing system. Such experimentation might change the operating characteristics of the system itself, and thus the risk that such experimentation might harm the system's performance is so great that the possibility is discarded. It is also possible that the system is just not available for experimentation. Alternatively, if the problem is to design an inventory control system for a planned facility, the system does not even exist prior to the time it is needed. In the second case, the complexity of many production systems precludes the application of analytic techniques, either deductive or algorithmic. If the system contains many stochastic elements of a complex nature, the resulting model probably resists analytic treatment. The two situations just discussed, where experimentation on the real-world system is not possible and where appropriate analytical techniques are not available, are the general *raison d'etre* behind any simulation study. This rationale suggests the following definition of simulation:

A technique of problem solving based upon experimentation performed on a model of the real-world system.

Developmental Activities

The first developmental activity is the *design and implementation* of the simulation model. The specific tasks in this activity will not be discussed in detail in the remaining sections of this chapter. However, an excellent discussion of this phase is found in many simulation textbooks [Emshoff and Sisson (8), Meier et al. (38), and Naylor et al. (41)]. Assuming for the time

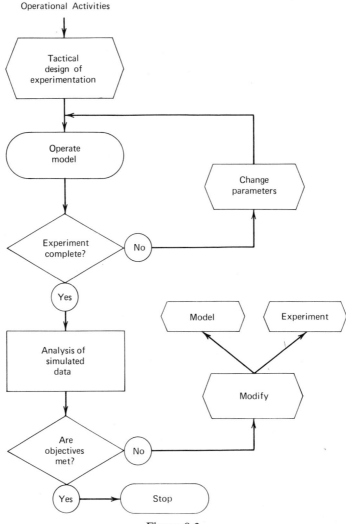

Figure 9.3

being that these tasks are completed, the next activity is *verification* of the model. A verified model is one that has been proven to behave as its designer intended. This is an important activity in that without satisfactory and explicit verification, it is possible to have a model that appears to work satisfactorily but which gives answers that are actually erroneous. Fishman and Kiviat (9) suggest techniques for verification, including statistical methods, that go far beyond the usual practices of simple comparative analysis and manual checking of calculations.

Fishman and Kiviat (9) also describe methods of *model validation*. Validation is one of the most critical activities performed in any simulation study. It is also one of the most difficult to accomplish satisfactorily. A validated model is one that has been proven to be a reasonable abstraction of the real-world system it is intended to represent. The usual approach to validation is to run the model with historical data and compare model results with actual system results for the same historical period. Such comparisons usually are not valid because of the fact that the model may be experimental or predictive in nature. It is also difficult to make a statistical comparison of results in many situations where such a comparison is appropriate, because of the requirement that equilibrium be reached before results are measured. It may take considerable time to reach equilibrium with the computer simulation model while the real-world system might never exist in a state of equilibrium—thereby severely complicating the comparison. Additional suggestions on validation techniques are provided by Van Horn's chapter in Naylor (57).

Strategic design refers to the activity of designing and planning the experimentation to be done with the simulation model and is the next activity. It includes specification of information to be determined and the accuracy of that information. The two classes of experimentation, as in the establishment of an objective, deal with exploration of system behavior and/or optimization of system parameters. Exploration of system behavior is undertaken in an attempt to explain the relationship between results and the controllable parameters of the simulation. Optimization is performed to find the combination of parameter levels which minimize or maximize the results of the simulation. Experimental designs, like full factorial, fractional factorial, etc., are appropriate for exploration experimentation. For optimization, optimum seeking techniques are available, and though in many cases they cannot guarantee a global optimum, they can give good practical results. The article by Hunter and Naylor (22) is a particularly good outline of experimental design for simulation studies, while Schmidt and Taylor (49) have a good discussion on simulation optimization techniques.

Operational Activities

At this stage in the simulation process the model has been designed, implemented, studied, and its use has been planned. The remaining activities are to carry out the actual simulation experimentation. This must include tactical design of the experiments that are to be performed as the first activity. Conway (7) describes this activity as determining how many simulation runs are to be executed and how data are to be collected from each run. This includes establishing initial conditions for variables in the model and estimating parameters so that the simulated system will reach a state of equilibrium as soon as possible. The user must also determine how equilibrium will be recognized so that data can be gathered without being biased by transients from start up of the run. Other considerations are the sample size required for the data to be gathered and the techniques to be used to compare alternative systems if this is the study objective. In this latter case, the user will be interested in relative results from the simulation runs. He can apply methods such as using the same sequence of random numbers for each run, which will reduce the residual variation between sets of results and thus will permit a reduction in length of the simulation runs themselves.

The simulation runs themselves can be represented as a loop, as shown in Fig. 9.3. In this loop, the model is run for the specific time, parameters changed, and the model run again. This is repeated until the specific experimentation has been completed. This is followed by an analysis activity in which the simulated data are processed and statistics are developed. Techniques such as regression analysis and analysis of variance are widely used methods of interpreting these data in respect of the original objective.

If the objective has been met, the simulation study is completed at this point. However, because simulation is a trial-and-error process, it will often be that the objective has not been satisfied, which leaves two general alternatives available. The first is to modify the model so that it will facilitate discrimination among simulated systems and then to rerun the experiment. The second alternative is to use the original model but to alter the design of the experimentation, using new search techniques or more powerful experimental designs.

9.3 DESIGN OF SIMULATION MODELS

A well-designed model is a key to meaningful simulation results. If the model builder overlooks the requisites of simulation that have previously been discussed, the simulation study may fall far short of accomplishing its objectives, or may indicate a false achievement when there is none. Likewise, if the model fails to take into consideration the important aspects of the real-world system, then the model cannot be validated. If such a model is used without validation, predictions of system behavior based on the model may be erroneous. The discussion of model design presented here will consider two groupings of design consideration: simulation technique related design considerations and practical restrictions due to computer software availability.

Simulation Related Considerations

The topics under this heading are generally given rather complete coverage in texts on simulation. Also, there may not be a design consideration if the user employs one of the generally available simulation languages. Each will be subsequently discussed in this chapter. The topics are:

> Time control
> Random number generation
> Stochastic variate generation
> Variance reduction techniques
> Simulation languages

Time control is generally divided into two classes, though Nance (58) advances the idea of a continuous time flow mechanism. The two typical types are *uniform time flow* and *variable time flow*. With uniform time flow, the model is advanced and processed through each and every time period simulated at fixed steps or intervals. Variable, or next-event, time-flow mechanism causes time to be incremented between only those periods that have events occurring. The model is processed only at these times and performance figures adjusted to account for the periods skipped. If the system has events that occur very frequently and with predescribed regularity (as in forecasting), then uniform time flow might be the best choice. However, if the events are irregular, then the time periods skipped will reduce computer running time and justify the additional programming generally required for variable time flow.

Simulation is a useful tool because of its ability to handle complex systems that require the modeling of interacting stochastic variates. These are the means for modeling empirical or theoretical distributions of real-world parameters. Stochastic treatment of relevant events greatly increases the realism and applicability of the simulation model. These stochastic variates are generated by manipulation of pseudorandom numbers calculated by the computer. Most computer facilities include such a generator in their software libraries, or can easily develop one. However, both random-number generation and stochastic-variate generation will be discussed in some detail as they are fundamental to any simulation analysis. Variance reduction methods, the next of the technique related topics, will not be discussed in any detail, even though this can be an important means of reducing the time and cost of using simulation. These methods are generally applied to the scheme in which the simulation model utilizes random numbers. The result is that the variance of response variables is reduced substantially which can be used as a basis for reducing the number of iterations required for developing results at the desired level of confidence.

The topics already discussed are often to some degree dependent on the simulation language chosen for the study. If a simulation language is utilized, the time-flow mechanism is already specified within the confines of the language, and often methods of random-number generation and stochastic-variate generation. Some of the general-purpose simulation languages being used today include the following:

> SIMSCRIPT 2.5
> GASP II/IV
> DYNAMO
> GPSS III
> SIMULA
> SOL

Many of the simulation textbooks contain detailed comparisons of the languages that can be helpful in selecting one to use. A brief discussion of simulation languages can be found in Section 9.18.

Conclusions

Simulation is a useful and appropriate management science technique for use in the analysis of complex problems. The technique permits the testing and evaluation of current, proposed, or conceptualized systems without risk to current system performance or need for real-world experimentation. It also permits the study of complex problems where direct analytic solution is not possible. Simulation is also an easy technique in which to develop proficiency, although it often requires a wide range of skills. The remainder of this chapter will be devoted to the task of developing these skills.

II. EXAMPLES OF SIMULATION MODELING

9.4 SALES OF LIFE INSURANCE

In order to illustrate the fundamental concepts in simulation analysis, consider the following illustrative example. Suppose that Joe Cool is working for the Cosmic Life Insurance Company. Cosmic Life sells insurance on a door-to-door basis, and has kept accurate records on their past sales history. Based on previous sales, there is a 50% chance that when Joe Cool makes a house call the resident will not be interested in purchasing a life insurance policy. In other words, approximately 50% of the time the resident will be willing to enter into further discussions regarding policy protection. However, this is not a guarantee of future sales. Even though Joe Cool is allowed the opportunity to discuss Cosmic policies, $\frac{1}{2}$ of the time the visit will result in a "no sale," $\frac{1}{3}$ of the time in the sale of a $10,000 life insurance policy, and $\frac{1}{6}$ of the time in the sale of a

$20,000 policy. Using a simulated sample of 20 household visits, determine the probability that a sale will be made at each house and the "expected" policy value for each policy holder assuming a sale is made.

In order to simulate the behavior of a salesman, two events must be defined probabilistically. The first event is an *interest* or *no interest* event at the door. The second event is a *dollar value* sale given that entrance to the house is granted. In order to simulate these events, suppose that we choose a sequence of 20 visits. At each visit, the outcome of the first event must be determined in such a way as to obey the rule established for interest/no interest. Since this is an event with two discrete outcomes, each with a probability of occurence equal to 0.50, a coin flip will be used to determine the outcome. If a *head* occurs, the salesman is allowed to further discuss the policies. If a *tail* occurs, he will proceed to the next customer. The following information is only relevant if the flip is a head. If interest is indicated by a prospective customer, subsequent discussions will result in one of three outcomes: (1) no sale, (2) sale of a $10,000 policy, or (3) sale of a $20,000 policy. Since there are three possible outcomes, a fair die will be rolled in order to randomly choose the appropriate result. Define "no sale" to occur if a 1, 2, or 3 appears on the die; "$10,000 sale" if a 4 or 5 appears, and "$20,000 sale" if a 6 appears. Note that the probability of these respective outcomes are 1/2, 1/3, and 1/6, respectively, which obey the sale probabilities previously defined. The results of twenty visits are given in Table 9.1.

From Table 9.1, 13 of the visits resulted in a "no sale." Hence P_r(no sale) $= 13/20 = 0.65$. In addition, there were four $10,000 policies sold and

Table 9.1
SIMULATION OF 20 INSURANCE CALLS.

Trial	Flip	Interest	No Interest	Roll	$ Value 0	$ Value 10	$ Value 20	Value
1	H	X		4		X		10,000
2	H	X		4		X		10,000
3	T		X					0
4	H	X		1	X			0
5	H	X		2	X			0
6	T		X					0
7	H	X		3	X			0
8	H	X		6			X	20,000
9	T		X					0
10	T		X					0
11	H	X		2	X			0
12	T		X					0
13	H	X		3	X			0
14	T		X					0
15	H	X		6			X	20,000
16	H	X		4		X		10,000
17	H	X		2	X			0
18	H	X		4		X	X	10,000
19	T		X					0
20	H	X		6			X	20,000

Table 9.2
COMPARISON OF SIMULATED AND THEORETICAL RESULTS.

			Given a Sale:		
	Probability of No Sale	Probability of Sale	Probability of $10.000	Probability of $20.000	Expected Value of Policy
Simulated	0.65	0.35	0.5714	0.4286	$14,286
Theoretical	0.75	0.25	0.667	0.333	$13,333

three $20,000 policies sold. Therefore, given that a policy is sold, there is a 57.14% chance that it will be a $10,000 policy and a 42.86% chance that it will be a $20,000 policy. Hence, the expected value of a policy given that a policy is sold is estimated as $E(V) = 0.5714(\$10,000) + 0.4286(\$20,000) = \$14,286$. Because of the simplicity of this illustrative problem, these results can be compared to the theoretical results. This comparison is made in Table 9.2.

Table 9.2 reveals that the simulated results agree favorably with the theoretical calculations. A moments reflection will reveal the source of the disagreement, that is, the period over which the results were calculated. It is intuitively clear that the number of visits simulated (20) could drastically effect the results, since the procedure actually relies on probabilistic sampling of stochastic events. Viewed as a sampling procedure, the more samples that are taken the more accurate are the desired results. In general, the interaction of several events might necessitate a large number of trials. It is also clear that extensive bookkeeping procedures might be needed if complex situations are to be simulated. In addition, a great number of "random deviates" might be required for complex event simulations over long periods of time.

In this example, the probabilistic nature of simulation modeling was illustrated, and due to the specialized structure of the (discrete) probability density functions used to describe the problem a simple coin flip and a single die were used to generate a random sequence of events. The following example will serve to illustrate the same procedure in an example too complex to represent in this fashion.

9.5 PRODUCTION LINE MAINTENANCE [Schmidt (59)]

Five production lines are to be maintained by one repair crew. When one of the lines fails it is repaired unless the repair crew is occupied on another line, in which case it must wait for service. The repair crew services the lines in the order in which they fail. The production system operates three shifts per day, 5 days per week.

The time elapsed between start-up of a line and its failure has been observed to vary from one run to another in an unpredictable or random manner. Similar variation has been observed for the time to repair a line when it fails. The observed frequency distribution of failure and service times for line number 1 are given in Table 9.3 and graphically in Figs. 9.4 and 9.5. This data is based on an observation period of 20 weeks. Data of a similar nature were collected on the remaining four lines during the same period but in

Table 9.3

**FREQUENCY DISTRIBUTION OF FAILURE AND SER-
VICE TIMES**

Failure Time		Service Time	
Time Interval (weeks)	Observed Frequency	Time Interval (weeks)	Observed Frequency
0.00–0.02	35	0.000–0.002	35
0.02–0.04	20	0.002–0.004	23
0.04–0.06	16	0.004–0.006	28
0.06–0.08	20	0.006–0.008	13
0.08–0.10	17	0.008–0.010	16
0.10–0.12	16	0.010–0.012	13
0.12–0.14	8	0.012–0.014	6
0.14–0.16	6	0.014–0.016	11
0.16–0.18	5	0.016–0.018	3
0.18–0.20	2	0.018–0.020	3
0.20–0.22	5	0.020–0.022	5
0.22–0.24	8	0.022–0.024	4
0.24–0.26	3	0.024–0.026	1
0.26–0.28	5	0.026–0.028	3
0.28–0.30	1	0.028–0.030	2
0.30–0.32	1	0.030–0.032	2
0.32–0.34	1	0.032–0.034	2
0.34–0.36	1	0.034–0.036	2
0.36–0.38	1	0.036–0.044	0
0.38–0.40	0	0.044–0.046	1
0.40–0.42	2	0.046–0.074	0
0.42–0.44	0	0.074–0.076	1
0.44–0.46	1		
Total	174	Total	174

order to avoid unnecessary complications in the model development they will not be presented.

In this system, once the times of failure and repair are known the status of all of the lines and the repair crew can be determined. Therefore, if the analyst can predict these times in some manner he can write a computer simulation program that will reproduce the characteristics of the system. Failure time and service time are random variables and cannot be predicted with certainty, however, and the simulation analyst therefore attempts to generate these times in a manner which will reproduce the variability observed in the past on the assumption that similar variability can be anticipated in the future. However this does not imply that behavior realized in the past will be reproduced identically in the future. The latter point is important. Twenty-week's data has been collected on the system considered here. If the system were observed for an additional 20 weeks one would not expect an identical repetition of the first 20 weeks. Assuming that the system does not change radically from the first 20 weeks to the second, however, one would expect to find similar distributions of service and failure times for the two periods. That is, one would not expect

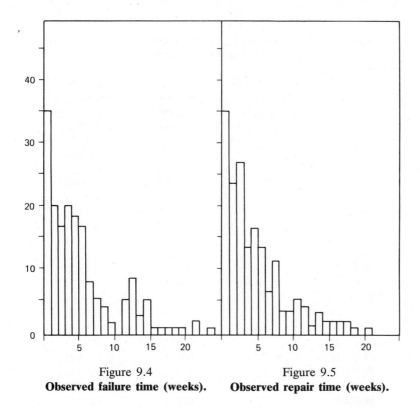

Figure 9.4
Observed failure time (weeks).

Figure 9.5
Observed repair time (weeks).

radical departures from Figs. 9.4 and 9.5 for the second 20 weeks. Therefore, for this problem the analyst would attempt to reproduce the variability of service time and failure time without reproducing identical values of these variables.

The variability of a random variable is generally represented by a *frequency distribution* such as those given in Table 9.3 and Figs. 9.4 and 9.5 or a relative frequency distribution. A relative frequency distribution is the same as a frequency distribution except that the frequency counts in each interval or category are divided by the total number of observations.

An elaboration of the methods for generating random variables will be discussed later in this chapter. The essential characteristic of a realistic random variable generator is that it will reproduce the variability observed in the random variable studied.

The first step in developing a random variable or process generator is calculation of the *cumulative distribution function* of the random variable. Assume that the range of values for the random variable has been broken into n intervals and that f_i is the frequency count for the ith interval. Then the cumulative frequency up to and including the jth interval, F_j, is given by;

$$F_j = \frac{1}{n} \sum_{i=1}^{j} f_i$$

To illustrate, calculation of the cumulative frequency distribution is summarized in Table 9.4 for the service-time data given in Table 9.3.

The next step in generating a random variable is to select or generate a random number. A random number will be defined as a random variable that is

Table 9.4
**DEVELOPMENT OF THE RELATIVE CUMULATIVE DISTRIBU-
TION OF SERVICE TIME.**

Time Interval (Weeks)	Observed Frequency Distribution	Relative Frequency Distribution	Relative Cumulative Frequency Distribution
0.000–0.002	35	0.2011	0.2011
0.002–0.004	23	0.1322	0.3333
0.004–0.006	28	0.1609	0.4942
0.006–0.008	13	0.0747	0.5689
0.008–0.010	16	0.0920	0.6609
0.010–0.012	13	0.0747	0.7356
0.012–0.014	6	0.0345	0.7701
0.014–0.016	11	0.0632	0.8333
0.016–0.018	3	0.0173	0.8506
0.018–0.020	3	0.0173	0.8679
0.020–0.022	5	0.0287	0.8966
0.022–0.024	4	0.0230	0.9196
0.024–0.026	1	0.0057	0.9253
0.026–0.028	3	0.0173	0.9426
0.028–0.030	2	0.0115	0.9541
0.030–0.032	2	0.0115	0.9656
0.032–0.034	2	0.0115	0.9771
0.034–0.036	2	0.0115	0.9886
0.036–0.044	0	0.0000	0.9886
0.044–0.046	1	0.0057	0.9943
0.046–0.074	0	0.0000	0.9943
0.074–0.076	1	0.0057	1.0000

uniformly distributed over the interval 0 to 1. That is, each number between 0 and 1 has an equal and independent chance of occurring. Let RN be the random number selected and let x_i be the upper limit of the ith interval. If

$$F_{i-1} < RN \leq F_i$$

then the value of the random variable will be defined (arbitrarily) as x_i.

In summary, random times to failure and line repair times can be generated through the use of the cumulative distribution functions associated with these random events. Random deviates are obtained through the use of *random numbers* distributed uniformly on the interval 0–1. Generation of random numbers is discussed in great detail in Section 9.3. For the present time, assume that an ample supply of these random numbers is available for use.

Returning to the illustration in Table 9.4, if the random numbers, RN, are uniformly distributed between 0 and 1, then we would expect 20.11% of these numbers to be less than 0.2011 and 20.11% of the service times generated would have a value of 0.002. We would expect 13.22% of the random numbers to fall between 0.2011 and 0.3333 leading to a value of service time of 0.004. Continuing in this manner, it is readily seen that the generative process given here will lead, in the long run, to proportions of times in each interval which correspond to the proportions observed. Although the use of the upper bound for each interval will create a slight bias with regard to the continuous time scale, this is used only for illustrative purposes and could be corrected through a continuous approximation.

To illustrate the simulation of this system, a 5.5 hour period beginning at midnight will be simulated. The logic of the simulation model is summarized in Fig. 9.6. The first step is to generate the time of the first failure for each line. These times are given as follows:

$$
\begin{aligned}
\text{First failure, line } 1 &= \quad 2\!:\!17 \\
\text{First failure, line } 2 &= \quad 4\!:\!12 \\
\text{First failure, line } 3 &= 10\!:\!24 \\
\text{First failure, line } 4 &= \quad 3\!:\!08 \\
\text{First failure, line } 5 &= \quad 3\!:\!21
\end{aligned}
$$

The first event which alters the operating status of the system is a failure on the first line at 2:17. As defined above, a repair of line one should commence. Therefore a service time for line 1 is generated and is 27 minutes. This creates the next status-changing event which occurs at 2:44. Since the line will fail again, a new failure time is generated for line 1 and is 30 hours and 15 minutes. Therefore line 1 fails again at 8:59 the next day.

The next event is a failure of line 4 at 3:08. Since no other lines are already down, a service time for line 4 is generated and is 32 minutes. Thus line 4 is up again at 3:40. Before line 4 is repaired, line 5 fails at 3:21 and is the next status-changing event. However, since the repair crew is busy on line 4, line 5 must wait for service. The next event is the repair of line 4 at 3:40, at which time repairs commence on line 5. Placing line 4 in service requires generation of its next failure time and is 31 hours 12 minutes, or at 10:52 the next day. Repair time for line 5 is 22 minutes and repairs are completed at 4:02 and is the next event. At 4:02 a new failure time is generated for line 5 and is 5 minutes or occurs at 4:07. Since all lines are operating at 4:02, the next status-changing event is a line failure. The next line to fail is 5 at 4:07. Repairs for line 5 commence at 4:07 since no other lines are down at this time. Repair time on line 5 is generated and is 18 minutes; line 5 going into operation again at 4:25. The next event which occurs is a failure of line 2 at 4:12. Since the repair crew will be occupied on line 5 until 4:25, line 2 must wait for repairs until this time. The next event in the simulation is a repair of line 5 at 4:25 requiring generation of a new failure time for line 5 and a service time for line 2 since repairs for line 2 start upon completion of repairs for line 5. Generated failure time for line 5 is 58 minutes and service time for line 2 is 19 minutes. Therefore line 2 starts operating at 4:44. At 4.44 a new failure is generated for line 2, is 9 minutes, occurs at 4:53, and is the next event. Service on line 2 starts at 4:53 since line 2 is the only line down at that time. Generated service time for line 2 is 83 minutes. Therefore line 2 is placed in operation at 6:16. At 5:23 line 5 fails but must wait for service since the repair crew is occupied on line 2 at this time.

The above sequence of events is summarized in Table 9.5.

Although an extensive simulation analysis of this system by hand could become tedious if continued for long periods of study, using Fig. 9.6 and the given data a computer program is easily constructed and extended analysis can be conducted. A computer program was utilized for this particular example,

Table 9.5
FIVE AND ONE-HALF-HOUR PERIOD OF SIMULATION FOR FIVE PRODUCTION LINES

Time of change in system Status hr. (min)	Event altering system Status	Status					Crew	Lines Down	Cumulative Time Repair (min)	Waiting (min)
		Line 1	Line 2	Line 3	Line 4	Line 5				
Midnight	None	Operating	Operating	Operating	Operating	Operating	Idle	0	0	0
2:17	Line 1 fails	Down (In service)					Line 1	1	0	0
2:44	Line 1 repaired	Operating					Idle	0	27	0
3:08	Line 4 fails				Down (In service)		Line 4	1	27	0
3:21	Line 5 fails					Down (Waiting)	Line 4	2	40	0
3:40	Line 4 repaired				Operating	Down (In service)	Line 5	1	59	19
4:02	Line 5 repaired					Operating	Idle	0	81	19
4:07	Line 5 fails					Down (In service)	Line 5	1	81	19
4:12	Line 2 fails		Down (Waiting)				Line 5	2	86	19
4:25	Line 5 repaired		Down (In service)			Operating	Line 2	1	99	32
4:44	Line 2 repaired		Operating				Idle	0	118	32
4:53	Line 2 fails		Down (In service)				Line 2	1	118	32
5:23	Line 5 fails					Down (Waiting)	Line 2	2	148	32

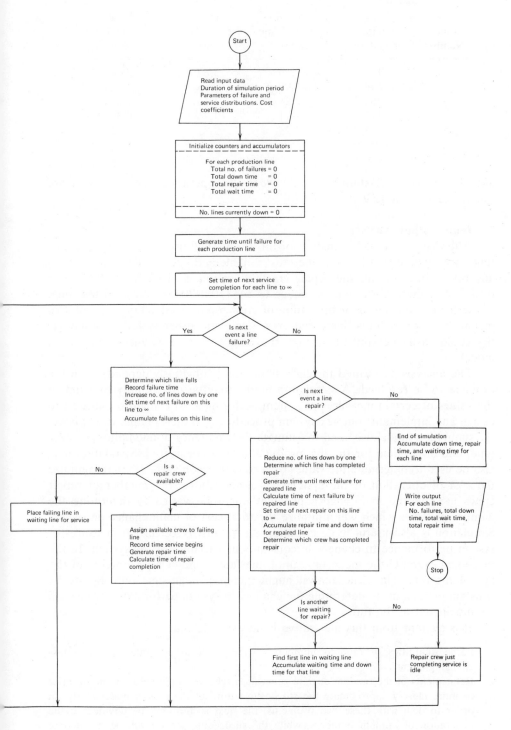

Figure 9.6
Flowchart for the maintenance simulator.

Table 9.6
RESULTS OF 20 WEEKS SIMULATION OF FIVE PRODUCTION LINES

Line Number	Number of Failures	Total Down Time (weeks)	Total Repair Time (weeks)	Total Waiting Time (weeks)
1	177	2.46	1.82	0.64
2	694	5.90	3.58	2.32
3	354	2.84	1.16	1.70
4	115	2.11	1.76	0.35
5	1093	6.25	2.72	3.53

and the system was studied for 20 weeks of operation. These results are summarized in Table 9.6.

Input-output Analysis

Although an extensive analysis of this output will not be performed at this time, it is evident that line 4 is the most reliable and line 5 is down more than any other. In addition, the repair crew utilization is given by $11.04/20.0 = 0.552$ while there are repairs in queue $(8.54)(100)/20.0 = 42.7\%$ of the time. These figures indicate poor utilization of crew repair availability. Preventative maintenance procedures, increased crew sizes, and other system characteristics could easily be studied through the use of a more extensive simulation model.

The analysis performed through simulation is obviously dependent on the problem to be resolved. A simulation model may be used simply to estimate the values of certain measures of system performance, or might be utilized to design and implement complex system procedures. In the example cited above, the simulation model was used to estimate the frequency of line failure, waiting time, and down time for the five production lines considered. Simulation may also be used to determine the values of certain decision variables that minimize the cost of operation of the system. As noted above, the number of repair crews used in the maintenance problem might be varied to determine the number of crews which will minimize the total cost of maintenance per week. Simulation is also useful in determining the sensitivity of certain measures of system performance to changes in constants or variables of the system. In the preceding example the mean time until line failure might be a function of the age of the line. Thus, the analyst might increase mean time until failure by constant increments to determine the changes in system performance which can be anticipated in the future.

It is evident from this illustrative hand example that:

1. Large quantities of random numbers are required to generate system status-changing events.
2. Refinements of the random deviate generation scheme would be desirable in order to more closely approximate the stochastic nature of the system under study. In order to deal with these two problems, the next section will be devoted to the generation of random numbers, while the succeeding section will be devoted to advanced techniques useful in generating a wide variety of random deviates.

III. PSEUDORANDOM NUMBERS

9.6 GENERATION OF RANDOM DEVIATES

In nearly all simulation experiments there exists a need for generating random statistical deviates from a certain distribution. The distribution will be the one that adequately describes and represents the physical process involved at that point in the experiment. During an actual simulation experiment, this process of generating a random deviate from a particular distribution may have to be done many times for many distributions, depending on the complexity of the model being investigated by the experiment.

This section will be concerned with the techniques of generating the required statistical deviates on a digital computer.

The general process for generating a random deviate from a specific distribution will nearly always follow this pattern:

1. Generate a random number from the uniform distribution.
2. Perform a mathematical transformation of the uniform random number or numbers which produces a random deviate from the desired distribution.
3. Use the transformed deviate in the experiment as required.

These three steps are then repeated many times for the chosen distribution (and other distributions as required) as the experiment proceeds in time. Of course, it should be realized that at times the simulation model will require variates directly from the random-number generator, in which case step 2 will not be necessary.

Since the generation of a random number is the beginning for the generation of deviates from the more complicated distributions, the uniform distribution on the interval $[0, 1]$ will be discussed first and then followed by discussions of (1) the techniques for transforming the uniform variate into a variate from a more complicated distribution, and (2) the more complicated distributions themselves.

9.7 THE UNIFORM DISTRIBUTION AND ITS IMPORTANCE TO SIMULATION

The uniform distribution over the interval $[0, 1]$ is given by:

$$f(x_0) = 1 \qquad \text{for } 0 \leq x_0 \leq 1 \qquad (9.1)$$

$$F(x_0) = x_0 \qquad \text{for } 0 \leq x_0 \leq 1 \qquad (9.2)$$

where the probability density function $f(x_0) = \text{probability } (x = x_0)$ and the cumulative distribution function $F(x_0) = \text{probability } (x \leq x_0)$. The uniform distribution will be used as described above in deriving statistical generators for other probability distributions throughout this chapter. The term *uniform distribution* will refer to the above distribution over the interval $[0, 1]$, and uniform random numbers or uniform random variates will refer to numbers generated from a uniform distribution over this range. Uniform deviates over a general range are easily generated through a scale transformation.

The probability density function (Fig. 9.7) and the cumulative distribution function (Fig. 9.8) are shown on p. 378.

The imporazance of the uniform distribution stems from its use as the foundation in generating random deviates (variates) from more complicated distributions required in simulation experiments. As a simulation experiment

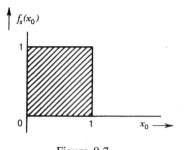

Figure 9.7
Uniform density function.

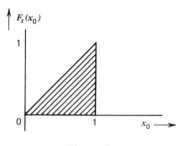

Figure 9.8
Uniform distribution function.

proceeds in time, uniformly distributed random numbers are repeatedly being generated, giving rise to various combinatorial operations on these deviates to produce random variates from any other statistical distribution required by the simulation.

Tocher (13) has suggested three modes of providing uniform random numbers on digital computers. These include (1) external provision, (2) internal generation by a random physical process, and (3) internal generation of sequences of digits by a recursive equation. The first method involves the recording of random-number (47) tables (*Rand* Tables) on magnetic tape for input into a digital computer and then treat these random numbers as data for the problem of interest. A major objection to this method is the slow process of input to the machine. The second method uses an outside physical process whose random results can be read into the computer as a sequence of digits. Among the external processes which have been used are the random decay of radioactive material and thermal noise in an electric valve circuit. The major objections to this method are that the results are not reproducible and that the random physical processes may develop a defect in their randomness. The third alternative, and the one that is most acceptable for digital computer simulations involves the generation of "pseudorandom numbers" by an algorithmic-recursive-type equation. Being algorithmic and recursive indicates that the results of the previous calculations will be used in determining the next calculation. The ith term is used in a formula to calculate the $(i+1)$st term; the $(i+1)$st term is used to calculate the $(i+2)$nd term, and so on. Any series of numbers created by this method can never be truly random but for all practical purposes formulas have been developed which prove highly satisfactory. To determine whether or not a given sequence is satisfactory, various statistical tests have been designed to test the properties of the variates in question. These tests are discussed in some detail after a brief discussion of current and historical methods used to generate these sequences of uniform deviates.

9.8 GENERATION OF RANDOM NUMBERS

Producing a number by some algorithm takes away some of the randomness that it should possess. A truly "random" number or occurrence can be produced only by some physical phenomenon, such as white noise. For this reason, numbers produced by algorithms are correctly referred to as "pseudorandom numbers." Understanding this, pseudorandom numbers shall from this point be referred to as random numbers.

Properties of Uniformly Distributed Numbers

A random number generator should have the following properties:

1. The numbers generated should have as nearly as possible a uniform distribution.
2. The generator should be fast.
3. The generator program should not require large amounts of core.
4. The generator should have a long period (i.e., it should produce a large sequence of numbers before the sequence begins to cycle).
5. The generator should be able to produce a different set of random numbers or to reproduce a series of numbers.
6. The method should not degenerate to repeatedly produce a constant value.

Several methods will now be examined which have been developed to generate sequences of pseudorandom numbers. The first three methods (Midproduct, Fibonacci, and Midsquare) are of historical significance but have detrimental, limiting characteristics. The remaining three techniques are currently utilized in varying forms and represent the class of generators belonging to *congruential methods*.

Midsquare Technique

We select a four-digit integer seed to initialize the generator. Our first random number is obtained from the seed in the following manner: The seed is squared and all digits except the middle four are ignored. The result is then normalized to give the first random number; this number is subsequently used as the new seed. Pseudorandom numbers can be generated in this manner, each time using the previous random number as the new seed.

The Midsquare technique is seldom used today. The method has a tendency to degenerate rapidly. If the number zero is ever generated, all subsequent numbers generated will also have a zero value unless steps are provided to handle this case. Furthermore, the method is slow since many multiplications and divisions are required to access the middle digits in a fixed-word binary computer.

Midproduct Technique

This method is similar to the Midsquare technique except that a successive number is obtained by multiplying the current number by a constant, K, and taking the middle digits. The formula is

$$S_{n+1} = K(S_n)$$

The Midproduct technique has the following properties:

1. A longer period than the Midsquare technique
2. More uniformly distributed than the Midsquare technique
3. The method tends to degenerate

Fibonacci Method

This generator is based on the Fibonacci sequence and is represented by:

$$X_{n+1} = (X_n + X_{n-1}) \bmod m$$

The method usually produces a period of length greater than m; however, the pseudorandom numbers obtained by using the Fibonacci method fail to pass the tests for randomness. Consequently the method does not give satisfactory results.

9.9 THE LOGIC IN GENERATING UNIFORM RANDOM VARIATES VIA A CONGRUENTIAL METHOD

Congruential methods of random number generation can be explained in the following manner. Consider the following relation.

$$D = N(\mod T)$$

Consider any two real numbers N and D. If the difference between two numbers D and N is *evenly* divisible by an *integer*-valued number T, then one defines D to be *congruent* to N with modulus M.

For example consider the following relationship.

$$31 = 1(\mod 10)$$

By the equation, $D = 31$, $N = 1$, and $T = 10$. Note that the difference between D and N is evenly divisible by T. The meaning of the above equation can also be explained in the following manner. If the expression $\left[\frac{(D-N)}{M}\right]$ is an integer, then D is congruent to N with modulus M. In general there are many values of M which satisfy the above definition. In most cases one is interested in the largest value of M which satisfies this definition. Given values of N and T this is easily determined through the following equation:

$$D = N - \left(\frac{N}{M}\right)M \tag{9.3}$$

where: (N/M) is a *truncated* value. For example, suppose:

$$D = 15(\mod 4)$$

By Eq. 9.3, $D = 15 - (15/4)4 = 3$.

Previous methods of generating uniform variates (Midsquare method, Fibonacci, and modifications) have given way to the near exclusive use today of the congruential methods based on a relationship of the form

$$r_{i+1} = (ar_i + c)(\mod T) \tag{9.4}$$

This says that the sum $(ar_i + c)$ is to be divided by T, and r_{i+1} is set equal to the remainder, where r_{i+1} is the new uniform deviate and r_i is the previous uniform deviate.

Much work has been done with the congruential methods. They have been found to produce numbers which are more uniformly distributed than any other method used thus far. They also have longer periods and can be computed faster, in general, than other methods. Congruential sequences, however, ultimately begin to cycle.

Rules for Choosing the Constants

a should be an odd integer, not divisible by either 3 or 5.

c can usually be taken to be any constant desired. However, to assure good results, choose c so that $c \mod 8 = 5$ (for a binary computer) or so that $c \mod 200 = 21$ (for a decimal computer).

T should be large; it is usually taken as the word size of the computer for convenience.

According to Naylor et al. (11), the sequence obtained by this method will have a full period of T numbers if:

1. c is odd and relatively prime to T,
2. $a = 1 \pmod{p}$ if p is a prime factor of T,
3. $a = 1 \pmod{4}$ if 4 is a factor of T.

Usually for a decimal computer we pick T as some power of 10 and on a binary computer we pick T as some power of 2. The most convenient choices for a are of the form $a = 2^s + 1$ for $s > 2$ for binary computers and $a = 10^s + 1$ for $s > 1$ for decimal computers. For binary computers, $T = 2^{35}$ has been an acceptable choice over a wide range of applications.

The form of Eq. 9.4 with $c \neq 0$ is called the *mixed congruential method*. With $c = 0$, we have the *multiplicative congruential method* where

$$r_{i+1} = ar_i \pmod{T} \tag{9.5}$$

According to Hull and Dobell (21), the best results for the multiplicative congruential method on a binary machine are achieved when:

1. $a = 8t \pm 3$
2. $t = $ an integer
3. r_0 is odd
4. $T = 2^b$, where $b > 2$

Here the period is $T/4$.

The values of these parameters are chosen to make the period as long as possible while minimizing the correlation coefficient between successive values of the generated sequence.

Other congruential schemes which have passed certain statistical tests can be found in Handbook of Mathematical Functions (20).

Several new versions of the congruential method have been suggested by those who claim shortcomings in the randomness of uniform random numbers created by a fixed congruential equation. MacLaren and Marsaglia (10) have proposed a combination of two congruential generators to produce uniform random sequences. In this method one generator is used to shuffle the sequence produced by the other. Bray (32) has developed a procedure using five multipliers that are alternated by use of a multiplicative random switch.

The following paragraphs will provide the reader with FORTRAN IV subroutines which serve to illustrate the (1) mixed, (2) multiplicative, and (3) quadratic congruential methods of random deviate generation. The generators presented in the following examples were written for a CDC-6500 computer (word size 60 bits). Since $2^{48} - 1$ is the value of the largest integer that can be represented in floating point form, this constant is used for T. Each number generated is normalized so that it can be represented as a fraction between 0 and 1. X_0 is chosen arbitrarily. The congruential methods are explained and illustrated below:

Mixed Method

This method has the form already mentioned; $c \neq 1$ and $a \neq 0$.

EXAMPLE 9.9-2

```
SUBROUTINE RANMIX (ISEED,RN)
K = 31623
IADD = 2178281829
ISEED = ISEED*K+IADD
RN = ISEED
RNORMAL = 281474976710655
RN = RN/RNORMAL
RETURN
END
```

Multiplicative Method

This method is obtained by setting $a = 0$, thus giving

$$X_{n+1} = cX_n \bmod m$$

EXAMPLE 9.9-1

```
  SUBROUTINE RANMUL (ISEED,RN)
  K = 31623
  ISEED = ISEED*K
  RN = ISEED
C 2**48-1 = 281474976710655
  RNORMAL = 281474976710655
  RN = RN/RNORMAL
  RETURN
  END
```

It should be noted that the multiplicative method given in the above example has proven itself very reliable in repeated applications on a wide range of digital computers. In order to use this generator on other machines, all that is necessary is to determine the computer word size and replace RNORMAL by that number.

Quadratic Congruential Method

This method is represented by the formula

$$X_{n+1} = (dX_n^2 + cX_n + a) \bmod m \tag{9.5}$$

Choose d using the same rules as used in choosing c. m should be a power of 2 for the method to give satisfactory results.

EXAMPLE 9.9-3

```
  SUBROUTINE RANQUAD (ISEED,RN)
  IC = 31623
  ID = 42613
  IADD = 27181829
  ISEED = ID*ISEED**2 + ID*ISEED + IADD
  RN = ISEED
C 2**48-1 = 281474976710655
  RNORMAL = 281474976710655
  RN = RN/RNORMAL
  RETURN
  END
```

9.10   TESTING A UNIFORM RANDOM-NUMBER GENERATOR

Since a random deviate from a certain distribution is created by performing a transformation on a uniform variate, the main emphasis on statistical testing will concern the ability of a random-number generator to accurately generate sequences of numbers uniformly distributed on the (0, 1) interval. It is assumed that the transformations involved in transforming deviates of the uniform distribution to deviates of the particular distribution desired are mathematically correct. Hence if anything is statistically wrong with the final distribution, it will be because of deficiencies in the original random-number generator. Therefore, the following statistical tests will be performed on the sequence of numbers generated by the uniform generator. Although there are many tests commonly used to determine the accuracy of a random-number generator [see, for example, Emshoff and Sisson (8), Naylor et al. (41), and Schmidt and Taylor (49)] only four will be presented for illustrative purposes.

The Frequency Test

Probably the most important testing is concerned with the uniformity of the distribution and is generally carried out by using the chi-square test and the Kolmogorov-Smirnov test. Both tests are based on the grouping of sample data into classes over the interval (0, 1). The chi-square goodness of fit test allows us to determine whether the observed frequencies in each class are sufficiently close to the frequencies expected if the data did, in fact, come from the uniform distribution. The test statistic is given by:

$$\bar{C} = \sum_{i=1}^{n} \frac{(O_i - E_i)^2}{E_i} \tag{9.7}$$

where:
O_i = observed number in ith class
E_i = expected number in ith class
  = T/n
T = total number of observations
n = number of classes

The value of $\bar{C}$ is to be compared with the value $X_\alpha^2(n-1)$ which comes from a chi-square distribution on $n-1$ degrees of freedom with a level of significance of α. If the test statistic given by the above summation is greater than $X_\alpha^2(n-1)$, then the uniform generator should be viewed with suspicion.

For example, consider the random-number table, Table 9.7: there are 100 numbers generated, so $N = 100$. Now we shall divide the unit interval into n equal intervals; let $n = 10$. The expected number of random numbers in each subinterval (0.10 in length) is $N/n = 100/10 = 10$. By counting the number of generated numbers falling in each subinterval, we obtain the following results:

Actual	10	11	11	11	8	11	10	13	10	5
Expected	10	10	10	10	10	10	10	10	10	10

　　　　 0　　 0.1　 0.2　 0.3　 0.4　 0.5　 0.6　 0.7　 0.8　 0.9　 1.0

Table 9.7
A RANDOM NUMBER TABLE

0.001213	0.898980	0.578800	0.676216	0.050106
0.499629	0.282693	0.730594	0.701195	0.182840
0.108501	0.386183	0.769105	0.683348	0.551702
0.557434	0.799824	0.456790	0.216310	0.876167
0.092645	0.589628	0.332164	0.031858	0.611683
0.762627	0.696237	0.170288	0.054759	0.915126
0.032722	0.299315	0.308614	0.833586	0.517813
0.352862	0.574100	0.265936	0.859031	0.433081
0.941875	0.240002	0.655595	0.385079	0.908297
0.199044	0.936553	0.888098	0.817720	0.369820
0.339548	0.543258	0.624006	0.091330	0.416789
0.155062	0.582447	0.858532	0.887525	0.337294
0.751033	0.239493	0.535597	0.333813	0.493837
0.634536	0.199621	0.650020	0.745795	0.791130
0.227241	0.191479	0.406443	0.081288	0.734352
0.721023	0.222878	0.072814	0.641837	0.442675
0.789616	0.052303	0.106994	0.558774	0.141519
0.760869	0.120791	0.277380	0.657266	0.792691
0.805480	0.826543	0.294530	0.208524	0.429894
0.585186	0.986111	0.344882	0.343580	0.115375

Using the chi-square test,

$$\bar{C} = \sum \frac{(\text{actual} - \text{expected})^2}{\text{expected}}$$

and summing over the ten subintervals, we have

$$\frac{(10-10)^2}{10} + \frac{(11-10)^2}{10} + \frac{(11-10)^2}{10} + \frac{(11-10)^2}{10} + \frac{(8-10)^2}{10} + \frac{(11-10)^2}{10}$$

$$+ \frac{(10-10)^2}{10} + \frac{(13-10)^2}{10} + \frac{(10-10)^2}{10} + \frac{(5-10)^2}{10} = 4.2$$

If we arbitrarily specify a value of $\alpha = 0.05$, (this signifies an error of Type I to be 5 percent) the computed value of $\bar{C} = 4.2$ can be compared to a critical value of $\chi^2_{0.05}(9) = 16.919$. Since $\chi^2_{0.05}(9) \gg \bar{C}$, the randomness of the numbers in Table 9.7 might be accepted.

The other test under the general category of goodness of fit is the Kolmogorov-Smirnov test which involves the use of a cumulative frequency distribution. Let $F(x_0) = x_0$ be the continuous cumulative distribution of a sample of T observations. For any given observation, x_0, $S_T(x_0) = m/T$ where m is the observed number of observations less than or equal to x_0. The Kolmogorov-Smirnov test statistic is that D which equals the largest single deviation between $F(x_0)$ and $S_T(x_0)$ over the range $(0, 1)$ at a specified number of equal intervals. This value of D must be compared with the critical value of $D_{1-\alpha}$ from the Kolmogorov-Smirnov goodness-of-fit table for the sample size given. If D (data) is greater than $D_{1-\alpha}$ (table) then the hypothesis that the data came from a true uniform distribution might be rejected.

Other considerations regarding the applications of the above two tests can be found in Schmidt and Taylor (49), as well as Phillips (43).

Two rough tests for randomness of N uniform random deviates R_i, $i = 1, 2, \ldots, N$ is to compute the mean and partial variance. The numbers are uniformly random if

$$\frac{1}{N} \sum_{i=1}^{N} R_i \approx \frac{1}{2}$$

$$\frac{1}{N} \sum_{i=1}^{N} R_i^2 \approx \frac{1}{3}$$

These are merely rough tests which may save time and further testing if the data does not approach these values.

The Gap Test

If the random numbers generated are considered as digits, then this test is performed by counting the number of digits that appear between successive occurrences of a particular specified digit. The number of gaps of each length k is recorded, then a chi-square test is utilized for cells defined at $k = 0, 1, 2, \ldots$. For example, 93649 illustrates a gap of length 3 between the two 9's.

For any k the probability of a gap of length k is:

$$P(k) = 0.1(0.9)^k$$

This says that $P(0) = 0.1$ or that one-tenth of the time pairs of digits will occur in a sequence of truly random digits, a somewhat surprising result.

This test can also be performed by treating the numbers generated as real numbers instead of treating them as digits. The logic behind such a test is as follows. A gap of length k is said to occur if k successive digits appear which are not between α and β, and the $(k+1)$st digit is between α and β for some specified $0 \leq \alpha < \beta \leq 1$. Since the probability that a number drawn from a uniform $(0, 1)$ population over the entire interval is one, the probability that a gap of length k occurs over a chosen interval is equal to the length of that interval. We will not illustrate this modification; the reader is referred to Knuth (27) for details. The standard gap test is given below.

EXAMPLE 9.10-1

First, we multiply each of our 100 pseudorandom numbers by 10 to give integer values (we may multiply by a larger number than 10 if more significance is desired). Next, choose a suitable sequence for k. We shall let $k = 0, 1, 2, \ldots, 10$. That is, we shall consider gaps of length k for each of the values 0 through 10. From the formula that gives the probability that a gap of length k will occur,

$P(0) = 0.1$	$P(6) = 0.053$
$P(1) = 0.09$	$P(7) = 0.048$
$P(2) = 0.081$	$P(8) = 0.043$
$P(3) = 0.072$	$P(9) = 0.039$
$P(4) = 0.066$	$P(10) = 0.035$
$P(5) = 0.059$	

To obtain the observed probabilities, we count the number of times a gap of length k, $(k = 0, 1, \ldots, 10)$ occurs and divide by 100 (the number of digits sampled). The resulting table of actual and expected occurrences is shown below. Gap occurrences were calculated by rows in Table 9.7.

Actual	0.11	0.07	0.02	0.1	0.09	0.1	0.05	0.06	0.08	0.13	0.12
Expected	0.1	0.09	0.08	0.07	0.07	0.06	0.05	0.05	0.04	0.04	0.04
Gap length	0	1	2	3	4	5	6	7	8	9	10

A chi-square test is now performed using 11 cells and Eq. 9.7.

The Runs Test

A slightly modified special case of the second gap test with $\alpha = 0$, $\beta = 0.5$ is the test of runs above and below the mean. A binary sequence is created whose ith term is 0 if the ith random number generated is less than 0.5, and 1 if the ith random number generated is greater than 0.5. A sequence of 1's bracketed by zeros constitutes a run as does a sequence of zeros bracketed by 1's. The expected number of runs is $(N+1)/2$ and the expected number of runs of length k is $(N-k+3)*2^{-k-1}$ where N is the number of numbers generated.

Another version of the runs test is a test of runs up and down. A sequence of random numbers, $r_1, \ldots r_N$ is generated. A binary sequence is created whose ith term is 0 if $r_i < r_{i+1}$, and 1 if $r_i > r_{i+1}$. In this case the expected number of runs is $(2N-1)/3$ and the expected number of runs of length k is

for $k < N-1$ $\qquad E(k) = \dfrac{2[(k^2+3k+1)N-(k^3+3k^2-k-4)]}{(k+3)!}$

for $k = N-1$ $\qquad E(k) = 2/N!$

In order to illustrate this version of the runs test, consider the following binary sequence produced from the 100 random number samples in Table 9.7.

```
0   1   0   1   0
1   0   1   1   1
0   0   1   1   1
0   1   1   0   1
0   1   1   0   0
1   1   1   0   1
0   0   0   1   1
0   1   0   1   0
1   0   1   0   1
0   1   1   1   1
0   0   1   0   1
0   0   0   1   0
1   0   1   0   0
1   0   0   0   1
0   0   1   0   1
1   1   0   1   0
0   0   0   1   0
1   0   0   0   0
0   1   1   0   0
0   1   1   1
```

We shall give k an arbitrary value, say $k = 1, 2, \ldots, 5$. Then

$$E(1) = \frac{2[(1)^2 + 3(1) + 1]100 - [1^3 + 3(1^2) - 1 - 4]}{(1+3)!}$$

$\qquad = 41.7 \qquad\qquad\qquad = 41.7$

$\qquad =$ approximately 42

Similarly $E(2) = 18$, $E(3) = 5$, $E(4) = 1$, $E(5) = 0$. Using these values and counting the runs in the binary sequence, we obtain the following table:

Actual	41	11	8	2	1
Expected	42	18	5	1	0
k	1	2	3	4	5

For example, when $k = 1$, there are 22 runs generated by a single 1 bracketed by zeros, and 19 runs generated by a single zero bracketed by 1's.

A chi-square goodness-of-fit test is again used. A common fault of random-number generators is an excess of long runs [Naylor (1966)].

The Poker Test

The poker test examines individual digits of the pseudorandom numbers. Taking five digits at a time, the digits are classified as a particular poker hand. Probabilities can be calculated for the number of times each hand is expected to occur. This was done through the use of two correction factors and combinatorial formulas. The first factor represents the probability of a particular configuration of the type of hand. The second factor represents the number of ways the hand can be arranged. In the case of two pair the extra factor of 1/2 is needed because, for example, the arrangements of AABBC and BBAAC produce the same outcomes but are counted as two different occurrences by the first factor. The correction factors essentially account for permutations. The probabilities are given by the following calculations:

All different $\qquad \dfrac{10 \cdot 9 \cdot 8 \cdot 7 \cdot 6}{10^5} \cdot 1 = 0.30240$

One pair $\qquad \dfrac{10 \cdot 1 \cdot 9 \cdot 8 \cdot 7}{10^5} \binom{5}{2} = 0.50400$

Two pair $\qquad \dfrac{1}{2} \dfrac{10 \cdot 1 \cdot 9 \cdot 1 \cdot 8}{10^5} \binom{5}{2}\binom{3}{2} = 0.10800$

Three of a kind $\qquad \dfrac{10 \cdot 1 \cdot 1 \cdot 9 \cdot 8}{10^5} \binom{5}{3} = 0.07200$

Four of a kind $\qquad \dfrac{10 \cdot 1 \cdot 1 \cdot 1 \cdot 9}{10^5} \binom{5}{4} = 0.00450$

Five of a kind $\qquad \dfrac{10 \cdot 1 \cdot 1 \cdot 1 \cdot 1}{10^5} \binom{5}{5} = 0.00010$

Full house $\qquad \dfrac{10 \cdot 1 \cdot 1 \cdot 9 \cdot 1}{10^5} \binom{5}{3}\binom{2}{2} = 0.0090$

EXAMPLE 9.10-2

For our sample of pseudorandom numbers, one first considers the first· five digits in each number generated and classifies it as to the type of hand it represents. A count is kept of the total occurrences for each type of hand and then the total is divided by 100 (the number of digits considered). This gives the observed probabilities for the numbers generated. The expected values are obtained from the above formulas. A simple chi-square test is now performed with the chart below and the seven categories of possible hands (seven cells).

Actual	0.25000	0.5600	0.080	0.1000	0.0000	0.0000	0.0100
Expected	0.30204	0.5040	0.108	0.0720	0.0045	0.0001	0.0090
Categories	All different	One pair	Two pair	Three of a kind	Four of a kind	Five of a kind	Full house

In summary, it should be noted that even if the numbers tested are truly uniform, the probability that they will fail at least one test may still be high. This is true since each test is actually a hypothesis test run at a level of significance (type I error) of α. By definition α is the probability of rejecting the null hypothesis even if it is true.

EXAMPLE 9.10-3
Perform five tests, each at level of significance $\alpha = 0.05$. The probability of failing at least one of the five tests is:

$$p(\text{fail at least one test}) = 1 - (1 - \alpha)^n$$
$$= 1 - (0.95)^5$$
$$= 0.226$$

even though the numbers are truly acceptable!

There are other tests which can be run to test the "randomness" in a set of pseudorandom numbers. Additional tests are:

1. Serial tests—serial tests are used to check the randomness of successive numbers in a sequence.
2. Product tests—product tests measure the independence (correlation) between sequences of random numbers.
3. Tests for autocorrelation—autocorrelation tests examine the dependency of a particular number on another number in a sequence. These tests attempt to discern whether there are patterns or relationships among sets of random numbers.
4. The Maximum Test—examines sequences of numbers to detect abnormally high or low numbers.

IV. TECHNIQUES FOR GENERATING RANDOM DEVIATES

9.11   THE INVERSE TRANSFORMATION METHOD

The inverse transformation technique deals with the cumulative distribution function, $F(x)$, of the distribution to be simulated. Since $F(x)$ is defined over the interval $(0, 1)$, we can generate a uniform random variate R [also defined over the interval $(0, 1)$] and set $F(x) = R$. Then x is uniquely determined by the relation $F(x) = R$ and $x = F^{-1}(R)$ is the variate desired from the given distribution. The difficulty with this technique lies in finding the inverse transformation such that $F^{-1}(R) = x$. If this inverse function can be established, we only need generate various uniform random numbers and perform the inverse function on them to obtain random deviates from the distribution desired.

EXAMPLE 9.11-1

Generate a random variate from:

$$f(x) = \begin{cases} 3x^2 & 0 \le x \le 1 \\ 0 & \text{Elsewhere} \end{cases}$$

then:

$$F(x) = \int_{t=0}^{x} 3t^2 \, dt$$

Hence,

$$F(x) = x^3$$

Since $F(x)$ is the cumulative distribution function of $f(x)$, we can replace $F(x)$ by a random number R. The inverse transformation is therefore:

$$x = F^{-1}(R) = (R)^{1/3}$$

Hence, in order to generate a random deviate from the probability density $f(x) = 3x^2$, a random deviate from the uniform distribution is generated (call it R) and the desired deviate $x = (R)^{1/3}$.

The problem with the inverse transformation technique is that for many distributions, the inverse function, $F^{-1}(R)$, does not exist or it is so complicated as to be impractical. When this is the case, either approximations or other techniques must be used.

The Exponential Distribution

In simulation experiments, the exponential distribution is used to describe the time interval between occurrences of like events, which are often arrivals in queueing problems. If the probability that an event will occur in a small-time interval is very small, and if the occurrence of this event is independent of the occurrence of other events, then the time interval between occurrence of these events is exponentially distributed and the process is a Poisson process. In addition to queueing processes, the exponential distribution is also used to describe component failure rates in reliability analysis.

The probability density function and cumulative distribution function are given as

$$f(x) = \lambda e^{-\lambda x} \qquad \text{for } x \ge 0$$
$$F(x) = 1 - e^{-\lambda x} \qquad \text{for } x \ge 0$$

To generate a random deviate from the exponential distribution, the inverse transform technique is easily applied. We have $F(x) = 1 - e^{-\lambda x}$; so we generate a uniform random deviate R_1 and let

$$R = F(x) = 1 - e^{-\lambda x}$$

To find the inverse transform:

$$R = 1 - e^{-\lambda x}$$

or:

$$1 - R = e^{-\lambda x}$$

but $1-R$ is also from the uniform distribution, so let:

$$R = e^{-\lambda x}$$

or:

$$x = -\frac{\ln R}{\lambda}$$

Hence

$$F^{-1}(R) = -\frac{\ln R}{\lambda} = x$$

The procedure is to generate uniform random deviates and apply $F^{-1}(R)$ to generate exponential variates.

Weibull Distribution

The Weibull distribution is a family of density functions widely used in describing failure rate characteristics in reliability analysis.

The density function is

$$f(x) = \alpha\beta x^{\beta-1} e^{-\alpha x^{\beta}} \qquad x \geq 0$$

for $x > 0$, $\alpha > 0$, $\beta > 0$, the Weibull density function generates a family of probability density curves as α and β change their values.

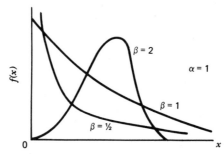

To generate a Weibull random deviate, the inverse transform technique can be used.

EXAMPLE 9.11-2

Define the cumulative distribution function.

$$F(x) = \alpha\beta \int_{t=0}^{x} t^{\beta-1} e^{-\alpha t^{\beta}} \, dt$$

let $y = \alpha t^{\beta}$

$$dy = \alpha\beta t^{\beta-1} \, dt$$

then:

$$F(x) = \alpha\beta \int_{0}^{\alpha x^{\beta}} t^{\beta-1} e^{-y} \frac{dy}{\alpha\beta t^{\beta-1}}$$

Hence,

$$F(x) = 1 - e^{-\alpha x^{\beta}}$$

We must now find the inverse transform $F^{-1}(R)$.

$$F(x) = R = 1 - e^{-\alpha x^{\beta}} \qquad \text{where } R \text{ is from the uniform distribution}$$

$$1 - R = e^{-\alpha x^{\beta}} \qquad \text{but } 1 - R \text{ is also from the uniform distribution, so}$$

$$R = e^{-\alpha x^{\beta}}$$

and

$$x = \left[-\frac{1}{\alpha} \ln R \right]^{1/\beta}$$

Hence in order to generate a series of deviates from the Weibull distribution, we only need to generate random deviates from the uniform distribution and apply the inverse transform

$$F^{-1}(R) = \left[-\frac{1}{\alpha} \ln R \right]^{1/\beta} = x$$

The Geometric Distribution

A random variable x, defined as the number of failures in a sequence of Bernoulli trials before the first success occurs, is known as a geometric random variable. This distribution is related to the binomial distribution and has been used in the area of quality control and for lag distributions in econometric models.

The probability density function for the geometric distribution is

$$f(x) = pq^x \qquad x = 0, 1, 2, \ldots$$

By definition, p is the probability of success for each Bernoulli trial and $q = 1 - p$. The cumulative distribution function is given by:

$$F(x) = \sum_{k=0}^{x} pq^k$$

To generate a random deviate from the geometric distribution, we make use of the fact that

$$1 - F(x) = q^{x+1}$$

and that $[1 - F(x)]/q$ has unit range. It will be left as an exercise for the student to show that these relationships are correct.

Once the above is accepted, let

$$R = q^x \qquad \text{(inverse technique)}$$
$$\ln R = x \ln q$$

and

$$x = \ln R / \ln q$$

is the desired geometric deviate where R is from the uniform distribution.

9.12 THE REJECTION TECHNIQUE

The rejection technique consists of drawing a random value from an appropriate distribution and subjecting it to a test to determine whether or not it will be accepted for use. To illustrate, let $f(x)$ be a frequency density function such that

$$f(x) = 0 \qquad \text{for } a > x > b$$

and

$$0 \leq f(x) \leq M \qquad \text{for } a \leq x \leq b$$

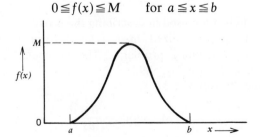

To carry out the method:

1. Generate two uniform random variates, R_1 and R_2.
2. Form the prospective random variate from $f(x)$; $x = a + (b-a)R_1$.
3. Test to see if $R_2 \leq f(a + (b-a)R_1)/M$.
4. If the inequality holds, then accept $x = a + (b-a)R_1$ as the variate generated from $f(x)$.
5. If the inequality is violated, generate two new random numbers and try again. Note that M is simply the *mode* of $f(x)$.

The theory behind this method is based on the fact that the probability of R_2 being less than or equal to $(1/M)f(x)$ is $(1/M)f(x)$. Hence, if the prospective candidate x is chosen at random according to $x = a + (b-a)R_1$ and rejected if $R_2 > (1/M)f(x)$, then the probability density function of the accepted x's will be exactly $f(x)$. Note that if no rejection were used, that is, just step 2 is executed, then x would be distributed uniformly between a and $a + b$. With the added rejection test, however, we are picking only those x's conforming to the original distribution $f(x)$.

EXAMPLE 9.12-1
Generate a random deviate from:

$$f(x) = 3x^2 \qquad 0 \leq x \leq 1$$

then $M = 3$, $a = 0$, $b = 1$

1. Generate R_1 and let $x = a + (b-a)R_1 = R_1$.
2. Generate R_2 and compare it with
3. If $R_2 \leq R_1^2$.

   then accept $x = R_1$ as a variate from $f(x)$
4. If $R_2 > R_1^2$, reject $x = R_1$ and repeat steps 1–3.

Tocher (52) has shown that the expected number of trials before a successful random deviate from $f(x)$ is generated is M. This suggests that the method may be quite inefficient for certain density functions.

The Beta Distribution
Consider the beta distribution defined by the following density function.

$$f(x) = \frac{\Gamma(\alpha + \beta)}{\Gamma(\alpha)\Gamma(\beta)} x^{\alpha-1}(1-x)^{\beta-1} \qquad 1 \geq x \geq 0$$

where α and β are the distribution parameters and

$$\Gamma(\phi) = \int_0^\infty x^{\phi-1} e^{-x} dx$$

The beta distribution is often used in describing the distribution of percentages, and has been extensively utilized in a related form in the analysis of PERT/CPM project scheduling problems. The particular shape of $f(x)$ is determined by α and β. (See Fig. 9.9.)
First determine the value of M.

$$M = \text{mode} = \frac{df(x)}{dx}\bigg|_{x=0}$$

Hence

$$M = \frac{\alpha - 1}{\alpha + \beta - 2}$$

Note that M is only defined for certain values of α and β. The procedure is as follows:

1. Choose (or determine) α and β.
2. Calculate $M = (\alpha - 1)/(\alpha + \beta - 2)$.
3. Proceed with the normal rejection scheme.
4. Generate two random numbers; $R1$ and $R2$.
5. If $R2*M \leq f(x \equiv R2) = \dfrac{\Gamma(\alpha + \beta)}{\Gamma(\alpha)\Gamma(\beta)} R2^{\alpha - 1}(1 - R2)^{\beta - 1}$

   Then Deviate $= R2$
   $\begin{cases} \text{if } R2*M > f(x \equiv R2) \\ \text{Then go to step 4 and start again.} \end{cases}$

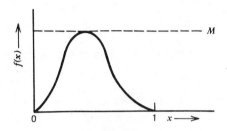

Figure 9.9
A particular beta form.

The Gamma Distribution

One of the most flexible distributions in engineering applications is the gamma density function. If a random variable is nonnegative and follows a unimodal distribution, the chances are good that a member of the gamma distribution can adequately describe the variable in question.

The gamma distribution is described by

$$f(x) = \frac{\beta^{\alpha}}{\Gamma(\alpha)} x^{\alpha - 1} e^{-x/\beta} \qquad x \geq 0$$

$$\Gamma(x) = \int_0^{\infty} X^{\alpha - 1} e^{-x} \, dx$$

where $\alpha > 0$, $\beta > 0$, and x is nonnegative. As α increases, the gamma distribution approaches a normal distribution asymptotically. If $\alpha = 1$, the gamma distribution is identical to the exponential distribution already discussed. A technique will now be discussed which generates general gamma variates. However, more efficient generation schemes for specialized related gamma forms will be given later in this section.

A Sampling Rejection Technique for Gamma Variates (Johnk's Method). A recently developed technique for generating stochastic gamma variates is one proposed by Johnk (3, 42). Establish the following fundamental theorems.

THEOREM 1

The sum of two gamma random variables with parameters $G_1(\alpha_1, \beta)$ and $G_2(\alpha_2, \beta)$ is also gamma with parameters $G(\alpha_1 + \alpha_2, \beta)$.

THEOREM 2

If U_1 and U_2 are continuous uniform random variables described by

$$f(U_i) = 1 \qquad i = 1, 2 \qquad 1 \geq U_i \geq 0$$

and

$$x = U_1^{1/A} \qquad y = U_2^{1/B}$$

and if it is true that

$$x + y \leq 1$$

then

$$z = \frac{x}{x + y}$$

is Beta distributed with distribution function:

$$f(z) = \frac{\Gamma(A + B)}{\Gamma(A)\Gamma(B)} z^{A-1}(1 - z)^{B-1} \qquad 1 \geq z \geq 0.$$

Note that this is a second method for generating Beta variates.

THEOREM 3

If x is a random variable gamma distributed with $\alpha = n + k$, $\beta = 1$; and if y is beta distributed with parameters $A = n$ and $B = k$; then $z = xy$ is gamma distributed with $\alpha = n$, $\beta = 1$.

Theorems 1, 2, and 3 are well known, and can be verified through the use of simple linear transformations and convolution theory [Johnk (42)].

The entire Johnk procedure depends on the ability to produce a random Beta deviate using Theorem 2, which is a rejection technique. In general, we can state

Lemma 1

Given a Beta distribution function with parameters A and B, if we define $x = u^{1/A}$ and $y = u_2^{1/B}$, then the probability that $x + y \leq 1$ is given by

$$Pr\{x + y \leq 1\} = \frac{AB\Gamma(A)\Gamma(B)}{\Gamma(A + B)(A + B)}$$

If we define $P = \{\Gamma(A, B)[AB \mid (A + B)]\}^{-1}$ then an expression is obtained for the expected number of rejections in obtaining one Beta variate. Various combinations of A and B are given below:

B \ A	1	3	5
1	1	4	6
3	4	30	56
5	6	56	252

A general conclusion is that if Johnk's technique is used in Beta generations *per se*, the time required to obtain a statistical deviate could prove prohibitive except for selected combinations of A and B. At this point let us consider the use of this technique to generate gamma variates via Theorem 3. Suppose that we desire to generate a gamma-distributed random variable with noninteger shape parameter, α. Now define $n = \alpha - (\alpha)$, where (α) is the largest truncated integer, and similarly define $k = 1 - \alpha + (\alpha)$. By Theorem 3 let $A = n$ and $B = k$. Under these rules, it is necessary that $\alpha \equiv n + k \equiv 1$. It follows that if a Beta variate is generated following the parameters A and B, and multiplied by a gamma variate with parameters $\alpha = 1$ and $\beta = 1$, then a gamma variate with $\alpha = n$ and $\beta = 1$ will be produced. Two facts are now significant and should be noted. A gamma distribution with parameters $\alpha = 1$, $\beta = 1$ is given by

$$f(x) = e^x \qquad \infty \geqq x \geqq 0$$

from which a variate is easily produced using an inverse transform. Since $A = n$ and $B = k$, A and B will always be less than one. By Lemma 1, the expected number of rejections in the beta generation phase would be:

$$R = [AB\Gamma(A)\Gamma(B)]^{-1} = [(1-B)B\Gamma(1-B)\Gamma(B)]^{-1} \approx \left[\frac{(1-B)B\Pi}{\sin n\Pi}\right]^{-1}$$

Hence, the expected number of rejections is approximated by $1.33 \geqq R \geqq 1$.

The fundamental ingredients have now been established to construct a random deviate generator for a gamma density with arbitrary noninteger shape parameter α and scale parameter β. The algorithm is as follows:

Define   (i) α is a noninteger shape parameter.

         (ii) $\alpha_1 = (\alpha)$ is the truncated integer root of α.

        (iii) u_i is the ith random number $1 \geqq u_i \geqq 0$.

1. Let $x = -\ln \prod_{i=1}^{\alpha_1} u_i$
2. Set $A = \alpha - \alpha_1$; $B = 1 - A$
   a. Set $j = 1$.
   b. Generate a random number, u_j, and set $y_1 = (u_j)^{1/A}$.
   c. Generate a random number, u_{j+1}, and set $y_2 = (u_{j+1})^{1/B}$.
   d. If $y_1 + y_2 \leqq 1$, go to (f).
   e. Set $j = j + 2$; go to (b).
   f. Let $z = y_1/(y_1 + y_2)$ so that z is a beta variable with parameters A and B by Theorem 2.
3. Generate a random number, u_N, and let $Q = -\ln(u_N)$.
4. The desired deviate is $D = (x + zQ)\beta$ by Theorem 1 and Theorem 3.

9.13 THE COMPOSITION METHOD

In this technique $f(x)$, the probability density function of the distribution to be simulated, is expressed as a probability mixture of properly selected density functions. This procedure is based on the definition of conditional probability or the law of compound probabilities.

Mathematically let $g(x|y)$ be a family of one-parameter density functions where y is the parameter identifying a unique $g(x)$. If a value of y is now drawn from a cumulative distribution function $H(y)$ and then if x is sampled from the $g(x)$ for that chosen y, the density function for x will be

$$f(x) = \int_{-\infty}^{\infty} g(x|y) \, dH(y)$$

By using this principle, more complicated distributions can be generated from simpler distributions which are themselves easily generated by the inverse transform technique or the rejection technique.

EXAMPLE 9.13-1
Taken from Butler (3). Generate a random variate from

$$f(x) = n \int_{1}^{\infty} y^{-n} e^{-xy} \, dy$$

let

$$dH(y) = n \, dy/y^{n+1} \qquad 1 < y < \infty, \ n \geq 1$$

and

$$g(x) = ye^{-yx}$$

A variate is now drawn from a density function whose cumulative distribution function is $H(y)$. Once this y is selected, it determines a particular $g(x) = ye^{-yx}$. The desired variate from $f(x)$ is then simply a generated variate from $g(x) = ye^{-yx}$. To carry out the above instructions, generate two uniform variates R_1 and R_2 and let

$$S_1 = R_1^{-1/n}$$

$$x = \frac{1}{S_1} \log R_2$$

then x is the desired variate from

$$f(x) = n \int_{1}^{\infty} y^{-n} e^{-yx} \, dy$$

This technique is appropriate when generating deviates of "higher" type distributions from simpler ones. The difficulty lies in identifying the $H(y)$ and $g(x|y)$ needed to produce a given $f(x)$ under the relationship

$$f(x) = \int_{-\infty}^{\infty} g(x|y) \, dH(y)$$

Fortunately, mathematical statisticians have provided us with several useful relationships called "convolutions" which can be used in generating certain random deviates. The following examples serve to illustrate the procedure.

The Poisson Distribution
If the time intervals between like events are exponentially distributed, the number of events occurring in a unit interval of time has the Poisson distribution. Applications of the Poisson random variable include such areas as

inventory control, queueing theory, quality control, traffic flow, and many other areas of management science.

The probability density function for the Poisson distribution is given by:

$$f(x) = \frac{\lambda^x e^{-\lambda}}{x!} \qquad x = 0, 1, 2, \ldots, \infty$$

where λ is the expected number of occurrences per unit time. This implies that the time between events is exponentially distributed with mean $1/\lambda$.

We can use this relationship between the exponential and Poisson distributions to generate deviates from the Poisson distribution. A Poisson deviate x can be defined in the following manner:

$$\sum_{i=1}^{x} y_i \leq 1 \leq \sum_{i=1}^{x+1} y_i$$

where $y_1, y_2, \ldots, y_{x+1}$ are random deviates from the exponential distribution having mean $1/\lambda$ and are generated by (inverse transform technique)

$$y_i = -\frac{1}{\lambda} \ln R_i$$

where R_i is from the uniform distribution. In summary, the cumulative sums are generated until the inequality holds. When this occurs, x is the Poisson random deviate desired.

Another form of this same procedure is to define the Poisson deviate x when

$$\sum_{i=1}^{x} y_i \leq \lambda \leq \sum_{i=1}^{x+1} y_i$$

where y_i are again deviates from the exponential distribution, but with mean 1, that is,

$$y_i = -\ln R_i$$

The two techniques are essentially the same, but the first inequality seems to be more in agreement with the definition of the exponential distribution since the y_i's actually have the true mean $1/\lambda$.

The Erlang Distribution

The Erlang distribution is a form of the gamma distribution with k equal to a positive integer. Mathematical statisticians have proven that this distribution is just the sum of k exponential variables, each with expected value $1/k$.

Hence, in order to generate an Erlang deviate we only need to sum k exponential deviates, each with expected value $1/k$. Therefore the Erlang variate x is expressed as

$$x = \sum_{i=1}^{k} y_i = -\frac{1}{\alpha} \sum_{i=1}^{k} \ln R_i$$

where y_i is an exponential deviate generated by the inverse transform technique and R_i is a random number from the uniform distribution.

The Binomial Distribution

A random variable x defined as the number of successful events in a sequence of n independent Bernoulli trials, each with probability of success p, is known as a binomial random variable. The binomial distribution is one of the most important statistical distributions used in the areas of statistical sampling and quality control.

The probability density function for the binomial distribution is given as

$$f(x) = \binom{n}{x} p^x q^{n-x} \qquad x = 0, 1, \ldots, n$$

where p = probability of success per trial
$\quad q = 1 - p$
$\quad n$ = number of trials
$\quad x$ = number of successes, an integer.

To generate a binomial deviate with parameters p and n the procedure is as follows:

1. Generate n uniform random deviates.
2. Count the number of uniform variates less than or equal to p.
3. The number found under step 2 is equal to the value of the binomial variate.

This procedure can then be repeated as many times as desired to generate other binomial deviates.

Another procedure involves using the normal distribution as an approximation to the binomial for cases where $n \geq 20$ and $np \leq 10$. Since the binomial variate is an integer, the normal variate used as an approximation must be rounded to the closest integer value. This method is faster but is only an approximation.

9.14 MATHEMATICAL DERIVATION TECHNIQUE

Under this technique, various functional relationships are used in order that certain complicated probability density functions can be represented in a simpler form from which deviates can easily be generated by the more common techniques. The normal distribution is one of the most widely used in applied statistics and has two parameters; μ = expected value, and σ^2 = variance. The cumulative distribution function of a normal random variable x is given by:

$$F(x) = \int_{-\infty}^{x} \frac{1}{\sigma\sqrt{2\pi}} e^{-\frac{1}{2}[(x-\mu)/\sigma]^2} dx \qquad \infty \geq x \geq -\infty$$

This function cannot be evaluated analytically; hence, many of the methods for generating normal deviates use approximation methods.

If the parameters μ and σ^2 have values of zero and 1, respectively, the distribution is known as the standard normal density with

$$f(z) = \frac{1}{\sqrt{2\pi}} e^{-z^2/2} \qquad \infty \geq z \geq -\infty$$

Any normal variate x with parameters μ and σ^2 can be converted to a standard normal variate z by using

$$z = (x - \mu)/\sigma$$

Conversely, in order to convert a standard normal deviate z to a normal deviate with parameters μ and σ^2, use

$$x = \sigma z + \mu$$

Hence to generate a normal deviate x with parameters μ and σ^2, we only need to generate a standard normal deviate and apply the preceeding equation. Many methods for generating standard normal deviates exist. Three examples will be given. The first is a mathematical derivation technique (Box and Muller), while the second and third will be explained in the section on approximation techniques (one technique attributed to Kahn and one to Hastings).

The Box and Muller Technique for Generating Normal Deviates [Box and Muller (4)]

The joint probability density function for two independent standard normal deviates x_1 and x_2 is

$$f(x_1, x_2) = \frac{1}{2\pi} e^{-1/2(x_1^2 + x_2^2)}.$$

Consider the substitutions

$$x_1 = r \cos \theta$$
$$x_2 = r \sin \theta$$

then

$$f(r, \theta) \, dr \, d\theta = \frac{1}{2\pi} e^{-r^2} r \, dr \, d\theta$$

so that θ has a uniform distribution over the interval $(0, 2\pi)$ and r^2 has an exponential distribution. So we generate two uniform random deviates R_1 and R_2 and let

$$r^2 = -\ln R_1 \quad \longleftrightarrow \text{(exponential generation}$$
$$r = (-\ln R_1)^{1/2} \qquad \text{by inverse transform technique)}$$
$$\theta = 2\pi R_2 \quad \longleftrightarrow \text{(scaled uniform generation)}$$

Then we have as the two desired normal deviates

$$x_1 = (\ln 1/R_1)^{1/2} \cos 2\pi R_2$$
$$x_2 = (\ln 1/R_1)^{1/2} \sin 2\pi R_2$$

The Box and Muller procedure generates two exact deviates from the standard normal distribution (usually requires approximation methods) by using a mathematical derivation (polar coordinates). Analytical manipulations reduce the procedure to the generation of an exponential deviate and a uniform deviate, and a combination of these results according to the original substitutions.

Another application of this technique is given by the *log normal* distribution. Since the log normal deviate x is related to the normal deviate y by the mathematical relationship $x = \ln y$, we need only to generate a normal deviate y and use the mathematical relationship $x = \ln y$ to find a deviate x from the log normal distribution.

9.15 APPROXIMATION TECHNIQUES

The approximation methods are all related to the inverse transform technique and are used when exact methods are either too complicated or, in fact, impossible. With approximation methods, one of three different quantities is approximated. These are:

1. The probability density function of the distribution to be simulated.
2. The cumulative distribution function of the distribution to be simulated.
3. The inverse transform to the cumulative distribution function of the distribution to be simulated.

Approximation methods are used when the cumulative distribution function cannot be obtained from the given probability density function, or when the inverse transform cannot be obtained even if $F(x)$ is available. When this is the case, an approximation for the probability density function must be made which facilitates the derivation of the cumulative distribution function, or an approximation must be made on $F(x)$ directly. Once the cumulative distribution function has been found to the approximated probability density function, the inverse transform can often then be applied and deviates are generated in the manner previously discussed.

Examples of Approximation Techniques

Suppose we wish to generate a deviate from the standard normal density function given by:

$$f(x) = \frac{1}{\sqrt{2\pi}} e^{-x^2/2} \qquad \infty \geq x \geq -\infty$$

An approximation has been given by Kahn (52):

$$e^{-x^2/2} \approx \frac{2e^{-kx}}{(1+e^{-kx})^2}$$

for

$$x > 0 \qquad \text{and} \qquad k = \sqrt{8/\pi}$$

The cumulative distribution function to the approximation is easily calculated as

$$F(x) = \frac{2}{1+e^{-kx}} - 1$$

The inverse to this approximation cumulative distribution function is then:

$$x = \frac{1}{k} \ln \frac{1+R_1}{1-R_1}$$

A random sign is then attached to this variate where R_1 is a deviate from the uniform distribution. Kahn's approximation derives a normal random deviate directly from an approximation to the density function, $f(x)$. The second method is to obtain an approximate inverse transform directly from this cumulative distribution function. When this occurs, an approximation for the cumulative distribution function is made which facilitates the derivation of the inverse transform. Once the inverse transform is found, deviates are again generated according to the inverse transform technique previously defined. Since this approximation method is not used as often as the following one, no examples will be given for this method.

Under the third approximation method, an approximation of the inverse transform itself is found and is applied directly to generate deviates from the distribution in question. One form often used for approximating the inverse function is

$$F(x) = a + bx + cx^2 + \alpha(1-x)^2 \ln(x) + Bx^2[\ln(1-x)]$$

a, b, c, α, and B are constants which give rise to the best approximation. From the cumulative distribution function, it is possible to construct a table giving the hypothetical frequencies for the various values of the variate from 0 to 1. The method of least squares can then be used to pass the curve through the series of points in the table. Tocher (14) illustrates that for the normal distribution with mean μ and standard deviation σ, this technique will yield the following:

$$a = (16834\mu - 13452.96\sigma) \times 2^{-11}$$
$$b = (26953.865\sigma) \times 2^{-11}$$
$$c = 0$$
$$\alpha = (-3772.769\sigma) \times 2^{-11}$$
$$B = (3772.769\sigma) \times 2^{-11}$$

Many other forms are used to approximate the inverse transform. One method attributed to Hastings for generating standard normal deviates is: (52)

let

$$y = [-2 \ln(1-R)]^{\frac{1}{2}}$$

then

$$x = F^{-1}(R) = y - \frac{a_0 + a_1 y}{b_0 + b_1 y + b_2 y^2}$$

where x is the desired standard normal deviate and R is from the uniform distribution. The approximated inverse transform is specified by

$$a_0 = 2.30753$$
$$a_1 = 0.27061$$
$$b_0 = 1.0$$
$$b_1 = 0.99229$$
$$b_2 = 0.04481$$

9.16 SPECIAL PROBABILITY DISTRIBUTIONS

The Chi-Square Distribution

The Chi-square distribution is a gamma distribution with $\alpha = 1/2$ and $k = v/2$, and therefore, has expected value equal to $(1/\alpha)k = 2k = v$ (where v is called the degree of freedom). The chi-square distribution is important for its use in testing of hypotheses regarding goodness of fit.

There are two cases to consider when generating chi-square deviates as the sum of k exponential deviates (gamma generation).

Case 1. If the expected value of x is even, then k is an integer and

$$x = -\frac{1}{\alpha} \sum_{i=1}^{k} \ln R_i$$

is used for the chi-square deviates.

Case 2. If expected value of x is odd then $k = E(x)/2 - 1/2$ and

$$x = -\frac{1}{\alpha} \sum_{i=1}^{k} \ln R_i + z^2$$

is used for the chi-square deviate where z^2 is the square of a standard normal variate whose generation was discussed previously. R_i is again a uniform random deviate.

Another technique for generating a chi-square variate makes use of the fact that a chi-square variable with v degrees of freedom can be represented as the sum of the squares of v standard normal deviates. Using this gives

$$x = \sum_{i=1}^{v} z_i^2$$

as a chi-square variate where the z_i are deviates generated from the standard normal distribution.

The Student's T Distribution
The T random variable is defined as the ratio of a standard normal variable to the square root of a chi-square variable divided by its degrees of freedom. The T distribution is used in testing statistical hypotheses.

Mathematically, the T random variable is given as:

$$x = \frac{z}{\sqrt{\dfrac{x_1}{v}}}$$

where z is a standard normal variable and x_1 is a chi-square variable with v degrees of freedom.

A deviate from the T distribution is given by

$$x = \frac{z_1}{\left(\sum_{i=2}^{v+1} \dfrac{z_i^2}{v}\right)^{1/2}}$$

where the z's are standard normal variates.

The F Distribution
If x_1 and x_2 are chi-square random variables with degrees of freedom of a and b, respectively, then

$$x = \frac{x_1/a}{x_2/b}$$

is an F random variable with degrees of freedom a and b.

To generate an F variate, we only need to use

$$x = \frac{\dfrac{\sum_{i=1}^{a} z_i^2}{a}}{\dfrac{\sum_{i=a+1}^{a+b} z_i^2}{b}} = \frac{b \sum_{i=1}^{a} z_i^2}{a \sum_{i=a+1}^{a+b} z_i^2}$$

where z_i are standard normal deviates used to produce a chi-square variate as shown in the section on the chi-square distribution.

V. SIMULATION LANGUAGES

9.17 AN OVERVIEW

Let us suppose that a simulation model is to be constructed in order to study a large industrial complex. Further suppose that there are many production lines similar to those studied in Section 9.2 with a large number of repair crews servicing the plant. Imbedded within this framework are various subsets of activities that also interact with the production lines. Machine centers, work forces, inventory systems, rework operations, and so on. It is obvious that if a simulation model is to be constructed and used to study proposed changes within this environment, there are a large number of interrelated events which will have to be processed as the simulation progresses through time. These events will have to be processed in proper order as they occur through time, and any related changes in the system due to event status will have to be properly executed. In addition, each event might be stochastic in nature such that many different probability density functions must be used along with literally thousands of random numbers. Furthermore, in order to assess the impact of selected operational changes; sequencing rules, various queue lengths or queue disciplines, and possible additional changes in the system, there will have to be a wide variety of statistical arrays maintained and continuously updated.

Although all of the above requirements can be handled through proper statement by statement computer coding, it would be extremely convenient and efficient to have many of these tasks "preprogrammed" and packaged in such a manner as to be easily accessible, versatile, and reliable for a wide variety of simulation applications.

A *simulation language* is the vehicle through which these required simulation tasks are supplied to potential systems analysts. Proper use of simulation languages can be crucial to the success or failure of a proposed simulation project. Proper language selection can determine the economic feasibility of a simulation study, and might result in manpower savings by a factor of 10 or more. Although simulation languages differ in their construction, logic, ease of usage, accessability, and flexibility, each attempts to supply to a potential user the following standard capabilities:

1. Structured data input
2. A predetermined time-flow mechanism
3. Echo checks and/or error checks for program inputs and logic structure
4. Random-number generation routine(s)
5. A variety (capability) of random deviate generators
6. A *clock routine* which automatically stores, sequences, and chronologically selects simulated events through time and maintains model equilibrium
7. Automatic statistical collection (generation) functions
8. Standard simulation output of relevant data and simulation statistics
9. Ease of usage
10. Proper documentation and instructions for any user

Although most simulation languages attempt to provide the above standard capabilities, there are many ways in which one simulation language might differ from another. Some of these differences are as follows:

1. Mode and nature of data entry
2. Degree of documentation
3. Procedures for obtaining random numbers and generating random deviates
4. Base code from which the language is constructed (FORTRAN IV, COBOL, SIMSCRIPT, PL-I, and so on)
5. Time-flow mechanisms (uniform or variable time flow)
6. Ease of usage and difficulty to learn
7. Initialization of the program
8. Methods of collecting, collating, and analyzing data
9. Format and extent of output reports
10. Basic intent of the language
11. Primary event classification (events discrete in time or continuous through time)

The advantage in using a preconstructed simulation language is best explained by considering the actual process of translating an abstract or real-world problem into a simulation program. In general, the analyst has the objectives of the study and the scope of the model well defined. He will usually be proficient in at least one computer programming language (usually FORTRAN IV or COBOL). The next step in the modeling process would be a clear definition of the problem either symbolically (flowcharts), descriptively (English, Spanish, etc.), or conceptually (prototype models, scaled figures, etc.). As soon as the problem to be studied is clearly defined and categorized, the analyst is ready to proceed with the construction of a simulation program. In the process of model construction, the program will have to be checked, debugged, and probably changed many times. If the analyst cannot program, but must relay on an outside programming source, serious communication problems might arise. If the analyst happens to know a common language such as FORTRAN IV, and does his own programming, the communication problems will be reduced; however, this does not eliminate the efforts required to prepare, test, and debug a simulation program after the basic situation is understood.

Simulation analysts had to face these problems repeatedly in the early years of simulation application. It was the repetition of these common processes which led to the development of simulation languages in the early 1960s by groups of people who understood the simulation process. The major advantage in using a simulation language is the savings in time and effort required to structure and debug the total simulation model. Although there will undoubtedly be a process of trial, error, and debugging, the total required for these functions is in general drastically reduced. Another primary advantage is that once the model has been debugged and constructed, it is generally easier to modify and perform experiments on a program constructed from a simulation language than one constructed from a multipurpose language such as FORTRAN IV.

In addition to the aforementioned benefits in terms of increased user flexibility, savings in total programming and debug time, and standardization of programming procedures, a rather unique change in modeling philosophy occurs simply because the modeler is using a dedicated and specifically designed simulation language. Many simulation languages are actually programming languages in their own right. That is, such a simulation language can be used for many purposes and has a vocabulary unique to that particular framework. If such a simulation language is repeatedly used for modeling purposes, the analyst begins to structure his thinking and the model-building process within the confines of that particular language. If a simulation language begins to be used in this manner, it actually becomes an aid in the problem-solving process and model formulation. This change in modeling philosophy often serves to reduce or eliminate a critical step in the problem-solving process—the task of converting conceptualization into computer code. This step is absorbed directly into the problem-solving process and becomes as natural as the verbal description of a problem. The analyst begins to "think" as a simulator.

9.18 COMPARISON OF SELECTED EXISTING SIMULATION LANGUAGES

All formal simulation languages have unique characteristics. Some are better suited to certain classes of problems than others. The relative importance and usefulness of a simulation language to a potential user is a function of the user's interests and modeling intent. In addition, pedagogical considerations can be quite diverse from one modeler to another. The interest of a learner might be different from those of an expert, the choice from a systems analyst's viewpoint might be quite different from that of higher management, and the language needed by a chemical engineer for process simulation might differ from that of an industrial engineer in a piece-part manufacturing plant. All users, however, are generally interested in the following common considerations [Emshoff and Sisson (8)].

- A language which facilitates model construction and formulation
- A language which is easy to learn and use
- A language which provides adequate debugging and error diagnostics
- A language which can be used on a wide range of problems

The first criterion relates to the moral, physical, and mental structure of the problem analyst. The statement or commands used in the modeling process should agree with the general conceptual framework under which the analyst might normally operate. The second and third criteria deal with the completeness, integrity, and physical structure of the language itself. These functions are normally embedded in the language structure and cannot be easily changed, if at all. The last criteria deals with the flexibility, completeness, and inherent purpose of the language itself. Several simulation languages will now be described in general terms.

GPSS III–GPSS (General Purpose Systems Simulator)

GPSS is a simulation language originally developed by G. Gordon for the IBM Corporation in the early 1960s (15). GPSS III is the third version of this language, and it requires the use of its own compiler. It is a system which constructs a logical model of the system under study through the use of *block commands*. These commands perform specific functions which are unique to the language. Time is advanced in fixed units as *transactions* flow through a specified sequence of block commands. Transactions might possess certain *attributes* which can be used to make logical decisions at chosen block commands. Each block type might have names, symbols, or numbers associated with it and each block consumes a specified amount of time to process a transaction. Block types can handle one item (facilities) or multiple items simultaneously (store). For example:

Typical block types
$\begin{cases} \textit{Originate:} & \text{Creates transactions} \\ \textit{Queue:} & \text{Creates storage space and maintains certain queueing statistics} \\ \textit{Split:} & \text{Creates multiple transactions from one transaction} \\ \textit{Hold:} & \text{Stores a transaction for a designated amount of time} \end{cases}$

GPSS III is particularly effective when studying inventory and queueing type problems. It provides a fixed format output, and collects predesignated statistics automatically. GPSS III advances time in fixed increments, but the time flow mechanism uses next event logic.

SIMSCRIPT 2.5

The simscript simulation language was developed at the Rand Corporation by H. M. Markowitz et al. in the early 1960s (31). SIMSCRIPT is a complete programming language. Although it was originally designed for simulation analysis, it can be used as a general purpose programming language. It also requires a special compiler, and is available only on certain computer systems. SIMSCRIPT views the world as one in which the status is unchanged except at certain points in time called *event times*. A system is described in terms of the status-changing events, and the components of which the system is composed are called *entities*. Properties or characteristics which are associated with entities are called *attributes*, and a group or groups of entities are called *sets*. The logic of the simulator is constructed through a series of user-constructed statements similar in nature to FORTRAN IV. These statements perform designated functions, but must be strung together in such a manner as to create the correct program sequencing. Events are normally of two types: those which are generated internally to the simulator (endogenous events) and those created outside the simulation framework (exogenous events). Each event that is desired for the simulation model requires the construction of a separate small event subroutine. The initial conditions, elements of the system, and other required input data are initially entered in the program through *definition cards*. SIMSCRIPT provides standard error diagnostics and has a fixed format output for common statistics. SIMSCRIPT 2.5 is a variable time event simulator, or a *next event* simulator.

GASP II

GASP II is a simulation language created by A. Alan B. Pritsker while at Arizona State University in the mid 1960s [Pritsker and Kiviat (44)]. The unique feature of GASP is that the language is entirely FORTRAN IV based, and can be used on any available digital computer with a standard FORTRAN compiler. The logic and construction of GASP II closely parallels that of SIMSCRIPT II, although it contains a unique event-processing routine constructed in FORTRAN. Like SIMSCRIPT 2.5, GASP II demands that the user construct several subroutines that govern the logic and event structure of the simulation process. The user should be quite familiar with FORTRAN IV. GASP II views the world as consisting of various status-changing entities called *elements* (men, machines, etc.). Each element may possess characteristics called *attributes*. Various programmed *decision rules* determine the occurrence or nonoccurrence of *events*. The occurrence of an event may depend on the *state* of the system or on the values of an attribute or set of attributes. GASP II provides extensive error-detection schemes, flexible output, and automatic generation of random numbers and statistical deviates. Fixed output is available for each simulation; however, being FORTRAN based, additional output is easily created. GASP II is a *next event* or variable time increment simulator.

SIMULA

SIMULA is a simulation language which was developed by O. Dahl (53) and K. Nygaard specifically for the Univac division of the Sperry Rand Corporation. SIMULA is among a class of simulation languages which translates chosen syntactic structure into an *ALGOL* base. [PROSIM also translates into an ALGOL base [Emshoff and Sisson (8)].] One of the unique features of SIMULA is the capability to create, destroy, and modify existing and new *processes* created by collections of SIMULA control statements. SIMULA creates a common data file which is accessable by all *processes*. SIMULA also deals with *activities* which can be created or destroyed through structured groups of SIMULA statements and commands. A transaction can be either created or destroyed by processes; however, the procedure must be constructed by the user for each individual case. Program logic is controlled by a master clock routine, and the SIMULA language provides preprogrammed logic to connect all components of the model. As in SIMSCRIPT 2.5 and GASP II, SIMULA provides a random number generator, several random variable generation schemes, a fixed format output, and error-checking devices. SIMULA also allows the user to program special capabilities into the language if so desired.

Up to this point our discussion of simulation and simulation languages has been limited to those simulation models which deal exclusively with *next event* simulation. That is, those events which are scheduled to occur within the time frame of the simulation study, and when they occur the *status* of the system is changed at that time. Most simulation languages advance from event to event, discretely updating time. There are certain processes which change *continuously* over time, and when a chosen *threshold level* is reached a status change is said to occur creating a time-dependent event. Such changes are usually expressed in terms of continuously time-varying equations—differential equations or difference equations. In many engineering design problems and in certain microeconomic models such relationships are quite prevalent. Several simulation languages have been constructed that are specifically designed to deal with continuously time-varying events. A discussion of the major languages is given below.

DYNAMO

The simulation language DYNAMO was created by P. Fox and A. L. Pugh at the Massachusetts Institute of Technology in the early 1960s (46). DYNAMO was created for the specific purpose of studying systems which can be described by a set of finite difference equations. The operating framework from which DYNAMO was derived was *Industrial Dynamics;* a language created by J. W. Forrester some years earlier to study individual companies or a consortium of industrial firms in response to alternative course of actions and management policies [Forrester (12)]. DYNAMO essentially attempts to discretize inherently continuous relationships and operating characteristics through fixed-time advance mechanisms. In doing so, continuously time-varying processes ideally solved via an analog computer can be discretely approximated on a digital computer. If the time advance is fine enough, the continuous time domain is accurately approximated. All DYNAMO models depend on the transfer of information and entities described in terms of *rates* of flow. Certain *decision* functions need to be created to describe how these *rates* of flow actually effect the system under study. The commands used in DYNAMO are very similar to FORTRAN-type statements. However, DYNAMO creates structured *levels* of modeling variables that can be used to describe a wide variety of process relationships. In general, DYNAMO will operate on practically any digital computer with three tape drives and one data channel. Documentation is readily available [Pugh (46)]. DYNAMO has to date been most effectively used in econometric modeling [Naylor et al. (41)], and simulation of industrial complexes [Pugh (46)] along with urban, social, and world-systems models.

There are two other languages specifically constructed to deal with simulation models involving differential or difference equations. Those languages are:

1. CSMP—(International Business Machines, 1967)
   Primarily created to solve engineering design problems
2. CONRAD—(GEC/AE I Automation, Inc. in England, 1970)
   A general language used for continuous processes; it is still in the last stages of development

GASP IV (23, 62)

GASP IV is a simulation language developed by A. Alan B. Pritsker and N. Hurst in 1973. GASP IV is a computer language which can be used for writing discrete, continuous, or combined simulation programs. *Discrete simulation* is simulation in which the dependent variables of the model change discretely at specified points in simulated time; *continuous simulation* is simulation in which the dependent-state variables of the model may change continuously over simulated time; and *combined simulation* is simulation in which the dependent variables of a model may change discretely, may change continuously, or may change continuously with discrete jumps superimposed.

GASP IV is a unique contribution to the simulation field in two primary ways.

1. GASP IV is entirely FORTRAN IV based and written in *ANSI FORTRAN*.
2. GASP IV is the first simulation language to completely integrate the concepts of discrete event simulation and continuous time-varying event simulation under a common framework.

In addition, GASP IV is well documented [Pritsker (62, 45)] and has already been applied to a wide variety of simulation studies [Pritsker (45)].

GASP IV embodies all of the concepts of GASP II, and is structured in the same manner. The primary difference is the definition of *state space* events that occur when a *threshold* value is reached by a *state* variable.

In GASP IV, it is necessary to describe events in terms of the mechanism by which they are scheduled. Those events occurring at a specified projected point in time are referred to as *time events.* They are the type of events commonly thought of in conjunction with "next-event" simulation. Events that occur when the system reaches a particular state are called *state events.* Unlike time-events, they are not scheduled in the future but occur when state variables meet prescribed conditions. In GASP IV, state events can initiate time events and time events can initiate state events.

The behavior of a state variable can be described through differential or difference equation representation.

GASP IV provides a formalized world view. This world view specifies that the status of a system be described in terms of a *set of entities, their associated attributes,* and *state variables.* The GASP IV simulation philosophy is that a dynamic simulation can be obtained by modeling the events of the system and by advancing time from one event to the next.

GASP IV promises to become a widely used and universally accepted simulation language due to its generalized modeling capabilities and its FOR-TRAN base. Having only recently been developed, it is just now becoming known to a wide user audience.

In addition to the simulation languages previously discussed, there exist several other languages which either serve special purposes or have been limited to a small interested group of users. An excellent summary of most available simulation languages is given by Emshoff and Sisson [8]. The interested reader is referred to their work for further references.

VI. ADVANCED CONCEPTS IN SIMULATION ANALYSIS

Although it is beyond the scope of this chapter to explore in any great detail the total spectrum associated with simulation analysis, it should be noted that the actual construction, debugging, and production of a workable simulation program might very well be only a starting point for more comprehensive simulation analysis. Several advanced areas of digital simulation analysis are as follows:

1. Design of computer simulation experiments
2. Variance reduction techniques
3. Statistical analysis of simulation output
4. Optimization of simulation parameters

9.19   DESIGN OF SIMULATION EXPERIMENTS

Once a simulation model has been constructed and meaningful system statistics are being generated, the experimenter may be interested in learning more about the underlying structure or properties of the system being studied. In particular, it might be desirable to quantify the effects of deliberately changing relevant factors over a given region of interest. Through an investigation of simulation output it is possible to create a *response surface* in which the various factors involved are designated at different levels of operation. In order to characterize these surfaces *experimental designs* are often used to analyze, quantify, and predict the effects of response-surface change. Experimental designs such as *full factorials, latin squares, fractional designs,* and *rotatable designs* have been successfully employed with digital simulation experiments

[Hunter and Naylor (22)]. Through the use of *linear and curvilinear* regression, the results of these experiments have been reduced to formulas which can *predict* system behavior over a wide range of changes. The primary purpose of experimental designs is to determine *which variables* are most important, *how* these variables influence the response of our simulation model, and *why* certain results occur as they do in the simulation experiment. Experimental designs are expected to play an increasingly important role in future analysis of digital simulation output.

9.20   VARIANCE REDUCTION TECHNIQUES

Simulation experiments are constructed in order to gain meaningful information about certain aspects of the system under study. For example, in simulating a single-channel queueing problem one might be primarily interested in the expected waiting line or expected queue which develops during the servicing period. Normally, one would observe the system at intervals of change, update all relevant queueing statistics, and print out desired information after a period of simulated time. The entire simulation might yield a result for *expected queue length*. Now, since the simulation itself is a random process, the output is by definition a *random variable*. Being a random variable, simulation output inherently contains statistical fluctuation and great care should be exercised in using these results. In words, we wish our output to be as accurate as possible considering statistical variation. A common way to reduce this measure of uncertainty is to *replicate* the experiment and *average* the simulation results. From elementary statistics we know that for a random variable x and an estimator $\bar{x}$ the following is true.

$$E(\bar{x}) = E(x)$$

$$\text{VAR}(\bar{x}) = \frac{\text{VAR}(x)}{n}$$

Hence, we reduce the variance of our estimator by a factor of $(1/n)$ by doing n times as much work. Since variance is obviously related to the amount of work involved, we can define efficiency as

$$\text{efficiency} = 1/(\text{variance})(\text{work})$$

A *variance reduction* technique is therefore one which reduces the inherent random deviation in our statistical output. Obviously, we would do well to seek methods that will reduce variance by factors proportionately more than the work involved to accomplish this reduction.

There have been several statistically based techniques which help to accomplish this goal. An excellent survey is given by Naylor (41, 57); while Hammersley and Handscomb (19) provide a theoretical basis for variance reduction techniques. Numerical examples are given for a few common techniques in Hillier and Liebermann (60). Some of these techniques are listed below.

1.   Use of Expected Values
2.   Stratified Sampling
3.   Importance Sampling
4.   Control Variates
5.   Antithetic Variates
6.   Quasirandom Numbers

Practical applications of these techniques are very few in number, and the investigation of their use and efficiency is a topic for further research.

9.21 STATISTICAL ANALYSIS OF SIMULATION OUTPUT

Closely related to the problems of variance reduction and simulation efficiency are the problems of relevant statistical analysis of simulation output.

A requirement exists for the development of a statistical technique or set of techniques to (1) validate, (2) authenticate, and (3) collate time series data generated by digital simulation models. *Validation* is an implication that the model adequately represents the "real-world" situation; *authentication* denotes the establishment of a measure of confidence in a single set of model results; *collation* connotes a critical comparison of two or more sets of model output. The process for validating, authenticating, and collating digital simulation models is designated as *verification*. This section addresses itself to this requirement for a subset of time-series data generated by simulation models.

Four main types of statistical functions have evolved for describing random data: (1) mean-square values, (2) probability density functions, (3) autocorrelation functions, and (4) power spectral density functions. In the case of describing joint properties of random data, three types of statistical functions have been developed to satisfy this descriptive requirement: (1) joint probability density functions, (2) cross-correlation functions, and (3) cross-spectral density functions for the amplitude, time, and frequency domains, respectively. Each of these areas are subject to certain weaknesses and strengths. Fishman and Kiviat (9) recently suggest spectral analysis as a superior technique for evaluating autocorrelated simulation results. Spectral analysis has been employed successfully in the study of the time-dependent nature of physical processes and, more recently, economic processes (57).

The initial requirement for either collation or validation of simulation results is the examination of the data for *stationarity, normality,* and *randomness.* It is assumed that *autocorrelation* exists and consequently, standard statistical techniques for analysis of simulation data cannot be accurately utilized. The assumption of autocorrelation is well founded, for it is well known that most digital simulation data is highly autocorrelated. The purpose of a statistical analysis of simulation output would be to remove the effects of autocorrelation from this data, and in the process detect other abnormalities which are not readily evident, such as influential noise and periodicities. Once these effects have been removed, the data should then exhibit the properties of randomness and independence necessary for conventional statistical analysis, and provide a more reliable basis for sound operating decisions.

Not only does the effect of autocorrelation bias most simulation results, but the problem is confounded by the interaction with initial conditions, modes of sampling, and external problems due to faulty deviate generators. The exploration and analysis of these problem areas is a source of current research. Fishman (10) has recently published an excellent text which explores the mathematical and practical aspects of the problem. Duket (61) has also investigated this area and concludes that the currently suggested techniques for the analysis of simulation output may be deficient. Certainly the problem is a highly complex one and will require much further research.

9.22 OPTIMIZATION OF SIMULATION PARAMETERS

Although simulation is primarily a tool for systems *analysis*, there is no reason why one should not employ it for systems *optimization* when the model is appropriate. For example, instead of determining the expected queue length of a servicing facility and analyzing the effects of such a queue, one might be interested in determining the *optimum* queue length with respect to minimized system costs. Optimization of simulation experiments can be achieved through an interface with the tools of linear and nonlinear programming. In addition, statistical techniques such as response surface analysis have been used within the "spirit" of simulation analysis for long periods of time. Direct search techniques which require only a "black box" response can be used to guide a simulation to an optimum response with respect to the chosen decision variables. Some of these optimization techniques are discussed in the next chapter (Golden Section Search, Hooke-Jeeves Search); others are available in books in the reference list. The primary problem appears to be in the interface between sound simulation technology and mathematical optimization. However, with the increasing popularity of the "team approach" to problem solving these difficulties are rapidly being resolved.

9.23   SUMMARY AND CONCLUSIONS

This chapter has attempted to present some of the major aspects of digital simulation analysis. Once viewed as a plaything for idle computer programmers, simulation now plays a major role in the solution of real-world problems from all phases of operations research. Fundamental to the development of any simulation model is the generation of random or "pseudorandom numbers"; and subsequently the generation and use of statistical random deviates. Sections 9.6 through 9.16 dealt in some detail with these two problems. Since a sound random number is an absolute necessity, general tests for determining the validity of a random number generator were explained in Section 9.10.

Simulation languages are now taking a central role in determining the scope and applicability of simulation modelling. Part V attempted to survey the major simulation languages in such a way as to impart general knowledge about their characteristics to the casual reader. Although simulation languages will continue to play a central role in large-scale systems simulation, there may exist problems which can be adequately formulated and solved by hand or on one of the ever increasing "hand computers" currently available on the market today. Part II was used to illustrate the logic and procedures of simulation analysis on two fundamental problems.

Simulation analysis provides a means by which the systems analyst can experiment in a representative problem area without having to deal directly with the real-world system itself. Since simulation is a sampling procedure used to produce relevant statistical results about complex problems, the most important thing about the simulation process is the production, collation, and interpretation of output data. Some of the ways in which this problem might be addressed were discussed in Section 9.21.

Regardless of the position which one wishes to take regarding the scope, purpose, and applicability of operations research, one thing is clear— simulation analysis now holds a central role in the study and solution of complex engineering problems, and it is a tool with which every systems analyst should be familiar.

EXERCISES

1. From the discussion and definitions of Part I, write out your *own* definition of simulation as you now perceive it.

2. List ten reasons for wanting to use simulation to model real-world problems.

3. List five disadvantages in using simulation analysis.

4. Explain the difference in deductive and algorithmic models. Give two examples of each type.

5. Explain the differences in *design activities* and *operational activities* in simulation modeling.

6. Explain the difference in *uniform* time-flow simulations and *variable* time-flow simulations. Discuss the merits of each, and indicate when one would be preferred over the other.

7. The Neetee-Eatee Hamburger Joint specializes in soybean burgers. However, soyburgers are not the only commodity sold. Customers may also buy cokes, fishburgers, and so on. Customers arrive according to the following interarrival rate distribution over the lunch period from 11:00 AM to 1:00 PM

Time Between Arrivals (minutes)	Probability
3	0.30
5	0.20
6	0.15
8	0.20
10	0.15

People who want burgers for lunch usually arrive in groups. The following distribution of arrivals has been observed over a period of past history:

Number of People	Probability
1	0.40
2	0.30
3	0.20
4	0.10

Each individual customer orders between none and two hamburgers according to the following:

Burgers per Person	Probability
0	0.20
1	0.65
2	0.15

Due to fluctuations in burger-eating per person, the average stay per person is a random variable given by the following:

Length of Stay (minutes)	Probability
10	0.10
15	0.40
20	0.30
25	0.20

If a group enters the restaurant, the time in the system for the group is determined by the longest length of stay for an individual in that group.

Using random number tables, simulate behavior of the hamburger joint for a period of 6 hours. Determine answers to the following questions:
1. How many burgers would have to be made on the average on an hourly basis?
2. What is the expected stay in the dining area per group of people?

8. Simulate a multiple-channel service system with three parallel channels, equal selection probabilities, exponential time between arrivals, and exponential service times. Assume an infinite queue length.

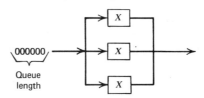

Service Times
Server 1:	6.2 minutes/unit
Server 2:	5.1 minutes/unit
Server 3:	4.8 minutes/units

Interarrival Time: 3.5 minutes/unit

Determine the percent utilization of each service facility for a period of simulated time equal to 3 hours. Compare this estimate to the exact answer using the appropriate formula from Chapter 7.

9. A conveyor-serviced production system consists of two operators in series performing essentially the same operation. A schematic of this operation is as follows:

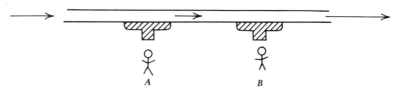

Items arrive via a continuous belt conveyor according to an exponential density function with mean equal to 2.8 minutes/item. Server A and Server B service these items according to a normal density function with the following parameters.

Server	μ	σ^2
A	5.2	1.0
B	5.0	1.0

Server A has in-process storage for two items, and Server B has in-process storage for one item (in addition to item being serviced). Simulate the behavior of this system from a completely idle state for a period of 300 time units and estimate the following:

a. Percent utilization of Server A.
b. Percent utilization of Server B.
c. Number of balkers per 100 time units.

10. List five desirable properties that a "good" random number generator should possess.

11. Explain the difference in "random numbers" and "pseudorandom numbers."

12. Demonstrate the procedure of random deviate generation using the midsquare technique starting with the number 3264. What is the period for this sequence of random numbers?

13. Repeat Exercise 12 using the same random-number seed for the midproduct technique. Use $k = 47$.

14. Using the table of random numbers given in Appendix B, run the following random number tests.
    a. The frequency test
    b. The gap test
    c. The poker test
    d. The runs test

15. Using the Box-Muller normal random generation scheme for standard normal variates ($\mu = 0; \sigma^2 = 1$), write a function to generate normal random deviates from the general normal density function ($\mu = \theta; \sigma^2 = \varphi$).

16. Use the fundamental theory and logic of the *rejection technique* to estimate the area under the following curve.

$$Y = 0.65 \sin(x) \qquad \pi \geq x \geq 0$$

Use 100 points to perform the required calculations.

17. Develop a random deviate generation scheme for the following probability density function.

$$f(x) = \begin{cases} x^2/2 & 1 \geq x \geq 0 \\ 2.3e^{-x} & \infty \geq x \geq 1 \end{cases}$$

18. The following probability density function is known as the *Raleigh* distribution.

$$f(x) = \begin{cases} x/\sigma^2 \exp\left(-\dfrac{x^2}{2\sigma^2}\right) & \begin{aligned} x &\geq 0 \\ \sigma &> 0 \end{aligned} \\ 0 & \text{elsewhere} \end{cases}$$

Develop a random deviate generator for this density function.

19. The *triangular* density function is a continuous density which follows the following general form:

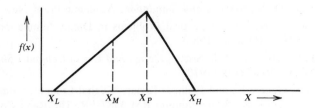

where: X_L = minimum value
X_H = maximum value
X_P = most likely value
X_M = mean value

The triangular density function is given with respect to the position of X_P, such that:

$$f(x) = \begin{cases} \dfrac{2(X - X_L)}{(X_H - X_L)(X_P - X_L)} & X \leq X_P \\[3mm] \dfrac{2(X_H - X)}{(X_H - X_L)(X_H - X_P)} & X > X_P \end{cases}$$

Develop a random deivate generator for the triangular density function.

20. Structure a new random deviate generation scheme for the standard normal density function using the *rejection technique.* Comment on your new method. Would it be efficient; if not, why?

21. According to the text, a Poisson deviate with parameter λ can be generated by finding the number of exponential random deviates used to satisfy the following inequality.

$$\sum_{i=1}^{x} y_i \leqq 1 \leqq \sum_{i=1}^{x+1} y_i$$

where: $y_i = 1/\lambda \ln (R_i)$

R_i = the ith random number in a sequence of random numbers.

Verify this fact.

22. List eight capabilities that a simulation language should provide.

23. What is *variance reduction*? Why is this important to digital simulation experiments?

24. Explain the difference in computer simulation model (1) verification and (2) validation.

REFERENCES

1. Aitchison, J., and J. A. C. Brown, *The Lognormal Distribution*, Cambridge University Press, Cambridge, 1957.

2. Allard, J. L., R. A. Dobell, and T. E. Hull, "Mixed Congruential Random Number Generators for Decimal Machines", *Journal of the ACM*, **10,** (2), 131–132, (April 1963).

3. Berman, M. G., "Generating Random Variates from Gamma Distributions with Non-Integer Shape Parameters", The Rand Corporation, R-641-PR, Santa Monica, Calif., November, 10970.

4. Box, G. E. P., and M. E. Muller, "A Note on the Generation of Normal Deviates", *Annals of Mathematical Statistics*, XXIX, 610–611, (1958).

5. Butler, James W., "Machine Sampling from Given Probability Distributions", in *Symposium on Monte Carlo Methods*, edited by H. A. Meyer, Wiley, New York, 1956.

6. Chorafas, D. N., *Systems and Simulation*, Academic Press, New York, 1965.

7. Conway, R. W., "Some Tactical Problems in Digital Simulation", *Manag. Sci.,* **10**(1), 47–61, (October 1963).

8. Emshoff, J. R., and R. L. Sisson, *Design and Use of Computer Simulation Models*, MacMillan, New York, 1970.

9. Fishman, George S., and Philip J. Kiviat, "Digital Computer Simulation: Statistical Considerations", Memorandum RM-5387-PR, The Rand Corporation, Santa Monica, Calif., November, 1967.

10. Fishamn, G. S., Concepts and Methods in Discrete Event Digital Simulation, Wiley, New York, 1973.

11. Fishman, G. S., and P. J. Kiviat, "The Analysis of Simulation-Generated Time Series", *Manag., Sci.,* **13,** 525–557, March, 1967.

12. Forrester, Jay, *Industrial Dynamics*, MIT Press, Cambridge, Mass., 1961.

13. Gaver, Donald P., "Statistical Methods for Improving Simulation Efficiency", Management Sciences Research Report No. 169, Graduate School of Industrial Administration, Carnegie-Mellon University, Pittsburgh, Pennsylvania, August, 1969.

14. Golden, D. G., and J. D. Schoeffler, "*GSL*-A Combined Continuous and Discrete Simulation Language", *Simulation*, **20,** pp. 1–8, (January 1973).

15. Gordon, Geoffrey, *System Simulation*, Prentice-Hall, Englewood Cliffs, New Jersey, 1969.

16. Greenberger, M., "Method in Randomness", *Communications of the ACM, VIII*(3) 177–179, (1965).

17. Grosenbaugh, L. R., "More on Fortran Random Number Generators", *Communications of the ACM, 12*(11), 639, (November 1969).

18. Gruenberger, Fred Joseph, *Problems for Computer Solution*, Wiley, New York, 1965.

19. Hammersly, J. M., and D. C. Handscomb, *Monte Carlo Methods*, Wiley, New York, 1964.

20. *Handbook of Mathematical Functions*, edited by M. Abramowitz and I. A. Stegun, Applied Mathematics Series 55, Department of Commerce, Government Printing Office, Washington D.C., 1967, p. 950.

21. Hull, T. E., and A. R. Dobell, "Random Number Generators", *Society for Industrial and Applied Mathematics*, 4(3), 320, (July 1962).

22. Hunter, J. S., and T. H. Naylor, "Experimental Designs for Computer Simulation Experiments", *Manag. Sci., 16*(7), 422–434, (March 1970).

23. Hurst, N. R., "GASP IV: A Combined Continuous/Discrete FORTRAN Based Simulation Language," unpublished Ph.D. Thesis, Purdue University, Lafayette, Ind., 1973.

24. IBN Corporation, General Purpose Simulation System/360 OS and DO5 Version 2 User's Manual, SH20-0694-0, White Plains, N.Y., 1969.

25. Kiviat, P. J., R. Villanueva, and H. Markowitz, *The SIMSCRIPT II Programming Language*, Prentice-Hall, Englewood Cliffs, N.J., 1969.

26. Kleine, Henry, "A Survey of Users' Views of Discrete Simulation Languages", *Simulation, 14*(5), 225–229, (May 1970).

27. Knuth, Donald E., *The Art of Computer Programming*, Vol. 2, Addison Wesley, Reading, Mass., 1968.

28. Kruskal, B., "Extremely Portable Random Number Generator", *Communications of the ACM, 12*(2), 93–94, (February 1969).

29. Larson, Harold J., *Introduction to Probability Theory and Statistical Inference*, Wiley, New York, 1969.

30. MacLaren, M. D., and G. Marsaglia, "uniform Random Number Generators", *Journal of the ACM, 12*(1), 83–89, (January 1965).

31. Markowitz, H. M., H. W. Karr, and B. Hausner, *SIMSCRIPT: A Simulation Programming Language*, Prentice-Hall, Englewood Cliffs, N.J., 1963.

32. Marsaglia, G., and T. A. Bray, "One-Line random number generators and their use in Combinations", *Communications of the ACM, 11*(11), 757–759, (November 1968).

33. Marsaglia, G., and M. D. MacLaren, "A Fast Procedure for Generating Normal Random Variables", *Communications of the ACM, VII*, 4–10, (1964).

34. Marsaglia, G., and M. D. MacLaren, "Uniform Random Number Generators", *Journal of the Association for Computing Machinery, XII*, 83–89, (1965).

35. Martin, F. F., *Computer Modelling and Simulation*, Wiley, New York, 1968.

36. McMillan, C., and R. F. Gonzales, *Systems Analysis: A Computer Approach to Decision Models*, Richard D. Irwin, Inc., Homewood, Ill., 1965.

37. Meier, Robert C., "The Application of Optimum-Seeking Techniques to Simulation Studies: A Preliminary Evaluation", *Journal of Financial and Quantitative Analysis*, 2(1), 31–51, (March 1967).

38. Meier, Robert C., W. T. Newell, and H. L. Pazer, *Simulation in Business and Economics*, Prentice-Hall, Englewood Cliffs, N.J., 1969.

39. Mihram, G. A., "On Antithetic Variates", Proceedings of the 1973 Summer Computer Simulation Conference, Montreal, July 17–19, 1973, pp. 91–95.

40. Mize, J. H., and J. C. Cox, *Essentials of Simulation*, Prentice-Hall, Englewood Cliffs, N.J., 1968.

41. Naylor, T. H., J. L. Balintfy, D. S. Burdick, and Kong Chu, *Computer Simulation Techniques*, Wiley, New York, 1966.

42. Phillips, D. T., and C. S. Beightler, "Procedures for Generating Gamma Variates with Non-Integer Parameter Sets", *J. Stat. Comput. Simul.*, 1, 197–208, (1972).

43. Phillips, D. T., "Applied Goodness of Fit Testing," AIIE Monograph Series, AIIE-OR-72-1, Atlanta, Georgia, 1972.

44. Pritsker, A. A. B., and P. J. Kiviat, *Simulation with GASP II*, Prentice-Hall, Englewood Cliffs, N.J., 1969.

45. Pritsker, A. A. B., *The GASP IV User's Manual*, Pritsker and associates, W. Lafayette, Ind., 1973.

46. Pugh, A. L. III DYNAMO II User's Manual, The M.I.T. Press, Cambridge, Mass.: 1970.

47. Rand Corporation, *A Million Random Digits with 1,000,000 Normal Deviates*, Free Press, New York, 1955.

48. Schriber, T., *A GPSS Primer* (preliminary printing), Ulrich's Books, Ann Arbor, Mich., 1972.

49. Schmidt, J. W., and R. E. Taylor, *Simulation and Analysis of Industrial Systems*, Richard D. Irwin, Inc. Homewood, Illinois, 1970.

50. SCi Simulation Software Committee, "The SCi Continuous System Simulation Language (CSSL)", *Simulation*, 9, 281–303, (December 1967).

51. Tocher, K. D., "The Application of Automatic Computers to Sampling Experiments", *Journal of the Royal Statistical Society*, B16, 39–61, (1954).

52. Tocher, K. D., *The Art of Simulation*, Van Nostrand, Princeton, N.J., 1963.

53. Tocher, K. D., "Review of Computer Simulation Languages", *Oper. Res. Quart.*, 16, 189–217, (June 1965).

54. Tramposch, H., and H. A. Jones, Jr., "Impact Problems Efficiently Solved with 1130 CSMP", *Simulation*, 14, 73–79, (February 1970).

55. Weibull, W., "A Statistical Distribution of Wide Applicability", *Journal of Applied Mechanics*, XVIII 293–297, (1951).

56. Wilson, Benjamin, *Integral Calculus*, London: 1891.

57. Naylor, T. H., *Computer Simulation Experiments with Models of Economic Systems*, Wiley, New York, 1971.

58. Nance, R. E:, "On Time Flow Mechanisms for Discrete System Simulation", Computer Science Center, Southern Methodist University, Dallas, Texas, 1969.

59. Schmidt, J. W., "Fundamentals of Simulation", *Proceedings 1974 Systems Engineering Conf.*, Minneapolis, Minn., November, 1974.

59. Schmidt, J. W., "Fundamentals of Simulation", *Proceedings 1974 Systems Engineering Conference*, Minneapolis, Minn., November, 1974.

60. Hillier, F. S., and G. J. Lieberman, *Introduction to Operations Research*, 2nd Ed., Holden-Day, San Francisco, 1974.

61. Duket, S. D., *Simulation Output Analysis*, unpublished Masters Thesis, Purdue University, Lafayette, Ind., 1974.

62. Pritsker, A. A. B., *The GASP-IV Simulation Language*, Wiley, New York, 1974.

CHAPTER 10
DYNAMIC PROGRAMMING

PART I. BASIC CONCEPTS

10.1 INTRODUCTION

In most operations research problems the objective is to find the optimal (maximum or minimum) values of the "decision variables"; that is, those variables which can change or be controlled within the problem structure. Usually, these variables are dealt with *simultaneously* or collectively. Each of us, however, has been faced with problems in which it might be possible to break our decisions up into smaller components or parts (decomposition) and then recombine our previous decisions in some form or another to obtain the desired answer (composition). This approach is called *multistage problem solving*, and dynamic programming is a systematic technique for reaching an answer in problems of this nature. Many techniques are found in this book for solving various optimization problems. Numerous algorithms have been developed to solve both linear and nonlinear objective functions subject to various constraint configurations. One might think that all procedures could be classified as those dealing with either linear or nonlinear functions, but dynamic programming cannot be uniquely classified in either category. Properly applied, dynamic programming cuts across all fields of mathematical programming. Important applications have surfaced in inventory control theory, network flows, job-shop scheduling, production control, integer programming, and many other areas. Dynamic programming has also proven useful in solving problems relevant to all fields of engineering. Although it might seem that we are about to produce the panacea of algorithmic procedures, the reader should be forewarned that this is not the case. Like all operations research techniques, dynamic programming has its limitations and weaknesses. However, when applicable the technique can be spectacular with regard to its computational savings.

10.2 HISTORICAL BACKGROUND

The founding father of dynamic programming, and the man primarily responsible for the current popularity of dynamic programming is Richard Bellman. Bellman first developed the concepts of dynamic programming in the late 1940s and early 1950s while working as a member of The Rand Corporation.

A number of papers subsequently evolved from Bellman's work, culminating in a book, *Dynamic Programming*, in 1957 (4). Since that time, the book has been a continuing source of unique applications and problem-solving logic for numerous engineering problems. A second book by Bellman appeared in 1961, and in 1962 (7) a third book was produced in collaboration with S. E. Dreyfus, a Rand colleague. As Bellman and his associates began to proliferate the techniques and methodologies of dynamic programming, important contributions were made by other authors. Aris (1, 2) authored two books on Dynamic Programming, the first in 1961 and the second in 1964. In late 1964, Aris, Nemhauser, and Wilde developed a generalized theory for dealing with branched, cyclic, and looping multistaged systems (3). L. G. Mitten also contributed greatly during this period (17, 18, 19), and supplied many of the underlying ideas for important future development. Mitten (18), Denardo (9), and Dreyfus (10) all independently contributed to the mathematical properties of the dynamic programming approach.

In 1966 G. L. Nemhauser produced an excellent text dealing with the applications of dynamic programming, *Introduction to Dynamic Programming* (21). Other references include the book by Wilde and Beightler, *Foundations of Optimization* and one by D. J. White, *Dynamic Programming* (26). Other important references are given in the bibliography which follows this chapter.

II. THE DEVELOPMENT OF DYNAMIC PROGRAMMING

10.3 MATHEMATICAL DESCRIPTION

Suppose that we are faced with a problem in which there are known input parameters and we desire to use these parameters (maximize or minimize a criterion) in an optimal fashion. Denote the point at which we make a decision as a *stage*, and our input parameters as the *state*. Let the decision itself be governed by some sort of equation or rule, called a *transformation*. Pictorially

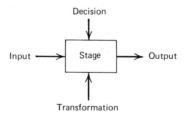

Let us imagine that at each *stage* we are forced to make a *decision*. Every decision that we make has a relative worth, or benefit, (good or bad!) reflected by a decision benefit equation. Let this equation be represented as a *return function*, since for every set of decisions we make we get a return on each decision. This *return function* will, in general, depend on both the *state variable* and the *decision* made at stage n. An *optimal* decision at stage n would be that decision which yields a maximum (or minimum) return for a given value of the state variable, S_n.

Functionally, for a single stage we have:

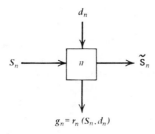

$$g_n = r_n\,(S_n, d_n)$$

where:

S_n = Input state $\tilde{S}_n$ = Output state

n = Stage number g_n = Return function = $r_n(S_n, d_n)$

d_n = Decision

It may be beneficial to clarify these definitions with a representative example. Consider a manager (the decision maker) at a particular point in time (the stage). He has at his disposal a certain amount of money to invest (state variable) in one of ten possible projects (decision variables). Each project would yield a return on his investment (return function). If one assumes that the possible investment alternatives are described by incrementally increasing costs, then the possible investment decisions obviously depend on the amount of investment money available and the project chosen. Hence, as previously stated, each possible return is a function of both the *state variable* and the feasible *decision variable*.

Suppose that we are faced with a number of decision points (stages) related in some manner by a *transition function*,

$$\tilde{S}_n = S_n \circledast d_n$$

(output of stage n) = (input to stage n) $\circledast$ (decision made at stage n)

In this general formulation $\circledast$ represents any operand dictated within the context of the problem at hand, and in addition might change from one stage to the next. For example, $\circledast$ might represent addition, subtraction, division, or multiplication ($+$, $-$, $\div$, $\times$, respectively).
Examples of stage transformations are given by:

$\circledast$	Transition Function
$+$	$\tilde{S}_n = S_n + d_n$
$-$	$\tilde{S}_n = S_n - d_n$
$\times$	$\tilde{S}_n = S_n \cdot d_n$
$\pm\sqrt{}$	$\tilde{S}_n = S_n \pm \sqrt{d_n}$

The units of S_n, d_n and $\tilde{S}_n$ must be homogeneous. These units might be dollars, machines, or any other designation. These units are determined by the particular problem being solved, as will be illustrated through the examples which fill this chapter.

Further suppose that there are exactly N stages at which a decision is to be made. These N stages are all linked by the transition function or functions previously described. Functionally,

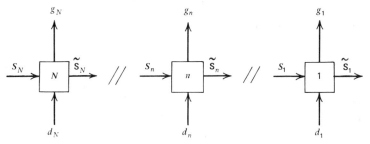

An N-stage multistage system.

Since a state variable is both the output from one stage and an input to another, it is sometimes represented by more than one symbol, namely:

$$\tilde{S}_{i+1} \equiv S_i \qquad i = 1, 2, \ldots, (N-1)$$

Note also that the stages are numbered in an *opposite direction* to the flow of information. The usefulness (or necessity) of such a convention will be made clearer as Dynamic Programming is explored.

In dynamic programming, one solves multivariable optimization problems *sequentially*, or one *stage* at a time. Hence, it will be necessary to keep track of all the returns accumulated in our decision process as we proceed from stage to stage. Denote by $f_n(S_n, d_n)$ the *accumulated* total return calculated over n stages, given a particular state variable, S_n. Similarly denote by $f_n^*(S_n)$ the *optimal* n-stage total return for a particular input state, S_n. That is, a particular value of S_n might give rise to many possible decisions, d_n, among which is a decision, d_n^*, which gives rise to an optimal n-stage total return $[f_n^*(S_n)]$.

Since $f_n^*(S_n)$ consists of accumulated optimal returns, then it can be written as

$$f_n^*(S_n) = \underset{d_n, d_{n-1}, \ldots, d_1}{\text{opt}} \{g_n \circledast g_{n-1} \circledast \cdots \circledast g_1\}$$

$$= \underset{d_n, d_{n-1}, \ldots, d_1}{\text{opt}} \{r_n(d_n, S_n) \circledast r_{n-1}(d_{n-1}, S_{n-1}) \circledast \cdots \circledast r_1(d_1, S_1)\}$$

Now suppose that we are dealing with a minimization problem, possessing additive transitions and additive returns. This implies that the optimization problem is represented as follows:

$$f_n^*(S_n) = \underset{d_n, d_{n-1}, \ldots, d_1}{\text{min}} \{r_n(d_n, S_n) + r_{n-1}(d_{n-1}, S_{n-1}) + \cdots + r_1(d_1, S_1)\}$$

10.4 DEVELOPING AN OPTIMAL DECISION POLICY

If our multistage system actually looks like the one just illustrated, then we can notice some interesting characteristics; namely,

1. There are exactly N points at which a decision must be made.
2. If we *start* at stage 1, then nothing affects an optimal decision except the knowledge of the *state* of the system at stage 1 and the choice of our *decision variable*.
3. Stage 2 only affects the decision at stage 1; the choice we make at stage 2 is governed only by the *state* of the system at stage 2 and the restrictions on our decision variable.
4. And so on to stage N.

To begin, suppose that we *knew* the optimal *policy* (the set of decisions which would lead to an optimal value of our *return function*) for every possible *state* at *stage 1*. It is true that if we make an optimal decision at stage 1 corresponding to a given state S_1, this decision is unaffected by whatever occurs at stages $2, 3, \ldots, N$. (Since they *precede* stage 1.) Now suppose that stages 1 and 2 are connected by the following relation (transition function):

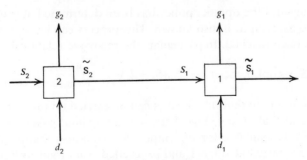

Transition function.

It is obvious from previous discussions that the one-stage return is given by:

$$g_1 = r_1(S_1, d_1)$$

and the *optimal* one-stage return is found by searching over all possible decision variables (defined by a particular state variable). Hence,

$$f_1^*(S_1) = \operatorname*{opt}_{d_1} \{r_1(S_1, d_1)\}$$

Now note that the range of d_1 is *determined* by S_1, but S_1 is determined by what has happened in the previous stage. Specifically, define $S_1 = S_2 - d_2$ for this example.* Consider now the total optimal two-stage return:

$$f_2^*(S_2) = \operatorname*{opt}_{d_2} \{r_2(S_2, d_2) + f_1^*(S_1)\}$$

or

$$f_2^*(S_2) = \operatorname*{opt}_{d_2} \{r_2(S_2, d_2) + f_1^*(S_2 - d_2)\}$$

since

$$S_1 = S_2 - d_2$$

An interesting fact is now observed, namely that $f_2^*(S_2)$ is only a function of S_2 and d_2! (provided $f_1^*(S_1)$ is known for all possible values of S_1). By continuing the above logic recursively, it is clear that for a general N-stage system one could write:

$$f_N^*(S_N) = \operatorname*{opt}_{d_N} \{r_N(d_N, S_N) + f_{N-1}^*(S_{N-1})\}$$

The entire procedure now reveals itself through the above equation. If one is given the input state S_N it is possible to recover $f_N^*(S_N)$ *provided* one has available $f_{N-1}^*(S_{N-1})$. Proceeding further, $f_{N-1}^*(S_{N-1})$ can only be determined by knowing $f_{N-2}^*(S_{N-2})$, and so on, until one finally needs $f_1^*(S_1)$. But this is where the entire procedure started!

From the above logic, the computational procedure is to determine $f_1^*(S_1)$ for all possible values of S_1. Hence $f_1^*(S_1)$ is defined for any state variable at

---

* There are many other possible relations, this particular one is considered only for illustrative purposes. Others will be dealt with later.

stage 1. Knowing $f_1^*(S_1)$, $f_2^*(S_2)$ is now determined for all possible values of S_2 through the following recursion:

$$f_2^*(S_2) = \operatorname*{opt}_{d_2} \{r_2(S_2, d_2) + f_1^*(S_1)\}$$

or

$$f_2^*(S_2) = \operatorname*{opt}_{d_2} \{r_2(S_2, d_2) + f_1^*(S_2 - d_2)\}$$

Notice that once the optimal policy has been determined at stage 2, for any incoming state S_2, then S_1 is also known. This process can be repeated until the Nth stage has been reached. In particular, the recursive relationship is given by

$$f_n^*(S_n) = \operatorname*{opt}_{d_n} \{r_n(S_n, d_n) + f_{n-1}^*(S_n - d_n)\} \qquad \begin{array}{l} n = 1, 2, \ldots, N \\ (\text{where } f_0^*(S_0) \equiv 0) \end{array}$$

The reader should note that this process can be carried on through any number of stages, N, and that at any stage $1 \leq n \leq N$ an *optimal policy* for the n-stage problem is readily available for *any* input, S_n. Note also that computationally the process was started at stage 1 and proceeded from right to left to stage N. In certain problems, it may be more desirable to start at stage N and proceed to stage 1 in the same fashion. The latter procedure is called *forward analysis* or *forward recursion* while the former is called *backward analysis* or *backward recursion*. Both procedures are essentially the same mathematically, but computationally one may be much easier than the other; the choice is largely dependent on the ability or ingenuity of the researcher and the form of the problem at hand. In addition, the mathematical formulations of the transition function and the return function will vary from problem to problem. In general, the recursive relationship is given by

$$f_n^*(S_n) = \operatorname*{opt}_{d_n} \{r_n(S_n, d_n) \circledast f_{n-1}^*(S_{n-1})\}$$

$$S_{n-1} = S_n \circledast d_n$$

Note that this gives rise to multiplicative, divisional, and other relationships from stage to stage. The key step in solving the general dynamic programming problem is the decomposition of the above equation into N separate optimizations involving $f_1^*(S_1)$, $f_2^*(S_2)$, ..., $f_N^*(S_N)$. This general decomposition is always possible for additive ± returns. For the general case, the properties of *separability* and *additivity* must hold. These concepts are beyond the scope of this introductory chapter but the interested reader can see Denardo and Mitten (9) and Dreyfus (10) for details. Finally the states of the system, the decisions, and the return function are generally known from the original problem formulation. Because each problem has a unique transition function, and the choice of states change from problem to problem, dynamic programming is largely an *art*, not primarily a *science*. The more exposure you have to dynamic programming problems, the better your understanding. Hence, we will look at a number of different problems.

10.5 DYNAMIC PROGRAMMING—IN PERSPECTIVE

Dynamic programming is a mathematical technique dealing with the optimization of multistage processes. The basic concept is contained within the "*principle of optimality*":

The optimal set of decisions in a multistage decision process has the property that whatever the initial stage, state, and decisions are, the remaining decisions must constitute an optimal sequence of decisions for the remaining problem, with the stage and state resulting from the first decision (or occurring naturally) considered as initial conditions.

Basic Features of a Dynamic Programming Problem

1. In dynamic programming problems, decisions regarding a certain problem are typically optimized at subsequent *stages* rather than simultaneously. This implies that if a program is to be solved using dynamic programming, it must be separated into N subproblems.

2. Dynamic programming deals with problems in which choices, or *decisions*, are to be made at each *stage*. The set of all possible choices is reflected, governed, or both, by the *state* at each stage.

3. Associated with each decision at every stage is a *return function* which evaluates the choice made at each decision in terms of the contribution that the decision can make to the overall objective (maximization or minimization).

4. At each stage the *total* decision process is related to its adjoining stages by a quantitative relationship called a *transition function*. This transition function can either reflect discrete quantities or continuous quantities depending upon the nature of the problem.

5. Given the current state, an optimal policy for the *remaining stages* in terms of a *possible input state* is independent of the policy adopted in previous stages.

6. The solution procedure always proceeds by finding the optimal policy for each possible input *state* at the present stage.

7. A recursive relationship is always used to relate the optimal policy at stage n to the $(n-1)$ stages that follow. This relationship is given by

$$f_n^*(S_n) = \operatorname*{opt}_{d_n} \{r_n(d_n) \circledast f_{n-1}^*(S_n \circledast d_n)\}$$

Here the symbol $\circledast$ denotes any mathematical relationship between S_n and d_n; including addition, subtraction, multiplication, and root operations.

8. By using this recursive relation, the solution procedure moves from stage to stage—each time finding an optimal policy for each *state* at that *stage*—until the optimal policy for the last stage is found. Once the N-stage optimal policy has been discovered, the N-component decision vector can be recovered by tracing back through the N-stage transition functions.

III. ILLUSTRATIVE EXAMPLES

10.6 A PROBLEM IN OIL TRANSPORT TECHNOLOGY

The concepts and computational procedures involved in solving dynamic programming problems are best illustrated through the use of an example. Consider the following problem.

The Black Gold Petroleum Company has recently found large deposits of oil on the North Slope of Alaska. In order to develop this field, a transportation network must be developed from the North Slope to one of ten possible shipping points in the United States. The total transmission line will require eight pumping stations between a North Slope ground oil storage plant and the shipping points. A number of sites are possible for each substation, but not every site in one area can be reached from every site in the next area for a number of reasons. These include (1) geographic inaccessibility due to terrain features such as mountains or lakes, (2) the inability to purchase lease right-of-ways, and (3) restricted wildlife areas. Associated with each pair of pumping stations is the cost of constructing the connecting transmission line. The construction cost between any two points is not a constant, but varies from a given origin to a given destination. The problem is to determine a feasible pumping configuration for the crude oil, while minimizing the attendant manufacturing costs. The following diagram represents the problem with accessible sites connected by arcs, labeled with the cost of constructing those arcs.

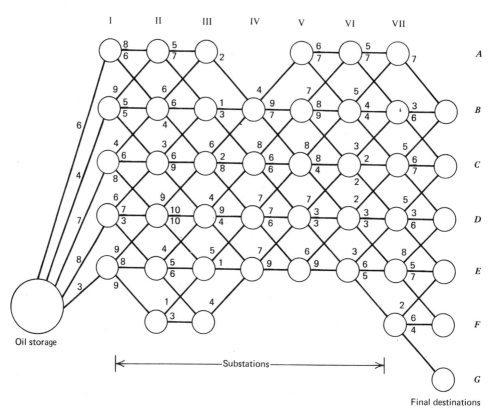

Figure 10.1
The distribution network.

Solution Procedure

The typical analyst might view this problem as one of a finite set of feasible shipping paths. Following this line of reasoning, one might determine that there are more than 100 feasible paths to consider. Each would have to be evaluated in order to guarantee an optimal solution. Furthermore, as the network grows linearly in size, the number of feasible alternatives to be examined grows at a combinatorial rate. Discarding this line of reasoning, one might decide to be "greedy" about the whole matter and develop a solution by choosing the path of least resistance (least-cost path) starting at the oil storage location and proceeding from left to right in Fig. 10.1. The following sequence of oil flow is then generated.* The numbers which appear in each node represent the total *accumulated* cost incurred in reaching that particular node. A quick check

---

* Note that this is not the only sequence one can generate under this criteria since at node IV-C one has two choices of where to go.

reveals that this sequence cannot be the optimal (least-cost) solution, since by

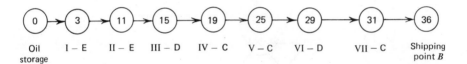

| Oil storage | I – E | II – E | III – D | IV – C | V – C | VI – D | VII – C | Shipping point *B* |

violating our selection rule at position VI-D, we obtain a solution costing only 35 units, namely,

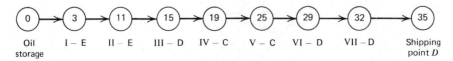

| Oil storage | I – E | II – E | III – D | IV – C | V – C | VI – D | VII – D | Shipping point *D* |

Suppose that we consider an entirely different approach to the problem solution. Let us assume that we have transported oil to some station in region VII. Further assume that we have no idea *how* we got there or what it has cost us to get there. Our primary concern is to pump the oil from whichever station we are at in region VII to a final shipping point at minimum cost. If we adopt the notation that the total cost of proceeding from the current point to a final shipping point will be written inside the node, we obtain the following:

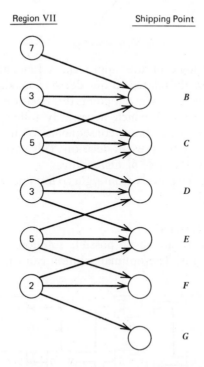

The following observation should now be obvious—*Regardless of where we might be in region VII, we have a minimum cost policy which leads us to our final destination.* Now suppose that we repeat this logic by assuming that the oil has been pumped to region VI and we wish to proceed to a final destination at minimum cost. Again, we do not know *where* we are at, but minimum costs can be calculated for every pumping station. These are given below.

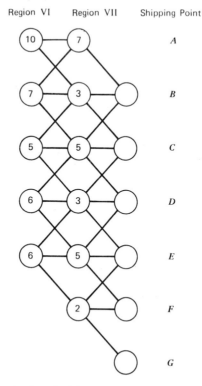

In examining the logic of this approach, a fundamental idea is readily conceived which is directly related to our decision making process.

If a decision is made at any given point, this decision must be optimal with respect to all other decisions which necessarily follow. In other words, all decisions which follow are a direct consequence of the one which was just made, and are dictated by the present decision. This basic principle has already been introduced as the *Principle of Optimality*.

Hence, proceeding recursively from right to left until the oil storage node is reached, Fig. 10.2 is produced.

Interpretation of Results

From Fig. 10.2, there are seven possible solutions, each of which yield a minimum cost of 30 units. The optimal solution can easily be illustrated by a tree diagram.

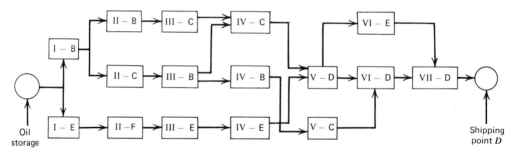

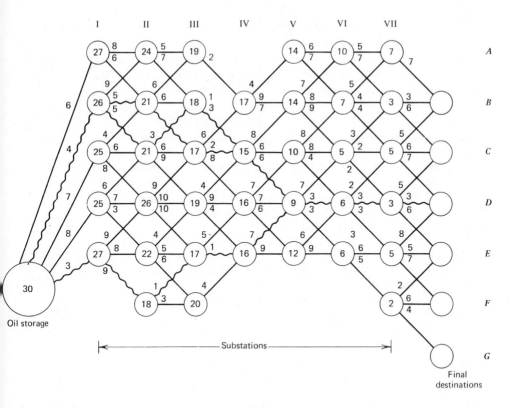

Figure 10.2
Final analysis.

From these results several interesting observations can be made.

1. Multiple optimal solutions have been obtained, not just a single solution. This is an extremely desirable result, since if there exist alternative solutions, they will be uncovered in the course of the problem solution.
2. The total number of paths evaluated in the problem solution increased in a linear fashion, proportional only to the number of pumping stations in each vertical region. Hence the original combinatorial problem has been dramatically reduced.
3. From any vertical region, the *optimal* policy is given from any pumping station within that region to a final shipping point. This could be extremely important as the project progresses.

For example, suppose that pumping stations have been constructed up to the station at node IV-C. Now suppose that we are unable to obtain building rights from node IV-C to node V-D. The new optimal policy is easily recovered since we know the optimal completion costs from any station in region V to final shipping. The optimal policy is to build link nodes IV-C to V-C and continue along the following path.

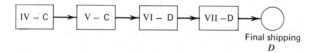

Final shipping
D

The new optimal cost is 31 units. This type of suboptimal evaluation is almost always available in dynamic programming results.

This type of problem is called a *serial dynamic programming problem,* and it can also be solved through the use of decision tables. In order to illustrate the use of decision tables let us define a few key terms.

1. Let each set of vertical nodes be called a *stage.* Thus each stage physically represents a particular pumping region.
2. At any given stage, we will find ourselves at a particular pumping station. Call this our *state.*
3. At each stage we are forced to make a *decision* at each possible state. In this case, we must decide where to proceed. Denote the set of possible decisions as either forward, right, or left from each state.
4. Each decision must have associated with it a tangible benefit or cost called a *return.* This return might in general be given by some constant value, an algebraic equation, or even a complex mathematical model. In this example the return would be a single number (cost).
5. The total cost (or benefit) as one proceeds from one stage to another is given by a *transition function.* This function might be additive, multiplicative, or any other numerical operation. In this example, the transition function is simply an addition of total project costs.

For regions I through VII, define the set of all decision variables at the kth stage as d_k $(k = 1, 2, \ldots, 7)$, where d_k signifies forward (F), right (R), and left (L). Denote $f_k(S_k, d_k)$ as the total *accumulated* cost, given that there are k pumping stations yet to build, we are at a state S_k, and we make a decision d_k. Now, if we are at a particular state S_k with k stages yet to go, a particular decision d_k^* will yield an optimal decision policy, $f_k^*(S_k) = \operatorname*{opt}_{d_k} f_k(S_k, d_k)$. If there exist N stages in a dynamic programming problem, the objective is to find a policy set $f_1^*(S_1), f_2^*(S_2), \ldots, f_N^*(S_3)$. Consider a decision table for region VII. We will call this stage 1 since it is the first decision point, and enter $r_1(S_1, d_1)$ in the body of the table.

Stage 1
(REGION VII)

S_1 \\ d_1	R	L	F	d_1^*	$f_1^*(S_1)$
A	7	—	—	R	7
B	6	—	3	F	3
C	7	5	6	L	5
D	6	5	3	F	3
E	7	8	5	F	5
F	4	2	6	L	2

Note that for any possible state we might be in, an optimal decision policy and return is given by d_1^* and $f_1^*(S_1)$ respectively. Proceeding to stage 2 (region VI) we obtain:

Stage 2
(REGION VI)

S_2 $\diagdown$ d_2	R	L	F	d_2^*	$f_2^*(S_2)$
A	12	—	10	F	10
B	9	12[a]	7	F	7
C	5	6	7	R	5
D	8	7	6	F	6
E	7	6	11	L	6

[a] If one is in state B at stage 2 and decides to go left, this will cost 5 units. This decision puts one at state A in stage 1. From the decision table at stage 1, state A, the optimal policy costs $f^*(A) = 7$ units. Hence the total cost is 12 units.

Note that the entries in the table for stage 2 contain the cumulative costs of progressing from region VI to a final destination. In mathematical terms,

$$f_2^*(S_2) = \min_{d_2} \{r_2(S_2, d_2) + f_1^*(S_1)\}.$$

It is important to note that $f_1^*(S_1)$ is *only* a function of the state variable S_1, and S_1 is uniquely determined once a particular decision, d_2, is known at stage 2. Proceeding recursively, the following tables are generated in a similar fashion.

Stage 3
(REGION V)

S_3 $\diagdown$ d_3	R	L	F	d_3^*	$f_3^*(S_3)$
A	14	—	16	R	14
B	14	17	15	R	14
C	10	15	13	R	10
D	9	12	9	R, F	9
E	—	12	15	L	12

$$f_3^*(S_3) = \min_{d_3} \{r_3(S_3, d_3) + f_2^*(S_2)\}$$

Stage 4
(REGION IV)

S_4 $\diagdown$ d_3	R	L	F	d_4^*	$f_4^*(S_4)$
B	17	18	23	R	17
C	15	22	16	R	15
D	18	17	16	F	16
E	—	16	21	L	16

$$f_4^*(S_4) = \min_{d_4} \{r_4(S_4, d_4) + f_3^*(S_3)\}$$

Stage 5
(REGION III)

S_5	d_5 R	L	F	d_5^*	$f_5^*(S_5)$
A	19	—	—	R	19
B	18	—	18	R, F	18
C	24	23	17	F	17
D	20	19	25	L	19
E	—	21	17	F	17
F	—	20	—	L	20

$$f_5^*(S_5) = \min_{d_5} \{r_5(S_5, d_5) + f_4^*(S_4)\}$$

Stage 6
(REGION II)

S_6	d_6 R	L	F	d_6^*	$f_6^*(S_6)$
A	25	—	24	F	24
B	21	25	24	R	21
C	28	21	23	L	21
D	27	26	29	L	26
E	26	23	22	F	22
F	—	18	23	L	18

$$f_6^*(S_6) = \min_{d_6} \{r_6(S_6, d_6) + f_5^*(S_5)\}$$

Stage 7
(REGION I)

S_7	d_7 R	L	F	d_7^*	$f_7^*(S_7)$
A	27	—	32	R	27
B	26	33	26	R, F	26
C	34	25	27	L	25
D	25	27	33	R	25
E	27	35	30	R	27

$$f_7^*(S_7) = \min_{d_7} \{r_7(S_7, d_7) + f_6^*(S_6)\}$$

The optimal solution is given by computing the minimum-cost routes from the oil storage depot to each possible state in stage 1. The results are given by:

Stage 8

S_8	d_8 A	B	C	D	E	d_8^*	$f_8^*(S_8)$
Oil Storage	33	30	32	33	30	B, E	30

At this point, our recrusive analysis is complete and from the above table an optimal cost route has been found which costs 30 units. However we do not know what this route will be until we retrace an optimal path successively through stages $8, 7, \ldots, 1$. This is easily done since we know an optimal decision for every possible input state at each subsequent stage. At stage 8, the optimal policy is to proceed to B or E. Looking at stage 7, the optimal policy starting in state B or E is to proceed right if $S_7 = E$; or right or forward if $S_7 = B$. Proceeding in this manner, seven optimal solutions are generated which correspond to those obtained previously.

Finally note that since there is only one fixed state for the last stage (*first decision point*), the analysis becomes trivial at this stage. Dynamic programming problems with a fixed initial state are usually called *initial value* problems. Such problems are, in general, easier to solve using computations that run against the sequence of physical decisions as this example illustrates. Such an analysis has previously been defined as *backward recursion*. In Section 10.10 we illustrate the use of *forward recursion* in solving dynamic programming problems.

10.7 THE OPTIMAL CUTTING STOCK PROBLEM

The 'Proper Printer' paper company has received orders for four different groups of informative literature. The following orders have been placed.

> 8 rolls of 2-foot paper at $2.50 per roll
>
> 6 rolls of 2.5-foot paper at $3.10 per roll
>
> 5 rolls of 4-foot paper at $5.25 per roll
>
> 4 rolls of 3-foot paper at $4.40 per roll

Due to heavy demands on the printing process, the paper company only has 13 feet of paper from which to fill these orders. If partial orders can be filled, which orders and how many of each should be filled in order to maximize total profits?

This problem is actually representative of a larger class of mathematical programming problems known as "Knapsack Problems" or the "Fly-Away Kit Problem." Mathematically the problem can be represented as an all-integer linear programming problem in the following manner:

$$\text{Maximize/Minimize:} \quad \{x_1 P_1 + x_2 P_2 + \cdots + x_n P_n\}$$

$$\text{Subject to:} \quad x_1 Q_1 + x_2 Q_2 + \cdots + x_n Q_n \leq U$$

$$x_1, x_2, \ldots, x_n \text{ integer}$$

$$x_i \geq 0 \qquad \text{all } i$$

$$\text{where:} \quad \left. \begin{array}{l} P_i = \text{profit/cost per unit} \\ Q_i = \text{consumption per unit} \end{array} \right\} i = 1, 2, \ldots, n$$

$$U = \text{upper limit on consumption}$$

This class of problems is explored in greater detail in Chapter 11, but it is now shown that this problem can be solved using dynamic programming. In order to do so, we must define the problem stages, decision variables, state variables, return function, and transition function. For this particular problem, we establish the following definitions.

Stages. The stages for this problem will be different orders. Since four orders are under consideration, a four-stage dynamic programming problem must be analyzed. Schematically, it can be represented by the following stage diagram.

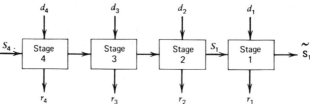

State Variables. The choice of a state variable is probably not immediately obvious for this problem. In general, the definition of the state variables in a particular dynamic programming problem will depend on the foresight and ingenuity of a given problem solver. For this example, a proper choice would be to define the state variable at stage n to be the *remaining* feet of paper left for the order being processed at stage n and *all* remaining stages.

Decision Variables. The decision variables will be how many rolls of paper to manufacture at each stage. A lower bound for the decision variable at each stage is obviously zero, and an upper bound is given by the number of rolls physically possible under the availability constraint. These upper bounds are given by $[F_o/L_n]$, where F_o is the feet of available paper, L_n is the desired length of the nth order, and $[\ ]$ denotes the largest-integer portion of the ratio F_o/L_n. However at stage n there is always exactly S_n feet of paper left for orders $n, (n-1), \ldots, 1$, hence, at each stage d_n will be given by $d_n \leq [S_n/L_n]$, with $d_n \leq [F_o/L_n]$ only when $S_n = F_o = 13$ ft.

Return Function. The return function at the nth stage will be the additional revenue gained by making d_n rolls of the nth order.

Transition Function. The transition function should reflect the amount of available paper left to use at the nth stage. Hence the transition function at the nth stage is the amount of paper left for consumption at stages $(n-1), (n-2), \ldots, 1$. This is given by

$$S_{n-1} = S_n - d_n L_n \qquad n = 2, 3, 4$$

Note that when $n = 1$

$$S_0 = S_1 - d_1 L_1$$

Since S_0 physically represents the amount of paper unused in the entire process, this should be as close to zero as possible. Therefore d_1 is uniquely determined by its maximum allowable value, given by $d_1 = [S_1/L_1]$, and so will be the integer part of this ratio.

The dynamic programming problem is therefore given by the following expression at the nth stage:

$$f_n^*(S_n) = \max_{0 \leq d_n \leq [S_n/L_n]} \{r_n(S_n, d_n) + f_{n-1}^*(S_{n-1})\}$$

$$\text{where:} \quad S_{n-1} = S_n - d_n L_n$$
$$\text{and} \quad f_0^*(S_0) \equiv 0$$
$$f_n(S_n, d_n) = r_n d_n$$
$$n = 1, 2, 3, 4$$

Since there is no reason to order our stages in any particular manner, we may associate any paper order with any stage. For illustrative purposes, let:

$$\text{Stage } 1 \Rightarrow 2.5 \text{ ft paper,}$$

$$\text{Stage } 2 \Rightarrow 4 \text{ ft paper,}$$

$$\text{Stage } 3 \Rightarrow 3 \text{ ft paper, and}$$

$$\text{Stage } 4 \Rightarrow 2 \text{ ft paper.}$$

The solution is given by the tables on pages 436 and 437.

The optimal solution results in a total profit of $f_4^*(S_4 = 13) = \$18.45$. The optimal policy is recovered by working backwards through stages 4, 3, 2, and 1. The results are summarized below

Stage n	S_n	Optimal Policy	Transition to Stage $(n-1)$
4	$S_4 = 13$	$d_4^* = 0$	$S_3 = S_4 - 2d_4^* = 13$
3	$S_3 = 13$	$d_3^* = 3$	$S_2 = S_3 - 3d_3^* = 4$
2	$S_2 = 4$	$d_2^* = 1$	$S_1 = S_2 - 4d_2 = 0$
1	$S_1 = 0$	$d_1^* = 0$	$S_0 = 0$

Since S_4 is known (specified) to be $S_4 = 13$, this is again an *initial value* dynamic programming problem. Note that all available paper was used since $S_0 \equiv 0$ in the final analysis. Now suppose you are told that due to tattered edges, only 12 feet of paper will be available to fill all orders. How is the analysis changed? In a general mathematical programming approach, it would probably require a re-solution of the entire problem. However note that in the dynamic program-ming approach, all that is changed is the value of S_4 (from $S_4 = 13$ to $S_4 = 12$). But by the principle of optimality, if S_4 changes to a lower value, all subsequent analysis at stages 3, 2, and 1 will still be valid since they have been computed for all possible input values of S_3, S_2, and S_1, respectively. (Note this will not be true for *all* values if S_4 is made larger.) Using this basic premise, the following tables yield optimal results for the range of input values $S_4 = 13$, 12, 11, and 10.

$$f_4^*(S_4) = \max_{0 \le d_4 \le [S_4/L_4]} \{r_4(S_4, d_4) + f_3^*(S_3)\}$$

where: $S_3 = S_4 - 2d_4$

d_4 \ S_4	13	12	11	10
0	18.45	17.60	15.0	13.20
1	17.50	15.70	15.70	13.10
2	18.20	15.60	14.65	13.80
3	17.15	16.30	13.70	12.95
4	16.20	15.25	14.40	10.0
5	16.90	12.50	12.50	12.50
6	15.0	15.0	—	—
$f_4^*(S_4)$	18.45	17.60	15.70	13.80
d_4^*	0	0	1	2

Input State S_4	d_4^*	d_3^*	d_2^*	d_1^*	$f_4^*(S_4)$
13	0	3	1	0	$18.45
12	0	4	0	0	$17.60
11	1	3	0	0	$15.70
10	2	2	0	0	$13.80

Stage 1

$$f_1(S_1, d_1) = \{3.10 d_1\}; \qquad f_1^*(S_1) = \max_{5 \geq d_1 \geq 0} \{3.10 d_1\}$$

S_1 ＼ d_1	0	1	2	3	4	5	6	7	8	9	10	11	12	13
0	0	0	0	0	0	0	0	0	0	0	0	0	0	0
1	—	—	—	3.10	3.10	→	→	→	→	→	→	→	→	→
2	—	—	—	—	—	6.20	6.20	→	→	→	→	→	→	→
3	—	—	—	—	—	—	—	—	9.30	9.30	→	→	→	→
4	—	—	—	—	—	—	—	—	—	—	12.40	12.40	12.40	→
5	—	—	—	—	—	—	—	—	—	—	—	—	—	15.50
$f_1^*(S_1)$	0	0	0	3.10	3.10	6.20	6.20	6.20	9.30	9.30	12.40	12.40	12.40	15.50
d_1^*	0	0	0	1	1	2	2	2	3	3	4	4	4	5

Stage 2

$$f_2^*(S_2) = \max_{3 \geq d_2 \geq 0} \{5.25 d_2 + f_1^*(S_2 - 4 d_2)\}$$

S_2 ＼ d_2	0	1	2	3	4	5	6	7	8	9	10	11	12	13
0	0	0	0	3.10	3.10	6.20	6.20	6.20	9.30	9.30	12.40	12.40	12.40	15.50
1	—	—	—	—	5.25	5.25	5.25	8.35	8.35	11.45	11.45	11.45	14.55	14.55
2	—	—	—	—	—	—	—	—	10.50	10.50	10.50	13.60	13.60	16.70
3	—	—	—	—	—	—	—	—	—	—	—	—	15.75	15.75
$f_2^*(S_2)$	0	0	0	3.10	5.25	6.20	6.20	8.35	10.50	11.45	12.40	13.60	15.75	16.70
d_2^*	0	0	0	0	1	0	0	1	2	1	0	2	3	2

Stage 3

$$f_3^*(S_3) = \max_{4 \geq d_3 \geq 0} \{4.40 d_3 + f_3^*(S_3 - 3d_3)\}$$

S_3 \ d_3	0	1	2	3	4	5	6	7	8	9	10	11	12	13
0	0	0	0	3.10	5.25	6.20	6.20	8.35	10.50	11.45	12.40	13.60	15.75	16.70
1	—	—	—	4.40	4.40	4.40	7.50	9.65	10.60	10.60	12.75	14.90	15.85	16.80
2	—	—	—	—	—	—	8.80	8.80	8.80	11.90	14.05	15.0	15.0	17.15
3	—	—	—	—	—	—	—	—	—	13.20	13.20	13.20	16.30	18.45
4	—	—	—	—	—	—	—	—	—	—	—	—	17.60	17.60
$f_3^*(S_3)$	0	0	0	4.40	5.25	6.20	8.80	9.65	10.60	13.20	14.05	15.0	17.60	18.45
d_3^*	0	0	0	1	0	0	2	1	1	3	2	2	4	3

Stage 4

$$f_4^*(S_4) = \max_{6 \geq d_4 \geq 0} \{2.50 d_4 + f_3^*(S_4 - 2d_4)\}$$

S_4 \ d_4	0	1	2	3	4	5	6	$f_4^*(S_4)$	d_4^*
13	18.45	17.50	18.20	17.15	16.20	16.90	15.0	18.45	0

Now suppose that $S_4 = 13$ and you receive a directive that at least one roll of 2-foot paper *must* be shipped. Since this type of order corresponds to stage 4, we are really saying that $d_4 \geq 1$; and because the optimal solution already derived violates this constraint, what further calculations are necessary to solve this problem? The answer is, None! Since we already have optimal policies for any set of input-state variables, stage 4 is examined for the best policy. From stage 4 calculations, it is clear that the best policy is to make exactly two rolls of 2-foot paper $(d_1^* = 2)$. This will lead to the following optimal policy:

Stage n	d_n^*
4	2
3	3
2	0
1	0

$$f_4^*(S = 13) = \$18.20$$

It is interesting to note that this solution is counter to engineering intuition, since logic would dictate that if we are forced to make a 2-foot roll, we should only make one. This decision, however, would result in a profit of $17.50. Following the optimal policy, this new restriction has cost us only 25¢.

10.8 A PRODUCTION PLANNING PROBLEM [Gibson (12)]

There is an East Texas manufacturing operation that produces "Blue Bird" boats. Required production rates for this operation are 100 boats per month. Each boat must be processed through three separate machine shops. Shop 1 contains four machines, shop 2 contains three machines, and shop 3 contains five machines. Each machine common to a single shop is capable of performing the same operation but the machines differ in their ability to perform satisfactory work. These differences can be attributed to age, operators, make of machine, and so on. The operating cost of each machine is composed of a fixed set-up cost and an operating cost per unit. In addition, it is known that each machine produces a certain percent defective. Because of certain complex interprocess relations, previous studies have shown that both the operating costs and the percentage of good units produced are a function of which machine is used in a particular shop to shop sequence. The basic data is given in the table on page 439. All defective units produced by any machine cannot be recovered. Defective units at shop 3 will result in a loss of $20.00 per unit, shop 2 defects cost $10 per unit, and defects at shop 1 result in a $5 loss per unit.

The problem is to determine which machine should be selected in each machine shop so as to minimize the total cost of production.

In order to utilize the technique of dynamic programming, we must first define the (1) stages, (2) state variables, (3) decision variables, (4) return function, and (5) transition function. The following definitions are established:

1. *Stages.* Each machine shop will constitute a stage.
2. *State variables.* The state variables at each stage will be the machine which precedes the present operation.
3. *Decision variables.* At each stage we should decide on which machine to use.

Table 10.1
JOB SHOP-COST DATA PROCESS

Machine Shop	Machine	Preceding Machine	(F) Fixed Cost ($)	(V) Variable Cost ($)	(D) Defect Percentage
1	A	—	50	50	10
	B	—	50	50	8
	C	—	54	48	9
	D	—	55	45	10
2	E	A	20	3	12
		B	320	2	10
		C	220	8	12
		D	220	8	10
	F	A	230	9	5
		B	330	4	10
		C	330	12	5
		D	280	4	10
	G	A	330	4	11
		B	420	2	8
		C	140	2	12
		D	300	6	10
3	H	E	480	52	8
		F	470	48	7
		G	490	44	6
	I	E	500	50	8
		F	500	51	8
		G	500	49	8
	J	E	550	50	8
		F	560	49	9
		G	570	41	9
	K	E	600	42	5
		F	610	40	10
		G	630	40	15
	L	E	800	41	5
		F	850	30	10
		G	820	45	8

Hence the choice of a particular machine at stages 1, 2, and 3 will be the decision variable.

4. *Return function.* Each decision will result in a total production cost (fixed, variable, and defect cost). This total return can be expressed mathematically as:

$$r_n(S_n, d_n) = F_n + V_n[U_n] + D_n[P_n \times U_n]$$

where:

r_n = total cost at nth stage

F_n = fixed cost at nth stage

V_n = variable cost at nth stage

D_n = percent defective

U_n = total units produced at nth stage

P_n = cost per defect at nth stage

S_n = appropriate state variable

d_n = appropriate decision variable

5. *Transition function and the optimization problem.* As one proceeds from shop to shop, the criteria to be minimized is that of total cost. Since the costs are additive from shop to shop, the transition function takes the form of

$$f_n^*(S_n) = \min_{d_n} \{r_n(S_n, d_n) + f_{n-1}^*(S_{n-1})\}$$

but the state variable at stage $(n-1)$ is completely determined once a particular decision is made at stage n, since any particular machine selection made at stage n would actually be the state variable at stage $(n-1)$ by definition. Thus the optimization problem becomes

$$f_n^*(S_n) = \min_{d_n} \{[F_n + V_n(U_n) + D_n(P_n \times U_n)] + f_{n-1}^*(d_n)\} \qquad n = 1, 2, 3$$

where:

$$f_0^*(d_1) \equiv 0$$

The solution is given by the following three-stage calculations.

Stage 1
UNITS REQUIRED

S_1 \ d_1	H	I	J	K	L
E	109	109	109	106	106
F	108	109	110	112	112
G	107	109	110	118	109

Stage 1
COST ANALYSIS

S_1 \ d_1	H	I	J	K	L	d_1^*	$f_1^*(S_1)$
E	6328	6130	6180	5172	5266	K	5172
F	5814	6239	6150	5330	4450	L	4450
G	5338	6021	5280	5710	5905	J	5280

Stage 2
UNITS REQUIRED

S_2 \ d_2	E	F	G
A	121	118	124
B	118	125	120
C	121	118	125
D	118	125	123

Stage 2
COST ANALYSIS

S_2 \ d_2	E	F	G	d_2^*	$f_2^*(S_2)$
A	5705	5802	6246	E	5705
B	5848	5410	6040	F	5410
C	6510	6256	5820	G	5820
D	6456	5360	6448	F	5360

Stage 3
UNITS REQUIRED

S_3 \ d_3	A	B	C	D
No machine	135	136	138	139

Stage 3
COST ANALYSIS

S_3 \ d_3	A	B	C	D	d_3^*	$f_3^*(S_3)$
No machine	12,575	12,315	12,563	11,740	D	11,740

In our analysis, the input to each stage is information about the machine used in the preceding stage, since this is the factor which differentially affects our cost function. We begin at stage 1 and decide on the best machine to use for each possible machine at stage 2. Tabulated results are shown in the stage 1 calculations. To compute the number of units to be processed by the machine in question, simply divide the required output by the percentage of good units produced for that machine. For example, if machine H is selected at stage 1, and the machine used at stage 2 was machine E, then the number of units that must be processed to obtain 100 units is $100/0.92 = 109$. Total cost is the sum of scrap, fixed, and variable costs. To choose machine H preceded by machine E, again as an example, we find the cost to be $9(\$20) + \$480 + 109(\$52) = \$6,328$. The rest of stage 1 is generated in like manner. Hence it is seen that if the machine selected at stage 2 is E, F, or G, then the best choice at stage 1 is K, L, or J, respectively.

Next we proceed to stage 2. Again, for each possible input (i.e., for each machine at stage 3), we decide on the best machine to use. At this stage, however, we must carry the corresponding best cost from stage 1 to derive the minimum total cost. For example, consider machine E when it is preceded by machine A. From the stage 1 analysis, we learned that if we select machine E at stage 2, then it is best to employ machine K at stage 1, which requires 106 units. Hence machine E will require $106/0.88 = 121$ units to be processed. The cost for operating machine E when preceded by machine A is calculated to be $15(\$10) + \$20 + 121(\$3) = \$533$.

To couple stages 2 and 1, we must add to the cost of operating machine E to the least cost at stage 3 when preceded by E which is given in stage 1 as $\$5172$ (corresponding to machine K). The least system cost of stages 2 and 1 when machine E is selected at stage 2 and it was preceded by machine A is $\$533 + \$5172 = \$5705$. The remainder of the stage 2 calculations is generated in similar manner. It is found that if machine A, B, C, or D is selected at stage 3, then the best machine to choose at stage 2 is machine E, E, G, or F, respectively.

Stage 3 is the last stage to be analyzed. If machine A is selected, then $121/0.90 = 135$ units must be processed. Operating costs for machine A are

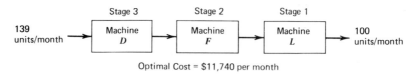

Optimal Cost = $11,740 per month

Figure 10.3
Optimal machine sequence.

then $14(\$5) + \$50 + 135(\$50) = \$6870$. Coupled with the optimal policies $f_2^*(S_2)$ from stage 2, the least cost of operating the system when machine A is selected at stage 1 is $\$6870 + \$5705 = \$12,575$. The same procedure is repeated for machines B, C, and D.

A forward pass through the stage analyses will now find the optimal solution. The stage 3 analysis shows that machine D should be selected. Hence the input to stage 2 is D and from stage 2 calculations, we see that the best machine is machine F. Moving to stage 1 we see that the best choice when $S_3 = F$ is machine L. The optimal sequence is then determined as shown in Fig. 10.3.

10.9 A PROBLEM IN INVENTORY CONTROL

The "Dry Feet Can't Be Beat" shoe store sells rubber shoes for protective use in snow. Past experience has indicated that the selling season is only 6 months long, and lasts from October 1 through March 31. The sales division has forecast the following demands for next year.

Month	Demand
October	40
November	20
December	30
January	40
February	30
March	20

All shoes sold by this store are purchased from outside sources. The following information is known about this particular shoe.

Purchasing Conditions. The unit purchasing cost is $4.00 per pair; however, the supplier will only sell in lots of 10, 20, 30, 40, or 50 pair. Any orders for more than 50 or less than 10 will not be accepted.

Quantity Discounts. The following quantity discounts apply on lot size orders.

Lot Size	Discount (percent)
10	5
20	5
30	10
40	20
50	25

Ordering Costs. For each order placed, the store incurs a fixed cost of $2.00. In addition, the supplier charges an average amount of $8.00 per order to cover transportation costs, insurance, packaging, and so on, irrespective of the amount ordered.

Storage Limitations. Due to large in-process inventories, the store will carry no more than 40 pair of shoes in inventory at the end of any one month. Carrying charges are $0.20 per pair per month, based on the end-of-month inventory. Since the sale of snowshoes is highly seasonable and subject to design changes, it is desired to have both incoming and outgoing seasonal inventory at zero.

Assuming that demand occurs at a constant rate throughout each month and that the holding cost is based on the end of the month inventory, find an ordering policy which will minimize total seasonal costs.

Define the following relevant terms.

Stages. Each month of the 6-month ordering cycle will constitute a single stage. The state diagram will be as shown below.

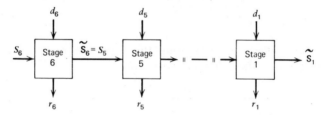

State Variables. At the nth stage, the state variable should be defined as the amount of entering inventory, given that there are n months remaining in the present selling period.

Decision Variables. At the nth stage, the decision to be made is how many pairs of shoes should be ordered to satisfy the demand during stages $n, (n-1), \ldots, 1$.

Transition Function. The transition function must relate the state variable at stage n to the state variable at stage $(n-1)$. This function is given by

$$S_{n-1} = S_n + d_n - D_n \qquad n = 1, 2, \ldots, 6$$

where:

$$S_0 = \tilde{S}_1 \equiv 0$$

$$S_6 \equiv 0$$

S_n = state variable at nth stage (entering material)

d_n = decision variable at nth stage (quantity ordered)

D_n = demand at nth stage

Note that $(S_n + d_n - D_n)$ will be the quantity of items for which a holding cost of $h_n = \$0.20$, $n = 1, 2, \ldots, 6$ per unit will be incurred.

Return Function. The return function at each stage should reflect the total cost resulting from the particular decision made at that stage. The return function at the nth stage is given by:

$$r_n(d_n, S_n) = \phi(d_n) + h_n(S_n + d_n - D_n) \qquad n = 1, 2, \ldots, 6$$

where:

$\phi(d_n) =$ order cost function at nth stage. In this problem $\phi(d_n)$; $n = 1, 2, \ldots, 6$ is composed of a fixed cost of $10.00 per order, plus a variable cost which depends upon the number of units ordered.

$h_n =$ holding cost per unit per month. This cost is the same for all stages and is equal to $0.20 per pair; $h_n = \$0.20$, $n = 1, 2, \ldots, 6$.

The dynamic programming formulation is therefore represented in the following mathematical form:

$$f_n^*(S_n) = \min_{d_n} \{\phi(d_n) + h_n(S_n + d_n - D_n) + f_{n-1}^*(S_{n-1})\} \qquad n = 1, 2, \ldots, 6$$

where:

$$f_0^*(S_0) \equiv 0$$

$$S_{n-1} = S_n + d_n - D_n \qquad n = 1, 2, \ldots, 6$$

$$S_0 \equiv 0$$

$$S_6 \equiv 0$$

Solution Technique. In computing this equation recursively, it will be convenient to refer to the following cost data:

Units Ordered	$\phi(d_n)$	Comment (percent discount)
10	48	5
20	86	5
30	118	10
40	138	20
50	160	25

Stage 1 (March)

Since it is desired to reduce all inventory to zero by the end of March, $S_0 \equiv 0$. Demand for stage 1 is 20 units, so it follows that S_1 will be either 0, 10 or 20 units, and $d_1^* = D_1 - S_1$

$$f_1^*(S_1) = \min_{d_1} \{\phi(d_1)\}$$

S_1	d_1^*	$f_1^*(S_1)$
0	20	86
10	10	48
20	0	0

Stage 2 (February)

$$f_2^*(S_2) = \min_{d_2} \{\phi(d_2) + 0.20(S_2 + d_2 - 30) + f_1^*(S_1)\}$$

where:

$$S_1 = S_2 + d_2 - 30$$

d_2 S_2	0	10	20	30	40	50	d_2^*	$f_2^*(S_2)$
0	—	—	—	204	188	164	50	164
10	—	—	172	168	142	—	40	142
20	—	134	136	122	—	—	30	122
30	86	98	90	—	—	—	0	86
40	50	52	—	—	—	—	0	50

Stage 3 (*January*)

$$f_3^*(S_3) = \min_{d_3} \{\phi(d_3) + 0.20(S_3 + d_3 - 40) + f_2^*(S_2)\}$$

where:

$$S_2 = S_3 + d_3 - 40$$

d_3 S_3	0	10	20	30	40	50	d_3^*	$f_3^*(S_3)$
0	—	—	—	—	302	304	40	302
10	—	—	—	282	282	286	30, 40	282
20	—	—	250	262	264	252	20	250
30	—	212	230	244	230	218	10	218
40	164	192	212	210	196	—	0	164

Stage 4 (*December*)

$$f_4^*(S_4) = \min_{d_4} \{\phi(d_4) + 0.20(S_4 + d_4 - 30) + f_3^*(S_3)\}$$

where:

$$S_3 = S_4 + d_4 - 30$$

d_4 S_4	0	10	20	30	40	50	d_4^*	$f_4^*(S_4)$
0	—	—	—	420	422	414	50	414
10	—	—	388	402	392	384	50	384
20	—	350	370	372	362	332	50	332
30	302	332	340	342	310	—	0	302
40	284	302	310	290	—	—	0	284

Stage 5 (*November*)

$$f_5^*(S_5) = \min_{d_5} \{\phi(d_5) + 0.20(S_5 + d_5 - 20) + f_4^*(S_4)\}$$

where:

$$S_4 = S_5 + d_5 - 20$$

d_5 S_5	0	10	20	30	40	50	d_5^*	$f_5^*(S_5)$
0	—	—	500	504	474	468	50	468
10	—	462	472	454	446	452	40	446
20	414	434	422	426	430	—	0	414
30	386	384	394	410	—	—	10	384
40	336	356	378	—	—	—	0	336

Stage 6 (October)

$$f_6^*(S_6) = \min_{d_6} \{\phi(d_6) + 0.20(S_6 + d_6 - 40) + f_5^*(S_5)\}$$

where:

$$S_5 = S_6 + d_6 - 40$$

Since the seasonal nature of the problem dictates a zero ending inventory, there will be no inventory carried from stage 6. Hence

d_6 S_6	0	10	20	30	40	50	d_6^*	$f_6^*(S_6 = 0)$
0	—	—	—	—	606	608	40	606

From stage 6, the optimal policy is easily recovered from the transition functions and is given by:

$$d_6^* = 40 \qquad d_3^* = 40$$
$$d_5^* = 50 \qquad d_2^* = 50$$
$$d_4^* = 0 \qquad d_1^* = 0$$

Total cost $= 138 + \{160 + 0.20(30)\} + 0 + 138 + \{160 + 0.2(20)\}$
Total cost $= 606 = f_6^*(S_6 = 0)$

10.10 INTERCHANGING OPTIMIZATION—FORWARD AND BACKWARD RECURSION

In all previous examples, the dynamic programming recursive relationship for an N-stage system has started from stage 1 (right) and proceeded to stage N (left). This has been called *backward recursion*, since the calculations were made in a direction opposite to material flow. In many problems, the solution

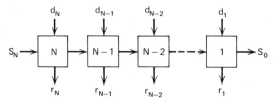

procedure can be developed from stage N (left) to stage 1 (right). This is called *forward recursion*, and generally involves a different definition of the state variables and the transition function than those used in backward recursion.

In order to illustrate the concepts and procedures of *forward recursion*, the previous example will be resolved starting with stage 6 (October) and ending with stage 1 (March). The stages and decision variables will remain the same. However the fundamental definitions of the input *state* variables, S_n, and the output state variables, $\tilde{S}_n$, will be changed in the decision-making process. This is accomplished by redefining the transition function. Recall that:

$$S_{n-1} = S_n + d_n - D_n \qquad n = 1, 2, \ldots, N$$

The state variable at the nth stage will now be defined as the number of shoes left to satisfy the demands for all *subsequent* stages after the demand at the nth stage has been satisfied.

The transition function must now relate the state variable at stage n to that of stage $(n + 1)$. (Note in backward recursion, the role of the transition function was to relate the state variable at stage n to the one at stage $(n - 1)$.) Hence, the transition function is given by

$$S_{n+1} = S_n + D_n - d_n \qquad n = 1, 2, \ldots, (N - 1)$$

where

$$N = \text{number of stages}$$

These relationships indicate the basic difference in state variable relationships inherent in forward-versus-backward recursion. *Backward recursion* starts at stage 1, and proceeds to stage N, computing the optimal stage returns for every possible *input state* component, S_n. In contrast, *forward recursion* starts at stage N and proceeds to stage 1, computing optimal stage returns for every possible *output state*. Note from the forward recursion formulation, the state variable S_n, as defined, is precisely the same as $\tilde{S}_n$ in the backward formulation.

The return function at stage n will still consist of a purchasing cost (subject to quantity discounts) and an inventory holding cost based on the amount of inventory left after the demand at stage n has been satisfied. The dynamic programming problem will therefore be stated as:

$$f_n^*(S_n) = \min_{d_n} \{\phi(d_n) + 0.20 S_n + f_{n+1}^*(S_{n+1})\}$$

where

$$S_{n+1} = S_n + D_n - d_n \qquad n = 1, 2, \ldots, 6$$
$$f_7^*(S_7) \equiv 0$$

Finally note that $f_{n+1}^*(S_{n+1})$ is not actually an $(n + 1)$ stage optimal return, but the *optimal accumulated policy* associated with stage $(n + 1)$. That is,

$$f_{n+1}^*(S_{n+1}) = \operatorname*{opt}_{d_{n+1}} \{r(S_{n+1}, d_{n+1})\} + f_{n+2}^*(S_{n+2}) + \cdots + f_N^*(S_N)$$

The complete solution using *forward recursion* is given by the following tables.

Stage 6 (October)

$$f_6^*(S_6) = \min_{d_6} \{\phi(d_6) + 0.20 S_6\}$$

Realizing that the beginning inventory must be zero, the first stage is decision-less since: $S_7 = 0 = S_6 + D_6 - d_6$. Therefore $d_6^* = S_6 + D_6 = S_6 + 40$

S_6	d_6^*	$f_6^*(S_6)$
0	40	138
10	50	162

Stage 5 (*November*)

$$f_5^*(S_5) = \min_{d_5} \{\phi(d_5) + 0.20S_5 + f_6^*(S_6)\}$$

where

$$S_6 = S_5 + 20 - d_5$$

S_5 \ d_5	0	10	20	30	40	50	d_5^*	$f_5^*(S_5)$
0	—	210	224	—	—	—	10	210
10	—	—	250	258	—	—	20	250
20	—	—	—	284	280	—	40	280
30	—	—	—	—	306	304	50	304
40	—	—	—	—	—	330	50	330

Stage 4 (*December*)

$$f_4^*(S_4) = \min_{d_4} \{\phi(d_4) + 0.20S_4 + f_5^*(S_5)$$

where

$$S_5 = S_4 + 30 - d_4$$

S_4 \ d_4	0	10	20	30	40	50	d_4^*	$f_4^*(S_4)$
0	304	328	336	328	—	—	0	304
10	332	354	368	370	350	—	0	332
20	—	382	394	402	392	374	50	374
30	—	—	422	428	424	416	50	416
40	—	—	—	456	450	448	50	448

Stage 3 (*January*)

$$f_3^*(S_3) = \min_{d_3} \{\phi(d_3) + 0.20S_3 + f_4^*(S_4)\}$$

where

$$S_4 = S_3 + 40 - d_3$$

S_3 \ d_3	0	10	20	30	40	50	d_3^*	$f_3^*(S_3)$
0	448	464	460	450	442	—	40	442
10	—	498	504	494	472	466	50	466
20	—	—	538	538	516	496	50	496
30	—	—	—	572	562	540	50	540
40	—	—	—	—	594	584	50	584

Stage 2 (February)

$$f_2^*(S_2) = \min_{d_2} \{\phi(d_2) + 0.20S_2 + f_3^*(S_3)\}$$

where

$$S_3 = S_2 + 30 - d_2$$

S_2 \ d_2	0	10	20	30	40	50	d_2^*	$f_2^*(S_2)$
0	540	544	552	560	—	—	0	540
10	586	590	584	586	582	—	20	584
20	—	636	630	618	608	606	50	606
30	—	—	676	664	640	632	50	632
40	—	—	—	710	686	664	50	664

Stage 1 (March)

$$f_1^*(S_1) = \min_{d_1} \{\phi(d_1) + f_2^*(S_2)\}$$

where

$$S_2 = S_1 + 20 - d_1$$

Since the ending inventory must always be zero, the stage 1 calculations are also simplified.

S_1 \ d_1	0	10	20	d_1^*	$f_1^*(S_1)$
0	606	632	626	0	606

$$d_1^* = 0$$
$$d_2^* = 50$$
$$d_3^* = 40$$
$$d_4^* = 0$$
$$d_5^* = 50$$
$$d_6^* = 40$$

This is, of course, the same results as those obtained previously using *backward recursion*.

Finally it should be noted that the mathematical basis of whether to use forward recursion or backward recursion depends on the general technique of *state inversion*, a process by which the roles of the input and output state variables are effectively interchanged. The reader interested in a detailed treatment of this subject is referred to in Ref. (25), Chapter 8.

IV. CONTINUOUS STATE DYNAMIC PROGRAMMING

In every problem presented thus far, a tabular decision table was required to list all possible combinations of the decision variable and the state variable at each stage. This solution technique was necessitated by the fact that we were dealing with integer-valued components at each stage. In many problems this restriction can be removed, so that both the decision variables and state variables are free to take on any value in the allowable range of values (the feasible alternatives). Such problems will be called *continuous-state dynamic programming* problems. Computationally the removal of the finite valued state and decision variable assumption allows us to use all the tools of continuous mathematical programming, including derivatives and direct search techniques. The following example will serve to illustrate the computational procedure.

10.11 A NONLINEAR PROGRAMMING PROBLEM

$$\text{Maximize} \quad \sum_{i=1}^{3} r_i$$

$$\text{Subject to} \quad S_{i-1} = 3S_i - d_i \qquad i = 1,2,3$$

$$S_i \geq d_i \geq 0$$

where

$$r_1 = 3d_1$$
$$r_2 = 2d_2$$
$$r_3 = d_3^2$$

The problem is one of maximizing the set of three stage returns, where the return at a given stage is a function of the decision made at that stage. The solution is as follows:

Stage 1

$$\max_{S_1 \geq d_1 \geq 0} \{r_1\} = \max_{S_1 \geq d_1 \geq 0} \{3d_1\}$$

Since d_1 can assume any value on the range $S_1 \geq d_1 \geq 0$, it is obvious that d_1^* (the optimal value of d_1) should be as large as possible. Therefore

$$d_1^* = S_1$$
$$f_1^*(S_1) = 3S_1$$

Stage 2

$$\max_{S_2 \geq d_2 \geq 0} \{r_2 + f_1^*(S_1)\} = \max_{S_2 \geq d_2 \geq 0} \{2d_2 + 9S_2 - 3d_2\}$$

$$= \max_{S_2 \geq d_2 \geq 0} \{9S_2 - d_2\}$$

$$\therefore \quad d_2^* = 0$$
$$f_2^*(S_2) = 9S_2$$

Stage 3

$$\max_{S_3 \geq d_3 \geq 0} \{r_3 + f_2^*(S_2)\} = \max_{S_3 \geq d_3 \geq 0} \{d_3^2 + 27S_3 - 9d_3\}$$

The objective at stage 3 is to maximize the function $f = d_3^2 - 9d_3 + 27S_3$. This is

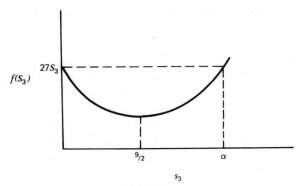

Figure 10.4

a convex function in d_3 as shown in Fig. 10.4. From Fig. 10.4 it is obvious that
the optimal decision policy would be:

$$
\begin{array}{lll}
\text{if:} & S_3 < \alpha & \text{Then;} \quad d_3^* = 0 \\
& S_3 > \alpha & d_3^* = S_3 \\
& S_3 = \alpha & d_3^* = 0 \quad \text{or} \quad S_3
\end{array}
$$

The point α is easily found, since

$$27S_3 = \alpha^2 - 9\alpha + 27S_3$$

$$\Rightarrow \alpha = 9$$

Hence

$$
f_3^*(S_3) = \begin{cases} 27S_3 & \text{for} \quad S_3 \leqq 9 \\ S_3^2 + 18S_3 & \text{for} \quad S_3 > 9 \end{cases}
$$

The optimal decision policy is now available for any input state S_3. Solution
values are given in Table 10.2 for selected inputs.

Table 10.2

S_3	d_1^*	d_2^*	d_3^*	Optimal Return $f_3^*(S_3)$
3	27	0	0	81.0
6	54	0	0	162
9	81(54)	0	0(9)	243
12	72	0	12	360

10.12   A PROBLEM IN MUTUAL FUND INVESTMENT STRATEGIES*

Continuous-Variable, Initial Value Problem

Suppose you are considering investment in two mutual funds. You have
$10,000 to invest right now and will be able to invest an additional $1000 per
year for each of the next 4 years. At the beginning of each investment period,
you must decide how much of your available capital to invest in each fund.
Once invested, the money cannot be withdrawn until the end of the 5-year
period. The investments will earn money in two different ways: (1) Each fund

* This problem was adapted from one presented by Wilde and Beightler (25); originally conceived by
Bellman (4).

has a long-term dividend potential realized as a percent return per year on accumulated capital, and the value of any investment left in the fund is expected to increase at this growth rate; (2) each fund also has a short-term interest-dividend rate, and any investment in some period will return cash to you at the end of the period at the particular rate of interest. This cash is available for reinvestment. Any money not invested in one of these funds earns you nothing.

What you need is a "5-year plan" for investment, the goal being to maximize total investment returns at the end of the fifth year.

Fund	Short-Term Rates (i)					Long Term Dividend (I)
	1	2	3	4	5	
A	0.020	0.0225	0.0225	0.025	0.025	0.04
B	0.060	0.0475	0.050	0.040	0.040	0.03

Use backward recursion and consider the last year first:

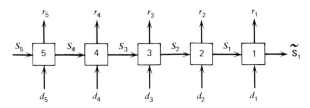

Define. Stage: each investment period

State: S_n = amount of capital available for investment at beginning of year $(6-n)$

Decision: d_n = amount of capital to invest in fund A at beginning of year $(6-n)$

$\therefore (S_n - d_n)$ = amount of money for fund B

Return: r_n = future value of long term earnings for stages $5, 4, 3, 2$.

r_1 = present value of all earnings for stage 1.

Transition Function: $S_{n-1} = i_A d_n + i_B (S_n - d_n) + 1000$

$= 1000 + i_B \cdot S_n + d_n (i_A - i_B)$ for $n = 1, 2, 3, 4$

and

$S_5 = 10{,}000$

The goal is to

$$\max R = \sum_{n=1}^{5} r_n$$

where

$r_n = (1 + I_A)^n \cdot d_n + (1 + I_B)^n (S_n - d_n)$

$= d_n [(1 + I_A)^n - (1 + I_B)^n] + S_n (1 + I_B)^n$ for $n = 2, 3, 4, 5$

$r_1 = (1 + I_A)^1 d_1 + (1 + I_B)^1 (S_1 - d_1) + i_A d_1 + i_B (S_1 - d_1)$

$= d_1 [I_A - I_B + i_A - i_B] + S_1 [1 + I_B + i_B]$

Stage 1

$$f_1^*(S_1) = \max_{0 \le d_1 \le S_1} \{d_1(0.04 - 0.03 + 0.025 - 0.040) + S_1(1 + 0.03 + 0.040)\}$$

$$= \max_{d_1} \{1.070S_1 - 0.005d_1\}$$

The optimal decision is therefore to make d_1 as small as possible. Hence

$$d_1^* = 0$$

$$f_1^*(S_1) = 1.070S_1$$

Stage 2

$$f_2^*(S_2) = \max_{0 \le d_2 \le S_2} \{r_2 + f_1^*(S_1)\}$$

$$= \max_{d_2} \{d_2(1.04^2 - 1.03^2) + S_2(1.03)^2 + 1.07(1000 + 0.04S_2 - 0.015d_2)\}$$

$$= \max_{d_2} \{1070 + 1.1037S_2 + 0.0046d_2\}$$

Hence

$$f_2^*(S_2) = 1070 + 1.108S_2 \qquad \text{and} \qquad d_2^* = S_2$$

Stage 3

$$f_3^*(S_3) = \max_{0 \le d_3 \le S_3} \{r_3 + f_2^*(S_2)\}$$

$$= \max_{d_3} \{d_3(1.04^3 - 1.03^3) + S_3(1.03)^3 + 1070$$

$$+ 1.108(1000 + 0.05S_3 - 0.0275d_3)\}$$

$$= \max_{d_3} \{2178 + 1.1481S_3 + 0.0018d_3\}$$

Hence

$$f_3^*(S_3) = 2178 + 1.15S_3 \qquad \text{and} \qquad d_3^* = S_3$$

Stage 4

$$f_4^*(S_4) = \max_{0 \le d_4 \le S_4} \{r_4 + f_3^*(S_3)\}$$

$$= \max_{d_4} \{d_4(1.04^4 - 1.03^4) + S_4(1.03)^4 + 2178$$

$$+ 1.15(1000 + 0.045S_4 - 0.025d_4)\}$$

$$= \max_{d_4} \{3328 + 1.1772S_4 + 0.0156d_4\}$$

Hence

$$f_4^*(S_4) = 3328 + 1.193S_4 \qquad \text{for} \qquad d_4^* = S_4$$

Stage 5

$$f_5^*(S_5) = \max_{0 \le d_5 \le S_5} \{r_5 + f_4^*(S_4)\}$$

But

$$S_5 = 10{,}000$$

Therefore

$$f_5^*(S_5) = \max_{d_5} \{d_5(1.04^5 - 1.03^5) + 10{,}000(1.03)^5$$

$$+ 3328 + 1.193(1000 + 0.05(10{,}000) - 0.04d_5)\}$$

or

$$f_5^*(S_5) = \max_{d_5} \{16{,}711 + 0.0097d_5\}$$

Hence

$$f_5^*(S_5) = 16,808 \quad \text{and} \quad d_5^* = S_5 = 10,000$$

Summary

	Investment in Fund	
Beginning of year	*A*	*B*
1	10,000	0
2	All available funds	0
3	All available funds	0
4	All available funds	0
5	0	All available funds

Optimal total return $= f_5^*(S_5 = \$10,000) = \$16,808$ at end of fifth year.

10.13 A SPECIAL CASE OF LINEAR ALLOCATIONS IN CONTINUOUS DYNAMIC PROGRAMMING [CRISP AND BEIGHTLER (8)]

Suppose that we consider a serial multistage system with linear return functions of the form, $r_n = a_n d_n + b_n S_n$, and linear transition functions given by $S_{n-1} = A_n d_n + B_n S_n$, all n. The specific optimization problem will be of the following form:

$$\text{Maximize}_{d_n \in S} \quad \sum_{n=1}^{N} r_n$$

$$\text{Subject to} \quad r_n = a_n d_n + b_n S_n$$

$$S_{n-1} = A_n d_n + B_n S_n \qquad n = 1, 2, \ldots, N$$

$$S_n \geq d_n \geq 0$$

Crisp and Beightler (8) have shown that under certain conditions, the dynamic programming approach is unnecessary, and the optimal solutions can be generated through simple algebraic manipulations. Crisp and Beightler have proved the following theorems.

THEOREM I

If a_n, b_n, A_n, and B_n are all greater than zero, then:

$$d_n^* = S_n \qquad n = 1, 2, \ldots, N$$

$$f_N^*(S_N) = \sum_{n=1}^{N} (a_n + b_n) S_n$$

Corollary 1. If: $a_n = \alpha \qquad A_n = A \qquad$ all n
$b_n = \beta \qquad B_n = B$

$$\alpha, \beta, A, B > 0$$

then: $d_n^* = S_n \qquad n = 1, 2, \ldots, N$

$$f_N^*(S_N) = (\alpha + \beta)\left[\frac{1 - (A+B)^n}{1 - (A+B)}\right]$$

THEOREM II

If:

$$\begin{cases} a_n = \alpha \\ b_n = \beta \\ A_n = A \\ B_n = B \end{cases} \text{all } n \text{ and} \quad \begin{cases} \alpha, \beta > 0 \\ A < 0 \\ B > 0 \\ A + B > 0 \end{cases}$$

then:

$$d_n^* = S_n \qquad n = 1, 2, \ldots, \phi$$
$$d_n^* = 0 \qquad n = \phi + 1, \phi + 2, \ldots, N$$

$$f_N^*(S_N) = \beta \sum_{n=1}^{N} S_n + \alpha \sum_{n=0}^{\phi} S_n$$

$$\Rightarrow f_N^*(S_N) = \left\{ B^{N-\phi} \left\{ (\alpha + \beta) \left[\frac{1 - (A+B)^N}{1 - (A+B)} \right] \right\} + \left[\frac{1 - B^{N-\phi}}{1 - B} \right] \right\} \cdot S_N$$

where:

$$\phi = T_r \left[\frac{\ln \left[\dfrac{A\beta + \alpha(1-B)}{A(\alpha + \beta)} \right]}{\ln(A+B)} + 1 \right]$$

and T_r indicates a truncation of the bracketed term: $[\cdots]$.

THEOREM III

If:

$$\begin{cases} a_n = \alpha \\ b_n = \beta \\ A_n = A \\ B_n = B \end{cases} \text{all } n \text{ and} \quad \begin{cases} A, B, \beta > 0 \\ \alpha < 0 \\ \alpha + \beta > 0 \end{cases}$$

then:

$$d_n^* = 0 \qquad n = 1, 2, \ldots, \phi$$
$$d_n^* = S_n \qquad n = \phi + 1, \phi + 2, \ldots, N$$

$$f_N^* = \beta \sum_{n=1}^{N} S_n + \alpha \sum_{n=\phi}^{N} S_n = \left\{ (A+B)^{N-\phi} \left\{ \beta \left[\frac{1 - B^\phi}{1 - B} \right] \right\} + (\alpha + \beta) \left[\frac{1 - (A+B)^{N-\phi}}{1 - (A+B)} \right] \right\} S_N$$

where:

$$\phi = T_r \left[\frac{\ln \left(\dfrac{A\beta + \alpha - \alpha\beta}{A\beta} \right)}{\ln B} \right]$$

EXAMPLE 13-1   LINEAR ALLOCATION PROBLEM

A numerical example will serve to illustrate the procedure. Consider the following 15-stage dynamic programming problem [Crisp and Beightler (8)].

$$\text{Maximize:} \qquad \sum_{i=1}^{15} r_n$$

$$\text{Subject to:} \qquad r_n = -2.0 d_n + 2.2 S_n$$

$$S_{n-1} = 0.1 d_n + 1.1 S_n$$

$$n = 1, 2, \ldots, 15$$

$$\text{and:} \qquad S_N = S_{15} = 100$$

This problem conforms to the conditions specified in Theorem III. Hence

$$\alpha = -2.00 \qquad \beta = 2.20 \qquad A = 0.10 \qquad B = 1.10$$

Therefore

$$\phi = T_r \left[\frac{\ln \left(\frac{0.22 + 2.0 - 2.2}{0.22} \right)}{\ln (1.1)} \right] = 7$$

Hence

$$d_1^* = d_2^* = \cdots = d_7^* = 0$$

$$d_8^* = d_9^* = \cdots = d_{15}^* = S_n$$

$$f_{15}^*(S_N = 100) = 2.2 \sum_{n=1}^{15} S_n - 2.0 \sum_{n=8}^{15} S_n$$

$$= \left\{ (1.20)^8 \left\{ 2.20 \left[\frac{1 - (1.10)^7}{1 - 1.10} \right] \right\} + 0.20 \left[\frac{1 - (1.2)^8}{1 - 1.2} \right] \right\} 0.100$$

$$= 9303$$

V. MULTIPLE-STATE VARIABLES

10.14   THE "CURSE OF DIMENSIONALITY"

In all the example problems solved thus far, each was characterized by the presence of a single-state variable at every stage in the dynamic programming formulation. Computationally, the presence of multiple-state variables creates major difficulties in the solution of dynamic programming problems. Consider a ten-stage problem with a single-state variable composed of five components at each stage. If a feasible decision can be made at every stage over all five components the solution procedure will require at most $(5 \times 5 \times 10) = 250$ calculations to be made in the problem solution. Now consider the addition of another state variable at each stage consisting of five components. Each stage might now require $(5 \times 5 \times 5)$ calculations, while the entire program could require as many as $(5 \times 5 \times 5 \times 10) = 1250$ separate calculations in the decision/state variable matrices. In addition, in order to compute an optimal solution to the complete problem, it is necessary to retain an optimal solution to *every* state variable combination at each stage. If one considers a problem with five state variables, each with ten components, the amount of information required to both be computed and stored would be astronomical! This dramatic increase in the amount of work (and storage) required to reach an optimal solution has been called the "curse of dimensionality" by Bellman (4).

The difficulties encountered in multiple-state dynamic programming will be illustrated through the solution of the following nonlinear, integer programming problem.

10.15   A NONLINEAR, INTEGER PROGRAMMING PROBLEM

$$\text{Maximize:} \quad 13x_1 - 5x_2^2 + 30.2x_2 - x_1^2 + 10x_3 - 2.5x_3^2$$

$$\text{Subject to:} \quad 2x_1 + 4x_2 + 5x_3 \leq 10$$

$$x_1 + x_2 + x_3 \leq 5$$

$$x_1, x_2, x_3 \geq 0 \quad \text{and integer}$$

Define the *decision variables* as $d_1 = x_1$, $d_2 = x_2$ and $d_3 = x_3$, and let the *stages* correspond to the variables x_i, $i = 1, 2, 3$.

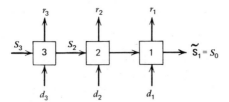

Since the present problem has two equality constraints, there will be two state variables to search over. Denote these two state variables at the nth stage as S_n and y_n, $n = 1, 2, \ldots, N$, such that

$$S_{n-1} = S_n - \alpha_n d_n \qquad n = 1, 2, \ldots, N$$
$$y_{n-1} = y_n - \nu_n d_n$$

The optimization problem now becomes

$$\text{Maximize:} \quad 13d_1 - 5d_2^2 + 30.2d_2 - d_1^2 + 10d_3 - 2.5d_3^2$$
$$\text{Subject to:} \quad 2d_1 + 4d_2 + 5d_3 \leq 10$$
$$d_1 + d_2 + d_3 \leq 5$$
$$d_1, d_2 \geq 0$$
$$d_1, d_2 = 0, 1, 2, \ldots$$

Stage 1:

$$f^*(S_1, y_1) = \max_{0 \leq d_1 \leq \min[10/2, 5]} \{13d_1 - d_1^2\}$$

Since

$$\frac{\partial f(S_1, y_1)}{\partial d_1} = 13 - 2d_1 = 0$$

This implies that $d_1 = 6.5$, and the second derivative verifies that this is a maximum. Note, however, from the bounds on the decision variable that $5 \geq d_1^* \geq 0$, so the optimal solution would be to make d_1 as large as possible. Hence, noting that only integer solutions are feasible.

$$d_1^* = \min I\left\{\frac{S_1}{2}, y_1\right\}$$

where

$$I = \text{integer values of } \frac{S_1}{2} \text{ and } y_1$$

The solution to the stage I problem is given by Table 10.3 for all feasible combinations of S_1 and y_1.

Stage 2:

$$f_2^*(S_2, y_2) = \underset{0 \leq d_2 \leq [10/4, 5]}{\text{Maximize}} \{30.2d_2 - 5d_2^2 + f_1^*(S_1, y_1)\}$$

$$\text{Subject to} \quad S_1 = S_2 - 4d_2$$
$$y_1 = y_2 - d_2$$

Since $f_2(S_2, y_2) = 30.2d_2 - 5d_2^2$

$$\frac{\partial f_2}{\partial d_2} = 30.2 - 10d_2 = 0$$

Table 10.3
TWO-TABLE VARIABLE COMPUTATIONS

S_1 \ y_1	0	1	2	3	4	5	6	7	8	9	10
0	0 / 0										
1	0 / 0	0 / 0	1 / 12								
2	0 / 0	0 / 0	1 / 12	1 / 12	2 / 22						
3	0 / 0	0 / 0	1 / 12	1 / 12	2 / 22	2 / 22	3 / 30				
4	0 / 0	0 / 0	1 / 12	1 / 12	2 / 22	2 / 22	3 / 30	3 / 30	4 / 36		
5	0 / 0	0 / 0	1 / 12	1 / 12	2 / 22	2 / 22	3 / 30	3 / 30	4 / 36	4 / 36	5 / 40

S_n d_n, which yields highest stage n return;

Y_n $f^*(S_n, y_n)$ for a given d_n;

⟶   indicates all entries in that row are the same as the last entry recorded in that row.

Table 10.4

STAGE TWO CALCULATIONS

S_2 \ y_2	0	1	2	3	4	5	6	7	8	9	10
0	0 / 0										
1	0 / 0	0 / 0	0 / 12	0 / 12	1 / 25.2						
2	0 / 0	0 / 0	0 / 12	0 / 12	1 / 25.2	1 / 25.2	1 / 37.2	1 / 37.2	2 / 40.4	2 / 40.4	2 / 52.4
3	0 / 0	0 / 0	0 / 12	0 / 12	1 / 25.2	1 / 25.2	1 / 37.2	1 / 37.2	2 / 47.2	2 / 40.4	2 / 52.4
4	0 / 0	0 / 0	0 / 12	0 / 12	1 / 25.2	1 / 25.2	1 / 37.2	1 / 37.2	1 / 47.2	2 / 40.4	1 / 52.2
5	0 / 0	0 / 0	0 / 12	0 / 12	1 / 25.2	1 / 25.2	1 / 37.2	1 / 37.2	1 / 47.2	2 / 40.4	1 / 55.2

Therefore $d_2 = 3$ $\left(\text{a maximum point since } \dfrac{\partial^2 f_2}{\partial f_2^2} < 0\right)$. However d_2 cannot assume a value of 3 since if d_1 is zero, $4d_2 \leq 10$, and max $\{d_2\} = 2$. In addition, it may not be optimal to choose d_2 as large as possible due to the variable dependencies. Feasible combinations are thus evaluated at stage 2 taking into account the stage 1 returns (see Table 10.4).

Stage 3:

$$f_3^*(S_3 - y_3) = \underset{0 \leq d_3 \leq [10/5,5]}{\text{Maximize}} \{10 d_3 - 2.5 d_3^2 + f_2^*(S_2, y_2)\}$$

Subject to $S_2 = S_3 - 5d_3$

$y_2 = y_3 - d_3$

But at stage 3, the state variables are known to be $S_3 = 10$ and $y_3 = 5$. The stage constraints therefore become

$$S_2 = 10 - 5d_3 \qquad \text{and} \qquad y_2 = 5 - d_3$$

since $f_3(S_3, y_3) = 10 d_3 - 2.5 d_3^2$

$$\frac{\partial f_3}{\partial d_3} = 10 - 5 d_3 = 0$$

which implies $d_3 = 2$ [a maximum stationary point]

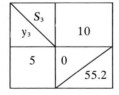

$$\begin{bmatrix} \text{Note that } d_3^* = 0 \text{ was} \\ \text{chosen, as usual, from} \\ \text{the entire set of} \\ \text{feasible } d_3 \end{bmatrix}$$

Hence

$$f_3^*(S_3 = 10, y = 5) = 55.20$$

Using the stage transition functions, it is easily found that the optimal solution is given by

$$d_3^* = x_3^* = 0$$
$$d_2^* = x_2^* = 1$$
$$d_1^* = x_1^* = 3$$

Although it was unnecessary to compute optimal returns for all possible state variable combinations (due to the decision restrictions), it is obvious that a great many more computations are necessary to solve a two-state variable problem than a one-state variable problem. In general, a dynamic programming formulation becomes quite unattractive when the number of state variables involved are three or more.

10.16   ELIMINATION OF STATE VARIABLES

Bellman and Dryfus (7) have suggested a procedure that can be used to considerably reduce this "curse of dimensionality" previously encountered. The technique is to introduce Lagrangian multipliers [Nemhauser (21)] into the problem. Consider the following N-stage dynamic programming problem with M-state variables.

Program I

$$\text{Maximize:} \quad f(\mathbf{d}) = \sum_{n=1}^{N} a_n d_n^{\phi_n}$$

$$\text{Subject to:} \quad h_1(\mathbf{d}) = \sum_{i=1}^{N} \alpha_i d_i^{\delta_i} \leq \beta_1$$

$$\cdot \qquad \cdot \qquad \cdot$$
$$\cdot \qquad \cdot \qquad \cdot$$
$$\cdot \qquad \cdot \qquad \cdot$$

$$h_{M-1}(\mathbf{d}) = \sum_{i=1}^{N} w_i d_i^{P_i} \leq \beta_{M-1}$$

$$h_M(\mathbf{d}) = \sum_{i=1}^{N} v_i d_i^{\phi_i} \leq \beta_M$$

Using a technique first proposed by the French mathematician Lagrange, $(M-1)$ Lagrangian multipliers, $\lambda_1, \lambda_2, \ldots, \lambda_{M-1}$, can be introduced reducing the above problem to a one-state variable dynamic programming problem consisting of $(N+M-1)$ decision variables.

The new problem would be

Program II

$$\text{Maximize:} \quad g(\mathbf{d}, \boldsymbol{\lambda}) = \sum_{n=1}^{N} \{ a_n d_n^{\phi_n} - \lambda_1[\alpha_n d^{\delta_n}] - \cdots - \lambda_{M-1}[w_n d_n^{P_n}] \}$$

$$\text{Subject to:} \quad \sum_{i=1}^{N} v_i d_i^{\phi_i} \leq \beta_M$$

$$\lambda_i \geq 0$$

The primary difference in these two formulations is that the $(M-1)$ Lagrangian multipliers in Program II replace the $(M-1)$ state variables in Program I. If the values of the $(M-1)$ Lagrange multipliers are set at some fixed values, then Program II becomes a standard one-state variable dynamic program. Everett (21) has shown that for any particular set of nonnegative Lagrangian multipliers chosen, a $\mathbf{d}^*$ which maximizes $g(\mathbf{d}, \boldsymbol{\lambda})$ also maximizes $f(\mathbf{d})$ subject to the constraints

$$\sum_{i=1}^{N} \alpha_i d_i^{\delta_i} \leq h_1(\mathbf{d}^*)$$

$$\cdot \qquad \cdot$$
$$\cdot \qquad \cdot$$

$$\sum_{i=1}^{N} v_i d_i^{\phi_i} \leq h_M(\mathbf{d}^*)$$

(10.1)

Note that by a particular choice of multipliers, we solve the original maximization problem, subject to the constraints of Eq. 10.1. If $h_m(\mathbf{d}^*) \equiv \beta_m$ $m = 1, 2, \ldots, M$ then we have solved the problem which we want to solve. However, if not all $h_m(\mathbf{d}^*)$ are less than or equal to β_m, then a new set of Lagrangian multipliers must be chosen and the entire problem resolved. Note that if $h_i(\mathbf{d}^*)$ is nonnegative, then as the Lagrangian multipliers of Program II *increase*, (1) the value of $g(\mathbf{d}, \boldsymbol{\lambda})$ *decrease*, and (2) the values of the $h_m(\mathbf{d}^*)$ *increase*. These and other heuristic relationships can help to guide the search for the optimal set of multipliers. A more sophisticated technique has been proposed by

Brooks and Geoffrion using linear programming, but it will not be discussed at this time.

Finally, it should be noted that if the function $f(\mathbf{d})$ is nonconcave, there may not be a set of nonnegative multipliers $\boldsymbol{\lambda}^*$ such that an optimal solution to $f(\mathbf{d})$ can be generated. This phenomena will occur if the optimal constrained solution to $f(\mathbf{d})$ occurs in a region of nonconcavity called a "*GAP*" (21). The difficulties in dealing with "gap problems" are still a subject of current research. For convex or concave optimization problems, "gaps" will not occur. The solution technique just discussed will now be illustrated through the solution of the previous example.

EXAMPLE 10.16-1
A problem with multiple-state variables.

The optimization problem is given by:

$$\text{Maximize:} \quad 13x_1 - 5x_2^2 + 30.2x_2 - x_1^2 + 10x_3 - 2.5x_3^2$$

$$\text{Subject to:} \quad 2x_1 + 4x_2 + 5x_3 \leq 10$$

$$x_1 + x_2 + x_3 \leq 5$$

$$x_1, x_2, x_3 \geq 0 \qquad \text{and integer}$$

The Lagrangian problem is given by

$$\text{Maximize:} \quad 13x_1 - 5x_2^2 + 30.2x_2 - x_1^2 + 10x_3 - 2.5x_3^2 - \lambda(2x_1 + 4x_2 + 5x_3)$$

$$\text{Subject to:} \quad x_1 + x_2 + x_3 \leq 5$$

$$x_1, x_2, x_3, \lambda \geq 0$$

$$x_1, x_2, x_3 \text{ integer}$$

Trial 1
Stage I

Let $\lambda = 0$

$$f_1(S_1) = \max_{0 \leq d_1 \leq 5} \{13d_1 - d_1^2\}$$

Since

$$\frac{\partial f_1}{\partial d_1} = 13 - 2d_1 = 0$$

This implies that $d_1 = 6.5$ (a maximum stationary point). Therefore, $d_1^* = S_1$

S_1	d_1^*	$f_1^*(S_1)$
0	0	0
1	1	12
2	2	22
3	3	30
4	4	36
5	5	40

Stage II

$$f_2(S_2) = \max_{0 \le d_2 \le 5} \{30.2x_2 - 5x_2^2 + f_1^*(S_2 - d_2)\}$$

S_2 \ d_2	0	1	2	3	4	5	$f_2^*(S_2)$	d_2^*
0	0	—	—	—	—	—	0	0
1	12	25.2	—	—	—	—	25.2	1
2	22	37.2	40.4	—	—	—	40.4	2
3	30	47.2	52.4	45.6	—	—	52.4	2
4	36	55.2	62.4	57.6	40.8	—	62.4	2
5	40	61.2	70.4	67.6	52.8	26	70.4	2

Stage III

S_3 \ d_3	0	1	2	3	4	5	$f_3^*(S_3)$	d_3^*
5	70.4	69.9	62.4				70.4	0

The optimal policy is therefore:

$$x_3^* = 0$$
$$x_2^* = 2 \qquad f_3^*(S_3 = 5) = 70.4$$
$$x_1^* = 3$$

Now evaluating the Lagrangian constraint at this optimal solution we find that

$$2x_1^* + 4x_2^* + 5x_3^* = 14$$

Since the constraint we seek is

$$2x_1 + 4x_2 + 5x_3 \le 10$$

the Lagrangian multiplier should be increased and the problem solved again. Note that although some energy has been expended in solving this problem, a particular problem has been solved (not the one we seek). In fact since $\lambda = 0$, we have solved the original optimization problem without the first constraint. In effect, a sensitivity analysis is being performed as we approach the optimal solution, and this can be quite valuable in many types of problems. Note that this implies a solution at which $\lambda \ne 0$ and the constraint is binding at optimality.

Trial 2

Let $\lambda = 1$.

With $\lambda = 1$, the problem now becomes

Maximize: $f_1(S_1) = 11x_1 - 5x_2^2 + 26.2x_2 - x_1^2 + 5x_3 - 2.5x_3^2$

Subject to: $x_1 + x_2 + x_3 \le 5$

Stage I

$$f^*(S_1) = \max_{0 \le d_1 \le 5} \{11d_1 - d_1^2\}$$

$$\frac{\partial f}{\partial d_1} = 11 - 2d_1 = 0$$

Therefore $d_1 = 5$, 6 [maximum]. Hence $d_1^* = S_1$

$$f_1^*(S_1) = 11S_1 - S_1^2$$

S_1	d_1^*	$f_1^*(S_1)$
0	0	0
1	1	10
2	2	18
3	3	24
4	4	28
5	5	30

Stage II

$$\max_{0 \le d_1 \le 5} \{26.2d_2 - 5d_2^2 + f_1^*(S_2 - d_2)\}$$

S_2 \ d_2	0	1	2	3	4	5	d_2^*	$f_2^*(S_2)$
0	0						0	0
1	10	21.2					1	21.2
2	18	31.2	32.4				2	32.4
3	24	39.2	42.4	33.6			2	42.4
4	28	45.2	50.4	43.6	24.8		2	50.4
5	30	39.2	56.4	51.6	34.8	6	2	56.4

Stage III

$$\max_{0 \le d_1 \le 5} \{5d_3 - 2.5d_3^2 + f_2^*(5 - d_3)\}$$

S_3 \ d_3	0	1	2	3	4	5	d_3^*	$f_3^*(S_3)$
5	56.4	52.9	42.4	24.9	1.2	−37.5	0	56.4

The optimal solution is:

$$x_1^* = 3$$
$$x_2^* = 2 \qquad f_3^*(S_3 = 5) = 56.4$$
$$x_3^* = 0$$

The Lagrangian constraint evaluated at $\mathbf{x}^*$ is:

$$2x_1^* + 4x_2^* + 5x_3^* = 14$$

Note that all we have done is change the Lagrangian and obtain the same solution. We will try a further increase in λ.

Trial 3

Let $\lambda = 5$.

The optimization problem becomes:

$$\text{Maximize:} \quad 3x_1 - x_1^2 + 10.2x_2 - 5x_2^2 - 15x_3 - 2.5x_3^2$$

$$\text{Subject to:} \quad x_1 + x_2 + x_3 \leq 5$$

It is obvious that $x_3^* = 0$. Hence a two-stage problem is given by:

Stage I

$$f_1^*(S_1) = \max_{5 \geq d_1 \geq 0} \{3x_1 - x_1^2\}$$

S_1 \ d_1	0	1	2	3	4	5	d_1^*	$f_1^*(S_1)$
0	0						0	0
1	0	2					1	2
2	0	2	2				1.2	2
3	0	2	2	0			1.2	2
4	0	2	2	0	-4		1.2	2
5	0	2	2	0	-4	-10	1.2	2

Stage II

$$f_2^*(S_2) = \max_{0 \leq d_2 \leq 5} \{12.2x_2 - 5x_2^2 + f_1^*(5 - d_2)\}$$

S_2 \ d_2	0	1	2	3	4	5	d_2^*	$f_1^*(S_2)$
5	2	9.2	6.2	-19.2	-30.8	-64	1	9.2

The optimal policy is:

$$x_3^* = 0$$
$$x_2^* = 1 \qquad f_3^*(S_3 = 5) = 9.2$$
$$x_1^* = 1, 2$$

The Lagrangian constraint becomes:

I. $2x_1^* + 4x_2^* + 5x_3^* = 6 \qquad (\mathbf{x} = 1, 1, 0)$

or

II. $2x_1^* + 4x_2^* + 5x_3^* = 8 \qquad (\mathbf{x} = 2, 1, 0)$

At this point, we note that λ has been increased too far, and so we decrease λ and try again.

Trial 4

$\lambda = 4.0$

$$\text{Maximize} \quad 5x_1 - x_1^2 + 14.2x_2 - 5x_2^2 - 10x_3 - 2.5x_3^2$$

Once again, it is obvious that $x_3^* = 0$. The two-stage solution is given by:

Stage I

$$f_1^*(S_1) = \max_{0 \le d_1 \le 5} \{5d_1 - d_1^2\}$$

S_1 \ d_1	0	1	2	3	4	5	d_1^*	$f_1^*(S_1)$
0	0						0	0
1	0	4					1	4
2	0	4	6				2	6
3	0	4	6	6			2,3	6
4	0	4	6	6	4		2,3	6
5	0	4	6	6	4	0	2,3	6

Stage II

$$f_2^*(S_2) = \max_{0 \le d_2 \le 5} \{14.2x_2 - 5x_2^2 + f_1^*(S_2 - d_2)\}$$

S_2 \ d_2	0	1	2	3	4	5	d_2^*	$f_2^*(S_2)$
5	6	15.2	14.4	3.6	−19.2	−54	1	15.2

The optimal solution is given by:

$$x_3^* = 0$$
$$x_2^* = 1 \qquad f_3^*(S_3 - 5) = 15.2$$
$$x_1^* = 2, 3$$

The Lagrangian constraint evaluated at this solution yields

I. $2x_1^* + 4x_2^* + 5x_3^* = 8$ $(\mathbf{x} = 2, 1, 0)$

II. $2x_1^* + 4x_2^* + 5x_3^* = 10$ $(\mathbf{x} = 3, 1, 0)$

Since the right-hand side of the Lagrangian constraint equals 10, an optimal solution has been found to the original problem. From the original objective function we have:

$$f(\mathbf{x}) = 13x_1 - 5x_2^2 + 30.2x_2 - x_1^2 + 10x_3 - 2.5x_3^2$$

which when evaluated at $x_1^* = 3$, $x_2^* = 1$ and $x_3^* = 0$ yields $f^*(\mathbf{x}) = 55.2$ as before.

Note that in the algorithmic process we also obtain a solution to the problem when the constraint is given by:

$$2x_1 + 4x_2 + 5x_3 \leqq 8$$

Namely:

$$x_1^* = 2 \quad x_2^* = 1 \quad x_3^* = 0 \quad f(\mathbf{x}) = 47.2$$

This can be verified by checking the solution through example 10.15.

10.17 SUMMARY AND CONCLUSIONS

This chapter has attempted to explain the optimization technique known as dynamic programming. Dynamic programming is not a mathematical algorithm, but a *solution procedure* which has been effectively applied to a wide variety of operations research problems. The successful application of dynamic programming is often based on the *art* of modeling rather than the mathematical aspects of problem solution. This chapter has attempted to develop the fundamental approach to problem solving via dynamic programming, while cultivating the art through a series of representative example problems. In concluding, it is important to place the entire contents of this chapter into its proper perspective. Although dynamic programming is an extremely powerful optimization technique when applied to a wide range of problems, it is not the panacea of all solution procedures. Quite to the contrary, dynamic programming is only one of many operations research techniques which should be contained in the engineers' repertoire of problem-solving capabilities. This chapter has illustrated the solution procedure for a wide range of engineering problems, each of which exhibited unique characteristics. In general, any optimization problem which can be decomposed by the principle of optimality is a candidate for efficient solution via dynamic programming. If the problem can also be formulated with three or less state variables, spectacular computational savings can often be realized. It is hoped that the material in this chapter will serve to facilitate increased applications of this powerful technique.

REFERENCES

1. Aris, R., *The Optimal Design of Chemical Reactors*, Academic, New York, 1961.
2. Aris, R., *Discrete Dynamic Programming*, Blaisdell Publishing Co., New York, 1964.
3. Aris, R., G. Nemhauser, and D. J. Wilde, "Optimization of Multi-stage Cycle and Branching Systems by Serial Procedures," *A.I.Ch.E. Journal, 10,* 913–919 (1964).
4. Bellman, R., *Dynamic Programming*, Princeton University Press, Princeton, N.J., 1957.
5. Bellman, R., *Adaptive Control Processes: A Guided Tour*, Princeton University Press, Princeton, N.J., 1961.
6. Bellman, R., "Some Problems in the Theory of Dynamic Programming," *Econometrica, 22,* 37–48 (1954).
7. Bellman, R., and S. E. Dreyfus, *Applied Dynamic Programming*, Princeton University Press, Princeton, N.J., 1962.
8. Crisp, R. M. and C. S. Beightler, "Closed-Form Solutions to Certain Linear Allocation Problems", *AIIE Transactions,* 323–327 (December 1969).
9. Denardo, E. V., and L. G. Mitten, "Elements of Sequential Decision Processes," *A.I.I.E. Journal, XVIII* (1), 106–112 (1967).

10. Dreyfus, S. E., *Dynamic Programming and the Calculus of Variations*, Academic, New York, 1965.

11. Dreyfus, S. E., "Computational Aspects of Dynamic Programming," *Operations Research*, 5, 409–415 (1957).

12. Gibson, David, "Dynamic Programming: A Process Design Tool," *Industrial Engineering*, 25–31 (December 1969).

13. Hadley, G., *Nonlinear and Dynamic Programming*, Addison-Wesley, Reading, Mass., 1964.

14. Hastings, N. A. J., *Dynamic Programming With Management Applications*, Crane, Russak, and Co., New York, 1973.

15. Kaufmann, A., *Graphs, Dynamic Programming, and Finite Games*, Academic, New York, 1967.

16. Kaufmann, A., and R. Cruon, *Dynamic Programming*, Academic, New York, 1967.

17. Mitten, L. G., "Composition Principles for Synthesis of Optimal Multistage Processes," *Operations Research*, 12, 610–619 (1964).

18. Mitten, L. G., and G. L. Nemhauser, "Multistage Optimization," *Chemical Engineering Progress*, 59, 52–60 (1963).

19. Mitten, L. G., and G. L. Nemhauser, "Optimization of Multistage Separation Processes by Dynamic Programming," *Canadian Journal of Chemical Engineering*, 41, 187–194 (1963).

20. Nemhauser, G. L., "Decomposition of Linear Programs by Dynamic Programming," *Naval Research Logistics Quarterly*, 11, 191–196 (1964).

21. Nemhauser, G. L., *Introduction to Dynamic Programming*, Wiley, New York, 1966.

22. Roberts, S. M., *Dynamic Programming in Chemical Engineering and Process Control*, Academic, New York, 1964.

23. Saaty, T. L., *Mathematical Methods of Operations Research*, McGraw-Hill, New York, 1959.

24. Wald, A., *Statistical Decision Functions*, Wiley, New York, 1950.

25. Wilde, D. J., and C. S. Beightler, *Foundations of Optimization*, Prentice-Hall, Englewood Cliffs, N.J., 1967.

EXERCISES

1. An electric utility is building a large generating station and a regional power distribution network to serve a large number of customers scattered over a wide area. Because of the large area to be served, they decide to build ten substations to handle the distribution of power to specific localities. The problem is where to locate the substations along the transmission line so as to minimize the cost of building high-tension lines, assuming that local distribution costs are roughly the same no matter where the substation is built in a given local area. A number of sites are possible for each substation, but not every site in one area can be reached from every site in the next area for a number of reasons including (1) geographic inaccessibility due to terrain features such as lakes and mountains and (2) the inability to purchase or lease right-of-way for the lines. The following diagram represents the problem with accessible sites connected by arcs labeled with the cost of connecting them (in appropriate units).

    a. Determine the minimum cost power distribution plan.

    b. Assume due to political considerations, you must end at C. Determine the new minimum-cost solution.

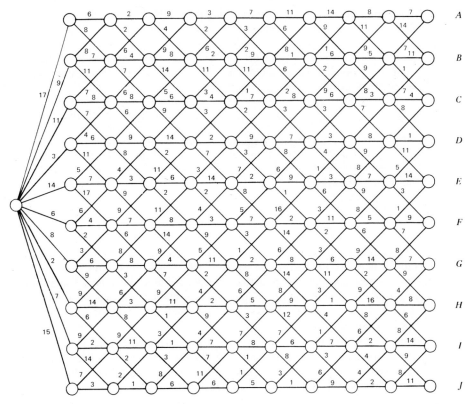

2. The shiek of Ali Condo has decided to take a vacation. Of course, he is taking his four wives with him. Now in spite of the fact that his profits from oil wells would allow him to take any size plane, the runway nearest his mountain retreat will only take a small plane. So to make a long story short, he only has room for 35 lb of luggage. Being a normal man, he needs only one 5-lb suitcase, so 30 lb are left to be split among his wives. Now each wife packs her own suitcase, so the weight of the suitcases varies among wives, however all of the suitcases for one wife are very close to the same weight. Now, as is true with all women, no luggage is too much, but there is the weight problem. So the shiek decided to rate the pleasure (we won't go into the details of how) he would get from each wife based on how many suitcases she was allowed to take (the more the better). This is what he came up with:

Wife	Weight per Suitcase	Total Pleasure Units per Suitcase				
		1	2	3	4	5
1	3	2	3	8	16	23
2	2	1	2	4	7	12
3	4	4	8	15	24	30
4	6	4	9	23	36	42

Now no wife could possibly go on a vacation without any luggage (and you can't have a wife mad at you), so each wife must have at least one suitcase. So, the question is, what should the shiek do to maximize pleasure?

3. A group of the local mafia is considering the establishment of a gaming house. The businessmen have already purchased a building with a floor space limitation of 25 square yards. These men are considering using four types of gambling. They include blackjack, poker, craps, and roulette. The estimated value per table and space required is given as follows (estimated by the mafias financial wizards):

		Space Required Per Table, S_i	Profit Added per Table			
	Game		First Table	Second Table	Third Table	Fourth Table
$i = 1$	Blackjack	4	10	7	4	1
$i = 2$	Poker	5	9	9	8	8
$i = 3$	Craps	6	11	10	9	8
$i = 4$	Roulette	3	8	6	4	2

It is important to note that the investors have realized that their marginal returns decrease for each game as more tables are added. This indicates that the clientele may fill one roulette table all the time but that a second table might be idle part of the time. Thus we have the varying values for each item (game). How many tables should be installed for each game in order to maximize profits?

4. The Davis Car Rental Agency has four cars available at Central Headquarters. There are requests from six marketing outlets for one car apiece. Based on customer satisfaction, mileage and transportation costs; the following cost matrix has been constructed for car delivery.

		Market					
		1	2	3	4	5	6
Cars	1	7	12	9	15	8	14
	2	5	10	5	12	6	13
	3	8	10	7	16	7	12
	4	9	11	8	14	7	11

a. Set up this problem as a mathematical programming problem. Can you identify this particular type of problem?
b. Solve this problem using dynamic programming.

5. Platinum has been discovered in two different countries. The mines are named A and B. Each dollar spent mining platinum in mine A (at the beginning of the year) yields at the end of that year and each succeeding year, 1 pound of platinum and $30 in backing capital which is generously "loaned" to the mine by another government. Each dollar spent mining platinum in mine B, in a similar fashion, yields 0.5 pound of platinum and $100 in backing capital. The governments of both countries have just been overthrown and the new ruler (of both countries) would like to know the best way to allocate his available money (S_3) so as to maximize the amount of platinum produced during the next 3 years.

6. A rancher wishes to build up his herd of cattle but has an initial capital of only $5000. The rancher can purchase two strains of cattle, A or B. For each $1000 invested in cattle A one obtains each year two calves and $500 in operating capital. Cattle type B yields three calves on the average and $200 capital. How

should money be allocated over the next 4 years in order to build up the herd maximally? How many cattle will the rancher have at the end of 4 years? *Note: Assume that this problem can be worked as a continuous dynamic programming problem, and round the optimal solution.*

7. A wine distiller produces wine in a process which consists of n stages. At each stage one faces the decision of whether to sell the yield from that stage or purify it further. Revenue derived from a vat of wine sold after the nth stage is $250n$. The cost of passing through stage n is $4n^2$.

    a. Through how many stages should the wine be passed in order to maximize profit?

    b. What is the maximum profit?

    Important: The number of stages must be treated as a discrete variable.

8. Solve the following problem using dynamic programming.

$$\text{Minimize:} \quad f(x) = 2x_1^2 - 3x_2 - 4x_3^2$$
$$\text{Subject to:} \quad 3x_1 + 2x_2 + 6x_3 \geq 16$$
$$x_2 \leq 4$$
$$x_3 \leq 5$$
$$x_1, x_2, x_3 \geq 0$$

9. Solve the following problem using dynamic programming.

$$\text{Maximize:} \quad f(x) = 2x_1^3 - 3x_1 + x_2^2 - 4x_2 + x_3$$
$$\text{Subject to:} \quad 4x_1 + 2x_2 + 3x_3 \leq 15.3$$
$$x_1, x_2, x_3 \geq 0$$

10. Re-solve Problem 9 under the assumption that x_1, x_2, and x_3 can only take on integer values.

11. Solve the following problem using dynamic programming.

$$\text{Minimize:} \quad f(x) = x_1(2x_1 - 4) + 3x_2(x_2 - 1) + x_3^2 - 7x_3 + 7$$
$$\text{Subject to:} \quad 2x_1 + 3x_2 + 2x_3 \geq 15$$
$$x_1, x_2, x_3 \quad \text{integer}$$
$$x_1, x_2, x_3 \geq 0$$

12. Solve the following problem using dynamic programming.

$$\text{Maximize:} \quad f(x) = 2x_1 - x_1^2 + x_2$$
$$\text{Subject to:} \quad 2x_1^2 + 3x_2^2 \leq 6$$
$$x_1, x_2 \geq 0$$

13. Develop a set of recursive equations to solve the following class of dynamic programming problems.

$$\text{Minimize:} \quad \sum_{n=1}^{N} a_i x_i^{b_i}$$
$$\text{Subject to:} \quad \prod_{n=1}^{N} c_i x_i^{d_i} \geq k$$
$$x_i \geq 0 \quad i = 1, 2, \ldots, N$$

14. Using the results of Exercise 13, solve the following problem.

$$\text{Minimize:} \quad 3x_1^2 + 4x_2^2 + x_3^2$$
$$\text{Subject to:} \quad x_1 x_2 x_3 \geq 9$$
$$x_1, x_2, x_3 \geq 0$$

15. A government analyst has identified five critical subsystems which are instrumental to the mission effectiveness of a new fighter aircraft that has been designed by the Aero-Astro aircraft company. It has been determined that the overall effectiveness of the aircraft is equal to the product of the individual effectiveness of each of the five subsystems.

   Although numerous bids have been received, Aero-Astro has identified two options for each subsystem which meet the design specifications. Only $100k are available for these subsystems.

   What is the maximum effectiveness that can be obtained for this amount?

TABLE OF AVAILABLE OPTIONS

	UHF Radio	TACAN	WPNS Delivery	Radar	Navigation System
Option A	Eff = 0.95	0.90	0.95	0.90	0.95
	Cost = 20k	15k	30k	40k	20k
Option B	Eff = 0.90	0.85	0.90	0.85	0.8
	Cost = 15k	10k	25k	30k	10k

16. Solve the following dynamic programming problems. (Hint: Examine closely the form of the problems.)

a. Maximize: $f(x) = \sum_{n=1}^{3} r_n$

$$r_1 = 3d_1 + 2S_1$$
$$r_2 = d_2 + S_1$$
$$r_3 = d_1 + S_1$$
$$S_n = S_{n-1} = 4S_n + 2S_n \qquad n = 1, 2, 3$$
$$S_3 = 20$$

b. Maximize: $f(x) = \sum_{n=1}^{10} r_n$

$$r_n = -3.7d_n + 1.6S_n$$
$$S_{n-1} = \frac{1}{2}d_n + 0.78S_n \qquad n = 1, 2, 3, \ldots, 10$$
$$S_{10} = 56$$

17. Solve the following two-state variable dynamic programming problem using the state variable reduction procedure of Lagrangian multipliers.

$$\text{Maximize: } \sum_{n=1}^{3} r_n$$
$$r_1 = 10x_3 - 0.50x_3^2$$
$$r_2 = 12x_2 - 0.60x_2^2$$
$$r_3 = 5x_1 - 0.40x_1^2$$
$$x_1 + x_2 + x_3 = 20$$
$$2x_1 + 3x_2 + 2.5x_3 = 40$$
$$x_1, x_2, x_3 \geq 0$$

CHAPTER 11
NONLINEAR PROGRAMMING

I: BASIC CONCEPTS

11.1 INTRODUCTION

In Chapter 2 the fundamentals of linear programming were explored in great detail. As the name indicates, all functional forms dealt with in that chapter were linear in nature. In several instances, one might have wondered about the validity of such assumptions. Indeed in many situations the assumption of linearity as applied to a real-world process might be questionable. In recent years, there has been a great deal of research applied to the solution of what we will call "nonlinear programming problems." Methods that are derived to solve the broad set of problems that make up this functional classification will be referred to as nonlinear programming algorithms. A major disadvantage in studying the field of nonlinear programming is the wide variety of techniques which are presently used to attack nonlinear programming problems. A nonlinear programming problem is characterized by terms or groups of terms which involve intrinsically nonlinear functions. For example: $\sin(x)$, $\cos(y)$, $e^{x_1+x_2}$, $\ln(x_3)$, and so on. Nonlinearities also arise as a result of interactions between two or more variables, such as: x_1x_2, $x_1 \ln(x_2)$, $x_2^{x_3}$, and so on. In studying linear programming solution techniques, there was a basic underlying structure which was exploited in solving those problems. Primarily this structure dictated that an optimal solution could be found by (cleverly) solving sets of linear equations. It was also known that an optimal solution would always be found at an extreme point of the feasible solution space. In solving nonlinear programming problems, an optimal solution might be found at an extreme point, a point *interior* to the feasible region, or at a point of discontinuity. In addition, algorithmic techniques might involve the solution of simultaneous linear equations, simultaneous nonlinear equations, or both. Many algorithmic procedures have been suggested for solving nonlinear programming problems, however, only a small subset of all procedures have actually proved useful in solving real-world problems. Indeed, some of the more successful techniques resort to approximation techniques using linear programming subproblems.

This chapter will attempt to define the basic characteristics of nonlinear programming, and to explain several useful algorithms employed in solving nonlinear programming problems. The algorithms explained in this chapter were chosen for three basic reasons: first, they are widely used in practice and have met with a measurable degree of success; secondly, each technique chosen illustrates a fundamental approach to the solution of nonlinear programming problems; and thirdly, they have all been programmed for the digital computer and are available without great difficulty. Finally, in attempting to convey the algorithmic methodology and underlying theory of nonlinear programming the major concepts are conveyed at a fundamental level for greater understanding of the student. In practice, there are many complex modifications to the basic underlying concepts presented here. These modifications are best classified as advanced nonlinear programming and will not be explained in this text.

Problem Definition. Define the following generalized mathematical program:

$$\text{Minimize:} \quad f(\mathbf{x}) \qquad \mathbf{x} \in E^n$$
$$\text{Subject to:} \quad H_j(\mathbf{x}) = 0 \qquad j = 1, 2, \ldots, M$$
$$G_k(\mathbf{x}) \leq 0 \qquad k = 1, 2, \ldots, \bar{M}$$
$$\mathbf{x} = (x_1, x_2, \ldots, x_N)$$

Without loss of generality, the following definitions will be directed at minimizing solutions to the above problem.

Note that there are N decision variables defined by M equality constraints and $\bar{M}$ inequality constraints. If both the objective function and all constraints are *linear*, then we have a linear programming problem. If any component of $f(\mathbf{x})$, $H_j(\mathbf{x})$, or $G_k(\mathbf{x})$ contains nonlinear functions then we have a nonlinear programming problem. All mathematical programs can be expressed in this form. Nonnegativity conditions on any of the solution variables are implicitly defined as part of the $\bar{M}$ inequality constraint set. Any solution vector $\mathbf{x}$ which satisfies all sets of M equality constraints and $\bar{M}$ inequality constraints is called an *admissible* or *feasible* solution. A particular set of solution variables which yield a minimizing value for $f(\mathbf{x})$ is called the *optimizing solution vector*. Such a solution vector will be denoted by $\mathbf{x}^*$ and need not necessarily be unique. Indeed, many nonlinear programming problems possess multiple solution vectors which yield the same optimal value for $f(\mathbf{x})$. The question of whether or not a nonlinear programming problem possesses a finite optimal solution at all depends on whether or not the problem is *bounded* in the solution variables. Determining if a (unique) optimal solution does exist to a bounded nonlinear programming problem is dependent on the shape of the objective function and the constraint set.

Consider a sequence of points $x_1 > x_2 > x_3 > \cdots > x_n$. If $f(x_1) > f(x_2) > \cdots > f(x_n)$, then the function is said to be monotonically increasing. If $f(x_1) < f(x_2) < \cdots < f(x_n)$, then the function is said to be monotonically decreasing. If $f(x_n) \geq f(x_{n+1})$ or $f(x_n) \leq f(x_{n+1})$, then the function is monotonically nonincreasing and monotonically nondecreasing, respectively. If over a given region a function increases (decreases) to a certain point and then decreases (increases) monotonically, the function is said to be *unimodal*. A unimodal function has only one peak (valley). Functions with two or more "peaks" are called *multimodal*.

A saddle point is one which *appears* to be an optimal solution from a local viewpoint, but is in fact inferior to some other point in the solution space. Since there might be many such points within a general nonlinear programming formulation, these points are called *stationary points* or in this case *local minima*.

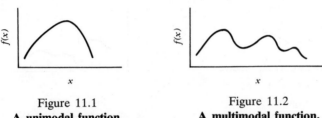

Figure 11.1	Figure 11.2
A unimodal function.	**A multimodal function.**

(See Figs. 11.1–11.3.) Stationary points might exist at a true minimum, a point of inflection, a saddle point, or even a maximum! The best optimizing solution is called a *global minimum.* Most nonlinear programming algorithms yield solutions which are *local minima.* This is caused primarily by algorithmic procedures which depend on the local properties of a nonlinear programming problem. Fortunately many real-world formulations possess only a global minimum. However when this is not the case, alternate local minima solutions must be examined to determine the best. Intimate knowledge of the problem at hand or a different set of starting procedures often help to find the global minimum. In certain cases, *any* solution identified as locally optimal is indeed a *global* optimal solution. Since such cases greatly enhance the power of nonlinear programming algorithmic procedures, it would be worth our time to examine those cases in which this property is true. In general, functions can be classified as (a) continuous, (b) discontinuous, or (c) discrete (see Figs. 11.4–11.6).

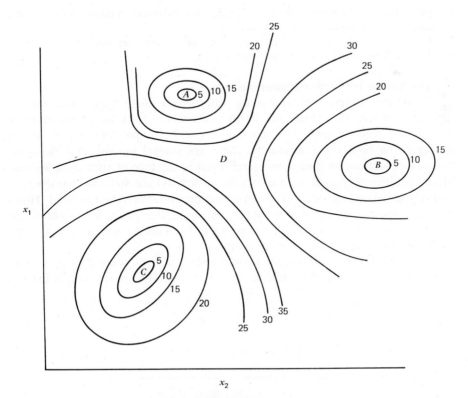

Figure 11.3
A multimodal function with a saddle point.

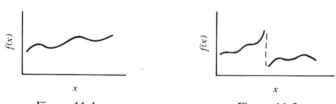

Figure 11.4	Figure 11.5
A continuous function.	**A discontinuous function.**

A special type of function which we will find extremely beneficial is a *concave* or *convex* function. Mathematically a *convex* function is defined as follows:

Definition of a Convex Function. Given any two points in n-dimensional space $(\mathbf{x}_1, \mathbf{x}_2)$, if the following inequality holds at all pairs of points the function is said to be *convex.*

$$f[(1-\theta)\mathbf{x}_1 + \theta\mathbf{x}_2] \leq [(1-\theta)f(\mathbf{x}_1) + \theta f(\mathbf{x}_2)] \qquad 1 \geq \theta \geq 0$$

A concave function is similarly defined with the inequality reversed. Although this definition will prove useful mathematically, what does it mean? Geometrically it means that if a function is convex (concave) and if a line is drawn between any two points on the surface of the function, the line segment joining these two points will lie entirely above (below) that function.

Note from Figs. 11.7–11.12 several important facts:

1. The definition of a convex (concave) function is not dependent on the definition of a function being continuous (discontinuous).
2. A function can be concave over one region and convex over another.
3. A linear function is *both* concave and convex.

The Search for Optimal Solutions

In solving nonlinear programming problems, it might appear that we are searching for the proverbial "needle in a haystack." With an infinite number of solution vectors and the possibilities of multiple optima, it might appear to be hopeless. Fortunately, there are several fundamental theorems that can be utilized to guide our search even in the face of such complexities. Moreover, if such conditions as convexity (concavity) are met, the characterization of the (unknown) optimal solution becomes relatively well defined. However, lest the reader become relatively secure at this point, let us state that although the characterization of the problem becomes easier, the actual solution procedure might be extremely complex.

If we are dealing with bounded continuous functions, a theorem by Weierstrass (21) guarantees us that a maximum or minimum will always exist, either at a

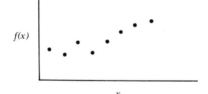

Figure 11.6
A discrete function.

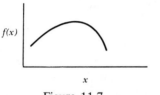

Figure 11.7
A concave function.

Figure 11.8
A convex function.

point interior to the boundaries of feasible solution variables or at the boundary itself. This is intuitively clear, since a bounded function must always possess a maximum or minimum value somewhere within the region of interest. If the function is *continuous* over the domain of interest, stationary points can be located through the use of differential calculus provided all derivatives can be found. The calculus tells us that a stationary point will exist in the interior or at a boundary if the partial derivatives of an unconstrained function vanish (become zero) at a particular solution vector. The constrained case is similarly treated through the use of constrained derivatives and will be discussed later in this chapter. In addition, if there are discontinuities in our function, then one (or more) of these derivatives might fail to exist. These points would then need to be considered separately. Finally an optimal solution might exist at a

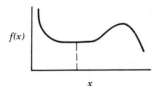

Figure 11.9
**A function neither concave
nor convex.**

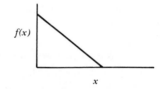

Figure 11.10
**A function which is both concave
and convex.**

boundary point defined by the constraints on the problem. For example, this is the case in linear programming which is a special (completely degenerate) case of nonlinear programming.

In summary, if we are to devise a procedure for solving nonlinear programming problems, we need to examine the following three candidates:

1. All points at which the continuous first derivatives are all zero.
2. All points interior to the region at which discontinuities exist for the continuous first derivatives.
3. Points on the boundaries of the solution space.

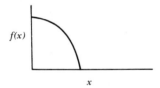

Figure 11.11
A monotonic concave function.

Figure 11.12
A discontinuous convex function.

The Effects of Concavity/Convexity on the Search for an Optimum

Case A: Maximum or Minimum—Unconstrained. If the nonlinear programming problem consists of only an objective function, $f(\mathbf{x})$, and if the objective function is convex (concave), then a unique (single) optimum solution will be found at a point (a) interior to the feasible region where all derivatives vanish or (b) at a boundary point (see Figs. 11.13 and 11.14).

Case B: Maximization—Constrained. If the nonlinear programming problem consists of both an objective function and constraints, the uniqueness of an optimal solution depends on the nature of both the objective function and the constraint set. If the objective function is *concave*, and the constraint set forms a *convex* region, there will be only one maximizing solution to the problem. Hence any stationary point must be a *global maximum* solution.

Case C: Minimization—Constrained. If the nonlinear programming problem consists of both an objective function and constraints, and if the objective function is *convex* and the constraint set also forms a *convex* region, then any stationary point will be a *global minimizing* solution.

Case D: Minimizing (Maximizing) A Concave (Convex) Function. If one is minimizing (maximizing) a concave (convex) function, then the optimal solution will only be found at one of the extreme points of the constraint set. For example, if one is *minimizing* the function given in Fig. 11.15, the points A and B are all that need to be examined. The problem in performing the required search is that for most nonlinear programming problems—especially real-world formulations—this set of (possible) solution points might be extremely large.

Case E: The Linear Function. A linear function forms a class of optimization problems all to itself. By previous definition, a linear function is both convex and concave. Thus if the solution space is convex, then a solution will always be found at a boundary. This observation is precisely what gave rise to the simplex algorithm of linear programming.

Case F: Nonconvex Regions. If the constraint set forms a nonconvex solution space, then any algorithmic procedure based on local properties of the nonlinear programming problem might produce a local stationary point which may be neither globally maximum or minimum. This

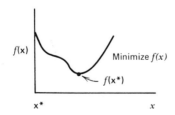

Figure 11.13
An interior solution to an unconstrained maximization problem.

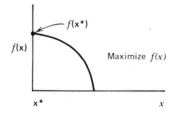

Figure 11.14
A boundary solution to an unconstrained maximization problem.

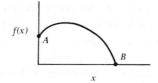

Figure 11.15
Minimizing a concave function.

observation is valid even if the objective function is linear in nature. Figure 11.16 illustrates this theory since points A, B, and C are all locally optimal to a maximizing procedure, with point B being the global maximizing solution.

The Quest for Optimality

Having identified some of the properties of nonlinear programming, we are now in a position to present some solution algorithms useful in solving nonlinear programming problems. As previously mentioned, the process of algorithmic development is still a very active research activity. Efficient algorithms have been derived for certain classes of problems, but it is doubtful that an algorithm will ever be developed which is universally accepted as a comprehensive solution technique. Hence unlike linear programming, there does not exist a *basic* underlying structure or concept such as the simplex algorithm.

Although the general problem remains extremely complex, the optimal solution will, in general, be found at an interior point at which first derivatives vanish, a boundary point, or a discontinuity. Except in certain special cases, the key as to where the optimal solution must be found will remain unknown. Hence, a comprehensive search must consider both interior points and boundary conditions. When possible, analytical techniques will be employed to guide our search. The most useful (and common) techniques will be first and second derivatives or a Taylor's series approximation. In the cases where analytical techniques cannot be used, such as in a "black box" response, a pattern or numerical search will have to be conducted. The problems of discontinuities can only be handled by examining the objective function value at each point of discontinuity, and retaining the maximum (minimum) solution. In general, this chapter will deal with what we will call "well-behaved" functions; that is, those which do not have any discontinuities or singularity points such as outward pointing cusps. These methods should be sufficient to attack many real-world applications. The remaining cases will be left to further study from the rapidly expanding technical literature and texts on nonlinear programming.

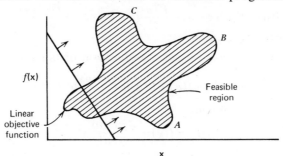

Figure 11.16
Linear optimization with a nonconvex solution space.

11.2 TAYLOR'S SERIES EXPANSIONS; NECESSARY AND SUFFICIENCY CONDITIONS

In developing the basic concepts of the techniques and goals of nonlinear programming, perhaps the most useful and fundamental development is the use and understanding of Taylor's series expansion. The use of this series surfaces in the recognition of optimal solutions, characterization of stationary points, and in linearizing (gradient) and quadratic approximation techniques.

Suppose that an arbitrary nonlinear function $f(x)$ having derivatives of all orders can be represented by a power series expansion of the form

$$f(x) = C_0 + C_1(x-a) + C_2(x-a)^2 + - + C_n(x-a)^n \tag{11.1}$$

THEOREM 1

A power series may be differentiated term by term within its interval of convergence.

By this theorem;

$$f'(x) = C_1 + 2C_2(x-a) + 3C_3(x-a)^2 + - + nC_n(x-a)^{n-1}$$
$$f''(x) = 2! \, C_2 + 3 \cdot 2C_3(x-a) + - + n(n-1)C_n(x-a)^{n-2}$$
$$f'''(x) = 3! \, C_3 + - - - + n(n-1)(n-2)C_n(x-a)^{n-3}$$

and in general

$$f^{(n-1)}(x) = (n-1)! \, C_{n-1} + n! \, C_n(x-a) + - + \tag{11.2}$$

If we substitute $x = a$ in these equations and also in $f(x)$, we can solve for the C's in the following manner:

$$\text{If} \qquad x = a; \qquad f(x) = f(a) = C_0$$

Hence

$$f'(a) = C_1 \qquad\qquad C_1 = f'(a)$$
$$f''(a) = 2! \, C_2 \qquad\qquad C_2 = f''(a)/2!$$
$$f'''(a) = 3! \, C_3 \qquad\qquad C_3 = f'''(a)/3!$$
$$\cdot \qquad\qquad\qquad \cdot$$
$$\cdot \qquad\qquad\qquad \cdot$$
$$\cdot \qquad\qquad\qquad \cdot$$
$$f^{(n-1)}(a) = (n-1)! \, C_{n-1} \qquad C_{n-1} = f^{(n-1)}(a)/(n-1)!$$

Thus $f(x)$ can be represented in a power series involving the differentials of $f(x)$ itself, namely:

$$f(x) = f(a) + f'(a)(x-a) + \frac{f''(a)}{2!}(x-a)^2 + - - + \frac{f^{(n-1)}(a)}{(n-1)!}(x-a)^{n-1} \tag{11.3}$$

This is called *Taylor's Series.**

Note if we let $x = a + h$ we get a useful form of this series

$$f(a+h) = f(a) + f'(a)h + \frac{f''(a)}{2!}h^2 + - + \tag{11.4}$$

and if we let $a \equiv 0$, we obtain

$$f(h) = f(x) = \sum_{n=0}^{\infty} \frac{f^n(0)}{n!} x^n \tag{11.5}$$

This is known as *Maclaurin's Series.*

* Brook Taylor (1685–1731).

Unconstrainted Optimization and Its Relationship to Taylor's Series

Recall that for Taylor's Series,

$$f(x) = f(a+h) = f(a) + f'(a)h + \frac{f''(a)}{2!}h^2 + - + \tag{11.6}$$

Now suppose we consider a small deviation, Δx, away from a point x_0 to a point x; if we associate Δx with h and x_0 with a;

$$f(x) = f(x_0 + \Delta x) = f(x_0) + f'(x_0)\,\Delta x + \frac{f''(x_0)}{2!}[\Delta x]^2 + - +$$

$$f(x) = f(x_0) + \left(\frac{df}{dx}\right)_{x_0}\Delta x + \frac{1}{2}\left(\frac{d^2f}{dx^2}\right)_{x_0}\Delta x^2 + - + \tag{11.7}$$

This equation says that if we are given the value of a function and all of its derivatives at some point x_0, the value of that function can be determined at any other nearby point. The accuracy of such a determination is dependent on the number of terms needed to adequately represent an arbitrary function. Two forms of Eq. 11.7 will be subsequently explored in great detail, those being the linear approximation (first two terms) and the quadratic approximation (first three terms).

EXAMPLE 11.2-1

Given $f(x) = 4 - 7x + x^2$
   a. Calculate the value of this function at $x_0 = 2$.
   b. Find the value of $f(x)$ at $x = 4$ by using (a) and the derivatives of $f(x)$ in Eq. 11.7.
   a. $f(x_0)|_{x_0=2} = 4 - 7(2) + 4 = -6$
   b. $f'(x) = 2x - 7 \qquad \Delta x = 2$
      $f''(x) = 2$
      $f'''(x) = 0$

Hence

$$f(x = 4) = f(x_0) + f'(x_0)(2) + \frac{f''(x_0)}{2!}(2)^2$$

$$= -6 + (-3)(2) + \frac{(2)(2)}{2}$$

or

$$f(x) = -8$$

The true value of the objective function is given by

$$f(x)|_{x=4} = 4 - 28 + 16 = -8$$

Note that since the function which we wish to approximate is actually a quadratic function, the first three terms of Eq. 11.7 gave an *exact* answer.

EXAMPLE 11.2-2

Calculate the value of $f(x) = 2X^3 - 3X^2 + X - 4$ at $x = 7$ starting from the point $x_0 = 3$

$$f(x_0)|_{x_0=3} = 26$$

From Eq. 11.7;

$$f(x) = f(x_0) + \left(\frac{df}{dx}\right)_{x_0}\Delta x + \frac{1}{2}\left(\frac{d^2f}{dx^2}\right)\Delta x^2 + \cdots +$$

Define:

$$x_0 = 3$$
$$\Delta x = 4$$

and

$$\frac{df}{dx} = 6x^2 - 6x + 1$$

$$\frac{d^2f}{dx^2} = 2x - 6$$

Hence

$$\left(\frac{df}{dx}\right)_{x_0} = 37 \qquad \Delta x = 4$$

$$\left(\frac{d^2f}{df^2}\right)_{x_0} = 30$$

Therefore

$$f(x) = 26 + (37)(4) + \tfrac{1}{2}(30)(16)$$
$$f(x) = 414$$

The true value of $f(x)$ at $x = 7$ is given by:

$$f(x) = 542$$

Note that the Taylor's series approximation underestimated the correct answer. The reason for this lies in the fact that the true expression is cubic, and we have used a quadratic approximation. The reader will be asked to show in Exercise 3 that a cubic approximation will yield the exact answer.

Conditions for a Local Minimum

Suppose that we are given a point x^* suspected to be a local minimum. How do we check to see if this hypothesis is true?

Consider an arbitrary deviation from x^* given by ε. This gives a *neighborhood* surrounding x^*; $x^* \pm \varepsilon$. Denote this neighborhood by δ. Therefore x will be contained in δ if

$$0 \leq |x - x^*| \leq \varepsilon$$

Now let:

$$x = x^* + \Delta x$$

where

$$0 \leq \Delta x \leq \varepsilon$$

x^* is a *local* minimum if

$$f(x^*) \leq f(x)$$

Hence for $x \in \delta$, if $x = x^* + \Delta x$ then using Eq. 11.7,

$$f(x) = f(x^*) + \left(\frac{df}{dx}\right)^* \Delta x + \left(\frac{d^2f}{dx^2}\right)^* \frac{\Delta x^2}{2!} + + - + \tag{11.8}$$

The expressions $(df/dx)^*$ and $(d^2f/dx^2)^*$ represent the first and second derivatives of $f(x)$ evaluated at the point x^*. Suppose we now define

$$\delta x = f(x) - f(x^*) = \left(\frac{df}{dx}\right)^* \Delta x + \frac{1}{2!}\left(\frac{d^2f}{dx^2}\right)^* \Delta x^2 \tag{11.9}$$

where we ignore terms of higher orders.

Since we have assumed x^* to be a local minimum, then $\delta x = f(x) - f(x^*)$ must be positive for all perturbations $\Delta x = x^* \pm \varepsilon$ in the neighborhood of x^*. Note at this point that Δx can either be $+$ or $-$ in the first term $[(df/dx)^* \Delta x]$; however, by the above arguments;

$$\left(\frac{df}{dx}\right)^* \Delta x + \frac{1}{2!}\left(\frac{d^2f}{dx^2}\right)^* \Delta x^2 \geq 0 \qquad (11.10)$$

In general, if Δx is very small, then Δx^2 will be even smaller and the first term will completely dominate the sign of the whole series (unless, of course, it is zero—this will be discussed later). Hence there are three possible cases:

Case I. If $(df/dx)^* > 0$, then Δx must also be > 0 for x^* to be a local minimum.

Case II. If $(dy/dx)^* < 0$, then Δx must also < 0 for x^* to be a local minimum.

Case III. If $(dy/dx)^* \equiv 0$, then Δx can be anything and the sign of the series is dominated by the second term, that is,

$$\frac{1}{2!}\left(\frac{d^2f}{dx^2}\right)^* \Delta x^2$$

Since $1/2!$ and Δx^2 are always positive regardless of Δx, then it is necessary that $(d^2f/dx^2)^* > 0$.

Now, suppose that *both* $(dy/dx)^* = 0$ and $(d^2f/dx^2)^* = 0$. In this case, no information is obtained from either the first or second derivatives. When this situation occurs, one is forced to obtain information from higher-order derivatives.

From Eq. 11.7, note that the next term in the Taylor's Series expansion contains Δx^3. This implies that by the same arguments previously applied to the first derivative term, the third term *must* also vanish if the point is either a minimum or a maximum. This is true because if it *did not* vanish, the value of the function could change signs with arbitrary changes in Δx. Such a situation exists in Figs. 11.17 and 11.18. Note from Figs. 11.17 and 11.18 that if the third-order terms fail to vanish, then the point is characterized as a *saddle point* or a *point of inflection*. Therefore if the third-order terms do vanish, then the nature of the stationary point is determined by the sign of the fourth-order

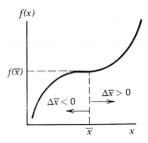

Figure 11.17
**A monotonically increasing
objective function.**

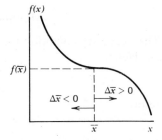

Figure 11.18
**A monotonically decreasing
objective function.**

terms. That is,

If: $\left(\dfrac{d^4f}{dx^4}\right)^* > 0$ the stationary point is a minimum   (11.11)

$\left(\dfrac{d^4f}{dx^4}\right)^* < 0$ the stationary point is a maximum   (11.12)

$\left(\dfrac{d^4f}{dx^4}\right)^* = 0$ higher-order terms must be examined   (11.13)

In continuing those arguments, it should now be clear that the first *non-vanishing derivative* must be *even*, and the sign of that derivative evaluated at the stationary point must be *positive* for a minimum and *negative* for a *maximum*. If the first nonvanishing derivative is *odd*, then the point is neither a maximum nor a minimum, but a point of inflection.

We can now summarize all this into compact rules which can easily be followed for finding or identifying minimum and maximum points for an unconstrained function which yields continuous derivatives.

Necessary Conditions for a Local Minimum.   If

$$\left(\dfrac{df}{dx}\right)^* = 0 \qquad \text{then} \qquad \left(\dfrac{d^2f}{dx^2}\right)^* \text{ must be} \geq 0 \qquad (11.14)$$

Sufficient Conditions for a Local Minimum.   If

$$\left(\dfrac{df}{dx}\right)^* = 0 \qquad \text{then} \qquad \left(\dfrac{d^2f}{dx^2}\right)^* > 0 \qquad (11.15)$$

The preceding arguments can easily be applied to *maximizing* stationary points so that

$$\text{If} \quad \left(\dfrac{df}{dx}\right)^* = 0 \qquad \text{then} \qquad \left(\dfrac{d^2f}{dx^2}\right)^* \leq 0 \qquad (11.16)$$

are *necessary conditions* and

$$\text{If} \quad \left(\dfrac{df}{dx}\right)^* = 0 \qquad \text{then} \qquad \left(\dfrac{d^2f}{dx^2}\right)^* < 0 \qquad (11.17)$$

are *sufficient conditions.*

Note that *all points* for which this is true must be minima (maxima), but there may exist some points for which this may not be true!

EXAMPLE 11.2-3

$$\text{Minimize:} \quad f(\mathbf{x}) = x_1^3 - 3x_1 + 6$$

The necessary condition for a minimzing solution is that the first derivative vanish. Hence

$$\frac{\partial f(\mathbf{x})}{\partial x_1} = 3x_1^2 - 3 = 0$$

Therefore

$$x_1^* = +1 \qquad \text{or} \qquad x_1^* = -1$$

Employing the second-derivative test in one dimension,

$$\left(\frac{\partial^2 f}{\partial x_1^2}\right)^* = 6x$$

Case I. At the point $x_1^* = 1.0$, the second derivative is positive. Therefore this solution is a minimizing stationary point.

Case II. At the point $x_1^* = -1.0$, the second derivative is negative. Therefore this solution is a maximizing point.

Multivariable Unconstrained Optimization

Define Taylor's series for an n-dimensional expansion as follows:

$$
\text{Let} \quad
\begin{aligned}
x_1 &= x_1^* + \Delta x_1 \\
x_2 &= x_2^* + \Delta x_2 \\
&\cdot \quad \cdot \quad \cdot \\
&\cdot \quad \cdot \quad \cdot \\
&\cdot \quad \cdot \quad \cdot \\
x_n &= x_n^* + \Delta x_n
\end{aligned}
\qquad
\mathbf{x} =
\begin{bmatrix} x_1 \\ x_2 \\ \cdot \\ \cdot \\ \cdot \\ x_n \end{bmatrix}
\qquad
\mathbf{x}^* =
\begin{bmatrix} x_1^* \\ x_2^* \\ \cdot \\ \cdot \\ \cdot \\ x_n^* \end{bmatrix}
\qquad
\Delta \mathbf{x} =
\begin{bmatrix} \Delta x_1 \\ \Delta x_2 \\ \cdot \\ \cdot \\ \cdot \\ \Delta x_n \end{bmatrix}
$$

Hence

$$
\mathbf{x} = \mathbf{x}^* + \Delta \mathbf{x}
$$

Assuming that the function $f(\mathbf{x})$ is continuous and possesses all nth-order partial derivatives, the following series expansion corresponds to Eq. 11.3:

$$
f(\mathbf{x}) = f(\mathbf{x}^* + \Delta \mathbf{x})
$$

$$
= f(\mathbf{x}^*) + \sum_{i=1}^{n} \left(\frac{\partial f}{\partial x_i} \right)^* \Delta x_i + \frac{1}{2!} \sum_{i=1}^{n} \sum_{j=1}^{n} \left(\frac{\partial f^2}{\partial x_i \, \partial x_j} \right)^* \Delta x_i \, \Delta x_j
$$

$$
+ \frac{1}{3!} \sum_{i=1}^{n} \sum_{j=1}^{n} \sum_{k=1}^{n} \left(\frac{\partial f^3}{\partial x_i \, \partial x_j \, \partial x_k} \right)^* \Delta x_i \, \Delta x_j \, \Delta x_k + - + \tag{11.18}
$$

For clarity, let us develop the concepts of necessary and sufficiency conditions for only two dimensions.

Taylor's Series Development in Two Dimensions. Consider the two-dimensional vector $\mathbf{x}$ in the neighborhood of $\mathbf{x}^*$. Define

$$
\mathbf{x} = \begin{bmatrix} x_1 \\ x_2 \end{bmatrix}
\qquad
\mathbf{x} = \begin{bmatrix} x_1^* \\ x_2^* \end{bmatrix}
\qquad
\Delta \mathbf{x} = \begin{bmatrix} \Delta x_1 \\ \Delta x_2 \end{bmatrix}
$$

By Taylor's Series;

$$
f(\mathbf{x}) = f(\mathbf{x}^* + \Delta \mathbf{x})
$$

$$
= f(\mathbf{x}^*) + \left(\frac{\partial f(x)}{\partial x_1} \right)^* \Delta x_1 + \left(\frac{\partial f(x)}{\partial x_2} \right)^* \Delta x_2
$$

$$
+ \frac{1}{2!} \left(\frac{\partial f^2(x)}{\partial x_1^2} \right)^* \Delta x_1^2 + \frac{1}{2!} \left(\frac{\partial f^2(x)}{\partial x_2^2} \right)^* \Delta x_2^2
$$

$$
+ (2) \frac{1}{2!} \left(\frac{\partial f(x)}{\partial x_1 \, \partial x_2} \right)^* \Delta x_1 \, \Delta x_2 + - - + \tag{11.19}
$$

Now define ∇f as follows:

$$
\nabla f = \left(\frac{\partial f}{\partial x_1}, \frac{\partial f}{\partial x_2} \right)
$$

and

$$
H \langle \mathbf{x} \rangle =
\begin{bmatrix}
\dfrac{\partial^2 f}{\partial x_1^2} & \dfrac{\partial^2 f}{\partial x_1 \, \partial x_2} \\[2mm]
\dfrac{\partial^2 f}{\partial x_1 \, \partial x_2} & \dfrac{\partial^2 f}{\partial x_2^2}
\end{bmatrix}
\tag{11.20}
$$

Using the above definitions, we can write:

$$f(\mathbf{x}) = f(\mathbf{x}^*) + [\nabla f]^* \, \Delta\mathbf{x} + \tfrac{1}{2}[H^*\langle\mathbf{x}\rangle] \, \Delta\mathbf{x}^2 + - + \tag{11.21}$$

The quantities $[\nabla f]^*$ and $[H^*(\mathbf{x}^2)]$ are the *gradient vector* and the *Hessian matrix* evaluated at the point $\mathbf{x}^*$. These two expressions will play an increasingly important role in future developments and should be carefully noted. For simplicity, we will often call ∇f the *gradient* and, $H(\mathbf{x})$ the *Hessian*.

EXAMPLE 11.2-4

Suppose $f(\mathbf{x}) = x_1^2 + x_1 x_2 + x_2^2$. Evaluated at $\mathbf{x}^* = [x_1, x_2] = [2, 3]$

$$f(\mathbf{x}) = 19$$

What is $f(\mathbf{x})$ at $\mathbf{x} = [3, 5]$? If

$$\mathbf{x}^* = [2, 3] \qquad \Delta\mathbf{x} = [1, 2]$$

then

$$\frac{\partial f}{\partial x_1} = 2x_1 + x_2 \qquad \frac{\partial f}{\partial x_2} = 2x_2 + x_1$$

$$\frac{\partial^2 f}{\partial x_1 \, \partial x_2} = 1 \qquad \frac{\partial^2 f}{\partial x_2^2} = 2 \qquad \frac{\partial^2 f}{\partial x_1^2} = 2$$

and

$$f(\mathbf{x}) = f(\mathbf{x}^*) + \left(\frac{\partial f}{\partial x_1}\right)^* \Delta x_1 + \left(\frac{\partial f}{\partial x_2}\right)^* \Delta x_2 + \tfrac{1}{2}\Delta\mathbf{x}^T[H^*\langle\mathbf{x}\rangle] \, \Delta\mathbf{x} \tag{11.22}$$

Equation 11.22 represents a second-order Taylor's Series expansion of $f(\mathbf{x})$. Using the vectors $\mathbf{x}^*$ and $\mathbf{x}$, one obtains

$$f(\mathbf{x}) = 19 + (7)(1) + 8(2) + \tfrac{1}{2}(2)(1) + \tfrac{1}{2}(2)(4) + \tfrac{1}{2}(1)(2)(2)$$
$$f(\mathbf{x}) = 49$$

Check:
$$f(\mathbf{x}) = [3]^2 + (3)(5) + [5]^2 = 49$$

Note that since $f(\mathbf{x})$ was actually a quadratic function, we exactly predicted the value of the function.

Sufficiency Conditions for a Local Minimum (Maximum). From previous discussions, we are sure that for a local minimum or maximum:

1. For a local minimum to exist, all local perturbations in the present solution vector must produce a *positive* change in the objective function.
2. For a local maximum to exist, all local perturbations in the present solution vector must produce a *negative* change in the objective function.

How can we guarantee that we have a local maximum or minimum? Since $\Delta\mathbf{x}$ is very small, then all first-order terms will dominate the sign of the entire Taylor's Series. Hence a necessary condition for a local *minimum* to exist is that the *gradient* vanish.

$$(\nabla f)^* \equiv 0$$

In addition, for a local minimum to exist it is *sufficient* to show that ∂f is positive for all points within the neighborhood of $\mathbf{x}^*$. Since the *gradient* must vanish, then the *Hessian* now controls the sign of the entire series. At this point, note that since we are dealing with real numbers the *Hessian* can be uniquely specified in terms of the controlling sign by means of the following five conditions:

The Hessian matrix $H\langle \mathbf{x} \rangle$ is said to be;

1. Positive definite if for all $\Delta \mathbf{x}$

$$(\Delta \mathbf{x})^T H^* \langle \mathbf{x} \rangle (\Delta \mathbf{x}) > 0 \tag{11.23}$$

2. Negative definite if for all $\Delta \mathbf{x}$

$$(\Delta \mathbf{x})^T H^* \langle \mathbf{x} \rangle (\Delta \mathbf{x}) < 0 \tag{11.24}$$

3. Indefinite if for all $\Delta \mathbf{x}$

$$\begin{array}{c} (\Delta \mathbf{x})^T H^* \langle \mathbf{x} \rangle (\Delta \mathbf{x}) \text{ can take both positive and negative} \\ \text{values for all changes in the neighborhood.} \end{array} \tag{11.25}$$

4. Positive semidefinite if for all $\Delta \mathbf{x}$

$$(\Delta \mathbf{x})^T H^* \langle \mathbf{x} \rangle (\Delta \mathbf{x}) \geqq 0 \tag{11.26}$$

5. Negative semidefinite if for all $\Delta \mathbf{x}$

$$(\Delta \mathbf{x})^T H^* \langle \mathbf{x} \rangle (\Delta \mathbf{x}) \leqq 0 \tag{11.27}$$

It then follows by examining the Taylor's Series expansion that the following rules can be used to identify a stationary point.

Sufficient Conditions for a Local Minimum at $\mathbf{x}^*$.
1. $(\nabla f)^* \equiv 0$
2. $H^* \langle \mathbf{x} \rangle$ *is positive definite* $\tag{11.28}$

Sufficient Conditions for a Local Maximum at $\mathbf{x}^*$.
1. $(\nabla f)^* \equiv 0$
2. $H^* \langle \mathbf{x} \rangle$ *is negative definite* $\tag{11.29}$

Sufficient Conditions for a Saddle Point.
1. $(\nabla f)^* \equiv 0$
2. $H^* \langle \mathbf{x} \rangle$ *is indefinite* $\tag{11.30}$

If $(\nabla f)^* \equiv 0$ and $H^* \langle \mathbf{x} \rangle$ is any semidefinite form, then higher-order terms must be examined to determine the nature of the solution vector. The reader should note that the nature of the Hessian matrix is easily determined from the functional second derivatives. For the reader who is unfamiliar with these tests, Appendix A has been included to facilitate the above rules.

Checking a Stationary Point for the n-Dimensional Unconstrained Optimization Problem. When dealing with functions of dimensions higher than two, it is convenient to define a procedure first presented by Endelbaum (3) that is useful in identifying a stationary point (one at which the *Gradient* vanishes). To this end, define the following n-dimensional matrix of second *partial derivatives*.

$$H^*(\mathbf{x}) = \begin{bmatrix} \left(\dfrac{\partial^2 f}{\partial x_1^2}\right)^* & \left(\dfrac{\partial^2 f}{\partial x_1, \partial x_2}\right)^* & \cdots & \left(\dfrac{\partial^2 f}{\partial x_n, \partial x_1}\right)^* \\[2ex] \left(\dfrac{\partial^2 f}{\partial x_2, \partial x_1}\right)^* & \left(\dfrac{\partial^2 f}{\partial x_2^2}\right)^* & \cdots & \left(\dfrac{\partial^2 f}{\partial x_n, \partial x_2}\right)^* \\[2ex] \cdot & \cdot & & \cdot \\ \cdot & \cdot & & \cdot \\ \cdot & \cdot & & \cdot \\[1ex] \left(\dfrac{\partial^2 f}{\partial x_n, \partial x_1}\right)^* & \left(\dfrac{\partial^2 f}{\partial x_n, \partial x_2}\right)^* & \cdots & \left(\dfrac{\partial^2 f}{\partial x_n, \partial x_n}\right)^* \end{bmatrix} \tag{11.31}$$

For this matrix, there exists exactly n-determinants formed from the single element in the upper-left-hand corner, successively through the entire matrix moving from upper left to lower right. Designate these determinates by D_1, $D_2, \ldots, D_n$. Endelbaum (3) has shown that the following tests are valid:

1. For a stationary point to be a *minimum*, it is sufficient that $D_1, D_2, \ldots, D_n$ all be *positive* quantities.
2. For a stationary point to be a *maximum*, it is sufficient that all *even* determinants are *positive* and all *odd* determinants are *negative*.

$$D_j < 0 \qquad j = 1, 3, 5, \ldots$$
$$D_j > 0 \qquad j = 2, 4, 6, \ldots$$

If these conditions are not exactly satisfied, then the point *may* or *may not* be an optimal solution. In this case, higher-order tests must be employed or all stationary points examined.

The Special Case of $n = 2$ (Two Dimensions). In the special case where there are only two decision variables, the above conditions reduce to a convenient test for a stationary point. Note that Eq. 11.31 reduces to the following sufficient conditions for a minimum.

$$\left(\frac{\partial^2 f}{\partial x_1^2}\right)^* > 0 \tag{11.32}$$

$$\left[\left(\frac{\partial^2 f}{\partial x_1^2}\right)^* \left(\frac{\partial^2 f}{\partial x_2^2}\right)^* - \left(\frac{\partial^2 f}{\partial x_1 \partial x_2}\right)^*\right] > 0 \tag{11.33}$$

In layman's terms, these conditions are sufficient because they guarantee that the function is convex over the solution space. In technical terms, these conditions must be met to guarantee a positive definite Hessian matrix. These conditions are sufficient for a maximizing point provided that $>$ can be replaced with $<$ in both cases. Weaker conditions can be stated in the following manner; if

$$\left(\frac{\partial^2 f}{\partial x_1^2}\right)^* \geq 0 \tag{11.34}$$

$$\left[\left(\frac{\partial^2 f}{\partial x_1^2}\right)^* \left(\frac{\partial^2 f}{\partial x_2^2}\right)^* - \left(\frac{\partial^2 f}{\partial x_1 \partial x_2}\right)^*\right] \geq 0 \tag{11.35}$$

Then the above conditions are necessary for a local minimum but not sufficient.

EXAMPLE 11.2-5

Minimize: $f(\mathbf{x}) = x_1^2 + x_2^2 - 2x_1 + x_1 x_2 + 1$

Is the point $\mathbf{x} = (x_1, x_2) = (\frac{4}{3}, -\frac{2}{3})$ a local minimum? From the above,

$$\frac{\partial f}{\partial x_1} = 2x_1 - 2 + x_2 \qquad \frac{\partial^2 f}{\partial x_1^2} = 2$$

$$\frac{\partial f}{\partial x_2} = 2x_2 + x_1 \qquad \frac{\partial^2 f}{\partial x_2^2} = 2$$

$$\frac{\partial^2 f}{\partial x_1 \partial x_2} = 1$$

From Eqs. 11.32 and 11.33, using the point $x_1 = \frac{4}{3}$, $x_2 = -\frac{2}{3}$, one obtains:

$$\left[\left(\frac{\partial^2 f}{\partial x_1^2}\right)^* \left(\frac{\partial^2 f}{\partial x_2^2}\right)^* - \left(\frac{\partial^2 f}{\partial x_1 \partial x_2}\right)^*\right] > 0$$

which yields,

$$(2)(2) - (1) = 3 > 0$$

and

$$\left(\frac{\partial^2 f}{\partial x_1^2}\right)^* = 2 > 0$$

Therefore, the point $x_1^* = \frac{4}{3}$ and $x_2^* = -\frac{2}{3}$ is a minimizing solution.

EXAMPLE 11.2-6

Consider the following objective function.

$$\text{Minimize:} \quad f(\mathbf{x}) = x_2^2 + 3x_1^6 + 5x_2^4$$

From $f(\mathbf{x})$, one obtains

$$\frac{\partial f}{\partial x_1} = 18x_1^5 \qquad \frac{\partial f}{\partial x_2} = 2x_2 + 20x_2^3 \qquad \frac{\partial^2 f}{\partial x_1 \partial x_2} = 0$$

$$\frac{\partial^2 f}{\partial x_1^2} = 90x_1^4 \qquad \frac{\partial^2 f}{\partial x_2^2} = 60x_2^2 + 2$$

From the first partial derivatives, it is evident that the point $x_1^* = 0$ and $x_2^* = 0$ is a stationary point. From the second partial derivatives, and the results of Eqs. 11.32 and 11.33,

$$\left[\left(\frac{\partial^2 f}{\partial x_1^2}\right)^* \left(\frac{\partial^2 f}{\partial x_2^2}\right)^* - \left(\frac{\partial^2 f}{\partial x_1 \partial x_2}\right)^*\right] = (0)(2) - 0 = 0 \tag{11.36}$$

Note that Eq. 11.36 satisfies the necessary conditions for a local minimum given by Eqs. 11.34 and 11.35. However, the point cannot be identified without reference to higher-order tests. The student will be asked to show in Exercise 4 that this point is indeed a global minimum solution.

II. UNCONSTRAINED OPTIMIZATION

11.3 FIBONACCI AND GOLDEN SECTION SEARCH

Fibonacci Search

Fibonacci Search is a univariate search technique which can be used to find the maximum (minimum) of an arbitrary unimodal, univariate objective function. The name Fibonacci Search has been attributed to this technique due to the search procedure's dependency on a numerical sequence called Fibonacci Numbers. Consider the following recursive relationship which generates an infinite series of numbers.

$$X_n = X_{n-1} + X_{n-2} \qquad n = 2, 3, \ldots.$$

Define:

$$X_0 = 1 \quad \text{and} \quad X_1 = 1$$

The above equation generates the following series of numbers which are known as a Fibonacci Sequence.

Sequence	Fibonacci Number
0	1
1	1
2	2
3	3
4	5
5	8
6	13
7	21
8	34
9	55
10	89
11	144
12	233
13	377
14	610
15	987
Etc.	Etc.

Although the name Fibonacci might be new to some readers, the Fibonacci sequence of numbers has a deep historical background. The derivation of this series goes back to Leonardo of Pisa, who was known as Fibonacci. The use of these numbers has appeared in such diverse areas as the reproduction of rabbits and the mathematical structure of pineapple scales! (22)

The Fibonacci Search technique is a sequential search technique which successively reduces the interval in which the maximum (minimum) of an arbitrary nonlinear function must lie. In order to apply this technique, the assumption of unimodality must be invoked or the technique may locate a stationary point or completely fail. If the assumption of unimodality holds, it can be shown that the Fibonacci search technique is an optimal search technique in the minimax sense. That is, compared to known univariate search techniques, in a sequence of N functional evaulations it will yield the minimum/maximum interval of uncertainty. The interval of uncertainty is defined as the interval in which the optimum solution is known to exist. The Fibonacci search technique can be derived from geometrical considerations, provided the goal of achieving a minimax search strategy is followed. The derivation follows that presented by Converse (4).

Suppose that a unimodal objective function is known to possess a maximum over a range of values from some point A to some point B (Fig. 11.20):

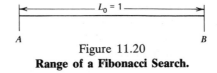

Figure 11.20
Range of a Fibonacci Search.

For convenience in calculations, further assume that this interval has been scaled to unity. (This assumption will be relaxed later.)

Define: L_n = Length of the interval of uncertainty
after n functional evaluations.

X_n = Value of X at the nth functional evaluation.

f_n = Value of the objective function at the nth point.

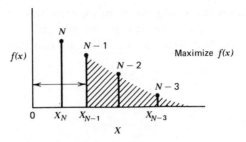

Figure 11.21
An increasing sequence of Fibonacci experiments.

Note that by previous assumptions, the initial interval of uncertainty is $L_0 = 1$. Furthermore if a single functional evaluation is made, then the interval of uncertainty is still unity, since we do not yet have enough information to eliminate any regions. Hence $L_0 = L_1 = 1$. Now suppose that a sequence of N functional evaluations has resulted in the pattern given by Fig. 11.21.

Note that as a result of this sequence of functional evaluations, the cross-hatched area in Fig. 11.21 has been eliminated under the assumption of unimodality. In contrast it is also possible that the following sequence might have occurred:

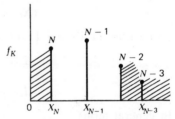

Figure 11.22
A nonincreasing sequence of Fibonacci experiments.

As a result of this sequence, the crosshatched area in Fig. 11.22 could be eliminated. Under the Minimax Principle, if we were optimizing our progression to the (ultimate) optimum solution, then the crosshatched areas in Figs. 11.21 and 11.22 should be equal. Therefore

$$L_N = X_{N-1} - 0 = X_{N-2} - X_N \tag{11.37}$$

Case I. Consider the sequence of experiments in Fig. 11.21. By construction, after $(N-1)$ functional evaluations,

$$f_{N-1} > f_{N-2} \tag{11.38}$$

Hence

$$L_{N-1} = X_{N-2} - 0 \tag{11.39}$$

From the definition of Eq. 11.37:

$$2L_N = [X_{N-2} - X_N] + [X_{N-1} - 0] \tag{11.40}$$

$$\therefore \quad 2L_N = [X_{N-2} - 0] + [X_{N-1} - X_N] \tag{11.41}$$

or

$$2L_N = L_{N-1} + \varepsilon \tag{11.42}$$

provided

$$\varepsilon \equiv [X_{N-1} - X_N]$$

Note that ε is actually the *resolution* of an experiment over the last two trials, or the distance between the last two experimental points. One can recursively repeat this same logic and arrive at the following conclusion:

If

$$f_{N-2} > f_{N-3} \tag{11.43}$$

then

$$L_{N-2} = X_{N-3}$$

These results correspond to those of Eqs. 11.38 and 11.39.

Case II.   Consider the sequence of experiments in Fig. 11.22. Suppose that the following occurred at the $(n-1)$st functional evaluation:

$$f_{N-1} < f_{N-2} \tag{11.45}$$

Hence

$$L_{N-1} = X_{N-3} - X_{N-1} \tag{11.46}$$

Since we are continually striving to minimize our current interval of uncertainty regardless of the functional evaluation results, we should require that L_{N-1} given by Eq. 11.46 be as good as the L_{N-1} given by Eq. 11.39. Hence

$$X_{N-3} - X_{N-1} = X_{N-2} - 0$$

or

$$(X_{N-3} - 0) = (X_{N-2} - 0) + (X_{N-1} - 0) \tag{11.47}$$

Using Eqs. 11.43 and 11.44, one implies that:

$$L_{N-2} = (X_{N-2} - 0) + (X_{N-1} - 0)$$

or

$$L_{N-2} = L_{N-1} + L_N \tag{11.48}$$

In general terms

$$L_{N-j} = L_{N-j+1} + L_{N-j+2} \qquad j = 2, 3, \ldots \tag{11.49}$$

Equation 11.49 represents a recursive relationship between successive intervals of uncertainty. Operating recursively on Eq. 11.49;

For $j = 2$; $$L_{N-2} = L_{N-1} + L_N$$

Hence from Eq. 11.42:

$$L_{N-2} = 3L_N - \varepsilon \tag{11.50}$$

For $j = 3$; $$L_{N-3} = L_{N-2} + L_{n-1}$$

Therefore from Eqs. 11.47 and 11.50;

$$L_{N-3} = 5L_N - 2\varepsilon \tag{11.51}$$

For $j = 4$; $$L_{N-4} = L_{N-3} + L_{N-2}$$

Hence

$$L_{N-4} = 8L_N - 3\varepsilon \tag{11.52}$$

One can now easily show by induction that the following series is established.

$$L_{N-j} = F_{j+1} L_N - F_{j-1} \varepsilon \qquad j = 1, 2, \ldots, (N-1) \tag{11.53}$$

Where

$$F_0 = 1 \qquad F_3 = 3$$
$$F_1 = 1 \qquad F_4 = 5 \qquad F_j = F_{j-1} + F_{j-2}$$
$$F_2 = 2 \qquad F_5 = 8 \qquad j = 2, 3, \ldots$$

The reader should notice that the values of F_j, $j = 0, 1, \ldots$; are the Fibonacci numbers previously introduced. What do we now have? Equation 11.53 is an expression from which the interval of uncertainty at any functional evaluation can be calculated from the following information.

1. The *resolution*, ε
2. The final interval of uncertainty, L_N
3. Fibonacci numbers

Consider now an arbitrary functional evaluation, $j = N - 1$ from Eq. 11.53;

$$L_1 = F_N L_N - F_{N-2}\varepsilon \Rightarrow L_N = \frac{L_1}{F_N} - \frac{F_{N-2}\varepsilon}{F_N}$$

But by definition, $L_1 \equiv L_0 \equiv 1$; hence

$$L_N = \frac{1}{F_N} + \frac{F_{N-2}\varepsilon}{F_N} \tag{11.54}$$

Substituting this expression back into Eq. 11.53;

$$L_N = \frac{L_{N-j} + F_{j-1}\varepsilon}{F_{j+1}} = \frac{1}{F_N} + \frac{F_{N-2}\varepsilon}{F_N}$$

Therefore

$$L_{N-j} = \frac{F_{j+1}}{F_N} + \frac{\varepsilon}{F_N}[F_{N-2}F_{j+1} - F_{j-1}F_N] \qquad j = 1, 2, \ldots$$

In particular, if $j = N - 2$

$$L_2 = \frac{F_{N-1}}{F_N} + \frac{\varepsilon}{F_N}[F_{N-2}F_{N-1} - F_{N-3}F_N]$$

By induction, one can show that

$$[F_{N-2}F_{N-1} - F_{N-3}F_N] \equiv [-1]^N$$

Hence

$$L_2 = \frac{1}{F_N}[F_{N-1} + \varepsilon(-1)^N] \tag{11.55}$$

Equation 11.55 is the key to an efficient univariate search technique, since it formally defines the interval of uncertainty after the second functional evaluation in terms of known Fibonacci numbers and the number of experiments one wishes to perform. For a minimax Fibonacci search procedure, the interval of uncertainty after the second functional evaluation should be the same length irrespective of previous results. Because the first functional evaluation will not reduce the initial interval of uncertainty, the minimax strategy is to place the first two functional evaluations a distance of L_2 units from each end of the initial interval. Subsequent experiments will be placed symmetrically within the existing interval of uncertainty according to the relation

$$L_{j+1} = L_{j-1} - L_j \qquad j = 2, 3, \ldots (N-1) \tag{11.56}$$

In general if L_0 is not scaled to 1, then the same sort of logic can be used to derive the following general expression corresponding to Eq. 11.54:

$$L_N = \frac{L_0}{F_N} + \frac{F_{N-2}\varepsilon}{F_N} \tag{11.57}$$

Finally, the important result of Eq. 11.55 is given by

$$L_2 = \frac{1}{F_N}(L_0 F_{N-1} + \varepsilon(-1)^N) \tag{11.58}$$

SUMMARY

Equation 11.58 is actually all that is needed in order to begin a Fibonacci Search. In order to utilize this equation, however, two factors must be specified in advance: (1) The minimum separation (resolution) between any two functional evaluations; (2) the number of experiments which will be run.

EXAMPLE 11.3-1

Maximize the function $f(x) = -3X^2 + 21.6X + 1.0$, with a minimum resolution of 0.50 over six functional evaluations. The optimal value of $f(x)$ is assumed to lie in the range $25 \geq X \geq 0$.

Solution

From Eq. 11.58:

$$L_2 = \frac{1}{F_N}[L_0 F_{N-1} + \varepsilon(-1)^N]$$

$$= \frac{1}{13}[25(8) + 0.50]$$

$$L_2 = 15.4231$$

Therefore the first two functional evaluations will be conducted over the range $25 \geq X \geq 0$, symmetrical within this interval. Therefore

$$X_1 = 15.4231$$
$$X_2 = 9.5769$$
$$f(X_1) = -379.477$$
$$f(X_2) = -67.233$$

Hence the region to the right of $X_1 = 15.42$ can be eliminated. Note that

$$L_0 = 25$$
$$L_1 = 25$$

and

$$L_2 = 15.4231$$

Thus

$$L_3 = L_1 - L_2 = 25 - 15.4231 = 9.5769$$

Symmetrically within the present interval of uncertainty, the two new points would be $X_3 = 9.5769$ and $X_4 = 5.8462$. Note that one of the new functional evaluations correspond to one of the old functional evaluations. This will always occur in a Fibonacci Search. The following table shows the progression through the first six functional evaluations.

Functional Evaluations (n)	Interval of Uncertainty	X_{n-1}	$f(X_{n-1})$	X_n	$f(X_n)$
2	$15.4231 \geq X \geq 0, [15.4231]$	9.5769	−67.233	15.4231	−379.477
3	$9.5769 \geq X \geq 0, [9.5769]$	5.8462	24.744	9.5769	−67.233
4	$5.8462 \geq X \geq 0, [5.8462]$	3.731	39.83	5.8462	24.744
5	$5.8462 \geq X \geq 2.115, [3.731]$	2.115	32.26	3.731	39.83
6	$4.2304 \geq X \geq 2.115, [2.115]$	3.731	39.83	4.2304	38.688

At the sixth functional evaluation, the interval of uncertainty is established as

$$I_6 = 2.115$$

The best estimate of the optimal solution is given by

$$X_5^* = 3.731$$

Hence

$$f^*(X_5) = 39.83$$

The resolution is

$$\varepsilon = 4.2304 - 3.731$$
$$\Rightarrow \varepsilon = 0.4994$$

Round-off errors in the fourth decimal place have caused us to fall below $\varepsilon = 0.50$. The optimal solution is $X^* = 3.60$ and will be approached through further searching, providing that the termination criteria is relaxed.

Golden Section Search

In performing a Fibonacci search, the two primary drawbacks are the a' priori specification of the resolution factor (ε) and the number of experiments to be performed (N). It is obvious that if the search is functioning properly, the successive experiments will gradually reduce the interval of uncertainty. From Eq. 11.53;

$$\lim_{\substack{\varepsilon \to 0 \\ N \to \infty}} \{L_N\} = \lim_{\substack{\varepsilon \to 0 \\ N \to \infty}} \left\{ \frac{1}{F_N} + \frac{F_{N-2}\varepsilon}{F_N} \right\} = 0 \qquad (11.59)$$

This simply says that the final interval of uncertainty will converge to zero as the number of functional evaluations increase to infinity.

From Eq. 11.58;

$$\lim_{\substack{N \to \infty \\ \varepsilon \to 0}} \{L_2\} = \lim_{\substack{N \to \infty \\ \varepsilon \to 0}} \left\{ \frac{1}{F_N} (L_0 F_{N-1} + \varepsilon(-1)^N \right\} = L_0 \left[\frac{F_{N-1}}{F_N} \right] \qquad (11.60)$$

One can show that in the limit $(4, 22)$ the ratio of F_{N-1}/F_N goes to 0.618.

This is known as the *golden ratio* or *golden section*, and has been used quite extensively in architectural applications. If we apply these results, it is immediately obvious that $L_2 = 0.618 \, L_0 = 0.618 \, L_1$. This is all we need to start a modified Fibonacci Search. This modified version is known as Golden Section Search [Wilde (22)]. Termination criteria can be based on a number of physical or mathematical considerations [Beveridge and Schecter (3) and Converse (4)]. For most practical purposes, the search can terminate when: (1) The functional evaluations X_n and X_{n-1} become arbitrarily close, or (2) changes in the objective function, $f(X)$, become negligible. In comparison to the Fibonacci Search procedure the Golden Section Search is less efficient. This is quite logical, since the Golden Section Search was derived from the Fibonacci Search. The primary difference lies in the goal of minimizing the maximum interval of uncertainty as the search proceeds. Since Eq. 11.60 is not dependent on resolution considerations nor the number of functional evaluations, the minimax principle is lost for early searches. However, part of this efficiency is regained as the number of search points increase. In practice, the Golden Section Search is often used because it requires less information to implement each search, and is by construction self-starting.

The general procedure is as follows:

Step I.   Define the initial interval of uncertainty as $L_0 = B - A$, where B is the upper bound of the search and A is the lower bound.

Step II.   Determine the first two functional evaluations at points X_1 and X_2 defined by:

$$X_1 = A + 0.618(B - A)$$
$$X_2 = B - 0.618(B - A)$$

Step III. Eliminate the appropriate region in which the optimum cannot lie.

Step IV.   Determine the region of uncertainty defined by:

$$L_{j+1} = L_{j-1} - L_j \qquad j = 2, 3, \ldots$$

Where

$$L_0 = B - A$$
$$L_1 = B - A$$
$$L_2 = X_1 - A$$

or

$$L_2 = B - X_2$$

depending on the region eliminated at Step III.

Step V.   Establish a new functional evaluation using the result of Step IV; Evaluate $f(x)$ at this point, and then go to Step III.

EXAMPLE 11.3-2

$$\text{Minimize:} \quad f(x) = x^4 - 15x^3 + 72x^2 - 1135x$$

Terminate the search when

$$|f(X_n) - f(X_{n-1})| \leq 0.50$$

The initial range of X is $1 \leq X \leq 15$.

Solution

The first two points are placed symmetrically within the interval $1 \leq X \leq 15$. The Golden Section ratio places these points at:

$$X_1 = 1 + 0.618(15 - 1) = 9.652$$

and
$$X_2 = 15 - 0.618(15 - 1) = 6.348$$
Hence

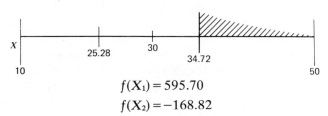

$$f(X_1) = 595.70$$
$$f(X_2) = -168.82$$

Therefore the region to the right of $X = 9.652$ can be eliminated, and the interval of uncertainty after two functional evaluations is given by

$$9.652 \geqq X \geqq 1$$

From this point on, the search procedure is exactly the same as a Fibonacci Search. The following table shows the progression of the Golden Section Search through ten iterations.

Functional Evaluations (n)	X_{n-1} (right)	$f(X_{n-1})$	X_n (left)	$f(X_n)$	Interval of Uncertainty	Length
2	9.652	595.70	6.346	-168.80	$9.652 \geqq X \geqq 1$	8.652
3	6.346	-168.80	4.304	-100.06	$9.652 \geqq X \geqq 4.304$	5.348
4	7.609	-114.64	6.346	-168.80	$7.609 \geqq X \geqq 4.304$	3.305
5	6.346	-168.80	5.566	-147.61	$7.609 \geqq X \geqq 5.566$	2.043
6	6.828	-166.42	6.346	-168.80	$6.828 \geqq X \geqq 5.566$	1.262
7	6.346	-168.80	6.048	-163.25	$6.828 \geqq X \geqq 6.048$	0.780
8	6.530	-169.83	6.346	-168.80	$6.828 \geqq X \geqq 6.346$	0.482
9	6.643	-169.34	6.530	-169.83	$6.643 \geqq X \geqq 6.346$	0.297

At iteration number 9, note that
$$f(X_9) = -169.34 \quad \text{and} \quad f(X_8) = -169.83$$
Hence
$$|f(X_9) - f(X_8)| = 0.49$$

Since termination criteria is satisfied, the Golden Section Search will stop at this point. The best answer is given by

$$X^* = \frac{6.643 + 6.346}{2} = 6.4945$$

$$f(X^*) = -169.80$$

11.4   THE HOOKE AND JEEVES SEARCH ALGORITHM

The Fibonacci and Golden Section Search algorithms are very effective in dealing with univariate nonlinear functions that are assumed to be unimodal. In practice, these searches can often be utilized over any bounded single variable search, but if the function is not unimodal, then global optimization is not guaranteed. In general, univariate search can be used in multivariable optimization through successive perturbations of each decision variable. The procedure for an N-variable optimization problem would be to fix $(N-1)$ variables at a chosen value, and search over the Nth decision variable until a maximizing (minimizing) solution is found with respect to that one variable. The procedure is then repeated by choosing one of the original fixed $(N-1)$ variables as a decision variable and finding a new optimal solution. The procedure is repeated until no change in any one variable will bring about an improvement in the current value of the objective function. This approach is called *sectioning*, and is perhaps the simplest of the multivariable optimization techniques. The sectioning approach works very well provided there is no strong interaction between the decision variables. Once strong interactions enter the optimization problem, there are long ridges and steep valleys often formed on the response surface, and the procedure tends to oscillate wildly as the one-dimensional searches are performed. Conceptually visualize a mountain climber trying to negotiate a steep ridge running from southwest to northeast, but he is restricted to small movements in the north-south directions only. Such would be the effect of search along coordinate axes over a function which runs diagonal to those axes. It is obvious that a better approach would be one that retains the simplicity of a coordinate axis search, but which provides an opportunity to change distance, direction, or a combination of both. The method of Hooke and Jeeves accomplishes those objectives. Without loss of generality, the method of Hooke and Jeeves will now be explained with reference to function minimization.

The Hooke-Jeeves algorithm consists of two distinct phases. The first is an *exploratory search* phase which serves to establish a direction of improvement, and a second is a *pattern move* which extracts the current solution vector to another point in the solution space. Using function minimization for illustrative purposes, the algorithm proceeds as follows: First, an initial solution vector is chosen $\mathbf{x}^{(0)} = (x_1^{(0)}, x_2^{(0)}, \ldots, x_n^{(0)})$. The initial value of the objective function is given by $f(\mathbf{x}^{(0)})$. Label this point *Set 1*. An initial *exploratory search* is now conducted about this point in order to find a direction of objective function improvement. Define a *perturbation* vector $\mathbf{P} = (\Delta x_1, \Delta x_2, \ldots, \Delta x_n)$ which will be used to systematically change the current solution vector. Choosing each variable in turn, an objective function evaluation is made at $x_k^{(0)} \pm \Delta x_k$; $k = 1, 2, \ldots, n$. In particular, suppose that $f(\mathbf{x})$ is evaluated at $\mathbf{x}_1^{(0)} = (x_1^{(0)} + \Delta x_1, x_2^{(0)}, \ldots, x_n^{(0)})$. If an improvement is found in $f(\mathbf{x})$ at $f(\mathbf{x}_1^{(0)})$ namely $f(\mathbf{x}_1^{(0)}) < f(\mathbf{x}^{(0)})$, then the current value of the objective function is updated to $f(\mathbf{x}_1^{(0)})$. If this move fails to improve the objective function, then the vector $\mathbf{x}_1^{(0)} = (x_1^{(0)} - \Delta x_1, x_2^{(0)}, \ldots, x_n^{(0)})$ is tried. This procedure is followed for each decision variable in turn, until the last decision variable has been changed. The final solution vector is accepted as a point in space which indicates a direction of objective function improvement. Call this point $\mathbf{x}^{(1)}$ and label it as *Base 1*. The *pattern move* phase is now implemented and consists of moving from $\mathbf{x}^{(0)}$ through $\mathbf{x}^{(1)}$ to a new point $\mathbf{x}^{(2)}$ defined by:

$$\mathbf{x}^{(2)} = \mathbf{x}^{(0)} + 2(\mathbf{x}^{(1)} - \mathbf{x}^{(0)})$$

or

$$\mathbf{x}^{(2)} = 2\mathbf{x}^{(1)} - \mathbf{x}^{(0)}$$

Call this point *Base 2*.

The point $\mathbf{x}^{(2)}$ is not immediately accepted. Before a decision is made to change the current accepted solution to *Base 2*, another *exploratory search* is conducted about *Base 2*. Performing this search as was done previously, a new point $\mathbf{x}^{(3)}$ will be established. At this time, a comparison is made between $f(\mathbf{x}^{(3)})$

and the *Base 1* solution vector. If $f(\mathbf{x}^{(3)}) < f(\mathbf{x}^{(1)})$, then $\mathbf{x}^{(3)}$ is accepted as the new solution and labeled *Base 1*. The point from which additional moves will now be made is updated to $\mathbf{x}^{(1)}$. Hence, $\mathbf{x}^{(1)}$ is now labeled *Set 1*. We are now ready to make another pattern move from point $\mathbf{x}^{(1)}$ (Set 1) through point $\mathbf{x}^{(3)}$ (Base 1) to a point $\mathbf{x}^{(4)}$ (Base 2). Exploratory searches will now be conducted about *Base 2* to determine if the pattern move was a success. This sequence of moves is repeated until an exploratory search about the point *Base 2* fails to yield objective function improvement. If this occurs, the pattern search is said to be a *failure*. When this occurs, the solution vector at *Base 1* is returned to the original status of *Set 1*, and the procedure begins anew around the point *Set 1* as if it were the initial solution vector. If an exploratory search about *Set 1* fails to yield an improved solution vector, then the change vector $\mathbf{P} = (\Delta x_1, \Delta x_2, \dots, \Delta x_n)$ should be reduced to $\mathbf{P} = (\Delta x_1/2. \Delta x_2/2, \dots, \Delta x_n/2)$ and another *exploratory search* conducted. When every component of $\mathbf{P}$ becomes less than a predetermined increment, the process terminates and *Set 1* is accepted as the optimal solution. Himmelblau (12) has suggested refined rules for termination, but our simple procedure will be used for illustrative purposes.

In general, after the *Initial exploratory search*, a point $\mathbf{x}^{(k)}$ is labeled *Set 1*. A point $\mathbf{x}^{(k+2)}$ is labeled *Base 1*. A projection is made from $\mathbf{x}^{(k)}$ through $\mathbf{x}^{(k+2)}$ to a point $\mathbf{x}^{(k+3)}$, labeled *Base 2*. If an exploratory search about point $\mathbf{x}^{(k+3)}$ is successful, then point $\mathbf{x}^{(k+1)}$ is accepted as *Set 1*, point $\mathbf{x}^{(k+3)}$ is accepted as *Base 1*, and the process repeated. If an exploratory search about *Base 2* results in failure, then *Base 1* is treated as if it were the initial solution vector, relabeled *Set 1*, and the entire procedure started anew.

EXAMPLE 11.4-1

$$\text{Minimize:} \quad f(\mathbf{x}) = 3x_1^2 + x_2^2 - 12x_1 - 8x_2$$

Suppose that we start from the point $\mathbf{x}^0 = (1, 1)$ with an initial change vector $\mathbf{P} = (0.50, 0.50)$. The value of $f(\mathbf{x})$ at the point $\mathbf{x}^0$ is given by $f(\mathbf{x}^0) = -10.0$.

Exploratory search from $\mathbf{x}^0 = (1, 1)$; Set $1 = (1, 1)$

$$x_1^{(1)} = 1 + 0.50 = 1.50 \qquad f(0.5, 0) = -18.25 \text{ (success)}$$
$$x_2^{(1)} = 1 + 0.50 = 1.50 \qquad f(1.5, 1.5) = -21.0 \text{ (success)}$$

The exploratory search is successful; hence,

$$\mathbf{x}^{(1)} = (1.5, 1.5); \qquad f(\mathbf{x}^{(1)}) = 21.0$$
$$\text{Set } 1 = (1, 1) = \mathbf{x}^{(0)}$$
$$\text{Base } 1 = (1.5, 1.5) = \mathbf{x}^{(1)}$$

A *pattern move* is now employed.

$$\mathbf{x}^{(2)} = 2\mathbf{x}^{(1)} - \mathbf{x}^{(0)} = \text{base } 1 - \text{set } 1$$

Hence

$$\mathbf{x}^{(2)} = (2.0, 2.0) \qquad f(\mathbf{x}^{(2)}) = -24.0$$
$$\text{Base } 2 = (2.0, 2.0)$$

The success or failure of the pattern move is now determined through a second exploratory search about Base 2. Functional comparisons will be based on $f(\mathbf{x}^{(2)}) = -24.0$.

Exploratory search from $\mathbf{x}^{(2)} = (2.0, 2.0)$

$x_1^{(3)} = 2.0 + 0.50 = 2.5$	$f(2.5, 2) = -23.8125$ (failure)
$x_1^{(2)} = 2.0 - 0.50 = 1.5$	$f(1.5, 2) = -23.8125$ (failure)
$x_2^{(3)} = 2.0 + 0.50 = 2.5$	$f(2.0, 2.5) = -25.75$ (success)

Hence

$$\mathbf{x}^{(3)} = (2.0, 2.5) \quad \text{and} \quad f(\mathbf{x}^{(3)}) = -25.75$$

At this point, Base 1 is accepted as the best possible solution to date. An algorithmic labeling update now occurs before proceeding.

$$\text{Set } 1 = (1.5, 1.5) = \mathbf{x}^{(1)}$$
$$\text{Base } 1 = (2.0, 2.5) = \mathbf{x}^{(3)}$$

A *pattern move* is now employed along the direction of function minimization. Since this direction is actually along the same line of improvement as before, the pattern move results in an *acceleration* in that direction.

$$\mathbf{x}^{(4)} = 2\mathbf{x}^{(3)} - \mathbf{x}^{(1)} = \text{Base } 1 - \text{Set } 1$$

Hence

$$\mathbf{x}^{(4)} = (2.5, 3.5) \quad f(\mathbf{x}^{(4)}) = -27$$

Again $f(\mathbf{x}^{(4)})$ is not immediately accepted or rejected, but an *exploratory search* is conducted about $\mathbf{x}^{(4)}$.

$x_1^{(5)} = 2.5 + 0.50 = 3.0$	$f(3.0, 3.5) = -24.75$ (failure)
$x_1^{(5)} = 2.5 - 2.0 = 2.0$	$f(2.0, 3.5) = -27.75$ (success)
$x_2^{(5)} = 3.5 + 0.50 = 4.0$	$f(2.0, 4.0) = -28.0$ (success)

At this point, Base $1 = (2.0, 2.5)$ is accepted as the best solution to date, and the following labels updated:

$$\text{Set } 1 = \mathbf{x}^{(3)} = (2.0, 2.5)$$
$$\text{Base } 1 = \mathbf{x}^{(5)} = (2.0, 4.0)$$

A *pattern move* now takes place from Set 1 through Base 1.

$$\mathbf{x}^{(6)} = 2\mathbf{x}^{(5)} - \mathbf{x}^{(3)} = \text{Base } 1 - \text{Set } 1$$

Hence,

$$\mathbf{x}^{(6)} = (2.0, 5.5) \quad \text{and} \quad f(\mathbf{x}^{(6)}) = -10.925$$

An exploratory search is compared to $f(\mathbf{x}^{(5)}) = -28.0$

$x_1^{(7)} = 2.0 + 0.50 = 2.5$	$f(2.5, 5.5) = -25$ (failure)
$x_1^{(7)} = 2.0 - 0.50 = 1.5$	$f(1.5, 5.5) = -25$ (failure)
$x_2^{(7)} = 5.5 + 0.5 = 6.0$	$f(2.0, 6.0) = -24$ (failure)
$x_2^{(7)} = 5.5 - 0.5 = 5.0$	$f(2.0, 5.0) = -27$ (failure)

At this point, the pattern search is deemed a failure. The algorithm now returns to point $\mathbf{x}^{(5)}$ and is begun anew as if $\mathbf{x}^{(5)}$ were $\mathbf{x}^{(0)}$ initially. If a pattern search about the point $\mathbf{x}^{(5)}$ is successful, then a pattern move will be made in the direction of improvement. If the pattern search about point $\mathbf{x}^{(5)}$ fails, then the step size vector $\mathbf{P} = (\Delta x_1, \Delta x_2, \ldots, \Delta x_n)$ is changed to $\mathbf{P} = (\Delta x_1/2, \Delta x_2/2, \ldots, \Delta x_n/2)$ and the process begins again. In this case, the procedure will terminate at point $\mathbf{x}^{(5)}$ since the (global) minimizing solution is

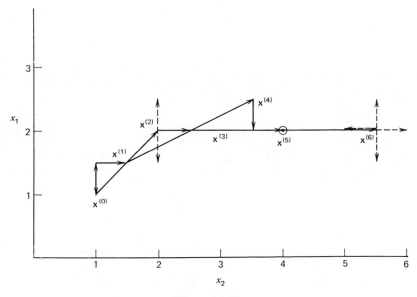

Figure 11.23
A Hooke and Jeeves Search.

$\mathbf{x}^* = (2.0, 4.0)$. The sequence of moves illustrating Example 11.4-1 are given in Fig. 11.23.

11.5 GRADIENT PROJECTION
Undoubtedly the most widely used component in nonlinear programming is the *gradient* of a function. In order to characterize and define the nature of a functional gradient, consider the point $\mathbf{x}_j$ in Fig. 11.24.

Suppose that we are at the point $\mathbf{x}_j$ and we seek to find the (unknown) maximum value of $f(\mathbf{x})$ which occurs at point A. Suppose further that the only properties which we can utilize in our search for the optimum are local values dependent on the coordinates of the current solution vector. Utilizing only this local information, suppose we wish to proceed from the current point $\mathbf{x}_j$ to a new point $\mathbf{x}_{j+1}$ in such a way that we approach the optimum at the fastest possible rate. In particular, suppose that we wish to move a distance s from a point $\mathbf{x}_j$ to a new point $\mathbf{x}_{j+1}$. $\mathbf{x}_{j+1}$ will be formed by moving a distance of s units

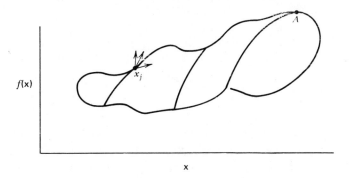

Figure 11.24
A multidimensional nonlinear function.

toward the optimum solution. In component form for i dimensional space;

$$x_{j+1}^{(i)} = x_j^{(i)} + sm_i$$

where m_i is the direction of move for the ith component (see Fig. 11.25). Suppose we wish to take a small step ds in such a way that an objective function $y = f(\mathbf{x})$ increases or decreases as much as possible. The distance of move is given by:

$$ds = \sqrt{dx_1^2 + dx_2^2 + \cdots + dx_n^2} \tag{11.61}$$

Assuming y to be differentiable, the change in y associated with a set of displacements dx_i is given by:

$$dy = \sum_{i=1}^{n} \left(\frac{\partial y}{\partial x_i}\right) dx_i \tag{11.62}$$

or

$$\frac{dy}{ds} = \sum_{i=1}^{n} \left(\frac{\partial y}{\partial x_i}\right) \frac{dx_i}{ds} \tag{11.63}$$

Now a particular set of displacements will make dy/ds as large or small as possible. This is the direction of steepest ascent or descent. Viewed as an optimization problem, we wish to maximize or minimize Eq. 11.63 subject to Eq. 11.61.

Maximize/Minimize: $\quad \dfrac{dy}{ds} = \sum\limits_{i=1}^{n} \left(\dfrac{\partial y}{\partial x_i}\right) \dfrac{dx_i}{ds}$

Subject to: $\quad ds = \sqrt{\sum\limits_{i=1}^{n} dx_i^2}$

Hence forming the Lagrangian function (see Section 11.6)

Maximize/Minimize: $\quad \sum\limits_{i=1}^{n} \left(\dfrac{\partial y}{\partial x_i}\right) \dfrac{dx_i}{ds} - \lambda\left[1 - \sum\limits_{i=1}^{n} \left(\dfrac{dx_i}{ds}\right)^2\right]$

Differentiating with respect to dx_i/ds,

$$\frac{\partial y}{\partial x_i} - 2\lambda\left(\frac{dx_i}{ds}\right) = 0 \qquad i = 1, 2, \ldots, n \tag{11.64}$$

and with respect to the Lagrangian multiplier, λ,

$$\sum_{i=1}^{n} \left(\frac{dx_i}{ds}\right)^2 = 1$$

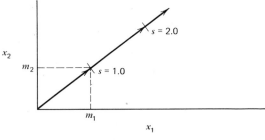

Figure 11.25
A two-dimensional move.

Therefore

$$\frac{1}{4\lambda^2} \sum_{i=1}^{n} \left(\frac{\partial y}{\partial x_i}\right)^2 = 1$$

or

$$2\lambda = \pm\sqrt{\sum_{i=1}^{n} \left(\frac{\partial y}{\partial x_i}\right)^2} \qquad (11.65)$$

As previously discussed, we are attempting to change our old point x_j to a new point x_{j+1} in an optimal manner. The change in the ith component is therefore given by

$$\frac{\partial x_i}{ds} = \frac{\partial y}{\partial x_i} \cdot \frac{1}{2\lambda} \qquad i = 1, 2, \ldots, n$$

In parametric form, this says for the ith component,

$$x_{j+1}^{(i)} = x_j^{(i)} + \left[\frac{\partial y}{\partial x_i} \cdot \frac{1}{2\lambda}\right] s = x_j^{(i)} + m_i s$$

Hence, using Eq. 11.64, a move giving the greatest *increase* in y is given by

$$m_i = \frac{\dfrac{\partial y}{\partial x_i}}{\sqrt{\sum\limits_{i=1}^{n} \left(\dfrac{\partial y}{\partial x_i}\right)^2}} \qquad i = 1, 2, \ldots, n$$

and that giving the maximum *decrease* is

$$m_i = \frac{-\dfrac{\partial y}{\partial x_i}}{\sqrt{\sum\limits_{i=1}^{n} \left(\dfrac{\partial y}{\partial x_i}\right)^2}} \qquad i = 1, 2, \ldots, n$$

Note that the numerator is the gradient, while the denominator is a normalizing factor.

EXAMPLE 11.5-1
A problem of steepest descent. Let the function be $y = (4 - x_1)^2 + x_2^2$ and our objective is to find the minimum point given an initial solution of $(0, 0)$.
That is,

$$x^{(1)} = (0, 0)$$
$$y = (4 - x_1)^2 + x_2^2$$

The direction of steepest descent for the ith component is given by

$$m_i = \frac{-\dfrac{\partial y_i}{\partial x_i}}{\sqrt{\sum\limits_{j=1}^{n} \left(\dfrac{\partial y}{\partial x_i}\right)^2}}$$

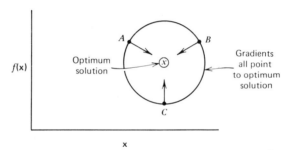

Figure 11.26
Gradient projection with circular contours.

For the given problem

$$\frac{\partial y}{\partial x_i} = -8 + 2x_1 \qquad \frac{\partial y}{\partial x_2} = 2x_2$$

$$\left.\frac{\partial y}{\partial x_i}\right|_{(0,0)} = -8 \qquad \left.\frac{\partial y}{\partial x_2}\right|_{(0,0)} = 0$$

$$m_1 = \frac{8}{\sqrt{64}} = 1 \qquad m_2 = \frac{0}{\sqrt{64}} = 0$$

$$\therefore \quad x_1^{(2)} = 0 + s(1) = s \qquad x_2^{(2)} = 0 + s(0) = 0$$

$$\therefore \quad y = (4-s)^2 \text{ is to be minimized with respect to } s$$

$$\frac{dy}{ds} = -8 + 2s = 0; \qquad \Rightarrow s = 4$$

$$\therefore \quad x_1^{(2)} = 4 \qquad x_2^{(2)} = 0$$

$$\mathbf{x}^{(2)} = (4, 0)$$

$$y|_{\mathbf{x}^{(2)}} = 0. \text{ Hence } \mathbf{x}^{(2)} \text{ is the minimum point}$$

The point $(4, 0)$ is the nucleus of a family of circles. Note we were able to obtain the optimal solution in one step. This is due to the special nature of the objective function (see Fig. 11.26).

EXAMPLE 11.5-2
Elliptical contours

$$\text{Minimize:} \quad y = 3x_1^2 + 4x_2^2$$

The direction of steepest descent is given by

$$m_i = \frac{-\dfrac{\partial y}{\partial x_1}}{\sqrt{\displaystyle\sum_{i=1}^{n}\left(\frac{\partial y}{\partial x_i}\right)^2}}$$

Let us start at the point $(1, 1)$.

It takes three iterations to reach the optimal solution and the appropriate values are tabulated on the next page.

EXAMPLE 11.5-3
Consider the following problem

$$\text{Minimize:} \quad y(x) = 2(x_1 + x_2)^2 + 2(x_1^2 + x_2^2)$$

Iteration Number	m_1	m_2	Optimal s	x_1	x_2
0	—	—	—	1	1
1	−0.6	−0.8	1.3736	0.1458	−0.0989
2	−0.8	0.6	0.2	0.0171	−0.0211
3	−0.518	0.8525	0.199	0	0

Pass 1. Let us start at the point $\mathbf{x}_0^{(1)} = \{5, 2\}$. Hence

$$y_1(\mathbf{x}) = 156.0$$

$$\frac{\partial y}{\partial x_1} = 4(x_1 + x_2) + 4x_1 \qquad \frac{\partial y}{\partial x_2} = 4(x_1 + x_2) + 4x_2$$

Evaluated at $\mathbf{x}_0^{(1)}$ we obtain

$$\left(\frac{\partial y}{\partial x_1}\right)\bigg|_{\mathbf{x}_0^{(1)}} = 48 \qquad \left(\frac{\partial y}{\partial x_2}\right)\bigg|_{\mathbf{x}_0^{(1)}} = 36$$

The direction of steepest descent is given by

$$m_1^{(1)} = \frac{-48}{\sqrt{48^2 + 36^2}} = \frac{-48}{60} = -0.8$$

$$m_2^{(1)} = \frac{-36}{\sqrt{48^2 + 36^2}} = \frac{-36}{60} = -0.6$$

Then, the position of a new point closer to the optimal value of $y(\mathbf{x})$ is

$$x_1^{(2)} = x_1^{(1)} + sm_1^{(1)} = 5 - 0.8s$$
$$x_2^{(2)} = x_2^{(1)} + sm_2^{(1)} = 2 - 0.6s$$

The optimal value of s is that which will minimize the value of $y(\mathbf{x})$ in the direction of steepest descent. Namely the value which minimizes

$$\bar{y}(\mathbf{x}) = 2[7 - 1.4s]^2 + 2[(5 - 0.8s)^2 + (2 - 0.6s)^2]$$

Using any one-dimensional search technique we find $s = 5.07$ yielding $\bar{y}(\mathbf{x}) = 3.97$. Thus the new base point is given by

$$x_1^{(2)} = 5 - 0.8(5.07) = 0.944$$
$$x_2^{(2)} = 2 - 0.6(5.07) = -1.042$$

Hence $Y_2(\mathbf{x}) = 3.977$ (note the significant decrease in the objective function).

Pass 2. Evaluating the partial derivatives at the new base point:

$$\left(\frac{\partial y}{\partial x_1}\right) = 3.384 \qquad \left(\frac{\partial y}{\partial x_2}\right) = -4.56$$

The direction of steepest descent:

$$m_1^{(2)} = \frac{-3.384}{\sqrt{(3.384)^2 + (-4.56)^2}} = \frac{-3.384}{5.678} = -0.5959$$

$$m_2^{(2)} = \frac{4.56}{\sqrt{(3.384)^2 + (-4.56)^2}} = \frac{4.56}{5.678} = 0.8030$$

Then the position of a new point closer to the optimum value of $y(\mathbf{x})$ is

$$x_1^{(3)} = x_1^{(2)} + sm_1^{(2)} = 0.944 - 0.5959s$$
$$x_2^{(3)} = x_2^{(2)} + sm_2^{(2)} = -1.042 + 0.8030s$$

Again s is defined by minimizing

$$y(\mathbf{x}) = 2[-0.098 + 0.2071s]^2 + 2[(0.944 - 0.5959s)^2 + (-1.042 + 0.8030s)^2]$$

which, again using the Fibonacci Search, yields $s = 1.36$ from which $\bar{y}(\mathbf{x}) = 0.11$

$$\begin{aligned} x_1^{(3)} &= 0.944 - 0.5959(1.36) = 0.1336 \\ x_2^{(3)} &= -1.042 + 0.8030(1.36) = 0.0501 \end{aligned} \Rightarrow Y_3(\mathbf{x}) = 0.11$$

Pass 3. Evaluating the partial derivatives at the new base point:

$$\left(\frac{\partial y}{\partial x_1}\right) = 1.2692 \qquad \left(\frac{\partial y}{\partial x_2}\right) = 0.9352$$

The direction of steepest descent is given by

$$m_1^{(3)} = \frac{-1.2692}{\sqrt{(1.2962)^2 + (0.9352)^2}} = \frac{-1.2692}{1.5765} = -0.8051$$

$$m_2^{(3)} = \frac{0.9352}{1.5765} = -0.5932$$

$$x_1^{(4)} = x_1^{(3)} + sm_1^{(3)} = 0.1336 - 0.8051s = 0.0289$$
$$x_2^{(4)} = x_2^{(3)} + sm_2^{(3)} = 0.0501 - 0.5932s = -0.027$$
$$y(\mathbf{x}) = 2[0.1837 - 1.3983s]^2 + 2[(0.1336 - 0.8051s)^2 + (0.0501 - 0.5932s)^2]$$

Again, using a one-dimensional search, we get $s = 0.13 \Rightarrow \bar{y}(\mathbf{x}) = 0.00$ to two decimal places. The procedure will terminate at this solution vector. The (accepted) optimal solution is $\mathbf{x}^* = (0.03, -0.03)$. The true optimal solution is $\mathbf{x}^* = (0.0, 0.0)$. This can easily be verified through further iterations.

Scaling and Oscillation

The difficulties encountered in solving the last problem arose due to the nonlinearities and elongated contours of the objective function. Strong interactions between solution variables also create great difficulties by forming long ridges or valleys which the gradient is not suited to negotiate. The problems associated with small oscillating movements through a long narrow valley or similar geometric configurations can sometimes be overcome by appropriate scaling of the objective function. Consider the following problem.

$$\text{Minimize:} \quad y = 100(x_2 - x_1^2)^2 + (1 - x_1)^2$$

This particular problem is called "Rosenbrock's Function," and it has been constructed to challenge the gradient procedure. The student will be asked to solve the problem in Exercise 11.9 in order to appreciate its difficulty. However consider the following transformation:

Let $\qquad\qquad z_1 = 10(x_2 - x_1^2); \qquad z_2 = 1 - x_1$

Hence we now wish to solve:

$$\text{Minimize:} \quad Y(\mathbf{z}) = z_1^2 + z_2^2$$

$$\left(\frac{\partial y}{\partial z_1}\right) = 2z_1 \qquad \left(\frac{\partial y}{\partial z_2}\right) = 2z_2$$

If $\mathbf{x}_0 = \{2, 2\}$; then $\mathbf{z}_0 = \{-20, -1\}$. Hence

$$\left(\frac{\partial y}{\partial z_1}\right)\Bigg|_{\mathbf{z}_0} = -40$$

$$\left(\frac{\partial y}{\partial z_2}\right)\Bigg|_{\mathbf{z}_0} = -2$$

$$m_1^{(1)} = \frac{40}{\sqrt{(-40)^2 + (-2)^2}} \qquad m_2 = \frac{+2}{\sqrt{(-40)^2 + (-2)^2}}$$

$$\Rightarrow m_1^{(1)} \approx 1.0 \qquad m_2^{(1)} \approx 0.050$$

Therefore

$$z_1^{(2)} = z_1^{(1)} + sm_1^{(1)}$$

$$z_2^{(2)} = z_2^{(1)} + sm_1^{(1)}$$

$$\Rightarrow z_1^{(2)} = -20 + s$$

$$z_2^{(2)} = -1 + 0.05s$$

The optimal s is given by

$$\text{Minimize:} \quad y = (-20 + s)^2 + (0.050s - 1)^2$$

which is minimized by $s = 20$. Therefore

$$z_1^{(2)} = -20 + 20 = 0$$

$$z_2^{(2)} = -1 + 1 = 0$$

At this point we note that the gradient will be zero and so we have reached an optimal solution in only one step; $z_1^* = 0$; $z_2^* = 0$. Translated into our original problem, this yields $x_1^* = x_2^* = 1.0$ which is a global minimum to Rosenbrock's function.

III. CONSTRAINED OPTIMIZATION PROBLEMS; EQUALITY CONSTRAINTS

11.6 LAGRANGE MULTIPLIERS

In most engineering problems—especially real-world formulations—the object is to optimize (maximize or minimize) a criterion (or objective) function subject to several constraints. Conceptually the introduction of side conditions that must be satisfied in an optimization problem presents no real difficulties; the feasible region of solutions is simply bounded or "constrained" by these side conditions. It seems that such a reduction of the feasible solution space would be highly beneficial; mathematically, however, it sometimes has devastating effects on rational solution techniques. For example, it can be relatively easy to solve a simple nonlinear optimization problem which is unconstrained, but if a few nonlinear *constraints* are imposed on the problem there are very few known solution techniques available. Certainly there are relatively few efficient solution techniques.

The mathematical technique of *Lagrange multipliers* has been developed to convert constrained optimization problems into unconstrained optimization problems. Of course, this can only be accomplished by creating a new problem of higher dimensions as will subsequently be made evident.

Consider the problem of maximizing a continuous and differentiable function $y_0 = f(x_1, x_2, \ldots, x_n)$ subject to the constraint $g(x_1, x_2, \ldots, x_n) = \alpha$ where $g(\mathbf{x})$ is also continuous and differentiable. The above conditions suggest that we could choose the variable x_n in the constraint and express it in terms of the remaining $(n-1)$ variables such that

$$x_n = H(x_1, x_2, \ldots, x_{n-1})$$

We could then substitute this into the objective function to obtain

$$y_0 = \hat{f}[x_1, x_2, \ldots, x_{n-1}, H(x_1, x_2, \ldots, x_{n-1})]$$

In this form, classical methods can be employed since the function is unconstrained. A necessary condition for extreme points (maximum or minimum) is that all the first derivatives vanish:

$$\frac{\partial y_0}{\partial x_j} = 0 \qquad j = 1, 2, \ldots, (n-1)$$

which yields by the chain rule

$$\frac{\partial y_0}{\partial x_j} = \frac{\partial \hat{f}}{\partial x_j} + \frac{\partial \hat{f}}{\partial x_n} \cdot \frac{\partial H}{\partial x_j} \qquad j = 1, 2, \ldots, (n-1)$$

However from $g(x_1, x_2, \ldots, x_n) = \alpha$ we see that

$$\frac{\partial g}{\partial x_j} + \frac{\partial g}{\partial x_n} \frac{\partial H}{\partial x_j} = 0 \qquad j = 1, 2, \ldots, (n-1)$$

$$\Rightarrow \frac{\partial H}{\partial x_j} = -\frac{\partial g}{\partial x_j} \Big/ \frac{\partial g}{\partial x_n} \quad \text{if} \quad \frac{\partial g}{\partial x_n} \neq 0 \qquad j = 1, 2, \ldots, (n-1)$$

Therefore

$$\frac{\partial y_0}{\partial x_j} = \frac{\partial \hat{f}}{\partial x_j} - \left[\frac{\partial \hat{f}}{\partial x_n} \cdot \frac{\partial g}{\partial x_j} \Big/ \frac{\partial g}{\partial x_n} \right] = 0 \qquad j = 1, 2, \ldots, (n-1)$$

If the solution vector obtained is the maximizing vector, then $x_1^*, x_2^*, \ldots, x_n^*$ are the maximizing values. Denote

$$\lambda = \frac{\partial \hat{f}}{\partial x_n} \Big/ \frac{\partial g}{\partial x_n}$$

so that

$$\frac{\partial \hat{f}}{\partial x_j} - \lambda \frac{\partial g}{\partial x_j} = 0 \qquad j = 1, 2, \ldots, n$$

and the enforced condition that

$$g(x_1, x_2, \ldots, x_n) = \alpha$$

Notice we now have $(n+1)$ equations in $(n+1)$ unknowns. These conditions are *necessary* for an optimum, provided that not all the derivatives $\partial g / \partial x_j$ vanish at $x_1^*, x_2^*, \ldots, x_n^*$. These necessary conditions can be obtained quite easily in practice, since we observe that we can write the following relation:

$$y_0 = f(x_1, x_2, \ldots, x_n) - \lambda [g(x_1, x_2, \ldots, x_n) - \alpha]$$

and then noting that

$$\frac{\partial y_0}{\partial x_j} = \frac{\partial f}{\partial x_j} - \lambda \frac{\partial g}{\partial x_j} = 0$$

$$\frac{\partial y_0}{\partial \lambda} = g(x_1, x_2, \ldots, x_n) - \alpha = 0$$

which are exactly the same conditions previously derived for optimality.

EXAMPLE 11.6-1

Maximize: $f(\mathbf{x}) = 3x_1^2 + x_2^2 + 2x_1x_2 + 6x_1 + 2x_2$

Subject to: $2x_1 - x_2 = 4$

Forming the *Lagrangian Function* one obtains:

Maximize: $L(x_1, x_2, \lambda) = 3x_1^2 + x_2^2 + 2x_1x_2 + 6x_1 + 2x_2 - \lambda[2x_1 - x_2 - 4]$

$$\frac{\partial L}{\partial x_1} = 6x_1 + 2x_2 + 6 - 2\lambda = 0$$

$$\frac{\partial L}{\partial x_2} = 2x_2 + 2x_1 + 2 + \lambda = 0$$

$$\frac{\partial L}{\partial \lambda} = 2x_1 - x_2 - 4 = 0$$

We now have three equations in three unknowns which we can solve simultaneously; and so, one obtains:

$$x_1^* = \frac{7}{11}$$

$$x_2^* = -\frac{30}{11}$$

$$\lambda^* = \frac{24}{11}$$

The original objective function yields the value: $f(x_1^*, x_2^*) = 85.7$.

Although we have found a stationary point for this maximization problem, there is actually no guarantee that this particular solution vector is the one we seek. In fact, any solution vector obtained by this constrained optimization technique might be a maximum, minimum, or a saddle point. For this particular problem, we can check our solution by referring to the results of Section 11.1. Recall that if the objective function is *concave*, and the constraints form a *convex* set, then the solution will be a global maximum. Using Appendix I, we know that if the Hessian matrix of a function is negative or negative definite, then the function is concave. From the objective function:

$$H(\mathbf{x}) = \begin{bmatrix} \dfrac{\partial f}{\partial x_1^2} & \dfrac{\partial f}{\partial x_1 x_2} \\[2mm] \dfrac{\partial f}{\partial x_2 x_1} & \dfrac{\partial f}{\partial x_2^2} \end{bmatrix}$$

Hence

$$H(\mathbf{x}) = \begin{bmatrix} 6 & 2 \\ 2 & 2 \end{bmatrix}$$

From Appendix I, since the matrix is symmetric and all principal diagonals are positive, the Hessian matrix is found to be *positive definite*. The objective function is thus *convex*, not concave. In addition, since the constraint is linear, it is convex and forms a convex set. Now recall from Section 11.1 that if a convex function is maximized, the solution will be found at an extreme point. In this example, the Lagrangian has located only a stationary point. The moral is to always check the nature of a Lagrangian stationary point.

Lagrangian Optimization; Everett's Method [Everett (9)]

Consider an arbitrary objective function $f(\mathbf{x})$, subject to K equality constraints of the form $g(\mathbf{x}) = b_1$, $i = 1, 2, K$, where $\mathbf{x}$ is a vector of j components, $j \geq K$. For simplicity, denote $H_i(\mathbf{x}) \equiv g(\mathbf{x})$ (note that we have deleted the resource specification). Now suppose we introduce K *nonnegative* $(\lambda_i \geq 0)$ real numbers, along with the assumption that there is a vector $\mathbf{x}^*$ which *maximizes* $f(\mathbf{x})$

$$\text{Maximize:}\quad f(\mathbf{x}) - \sum_{i=1}^{K} \lambda_i H_i(\mathbf{x}) \qquad \mathbf{x}^* \in S$$

over all $\mathbf{x} \in S$. It is not necessary that this vector be unique, only that there is some $\mathbf{x}^*$ which maximizes the above function. We will call this function the *Everett Lagrangian*. The above assumptions imply that

$$f(\mathbf{x}^*) - \sum_{i=1}^{K} \lambda_i H_i(\mathbf{x}^*) \geq f(\mathbf{x}) - \sum_{i=1}^{K} \lambda_i H_i(\mathbf{x})$$

Hence

$$f(\mathbf{x}^*) \geq f(\mathbf{x}) + \sum_{i=1}^{K} \lambda_i [H_i(\mathbf{x}^*) - H_i(\mathbf{x})] \qquad \text{for all } \mathbf{x} \in S$$

Now since $\mathbf{x}^*$ is a maximizing vector, it must be true for all feasible values in the neighborhood of $\mathbf{x}^*$ that

$$\sum_{i=1}^{K} \lambda_i [H_i(\mathbf{x}^*) - H_i(\mathbf{x})]$$

be nonnegative; therefore it must be true that $f(\mathbf{x}^*) \geq f(\mathbf{x})$. This leads us to the main theorem:

THEOREM 1

1. λ_i, $i = 1, 2, \ldots, K$ are nonnegative real numbers.
2. If $\mathbf{x}^* \in S$ maximizes the function $f(\mathbf{x}) - \sum_{i=1}^{K} \lambda_i H_i(\mathbf{x})$ $\mathbf{x} \in S$ then
3. $\mathbf{x}^*$ maximizes $f(\mathbf{x})$ for all feasible $\mathbf{x}$.

What does this tell us? It says that for *any* choice of nonnegative λ_i $i = 1, 2, \ldots, K$ that if an unconstrained maximum to the new Lagrangian function $f(\mathbf{x}) - \sum_{i=1}^{K} \lambda_i H_i(\mathbf{x})$ can be found, then this solution is also a valid solution to an original constrained optimization problem, but valid in the sense that the problem that we have solved by choosing a set of nonnegative λ_i may not be the problem that we wish to solve! In fact, corresponding to the optimal solution of the Lagrangian after choosing a set of λ's is a set of constraints which use only a specified amount of resources—the amount required to produce the present solution. In other words, we have solved a constrained problem but perhaps not the problem we wanted to solve. The problem that we wish to solve is one in which all resources (the **b** vector) are completely used. Now it is true that if we choose another set of λ's we will solve another problem—the trick is to choose this new set of λ's in such a way as to approach our original constraint set. One possible way is to exhaustively search all possible combinations until the right one is chosen, but in most cases one can tell how to change the multipliers by simply observing the changes in the resource vector.

The procedure is as follows:

1. Choose a set of nonnegative multiplers and transform the constrained problem to an unconstrained one.
2. Find a vector $\mathbf{x}^*$ which maximizes this new function.
3. Use this maximizing vector $\mathbf{x}^*$ to calculate the values for each constraint $H_i(\mathbf{x}^*)$ $i = 1, 2, \ldots, K$.
4. If $H_i(\mathbf{x}^*) \equiv b_i$ all i then an optimal solution has been found. If $H_i(\mathbf{x}^*) \neq b_i$ then go to 1 and repeat the procedure.

Putting the entire procedure into perspective, at each iteration we always solve *some* optimization problem. However, the problem which we have solved may not force $g(\mathbf{x}) - b_i = 0$. If we haven't solved the desired problem, then we should choose a new set of $\{\lambda_i\}$ in such a way as to approach the solution we seek.

For completeness, it should be noted that there may not be a set of λ's that will generate $H_i(\mathbf{x}^*) \equiv b_i$. These conditions are known as *gaps*, and they are a subject of considerable interest. It has been noted, however, that these are relatively rare in real-world problems. The above procedure will always converge to an optimal solution in a finite number of steps provided there are no gaps at the optimal solution and a solution exists. Hence the real value of this technique is that it can be used on (1) nondifferentiable functions and (2) special nondifferentiable functions such as integer programming problems.

EXAMPLE 11.6-2

An astronaut's water container is to be stored in a space capsule wall. The container is made in the form of a sphere surmounted by a cone, the base of which is equal to the radius of the sphere. If the radius of the sphere is restricted to exactly 6 feet and a surface area of 450 square feet is all that is allowed, find the dimensions x_1 and x_2 such that the volume of the container is a maximum.

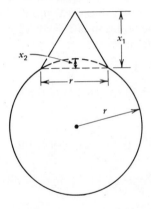

Volume of the conical top $= \frac{1}{3}\Pi \frac{r^2}{4} x_1 = \frac{\Pi r^2}{12} x_1$

Volume of the cut sphere $= \left[\frac{4}{3}\Pi r^3 - \frac{1}{6}\Pi x_2 \left(\frac{3r^2}{4} + x_2^2 \right) \right]$

$\therefore$ Volume of the capsule $= \frac{\Pi}{12} r^2 x_1 + \frac{4}{3}\Pi r^3 - \frac{\Pi}{6} x_2 \left(\frac{3r^2}{4} + x_2^2 \right)$

Surface area of cone $= \frac{\Pi r}{2} \left[\sqrt{\frac{r^2}{4} + x_1^2} \right]$

Surface area of spherical portion $= \left[4\Pi r^2 - \Pi \left(\frac{r^2}{4} + x_2^2 \right) \right]$

$\therefore$ Total surface area $= \frac{\Pi r}{2} \left[\sqrt{\frac{r^2}{4} + x_1^2} \right] + 4\Pi r^2 - \Pi \left(\frac{r^2}{4} + x_2^2 \right)$

From the above information, the following problem can be constructed:

Maximize: $f(\mathbf{x}) = \frac{\Pi}{12} r^2 x_1 + \frac{4}{3}\Pi r^3 - \frac{\Pi}{6} x_2 \left(\frac{3r^2}{4} + x_2^2 \right)$

Subject to: $\frac{\Pi r}{2} \left[\sqrt{\frac{r^2}{4} + x_1^2} \right] + 4\Pi r^2 - \Pi \left(\frac{r^2}{4} + x_2^2 \right) = 450$

or

Maximize: $f(\mathbf{x}) = \frac{\Pi}{12} (36)x_1 + \frac{4}{3}\Pi(216) - \frac{\Pi}{6} x_2(\frac{3}{4}r^2 + x_2^2)$

Subject to: $\frac{\Pi(6)}{2} [\sqrt{\frac{36}{4} + x_1^2}] + 4\Pi(36) - \Pi(\frac{36}{4} + x_2^2) = 450$

or

Maximize: $f(\mathbf{x}) = 9.43x_1 - 14.14x_2 - 0.52x_2^3 + 905.143$

Subject to: $9.43\sqrt{x_1^2 + 9} - 3.14x_2^2 = 25.714$

The Lagrangian function is given by:

Maximize: $L(\lambda_1, x_1, x_2) = 9.43x_1 - 14.14x_2 - 0.52x_2^3 - \lambda(9.43\sqrt{x_1^2 + 9} - 3.14x_2^2)$

The problem is now one of solving a two-variable, unconstrained maximization problem. This maximization can be carried out in any convenient manner. The Lagrangian technique suggested by Everett will now now be applied.

Phase 1. A common starting point is to choose $\lambda = 0$ and solve the original unconstrained problem for the solution variables. If this solution (fortuitously) satisfies the problem constraints as equalities, the problem is solved. If not, then a nonzero value of λ should be chosen and the problem solved again. For $\lambda = 0$, the solution is clearly $x_1^* = \infty$. This is logical because it will create an infinite container.

Phase 2. Assume $\lambda = 3$.

Maximize: $L(x_1, x_2) = 9.43x_1 - 14.14x_2 - 0.52x_2^3 - 3(9.43\sqrt{x_1^2 + 9} - 3.14x_2^2)$

Using the calculus;

$$\frac{\partial L(x_1, x_2)}{\partial x_1} = 9.43 - 3(9.43)(x_1^2 + 9)^{-1/2}x_1 = 0$$

$$\frac{\partial L(x_1, x_2)}{\partial x_2} = -14.14 - 1.56x_2^2 + 6(3.14)x_2 = 0$$

Note that both equations are simply quadratic functions. Solving, one obtains:

$$x_1^* = 1.06$$
$$x_2^* = 0.80$$

The constraint yields

$$9.43\sqrt{10.125} - 3.14(0.8)^2 \equiv 27.99$$

Note that we have found the solution to a *particular* optimization problem. Specifically, the problem where the right-hand side of the constraint is exactly 27.99. However, this is not the problem we wish to solve. In order to solve the problem as stated, it is necessary to modify λ and try again. Hence we will *decrease* the value of λ to 2.0 in an attempt to decrease the available resource. The following table gives the result of Phase 3. Note that the constraint evaluated at $\lambda = 2.0$ is equal to 26.94, which is closer to the value we seek. Further iterations are also shown.

Phase	λ	x_1^*	x_2^*	Constraint (Right-hand side)
1	0	∞	—	∞
2	3.0	1.06	0.80	27.99
3	2.0	1.73	1.35	26.94
4	1.5	2.68	2.79	13.52

Note that since at Phase 4 the resource requirement is too small, we will increase the value of λ (we have passed the value we seek). Continuing in this fashion).

Phase	λ	x_1^*	x_2^*	Constraint (Right-hand side)
5	1.9	1.86	1.47	26.48
6	1.8	2.00	1.61	25.89

We are sufficiently close to the answer to terminate. The optimal solution is

$$x_1^* = 2.0 \text{ feet}$$
$$x_2^* = 1.61 \text{ feet}$$

11.7 EQUALITY CONSTRAINED OPTIMIZATION: CONSTRAINED DERIVATIVES

Wilde and Beightler (21) have devised a direct method for handling nonlinear optimization problems subject to equality constraints.

Consider the problem of finding a stationary point of an arbitrary function $f(\mathbf{x})$ subject to M differentiable constraints:

$$g_j(\mathbf{x}) = 0 \qquad j = 1, 2, \ldots, M$$

where

$$\mathbf{x} = (x_1, x_2, \ldots, x_N)$$

We desire to find an expression for the first partial derivatives of $f(\mathbf{x})$ at all the points which satisfy $g_j(\mathbf{x}) = 0$.

By Taylor's Theorem, for the points $(\mathbf{x} + \Delta\mathbf{x})$ in the neighborhood of $\mathbf{x}$, we have

$$f(\mathbf{x} + \Delta\mathbf{x}) - f(\mathbf{x}) = \nabla f(\mathbf{x}) \cdot \Delta\mathbf{x} + \text{higher order terms}$$

and

$$g(\mathbf{x} + \Delta\mathbf{x}) - g_i(\mathbf{x}) = \nabla g_i(\mathbf{x}) \cdot \Delta\mathbf{x} + \text{higher order terms}$$

(Note that $\nabla f(\mathbf{x})$ and $\nabla g_i(\mathbf{x})$ are gradient vectors as defined in Section 11.5.)

as $\Delta x_j \to 0,$ then higher order terms rapidly vanish

Therefore to a first-order approximation,

$$\partial f(\mathbf{x}) = \nabla f(\mathbf{x}) \cdot \partial\mathbf{x}$$

and

$$\partial g_i(\mathbf{x}) = \nabla g_i(\mathbf{x}) \cdot \partial\mathbf{x} \qquad j = 1, 2, \ldots, M$$

Since $g_i(\mathbf{x}) = 0$, then $\partial g_i(\mathbf{x}) = 0$ so we obtain at a stationary point

$$\partial f(\mathbf{x}) = \nabla f(\mathbf{x}) \cdot \partial\mathbf{x} \tag{11.66}$$
$$0 = \nabla g_i(\mathbf{x}) \cdot \partial\mathbf{x} \qquad j = 1, 2, \ldots, M \tag{11.67}$$

At $\mathbf{x}$ the partial derivatives become known constants so that Eqs. 11.66 and 11.67 give rise to $(M+1)$ equations in $(N+1)$ unknowns. That is, $\partial f(\mathbf{x})$ and the N components of the vector $\partial\mathbf{x}$. Three cases may exist:

1. $M = N$
2. $M > N$
3. $M < N$

Cases 1 and 2 are of no importance, since if $M = N$ the solution would be $\partial\mathbf{x} = 0$, and if $M > N$, then $(M - N)$ equations are redundant. Hence we will concentrate on Case 3.

Partition $\mathbf{x}$ into two mutually exclusive sets, $\mathbf{Y}$ and $\mathbf{Z}$, such that $\mathbf{x} = (\mathbf{Y}, \mathbf{Z})$. Designate the vector $\mathbf{Y}$ as a set of M-independent or *decision* variables, and $\mathbf{Z}$ as a set of $(N - M)$-dependent or *state* variables. For simplicity, suppose that we define a partition of the gradient vector $f(\mathbf{x})$ into two parts defined by $\mathbf{Y}$ and $\mathbf{Z}$. The gradient vectors can now be rewritten as

$$\nabla f(\mathbf{x}) = \nabla f(\mathbf{Y}, \mathbf{Z}) = [\nabla f(\mathbf{Y}), \nabla f(\mathbf{Z})]$$

and

$$\nabla g_i(\mathbf{x}) = \nabla g_i(\mathbf{Y}, \mathbf{Z}) = [\nabla g_i(\mathbf{Y}), \nabla g_i(\mathbf{Z})] \qquad j = 1, 2, \ldots, M$$

Furthermore, define a nonsingular Jacobian matrix $\mathbf{J}$ by

$$\mathbf{J} = \nabla g(\mathbf{Y}) = \begin{bmatrix} \nabla g_1(\mathbf{Y}) \\ \nabla g_2(\mathbf{Y}) \\ \cdot \\ \cdot \\ \cdot \\ \nabla g_M(\mathbf{Y}) \end{bmatrix}$$

and a control matrix $\mathbf{C}$ by

$$\mathbf{C} = \nabla g(\mathbf{Z}) = \begin{bmatrix} \nabla g_1(\mathbf{Z}) \\ \nabla g_2(\mathbf{Z}) \\ \cdot \\ \cdot \\ \cdot \\ \nabla g_M(\mathbf{Z}) \end{bmatrix}$$

Equations 11.66 and 11.67 can now be rewritten as

$$\partial f(\mathbf{Y}, \mathbf{Z}) = f(\mathbf{Y})\partial + f(\mathbf{Z})\,\partial \mathbf{Z}$$

$$\mathbf{J}(\partial \mathbf{Y}) = -\mathbf{C}(\partial \mathbf{Z})$$

Since $\mathbf{J}$ is chosen nonsingular, we can immediately see that

$$\partial f(\mathbf{x}) = [-f(\mathbf{Y})\mathbf{J}^{-1}\mathbf{C} + f(\mathbf{Z})]\,\partial \mathbf{Z} \tag{11.68}$$

Note that Eq. 11.68 reflects how the rate of change in $f(\mathbf{x})$ behaves with respect to a rate of change in the decision vector. This is analogous to conventional first derivatives, but these rate of changes are *constrained*. The quantity in brackets will be denoted by $\boldsymbol{\nabla}_{YZ}$ and is formally a *constrained derivative*. Wilde and Beightler have shown that whenever constrained derivatives are used, the classical theory of *interior optima* may be employed. Therefore at the desired stationary point, $\mathbf{x}^*$, a necessary condition for optimality is that $\boldsymbol{\nabla}_{YZ} \equiv 0$. Formally, a constrained derivative is the rate of change of the objective function with respect to a certain decision variable, while holding all other decision variables constant. The state variables continually adjust to maintain feasibility. Note that by the construction of $\boldsymbol{\nabla}_{YZ}$, only *feasible*, not arbitrary perturbations, are allowed. The above procedure is a Jacobian method for obtaining the constrained derivative. For further use, it will be convenient to develop the above results in matrix notation.

If Z_i represents the ith element of $\mathbf{Z}$ and Y_i the ith element of $\mathbf{Y}$, then we can express the components of Eq. 11.68 as follows:

$$\nabla f(\mathbf{Y}) = \left(\frac{\partial f}{\partial Y_1} \quad \frac{\partial f}{\partial Y_2} \quad \cdots \quad \frac{\partial f}{\partial Y_M} \right) \tag{11.69}$$

$$\nabla f(\mathbf{Z}) = \left(\frac{\partial f}{\partial Z_1} \quad \frac{\partial f}{\partial Z_2} \quad \cdots \quad \frac{\partial f}{\partial Z_{M-N}} \right) \tag{11.70}$$

$$\mathbf{C} = \begin{bmatrix} \dfrac{\partial g_1}{\partial Z_1} & \dfrac{\partial g_1}{\partial Z_2} & \cdots & \dfrac{\partial g_1}{\partial Z_{M-N}} \\ \cdot & & & \cdot \\ \cdot & & & \cdot \\ \cdot & & & \cdot \\ \dfrac{\partial g_M}{\partial Z_1} & \dfrac{\partial g_M}{\partial Z_2} & \cdots & \dfrac{\partial g_M}{\partial Z_{M-N}} \end{bmatrix} \tag{11.71}$$

and

$$\mathbf{J} = \begin{bmatrix} \dfrac{\partial g_1}{\partial Y_1} & \dfrac{\partial g_1}{\partial Y_2} & \cdots & \dfrac{\partial g_1}{\partial Y_M} \\ \cdot & & & \cdot \\ \cdot & & & \cdot \\ \cdot & & & \cdot \\ \dfrac{\partial g_M}{\partial Y_1} & \dfrac{\partial g_M}{\partial Y_2} & \cdots & \dfrac{\partial g_M}{\partial Y_M} \end{bmatrix} \tag{11.72}$$

We now have all the necessary ingredients to solve equality-constrained optimization problems.

EXAMPLE 11.7-1

$$\text{Minimize:} \quad f(\mathbf{x}) = 5x_1^2 + x_2^2 + 2x_1x_2$$
$$\text{Subject to:} \quad g_1(\mathbf{x}) = x_1x_2 - 10$$

Since there are two variables in the problem and only one constraint, one must designate one of the variables as a *decision* variable, and the other as a *state* variable.

$$\text{Let:} \quad x_1 = \text{state variable}$$
$$x_2 = \text{decision variable}$$

Hence

$$\mathbf{Z} = (x_1)$$
$$\mathbf{Y} = (x_2)$$
$$\nabla f(\mathbf{x}) = \nabla f(\mathbf{Z}) = (10x_1 + 2x_2)$$
$$\nabla f(\mathbf{Y}) = (\ 2x_2 + 2x_1)$$
$$\mathbf{J} = [\nabla g_1(\mathbf{Y})] = [x_1]$$

Hence,

$$\mathbf{J}^{-1} = [x_1^{-1}]$$
$$\mathbf{C} = [\nabla g_1(\mathbf{Z})] = [x_2]$$

From Eq. 11.68

$$\blacktriangledown_{YZ} = [-\nabla f(\mathbf{Y})\mathbf{J}^{-1}\mathbf{C} + \nabla f(\mathbf{Z})]$$

Therefore

$$\blacktriangledown_{YZ} = (10x_1 + 2x_2) - (2x_2 + 2x_1)(x_1^{-1})(x_2)$$

or

$$\blacktriangledown_{YZ} = 10x_1 - 2x_2^2x_1^{-1}$$

A necessary condition for optimality is that $\blacktriangledown_{YZ}$ vanish. Therefore,

$$\blacktriangledown_{YZ} = 0 \Rightarrow 2x_2^2 - 10x_1^2 = 0$$

We now have two equations in two unknowns which must be satisfied:

$$x_2^2 - 5x_1^2 = 0$$

and

$$x_1x_2 - 10 = 0$$

Solving simultaneously one obtains:

$$x_2^4 = 500$$
$$\Rightarrow x_2^* = \pm 4.7287$$

and

$$x_1^* = \pm 2.1147$$

Hence we have two possible stationary points

$$\mathbf{x}_1^* = (2.1147, 4.7287)$$
$$\mathbf{x}_2^* = (-2.1147, -4.7287)$$

The reader can verify by examining the Hessian matrices of the objective function and constraint that both these points are minimizing solution vectors.

11.8 PROJECTED GRADIENT METHODS WITH EQUALITY CONSTRAINTS

Consider the problem of maximizing/minimizing a nonlinear objective function subject to linear or nonlinear constraints.

$$\text{Maximize/Minimize:} \qquad y = f(\mathbf{x})$$

$$\text{Subject to:} \quad g_i(\mathbf{x}) = b_i \qquad i = 1, 2, \ldots, m$$

$$\mathbf{x} = (x_1, x_2, \ldots, x_n)$$

The classical method of gradient optimization cannot be used in this problem, since variations in the vector $\mathbf{x}$ might lead to inadmissible regions violating one or more constraints. Thus any perturbation in the solution vector $\mathbf{x}$ must be made in such a way as to automatically satisfy the constraints. Therefore for any small displacement dx_i the following must be satisfied at an optimal solution.

$$dg_k = \sum_{i=1}^{n} \left(\frac{\partial g_k}{\partial x_i} \right) dx_i = 0 \qquad k = 1, 2, \ldots, m$$

The search for an optimal value must proceed in a restricted manner satisfying the constraints. As before, let us seek feasible perturbations that will make the rate of change in the objective function the greatest. Along a particular direction this rate of change is given by:

$$\frac{dy}{ds} = \sum_{i=1}^{n} \left(\frac{\partial y}{\partial x_i} \right) \frac{dx_i}{ds}$$

where we require:

$$ds = \sqrt{(dx_1)^2 + (dx_2)^2 + \cdots + (dx_n)^2}$$

while at the same time satisfying

$$\frac{dg_k}{ds} = \sum_{i=1}^{n} \left(\frac{\partial g_k}{\partial x_i} \right) \frac{dx_i}{ds} \equiv 0 \qquad k = 1, 2, \ldots, m$$

Formulated in this manner, the optimal rate of changes dx_i/ds are those which make the following Lagrangian function take on a stationary value.

$$F = \frac{dy}{ds} + \lambda_0 \left[1 - \sum_{i=1}^{n} \left(\frac{dx_i}{ds} \right)^2 \right] + \sum_{k=1}^{m} \lambda_k \left[\sum_{i=1}^{n} \left(\frac{\partial g_k}{\partial x_i} \right) \frac{dx_i}{ds} \right]$$

The necessary conditions are given by:

$$\frac{\partial F}{\partial \left[\dfrac{dx_i}{ds} \right]} = \frac{\partial y}{\partial x_i} - 2\lambda_0 \left(\frac{dx_i}{ds} \right) + \sum_{k=1}^{m} \lambda_k \left(\frac{\partial g_k}{\partial x_i} \right) = 0 \qquad i = 1, 2, \ldots, n \tag{11.73}$$

$$\frac{\partial F}{\partial \lambda_0} = \left[1 - \sum_{i=1}^{n} \left(\frac{dx_i}{ds} \right)^2 \right] = 0 \tag{11.74}$$

$$\frac{\partial F}{\partial \lambda_k} = \left[\sum_{i=1}^{n} \left(\frac{\partial g_k}{\partial x_i} \right) \frac{dx_i}{ds} \right] = 0 \qquad k = 1, 2, \ldots, m \tag{11.75}$$

From Eq. 11.73 we obtain

$$\frac{dx_i}{ds} = \frac{1}{2\lambda_0} \left[\frac{\partial y}{\partial x_i} + \sum_{k=1}^{m} \lambda_k \left(\frac{\partial g_k}{\partial x_i} \right) \right] \qquad i = 1, 2, \ldots, n \tag{11.76}$$

Equation 11.76 is the rate of change in x_i which results in the greatest change in $f(\mathbf{x})$ subject to the m equality constraints.

If we substitute Eq. 11.76 into Eq. 11.75 we obtain

$$\sum_{i=1}^{n}\left(\frac{\partial g_j}{\partial x_i}\right)\left[\frac{\partial y}{\partial x_i}+\sum_{k=1}^{m}\lambda_k\left(\frac{\partial g_k}{\partial x_i}\right)\right]\frac{1}{2\lambda_0}=0 \qquad j=1, 2, \ldots, m \tag{11.77}$$

or

$$\sum_{i=1}^{n}\left(\frac{\partial g_j}{\partial x_i}\right)\left(\frac{\partial y}{\partial x_i}\right)=-\sum_{i=1}^{n}\frac{\partial g_j}{\partial x_i}\sum_{k=1}^{m}\lambda_k\left(\frac{\partial g_k}{\partial x_i}\right) \qquad j=1, 2, \ldots, m \tag{11.78}$$

Now, if we substitute Eq. 11.76 into Eq. 11.74:

$$\sum_{i=1}^{n}\left[\frac{1}{2\lambda_0}\left(\frac{\partial y}{\partial x_i}\right)+\sum_{k=1}^{m}\lambda_k\left(\frac{\partial g_k}{\partial x_i}\right)\right]^2=1$$

or

$$\sum_{i=1}^{n}\left[\left(\frac{\partial y}{\partial x_i}\right)+\sum_{k=1}^{m}\lambda_k\left(\frac{\partial g_k}{\partial x_i}\right)\right]^2=4\lambda_0^2$$

From which we can obtain using Eq. 11.78:

$$2\lambda_0=\pm\sqrt{\sum_{i=1}^{n}\left[\left(\frac{\partial y}{\partial x_i}\right)^2+\frac{\partial y}{\partial x_i}\sum_{k=1}^{m}\lambda_k\left(\frac{\partial g_k}{\partial x_i}\right)\right]} \tag{11.79}$$

It should also be noted that $2\lambda_0$ is essentially a *constrained derivative*. Hence when λ_0 becomes very small we must be near an optimum solution. This will serve to guide our actions as we converge to an optimum. As before, the positive component of Eq. 11.79 represents the rate of maximum increase in the objective function, while the negative portion is the rate of maximum decrease.

As in the unconstrained case, our objective is to start with a feasible base point, $x_j^{(8)}$, and construct a new base point $x_j^{(8+1)}$ in such a manner that the objective function (1) increases/decreases at an optimum rate and (2) satisfies all constraints. The new base point will, as before, be some point at distance s along solution vector components $(\Delta x_1, \Delta x_2, \ldots, \Delta x_2)$. Algebraically

$$x_j^{(8+1)}=x_j^{(8)}+sm_j \qquad j=1, 2, \ldots, n \tag{11.80}$$

Using Eq. 11.73 this becomes:

$$x_j^{(8+1)}=x_j^{(8)}+s\left\{\frac{1}{2\lambda_0}\left[\frac{\partial y}{\partial x_j}+\sum_{k=1}^{m}\lambda_k\frac{\partial g_k}{\partial x_j}\right]\right\} \qquad j=1, 2, \ldots, n \tag{11.81}$$

By the previous derivation, this will be an improved solution vector for small movements, s. The computational scheme is as follows:

1. Enumerate the n partial derivatives of $y=f(x)$ and the $(m \cdot n)$ partial derivatives $\partial g_k/\partial x_i$ $k=1, 2, \ldots, m; i=1, 2, \ldots, n$.
2. Determine an initial feasible base point $x_j^{(1)}$.
3. Using Eq. 11.78, and the above results, calculate the m Lagrangian multipliers $\lambda_1, \lambda_2, \ldots, \lambda_m$.
4. Using the results of (3), calculate λ_0 from Eq. 11.79.
5. Calculate the new constrained base point $x_j^{(2)}$ using Eq. 11.81.
6. If the value of λ_0 at (5) becomes zero, then the last base point represents the optimal solution. Otherwise, return to (3) with the new base point and continue.

EXAMPLE 11.8-1

Minimize: $f(\mathbf{x})=(x_1-3)^2+(x_2-4)^2$
Subject to: $2x_1+x_2=3$

Phase 1

Step I. $\dfrac{\partial f}{\partial x_1} = 2(x_1 - 3)$ $\dfrac{\partial f}{\partial x_2} = 2(x_2 - 4)$

$\dfrac{\partial g}{\partial x_1} = 2$ $\dfrac{\partial g}{\partial x_2} = 1$

Step II.   A feasible starting solution is obviously given by $x_1 = (1, 1)$. Hence

$$x_1^{(1)} = 1.0; \quad x_2^{(1)} = 1.0; \quad f(x_1) = 13.$$

Step III. $\left(\dfrac{\partial f}{\partial x_1}\right)_{x_1} = -4$ $\left(\dfrac{\partial f}{\partial x_2}\right)_{x_1} = -6$

$\left(\dfrac{\partial g}{\partial x_1}\right)_{x_1} = 2$ $\left(\dfrac{\partial g}{\partial x_2}\right)_{x_1} = 1$

Hence from Eq. 11.78

$$(2)(-4) + (1)(-6) = -\{(2)[\lambda_1(2)] + (1)[\lambda_1(1)]\}$$

from which, $\lambda = 14/5$

Step IV.   Using Eq. 11.79;

$$4\lambda_0^2 = \left\{(-4)^2 + (-4)\left(\frac{14}{5}\right)(2)\right\}^2 + \left\{(-6)^2 + (-6)\left(\frac{14}{5}\right)(1)\right\}^2 = 409.6$$

or $2\lambda_0 = -20.24$

Step V. $x_1^{(2)} = 1 + s\left\{\dfrac{1}{-20.24}\left[-4 + \dfrac{14}{5}(2)\right]\right\}$

$x_2^{(2)} = 1 + s\left\{\dfrac{1}{-20.24}\left[-6 + \dfrac{14}{5}(1)\right]\right\}$

Suppose that we arbitrarily choose a step size $s = 2.0$, then

$$x_1^{(2)} = 0.763$$
$$x_2^{(2)} = 1.474$$
$$x_2 = (0.763, 1.474)$$

Note that at this new base point the objective function changes from $f(x_1) = 13$ to $f(x_2) = 11.381$. Note also that the new solution still lies along the equality constraint. Since $\lambda_0 \neq 0$ we should proceed to a new base point.

Phase 2

Step III. $\left(\dfrac{\partial f}{\partial x_1}\right)_{x_2} = -4.47$

$\left(\dfrac{\partial f}{\partial x_2}\right)_{x_2} = -5.052$

$\left(\dfrac{\partial g_1}{\partial x_1}\right)_{x_2} = 2.0$

$\left(\dfrac{\partial g_1}{\partial x_2}\right)_{x_2} = 1.0$

Hence from Eq. 11.78

$$(2)(-4.47)+(1)(-5.052)=-\{(2)(\lambda_1)(2)+(1)(\lambda_1)(1)\}$$

$$\lambda_1=\frac{14}{5}$$

Step IV.   Using Eq. 11.79

$$4\lambda_0^2=\left\{(-4.47)^2+(-4.47)\left(\frac{14}{5}\right)(2)\right\}^2+\left\{(-5.052)^2\right.$$

$$\left.+(-5.052)\left(\frac{14}{5}\right)(1)\right\}^2$$

Therefore $2\lambda_0=-12.43$

Step V. $x_1^{(3)}=0.763+s\left\{\frac{1}{-12.43}\left[-4.47+\frac{14}{5}(2)\right]\right\}$

$x_2^{(3)}=1.474+s\left\{\frac{1}{-12.43}\left[-5.052+\frac{14}{5}(1)\right]\right\}$

Therefore

$$x_1^{(3)}=0.49$$
$$x_2^{(3)}=2.02$$ $\mathbf{x}=(0.49, 2.02)$

The objective function is now $f(\mathbf{x}_3)=10.25$. Since we are still making improvements we proceed further.

Phase 3

Step III. $\left(\dfrac{\partial f}{\partial x_1}\right)_{\mathbf{x}_3}=-5.02$ $\left(\dfrac{\partial f}{\partial x_2}\right)_{\mathbf{x}_3}=-3.96$

$\left(\dfrac{\partial g}{\partial x_1}\right)_{\mathbf{x}_3}=2$ $\left(\dfrac{\partial g}{\partial x_2}\right)_{\mathbf{x}_3}=1$

Using Eq. 11.78;

$$(2)(-5.02)+(1)(-3.96)=-5\lambda_1$$

$$\lambda_1=\frac{14}{5}$$

Step IV.   Using Eq. 11.79

$$4\lambda_0^2=\left\{(-5.02)^2+(-5.02)\left(\frac{14}{5}\right)(2)\right\}^2+\left\{(-3.96)^2\right.$$

$$\left.+(-3.96)\left(\frac{14}{5}\right)(1)\right\}^2$$

$2\lambda_0=-5.44$

Step V. $x_1^{(4)}=0.69+s\left\{\frac{1}{-5.44}\left[-5.02+\left(\frac{14}{5}\right)(2)\right]\right\}$

$x_2^{(4)}=1.62+s\left\{\frac{1}{-5.44}\left[-3.96+\left(\frac{14}{5}\right)(1)\right]\right\}$

Therefore

$$x_1^{(4)}=0.37$$
$$x_2^{(4)}=2.26$$ $\mathbf{x}_4=(0.37, 2.26)$

The objective function is now $f(\mathbf{x}_4)=9.95$

Phase 4

Step III. $\left(\dfrac{\partial f}{\partial x_1}\right)_{\mathbf{x}_4} = -5.26$ $\left(\dfrac{\partial f}{\partial x_2}\right)_{\mathbf{x}_4} = -3.48$

$\left(\dfrac{\partial g}{\partial x_1}\right)_{\mathbf{x}_4} = 2.0$ $\left(\dfrac{\partial g}{\partial x_2}\right)_{\mathbf{x}_4} = 1.0$

Using Eq. 11.78;

$$(2)(-5.26) + (1)(3.48) = -5\lambda_1$$

$$\lambda_1 = \frac{14}{5}$$

Step IV. Using Eq. 11.79;

$$4\lambda_0^2 = \left\{(-5.26)^2 + (-5.26)\left(\frac{14}{5}\right)(2)\right\}^2 + \left\{(-3.48)^2\right.$$

$$\left. + (-3.48)\left(\frac{14}{5}\right)(2)\right\}^2$$

$$2\lambda_0 = -2.96$$

Step V. $x_1^{(5)} = 0.37 + 5\left\{\dfrac{1}{-2.96}\left[-5.26 + \left(\dfrac{14}{5}\right)(2)\right]\right\}$

$x_2^{(5)} = 2.26 + 5\left\{\dfrac{1}{-2.96}\left[3.48 + \left(\dfrac{14}{5}\right)(1)\right]\right\}$

Therefore

$$x_1^{(5)} = 0.025$$

$$x_2^{(5)} = 2.95$$

The objective function is now $f(\mathbf{x}_5) = 9.98$. At this point, note that we have not improved our objective function at the last move. The reason for this is that we have moved too far and passed the optimum. The procedure would now be to return to the last base point, reduce the step size, and proceed again. Further iterations will not be given since the procedure should be clear from the previous iterations.

IV. CONSTRAINED OPTIMIZATION PROBLEMS: INEQUALITY CONSTRAINTS

11.9 NONLINEAR OPTIMIZATION—THE KUHN-TUCKER CONDITIONS

In the previous section, it was found that Lagrangian multipliers could be utilized in solving equality constrained optimization problems. Kuhn and Tucker have extended this theory to include the general nonlinear programming problem with both equality and inequality constraints. Consider the following general nonlinear programming problem.

Program I

$$\text{Minimize } f(\mathbf{x})$$

$$\text{Subject to } h_j(\mathbf{x}) = 0 \qquad j = 1, 2, \ldots, m$$
$$g_j(\mathbf{x}) \geq 0 \qquad j = m + 1, \ldots, p$$

THEOREM 1

If $\mathbf{x}^*$ is a solution to Program I, and the functions $f(\mathbf{x})$, $h_j(\mathbf{x})$, and $g_j(\mathbf{x})$ are once differentiable, then there exists a set of vectors $\boldsymbol{\mu}^*$ and $\boldsymbol{\lambda}^*$ such that $\mathbf{x}^*$, $\boldsymbol{\mu}^*$, and $\boldsymbol{\lambda}^*$ satisfy the following relations:

$$h_j(\mathbf{x}) = 0 \qquad j = 1, \ldots, m \tag{11.82}$$

$$g_j(\mathbf{x}) \geq 0 \tag{11.83}$$

$$\mu_j[g_j(\mathbf{x})] = 0 \tag{11.84}$$

$$\mu_j \geq 0 \tag{11.85}$$

$$\frac{\partial f(\mathbf{x})}{\partial x_k} + \sum_{j=1}^{m} \lambda_j \left[\frac{\partial h_j(\mathbf{x})}{\partial x_k} \right] - \sum_{j=m+1}^{P} \mu_j \left[\frac{\partial g_j(\mathbf{x})}{\partial x_k} \right] = 0 \tag{11.86}$$

$$k = 1, 2, \ldots, N$$

Equations 11.82 through 11.86 represent relationships which when satisfied are necessary conditions for an optimal solution to Program I. These relationships are known as the *Kuhn-Tucker Conditions* after the men who first derived them. Note that Eqs. 11.82 and 11.83 specify primal feasibility. Equations 11.84 are complementary slackness conditions, analogous to those in linear programming; Eq. 11.85 contains nonnegative dual variables corresponding to the Lagrangian multipliers previously introduced in Section 11.6.

In most real-world formulations of nonlinear programming problems, there exist nonnegativity conditions on all solution variables. These are also accommodated in Program I, since they are of the same form as the stated inequality constraints. However we will consider this case separately in order to clarify certain notational problems which commonly appear in the literature. Consider the following statement of Program I with nonnegativity restraints on the solution variables.

Program II

$$\text{Minimize } f(\mathbf{x})$$

$$\text{Subject to } h_j(\mathbf{x}) = 0 \qquad j = 1, 2, \ldots, m$$
$$g_j(\mathbf{x}) \geq 0 \qquad j = m + 1, \ldots, p$$
$$x_k \geq 0 \qquad k = 1, 2, \ldots, N$$

THEOREM 2

If $\mathbf{x}^*$ is a solution vector to Program II, and if $f(\mathbf{x})$, $h_j(\mathbf{x})$, and $g_j(\mathbf{x})$ are once differentiable functions, then there exists a set of vectors $\boldsymbol{\mu}^*$, $\boldsymbol{\lambda}^*$, and $\mathbf{V}^*$ such that $\mathbf{x}^*$, $\boldsymbol{\mu}^*$, $\boldsymbol{\lambda}^*$, and $\mathbf{V}^*$ satisfy the following relations.

$$h_j(\mathbf{x}) = 0 \qquad j = 1, 2, \ldots, m \tag{11.87}$$

$$g_j(\mathbf{x}) \geqq 0 \qquad j = m+1, \ldots, p \tag{11.88}$$

$$x_k \geqq 0 \qquad k = 1, 2, \ldots, N \tag{11.89}$$

$$\mu_j[g_j(\mathbf{x})] = 0 \qquad j = m+1, \ldots, p \tag{11.90}$$

$$\mu_j \geqq 0 \tag{11.91}$$

$$V_k[x_k] = 0 \qquad k = 1, 2, \ldots, N \tag{11.92}$$

$$V_k \geqq 0 \tag{11.93}$$

$$\frac{\partial f(\mathbf{x})}{\partial x_k} + \sum_{j=1}^{m} \lambda_j \left[\frac{\partial h_j(\mathbf{x})}{\partial x_k} \right] - \sum_{j=m+1}^{p} \mu_j \left[\frac{\partial g_j(\mathbf{x})}{\partial x_k} \right] - V_k = 0 \tag{11.94}$$

$$k = 1, 2, \ldots, N$$

Note, however, that by Eqs. 11.94 and 11.92, these conditions imply that:

$$\Delta L_k(\mathbf{x}, \boldsymbol{\mu}, \boldsymbol{\lambda}) = \frac{\partial f(\mathbf{x})}{\partial x_k} + \sum_{j=1}^{m} \lambda_j \left[\frac{\partial h_j(\mathbf{x})}{\partial x_k} \right] - \sum_{j=m+1}^{p} \mu_j \left[\frac{\partial g_j(\mathbf{x})}{\partial x_k} \right] \geqq 0 \tag{11.95}$$

and:

$$x_k[\Delta L_k(\mathbf{x}, \boldsymbol{\mu}, \boldsymbol{\lambda})] = 0 \qquad k = 1, 2, \ldots, N \tag{11.96}$$

The reader should compare these equations to the more general results of Theorem 1. Let us now consider a series of examples explaining these conditions.

Discussion of the Kuhn-Tucker Conditions
Consider the following problem:

Program III

Minimize: $f(\mathbf{x})$ Note that $x_j \geqq 0$ is
Subject to: $x_j \geqq 0$ a *special* requirement
and not a *general* one

Now, if the constraints did not exist a necessary condition for an optimal solution would be

$$\frac{\partial f(\mathbf{x})}{\partial x_j} \bigg|_{\mathbf{x}^*} = 0 \qquad \text{all } j$$

The following example clearly shows why this need not be the case in the present problem.

We see that in Case II the constrained minimum is obviously not the free minimum as in Case I. In Case II the free minimum occurs at a negative value of $\mathbf{x}$, which is infeasible. Clearly, $\mathbf{x} \equiv 0$ is the solution to this problem. It is also clear that regardless of the functional form of $f(\mathbf{x})$, one of the quantities $(\mathbf{x}, [dF(\mathbf{x})/d\mathbf{x}])$ will be zero. Note also from the pictures that $dF/d\mathbf{x} \geq 0$. Thus, the optimality conditions are:

   a. $\mathbf{x} \geq 0$

   b. $x_j \cdot \dfrac{df(\mathbf{x})}{dx_j} = 0$ all j

   c. $\dfrac{df(\mathbf{x})}{dx_j} \geq 0$ all j

If $f(\mathbf{x})$ is *convex*, then these conditions are both *necessary and sufficient*.

    Using our newly acquired knowledge, let us proceed to a more general case.

Program IV

$$\text{Minimize } f(\mathbf{x})$$

$$\text{Subject to } g_i(\mathbf{x}) \geq 0 \quad i = 1, 2, \ldots, m$$

$$\mathbf{x} \geq 0$$

A *Partial Lagrangian Function* would be:

$$\text{Minimize } L(\mathbf{x}, \boldsymbol{\mu}) = f(\mathbf{x}) - \sum_{i=1}^{m} \mu_i[g_i(\mathbf{x})]$$

$$\mathbf{x} \geq 0$$

$$\boldsymbol{\mu} \geq 0$$

Since the Partial Lagrangian is now of the same form as Problem II, we can apply those results directly.

   A. $x_j \geq 0$ $j = 1, 2, \ldots, n$

   B. $x_j \left[\dfrac{\partial L(\mathbf{x}, \boldsymbol{\mu})}{\partial x_j} \right] = 0$ or $x_j \left[\dfrac{\partial f(\mathbf{x})}{\partial x_j} - \sum_{i=1}^{m} \mu_i \dfrac{\partial g_i(\mathbf{x})}{\partial x_j} \right] = 0$

   C. $\dfrac{\partial f(\mathbf{x})}{\partial x_j} - \sum_{i=1}^{m} \mu_i \dfrac{\partial g_i(\mathbf{x})}{\partial x_j} \geq 0$ $j = 1, 2, \ldots, n$

These conditions are completely analogous to Eqs. 11.89, 11.95, and 11.96 in Program II, but they are not enough to characterize a solution since the variables μ_i have not been dealt with completely. However we can repeat these arguments for the $\boldsymbol{\mu}$ vector, provided we treat μ_j as simply another independent variable. (This is actually what we do in Lagrangian optimization.)

   The conditions are therefore:

   D. $\mu_i \geq 0$ $i = 1, 2, \ldots, m$

   E. $\mu_i \left[\dfrac{\partial L(\mathbf{x}, \boldsymbol{\mu})}{\partial \mu_i} \right] = \mu_i g_i(\mathbf{x}) = 0$ $i = 1, 2, \ldots, m$ (11.96)

   F. $\dfrac{\partial L(\mathbf{x}, \boldsymbol{\mu})}{\partial \mu_i} = g_i(\mathbf{x}) \geq 0$

It will be left as an exercise for the student to show that the most general problem, stated on p. 522, can similarly be derived using the same logic.

Before using the Kuhn-Tucker conditions, one must assume that certain irregular conditions will not occur in the solution space—particularly at a stationary point. These irregular conditions are specified in what Kuhn and Tucker call the *constraint qualification*.

A rigorous discussion of the constraint qualification is beyond the scope of this text. However, it essentially guarantees that over the region of interest there will be no singularities or other anomalies, such as outward pointing cusps. For the interested reader, an excellent discussion of the constraint qualification is contained in Himmelblau (12). For completeness, the following theorem specifies the conditions under which the Kuhn-Tucker conditions are not only necessary but also sufficient.

The Kuhn-Tucker Sufficiency Theorem

Consider the nonlinear programming problem as stated in Program I. Let the objective function $f(\mathbf{x})$ be convex, $g_i(\mathbf{x})$ be concave for all $j = m+1, \ldots, p$; and $h_j(\mathbf{x})$ be linear for all $j = 1, 2, \ldots, m$. If there exists a solution $(\mathbf{x}^*, \boldsymbol{\mu}^*, \boldsymbol{\lambda}^*)$ satisfying the Kuhn-Tucker conditions (Eqs. 11.82 through 11.86), then $\mathbf{x}^*$ is an optimal solution to Program I.

EXAMPLE 11.9-1

Consider the following nonlinear programming problem:

$$\text{Minimize} \quad f(\mathbf{x}) = x_1^2 - x_2$$
$$\text{Subject to:} \quad x_1 + x_k = 6$$
$$x_1 \quad \geq 1$$
$$x_1^2 + x_2^2 \leq 26$$

Following Eqs. 11.80 and 11.81 we find:

$$f(\mathbf{x}) = x_1^2 - x_2; \qquad \nabla f(\mathbf{x}) = (2x_1, -1)$$
$$h_1(\mathbf{x}) = x_1 + x_2 - 6; \qquad \nabla h_1(\mathbf{x}) = (1, 1)$$
$$g_1(\mathbf{x}) = x_1 - 1; \qquad \nabla g_1(\mathbf{x}) = (1, 0)$$
$$g_2(\mathbf{x}) = 26 - x_1^2 - x_2^2; \qquad \nabla g_2(\mathbf{x}) = (-2x_1, -2x_2)$$

The Kuhn-Tucker conditions are given below:

$$x_1 + x_2 = 6$$
$$x_1 \geq 1$$
$$x_1^2 + x_2^2 \leq 26$$
$$\mu_1(x_1 - 1) = 0$$
$$\mu_2(x_1^2 + x_2^2 - 26) = 0$$
$$\mu_1 \geq 0, \quad \mu_2 \geq 0$$
$$2x_1 + \lambda_1 - \mu_1 + 2\mu_2 x_1 = 0$$
$$-1 + \lambda_1 + 2\mu_2 x_2 = 0$$

The Hessian matrix of $f(\mathbf{x})$, denoted by $H(\mathbf{x})$, is given by the following:

$$H(\mathbf{x}) = \begin{bmatrix} 2 & 0 \\ 0 & 0 \end{bmatrix}$$

Since $H(\mathbf{x})$ is positive semidefinite, the objective function $f(\mathbf{x})$ is convex (see Appendix A). Similarly, we can show that $g_2(\mathbf{x})$ is concave since its Hessian matrix is negative definite. Since $h_1(\mathbf{x})$ and $g_1(\mathbf{x})$ are linear, the conditions of the Kuhn-Tucker sufficiency theorem are satisfied. Hence if there exists a solution $(\mathbf{x}^*, \boldsymbol{\mu}^*, \boldsymbol{\lambda}^*)$ satisfying the Kuhn-Tucker conditions, then $\mathbf{x}^*$ is optimal to the nonlinear program. By inspection we find the following solution:

$$x_1^* = 1, \qquad x_2^* = 5, \qquad \lambda_1 = 0, \qquad \mu_1 = 2.2$$

and $\mu_2 = 0.1$. This solution satisfies the Kuhn-Tucker conditions. Hence, $x_1^* = 1$ and $x_2^* = 5$ is optimal and the minimum value of $f(\mathbf{x}) = -4.0$.

11.10 QUADRATIC PROGRAMMING

A quadratic programming problem will be formally defined in the following manner. ("Prime" denotes the transpose of a matrix or vector)

$$\text{Minimize:} \qquad f(\mathbf{x}) = \mathbf{c}\mathbf{x} + \mathbf{x}'\mathbf{Q}\mathbf{x} \tag{11.97}$$

$$\text{Subject to:} \qquad \mathbf{A}\mathbf{x} \geq \mathbf{b} \tag{11.98}$$

$$\mathbf{x} \geq 0 \tag{11.99}$$

$$\mathbf{c} = (c_1, c_2, \dots, c_n) \qquad\qquad \mathbf{b} = (b_1, b_2, \dots, b_m)$$

$$\mathbf{x} = (x_1, x_2, \dots, x_n)$$

$$\mathbf{Q} = \begin{bmatrix} q_{11} & q_{12} & \cdots & q_{1n} \\ q_{21} & q_{22} & \cdots & q_{2n} \\ \cdot & \cdot & & \cdot \\ \cdot & \cdot & & \cdot \\ \cdot & \cdot & & \cdot \\ q_{n1} & q_{n2} & \cdots & q_{nn} \end{bmatrix} \qquad \mathbf{A} = \begin{bmatrix} a_{11} & a_{12} & \cdots & a_{1n} \\ a_{21} & a_{22} & \cdots & a_{2n} \\ \cdot & \cdot & & \cdot \\ \cdot & \cdot & & \cdot \\ \cdot & \cdot & & \cdot \\ a_{m1} & a_{m2} & \cdots & a_{mn} \end{bmatrix}$$

The objective function (Eq. 11.97) is usually designated as a *quadratic form*, hence the name Quadratic Programming for this class of problems. Note that the region of feasible solutions is defined over a set of *linear* inequality constraints and a set of nonnegativity constraints on the solution variables.

Before we attempt to solve this nonlinear programming problem, let us define the conditions under which a problem solution might be obtained, and how such a solution might be characterized. Since the constraint set of Eqs. 11.98 and 11.99 is linear, it is convex. Thus if the objective function $f(\mathbf{x})$ is convex, we know that if a local minimizing solution exists to the quadratic programming problem it will also be a global minimizing solution. The quadratic function is convex provided that the matrix $\mathbf{Q}$ in Eq. 11.97 is positive definite or positive semidefinite.* In order to insure convergence to a global minimum, the elements of $\mathbf{Q}$ are required to satisfy the above conditions. The elements of $\mathbf{c}$, $\mathbf{A}$, and $\mathbf{b}$, however, are arbitrary. At the present time, there are

---

* For illustrative purposes, the quadratic programming problem has been presented as a minimization problem. If the objective function is to be maximized, the same arguments apply. In that case, the requirement would be for Q to appear as a negative definite or negative semidefinite matrix. See Appendix A for details.

no computationally efficient methods for finding a (global) optimal solution to the quadratic programming problem when $\mathbf{Q}$ is a general symmetric matrix. In the general case, any algorithm might converge to a local maximum, a local minimum, or even a saddle point. For the present time, we will consider only the case where $\mathbf{Q}$ is positive (semi)definite. In the next section, an algorithm will be presented which can be used to efficiently solve the quadratic programming problem.

Before proceeding, it would be most desirable to point out the major difference in finding a solution to a linear programming problem and a quadratic programming problem. In linear programming, if a feasible optimizing solution exists to a particular linear programming problem, this solution will always occur at a vertex of the feasible solution space. Furthermore, if the problem possesses N decision variables, there will be exactly M of, say, $M \leq N$ constraint inequalities satisfied as strict equalities at a nondegenerate optimal solution. In the quadratic programming problem, this need not be the case. In fact, optimality may occur at the intersection of $n \leq M$ inequalities holding at equality, or at a point strictly interior to all constraint equations. Consider Figs. 11.27–11.30 for a two-dimensional quadratic programming problem.

$$\text{Minimize:} \quad f(\mathbf{x}) = x_1^2 - 2x_1 + 4 + x_2^2 - 2x_2 + 1.$$

Note that the following optimal solutions occur for Figs. 11.27–11.30. (The objective function of Fig. 11.27 applies to Figs. 11.28–11.30)

Figure	x_1^*	x_2^*	Constraints	Binding Constraints
11.27	2.0	1.0	0	0
11.28	2.0	1.0	2	0
11.29	2.0	1.0	2	1
11.30	1/2	1/2	2	2

These considerations should be noted, for we will subsequently deal with them directly. For the present time, recall the following useful observation. If the objective function is convex and the constraints linear, then the problem is a *convex programming* problem. Hence if the Kuhn-Tucker conditions of Section 11.9 are applied to this program, then any set of solution variables satisfying the Kuhn-Tucker conditions must be a global minimizing solution. Let us

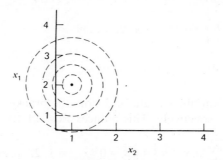

Figure 11.27
Circular contours.

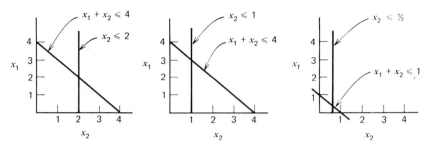

Figure 11.28   Figure 11.29   Figure 11.30

therefore develop an algorithm capable of finding a solution to the Kuhn-Tucker conditions generated from the quadratic programming problem of Eqs. 11.97–11.99.

For clarity, consider the following algebraic representation of the above equations. (Without loss of generality, assume q is symmetric.)

$$\text{Minimize:} \quad f(\mathbf{x}) = \sum_{j=1}^{n} c_j x_j + \sum_{j=1}^{n} \sum_{k=1}^{n} x_j q_{jk} x_k \tag{11.100}$$

$$\text{Subject to:} \quad g_i(\mathbf{x}) = \sum_{j=1}^{n} a_{ij} x_j \geq b_i \quad i = 1, 2, \ldots, m \tag{11.101}$$

$$\mathbf{x} \geq 0$$

Comparing this quadratic programming problem to Program IV (Section 11.9)

$$g_i(\mathbf{x}) = \sum_{j=1}^{n} a_{ij} x_j - b_i \quad i = 1, 2, \ldots, m$$

$$L(\mathbf{x}, \mathbf{u}) = \sum_{j=1}^{n} c_j x_j + \sum_{j=1}^{n} \sum_{k=1}^{n} x_j q_{jk} x_k - \sum_{i=1}^{m} \mu_i \left[\sum_{j=1}^{n} (a_{ij} x_j - b_i) \right]$$

The associated Kuhn-Tucker conditions are given by equations A through F.

A. $\mathbf{x} \geq 0$

B. $x_j \left[c_j + 2 \sum_{k=1}^{n} q_{jk} x_k - \sum_{i=1}^{m} \mu_i a_{ij} \right] = 0 \tag{11.102}$

C. $c_j + \sum_{k=1}^{n} q_{jk} x_k - \sum_{i=1}^{m} \mu_i a_{ij} \geq 0 \quad j = 1, 2, \ldots, n \tag{11.103}$

D. $\mu_i \geq 0$

E. $\mu_i \left[\sum_{j=1}^{n} a_{ij} x_j - b_i \right] = 0 \quad i = 1, 2, \ldots, m \tag{11.104}$

F. $\sum_{j=1}^{n} a_{ij} x_j - b_i \geq 0 \quad i = 1, 2, \ldots, m \tag{11.105}$

Let the nonnegative variables v_j and s_i denote the bracketed quantities in Eqs. 11.102 and 11.104 respectively. This reduces Eqs. 11.102 and 11.104 to

$$\mu_i \left[\sum_{j=1}^{n} a_{ij} x_j - b_i \right] = \mu_i s_i = 0 \quad i = 1, 2, \ldots, m \tag{11.106}$$

$$v_j [x_j] = 0 \quad j = 1, 2, \ldots, n \tag{11.107}$$

Note from Eq. 11.106 that since $g_i(\mathbf{x})$ is simply the ith inequality constraint in the original problem formulation, this implies that either μ_i or $g_i(\mathbf{x})$ or both must be zero at optimality. This condition is known as *complementary slackness*, and has the following interpretation: If the Lagrangian multiplier for the ith constraint is positive, then that constraint must be binding at optimality $(g_i(\mathbf{x}) \equiv 0)$. Conversely, if the ith constraint is *nonbinding* at optimality $(g_i(\mathbf{x}) > 0)$ this implies that the Lagrangian multiplier must be *zero* at optimality. Finally, note that Eq. 11.104 is actually stating that the original m constraints must be satisfied once we find an (optimal) solution. In summary, the Kuhn-Tucker conditions are as follows:

$$2 \sum_{k=1}^{n} q_{jk} x_k - \sum_{i=1}^{m} \mu_i a_{ij} - v_j = -c_j \qquad j = 1, 2, \ldots, n \qquad (11.108)$$

$$\sum_{j=1}^{n} a_{ij} x_j - s_i = b_i \qquad i = 1, 2, \ldots, m \qquad (11.109)$$

$$\mu_i s_i \equiv 0 \qquad i = 1, 2, \ldots, m \qquad (11.110)$$

$$v_j x_j = 0 \qquad j = 1, 2, \ldots, n \qquad (11.111)$$

$$\mathbf{x} \geq 0 \qquad \boldsymbol{\mu} \geq 0 \qquad \mathbf{v} \geq 0 \qquad \mathbf{s} \geq 0$$

We now have a total of $(m + n)$ additional *nonlinear* equations which if observed would yield a stationary point to the original quadratic program. In this case, since $\mathbf{Q}$ is positive (semi)definite, the solution is guaranteed to be the global (optimum) solution. Wolfe (23) has exploited this structure to form a simplex-based algorithm to solve this problem. Note that if a feasible solution can be found to Eqs. 11.108 and 11.109, while maintaining the relations of Eqs. 11.110 and 11.111 the problem is solved. Solutions to the $(m + n)$ linear equations are easily obtained through a simplex operation on Eqs. 11.108 and 11.109 using a Phase I procedure (see Chapter 2). The conditions of Eqs. 11.110 and 11.111 can be maintained by noting that when a change of basis occurs, and for the present time assuming nondegeneracy, the following rules must be strictly satisfied:

1. If a decision variable x_j is a basic variable, the variable v_j may not be considered as a candidate for entering the basis, and vice versa.
2. If the variable μ_i is a basic variable, the variable s_i may not be considered as a candidate for entering the basis and vice versa.

Since this technique uses the basic simplex algorithm, it is called the Simplex Method for Quadratic Programming. A damaging characteristic of this procedure is that this method may fail to converge when the matrix of the quadratic form (Q) is positive semidefinite (instead of positive-definite). A more efficient and simple method for solving the Kuhn-Tucker conditions 11.108 through 11.111 has been developed and is known as the *complementary pivot method*. This is computationally more attractive than most of the methods available for solving quadratic programming problems when Q is positive semidefinite. This method has been developed as a general procedure for solving a special class of problems known as the *complementary problem* which is discussed in detail in Section 11.11.

11.11   COMPLEMENTARY PIVOT ALGORITHMS

Consider the general problem of finding a nonnegative solution to a system of equations of the following form:

Find vectors $\mathbf{w}$ and $\mathbf{z}$ such that

$$\mathbf{w} = \mathbf{Mz} + \mathbf{q} \tag{11.112}$$

$$\mathbf{w} \geq 0, \qquad \mathbf{z} \geq 0 \tag{11.113}$$

$$\mathbf{w'z} = 0 \tag{11.114}$$

where $\mathbf{M}$ is an $(n \times n)$ square matrix and $\mathbf{w}$, $\mathbf{z}$, $\mathbf{q}$ are n-dimensional column vectors.

The above problem is known as a *complementary problem*. Note that there is no objective function to minimize or maximize in this formulation. Condition 11.112 represents a system of simultaneous linear equations; Condition 11.113 requires the solution to Condition 11.112 be nonnegative; Condition 11.114 implies $w_i z_i = 0$ for all $i = 1, 2, \ldots, n$ since w_i, $z_i \geq 0$. Thus we have a single nonlinear constraint.

As an illustration, consider a problem with

$$\mathbf{M} = \begin{pmatrix} 1 & 2 & 3 \\ 4 & 5 & 6 \\ 6 & 7 & 8 \end{pmatrix}$$

and

$$\mathbf{q} = \begin{pmatrix} 2 \\ -5 \\ -3 \end{pmatrix}$$

The *complementary problem* is given by

Find $w_1, w_2, w_3, z_1, z_2, z_3$

Such that

$$
\begin{aligned}
w_1 &= z_1 + 2z_2 + 3z_3 + 2 \\
w_2 &= 4z_1 + 5z_2 + 6z_3 - 5 \\
w_3 &= 6z_1 + 7z_2 + 8z_3 - 3 \\
w_1, w_2, w_3, & z_1, z_2, z_3 \geq 0 \\
w_1 z_1 + w_2 z_2 & + w_3 z_3 = 0
\end{aligned}
$$

Applications

The two important applications of the complementary problem are to solve linear and convex quadratic programming problems by converting them to an equivalent complementary problem.

Linear Programming.   Consider the linear program:

$$\text{Minimize} \qquad \mathbf{c'x}$$

$$\text{Subject to} \qquad \mathbf{Ax} \geq \mathbf{b}$$

$$\mathbf{x} \geq 0$$

where $\mathbf{A}$ is an $(m \times n)$ matrix, $\mathbf{c}$ and $\mathbf{x}$ are $(n \times 1)$ column vectors, and $\mathbf{b}$ is an $(m \times 1)$ column vector ("prime" denotes the transpose of a vector or matrix).

From duality theory, the dual of the above linear program is given by:

Maximize **b'y**

Subject to **A'y** $\leq$ **c**

y $\geq$ 0

According to the complementary slackness theorem (see Section 4.2), if there exists feasible solutions to the primal and the dual problems satisfying the complementary slackness conditions, then the feasible solutions are in fact optimal to their respective problems. Thus to find an optimal solution to the linear program, we can solve the following problem:

Find vectors **x**, **y**, **u**, **v** such that:

$$\mathbf{v} = -\mathbf{A'y} + \mathbf{c} \tag{11.115}$$

$$\mathbf{u} = \mathbf{Ax} - \mathbf{b} \tag{11.116}$$

$$\mathbf{x}, \mathbf{y}, \mathbf{u}, \mathbf{v} \geq 0 \tag{11.117}$$

$$\mathbf{v'x} + \mathbf{u'y} = 0 \tag{11.118}$$

u and **v** denote the vectors of slack variables of the primal and dual problems respectively.

Note that Eqs. 11.115 through 11.117 represent the primal-dual feasibility while Eq. 11.118 represents the complementary slackness condition. Comparing Eqs. 11.115 through 11.118 to the complementary problem previously defined, we get the equivalent complementary problem for a linear program as:

$$\mathbf{M} = \begin{pmatrix} \mathbf{0} & -\mathbf{A'} \\ \mathbf{A} & \mathbf{0} \end{pmatrix} \qquad \mathbf{w} = \begin{pmatrix} \mathbf{v} \\ \mathbf{u} \end{pmatrix} \qquad \mathbf{z} = \begin{pmatrix} \mathbf{x} \\ \mathbf{y} \end{pmatrix}$$

and

$$\mathbf{q} = \begin{pmatrix} \mathbf{c} \\ -\mathbf{b} \end{pmatrix}$$

It should be noted that **M** is a square, asymmetric, positive semidefinite matrix of order $(m + n)$.

Convex Quadratic Programming. Consider a convex quadratic programming problem of the form:

Minimize $f(\mathbf{x}) = \mathbf{cx} + \mathbf{x'Qx}$

Subject to $\mathbf{Ax} \geq \mathbf{b}$

$\mathbf{x} \geq 0$

where: **Q** is an $(n \times n)$ matrix.

Assume **Q** is symmetric and is positive-definite or positive semidefinite.

In matrix notation, the Kuhn-Tucker optimality conditions to the above convex quadratic program can be written as follows. (See Eqs. 11.108 through 11.111 in Section 11.10):

Find vectors **x**, **μ**, **v**, **s** such that

$$\mathbf{v} = 2\mathbf{Qx} - \mathbf{A'\mu} + \mathbf{c} \tag{11.119}$$

$$\mathbf{s} = -\mathbf{Ax} + \mathbf{b} \tag{11.120}$$

$$\mathbf{x}, \mathbf{\mu}, \mathbf{v}, \mathbf{s} \geq 0$$

$$\mathbf{v'x} + \mathbf{s'\mu} = 0$$

comparing the above system of equations to the complementary problem, we note that

$$\mathbf{w} = \begin{pmatrix} \mathbf{v} \\ \mathbf{s} \end{pmatrix}, \quad \mathbf{z} = \begin{pmatrix} \mathbf{x} \\ \mathbf{\mu} \end{pmatrix}, \quad \mathbf{M} = \begin{pmatrix} 2\mathbf{Q} & -\mathbf{A}' \\ \mathbf{A} & 0 \end{pmatrix}, \quad \text{and} \quad \mathbf{q} = \begin{pmatrix} \mathbf{c} \\ -\mathbf{b} \end{pmatrix}$$

Thus an optimal solution to the convex quadratic program may be obtained by solving the equivalent complementary problem shown above. It should be again noted that the matrix $\mathbf{M}$ is positive semidefinite, since $\mathbf{Q}$ is positive definite or positive semidefinite.

We shall illustrate the transformation of a linear and quadratic program to a complementary problem with the following examples.

EXAMPLE 11.11-1

Consider the linear program:

$$\begin{aligned}
\text{Minimize:} \quad & f(\mathbf{x}) = 2x_1 + 3x_2 - x_3 \\
\text{Subject to:} \quad & 2x_1 - x_2 + 5x_3 \geq 1 \\
& 3x_1 + x_2 - x_3 = 4 \\
& x_1 - x_2 + x_3 = 2 \\
& x_1, x_2, x_3 \geq 0
\end{aligned}$$

Before the linear program can be converted to a complementary problem, the equality constraints have to be converted to inequalities as follows:

$$\begin{aligned}
3x_1 + x_2 - x_3 &\geq 4 \\
x_1 - x_2 + x_3 &\geq 2 \\
(3x_1 + x_2 - x_3) + (x_1 - x_2 + x_3) &\leq 6
\end{aligned}$$

The last inequality simplifies to $4x_1 \leq 6$. The linear program may thus be rewritten as

$$\begin{aligned}
\text{Minimize:} \quad & f(\mathbf{x}) = 2x_1 + 3x_2 - x_3 \\
\text{Subject to:} \quad & 2x_1 - x_2 + 5x_3 \geq 1 \\
& 3x_1 + x_2 - x_3 \geq 4 \\
& x_1 - x_2 + x_3 \geq 2 \\
& -4x_1 \geq -6 \\
& x_1, x_2, x_3 \geq 0
\end{aligned}$$

Comparing the above linear program to the notations previously introduced, we obtain:

$$\mathbf{A}_{(4\times3)} = \begin{bmatrix} 2 & -1 & 5 \\ 3 & 1 & -1 \\ 1 & -1 & 1 \\ -4 & 0 & 0 \end{bmatrix}, \quad \mathbf{b} = \begin{pmatrix} 1 \\ 4 \\ 2 \\ -6 \end{pmatrix} \quad \text{and} \quad \mathbf{c} = \begin{pmatrix} 2 \\ 3 \\ -1 \end{pmatrix}$$

The equivalent complementary problem is given below:

$$\mathop{\mathbf{M}}_{(7\times7)} = \begin{bmatrix} 0 & -\mathbf{A} \\ \mathbf{A} & 0 \end{bmatrix} = \begin{bmatrix} 0 & 0 & 0 & -2 & -3 & -1 & 4 \\ 0 & 0 & 0 & 1 & -1 & 1 & 0 \\ 0 & 0 & 0 & -5 & 1 & -1 & 0 \\ 2 & -1 & 5 & 0 & 0 & 0 & 0 \\ 3 & 1 & -1 & 0 & 0 & 0 & 0 \\ 1 & -1 & 1 & 0 & 0 & 0 & 0 \\ -4 & 0 & 0 & 0 & 0 & 0 & 0 \end{bmatrix}$$

$$\mathop{\mathbf{q}}_{(7\times1)} = \begin{bmatrix} \mathbf{c} \\ -\mathbf{b} \end{bmatrix} = \begin{bmatrix} 2 \\ 3 \\ -1 \\ -1 \\ -4 \\ -2 \\ 6 \end{bmatrix}$$

The values of z_1, z_2, and z_3 produce the solution to x_1, x_2, and x_3; while z_4, z_5, z_6 and z_7 correspond to the dual solution.

EXAMPLE 11.11-2

Consider a convex quadratic programming problem:

$$\text{Minimize:} \quad f(\mathbf{x}) = -6x_1 + 2x_1^2 - 2x_1x_2 + 2x_2^2$$

$$\text{Subject to:} \quad -x_1 - x_2 \geq -2$$

$$x_1, x_2 \geq 0$$

For this problem

$$\mathbf{A} = (-1 \quad -1), \qquad \mathbf{b} = (-2), \qquad \mathbf{c} = \begin{pmatrix} -6 \\ 0 \end{pmatrix}, \qquad \text{and} \qquad \mathbf{Q} = \begin{bmatrix} 2 & -1 \\ -1 & 2 \end{bmatrix}$$

The equivalent complementary problem is given by

$$\mathop{\mathbf{M}}_{(3\times3)} = \begin{pmatrix} \mathbf{Q} + \mathbf{Q}' & -\mathbf{A}' \\ \mathbf{A} & 0 \end{pmatrix} = \begin{pmatrix} 4 & -2 & 1 \\ -2 & 4 & 1 \\ -1 & -1 & 0 \end{pmatrix}$$

and

$$\mathbf{q} = \begin{pmatrix} \mathbf{c} \\ -\mathbf{b} \end{pmatrix} = \begin{pmatrix} -6 \\ 0 \\ 2 \end{pmatrix}$$

The solution to z_1 to z_2 correspond to the optimal values of x_1 and x_2 since the matrix of the quadratic form $(\mathbf{Q})$ is positive definite.

An Algorithm to Solve the Complementary Problem

Consider the complementary problem:
Find vectors $\mathbf{w}$ and $\mathbf{z}$ such that

$$\mathbf{w} = \mathbf{Mz} + \mathbf{q}$$

$$\mathbf{w}, \mathbf{z} \geq 0$$

$$\mathbf{w}'\mathbf{z} = 0$$

Definitions

1. *Feasible Solution.* A nonnegative solution $(\mathbf{w}, \mathbf{z})$ to the system of the equation $\mathbf{w} = \mathbf{Mz} + \mathbf{q}$ is called a feasible solution to the complementary problem.
2. *Complementary Solution.* A feasible solution $(\mathbf{w}, \mathbf{z})$ to the complementary problem which also satisfies the complementarity condition $\mathbf{w}'\mathbf{z} = 0$ is called a complementary solution.

The condition $\mathbf{w}'\mathbf{z} = 0$ is equivalent to $w_i z_i = 0$ for all i. The variables w_i and z_i for each i is called a *complementary pair* of variables. Note that if the elements of the vector $\mathbf{q}$ are nonnegative, then there exists an obvious complementary solution given by $\mathbf{w} = \mathbf{q}$, $\mathbf{z} = 0$. Hence the complementary problem is nontrivial only when at least one of the elements of $\mathbf{q}$ is negative. This means that the initial basic solution given by $\mathbf{w} = \mathbf{q}$, $\mathbf{z} = 0$ is *infeasible* to the complementary problem even though it satisfies the complementary condition $\mathbf{w}'\mathbf{z} = 0$.

At present there exists no general algorithm to solve all the complementary problems. When the matrix $\mathbf{M}$ satisfies certain special properties, a *Complementary Pivot Method* has been developed by Lemke to determine the complementary solution if one exists. Specifically, the complementary pivot method is guaranteed to find a complementary solution when $\mathbf{M}$ satisfies any one of the following properties.

1. All the elements of $\mathbf{M}$ are positive.
2. The matrix $\mathbf{M}$ is positive definite.
3. All the principal determinants* of the matrix $\mathbf{M}$ are positive.

In other words, when $\mathbf{M}$ satisfies any of the above conditions, there always exists a complementary solution to the complementary problem irrespective of what values the elements of $\mathbf{q}$ assume.

We have previously stated that linear and convex quadratic programming problems give rise to a complementary problem where the matrix $\mathbf{M}$ is positive semidefinite. Under this case the complementary pivot method is quaranteed to terminate with a complementary solution only when a solution exists for that particular problem. In other words, it is possible for the complementary problem not to have a solution since some linear and quadratic programs may not have optimal solutions.

The Complementary Pivot Method

The complementary pivot method starts with the infeasible basic solution given by $\mathbf{w} = \mathbf{q}$; $\mathbf{z} = 0$. In order to make the solution nonnegative, an artificial variable z_0 is added at a sufficiently positive value to each of the equations in the $\mathbf{w} - \mathbf{Mz} = \mathbf{q}$ system, so that the right-hand-side constants $(q_i + z_0)$ become nonnegative. The value of z_0 will be the absolute value of the most negative q_i. We now have a basic solution given by:

$$w_i = q_i + z_0, \qquad z_i = 0 \qquad \text{for all } i = 1, \ldots, n,$$

and

$$z_0 = -\min_i(q_i)$$

Note as previously discussed that even though this solution is nonnegative,

---

* See Appendix A for the definition of principal determinants.

satisfies the constraints and is complementary ($w_i z_i = 0$), it is not feasible due to the presence of the artificial variable z_0 at a positive value. We shall call such a solution an *almost complementary solution*.

The first step in the complementary pivot method is to find an almost complementary solution, by augmenting the original system of Eq. ($\mathbf{w} = \mathbf{Mz} + \mathbf{q}$) by an artificial variable z_0 as follows:

$$\mathbf{w} - \mathbf{Mz} - \mathbf{e}z_0 = \mathbf{q}$$

$$\mathbf{w}, \mathbf{z}, z_0 \geqq 0$$

$$\mathbf{w'z} = 0$$

where

$$\mathbf{e}_{(n \times 1)} = (1, 1, \ldots, 1)'$$

Thus, the initial tableau becomes:

Basis	$w_1 \cdots w_s \cdots w_n$	$z_1 \cdots z_s \cdots z_n$	z_0	$\mathbf{q}$
w_1	1	$-m_{11} \quad -m_{1s} \quad -m_{1n}$	-1	q_1
w_s	$\quad 1$	$-m_{s1} \quad -m_{ss} \quad -m_{sn}$	-1	q_s
w_n	$\qquad 1$	$-m_{n1} \quad -m_{ns} \quad -m_{nn}$	-1	q_n

where the m_{ij}'s are the elements of the $\mathbf{M}$ matrix.

Step I. To determine the initial almost complementary solution, the variable z_0 is brought into the basis replacing the basic variable with the most negative value. (Let $q_s = \min q_i < 0$.) This implies that z_0 replaces w_s from the basis. Performing the necessary pivot operation yields the following tableau:

Tableau 1

Basis	$w_1 \cdots w_s \cdots w_n$	$z_1 \cdots z_s \cdots z_n$	z_0	$\mathbf{q}$
w_1	$1 \quad -1 \quad 0$	$m'_{11} \quad m'_{1s} \quad m'_{1n}$	0	q'_1
z_0	$0 \quad -1 \quad 0$	$m'_{s1} \quad m'_{ss} \quad m'_{sn}$	1	q'_s
w_n	$0 \quad -1 \quad 1$	$m'_{n1} \quad m'_{ns} \quad m'_{nn}$	0	q'_n

where

$$q'_s = -q_s; \quad q'_i = q_i - q_s \qquad \text{for all } i \neq s;$$

$$m'_{sj} = \frac{-m_{sj}}{-1} = m_{sj} \qquad \text{for all } j = 1, \ldots, n;$$

$$m'_{ij} = -m_{ij} + m_{sj} \qquad \text{for all } j = 1, \ldots, n \qquad \text{and } i \neq s.$$

Note that:

1. $q'_i \geqq 0 \quad i = 1, \ldots, n$
2. The basic solution $w_1 = q'_1, \ldots, w_{s-1} = q'_{s-1}, z_0 = q'_s, w_{s+1} = q'_{s+1}, \ldots, w_n = q'_n$, and all other variables initially zero is an almost complementary solution.

3. The almost complementary solution becomes a complementary solution as soon as the value of z_0 is reduced to zero.

In essence, the complementary pivot algorithm proceeds to find a sequence of almost complementary solutions (tableaus) until z_0 becomes zero. To do this, the basis changes must be done in such a way that the following conditions are met:

A. The complementarity between the variables must be maintained (i.e., $w_i z_i = 0$ for all $i = 1, \ldots, n$).
B. The basic solution remains nonnegative (i.e., the right-hand-side constants must be nonnegative in all tableaus).

Step II.   In order to satisfy Condition A, we observe that the variables w_s and z_s are both out of the basis in Tableau 1. As long as either one of them is made basic, the complementarity between **w** and **z** variables will still be maintained. Since w_s just came out of the basis, the choice is naturally to bring z_s into the basis. Thus we have a simple rule for selecting the nonbasic variable to enter the basis in the next tableau. It is always the complement of the basic variable which just left the basis in the last tableau. This is called the *complementary rule*.

After selecting the variable to enter the basis, we have to determine the basic variable to leave. This is done by applying the *Minimum Ratio Test* similar to the one used in the simplex method so that Condition B is satisfied. Therefore to determine the variable to leave the basis, the following ratios are formed:

$$\frac{q'_i}{m'_{is}} \qquad \text{for those } i = 1, \ldots, n \text{ for which } m'_{is} > 0$$

Let

$$\frac{q'_k}{m'_{ks}} = \underset{m'_{is} > 0}{\text{Minimum}} \left(\frac{q'_i}{m'_{is}} \right)$$

This implies that the basic variable w_k leaves the basis, to be replaced by z_s. We now obtain the new tableau by performing the pivot operation with m'_{ks} as the pivot element.

Step III.   Since w_k left the basis, the variable z_k is brought into the basis by the complementary rule, and the basis changes are continued as before until one of two things happens which indicates termination of the algorithm:

1. The minimum ratio is obtained in row s and z_0 leaves the basis. The resulting basic solution after performing the pivot operation is the complementary solution.
2. The minimum ratio test fails, since all the coefficients in the pivot column are nonpositive. This implies that there exists *no* solution to the complementary problem. In this case, we say that the complementary problem has a *Ray Solution* (26).

Remarks
1. It has been shown that the complementary pivot method always terminates with a complementary solution in a finite number of steps whenever (a) all the elements of **M** are positive, or (b) **M** has positive principal determinants (includes the case where **M** is positive definite).

2. The most important application of complementary pivot theory is in solving linear and convex quadratic programming problems. We have seen that under these cases, **M** is a positive semidefinite matrix. It has been proved that whenever **M** is positive semidefinite, the algorithm will terminate with a complementary solution if one exists for that problem. In other works, termination 2 implies that the given linear program or quadratic program has no optimal solution.

For a proof of the above remarks the reader is referred to Cottle and Dantzig (25).

Let us illustrate the complementary pivot method for solving a convex quadratic program using Example 11.11-2.

$$\text{Minimize:} \quad f(\mathbf{x}) = -6x_1 + 2x_1^2 - 2x_1x_2 + 2x_2^2$$

$$\text{Subject to:} \quad -x_1 - x_2 \geq -2$$

$$x_1, x_2 \geq 0$$

The equivalent complementary problem is given below:

$$\mathbf{M}_{(3\times3)} = \begin{pmatrix} 4 & -2 & 1 \\ -2 & 4 & 1 \\ -1 & -1 & 0 \end{pmatrix} \quad \text{and} \quad \mathbf{q} = \begin{pmatrix} -6 \\ 0 \\ 2 \end{pmatrix}$$

Since all the elements of **q** are not nonnegative, an artificial variable z_0 is added to every equation. The initial tableau is given below:

Tableau 1

Basis	w_1	w_2	w_3	z_1	z_2	z_3	z_0	q
w_1	1	0	0	-4	2	-1	$\boxed{-1}$	-6
w_2	0	1	0	2	-4	-1	-1	0
w_3	0	0	1	1	1	0	-1	2

The initial basic solution is $w_1 = -6$, $w_2 = 0$, $w_3 = 2$, $z_1 = z_2 = z_3 = z_0 = 0$. An almost complementary solution is obtained by replacing w_1 by z_0 as shown in Tableau 2. The almost complementary solution is given by $z_0 = 6$, $w_2 = 6$, $w_3 = 8$, $z_1 = z_2 = z_3 = w_1 = 0$. Since the complementary pair (w_1, z_1) is out of the basis, either w_1 or z_1 can be made a basic variable without affecting the complementarity between all pairs of variables ($w_i z_i = 0$). Since w_1 just left the basis, we bring z_1 into the basis. Applying the minimum ratio test, we obtain the ratios as (6/4, 6/6, 8/5). This implies that z_1 replaces w_2 in the basis. Tableau 3 gives the new almost complementary solution after the pivot operation. By applying the complementary rule, z_2 is selected as the next basic variable (w_2 just left the basis). The minimum ratio test determines w_3 as the

Tableau 2

Basis	w_1	w_2	w_3	z_1	z_2	z_3	z_0	q
z_0	-1	0	0	4	-2	1	1	6
w_2	-1	1	0	$\boxed{6}$	-6	0	0	6
w_3	-1	0	1	5	-1	1	0	8

Tableau 3

Basis	w_1	w_2	w_3	z_1	z_2	z_3	z_0	q
z_0	$-\dfrac{1}{3}$	$-\dfrac{2}{3}$	0	0	2	1	1	2
z_1	$-\dfrac{1}{6}$	$\dfrac{1}{6}$	0	1	-1	0	0	1
w_3	$-\dfrac{1}{6}$	$-\dfrac{1}{5}$	1	0	④	1	0	3

basic variable to leave. The next almost complementary solution after the pivot operation is shown in Tableau 4.

By the complementary rule, z_3 becomes the next basic variable. Application of the minimum ratio test results in the replacement of z_0 from the basis. This implies that the next tableau will correspond to a complementary solution as shown in Tableau 5.

Tableau 4

Basis	w_1	w_2	w_3	z_1	z_2	z_3	z_0	q
z_0	$-\dfrac{1}{4}$	$-\dfrac{1}{4}$	$-\dfrac{1}{2}$	0	0	$\left(\dfrac{1}{2}\right)$	1	$\dfrac{1}{2}$
z_1	$-\dfrac{5}{24}$	$-\dfrac{1}{24}$	$\dfrac{1}{4}$	1	0	$\dfrac{1}{4}$	0	$\dfrac{7}{4}$
z_2	$-\dfrac{1}{24}$	$-\dfrac{5}{24}$	$\dfrac{1}{4}$	0	1	$\dfrac{1}{4}$	0	$\dfrac{3}{4}$

The complementary solution is given by $z_1 = 3/2$, $z_2 = 1/2$, $z_3 = 1$, $w_1 = w_2 = w_3 = 0$.

Hence the optimal solution to the given quadratic program becomes:

$$x_1^* = \frac{3}{2}, \qquad x_2^* = \frac{1}{2}, \qquad \text{and} \qquad f(\mathbf{x}^*) = -\frac{11}{2}$$

Tableau 5

Basis	w_1	w_2	w_3	z_1	z_2	z_3	z_0	q
z_3	$-\dfrac{1}{2}$	$-\dfrac{1}{2}$	-1	0	0	1	2	1
z_1	$-\dfrac{1}{12}$	$-\dfrac{1}{12}$	$\dfrac{1}{2}$	1	0	0	$-\dfrac{1}{2}$	$\dfrac{3}{2}$
z_2	$-\dfrac{1}{12}$	$-\dfrac{1}{12}$	$\dfrac{1}{2}$	0	1	0	$-\dfrac{1}{2}$	$\dfrac{1}{2}$

Efficiency of the Complementary Pivot Method

A computer program to solve a complementary problem is given in Ravindran (28). In an experimental study conducted by Ravindran (29), the complementary pivot method has been tested against the simplex method for solving linear programming problems. The study reveals the superiority of the complementary pivot method over the simplex method in a number of randomly generated problems, both with regard to the number of iterations and computation time. Recent studies by Polito (27) and Lee (30) have shown the superiority of the complementary pivot method for solving convex quadratic programming problems as well.

11.12 SEPARABLE PROGRAMMING

Separable programming was first introduced by C. E. Miller in 1963. Beale (1) refers to separable programming as "probably the most useful nonlinear programming technique."

In separable programming, nonlinear programming problems are solved by approximating the nonlinear functions with piecewise linear functions and then solving the optimization problem through the use of a modified simplex algorithm of linear programming, or in special cases, the ordinary simplex algorithm.

A basic assumption in separable programming is that all functions in the problem be separable. Consider the following function of two variables:

$$f(x_1, x_2) = x_1^3 - 2x_1^2 + x_1 + x_2^4 - x_2 \tag{11.121}$$

This function is separable because it can be "separated" into two functions, each a function of one variable:

$$f(x_1, x_2) = f_1(x_1) + f_2(x_2) \tag{11.122}$$

where

$$f_1(x_1) = x_1^3 - 2x_1^2 + x_1 \tag{11.123}$$

and

$$f_2(x_2) = x_2^4 - x_2 \tag{11.124}$$

Hadley (11) shows how one can approximate a nonlinear separable function. Consider an arbitrary continuous function $f(x)$ of a single variable x which is defined for all x, $0 \le x \le a$. This function might have the form illustrated in Fig. 11.31. Suppose we arbitrarily choose some points (refer to them as grid points) within the range of possible values for x, as shown in Fig. 11.31. Now, if for each x_k we compute $f_k = f(x_k)$ and connect the points (x_k, f_k) and (x_{k+1}, f_{k+1}) we will have formed our approximation function $\bar{f}(x)$, which is a piecewise linear function.

From Fig. 11.31 we can see that depending on the function being approximated and the distance between the grid points, the approximation is very close to the original function in some regions and in other regions it is not close at all. A better approximation can be achieved by adding more grid points to the grid and making the grid points closer together. The grid points do not have to be equally spaced.

In order to make use of our approximating function $\bar{f}(x)$ we must show how to express it analytically. Referring again to Fig. 11.31 when x is in the

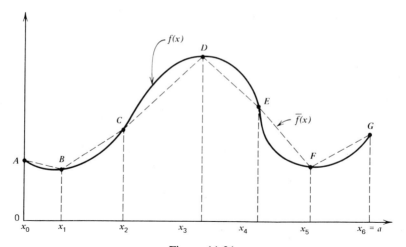

Figure 11.31
Approximination of a nonlinear function.

interval $x_k \leqq x \leqq x_{k+1}$, $f(x)$ is being approximated by $\bar{f}(x)$ where

$$\bar{f}(x) = f_k + \frac{f_{k+1} - f_k}{x_{k+1} - x_k}(x - x_k) \tag{11.125}$$

If x lies in the interval $x_k \leqq x \leqq x_{k+1}$ then it can be written

$$x = \lambda x_{k+1} + (1 - \lambda) x_k \tag{11.126}$$

for some λ, $0 \leqq \lambda \leqq 1$.

Solving Eq. 11.126 for $(x - x_k)$ we obtain

$$(x - x_k) = \lambda(x_{k+1} - x_k) \tag{11.127}$$

and substituting into Eq. 11.125 we have:

$$\bar{f}(x) = \lambda f_{k+1} + (1 - \lambda) f_k \tag{11.128}$$

Now, letting $\lambda = \lambda_{k+1}$ and $1 - \lambda = \lambda_k$ we see that when $x_k \leqq x \leqq x_{k+1}$, there exist a unique λ_k and λ_{k+1} such that:

$$x = \lambda_k x_k + \lambda_{k+1} x_{k+1} \tag{11.129}$$

$$\bar{f}(x) = \lambda_k f_k + \lambda_{k+1} f_{k+1} \tag{11.130}$$

$$\lambda_k + \lambda_{k+1} = 1 \tag{11.131}$$

where λ_k, $\lambda_{k+1} \geqq 0$.

In fact, for any x, $0 \leqq x \leqq a$, we can write the following:

$$x = \sum_{k=0}^{r} \lambda_k x_k \tag{11.132}$$

$$\bar{f}(x) = \sum_{k=0}^{r} \lambda_k f_k \tag{11.133}$$

where

$$\sum_{k=0}^{r} \lambda_k = 1, \qquad \lambda_k \geqq 0; \qquad k = 0, \ldots, r \tag{11.134}$$

and r is any suitable integer representing the number of segments into which the domain of x is divided. In addition, it is required that no more than two of the λ_k be positive, and if two are positive, say λ_k and λ_s, $s > k$, it must also be true that $s = k + 1$, or in other words, the λ's must be adjacent. These restrictions ensure that the approximating function will indeed be the dashed curve in Fig. 11.31.

Referring to Fig. 11.31 again, if λ_0 and λ_1 were positive and $\lambda_2, \ldots, \lambda_6$ were zero, then Eqs. 11.132 and 11.133 would give us a point on the line segment joining points A and B, a portion of our approximation function. However, if for instance λ_0 and λ_2 were allowed to be positive with λ_1, $\lambda_3, \ldots, \lambda_6$ equal to zero, we would then have a point on a line connecting A and C, which is not part of the approximation function, $\bar{f}(x)$; and if only λ_3 were positive, it must then equal 1, all other λ's would equal zero, and we would have point D, both on $f(x)$ and $\bar{f}(x)$.

McMillan (16) states that any continuous, nonlinear, and separable function $f(x_1, x_2, \ldots, x_n)$ can be approximated by a piecewise linear function and solved using a linear programming solution technique provided that the following prescription is applied.

$$f(\mathbf{x}) \approx \bar{f} = \sum_{k=0}^{r} \lambda_{k1} f_{k1} + \sum_{k=0}^{r} \lambda_{k2} f_{k2} + \cdots + \sum_{k=0}^{r} \lambda_{kn} f_{kn} \tag{11.135}$$

where

$$x_n = \sum_{k=0}^{r} \lambda_{kn} x_{kn} \qquad (r \text{ is defined as above}) \tag{11.136}$$

given that:

1. $\displaystyle\sum_{k=0}^{r} \lambda_{kj} = 1; \qquad j = 1, \ldots, n$ $\hspace{2cm}$ (11.137)

2. $\lambda_{kj} \geq 0; \qquad k = 0, \ldots, r, \qquad j = 1, \ldots, n$ $\hspace{1cm}$ (11.138)

3. No more than two of the λ's that are associated with any one variable j are greater than zero, and if two are greater than zero, they must be adjacent.

The following example will illustrate the use of the above approximation method and the use of the simplex algorithm of linear programming (modified to maintain Restriction 3 above) to solve the following nonlinear programming problem:

$$\text{Maximize:} \quad f(\mathbf{x}) = 3x_1 + 2x_2$$
$$\text{Subject to:} \quad (1) \ g(\mathbf{x}) = 4x_1^2 + x_2^2 \leq 16$$
$$(2) \ x_1, x_2 \geq 0$$

Notice that x_1 and x_2 enter the problem linearly in the objective function. In Constraint 1, however, they are nonlinear in nature. Thus we must write both x_1 and x_2 in terms of the λ's. If a variable is linear throughout the entire problem it is not necessary to write it in terms of the λ's; it can be used as a variable itself. Both the objective function and constraint 1 are separable functions.

$$f = f_1(x_1) + f_2(x_2)$$

where

$$f_1(x_1) = 3x_1$$

and

$$f_2(x_2) = 2x_2$$

Also,

$$g = g_1(x_1) + g_2(x_2)$$

where

$$g_1(x_1) = 4x_1^2$$

and

$$g_2(x_2) = x_2^2$$

Now in order to approximate our problem by using piecewise linear functions of the form Eq. 11.135 we must first determine the domains of interest for the variables x_1 and x_2. From Constraints 1 and 2 the possible values for x_1 and x_2 are $0 \leq x_1 \leq 2$ and $0 \leq x_2 \leq 4$, respectively. Dividing the domains of interest for x_1 and x_2 arbitrarily into four segments each, we obtain the grid points shown in Table 11.1. The column labeled x_{k1} shows the grid points for variable x_1, and the column labeled x_{k2} shows the grid points for variable x_2.

The piecewise linear function to be used to approximate f is

$$\bar{f} = \sum_{k=0}^{4} \lambda_{k1} f_{k1} + \sum_{k=0}^{4} \lambda_{k2} f_{k2} \tag{11.139}$$

The approximation function for g is

$$\bar{g} = \sum_{k=0}^{4} \lambda_{k1} g_{k1} + \sum_{k=0}^{4} \lambda_{k2} g_{k2} \tag{11.140}$$

In order to evaluate Eqs. 11.139 and 11.140 we must compute f_{k1}, f_{k2}, g_{k1}, and g_{k2} at each of the grid points for x_1 and x_2. These values are given in Table 11.1.

Table 11.1
**GRID POINTS AND VALUES OF FUNCTIONS
AT GRID POINTS**

K	x_{k1}	$f_{k1} = 3x_{k1}$	$g_{k1} = 4x_{k1}^2$	x_{k2}	$f_{k2} = 2x_{k2}$	$g_{k2} = x_{k2}^2$
0	0.0	0.0	0.0	0.0	0.0	0.0
1	0.5	1.5	1.0	1.0	2.0	1.0
2	1.0	3.0	4.0	2.0	4.0	4.0
3	1.5	4.5	9.0	3.0	6.0	9.0
4	2.0	6.0	16.0	4.0	8.0	16.0

We can now evaluate Eqs. 11.139 and 11.140 and write our approximation problem as

$$\text{Maximize } \bar{f} = 0.0\lambda_{01} + 1.5\lambda_{11} + 3.0\lambda_{21} + 4.5\lambda_{31} + 6.0\lambda_{41}$$
$$+ 0.0\lambda_{02} + 2.0\lambda_{12} + 4.0\lambda_{22} + 6.0\lambda_{32} + 8.0\lambda_{42}$$

Subject to:

(1) $\bar{g} = 0.0\lambda_{01} + 1.0\lambda_{11} + 4.0\lambda_{21} + 9.0\lambda_{31} + 16.0\lambda_{41}$
$$+ 0.0\lambda_{02} + 1.0\lambda_{12} + 4.0\lambda_{22} + 9.0\lambda_{32} + 16.0\lambda_{42} \leq 16$$

To this problem we must add constraints of the form Eq. 11.137.

(2) $\lambda_{01} + \lambda_{11} + \lambda_{21} + \lambda_{31} + \lambda_{41} = 1$

(3) $\lambda_{02} + \lambda_{12} + \lambda_{22} + \lambda_{32} + \lambda_{42} = 1$

Table 11.2
FIRST TABLEAU

c_j	0	1.5	3.0	4.5	6.0	0	2	4	6	8	0	
Basis	λ_{01}	λ_{11}	λ_{21}	λ_{31}	λ_{41}	λ_{02}	λ_{12}	λ_{22}	λ_{32}	λ_{42}	s	b
s	0.00	1.00	4.00	9.00	16.00	0.00	1.00	4.00	9.00	16.00	1.00	16.00
λ_{01}	1.00	1.00	1.00	1.00	1.00	0.00	0.00	0.00	0.00	0.00	0.00	1.00
λ_{02}	0.00	0.00	0.00	0.00	0.00	0.00	1.00	1.00	1.00	1.00	0.00	1.00
$\bar{c}$ Row	0.00	1.50	3.00	4.50	6.00	0.00	2.00	4.00	6.00	8.00	0.00	0.00

$$\bar{f} = 0.0$$

and the nonnegativity conditions of Eq. 11.138:

$$\lambda_{kj} \geq 0; \quad k = 0, \ldots, 4, \quad j = 1, 2$$

Note that this approximating problem to our original nonlinear problem is linear. Thus, we can solve this problem using the simplex algorithm of linear programming if we modify it to ensure that in any basic solution no more than two of the λ's that are associated with either of the x_j variables are greater than zero and if two (rather than one) are greater than zero, then they must be adjacent. These restrictions will be incorporated into a "restricted basis rule" for the simplex algorithm.

Adding slack variables to convert Constraint 1 of the approximating problem to an equality, we have our first simplex tableau in Table 11.2.

The first tableau shows an initial basic feasible solution of: $\lambda_{01} = 1.0$, $\lambda_{02} = 1.0$, $s = 16.0$, giving a value for the objective function of $\bar{f} = 0.0$. The relative profit ($\bar{c}$) row indicates that the problem is not yet optimal and that bringing λ_{42} into the basis will make the largest contribution to the objective function. However, under the restricted basis rule we can not bring λ_{42} into the basis unless it replaces λ_{02} in the basis. This is because we would have two nonadjacent λ's in the basis corresponding to the variable x_2. The minimum ratio rule of selecting the pivot row suggests that we can pivot either in row 1 or row 3. If we pivot in row 1, then λ_{02} will not leave the basis. We can pivot in row 3 to satisfy our restricted basis rule; the result of this pivot is shown in Table 11.3.

Checking the bottom row of the second tableau we see that the problem is not yet optimal. Bringing λ_{41} into the basis would make the largest contribution to the objective function; however, we would have to pivot in row 1 and this would violate the restricted basis rule because we would then have λ_{01} and λ_{41} in the basis. λ_{31} and λ_{21} cannot enter the basis for the same reason. Thus we finally pivot on the circled element. The result is shown in Table 11.4.

Table 11.3
SECOND TABLEAU

Basis	λ_{01}	λ_{11}	λ_{21}	λ_{31}	λ_{41}	λ_{02}	λ_{12}	λ_{22}	λ_{32}	λ_{42}	s	b
s	0.00	1.00	4.00	9.00	16.00	−16.00	−15.00	−12.00	−7.00	0.00	1.00	0.00
λ_{01}	1.00	1.00	1.00	1.00	1.00	0.00	0.00	0.00	0.00	0.00	0.00	1.00
λ_{42}	0.00	0.00	0.00	0.00	0.00	1.00	1.00	1.00	1.00	1.00	0.00	1.00
$\bar{c}$ Row	0.00	1.60	3.00	4.50	6.00	−8.00	−6.00	−4.00	−2.00	0.00	0.00	8.00

$$\bar{f} = 8.0$$

Table 11.4
THIRD TABLEAU

Basis	λ_{01}	λ_{11}	λ_{21}	λ_{31}	λ_{41}	λ_{02}	λ_{12}	λ_{22}	λ_{32}	λ_{42}	s	b
λ_{11}	0.00	1.00	4.00	9.00	16.00	−16.00	−15.00	−12.00	−7.00	0.00	1.00	0.00
λ_{01}	1.00	0.00	−3.00	−8.00	−15.00	16.00	15.00	12.00	7.00	0.00	−1.00	1.00
λ_{42}	0.00	0.00	0.00	0.00	0.00	1.00	1.00	1.00	1.00	1.00	0.00	1.00
$\bar{c}$ Row	0.00	0.00	−3.00	−9.00	−18.00	16.00	16.50	14.00	8.50	0.00	1.50	8.00

$$\bar{f} = 8.0$$

Using the restricted basis rule again we find that we can pivot on the circled element in the third tableau and it will improve the value of the objective function. Doing this, we obtain the tableau in Table 11.5.

Following this same procedure, after three more pivot operations we obtain the final tableau shown in Table 11.6.

Notice, by looking at the bottom row of the final tableau that further basis changes will not increase the value of the objective function. It is possible to reach a stage in the solution of such a problem where no further pivot operations are possible because of the restricted basis rule, but positive

Table 11.5
FOURTH TABLEAU

Basis	λ_{01}	λ_{11}	λ_{21}	λ_{31}	λ_{41}	λ_{02}	λ_{12}	λ_{22}	λ_{32}	λ_{42}	s	b
λ_{11}	1.00	1.00	1.00	1.00	1.00	0.00	0.00	0.00	0.00	0.00	0.00	1.00
λ_{32}	0.14	0.00	−0.43	−1.14	−2.14	2.28	2.14	1.71	1.00	0.00	−0.14	0.14
λ_{42}	−0.14	0.00	0.43	1.14	2.14	−1.28	−1.14	−0.71	0.00	1.00	0.14	0.86
$\bar{c}$ Row	−1.21	0.00	0.64	0.71	0.21	−3.43	−1.73	−0.57	0.00	0.00	−0.29	9.21

$$\bar{f} = 9.21$$

elements (for maximization problems) still appear in the bottom row of the tableau. Hadley (11) proves, however that when such a stage is reached, as long as every λ vector that could enter the basis has a negative element in its bottom row (for maximization problems), then we have obtained a relative maximum of the approximating problem with respect to the original variables (x's).

Now from the final tableau we see that $\lambda_{21} = 0.40$, $\lambda_{31} = 0.60$, and $\lambda_{32} = 1.00$. Note that this solution is consistent with conditions of Eqs. 11.137 and 11.138 and the restricted basis rule. Using Eq. 11.136 to recover the values of

Table 11.6
FINAL TABLEAU

Basis	λ_{01}	λ_{11}	λ_{21}	λ_{31}	λ_{41}	λ_{02}	λ_{12}	λ_{22}	λ_{32}	λ_{42}	s	b
λ_{21}	1.79	1.59	1.00	0.00	−1.39	1.79	1.59	1.00	0.00	−1.39	−0.20	0.40
λ_{32}	0.00	0.00	0.00	0.00	0.00	1.00	1.00	1.00	1.00	1.00	0.00	1.00
λ_{31}	−0.80	−0.60	0.00	1.00	2.40	−1.79	−1.59	−1.00	0.00	1.39	0.20	0.60
$\bar{c}$ Row	−1.79	−0.60	0.00	0.00	−0.60	−3.30	−1.59	−0.50	0.00	−0.10	−0.30	9.90

$$\bar{f} = 9.9$$

x_1 and x_2 we have

$$x_1 = \lambda_{01} x_{01} + \lambda_{11} x_{11} + \lambda_{21} x_{21} + \lambda_{31} x_{31} + \lambda_{41} x_{41}$$
$$= (0.00)(0.00) + (0.00)(0.50) + (0.40)(1.00) + (0.60)(1.50)$$
$$+ (0.00)(2.00) = 1.30$$
$$x_2 = \lambda_{02} x_{02} + \lambda_{12} x_{12} + \lambda_{22} x_{22} + \lambda_{32} x_{32} + \lambda_{42} x_{42}$$
$$= (0.00)(0.00) + (0.00)(1.00) + (0.00)(2.00) + (1.00)(3.00)$$
$$+ (0.00)(4.00) = 3.0$$

Substituting in these values for x_1 and x_2 we get the value of the objective function:

$$f(\mathbf{x}) = 3(1.30) + 2(3.00) = 9.90$$

Notice that this value also appears in the lower right-hand corner of the final tableau in Table 11.6 as the value of the objective function of our approximating problem, $\bar{f}$. This illustrates that the two objective functions are approximately equal.

Figure 11.32 gives a graphical solution to the above problem to illustrate that the solution is approximately correct.

Thus we have seen that separable programming can be used to solve nonlinear programming problems with separable functions.

The following pertinent comments are made by Hadley on separable programming:

1. Adding more grid points to an approximation of a nonlinear function will improve the approximation but at the expense of increasing the number of variables in the

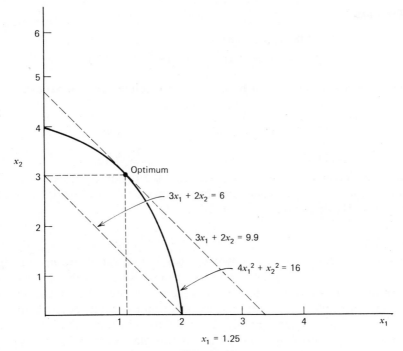

Figure 11.32
Graphical solution of Example.

approximating problem. This may, because of the restricted basic rule, considerably increase the number of iterations required in the simplex algorithm solution to the approximating problem.

2. If the set of feasible solutions to the original problem is convex, then any feasible solution to the approximating problem will also be a feasible solution to the original problem.

3. For more accurate solutions, it may be advantageous to solve a problem initially with a rather coarse grid (grid points widely spread) and then resolve it, using a finer grid only in the neighborhood of the solution to the first approximation. This would allow a closer approximation without increasing the number of grid points.

4. If we are maximizing, the objective function of the original problem is concave, and the constraint set is convex, then the same will be true for the approximating problem. The solution will be an approximation to a point at which the original problem assumes its global maximum. By solving a series of approximating problems, using finer and finer grids, the sequence of optimal values for the objective function of the approximating problem will approach, in the limit, the optimal value of the objective function for the original problem.

V. THE GENERAL NONLINEAR PROGRAMMING PROBLEM

11.13   NONLINEAR OBJECTIVE FUNCTION SUBJECT TO LINEAR OR NONLINEAR CONSTRAINTS: A CUTTING PLANE ALGORITHM

Consider the following general nonlinear programming problem:

Program I

$$\text{Maximize:} \quad f(\mathbf{x})$$

$$\text{Subject to:} \quad h_i(\mathbf{x}) \leq 0 \qquad i = 1, 2, \ldots, m$$

Define the feasible region which contains all possible solution vectors by the set S.

$$S = \{\mathbf{x} \mid h_i(\mathbf{x}) \leq 0\} \qquad i = 1, 2, \ldots, m$$

It will be assumed that $f(\mathbf{x})$ is a concave function, $h_i(\mathbf{x})$ $i = 1, 2, \ldots, m$ are linear or nonlinear convex functions, and that the region S forms a closed and bounded *convex set*. The reader not familiar with this concept is referred to Appendix A for definition and properties.

THEOREM 1

A sufficient condition for the convexity of S is that the constraint functions $h_j(\mathbf{x})$ $j = 1, 2, \ldots, m + 1$ are all convex functions. (Note that the negative of a concave function is a convex function.) Keeping Theorem 1 in mind, the basic underlying principle behind the Kelly algorithm is that even though the constraints are individually nonlinear, if they are all convex then they form a convex set. In addition, *any* convex set of feasible solutions (S for example) can be totally enclosed within a set of *linear* constraints (sometimes referred to as *half spaces*).

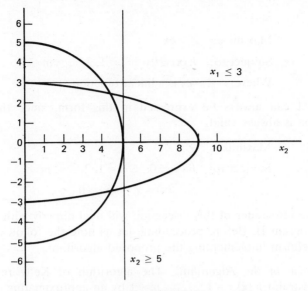

Figure 11.33
A constrained optimization problem.

For example, consider the following constraint set.

$$h_1(\mathbf{x}) = x_1^2 + x_2^2 - 25 \leq 0$$
$$h_2(\mathbf{x}) = x_1^2 + x_2 - 9 \leq 0$$
$$h_3(\mathbf{x}) = -x_1 \leq 0$$
$$h_4(\mathbf{x}) = -x_2 \leq 0$$

It is clear from Fig. 11.33 that the feasible region defined by:

$$K = \{(x_2, x_2) \mid x_1 \leq 3; \ x_2 \leq 5\}$$
$$x_1 \geq 0; \ x_2 \geq 0$$

Contains all possible solution vectors defined by:

$$\mathbf{s} = \{(x_1, x_2) \mid x_1^2 + x_2^2 \leq 25; \ x_1^2 + x_2 \leq 9\}$$
$$x_1 \geq 0; \ x_2 \geq 0$$

Of course, the set K would contain certain solution vectors which would not be defined by the set **s**, but every feasible solution to the original set **s** is also feasible to the (approximating) set K.

Kelly's Cutting Plane Algorithm

A method which can be employed to solve the above problem is a cutting plane algorithm developed by Kelly (14). The method is exceedingly simple in concept, and can be explained and implemented rather easily. The algorithm develops a series of ever-improving linear programming problems, whose solutions converge to the optimal solution of the original nonlinear programming problem. The procedure actually solves the following transtormed problem.

Program II

$$\text{Maximize:} \quad Z = \mathbf{cx}$$

$$\text{Subject to:} \quad h_i(\mathbf{x}) \leqq 0 \qquad i = 1, 2, \ldots, m$$

$$\text{Where:} \quad Z = \mathbf{cx} \text{ is a linear function.}$$

Program I can always be expressed in this form, since the following transformation is always valid.

$$\text{Maximize:} \quad Z$$

$$\text{Subject to:} \quad h_i(\mathbf{x}) \leqq 0 \qquad i = 1, 2, \ldots, m$$

$$h_{m+1}(\mathbf{x}) = Z - f(\mathbf{x}) \leqq 0$$

Hence the remainder of this discussion will deal directly with an approximation to Program II. Before proceeding, let us note the following theorems which are useful in implementing the proposed algorithm.

Basic Logic of the Algorithm. The algorithm of Kelly replaces each nonlinear constraint $h_i(\mathbf{x})$ $i = 1, 2, \ldots, m + 1$ by an approximating (linear) constraint $g_i(\mathbf{x})$ $i = 1, 2, \ldots, m + 1$ such that the solution to the original problem is always contained in the approximating (linear programming) problem.

THEOREM 2

If $\mathbf{x}_0$ is an optimal solution to the approximating linear programming problem, and if the solution vector $\mathbf{x}_0$ also satisfies the (original) nonlinear constraint set, then $\mathbf{x}_0$ is also an optimal solution to the (original) nonlinear programming problem.

Consider the case where $\mathbf{x}_0$ is *not* feasible to the original nonlinear programming problem. If this occurs, then a new linear constraint is introduced which *eliminates* the previous linear programming optimal solution $\mathbf{x}_0$, but simultaneously preserves *all* feasible solutions (not yet attained) of the original nonlinear programming problem. Geometrically, this new constraint acts as a "cutting plane" which "cuts off" the previous linear programming solution. Thus the algorithm which we are describing is sometimes referred to as "Kelly's Cutting Plane" algorithm. We will continue to add "cutting plane" constraints until the optimal solution is reached.

THEOREM 3

In order to converge to a feasible, optimal solution, an optimal solution to the original nonlinear programming problem must be a *boundary point* solution, since all approximating functions are linear.

In summary, the algorithm selects a sequence of approximating solutions which are infeasible to the original problem that converges towards feasibility. The procedure is essentially for nonlinear constraints; any linear constraints in the original constraint set remain unchanged.

Determination of the Cutting Plane. Since the constraints $h_i(\mathbf{x})$ $i = 1, 2, \ldots, m + 1$ are convex and assumed differentiable, by a Taylor's Series expansion:

$$h_i(\mathbf{x}) - h_i(\bar{\mathbf{x}}) \geqq \nabla h_i(\bar{\mathbf{x}})(\mathbf{x} - \bar{\mathbf{x}}) \qquad \text{for any} \quad \bar{\mathbf{x}} \in E^n \qquad (11.141)$$

When the optimal solution $\bar{\mathbf{x}}$ to the approximating problem does not satisfy the original constraint set, determine the constraint $h_K(\mathbf{x}) \leq 0$ which is most violated. That is;

$$\text{Max} \{h_j(\bar{\mathbf{x}})\} = h_k(\bar{\mathbf{x}}) \quad \text{for all } j \text{ for which } h_j(\bar{\mathbf{x}}) > 0$$

From Eq. 11.141, the new cutting plane constraint is given by the following:

$$g_K(\mathbf{x}) = h_K(\bar{\mathbf{x}}) + \nabla h_K(\bar{\mathbf{x}})(\mathbf{x} - \bar{\mathbf{x}}) \leq 0 \tag{11.142}$$

Note that the new constraint must satisfy two conditions.

1. The current solution vector $\bar{\mathbf{x}}$ should violate the new constraint.
2. All feasible solutions to the original nonlinear constraint $h_K(\mathbf{x}) \leq 0$ should satisfy the new constraint.

Proposition 1. For $\mathbf{x} = \bar{\mathbf{x}}$, the left-hand-side of Eq. 11.142 is $h_K(\bar{\mathbf{x}}) > 0$. Hence, Condition 1 is satisfied.

Proposition 2. Consider *any* $\mathbf{x}$ feasible to the original constraint $h_k(\mathbf{x})$. By the convexity assumption on $h_K(\mathbf{x})$,

$$h_K(\bar{\mathbf{x}}) + \nabla h_K(\bar{\mathbf{x}})(\mathbf{x} - \bar{\mathbf{x}}) \leq h_K(\mathbf{x}) \leq 0.$$

Hence any $\mathbf{x}$ feasible to the original constraint set also satisfy the approximating constraint.

Note that with the addition of the new constraint to the previous problem, the previous solution vector $\bar{\mathbf{x}}$ is now *infeasible* to the new problem. A new optimal solution is easily obtained through a *dual simplex* procedure (see Chapter 4).

Steps of the Algorithm.

Step I.   Find an approximating linear constrained region which contains the (optimal) solution to the nonlinear programming problem to solved. We can always choose large values of $x_j = \delta_j \quad j = 1, 2, \ldots, h$ such that s is enclosed in the set $\mathbf{k} = \{\mathbf{x} \mid x_j \leq \delta_j\}$.

Step II.   Solve the linear programming problem:

$$\text{Maximize:} \quad \text{LP1} = \mathbf{cx}$$

$$\text{Subject to:} \quad x_n \leq \delta_n \quad n = 1, 2, \ldots, n$$

Let $\bar{\mathbf{x}}$ be optimal for LP-1.

Step III. Check whether $h_i(\bar{\mathbf{x}}) \leq 0 \quad i = 1, 2, \ldots, m+1$
If yes, terminate.
If no, go to Step IV.

Step IV.   Find $h_K(\bar{\mathbf{x}}) = \max_{j \in m+1} \{h_j(\bar{\mathbf{x}})\} \ h_j(\bar{\mathbf{x}}) > 0$.

Step V.   Define a new constraint

$$g_{\text{new}}(\mathbf{x}) = h_K(\bar{\mathbf{x}}) + \nabla h_K(\mathbf{x} - \bar{\mathbf{x}}) \leq 0$$

Step VI.   Append this constraint to the previous LP problem and find a new optimal solution via a dual-simplex procedure. Call this the new $\bar{\mathbf{x}}$. Go to Step III.

Summary and Conclusions. Kelly's cutting plane method is widely used both as a direct solution technique, and as an auxiliary algorithm useful in implementing other related methods. There are several advantages and disadvantages associated with this technique.

Advantages
1. The technique uses a direct extension of the standard simplex algorithm (Dual Simplex). Therefore, it is very efficient for convex programming problems which are very nearly linear in structure.
2. There is relatively little work per algorithmic step. A simple dual simplex routine and a Taylor's Series approximation is all that is normally required.
3. The algorithm is easy to implement and program, and it is computationally sound.

Disadvantages
1. The algorithm requires convexity to guarantee convergence, hence it is not applicable to non-convex programming problems.
2. None of the intermediate solutions are feasible to the original problem.
3. The algorithm often exhibits slow convergence as the optimum is approached.
4. The size of the problem grows as more constraints are added, thus creating potential difficulties in computer core storage. Although this disadvantage might prove serious for larger problems there has been some work done on schemes to drop from the solution procedure old, previously generated constraints.

EXAMPLE 11.13-1

$$\text{Maximize:} \quad f(\mathbf{x}) = x_1 + x_2$$
$$\text{Subject to:} \quad h_1(\mathbf{x}) = x_1^2 + x_2^2 \leq 25$$
$$h_2(\mathbf{x}) = x_1^2 + x_2 \leq 9$$
$$x_1 \geq 0$$
$$x_2 \leq 0$$

Step I.   Suppose that the values of x_1 and x_2 are set to zero.

$$\text{Set } x_1 = 0 \quad \max\{x_2\} = \max\{5, 9\} = 9$$
$$\text{Set } x_2 = 0 \quad \max\{x_1\} = \max\{5, 3\} = 5$$

Hence the feasible solution space is bounded by the half-space defined by

$$K = \{(x_1, x_2) | x_1 \leq 5; \quad x_2 \leq 9; \quad x_1, x_2 \geq 0\}$$

Step II.   Maximize: $z = x_1 + x_2$
$$\text{Subject to:} \quad g_1(\mathbf{x}) = x_1 \leq 5$$
$$g_2(\mathbf{x}) = x_2 \leq 9$$
$$x_1, x_2 \geq 0$$
$$x_1^{(0)} = 5.0, \quad x_2^{(0)} = 9.0, \quad Z^{(0)} = 14.0$$

Step III.   Constraints are not satisfied

Step IV.   Max $\{h_1(\mathbf{x}), h_2(\mathbf{x})\} = $ Max $\{81, 25\} = h_1(\mathbf{x})$

Step V.   Generate a cutting plane constraint

$$g_3(\mathbf{x}) = h_1(\mathbf{x}^{(0)}) + \nabla h_i(\mathbf{x}^{(0)})(\mathbf{x} - \mathbf{x}^{(0)}) \leq 0$$

Since $\nabla h_i(\mathbf{x}^{(0)}) = (2x_1, 2x_2)$

$$g_3(\mathbf{x}) = 81 + (10, 18)\begin{pmatrix} x_1 \\ x_2 \end{pmatrix} - (10, 18)\begin{pmatrix} 5 \\ 9 \end{pmatrix}$$

$$\Rightarrow g_3(\mathbf{x}) = x_1 + 1.8x_2 \leq 13.1$$

Step VI.   The problem now becomes:

Maximize: $z = x_1 + x_2$

Subject to: $g_1(\mathbf{x}) = x_1 \leq 5$

$g_2(\mathbf{x}) = x_2 \leq 9$

$g_3(\mathbf{x}) = x_1 + 1.8x_2 \leq 13.1$

$x_1, x_2 \geq 0$

The reader will be asked to verify in Exercise 11.20 that the optimal solution to this problem is given by:

$x_1^* = 5.0$

$x_2^* = 4.5$

$Z^* = 9.5$

$\mathbf{x}^{(1)} = (5.0, 4.5)$

Return to Step III

Step III. $h_1(\mathbf{x}^{(1)}) = 20.2$

$h_2(\mathbf{x}^{(2)}) = 20.5$

Thus $h_2(\mathbf{x})$ is violated.

Step IV.   Max $\{h_1(\mathbf{x}), h_2(\mathbf{x})\} = \max \{0, 11.5\} = h_2(\mathbf{x})$

Step V.   Generate a new "cut"

$$g_4(\mathbf{x}) = h_2(\mathbf{x}^{(1)}) + \nabla h_2(\mathbf{x}^{(1)})(\mathbf{x} - \mathbf{x}^{(1)})$$

Since

$$\nabla h_2(\mathbf{x}) = (2x_1, 1)$$

$$g_4(\mathbf{x}) = 20.5 + (10, 1)\begin{pmatrix} x_1 \\ x_2 \end{pmatrix} - (10, 1)\begin{pmatrix} 5 \\ 4.5 \end{pmatrix} \leq 0$$

$$\Rightarrow g_4(\mathbf{x}) = 10x_1 + x_2 \leq 34$$

Step VI.   The problem now becomes:

Maximize: $z = x_1 + x_2$

Subject to: $g_1(\mathbf{x}) = x_1 \leq 5$

$g_2(\mathbf{x}) = x_2 \leq 9$

$g_3(\mathbf{x}) = x_1 + 1.8x_2 \leq 13.1$

$g_4(\mathbf{x}) = 10x_1 + x_2 \leq 34$

$x_1, x_2 \geq 0$

At this point, it should once again be emphasized that one would not completely resolve the above problem. Instead, $g_4(\mathbf{x})$ would be appended to the previous (optimal) linear programming tableau, and the new problem solved via a dual-simplex procedure.

The solution is given by:

$$x_1^* = 2.83$$
$$x_2^* = 5.70$$
$$z^* = 8.53$$
$$\mathbf{x}^{(2)} = (2.83, 5.7)$$

Step III

$$h_1(\mathbf{x}^{(2)}) = 40.499$$
$$h_2(\mathbf{x}^{(2)}) = 13.71$$

Since both constraints are violated, the algorithm would add a new cutting-plane constraint and proceed as in previous iterations. Since the procedure should be clear at this point, further iterations will not be shown. Progression of the algorithm to the present solution vector is shown in Figure 11.34, and is evident that the optimal solution of $x_1^* = 2.114$ and $x_2^* = 4.531$ is being approached.

11.14   OPTIMIZATION BY GEOMETRIC PROGRAMMING†

The increased use of mathematical models in the analysis and optimization of industrial systems is one of the significant developments of modern engineering practice. Unfortunately, most real-life systems are such that models which describe them accurately usually prove too complex for solution by the algorithms available. This is especially true of problems in which the constraints are nonlinear or the objective function is of more than second degree.

In 1961, however, Zener (24) observed that a sum of component costs sometimes may be minimized almost by inspection when each cost depends on products of the design variables, each raised to arbitrary but known powers. Duffin (6) and Peterson (7) extended Zener's work, and Passy and Wilde (17) further generalized the method to include negative coefficients and reversed inequalities. Zener and Duffin called their method *geometric programming*, since it was based on a generalization of the arithmetic-geometric mean inequality. The basic theory and formal proofs for this new optimization technique can be found in (3) and (21).

Geometric Programming

Consider first a hypothetical, unconstrained problem wherein we want to minimize the total inventory and production cost associated with the manufacture of a certain product. Let this cost be denoted by y:

$$y = c_1 q^{-3} s^{-2} + c_2 q^3 s + c_3 q^{-3} s^3 \qquad (11.143)$$

where

q = tons of product manufactured during a given period

s = fraction of production to be stored in inventory

c_1, c_2, and c_c are cost coefficients which vary with the time period and the production facilities.

† The authors would like to express their appreciation to Dr. C. S. Beightler, Dr. R. M. Crisp, Jr., and Dr. W. L. Meier for contributing the material which comprises this section.

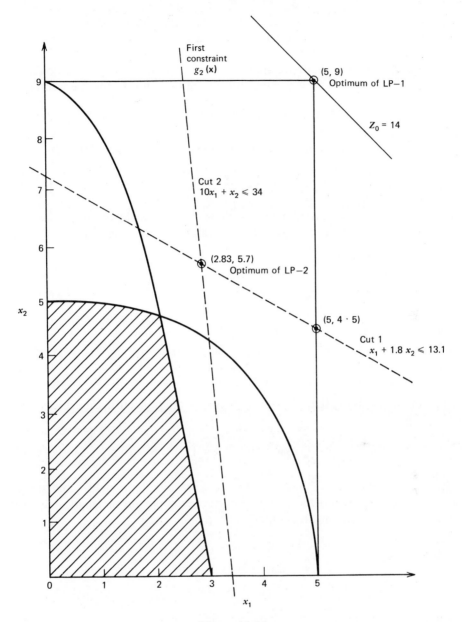

Figure 11.34
Cutting plane example.

The first term represents the setup and down-time costs; the second, the idle-time and fixed-production costs; the third, the inventory and handling costs.

Equation 11.143 is not a polynomial since the exponents are not restricted to the positive integers. However, the c_j must be positive, and this requirement led Zener and Duffin to call such functions *posynomials*. The classical method for minimizing such a function involves setting to zero the first partial derivatives of y with respect to both q and s. This produces nonlinear simultaneous equations which, in general, are quite difficult to solve. In addition, the vanishing of these first derivatives is only a necessary condition for a minimum; sufficient conditions are more complicated, involving functions of higher order partial derivatives.

Consider now a different approach to the solution of this problem. A posynomial containing N variables and a total of T terms may be written as

$$y = \sum_{t=1}^{T} c_t \prod_{n=1}^{N} x_n^{a_{tn}} \tag{11.144}$$

As in the classical method, one sets the first partial derivatives to zero:

$$\left(\frac{\partial y}{\partial x_k}\right)^* = \frac{1}{x_k^*} \sum_{t=1}^{T} a_{tk} c_t \prod_{n=1}^{N} (x_n^*)^{a_{tn}} = 0; \qquad k = 1, \ldots, N \tag{11.145}$$

Instead of solving these nonlinear equations directly for the optimal values, x_k^*, Zener and Duffin made a substitution of variables based on a duality theory. Define the optimal weights:

$$w_t \equiv \frac{c_t \prod_{n=1}^{N} (x_n^*)^{a_{tn}}}{y^*}; t = 1, \ldots, T \tag{11.146}$$

These weights must sum to unity:

$$\prod_{t=1}^{T} w_t = 1 \tag{11.147}$$

In addition (assuming that y^* and all of the x_k^* are nonzero), Eqs. 11.145 and 11.146 give

$$\sum_{t=1}^{T} a_{tk} w_t = 0; \qquad k = 1, \ldots, N \tag{11.148}$$

Notice that Eqs. 11.147 and 11.148 are *linear* in the weights, and do *not* depend on the cost coefficients c_t. For the example problem given by Eq. 11.143, these equations are simply

$$w_1 + w_2 + w_3 = 1$$
$$-3w_1 + 3w_2 - 3w_3 = 0$$
$$-2w_1 + w_2 + 3w_3 = 0$$

from which it follows at once that

$$w_1 = 0.4, \qquad w_2 = 0.5, \qquad w_3 = 0.1.$$

Thus without knowing the optimal production rate or optimal inventory, it is nevertheless possible to state definitely that these optimal values must always be such as to make the down-time and setup costs four times as large as the inventory and handling costs, and also such as to make the idle time and fixed production costs five times as large as the inventory and handling costs. Furthermore, this optimal distribution is totally unaffected by changes in the cost coefficients c_1, c_2, and c_3. This separation of technological effects, as reflected by the exponents a_{tn}, from the economic effects, as measured by the coefficients c_t, is unique to the geometric programming algorithm.

Since the weights sum to unity,

$$y^* = \prod_{t=1}^{T} (y^*)^{w_t}$$

$$= \prod_{t=1}^{T} \left(c_t \prod_{n=1}^{N} (x_n^*)^{a_{tn}} \right)^{w_t}$$

$$= \prod_{t=1}^{T} \left(\frac{c_t}{w_t} \right)^{w_t} \prod_{t=1}^{T} \prod_{n=1}^{N} (x_n^*)^{a_{tn} w_t} \qquad (11.149)$$

But, by Eq. 11.148,

$$\prod_{t=1}^{T} \prod_{n=1}^{N} (x_n^*)^{a_{tn} w_t} = \prod_{n=1}^{N} \prod_{t=1}^{T} (x_n^*)^{a_{tn} w_t}$$

$$= \prod_{n=1}^{N} (x_n^*)^{\sum_{t=1}^{T} a_{tn} w_t}$$

$$= 1$$

Therefore Eq. 11.149 becomes

$$y^* = \prod_{t=1}^{T} \left(\frac{c_t}{w_t} \right)^{w_t} \qquad (11.150)$$

and hence the minimal cost can be found, still without knowledge of the optimal values of the decision variables. In the illustrative example of Eq. 11.143, suppose that, for a particular time period and a given production facility, the unit costs are $c_1 = 60$, $c_2 = 50$, and $c_3 = 20$. Then from Eq. 11.150, the minimal cost is

$$y^* = \left(\frac{60}{0.4} \right)^{1.4} \left(\frac{50}{0.5} \right)^{0.5} \left(\frac{20}{0.1} \right)^{0.1}$$

$$= 125.8$$

If this is an acceptable cost, Eq. 11.146 can be used to find the optimal values of the decision variables:

$$60 q^{-3} s^{-2} = 0.4(125.8) = 50.32$$

$$20 q^{-3} s^{3} = 0.1(125.8) = 12.58$$

so that

$$q^3 = 1.19 s^{-2}$$

and

$$s^5 = 0.75, \quad \text{or} \quad s^* = 0.944$$

from which it follows that

$$q^3 = 1.34; \quad q^* = 1.12 \text{ tons}$$

Notice that the only *nonlinear* equations encountered in this analysis are those of Equation 11.147, each of which contain only one term, and therefore *linear* in the logarithm of x_n.

The preceding example was special in that it had exactly one more term than variable; that is, $T = N + 1$. Thus there were exactly as many linear equations (Eqs. 11.147 and 11.148) as there were variables, w_t, so that a unique set of weights satisfied these equations. When T is greater than $N + 1$, further steps must be taken to find the optimum weights.

Before leaving this special situation, however, it will be interesting to examine a problem familiar to all readers: finding the economic lot size for a purchased product. A simple form of this problem may be stated as follows: For a given product, a wholesaler must decide what size lots he will put into stock periodically. The total variable cost associated with the purchase and storage of this product is

$$y = \tfrac{1}{2}Qh + ad/Q + \frac{(c+kQ)d}{Q} \tag{11.151}$$

where

Q = lot size (pieces per order).

h = carrying cost per piece per year

d = annual requirements (pieces per year)

a = cost of processing an order

c, k = given constants.

The first term in this objective function represents the total carrying costs, the second term gives the total ordering costs, and the third term is the total purchasing costs. This last term includes quantity discounts, where $P + kQ$ is the price which the vendor charges for an order of Q pieces. Since Q is the only unknown, the constant term may be dropped, and Eq. 11.151 takes the form

$$y = c_1 Q + c_2 Q^{-1} \tag{11.152}$$

The optimal lot size, Q^*, can now be found directly by *inspection*, since Eqs. 11.147 and 11.148 are simply

$$w_1 + w_2 = 1$$

$$w_1 - w_2 = 0$$

Therefore, Q^* must be such as to make the two terms in Eq. 11.152 equal:

$$c_1 Q^* = c_2 Q^{*-1}$$

or

$$Q^* = \sqrt{\frac{c_2}{c_1}}$$

for *any* values of c_1 and c_2. From Eq. 11.151, $c_1 = (1/2)I$ and $c_2 = R(s+P)$, so that

$$Q^* = \sqrt{\frac{2d(a+c)}{h}}$$

Degrees of Difficulty
The difference between the number of variables and the number of independent linear equations is usually called the number of *degrees of freedom*. For Eqs. 11.148 and 11.149, this number is $T - (N+1)$. Zener and Duffin suggest calling this quantity the number of *degrees of difficulty*, since they make the problem harder to solve.

Consider the objective function

$$y = 1000x_1 + 4 \times 10^9 x_1^{-1} x_2^{-1} + 2.5 \times 10^5 x_2 + 9000 x_1 x_2 \tag{11.153}$$

This cost function is to be minimized by choosing positive values for x_1 and x_2. Using geometric programming, weights are introduced, and Eqs. 11.147 and 11.148 become:

$$w_1 + w_2 + w_3 + w_4 = 1$$
$$w_1 - w_2 \qquad + w_4 = 0$$
$$- w_2 + w_3 + w_4 = 0$$

Here, $N = 2$, $T = 4$, so that one degree of difficulty is present and the equations do not have a unique solution. There are, in fact, an infinity of solutions as can be seen by solving for the first three weights in terms of the fourth:

$$w_1 = \frac{1}{3}(1 - 2w_4) \qquad (11.154)$$

$$w_2 = \frac{1}{3}(1 + w_4) \qquad (11.155)$$

$$w_3 = \frac{1}{3}(1 - 2w_4) \qquad (11.156)$$

Any choice of w_4 will produce values for the other weights that will satisfy Eqs. 11.147 and 11.148. The problem is to select the optimal weights from among these infinite possibilities.

Although Eq. 11.150 holds for any number of degrees of difficulty, the minimum cost y^* cannot be computed until the optimal weights are known. If Eqs. 11.154, 11.155, and 11.156 are substituted into Eq. 11.150, the minimum cost will be given as a function, $d(w_4)$, of w_4 alone. Duffin has proved that $d(w_4)$, the *substituted dual function*, is *maximized* by the optimal weight, w_4^*, and that this maximum value is equal to the minimum cost y^*. Therefore,

$$d(w_4^*) = \max_{w_4 > 0} d(w_4) = y^* \qquad (11.157)$$

In general, he showed that a sufficient condition for y to be minimized is that the dual function defined by

$$d(w_1, \ldots, w_T) \equiv \prod_{t=1}^{T} \left(\frac{c_t}{w_t} \right)^{w_t} \qquad (11.158)$$

be maximum with respect to the w_t, subject to the conditions given by Eqs. 11.147 and 11.148.

The numerical value of w_4^* can be found most easily by setting to zero the first derivative of the logarithm of $d(w_4)$. When this is done (see 11.150), the optimal weight is found to be

$$w_4^* = 0.453$$

The other weights are found from Eqs. 11.154, 11.155, and 11.156:

$$w_1^* = w_3^* = 0.031; \qquad w_2^* = 0.484$$

and

$$y^* = \$12.6 \times 10^6$$

Although the weights are not independent of the cost coefficients c_t when there are degrees of difficulty, *bounds* on the weights can be found which do not depend on the cost coefficients. In this illustrative problem, for example, w_4 is bounded above by 1/2, since, at that value, w_1 and w_3 would vanish. Hence for *any* cost coefficients,

$$0 \le w_t = w_2 \le \frac{1}{3}$$

$$\frac{1}{3} \le w_2 \le \frac{1}{2}$$

$$0 \le w_4 \le \frac{1}{2}.$$

More degrees of difficulty, of course, complicate the problem still further. However, the following relationship,

$$y(x_1, \ldots, x_N) \ge y^* = d^* \ge d(w_1, \ldots, w_T), \qquad (11.159)$$

can be used for obtaining quick estimates of the optimal value of the objective function. This is accomplished by neglecting $T - (N+1)$ of the terms in y_1 thereby producing a problem with no degrees of difficulty. This zero degree problem is very easy to solve for the weights, which are then substituted into the original dual function to obtain a lower bound on the true optimum cost. The corresponding x_n can then be used to construct an upper bound by substituting them into the objective function.

In the objective function given by Eq. 11.153, for example, if the third term is discarded ($w_3 = 0$), the resulting zero-degree problem satisfies Eqs. 11.147 and 11.148 when $w_1 = w_3 = 0$ and $w_2 = w_4 = 1/2$. The dual function gives a lower bound as

$$d\left(0, \frac{1}{2}, 0, \frac{1}{2}\right) = \left(\frac{4 \times 10^9}{\frac{1}{2}}\right)^{\frac{1}{2}} \left(\frac{9000}{\frac{1}{2}}\right)^{\frac{1}{2}}$$

$$= 12.0 \times 10^6$$

Corresponding to these dual variables (weights) are the primal variables $x_1 = 411$ and $x_2 = 1.63$. Substitution of these values into the original objective function yields $y = 12.8 \times 10^6$. Hence, the use of Eq. 11.159 has produced tight bounds on the optimal value of the objective function:

$$12.0 \times 10^6 \le y^* \le 12.8 \times 10^6$$

Generalized Geometric Programming

Geometric programming has recently been generalized beyond the preceding description to allow the use of negative coefficients in both objective function and constraints, and also to permit reversed inequality constraints. The following is a summary of the most general formulation of the geometric programming problem. A complete discussion and derivation of these results may be found in (21).

Define the *generalized posynomial* $y_m(x)$ as

$$y_m \equiv \sum_{t=0}^{T_m} \sigma_{mt} C_{mt} \prod_{n=1}^{N} x_n^{a_{mtn}} \qquad m = 0, 1, \ldots, M \qquad (11.160)$$

where

$$\sigma_{mt} = \pm 1$$

is a signum function, and the coefficients c_{mt} are all positive.

The primal problem is to minimize

$$y \equiv y_o \tag{11.161}$$

subject to the constraints

$$y_m \leqq \sigma_m (\equiv \pm 1); \qquad m = 1, \dots, M \tag{11.162}$$

and

$$x_n > 0; \qquad n = 1, \dots, N \tag{11.163}$$

For the associated dual problem, consider a set of T variables ω satisfying a normality condition

$$\sum_{t=1}^{T_q} \sigma_{ot}\omega_{ot} = \sigma (\equiv \pm 1) \tag{11.164}$$

and N orthogonality conditions

$$\sum_{m=0}^{M} \sum_{t=1}^{T_m} \sigma_{mt}a_{mtn}\omega_{mt} = 0 \tag{11.165}$$

as well as T nonnegativity conditions

$$w_{mt} \geqq 0; \qquad m = 0, 1, \dots, M; \qquad t = 1, \dots, T_m \tag{11.166}$$

and M linear inequality constraints

$$\omega_{mo} \equiv \sigma_m \sum_{t=1}^{T_m} \sigma_{mt}\omega_{mt} \geqq 0; \qquad m = 1, \dots, M \tag{11.169}$$

where

$$T \equiv \sum_{m=0}^{M} T_m$$

From these variables, plus the c_{mt}, σ_{mt} and σ, the dual function can be formed as follows

$$d(\boldsymbol{\omega}) \equiv \sigma \left[\prod_{m=0}^{M} \prod_{t=1}^{T_m} \left(\frac{c_{mt}\omega_{mo}}{\omega_{mt}} \right)^{\sigma_{mt}\omega_{mt}} \right]^{\sigma} \tag{11.168}$$

In this function, ω_{00} is defined to be equal to $+1$ and, in addition,

$$\lim_{\omega_{mt} \to 0} \left(\frac{c_{mt}\omega_{mo}}{\omega_{mt}} \right)^{\sigma_{mt}\omega_{mt}} = 0 \tag{11.169}$$

Then for every point x^o where y is locally minimum there exists a set of dual variables $\boldsymbol{\omega}^o$ satisfying Equations 11.164 through 11.167 and such that

$$d(\omega^o) = y(x^o) \tag{11.170}$$

The dual function is stationary at $\boldsymbol{\omega}^o$ with respect to all nonnegative ω_{mt}; in particular at the global minimum x^*, if it exists, the corresponding dual variables $\boldsymbol{\omega}^*$ are such that

$$d(\omega^*) = y(x^*) \tag{11.171}$$

Once the dual variables $\boldsymbol{\omega}$ and $\boldsymbol{\delta}$ are known, the corresponding values of the primal variables x are found from the following relations:

$$c_{ot} \prod_{n=1}^{N} x_n^{a_{otn}} = \omega_{ot}\sigma y^o; \qquad t = 1, \dots, T_o \tag{11.172}$$

and

$$c_{mt} \prod_{n=1}^{N} x_n^{a_{mn}^{tn}} = \frac{\omega_{mt}}{\omega_{mo}}; \qquad t = 1, \ldots, T_m$$

$$m = 1, \ldots, M \tag{11.173}$$

From Eq. 11.172, it can be seen that σ will have the same sign as y^o. Since there will always be more terms than variables x, N equations can be found which are solvable for the N primals. In addition, the solution of these equations is not difficult since they are linear in $\log x_n$.

The following example will serve to illustrate the use of the above equations. Assume that it is desired to maximize the functional

$$y' = 5x_1^2 - x_2^2 x_3^4$$

subject to the usual nonnegativity conditions and the inequality

$$-5x_1^2 x_2^{-2} + 3x_2^{-1}x_3 \geq 2$$

To get this into the proper form given by Eqs. 11.161 and 11.162, the negative of y' must be minimized, and all terms in the constraint multiplied by $-(1/2)$ in order to reverse its sense. The equivalent problem is to minimize $y(\equiv -y')$

$$y = -5x_1^2 + x_2^2 x_3^4$$

subject to

$$\frac{5}{2}x_1^2 x_2^{-2} - \frac{3}{2}x_2^{-1}x_3 \leq -1$$

The dual variables must satisfy Eqs. 11.164 and 11.165:

$$-\ \omega_{01} + \ \omega_{02} \qquad\qquad = \sigma$$

$$-2\omega_{01} \qquad + 2\omega_{11} \qquad = 0$$

$$2\omega_{02} - 2\omega_{11} + \omega_{12} = 0$$

$$4\omega_{02} \qquad\quad - \omega_{12} = 0$$

The solution is $\sigma = -1$, $\omega_{01} = 3/2$, $\omega_{02} = 1/2$, $\omega_{11} = 3/2$, and $\omega_{12} = 2$. By definition, $\omega_{oo} \equiv 1$ and, from Eq. 11.167, $\omega_{10} = \sigma_1(\omega_{11} - \omega_{12}) = 1/2$.

The value of y at the stationary point x^o is given by $d(\omega^o)$:

$$y^o = -\left[\left(\frac{5 \cdot 1}{\frac{3}{2}}\right)^{-3/2}\left(\frac{1 \cdot 1}{\frac{1}{2}}\right)^{1/2} \cdot \left(\frac{\frac{5}{2} \cdot \frac{1}{2}}{\frac{3}{2}}\right)^{3/2}\left(\frac{\frac{3}{2} \cdot \frac{1}{2}}{2}\right)^{-2}\right]^{-1}$$

$$= -0.796$$

The optimal policy is found from Eqs. 11.172 and 11.173; the (absolute) value of the first term of the objective function is

$$5x_1^2 = \omega_{01}\sigma y^o = \frac{3}{2}(-1)(-0.796) = 1.19$$

so that

$$x_1^* = 0.489$$

The first term of the constraint is

$$\frac{5}{2}(0.488)^2 x_2^{-2} = \frac{\omega_{11}}{\omega_{10}} = \frac{\frac{3}{2}}{\frac{1}{2}} = 3$$

and thus

$$x_2^o = 0.445.$$

The second term of the constraint gives

$$\frac{3}{2}(0.455)^{-1}x_3 = \frac{\omega_{12}}{\omega_{10}} = \frac{2}{1} = 4$$

whence

$$x_2^* = 1.19.$$

Since there are zero degrees of difficulty, this is the only stationary point and, in fact, it is also the true minimum value of y under the inequality constraint. Hence the true maximum of the original problem is $y'^* = 0.796$.

This example points up the power of geometric programming in the analysis of systems described by complex mathematical models. No other algorithm could solve such a highly nonlinear problem as this so easily. Also, since the dual variables depend only on the exponents and signs, and not on the magnitudes of the coefficients, a study of these invariants gives valuable insight into the economics of the process.

Discussion and Comments

The geometric programming algorithm in its present form can handle a large class of problems often found in practice without the necessity of using questionable linear or quadratic approximations. Thus highly nonlinear systems can be analyzed using this technique and accurate answers obtained. In addition, important invariance properties of the system are often discovered, giving optimal component proportions that are completely independent of fluctuating prices and unit charges. Geometric programming has great potential in engineering design and systems analysis; it is a technique which can be applied to a wide variety of practical situations.

REFERENCES

1. Beale, E. M. L., P. J. Coen, and A. D. J. Flowerdew, "Separable Programming Applied to an Ore Purchasing Problem", *Journal of Applied Statistics*, July, 1965.

2. Beale, E. M. L., "Numerical Methods", in *Nonlinear Programming*, J. Abadie, Ed., North-Holland, Amsterdam, 1967, pp. 182–205.

3. Beveridge, G. S. and R. S. Schecter, *Optimization: Theory and Practice*, McGraw-Hill, New York, 1970.

4. Converse, A. D., *Optimization*, Holt, Rinehart and Winston, New York, 1970.

5. Cooper, Leon and D. Steinberg, *Introduction to Methods of Optimization*, W. B. Saunders Company, Philadelphia, 1970.

6. Duffin, R. J., "Dual Programs and Minimum Cost," *Journal of the Society of Industry and Applied Mathematics*, 10 (March 1962).

7. Duffin, R. J., and E. L. Peterson, "Constrained Minima Treated by Geometric Means," Westinghouse Scientific Paper 64-158-129-P3, March, 1974.

8. Duffin, R. J., E. L. Peterson, and C. Zener, *Geometric Programming*, Wiley, New York, 1966.

9. Everett, H., "Generalized Lagrangian Multipliers for Solving Problems of Optimal Allocation of Resources, *Operations Research*, 11, 399 (1969).

10. Gottfried, B. S. and Joel Weisman, *Introduction to Optimization Theory*, Prentice-Hall, Englewood Cliffs, N.J., 1973.

11. Hadley, G., *Nonlinear and Dynamic Programming*, Addison-Wesley, Reading Massachusetts, 1974.

12. Himmelblau, D. L., *Applied Nonlinear Programming*, McGraw-Hill, New York, 1972.

13. Hooke, R. and T. A. Jeeves, "Direct Search Solution of Numerical and Statistical Problems," *J. Assoc. of Comp. Machines*, 8, 212–229 (1061).

14. Kelley, J. E., "The Cutting Plane Method for Solving Convex Programs," *J. Soc. Ind. Appl. Math*, 8, 703–712 (1960).

15. Kunzi, H. P. and J. Krelle, *Nonlinear Programming*, Blaisdell Publishing Company, New York, 1966.

16. McMillan, Claude, Jr., *Mathematical Programming*, Wiley, New York, 1970.

17. Passy, U., and Wilde, D. J., "Generalized Polynomial Optimization," *SIAM Journal on Applied Mathematics*, 15 (5) (September 1967).

18. Rosen, J. B., "The Gradient Projection Method for Nonlinear Programming, Part I, Linear Constraints," *J. Soc. Ind. Appl. Math.*, 8, 181–217 (1960).

19. Saaty, T. L. and J. Bram, *Nonlinear Mathematics*, McGraw-Hill, New York, 1964.

20. Sokolnikoff, I. S. and R. M. Redheffer, *Mathematics of Physics and Modern Engineering*, 2nd Edn, McGraw-Hill, New York, 1966.

21. Wilde, D. J., and C. S. Beightler, *Foundations of Optimization*, Prentice-Hall, Englewood Cliffs, N.J., 1967.

22. Wilde, D. J., *Optimum Seeking Methods*, Prentice-Hall, Englewood Cliffs, N.J., 1964.

23. Wolfe, P., "The Simplex Method for Quadratic Programming," *Econometrica*, 27, 382–398 (1959).

24. Zener, C., "A Mathematical Aid in Optimizing Engineering Designs," *Proceedings of the National Academy Science*, 47, (April 1961).

25. Cottle, R. W. and G. B. Dantzig, "Complementary Pivot Theory and Mathematical Programming," *Journal of Linear Algebra and Applications*, 1, 105–125 (1968).

26. Lemke, C. E., "Bimatrix Equilibrium Points and Mathematical Programming," *Management Science*, 11, 681–689 (1965).

27. Polito, J., "A Comparison of Four Versions of a Modified Cottle-Dantzig Algorithm with the Lemke Method on Convex Quadratic Programs," Unpublished M. S. Thesis, School of Industrial Engineering, Purdue University, Lafayette, Indiana, December, 1974.

28. Ravindran, A., "A Computer Routine for Solving Quadratic and Linear Programming Problems," *Communications of the Association for Computing Machines*, 15, 818–820 (1972).

29. Ravindran, A., "A Comparison of Primal Simplex and Complementary Pivot Methods for Linear Programming," *Naval Research Logistics Quarterly*, 20, 95–100 (1973).

30. Lee, Harvey, "An Experimental Study on Solving Convex Quadratic Programming Problems," Unpublished M. S. Project, School of Industrial Engineering, Purdue University, W. Lafayette, Ind., August, 1975.

EXERCISES

1. Define the following terms:
   a. Linear function
   b. Nonlinear function

  c. Convex set/nonconvex Set
  d. Gradient vector
  e. Hessian matrix
  f. Necessary conditions
  g. Sufficiency conditions

2. A problem is described by a forth-order equation, $f(x)$. Write out the Taylor's series expansion which will predict $f(x)$ at a point B given $f(x)$ at any point A.

3. Show that if a cubic approximation to $f(x) = 2x^3 - 3x^2 + x - 4$ is used from Eq. 11.7, the exact value of $f(x)$ at $x = 7$ can be predicted.

4. Show that the point $\mathbf{x} = (0, 0)$ is a global minimum solution to:

$$f(\mathbf{x}) = x_2^2 + 3x_1^6 + 5x_2^4.$$

5. Minimize the following objective functions using a Golden Section Search. Use a resolution of $\epsilon = 0.10$.
   a. Minimize: $f(x) = 3x^4 + (x - 1)^2$

$$4 \geq x \geq 0$$

   b. Minimize: $f(x) = 4x \sin(x) \pi \geq x \geq 0$

   c. Minimize: $f(x) = 2(x - 3)^2 + e^{0.5x^2}$

$$100 \geq x \geq 0$$

6. An experimenter has obtained the following equation used to describe the trajectory of a space capsule:

$$f(x) = 4x^3 + 2x - 3x^2 + e^{x/2}$$

   Use the Golden Section Search technique to find a root of the above equation. *Hint: A new problem needs to be formulated to facilitate solution.*

7. Solve the following optimization problems using a Hooke-Jeeves Search. Start your search with unit moves along the co-ordinate axis and continue until the percent change in the objective function is 2 percent or less. Plot the trajectory of search.
   a. Minimize: $f(\mathbf{x}) = 50 + (2.71 - x_1)^2 + (1 - x_2)^2$
      start from the point $x = (0.5, 0)$

   b. Maximize: $f(\mathbf{x}) = \dfrac{1}{2x_1 + 6(x_2 + 1)^2}$

      start from the point $\mathbf{x} = (0, 0)$

8. Solve the following problem using gradient projection:

   Minimize: $f(\mathbf{x}) = 25(x_1 - 3x_2)^2 + (x_1 - 3)^2$
      start the search from the point $\mathbf{x} = (1, 2)$

9. Search for the optimum solution to Rosenbrock's function using gradient projection. Proceed through only five steps, and graph the progress of the search toward the optimum solution of $\mathbf{x} = (1, 1)$. Start at the point $\mathbf{x} = (-1, 1)$.

10. Solve the following problems through the classical Lagrangian technique. (Do not search the Lagrangian multiplier.)
    a. Minimize: $f(\mathbf{x}) = x_1^2 + x_2^2 - 4x_1 + 2x_2 + 5$
    Subject to: $g(x) = x_1 + x_2 = 4$
    b. Minimize: $f(\mathbf{x}) = (x_1 - 2)^2 + (x_2 - 1)^2$
    Subject to: $g(\mathbf{x}) = x_1 - 2x_2 + 1 = 0$
    (Himmelblau, 1972)

11. A problem which arises in oil-storage purchasing problems is that of determining how many gallons of each item to purchase for a minimum cost policy

under restricted tank space requirements. The following formula describes system costs.

Minimize:

$$f(\mathbf{x}) = \sum_{n=1}^{N} \left(\frac{\alpha_n \beta_n}{x_n} + \frac{\phi_n x_n}{2} \right)$$

where: α_n = fixed cost for nth item

β_n = withdrawal rate per unit of time for nth item

ϕ_n = the holding cost per unit time for nth item.

The floor space constraint is given by:

$$g(\mathbf{x}) = \sum_{n=1}^{N} f_n x_n \leq F$$

where: f_n = space requirement for nth item

F = available space

Suppose that the following costs are determined:

Item (n)	α_n ($)	β_n	ϕ_n ($)	f_n (cubic feet)
1	9.60	3	0.47	1.4
2	4.27	5	0.26	2.62
3	6.42	4	0.61	1.71

a. Verify that the positive optimal solution to the unconstrained problem is given by: $\mathbf{x} = (11.07, 12.82, 9.176)$.

b. If there is only 22 cubic feet of space available, solve the constrained problem as an equality constrained optimization problem using Everett's method of generalized Lagrangian multipliers.

12. Solve the following problem using constrained derivatives:

Minimize: $f(\mathbf{x}) = 7x_1 - 6x_2 + 4x_3$

Subject to: $x_1^2 + 2x_2^2 + 3x_3^2 = 1$

$x_1 + 5x_2 - 3x_3 = 6$

13. Solve the following problem using constrained derivatives:

Minimize: $f(\mathbf{x}) = 4x_1 - \frac{1}{2}x_2^2 - 12$

Subject to: $x_1 x_2 = 4$

14. Solve the following problems using the projected gradient method:

a. Minimize: $f(\mathbf{x}) = 4x_1 - x_2^2 - 6$

Subject to: $26 - x_1^2 - x_2^2 = 0$

b. Minimize: $f(\mathbf{x}) = 25(x_1 - 3x_2)^2 + (x_1 - 3)^2$

Subject to: $x_1 + 2x_2 = 9$

15. Solve the following problem using only the Kuhn-Tucker Conditions:

$$f(\mathbf{x}) = 100 - 1.2x_1 - 1.5x_2 + 0.3x_1^2 + 0.05x_2^2$$

Subject to: $g_1(\mathbf{x}) = x_1 + x_2 \geq 35$

$g_2(\mathbf{x}) = x_1 \geq 0$

$g_3(\mathbf{x}) = x_2 \geq 0$

16. Consider the following problem:

$$f(\mathbf{x}) = 100(x_2 - x_1^2)^2 + (1 - x_1)^2$$

Subject to: $g_1(\mathbf{x}) = x_1 + 1 \geq 0$

$g_2(\mathbf{x}) = 1 - x_2 \geq 0$

$g_3(\mathbf{x}) = 4x_2 - x_1 - 1 \geq 0$

$g_4(\mathbf{x}) = 1 - 0.5x_1 - x_2 \geq 0$

What can you say about the following two solution vectors?

$$\mathbf{x} = (-1, 1) \quad \text{and} \quad \mathbf{x} = (-0.3773, 0.1557)$$

17. Solve the following quadratic programming problems.
   a. Minimize: $f(\mathbf{x}) = x_1^2 - x_1 x_2 + 3x_2^2 - 4x_2 + 4$
      subject to: $x_1 + x_2 \leq 1$

      $x_1, x_2 \geq 0$
   b. Minimize: $f(\mathbf{x}) = 2x_2^2 + 3x_1^2 + 3x_1 x_2 - 25(x_1 + x_2)$

      Subject to: $2x_1 + x_2 \leq 5$

      $x_1, x_2 \geq 0$

18. Solve the following problem using separable programming.
   Maximize: $f(\mathbf{x}) = x_1^2 - 2x_2^2 + 3x_3^2 + 4x_2 - 9x_3$
   Subject to: $2x_1^2 + x_2 + x_3^2 \leq 2.5$
                    $x_1, x_2 \geq 0$

19. Show how the following problems can be solved using separable programming.
   a. Minimize: $f(\mathbf{x}) = x_1 + 3x_1 x_2 + x_2 x_3$
       subject to: $x_1 x_2 + x_3 + x_2 x_3 \geq 4$

       $x_1, x_2, x_3 \geq 0$
   b. Minimize: $f(\mathbf{x}) = 2e^{x_1^2 + x_2^2} + (x_1 - x_2)^2$
       Subject to: $x_1 + x_2 \geq 5$
                          $x_1, x_2 \geq 0$

20. Finish the example problem of Section 11.13 and verify that the optimal solution is given by: $\mathbf{x} = (5.0, 4.5)$ to an accuracy of ± 0.10.

21. Solve the following problem using Kelly's Cutting Plane algorithm.
   Minimize: $f(\mathbf{x}) = x_1^2 + x_2$
   Subject to: $x_1 + x_2 \geq 4$
                     $x_1, x_2 \geq 0$

22. Solve the following problem using Kelly's Cutting Plane algorithm.
   Minimize: $f(\mathbf{x}) = 3x_1^2 + x_2^2$
   Subject to: $h_1(\mathbf{x}) = 2x_1^2 + 3x_2^2 \leq 50$
                     $h_2(\mathbf{x}) = 4x_1^2 - x_2^2 \leq 35$
                     $x_1, x_2 \geq 0$

23. Solve the following problems using geometric programming.
   a. Minimize: $f(\mathbf{x}) = 5x_1^2 x_2^{-1} x_3 + 10x_1^{-3} x_2^2 x_3^{-2}$
       Subject to: $0.357 x_1^{-1} x_3 + 0.625 x_1^{-1} x_3^{-1} \leq 1$
                      $x_1, x_2, x_3 > 0$
   b. Minimize: $f(\mathbf{x}) = x_1^{-1} x_2^{-1} x_3^{-1}$
      Subject to: $2x_1 + x_2 + 3x_3 \leq 1$
                      $x_1, x_2, x_3 > 0$

24. Find the dimensions of an open rectangular tank that give a minimum surface area if the capacity of the tank is equal to 1000 cubic feet. Solve this problem using:
   a. Lagrangian multipliers
   b. Constrained derivatives
   c. Projected gradient
   d. Geometric programming
   Comment on the relative effectiveness of the solution techniques.

APPENDICES

REVIEW OF LINEAR ALGEBRA

A.1 SET THEORY

A *set* is a well defined collection of things. By well defined we mean that given any object it is possible to determine whether or not it belongs to the set.

The set $S = \{x \mid x \geq 0\}$ defines the set of all nonnegative numbers. $x = 2$ is an element of the set S, and is written as $2 \in S$ (2 belongs to S).

The *union* of two sets P and Q defines another set R such that $R = P \cup Q = \{x \mid x \in P \text{ or } x \in Q, \text{ or both}\}$.

The *intersection* of two sets, written $P \cap Q$, defines a set $R = \{x \mid x \in P \text{ and } x \in Q\}$.

P is a *subset* of Q, written $P \subset Q$, if every element of P is in Q.

Disjoint sets have no elements in common. If P and Q are disjoint sets, then $x \in P$ implies $x \in Q$ and vice versa.

The *empty* set, denoted by Φ, is a set with no elements in it.

A.2 VECTORS

A *vector* is an ordered set of real numbers. For instance, $\mathbf{a} = (a_1, a_2, \ldots, a_n)$ is a vector of n elements or components.

If $\mathbf{a} = (a_1, a_2, \ldots, a_n)$, and $\mathbf{b} = (b_1, b_2, \ldots, b_n)$, then

$$\mathbf{a} + \mathbf{b} = \mathbf{c} = (a_1 + b_1, a_2 + b_2, \ldots, a_n + b_n)$$
$$\mathbf{a} - \mathbf{b} = \mathbf{d} = (a_1 - b_1, a_2 - b_2, \ldots, a_n - b_n)$$

$\alpha \mathbf{a} = \mathbf{e} = (\alpha a_1, \alpha a_2, \ldots, \alpha a_n)$ for any scalar α positive or negative.

The vector $\mathbf{0} = (0, 0, \ldots, 0)$ is called the *null* vector.

The inner product of two vectors, written $\mathbf{a} \cdot \mathbf{b}$ or simply $\mathbf{ab}$ is a number given by

$$a_1 b_1 + a_2 b_2 + \cdots + a_n b_n$$

For example, if $\mathbf{a} = (1, 2, 3)$ and $\mathbf{b} = \begin{pmatrix} 4 \\ 5 \\ 6 \end{pmatrix}$, then $\mathbf{a} \cdot \mathbf{b} = 4 + 10 + 18 = 32$.

A set of vectors $\mathbf{a}_1, \mathbf{a}_2, \ldots, \mathbf{a}_n$, is *linearly dependent* if there exists scalars $\alpha_1, \alpha_2, \ldots, \alpha_n$ not all zero, such that

$$\sum_{i=1}^{n} \alpha_i \mathbf{a}_i = 0$$

In this case, at least one vector can be written as a *linear combination* of the others. For example,

$$\mathbf{a}_1 = \lambda_2 \mathbf{a}_2 + \lambda_3 \mathbf{a}_3 + \cdots + \lambda_n \mathbf{a}_n$$

If a set of vectors is not dependent, then it must be *independent*.

A *vector space* is the set of all n-component vectors. This is generally called the *euclidean n-space*.

A set of vectors is said to *span* a vector space **V** if every vector in **V** can be expressed as a linear combination of the vectors in that set.

A *basis* for the vector space **V** is a set of linearly independent vectors that spans **V**.

A.3 MATRICES

A *matrix* **A** of size $(m \times n)$ is a rectangular array (table) of numbers with m rows and n columns.

Example A.3-1

$$\underset{(2 \times 3)}{\mathbf{A}} = \begin{bmatrix} 1 & 2 & 3 \\ 4 & 5 & 6 \end{bmatrix}$$

is a matrix of two rows and three columns. The (i, j)th element of **A**, denoted by a_{ij}, is the element in the ith row and jth column of **A**. In Example A.3-1, $a_{12} = 2$ while $a_{23} = 6$. In general, a matrix of size $(m \times n)$ is written as,

$$\underset{(m \times n)}{\mathbf{A}} = [a_{ij}]$$

The elements a_{ij} for $i = j$ are called the *diagonal* elements; while the a_{ij} for $i \neq j$ are called the *off-diagonal* elements.

The elements of each column of a matrix define a vector called a *column vector*. Similarly, each row of a matrix defines a *row vector*. In Example A.3-1, the vectors $\mathbf{a}_1 = \begin{pmatrix} 1 \\ 4 \end{pmatrix}$, $\mathbf{a}_2 = \begin{pmatrix} 2 \\ 5 \end{pmatrix}$, and $\mathbf{a}_3 = \begin{pmatrix} 3 \\ 6 \end{pmatrix}$ are the column vectors of the matrix **A**; while the vectors $\mathbf{b}_1 = (1\ 2\ 3)$ and $\mathbf{b}_2 = (4\ 5\ 6)$ are the row vectors of **A**.

Thus a vector may be treated as a special matrix with just one row or one column. A matrix with an equal number of rows and columns is called a *square matrix*.

The transpose of a matrix $\mathbf{A} = [a_{ij}]$, denoted by $\mathbf{A}'$ or $\mathbf{A}^T$ is a matrix obtained by interchanging the rows and columns of **A**. In other words, $\mathbf{A}' = [a'_{ij}]$ where $a'_{ij} = a_{ji}$. The transpose of **A** defined in Example A.3-1 is given by

$$\underset{(3 \times 2)}{\mathbf{A}'} = \begin{bmatrix} 1 & 4 \\ 2 & 5 \\ 3 & 6 \end{bmatrix}$$

The matrix **A** is said to be *symmetric* if $\mathbf{A}' = \mathbf{A}$. The *identity* matrix, denoted by **I**, is a square matrix whose diagonal elements are all one and the off-diagonal elements are all zero.

A matrix whose elements are all zero is called a *null matrix*.

Matrix Operations

The *sum* or *difference* of two matrices **A** and **B** is a matrix **C** (written $\mathbf{C} = \mathbf{A} \pm \mathbf{B}$) where the elements of **C** are given by

$$c_{ij} = a_{ij} \pm b_{ij}$$

For two matrices **A** and **B**, the product **AB** is defined if and only if the number of columns of **A** is equal to the number of rows of **B**. If **A** is an $(m \times n)$ matrix and **B** is an

$(n \times r)$ matrix, then the product $\mathbf{AB} = \mathbf{C}$ is defined, whose size is $(m \times r)$. The (i, j)th element of $\mathbf{C}$ is given by,

$$c_{ij} = \sum_{k=1}^{n} a_{ik} b_{kj}$$

Example A.3-2

$$\underset{(2\times3)}{\mathbf{A}} = \begin{bmatrix} 1 & 2 & 3 \\ 4 & 5 & 6 \end{bmatrix}, \qquad \underset{(3\times2)}{\mathbf{B}} = \begin{bmatrix} 1 & 2 \\ 3 & 4 \\ 5 & 6 \end{bmatrix}$$

$$\mathbf{AB} = \underset{(2\times2)}{\mathbf{C}} = \begin{bmatrix} 22 & 28 \\ 49 & 64 \end{bmatrix}$$

Example A.3-3

Let $\mathbf{A} = \begin{bmatrix} 1 & 2 & 3 \\ 4 & 5 & 6 \end{bmatrix}$, $\mathbf{x} = \begin{bmatrix} 2 \\ 3 \\ 4 \end{bmatrix}$, and $\mathbf{y} = (2, 3)$. Then,

$$\mathbf{Ax} = \underset{(2\times1)}{\mathbf{b}} = \begin{bmatrix} 20 \\ 47 \end{bmatrix},$$

while

$$\mathbf{yA} = \underset{(1\times3)}{\mathbf{d}} = (14 \ 19 \ 24)$$

Note that $\mathbf{b}$ is a column vector, and $\mathbf{d}$ is a row vector. For any scalar α,

$$\alpha \mathbf{A} = [\alpha a_{ij}]$$

Matrix operations satisfy the following properties:

1. $(\mathbf{A} + \mathbf{B}) + \mathbf{C} = \mathbf{A} + (\mathbf{B} + \mathbf{C})$
2. $\mathbf{A} + \mathbf{B} = \mathbf{B} + \mathbf{A}$
3. $(\mathbf{A} + \mathbf{B})\mathbf{C} = \mathbf{AC} + \mathbf{BC}$
4. $(\mathbf{AB})\mathbf{C} = \mathbf{A}(\mathbf{BC})$
5. $\mathbf{IA} = \mathbf{AI} = \mathbf{A}$
6. $(\mathbf{A} + \mathbf{B})' = \mathbf{A}' + \mathbf{B}'$
7. $(\mathbf{AB})' = \mathbf{B}'\mathbf{A}'$

In general $\mathbf{AB} \neq \mathbf{BA}$.

Determinant of a Square Matrix

The determinant of a square matrix $\mathbf{A}$, denoted by $|\mathbf{A}|$, is a number obtained by certain operations on the elements of $\mathbf{A}$. If $\mathbf{A}$ is a (2×2) matrix, then,

$$|\mathbf{A}| = \begin{vmatrix} a_{11} & a_{12} \\ a_{21} & a_{22} \end{vmatrix} = a_{11} a_{22} - a_{12} a_{21}$$

If $\mathbf{A}$ is an $(n \times n)$ matrix, then

$$|\mathbf{A}| = \sum_{i=1}^{n} a_{i1}(-1)^{i+1} |\mathbf{M}_{i1}|$$

where $\mathbf{M}_{i1}$ is a submatrix obtained by deleting row i and column 1 of $\mathbf{A}$. For example,

$$\text{if} \qquad \underset{(3\times3)}{\mathbf{A}} = \begin{bmatrix} 1 & 2 & 3 \\ 4 & 5 & 6 \\ 7 & 8 & 9 \end{bmatrix}$$

then

$$|\mathbf{A}| = 1 \begin{vmatrix} 5 & 6 \\ 8 & 9 \end{vmatrix} - 4 \begin{vmatrix} 2 & 3 \\ 8 & 9 \end{vmatrix} + 7 \begin{vmatrix} 2 & 3 \\ 5 & 6 \end{vmatrix}$$

$$= (45 - 48) - 4(18 - 24) + 7(12 - 15) = 0$$

A matrix is said to be *singular* if its determinant is equal to zero. If $|\mathbf{A}| \neq 0$, then $\mathbf{A}$ is called *nonsingular*.

Inverse of a Matrix

For a nonsingular square matrix $\mathbf{A}$, the inverse of $\mathbf{A}$ denoted by $\mathbf{A}^{-1}$, is a nonsingular square matrix such that

$$\mathbf{A}\mathbf{A}^{-1} = \mathbf{A}^{-1}\mathbf{A} = \mathbf{I} \text{ (identity matrix)}$$

The inverse matrix ($\mathbf{A}^{-1}$) may be obtained by performing row operations on the original matrix ($\mathbf{A}$). The row operations consist of:

1. Multiply or divide any row by a number.
2. Multiply any row by a number and add it to another row.

To find the inverse of a matrix $\mathbf{A}$, one starts by adjoining an identity matrix of similar size as $[\mathbf{A}]$. By a sequence of row operations $\mathbf{A}$ is reduced to $\mathbf{I}$. This will reduce the original $\mathbf{I}$ matrix to $\mathbf{A}^{-1}$ since

$$\mathbf{A}^{-1}[\mathbf{A}\ \mathbf{I}] = [\mathbf{I}\ \mathbf{A}^{-1}]$$

Example A.3-4

$$\mathbf{A} = \begin{bmatrix} 1 & 1 \\ 1 & -1 \end{bmatrix}$$

Since $|\mathbf{A}| = -2$, $\mathbf{A}$ is nonsingular, and hence $\mathbf{A}^{-1}$ exists. To compute $\mathbf{A}^{-1}$ start with the following matrix:

$$(\mathbf{A}\ \mathbf{I}) = \begin{bmatrix} 1 & 1 & 1 & 0 \\ 1 & -1 & 0 & 1 \end{bmatrix}$$

subtract row 1 from row 2:

$$\begin{bmatrix} 1 & 1 & 1 & 0 \\ 0 & -2 & -1 & 1 \end{bmatrix}$$

Divide row 2 by -2

$$\begin{bmatrix} 1 & 1 & 1 & 0 \\ 0 & 1 & 1/2 & -1/2 \end{bmatrix}$$

Subtract row 2 from row 1:

$$\begin{bmatrix} 1 & 0 & 1/2 & 1/2 \\ 0 & 1 & 1/2 & -1/2 \end{bmatrix}$$

Thus

$$\mathbf{A}^{-1} = \begin{bmatrix} 1/2 & 1/2 \\ 1/2 & -1/2 \end{bmatrix}$$

Verify that $\mathbf{A}\mathbf{A}^{-1} = \mathbf{A}^{-1}\mathbf{A} = \mathbf{I}$.

A.4 QUADRATIC FORMS

A function of n variables $f(x_1, x_2, \ldots, x_n)$ is called a *quadratic form* if

$$f(x_1, x_2, \ldots, x_n) = \sum_{i=1}^{n} \sum_{j=1}^{n} q_{ij} x_i x_j = \mathbf{x}'\mathbf{Q}\mathbf{x}$$

where $\mathbf{Q}_{(n \times n)} = [q_{ij}]$ and $\mathbf{x}' = (x_1, x_2, \ldots, x_n)$. Without any loss of generality, $\mathbf{Q}$ can always be assumed symmetric. Otherwise $\mathbf{Q}$ may be replaced by the symmetric matrix $\dfrac{\mathbf{Q} + \mathbf{Q}'}{2}$ without changing the value of the quadratic form.

Definitions:

1. A matrix $\mathbf{Q}$ is *positive definite* if and only if the quadratic form $\mathbf{x'Qx} > 0$ for all $\mathbf{x} \neq 0$.
    For example, $\mathbf{Q} = \begin{bmatrix} 2 & -1 \\ -1 & 2 \end{bmatrix}$ is positive definite.

2. A matrix $\mathbf{Q}$ is *positive semidefinite* if and only if the quadratic form $\mathbf{x'Qx} \geq 0$ for all $\mathbf{x}$
    and there exists an $\mathbf{x} \neq 0$ such that $\mathbf{x'Qx} = 0$. For example, $\mathbf{Q} = \begin{bmatrix} 1 & -1 \\ -1 & 1 \end{bmatrix}$ is positive
    semidefinite.

3. A matrix $\mathbf{Q}$ is *negative definite* if and only if $-\mathbf{Q}$ is positive definite. In other words,
    $\mathbf{Q}$ is negative definite when $\mathbf{x'Qx} < 0$ for all $\mathbf{x} \neq 0$. For example, $\mathbf{Q} = \begin{bmatrix} -2 & 1 \\ 1 & -3 \end{bmatrix}$ is
    negative definite.

4. A matrix $\mathbf{Q}$ is *negative semidefinite* if $-\mathbf{Q}$ is positive semidefinite. For example,
    $\mathbf{Q} = \begin{bmatrix} -1 & 1 \\ 1 & -1 \end{bmatrix}$.

5. A matrix $\mathbf{Q}$ is *indefinite* if $\mathbf{x'Qx}$ is positive for some $\mathbf{x}$ and negative for some other $\mathbf{x}$.
    For example, $\mathbf{Q} = \begin{bmatrix} 1 & -1 \\ 1 & -2 \end{bmatrix}$ is indefinite.

Principal Minor

If $\mathbf{Q}$ is an $(n \times n)$ matrix, then the *principal minor* of order k is a submatrix of size
$(k \times k)$ obtained by deleting any $(n - k)$ rows and their corresponding columns from the
matrix $\mathbf{Q}$.

Example A.4-1

$$\mathbf{Q} = \begin{bmatrix} 1 & 2 & 3 \\ 4 & 5 & 6 \\ 7 & 8 & 9 \end{bmatrix}$$

Principal minors of order 1 are essentially the diagonal elements 1, 5, and 9. The
principal minor of order 2 are the following (2×2) matrices:

$$\begin{bmatrix} 1 & 2 \\ 4 & 5 \end{bmatrix}, \quad \begin{bmatrix} 1 & 3 \\ 7 & 9 \end{bmatrix}, \quad \text{and} \quad \begin{bmatrix} 5 & 6 \\ 8 & 9 \end{bmatrix}$$

The principal minor of order 3 is the matrix $\mathbf{Q}$ itself.

The determinant of a principal minor is called the *principal determinant*. For an
$(n \times n)$ square matrix, there are in all $2^n - 1$ principal determinants.

Leading Principal Minor of order k of an $(n \times n)$ matrix is obtained by deleting the
last $(n - k)$ rows and their corresponding columns. In Example A.4-1, the leading
principal minor of order 1 is one (delete the last two rows and columns). The leading
principal minor of order 2 is $\begin{bmatrix} 1 & 2 \\ 4 & 5 \end{bmatrix}$, while that of order 3, is the matrix $\mathbf{Q}$ itself. The
number of leading principal determinants of an $(n \times n)$ matrix is n.

There are some easier tests to determine whether a given matrix is positive definite,
negative definite, positive semidefinite, negative semidefinite or indefinite. *All these tests
are valid only when the matrix is symmetric* (If the matrix $\mathbf{Q}$ is not symmetric, change $\mathbf{Q}$
to $\dfrac{\mathbf{Q} + \mathbf{Q'}}{2}$ and then apply the tests).

Tests for Positive Definite Matrices
a. All diagonal elements must be positive.
b. All the leading principal determinants must be positive.

Tests for Positive Semi-Definite Matrices
a. All diagonal elements are nonnegative.
b. All the principal determinants are nonnegative.

Remarks

1. To prove that a matrix is negative definite (negative semidefinite) test the negative of that matrix for positive definite (positive semidefinite).
2. A sufficient test for a matrix to be indefinite, is that at least two of its diagonal elements are of the opposite signs.

A.5 CONVEX AND CONCAVE FUNCTIONS

A function of n variables $f(x_1, x_2, \ldots, x_n)$ is said to be a *convex function* if and only if for any two points $\mathbf{x}^{(1)}$ and $\mathbf{x}^{(2)}$ and $0 \leq \lambda \leq 1$,

$$f[\lambda \mathbf{x}^{(1)} + (1-\lambda)\mathbf{x}^{(2)}] \leq \lambda f(\mathbf{x}^{(1)}) + (1-\lambda)f(\mathbf{x}^{(2)})$$

A function $f(x_1, \ldots, x_n)$ is a concave function if and only if $-f(x_1, \ldots, x_n)$ is a convex function.

The gradient of a function $f(x_1, \ldots, x_n)$ is given by

$$\nabla \mathbf{f}(x_1, \ldots, x_n) = \left[\frac{2f}{2x_1}, \frac{2f}{2x_2}, \ldots, \frac{2f}{2x_n} \right]$$

The *hessian matrix* of a function $f(x_1, \ldots, x_n)$ is an $(n \times n)$ symmetric matrix given by

$$\mathbf{H}_f(x_1, \ldots, x_n) = \left[\frac{2^2 f}{2x_i 2x_j} \right]$$

Test for Convexity of a Function

A function f is a convex function if the hessian matrix of f is positive definite or positive semidefinite for all values of $x_1, \ldots, x_n$.

Test for Concavity of a Function

A function f is concave if the hessian matrix of f is negative definite or negative semidefinite for all values of $x_1, \ldots, x_n$.

Example A.5-1

$$f(x_1, x_2, x_3) = 3x_1^2 + 2x_2^2 + x_3^2 - 2x_1 x_2 - 2x_1 x_3 + 2x_2 x_3 - 6x_1 - 4x_2 - 2x_3$$

$$\nabla \mathbf{f}(x_1, x_2, x_3) = \begin{pmatrix} 6x_1 - 2x_2 - 2x_3 - 6 \\ 4x_2 - 2x_1 + 2x_3 - 4 \\ 2x_3 - 2x_1 + 2x_2 - 2 \end{pmatrix}$$

$$\mathbf{H}_f(x_1, x_2, x_3) = \begin{bmatrix} 6 & -2 & -2 \\ -2 & 4 & 2 \\ -2 & 2 & 2 \end{bmatrix}$$

To show that f is a convex function, we test $\mathbf{H}$ for positive definite or positive semidefinite property. Note that

1. $\mathbf{H}$ is symmetric
2. All diagonal elements are positive.
3. The leading principal determinants are

$$|6| > 0, \qquad \begin{vmatrix} 6 & -2 \\ -2 & 4 \end{vmatrix} = 20 > 0, \qquad |H_f| = 16 > 0$$

Hence $\mathbf{H}$ is a positive definite matrix, which implies f is a convex function. (As a matter of fact, when $\mathbf{H}_f$ is positive definite, f is said to be strictly convex with a unique minimum point.)

A.6 CONVEX SETS

A set **S** is said to be a convex set if for any two points in the set the line joining those two points is also in the set. Mathematically, **S** is a convex set if for any two vectors $\mathbf{X}^{(1)}$ and $\mathbf{X}^{(2)}$ in **S**, the vector $\mathbf{X} = \lambda\mathbf{X}^{(1)} + (1-\lambda)\mathbf{X}^{(2)}$ is also in **S** for any number λ between 0 and 1.

Examples

Figures 1 and 2 represent convex sets, while Figure 3 is not a convex set.

Theorem 1:   The set of all feasible solutions to a linear programming problem is a convex set.

Theorem 2:   The intersection of convex sets is a convex set.

Theorem 3:   The union of convex sets is not necessarily a convex set.

Definition:

A convex combination of vectors $\mathbf{X}^{(1)}, \mathbf{X}^{(2)}, \ldots, \mathbf{X}^{(k)}$ is a vector **X** such that

$$\mathbf{X} = \lambda_1\mathbf{X}^{(1)} + \lambda_2\mathbf{X}^{(2)} + \cdots + \lambda_k\mathbf{X}^{(k)}$$

$$\lambda_1 + \lambda_2 + \cdots + \lambda_k = 1$$

$$\lambda_i \geq 0 \quad \text{for } i = 1, 2, \ldots, k.$$

Extreme point or vertex of a convex set is a point in the set that cannot be expressed as the midpoint of any two points in the set.

For example, consider the convex set $\mathbf{S} = \{(X_1, X_2) \mid 0 \leq X_1 \leq 2, 0 \leq X_2 \leq 2\}$. This set has four extreme points given by $(0, 0)$, $(0, 2)$, $(2, 0)$, and $(2, 2)$.

A *hyperplane* is the set of all points **X** satisfying $\mathbf{CX} = Z$ for a given vector $\mathbf{C} \neq \mathbf{0}$ and scalar Z. The vector **C** is called the *normal* to the hyperplane. For example, $H = \{(X_1, X_2, X_3) \mid 2X_1 - 3X_2 + X_3 = 5\}$ is a hyperplane.

A *half space* is the set of all points **X** satisfying $\mathbf{CX} = Z$ or $\mathbf{CX} = Z$ for a given vector $\mathbf{C} \neq \mathbf{0}$ and scalar Z.

Theorem 4:   A hyperplane is a convex set.

Theorem 5:   A half space is a convex set.

Theorem 6:   Every basic feasible solution to a linear-programming problem corresponds to an extreme point of the convex set of feasible solutions.

Theorem 7:   If there exists an optimal solution to a linear program, then at least one of the extreme points of the convex set of feasible solutions will qualify to be an optimal solution.

Theorem 8:   The set of all optimal solutions to a linear program forms a convex set.

Remarks

1. The fundamental theory of the simplex method is based on Theorems 1, 6, and 7.
2. Theorem 8 is extremely useful in practice. If we have two optimal solutions to a

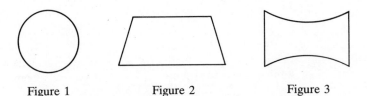

Figure 1   Figure 2   Figure 3

linear program, given by $X^{(1)}$ and $X^{(2)}$, then every solution X obtained by

$$\mathbf{X} = \lambda \mathbf{X}^{(1)} + (1 - \lambda) \mathbf{X}^{(2)} \qquad \text{for } 0 \leqq \lambda \leqq 1$$

is also an optimal solution. Thus a linear program may have (a) no optimal solution, (b) a unique optimal solution, or (c) an infinite number of optimal solutions.

REFERENCE

1. G. Hadley, *Linear Algebra*, Addison-Wesley, Reading, Mass., 1961.

APPENDIX B

The following congruential random-number generator was developed from the material in Chapter 9. This particular generator is applicable to the CDC 6500/6600 series of computers.

```
FUNCTION RAND (NR)
K=31623
NR=NR*K
RN=NR
SHIFT=2.0**48-1.0
RAND=RN/SHIFT
RETURN
END
```

The following sequence of random numbers was generated by this method.

0.2537	0.6767	0.3273	0.2178	0.8016
0.5962	0.7084	0.1520	0.2100	0.3364
0.1900	0.3001	0.5401	0.5548	0.4654
0.9124	0.4687	0.5940	0.0994	0.4848
0.6162	0.5216	0.8403	0.4257	0.6029
0.1441	0.1607	0.2950	0.2061	0.7591
0.1523	0.8092	0.7789	0.9791	0.6894
0.1541	0.6542	0.8866	0.0280	0.7688
0.9264	0.9548	0.8912	0.3455	0.9875
0.4595	0.9688	0.6479	0.1016	0.0396
0.8296	0.3852	0.0360	0.4227	0.8848
0.5094	0.3384	0.5954	0.8163	0.0180
0.7222	0.9673	0.6753	0.7680	0.6065
0.7483	0.1145	0.2270	0.7541	0.4235
0.5356	0.7623	0.5197	0.7585	0.8820
0.2672	0.6601	0.1400	0.9107	0.3606
0.8566	0.1277	0.6068	0.8044	0.2180
0.3903	0.7651	0.0546	0.2404	0.2012
0.4146	0.4226	0.3791	0.4881	0.8793
0.7885	0.4261	0.1267	0.0337	0.8038

INDEX